* *

VISION---Like *Visions of Neal, Visions* [...] length prose works concentrati[...] [...] ne individual, with no other form tha[...] [...]luding verse and any thing, even pictures. BOO[...] OF VISIONS

FLASH---"Dreamflashes," short sleepdreams or drowse daydreams of an enlightened nature describable in a few words, BOOK OF FLASHES. Example: *"Bringing gray suitcases down from the attic of heaven I say 'Me I'm not comin down any more!'"*

DAYDREAM---Prose description of daydreams, wish-dreams during waking hours, example: *"Wearing top hat with black cloak with red lining, with T.S. Eliot, walking into premiere of DOCTOR SAX, through crowd of queers, handsome."*

ROUTINE---William (Burroughs) Lee's invention---the prose acting-out of a daydreamed role, a complete wild explosive extenuation of a daydream

DHARMA-------Notes in any form about the Dharma.   BOOK OF DHARMAS
   All takes place in present tense

----

* * * * * * * O O O O O O O O O O O O O O O O O * * * * * * * *

POP
The sun keeps getting
   dimmer---foghorns
began to blow in the bay

POP
Time keeps running out
   -----sweat
On my brow, from playing

Also   *PRAYER,* for BOOK OF PRAYERS

Example:- "O Lord Avalokitesvara
   Emptiness Without End
   Bless all living & dying
      things
   In the endless past
   In the endless present
   In the endless future
                  amen."

* *

* *

some

of the

dharma

by jack kerouac

some
of the
dharma

jack kerouac

viking

VIKING
Published by the Penguin Group
Penguin Putnam Inc., 375 Hudson Street,
New York, New York 10014, U.S.A.
Penguin Books Ltd, 27 Wrights Lane,
London W8 5TZ, England
Penguin Books Australia Ltd, Ringwood,
Victoria, Australia
Penguin Books Canada Ltd, 10 Alcorn Avenue,
Toronto, Ontario, Canada M4V 3B2
Penguin Books (N.Z.) Ltd, 182–190 Wairau Road,
Auckland 10, New Zealand

Penguin Books Ltd, Registered Offices:
Harmondsworth, Middlesex, England

First published in 1997 by Viking Penguin,
a member of Penguin Putnam Inc.

1 2 3 4 5 6 7 8 9 10

LIBRARY OF CONGRESS CATALOGING IN PUBLICATION DATA
Kerouac, Jack, 1922–1969.
Some of the dharma / Jack Kerouac.
p.   cm.
ISBN *0–670–84877–8 (alk. paper)*
1. Buddhism.   I. Title.
BQ4012.K47   1997
294.3—dc21   97–12870

This book is printed on acid-free paper. ∞

Printed in the United States of America
Set in Sabon and Industrial
Designed by Brian Mulligan

to allen ginsberg

"I love Allen Ginsberg—
Let that be recorded in heaven's unchangeable
heart—"

—*Jack Kerouac*

contents

foreword

Jack Kerouac was born in 1922 in the New England mill town of Lowell, Massachusetts. Growing up in a Franco-American family with a mother, Gabrielle Kerouac, who was a devout and fervent Roman Catholic, he was immersed in the mystery and worship of the Holy child, Jesus Christ. It was a lasting influence: Forty years later, near the end of his life, he was painting pictures of angels, God, and the Madonna and child.

Another formative part of Jack's childhood was the tragedy of losing his older and only brother, Francis Gerard Kerouac, to rheumatic heart disease. In *Visions of Gerard* Jack later wrote: "For the first four years of my life, while he lived, I was not Ti Jean Duluoz, I was Gerard, the whole world was his face, the flower of his face, pale stooped disposition, the heartbreakingness and the holiness and his teachings of tenderness to me, and my mother constantly reminding me to pay attention to his goodness and advice. . . ." Gerard suffered through a lingering and painful illness that finally, to quote Gabrielle, carried him "off to heaven and the angels." This experience of loss was seminal to Jack's understanding of life.

He became seriously interested in Buddhism in 1953, and *Some of the Dharma* documents his Buddhist study. It begins with Buddhism's "Four Noble Truths," the first of which is "All life is sorrowful." The third is "The suppression of suffering can be achieved."

In June, 1993, I placed the finished manuscript of *Some of the Dharma* and the eleven spiral notebooks in which Jack originally wrote the book in the New York Public Library's Berg Collection. They are available there for study by literary scholars.

I would like to thank my nephew Jim Sampas, for his assistance with the Estate and work on this book in particular. Thanks to George Tobia, Jr. Thanks also to Kathleen Richards, David Ershun, and Nancy Howard of NK Graphics for their hard work on a difficult typesetting and proofreading job, and to the people at Viking Penguin who worked on the project: Beena Kamlani, Gail Belenson, Brian Mulligan, Alix McGowen, Roni Axelrod, Paul Morris, and Paul Slovak. Thanks to Jack's longtime agent Sterling Lord ("The Lord is my agent," Jack was fond of saying), and to Jack's current editor at Viking, David Stanford, the consummate diplomat, for his patience, tact, and great labor on behalf of Jack's work.

This book began as a series of notes for Allen Ginsberg and I have taken the liberty of dedicating it to him, Jack's dear and lifelong friend.

John Sampas, Executor
The Estate of Jack Kerouac
Lowell, Massachusetts
May 1997

about the manuscript

Many words will eventually be written about *Some of the Dharma*. This note is simply to introduce it and place it within the chronology of Jack Kerouac's work, largely through his own comments in letters and notes.

Kerouac was twenty-six when he completed his first novel, *The Town and The City*, in May 1948. It was published in 1950 and received good reviews, though it did not sell well. Over the next several years Kerouac worked on numerous preliminary versions of the book that ultimately emerged as *On The Road*. The first complete manuscript was typed during a three-week period in April 1951, and revised and re-typed in the weeks that followed. Kerouac later referred to *On The Road* as being written in his "middle style," between that of *The Town and the City* and the "spontaneous prose" which he committed himself to in the fall of 1951. Over the next two years Kerouac wrote *Visions of Cody, Doctor Sax, Maggie Cassidy,* and *The Subterraneans*. He considered these four books and *On The Road* to be "true story novels," all "chapters" of the "one vast book" of his multi-volume autobiographical *Legend of Duluoz*. Despite the efforts of literary agent Sterling Lord, the New York publishing world rejected his work, and by the fall of 1953 Kerouac was discouraged.

He had also become fascinated by Buddhism, and that fall he began a period of concentrated Buddhist reading, study, and practice which was to become central to his life and writing for the next few years. In December 1953 he enthusiastically began *Some of the Dharma* as a set of reading notes, but as the months passed, it evolved into a vast and complex all-encompassing work of nonfiction into which he poured his life, chronicling his thinking, incorporating reading notes, prayers, poems, blues poems, haiku, meditations, letters, conversations, journal entries, stories, and more. Kerouac felt he had discovered a powerful new form, and the Buddhism he explored with it became an important element of his worldview.

He finished *Some of the Dharma* on March 15, 1956. By that time he had also written *Mexico City Blues, Tristessa, Visions of Gerard, The Scripture of the Golden Eternity,* and some of *Desolation Angels*. Nine months later Sterling Lord sold *On The Road*.

The extraordinary success of *On The Road,* published in 1957, gave Kerouac the readership and recognition he had long sought, and at the same time unleashed the criticism and overwhelming fame which made it so difficult for him to continue his mission as a writer. His deep interest in Buddhism became clear to readers in 1958 with the publication of *The Dharma Bums*, written in 1957. That book played an important part in the growth of Buddhism in America—and it was born out of the two-and-a-half year period of intense study chronicled in *Some of the Dharma*.

Kerouac wrote *Some of the Dharma* (which he sometimes referred to as *Book of Dharmas*) in notebooks, typing up completed portions as he continued to write new material by hand. He started the project as notes on Buddhism to send to poet Allen Ginsberg. In May of 1954 Kerouac wrote to Ginsberg about his "discovery and espousal of sweet Buddha . . . I always did suspect that life was a dream, now I am assured by the most brilliant man who ever lived, that it is indeed so . . . I will and would go to El Paso Texas at first, to wash dishes and live across the river in $4 a month dobe cottage where with my Buddha Bibles and bean stews I would live life of mendicant thinker in this humble earth dream."

In the years to come Kerouac wrote many long letters to Ginsberg, detailing his thoughts on Buddhism and his developing practice. In another May 1954 letter he told Ginsberg that a few months before, in February, he had "typed up a 100-page account of Buddhism for you, gleaned from my notes . . . If you really want to see it, I will send it importantly stamped, it's the only copy, we must take special care with it, right?" He gave Ginsberg a list of nine books on Buddhism, and instructed him, " . . . Of course, for your beginning studies of Buddhism, you must listen to me carefully and implicitly as tho I was Einstein teaching you relativity or Eliot teaching the Formulas of Objective Correlation on a blackboard in Princeton."

On July 30, Kerouac still had not mailed the manuscript to Ginsberg, although he promised to do so in a few days. "I hope you like it; I hope it instructs you. . . . Myself, having really just reach'd the nadir of Nirvana-understanding, am probably depressed as an aftermath. . I tell you I had a vision of emptiness to put an end to all of em . . ."

Some of the Dharma continued to grow, and in November Kerouac wrote Ginsberg again: "I havent sent you the Notes on the Dharma because I keep reading it myself, have but one copy, valuable, sacred to me—will show it to you Dec 18 tho it isnt really much to someone else—Besides it is not finished, I keep adding every day . . ."

Near the end of a long letter to Ginsberg in January 1955, which included extensive commentary on Buddhism, Kerouac wrote: "I think the best thing to do next out is just send you my personal dharma notes with no comments because these letters are getting too much. A million things in my notes, why re-word them for you?"

That same month he wrote to his literary agent Sterling Lord: "I think the time has come for me to pull my manuscripts back and forget publishing." He asked Lord to return all his projects—four novels and some short pieces, adding, ". . . Publishing to me (the big kind like Town & City) is like a threat over my head, I know I'll write better when that whole arbitrary mess is lifted out of my thoughts and it's like early morning again, Saturday, no school, overalls and nothing to do but let the imagination play. Besides I wont need the money the way I'm going to live. And from now on all my writing is going to have a basis of Buddhist Teaching free of all worldly & literary motives so everything has actually worked out fine because in all conscience I couldn't publish Beat G.[eneration, eventually published as *On The Road*] except as 'Pre-enlightenment' work." Lord convinced Kerouac to let him keep working to get the manuscripts published, and Kerouac wrote him again on February 2: "You go on as you've been doing and excuse me for impatience & etc."

On March 4 Kerouac wrote Ginsberg again, from his sister Nin's house in North Carolina, and gave him an update on the project that was by now much more than notes: "*Some of the Dharma* is now over 200 pages, & taking shape as a great valuable book in itself. I haven't even started writing . . . I intend to be the greatest writer in the world and then in the name of Buddha I shall convert thousands, maybe millions: 'Ye shall be Buddhas, rejoice!' . . . I've realized something utterly strange and yet common, I think I've experienced the deep turning-about. At present I am completely happy and feel completely free. I love everybody and intend to go on doing so. I know that I am an imaginary blossom and so is any literary life and my literary accomplishments are so many useless imaginary blossoms . . . I have been having long wild samadhis in the ink black woods of midnight, on a bed of grass."

By April 1955 Kerouac was also working on *Buddha Tells Us,* which he described to Allen Ginsberg as "materially (and mostly) a kind of American transcript, American explanation in plain clear words, of the grand and mysterious Surangama Sutra. I dug Suzuki in NY public library, and I guarantee you I can do everything he does and better, in intrinsic Dharma teaching by words." At various stages Kerouac also referred to *Buddha Tells Us* as *Your Essential Mind: The Story of the Buddha; Buddhahood: The Essence of Reality; Wake Up;* and "my Buddhist handbook."

Kerouac's enthusiasm for Buddhism was not shared by everyone. His devoutly Catholic mother, Gabrielle, and his sister Nin and her family, with whom he often stayed during this period, were critical of his Buddhist studies and his meditation. He also felt that neither his literary agent, Sterling Lord, nor Robert Giroux, one of the New York editors who had shown an interest in his work, were supportive of his writing on Buddhism. On May 27 he shared his frustrations with Allen Ginsberg: "Lissen I wrote a full length Buddhist Handbook called *Buddha Tells Us* and here these rats in New York like, Lord says, 'Is it any good?' when I spend my last 2 dollars longdistancing him, and then Giroux, who'd earlier asked to see my Buddhist works (NOT the others, he was careful to emphasize to Lord) now lets it be known via Lord that he's changed his mind. Meanwhile the ms. has been sitting neatly typed and ready and idle for a whole month. . . . [*Buddha Tells Us*] is a Lake of Light, really great, and guess what it is?--an embellished precis of the Surangama Sutra, just what the doctor ordered for you hey? a real simple explanation guaranteed to explain the inside secret of emptiness., how come etc."

On June 7, he wrote Lord to say he was sending him *Buddha Tells Us,* describing it as "by far the most important thing I've ever done." That same day editor Malcolm Cowley, who had also shown interest in Kerouac's work (and who, with editor Keith Jennisen, later bought *On The Road* and *The Dharma Bums* for Viking) rejected the idea of the "lake of light," advising Jack, "There is no great interest here in the Buddha's Handbook. You are such a natural storyteller that I think stories are what you should tell." Sterling Lord also tried, unsuccessfully, to interest Harvard University Press in the book, which he described in a query letter.

Kerouac wrote to Ginsberg: "*Buddha Tells Us* has been received coldly by Cowley, Giroux, Sterling L.—a great book. It will convert many when it is published and read. If I can get it thru the Money changers, the people who sincerely read it will dig. I mean, I've read it over three times and it definitely has magical powers of enlightenment. I wish I had extry copy for you. It is now (supposedly) at Philosophical Lib. in NY, people who publish Suzuki."

On September 2nd Kerouac reported to Ginsberg that "publishers of Suzuki in N.Y. (Philos. Library) wanted me to guarantee 600 copies before publishing my 'very well written' Buddha-book. I dont know no 600 people with $3.50. Will change title to *Wake Up*."

In a letter to Malcolm Cowley on September 11th, Kerouac included, in a P.S. about his theory of writing, "I'm writing the Duluoz Legend as tho it were one great dream and the whole thing, whether in the section of it dealing with dreams-of-sleep called *Book of Dreams* or section of it dealing with the Samadhi meditation reports (*Book of Ecstasies*) or section of it dealing with adventures past or present or to come (like *Doctor Sax*, or my present *Tristessa* story or my future *Brakeman on the Railroad*)—the whole Duluoz Legend is regarded as one great dream with a unified spontaneous language lulling out the report forever so that in my sleep-bed the uproar continues—and the uproar, like uproar of *Finnegan's Wake*, has no beginning and no end—so that in the end the WRITTEN Duluoz Legend is only a tiny fragment of the huge ignorance of consciousness in the Tathagata's Womb."

In the fall of 1955 Kerouac was living with Allen Ginsberg in Berkeley, and through Ginsberg met poet and Zen student Gary Snyder, who later studied and practiced Zen in Japan for many years. He also met poet Philip Whalen, who went on to become a Zen Buddhist priest in San Francisco. Kerouac exchanged numerous letters with both Whalen and Snyder about Buddhism. On January 18, 1956, he wrote to Whalen: "Did you see where Alan Watts (in an 'impertinent interview' in the Realist magazine) said I had Zen flesh but no Zen bones. It made me shudder. 'No Zen bones yet,' he said. It must mean that when I have a bellyache I moan. I cant stand pain, I admit it. I'd like to found a kind of monastery in the plateau country outside Mexico city, if I had the money . . . But I cant imagine what my rules would be, what rules would conform with pure essence Buddhism, say. That would be, I spose, NO RULES. Pure Essence Buddhism is what I think I want . . . lay aside all the arbitrary rest of it, Hinayana, Shinayana, etc. Mahayana, Zen, Shmen. . ." On February 7, Kerouac wrote Whalen again:

> Only two things to do, One, train our mind on the emptiness aspect of things, and, Two, take care of our body. Because all things are different appearances of the same emptiness. Just no more to it than that. And the knowing of this, that all things are different appearances of the same emptiness, this is bhikkuhood . . . . . . the continual striving to know it continually, and the consequent earnest teaching of it, this is bodhisattvahood . . . . . and the perfect success in perfect and continual knowing of this so that it is no longer "knowing" but the Emptiness-hood itself, this is Buddhahood. The Path is knowing and struggling to know this . . .

> . . . How dreary my "return to N.Y." was, Jesus, my friends gettin older and vaguer and treating me with vaguer neglect and unconcern so much so I'm speechless among them—I felt like a bum among them—didnt even bother to explain the Dharma anymore, couldnt even open my mouth . . .

On March 8, 1956, Kerouac wrote to Gary Snyder from his sister's in North Carolina, predicting that one day "the President of the United States will meditate in the Meditation Room." He described a prayer technique, adding, "I know this works because it's worked for me, alone, with dogs, in my Twin Tree Grove here, every night now for the past 6 weeks." With the letter, he also sent Snyder a sample page from *Some of the Dharma*. As Kerouac worked his way through the handwritten notebooks, creating the finished typescript, the pages had become more and more complex and elaborate, the various blocks of text arranged in intricate patterns.

In the spring of 1956 Kerouac returned to the Bay Area and lived with Gary Snyder in Mill Valley. Snyder, who was the inspiration for the character Japhy Ryder in *The Dharma Bums*, suggested that Kerouac should write a sutra. He composed *The Scripture of the Golden Eternity*.

In the summer of 1956, poet and founder of City Lights Books Lawrence Ferlinghetti published Allen Ginsberg's poem *Howl*. The dedication page of the book began:

> To - Jack Kerouac, new Buddha of American prose, who spit forth intelligence into eleven books written in half the number of years (1951-1956)—ON THE ROAD, VISIONS OF NEAL, DOCTOR SAX, SPRINGTIME MARY, THE SUBTERRANEANS, SAN FRANCISCO BLUES, SOME OF THE DHARMA, BOOK OF DREAMS, WAKE UP, MEXICO CITY BLUES, and VISIONS OF GERARD—creating a spontaneous bop prosody and original classic literature. Several phrases and the title of HOWL are taken from him."

In early December, 1956, Sterling Lord sold *On The Road* to Viking. Publication was scheduled for Fall 1957. By the end of the year Kerouac had finished typing *Some of the Dharma*. On December 26, 1956, he wrote to Sterling Lord from Florida: "I'm going to bring you four huge manuscripts besides these others we had. *Some of the Dharma, Visions of Neal, Book of Dreams* and *Book of Blues* (poems) . . . Anyway, you might as well have the whole cannon in your closet as we're starting to bombard . . ."

On September 5, 1957, *On The Road* received a glowing review in *The New York Times*. From that morning on, Kerouac was famous, and most of the books he had written in the years before were eventually published.

In 1958 *The Subterraneans* and *The Dharma Bums* were published. In January of that year Kerouac wrote enthusiastically to Philip Whalen: "I mean 1958 will be great year, year of buddhism, already big stir in ny about zen, allen watts big hero of madison avenue now, and nancy wilson ross big article about zen in mademoiselle mentions me and allen and knows her buddhism good, now with dharma bums i will crash open whole scene to sudden buddhism boom and look what'll happen closely soon . . . . everybody going the way of the dharma, this no shit . . . reached dead head block . . . . then with arrival of gary, smash! watch. you'll see. it will be a funny year of enlightenment in america . . i dunno about 1959 but 58 is going to be dharma year in america . . . . everybody reading suzuki on madison avenue."

Doctor Sax, Maggie Cassidy, Mexico City Blues, and a portion of *Visions of Cody* were published in 1959. Kerouac had not given up on *Some of the Dharma,* and in December of that year included the idea of publishing selections from it in correspondence with Lawrence Ferlinghetti at City Lights. But Buddhism was no longer the central focus it had been for Kerouac. On June 10th he wrote to Philip Whalen: "Myself, the dharma is slipping away from my consciousness and I cant think of anything to say about it any more. I still read the diamond sutra, but as in a dream now. Dont know what to do. Cant see the purpose of human or terrestrial or any kinda life without heaven to reward the poor suffering fucks. The Buddhist notion that Ignorance caused the world leaves me cold now, because I feel the presence of angels. Maybe rebirth is simply HAVING KIDS."

The pressures of his fame and notoriety and his drinking all took a heavy toll on Kerouac. In May 1960 he wrote to Philip Whalen: "The trouble is I don't write any more, havent written since I saw you summer of 57 because of all the hoorabooloo around publishing and being called messiah with thousands of pains in the ass interrupting me . . ." But he did continue to write, and to publish. By 1964 seven more books had come out— *The Scripture of the Golden Eternity, Tristessa, Lonesome Traveler, Book of Dreams, Pull My Daisy, Visions of Gerard,* and *Big Sur,* some completed years before, some written or finished recently. In December 1964 Kerouac checked in with Sterling Lord again on the status of *Some of the Dharma:* it had suffered further rejection. Kerouac suggested they try New Directions, but nothing came of it.

By 1966 Kerouac had published *Desolation Angels* and *Satori in Paris,* and started *Vanity of Duluoz.* In August he wrote to Sterling Lord: ". . . Please have your secretaries wrap up *Some of the Dharma* (black binding) *Pomes all Sizes* (black binder) (also) and have them mail that to me . . . Need that for research on new novel."

By the time he died in 1969, Kerouac had published three more of the *Legend of Duluoz* novels—*Desolation Angels, Satori in Paris,* and *Vanity of Duluoz.* But *Some of the Dharma* remained unpublished, as did *Wake Up.* A few poems from *Some of the Dharma* found their way into print in *Scattered Poems,* published in 1971, *Pomes all Sizes,* published in 1992, and *Selected Letters: 1940–1956,* published in 1995. And the magazine *Tricycle: A Buddhist Review* published *Wake Up* in serialized form between 1993 and 1995.

After Kerouac's death the meticulously typed manuscript of *Some of the Dharma,* with a few handwritten annotations and drawings by Kerouac, remained in his literary archive until 1991, when John Sampas, the executor of his Estate, sent it to Viking Penguin via Sterling Lord. In preparing the manuscript for publication we have clarified a few of the handdrawn arrows and boxes, corrected obvious typographical errors and misspellings, and otherwise made changes only to establish consistency. Kerouac's eccentricities of language, and the patois and Spanish are untouched. *Some of the Dharma* is published here in a typeset facsimile, recreating the form which Kerouac so painstakingly gave it on his manual typewriter.

There is now widespread serious interest in Jack Kerouac's work and in Buddhism. It seems appropriate that this, his least known book, should finally see the light of day on the fortieth anniversary of the publication of his best-known book, *On The Road.*

David Stanford, Editor
Viking Penguin

March 12, 1997

book one

BUDDHA

FOUR NOBLE TRUTHS

1. All Life is Sorrowful
2. The Cause of Suffering is Ignorant Craving
3. The Suppression of Suffering can be Achieved
4. The Way is the Noble Eightfold Path

8 Fold Path

1. Right Views—Ideas Buddhistic
2. Right Aspirations—Resolution to Follow
3. Right Speech—Gentle Speech
4. Right Conduct—Kind Circumspect Behavior
5. Right Means of Livelihood—Harmless Foodgathering
6. Right Endeavor—Perseverance in Supernormal States
7. Right Mindfulness—Realization of Supernormal States
8. Right Contemplation—Holy Ecstasy in Supernormal States

DIGHA NIKAYA   Long dialogs
NIRVANA   Extinction-"snapped relationship"
KARMA   The universal law involving rebirth (samsara)
YANA   Ferryboat
DHYANA   Ecstasy (of contemplation)
BODHI   Enlightenment
DHARMA   The law of things
TIRTHA   A ford, crossing
TIRTHANKARAS   Those providing a ford
VIDYA   Yonder bank of wisdom
KAMA   Desire
MARA   Death
AVIDYA   spiritual ignorance
MOKSAR   Liberation
    The ferryboat: "The gunwale framing, protecting and defining the
                        perfect ascetic life"

Life is nothing but a short vague dream encompassed round by flesh and tears

"He hath set the world in their heart, so that no man can find out the work
that God maketh from the beginning to the end"   --Ecclesiastes 3.11

"But Jesus held his peace"   --did not let it fly off the handle

REPOSE BEYOND FATE
    REST BEYOND HEAVEN

                    Buddha goes beyond Christ for I have had a vision of
                    the anxieties of Heaven in Mexico City Benzedrine
                    Visions Dec 1952 and I dont want to go there

THEIR TIME . . . their time is running out
                And they're arguing
                "Time's not so slow
                as you think;
                You're not counting calamity"

Lends his graceful pearl to the heavens, Buddha

        Buddha has a heavenly mind . . .

    Great Shifts, religions . . .

      The World does everything wrong on purpose----then why ever give it
      further consideration?

". . .through the knowledge born of sense and object, the lord of knowledge
(self) is born. The shoot springs from the seed"

THE SOUL IS DEAD

". . intervolved effects of recollection " (like knowing the sweetness of
sugar ahead of time) "lead to development of Self . . . infants desire nothing
but an end to birth",,,

SAINT SHIP   SPAMANA SHIP   in India   (terms, names for Monks)

A Rishi-hermit	A Brahmana
A Sramana	An Arhat or Arahat
A Bhikkshu	A Buddha a Muni
(Bhikkshuni, woman)	A Tathagata
A Pratyeka	A Pravragita
An Elder	A Teacher
An Ariya (Ignu)	A Rahan
(meaning an "Elect")	A Phralaong (Burma)
A Rathee, or Raci	A Rahanda

In Burma they think they live on mountain a million miles high named
Mien-Mo (82,000 youdzanas high) (each y. is 12 miles) and that to the South
is an island, Dzapoudiba, or, India---

Day by day
Haggard and dull signs on
the sheen of this skin---
the sheath of proud self
cracks, the sword rusts,
the swordsman falls sighing
in the fault sour sea.

"Why do you permit your thoughts to rise and fall . . . why do you let your senses deceive you as to the true unchanging nature of . . . the eternal and tranquil Mind, and then to do things in a reversed order which leads to motion and confusion and suffering? As one forgets the true nature of Mind, so he mistakes the reflections of objects as being his own mind, thus binding him to the endless movements and changes and sufferings of the recurring cycles of deaths and re births that are of his own causing. You should regard all that changes as dust particles and that which is unchanging as being your own true Nature of Mind."
                        ---From the SURANGAMA SUTRA
    "In the perception of your eyes there are no signs of age, no wrinkles . . . wrinkles are the symbol of change and the un wrinkled is the symbol of the un changing."
    First sight of the sea, second sight of the sea, Newport Madhouse sight of the sea, now sight of the sea---

The world and everything in it
One vast body seen and hassled
By sentient embodied thinking
Bearers of Mind
Which is the manifestation
Of the tranquil and eternal
Radiant bright Essence-
Mind of perfect Purity
Beyond all body
Neither light nor eyes
Alone reveal.
Moveless mind sees motion,
Yen, shape, shadow, clock;
Changeless mind sees change,
Reflections, Particles of Dust.

Buddhism is a return to the Original mind.

Return those shoes
    to the shoemaker
Return this hand to my father
This pillow to the pillowmaker
Those slippers to the shop
That wainscot to the carpenter,
But my mind
    my tranquil and eternal Mind
Return it to whom?

    The perceiving that your mind is doing is not caused by the light, otherwise you wouldnt be able to perceive darkness, which you do; the cause of the perceiving that you are doing is the true Mind. (Neither the lamp nor the eyes.)

The fact that people
Put up walls
In front of us
Or take them Down
Is not an attribute of
Our perception of sight.

The tranquil and Eternal mind
Does not discriminate
In shapes or forms
But has a brightness of its own
And imageless.

My eyes look west
My eyes look north
My eyes look east
But my tranquil and eternal Mind
Which way?

BUDDHA "Your mind has its own mysterious nature of brightness and purity, and when you try to refer your Mind to the various classes of phenomena you simply deceive and bewilder yourself, and, by so doing, you have lost your own true nature and have suffered endless mis fortunes, like a vagrant, adrift on the ocean of deaths and re births, that is why I look on you as being most pitiable, Ananda"   from *Surangama Sutra*

In India in a bamboo grove
Where it was said:
"All the Buddhalands of purity
Greater in number
Than the fine particles of dust"

"Under . . . Heavenly conditions you would still have to continue making distinctions between yourself and objects " (almost sarcastically said)

The dark Scorpion bit me
On the bright mountain
My flesh was fevered
I bathed it in the river
My perception never changed
My heart was angered
Hand insulted, Mind unmoved,
Skin was put in cold night water

In a straw hat
I listened to the musicians
Shaded from the sun---
Thoughts fixed on brilliance
    I got deaf---
    Night fall
They folded up their guitars.

"Or, Ananda, suppose you fill the square vessel with objects and then remove the vessel's squareness; are you still troubled as to the existence of shape in open space?"

Marijuana simulates the conditions of perfect and pure bodiless contemplation, because the alkaloid stuns the nervous centers, but panic is
caused, by the poison, to overcome peace and sense of rest   So natural contemplation induced by serious self disciplinary trance methods is far better.

Remove all attachments to the body save refreshing food and beverage, even
if the attachment has for its purpose the disembodying effect so desirable
to the tranquil meditator.

SPACE

"If it is space that is perception of sight, you ought to know,
and if we were to remove perception of sight, what would you
substitute for space?" (Surangama)

Me . . . . "a junior Arhat not yet free from the intoxicants"

SUPREME BODHI

Yonder mountain
Solid object
As we perceive it
Is but a manifestation
Arising from our senses
In contact with it.
Remember therefore
That it is illusion
No ambiguity about that.
The Eternal and tranquil Mind
Is bringing you this Program
Direct from Rosy Essence.

A note on Helen Keller:

"Perception of Sight is Pure
Reality itself . . ."
(She doesnt perceive the discriminating phenomena of the mountain,
which swims before our eyes, her eternal and Tranquil Mind perceives
only Rosy Pure Essence without shadow or shape)---

SIGHT

The perception of eyes
Is a condition
Dependent on causes---
Morbid and sick eyes
See snow and automobiles
Where elephants of India
Pass infinitesimally--
Morbid & sick's the condition,
The inflamed Karma eye;
Morbid and misty's the cause,
The perception of sight
Of the inflamed Eye.

Or--

If you were not here
To see the world
With your special
Conditioned eyes
What makes you think
It would look like that?

There is a difference between the perception of the sight of the inflamed eye, and the perception of the sight of the intuitive, enlightening, non-intoxicating, mysterious, intrinsic Mind.

Religions appear to be schismatic technical haranguish corruptions of some original pure Vision...Gotama Buddha broke from Vedic clutter to Pure Sorrow, and in spite of his Rationalism, 1000 Sects like the Lokottaravādins sprang up.

BIBLIOGRAPHY

TEXTS FROM THE BUDDHIST CANON KNOWN AS DHAMMAPADA   Samuel Beal, London and Boston 1878

LIFE OF BUDDHA , or BUDDHA CHARITA, by Asvaghosha, trans. S.Beal (Sacred Books of the East Vol 19)

THE GOSPEL OF BUDDHA   by Paul Carus (Open Court, Chicago 1894)

BUDDHISM IN TRANSLATIONS   by Henry Clarke Warren (Harvard Oriental Series Vol 3, Harvard Univ Press 1896)

ALSO IN HARVARD CLASSICS

THE BUDDHIST BIBLE   Dwight Goddard (Goddard, Thetford, Vt)
        (Including the Surangama Sutra)

BUDDHIST LEGENDS,   E W Burlingame   Harvard Oriental Series Vol 28 30
        (Complete *Commentary* on Dhammapada's 423 Aphorisms)

THE DIALOGS OF THE BUDDHA
        DIGHA-NIKAYA   Rhys Davids, 3 Vols, Oxford

VISSUDHI MAGGA   by Buddhaghosha, trans P M Tin (The Path of Purity, Pali Text Society, Trans. Series, 11, 17, 21)

THE SACRED BOOKS AND EARLY LITERATURE OF THE EAST   Volume 10 India and Buddhism   Parke, Austin and Lipscomb   New York London

(I have last named book and Goddard's Buddhist Bible)

THE FOUR PRECEPTS

1. No lust and avarice *UNCHASTITY* (Adultery without Consent) (Rapacity)
2. No cruelty and egoism *KILLING* (Brutalizing)
3. No insincerity and proud deceit *LYING*
4. No covetousness and stealing *STEALING*

a. Concentrate the Mind   b. Keep the precepts   c. Practice dhyana (meditative ecstasy) for samadhi (transcendental intelligence)

"Walt Whitman is Chinese" and "When one asks about contemporary philosophy in America one thinks of Professor Whitehead. But what has the philosophy of Professor Whitehead got to do with the common man?" (Lin Yutang, and it's *funny*)

All over America, truckdrivers, and the only philosopher   Professor
Whitehead   And everybody mad as hell   and black is ignorance   But not
Professor Whitehead

            Taoism is a human religion rather than divine like
      Buddhism   Tao can be "used" (as by the Giggling Lings
      and Laundrymen) (and cackling architects of the eternal nod)

Body views body in a certain way, the bodiful way; but bodiless Eternal
  and Tranquil Mind, when disembodied and pure in its Original pre World
State, views body in a way which body cannot know and which is only hinted
in the body's mind which is my thinking discriminating mind . . . so in reality
this plant is on fire and violently moving (and swimming in the sea of time
like the tic tic tic awe-awry-waving-around clock) . . . body views body
as body, mind views body as mind, body views mind as body, mind views mind
as mind of course.

      Stran to gesay . . . the future is ah bubble

    Perceive, if you will, that you dont have to worry . . . solid table,
eyeball blue moist perception (liquid eternal view)----let yr eyes cross
and wander, the table varies, wavers, wanders, but it's still there and so's
your perception and you dont have to deal in anxieties of the mind, try
selling rugs in pornographic brown Paree

     BUDDHA AND JESUS BOTH FREED THEMSELVES OF THE
    SUBCONSCIOUS DREAMFLOOD WHICH IS THE SOURCE OF "RELIGIOUS
    VISION" AND AVAILABLE TO ANY DOZING MAN . . .

From the most Frantic Railroad Book-of-Rules of All:
    "There is no offence if there is a view as to what is impure in
   what is pure, if there is a view as to what is impure in what is impure,
  if he is mad, if he is a beginner. //6//4//"
                --BOOK OF THE DISCIPLINE Vinaya Pitaka

        A MAGICAL DHARANI (or ,prayer)
   Tutte, tutte---vutte, vutte, patte, patte---katte, katte,---amale, amale-
--vimale, vimale----nime, nime,----hime, hime---vame, vame---kale, kale,
kale, kale---attc, mattc----vatte, tutte----jnette, sputte---katte, katte---
latte, patte----dime, dime----cale, cale----pace, pace---badhe, bandhe---
ance, mance----dutare, dutare-----patare, patare----arkke, arkke----sarkke,
sarkke---cakre, cakre----dime, dime---hime, hime----tu tu tu tu (4)----du
du du du (4)----ru ru ru ru (4)---phu phu phu phu (4)----svaha.

    From the MAHAVISTU ". . . the . . . Exalted One . . . possessed the Monk's
   requisites of robe, bowl, bed, seat and medicines for use in sickness."
(in 300 B C this written and reported)
   ". . . the jungle of rebirth in an incessant round . . ."
   Some are reborn in hell as "brutes and ghosts"---(and "female fiends").

   "The whole world is fraught with peril. The whole world is on fire; the
  whole world is ablaze. The whole world is quaking"
   THE FOUR DHYANAS:-
   ". . . THE FIRST MEDITATION is aloof from sense-desires and from
   sinful and evil ideas, is attended by applied and sustained

thought, and is born of solitude and is full of zest and ease."

",. the SECOND MEDITATION is free from applied and sustained thought, and is born of solitude and is full of zest and ease, one pointed, born of concentration"

". . . the THIRD MEDITATION . . . is free of the fervor of zest, indifferent and mindful dwelling at ease"

". . . the FOURTH MEDITATION is indifferent to ease and ill, past happiness and misery . . . utter purity of equanimity and mindfulness (zero point between joy and sorrow)"

"Then with heart composed, purified, cleansed, without blemish, free of the lusts, supple, ready to act, firm and unperturbed, he, in the first watch of the night, turned and applied his mind to acquire the sight of the deva eye (angel eye). . . . sees fair beings and foul beings passing away and coming to birth . . . how they go to bournes of good . . . and ill . . . in accordance with their Karma--" DIPAMKARA

BENARES, the Capital of the World . . .

WHAT happens on High: The celestial nymph who passed from that state like a flame while she and 999 other nymphs were decking their Garland-wearer God husband, and lived, and suffered, and gave birth, and earnest-wished to return to her celestial husband and so practised kindness to Arhats, and died, and came back to the Celestial Garden, and they were still decking the God and he said "Where have you been?/ We have not seen you since morning"

FANTASY: Abraham Lincoln reborn as a little tiny live doll in black coat and top hat begging at kitchen tables for food, with Asvaghosha's Buddha Charita under his arm (because he read Life of Buddha but tolerated War) (tolerated rancor, rivalry, history)
Put that in yr cornfield Carl

The Sea Shroud's conception of the Sea is a seaweed conception of the Sea, the Igsea---

Bibliography→   (Sacred Books of the Buddhists LUZAC and Co. 46 Great Russell
                   St London W C 1 1949 ----the best literary gems)

THE DIAMOND STANZA
HE THAT HAS NO LONGINGS   HE THAT FULLY UNDERSTANDS   HE THAT ENTERTAINS
NO DOUBTS   HE THAT HAS PLUNGED INTO THE DEATHLESS   HIM I CALL A
BRAHMIN

"Affection" in the sense of grasping or covetous stinging itch to caress a favored object or being, like a fickle paramour her siamese cat, or a fickle timed tonguelicking girl her boy lover, the nervous twitch to "hold" "keep" "possess" "caress" "fondle" "stroke" "hug" ---all transient as a bubble in the sea of time and not anything more than the transient craving for a candy bar, not any nobler or exaltable as human love, just a lot of nerve wracked twaddle of the restless fingers . . For behold, it's because they're in love with themselves that they want you to look at them all the time and keep drawing your attention--in love with themselves and not with you, for if they really loved you, they would not disturb your natural tranquillity of mind---Therefore the most beneficial teaching in this world is the teaching by silence and example of silence and repose-----But some

must bake the bread, and some eat it, and the bakers are agitated--- Bake
therefore yr own bread, calm . . . If you dote on the love of another human
being, every time you disturb (her him) to draw attention to your loving,
you do her a disservice as of hating. Beware of lechery and then beware
of the conspiring earnestness. . Be like a junk drunk punk, hang motionless
in the wait for the time to wheel around . . . This is why a man doesnt need a
woman, or a cigarette, or a house. He needs just food for sustenance and
a decision to exercise his free will in thought, and action, and thought
is the shadow of action, which is a shadow also.

> Warm hand and cold hand
> held together manifest
>   The phenomena of contamination
>   Setting up the condition
>   For a perception of 2 sensations

The great mystery and astonishing discovery of Indian Philosophy
or Buddha is, that in reality there is only perfect emptiness and silence
and all this rigamarole we see, hear, feel, taste, smell, touch and think
about is originating from that first defilement of individuation that took
place in the heavens when Mind fell to Discriminate phenomena and but why?
(MINDFALL) Why did Mind fail? fall? Christianity says, to bring disgrace
and then grace (via Son of God) to Universe'''--Indians dont say---Since
we are not "children of God" helplessly originated in clay-form and promised
reprieve back in Essence heaven if we're good, but God ourselves, Buddha
holds us directly responsible for all the defilements including the first
(in Emptiness discriminating phenomena) on down to the defilements of
  differentiating seen form (we could have ignored) on down to the klesas,
the various "needs" such as, Tiger needs meat, on down to grasping of
things we desire (itself) on down to the final defilement of consequent
conflict, bewilderment and weariness leading to decay, growing old, suffering and death---
    Now I remember: The state of my Mind was pure water before I was
born; at birth the sediment defilements of the evil passions troubled it
Not "my" Mind,----Mind-----
    Tranquillize the body now and let the sediment settle.
    Carefully strain off top for perfect purity and all things will be
seen not in separateness but in unity wherein there is no place for evil
passions to enter--- This purity is in full conformity with the mysterious
and indescribable purity of Nirvana ---

    This means that you must go, and devote yourself entirely to
thought, for Two goals
    1. Emptying yr mind, transmuting false Mind of death and re birth
    into true and clear Essence Mind, tranquillizing and straining off the
      pure, harmonizing starting point with Goal of perfect Enlightenment

    2.Attain Bodhisattva-Mahasattvaship by abandoning all dependence
    upon conceptions of ego-selfness by running passionate desires thru
    the wringer of the 5 defilements and understanding the deceptiveness of
    the sense-organs and sense-minds and the discriminating thoughts
    relating to them and to the objects of sense, and to the general topsy-
    turviness of Mind, subduing vagrant thoughts and vexations of mind
    and successfully ascending to the throne of Tathagata.

MORE SIMPLY   Go somewhere to limitless solitude in the tolerant open
                 and where yr food is cheap, and devote all time to thot
                    1.Clear the mind of all post-birth defilement
                    2.Get rid of Ego Selfness to help all sentient
                                                                 life

ONE GOOD METHOD

> Dont use yr eyes
> Dont use yr ears
> Dont use yr nose
> Dont use yr tongue
> Dont use yr body
> Dont use yr discriminating mind

POEM

If he can be call'd meek
    who has no wishes
--or hiding who needs never
    be found--
    or scared who never
attacks---
    forgotten, who watches up
the night---
    If he can be called "he,"
who has no self
    Writes "One is All"
    On every wall.

"Literature" is no longer Necessary
    Teaching is left . . .

Unquestionably, the extraordinary private will-to-live in even a cat, the
impossibility of his accepting death or of escaping from the infolded grati-
fication of his Self, the inward smile and satisfied sleep, the unbounded
confidence inside his Ego, the certainty that it is so, proves that he is
God, in a cat body, and ever so, till rebirth in another higher or lower
earthly sentience; the mere cupness, form-ness, of a plastic cup, proves
that it is God, in a cup-form-body, temporarily regnant there.
    But "God" is a Faustian, false concept.

TRANSMUTED; SEXUALIS SAMPLE

    Allen, suppose a man speaks of a sex girl, he immediately is conscious
of spittle throbbing out of the tip of his penis . . . It neither comes from the
girl, nor from the actual girl being in contact with the penis. If throbbing
penis-spittling is manifested by a girl, then she must be speaking for herself, how is it that she was perceived in this case by just of speaking *about*
her. Or if the perception arises from the going into the tip of the penis,
then it should be heard by the penis; why did the throbbing and spittle have
to wait until the ear heard of the sex of the girl? If it was the ear that
heard it why did not the spittle throb up out of the ear? Therefore Allen
you should know that the thinking ingredients of perception are fanciful
and illusion, they are neither manifested naturally by causes and conditions
nor spontaneously by their own nature.

BRIGHTNESS AND DARKNESS conflict, are opposing and therefore false notions
    placing a constraint upon the Bodhi Wisdom Nature, which is contamination
causing the perception of sight (which has no substantiality of existence)
to perceive---

The thought-material manifested during sleep is still the same material as
that during waking, but uncontrolled by mind laws. This disproves the
theory of conscious and subconscious, which is a false duality placing a
constraint upon the original intelligence nature, which is contamination

causing the perception of dual-mind-sensing (which has no substantiality
of existence) to go on perceiving, so out of opposing conflicting notions
comes same.

In the Beginningless Beginning it would be called Emptiness and now it
would have to be called Space because things have been dreamed and discriminated into being to fill her up----Things that when arbitrarily fanned
blow up a wind the intrinsic nature of which was just asleep and is the
real Emptiness (the intrinsic nature of space is the real wind-essence);
things that when arbitrarily fired up burn up a fire the intrinsic nature
of which is the real emptiness (the intrinsic nature of space is the real
fire-essence); things that form molds creating water (the intrinsic nature
of space, emptiness, is the real water-essence); things like sight, the see
and the seeableness, the 2-fold hassle of Emptiness "Self"-viewing the dust
mote-fruit of the First contaminating conflict

    Unweaving the world back

     Realizing that water is made

     Fire and wind---Invisible

     The "devil" is matter, earth,
       Filling emptiness with Dust
     Defiling inconceivable purities
       Where space and sight were One

Earth, Fire, Water, Air are
Invisible servants of some
Hasslous action (which is
Discriminating Ignorance)

  ---Water fills the molds
   --Fire obliges
  ---Air responds from sleep
  --Earth is the only sight you see
       Earth filled the mold of seeing
       Obliged
       Responded from sleep
       Was all the sight to see.

RIGHT MINDFULNESS

     Eyeball leaps to see
     Ego leaps to vain
     Worry leaps to gnaw
     Tongue to tattle, taste,
     Brain to frame
     Imagination draw---
     Foot leaps to walk
     Finger to feel, grab, claw,
     Cock to throb, think,
     Mind to think up thoughts,
     Choice to choose up choices,
     But Right Mindfulness
     Leaps to avoid:
       This is the true Morphine.

Those who apprehend the eternal principles (Tao) do not suffer material
things to injure them.

"Do not let the artificial obliterate the natural; do not let will obliterate
destiny; do not let virtue be sacrificed to fame"
                                    CHUANGTSE

"Rest in inaction, and the world will be reformed of itself; Forget your
body and SPIT FORTH INTELLIGENCE. Ignore all differences and become one
with the Infinite. Release yr mind, and free yr spirit. Be vacuous, be
devoid of soul. Thus will things grow and prosper and return to their
Rust and Rest. Returning to their Root. Returning to their Root without
their knowing it, the result will be a formless whole which will never be
cut up, to know it is to cut it up"   GREAT NEBULOUS says to GENERAL CLOUDS
in Chuangtse

KUANG CH'ENGTSE-----
            "The essence of perfect Tao is profoundly mysterious; its
      extent is lost in obscurity.
            "See nothing, hear nothing; guard yr spirit in quietude,
and yr body will go right of its own accord.
            "Be quiet, be pure; toil not yr body, perturb not yr
vital essence, and you will live forever.
            "For if the eye sees nothing, and the ear hears nothing, and
the mind thinks nothing, yr spirit will stay in yr body, and the body will too
thereby live forever.
            "Cherish that which is within you, and shut off that which is
without; for much knowledge is a curse.
            "Then I will take you to that abode of Great Light to reach
the Plateau of Absolute YANG   I will lead you through the door of the
Dark Unknown to the Plateau of the Absolute YIN   I will lead you through
Eternity to wander in the great wilds of Infinity"   CHUANGTSE

        Taoism is believed to be the Chinese transmutation of Buddhism
    filtering in from India in about 300 B C

        "How did the great rivers and seas become the lords of the
          ravines? By being good at keeping low. . . . Because the Sage
          does not contend, no one in the world can contend against him"
        LAOTSE   Lin Yutang trans.

          "Because it is great
            therefore it resembles folly"

      "He who knows does not speak;
        He who speaks does not know."

          "Accomplish do-nothing
          Attend to no-affairs.
          Taste the flavorless"

    "Not knowing the union of male and female, yet his organs are complete,
which means his vigor is unspoiled" (Reich?)

          "Who is rich in virtue
            Is like a child"

        "Stop its apertures, close its doors, and one's whole life is
                                    without toil"

"The teaching without words
    And the benefit of taking no
            action
  Are without compare in the universe"

"The greatest abundance
        seems meagre
  And its use will never fail.
  What is most straight
        appears devious"

"He who is aware of the Male
But keeps to the Female
Becomes the ravine of the world.
Being the ravine of the world,
He has the Eternal power which
        never fails,
And returns again to the babe."

"He who is conscious of the bright
But keeps to the dark
Becomes the model for the world.
Being the model for the world,
He has the eternal power which
        never errs,
And returns again to the Primordial Nothingness"

"He who is familiar with honor and glory
But keeps to obscurity
Becomes the valley of the world.
Being the valley of the world
He has an eternal power which
        always suffices,
And returns again to pristine simplicity"

    ''

ASVAGHOSHA'S AWAKENING OF FAITH

    1. Greatness of Mind's Emptiness
    2. Greatness of Mind's Trueness
    3. Greatness of Mind's Freedom

    In all 3 cases considered as a clear (empty) mirror

    4. Greatness of Mind's Compassionate Helpfulness

    Because free from all bodiful limitations of selfness

That thought, any thought, (name it).   , the pristine stuff that made it!

SO,
    After the exercise of the 5 Defilements run the thought (*that has arisen
to disturb yr tranquillity by just appearing*) one more wringer dry through
egoism, which comes from the mind perceiving those differences that awakened
desire, grasping and decrepit suffering----"and then the mind notes that some

relate to himself and some to not-self, from which rises the conception
of an actor, an ego self" and the following conception of a surrounding world
that is not-self.

Discover that great secret heart of compassion----which
is in All held second to body-need and world desire.

EL DORADO ARKANSAS
Release yourself, sweet escapee,
Death owns bones;
But infinite emptiness
And eternal silence
Of Pure Perfect Mind
Who how much owns?
All, all of it.

Death is Truth.

Death the Golden Age.

The Infinite reaching itself returning to Golden Age

To look everywhere and see nothing, that's the aim of wisdom---removing
from free perfect Mind's reflection the contaminations of sight, leaving
instead the Snowy Nothingness

Walking with eyes self blinkered in perfect

"THE GREAT OCEAN is also in reciprocal development with the illusive
conception of fire within the mind, and reveals the fact that the
blazing Fire is arising continuously" (Surangama Sutra)

MAD
The only perfect realization of personality coming when raving insane
in a madhouse, saint guarded by sinners----every moment perfect ecstasy of
self-expression, Rosy Golden Flawlessness and Glamor---and when in glimmer
of knowledge that one is now adjudged "insane" the world makes no difference
any moreanyhow- -The Messianic complex. "Father forgive them for they know not
what they do " ---Jesus is in a padded cell, Mahomet has paraldehyde shoved
down his throat, Zoroaster is beaten by special guards of civilization,
Buddha is alone and catatonic.

"All the activities of the mind are but the working over of material
that has originated within its own nature"

The Dharma can save the world by extinguishing it---only in that
sense it is not useless, as all other things are useless or only useful
for useless ends. "Useless" is however the ideal state because it does not
relate to things of worldly nature. That is why the Dharma, the Teaching of
Eternity, cannot be called useful and yet can be called not useless. Extinguishing the world the thread will end which holds us weaved now to the
notion of anything being useful for some succeeding reason.
Death is the golden age. The extinction in Nirvana, the living suicide, freezes us in the ecstasy of body-stopped and body-surpassed and all
understood, and death the moreso as even the bondage of the brain-cells
is undone, and Essence Silence in emptiness permeates every square inch of

the space that once was named because it had motility, or hassle of motion, and encarnadined bone and vein and was (tho slated to last 70 years, or 2 seconds in Time) called "my body."

     Fearing death, one will fear the heedless perfection which shall surpass the anxious flaw of life, the nerve-flow so dependent on cause and conditions of knowledge which we know in life and are bewildered by because of sheer multiplicity. Doubt is a condition of life quaking in the bone because the bone is on fire.

     Beyond fire is emptiness, beyond fear is nothing. Dead is the best age because it is beyond the conditions of young and old, subject to neither flaw, complaint, harassment or transient soon-to-be-saddened advantage. The return, later, to the original state, desired now, is the golden age reached. In the time of death reign perfection and bliss, not the least reason for this being that the ego that once grasped at the notion of fear of death and love of life is now dissolved in a rotten chemic proving. When the body is returned without complaint to the body-world, and "soul" is dead, Mind, undergoing another impulse of vibration, but otherwise unmoved, has cast off ego too as a husk. Ego divested of a husk itself hardens and dies, by which the graveyards are filled with diamonds of dead egos celebrated in carved stone above. No less than the diamond on the world's dowageress dead finger, is the hardness, deadness, and lack-value of the dead and castoff ego in the grave. The dead men's pressed lips would taste dry musk if taste werent made to accommodate some mortal mouth awhile in a transient stress as dependent on causes and conditions as electricity; beyond taste is the ideal, the untastable.

     THE FACT THAT you can hear, see, feel, doesnt mean that you have to listen, watch, suffer pain or enjoy pleasure; the fact that you can taste and smell is an attribute of your Universal Mind, not ne-cessarily subject to the causes and savors of the world unless you want it so.

     Life is an unreal ride. The starting point takes you to the terminal and all's forgotten and you dont even remember what made you start the trip at all. Einstein and Freud will analyze and explain, but the Fascist factories are manifestations of the Universal Mind and World Wars the crash of factories head-on, all better unborn in create-less essence, as at First.

When a scientist says "emotion" he means mystery, he means like the mystic mudra of the hand pointed up or down, (in the bleak), he means Unknown ---and that is why he dismissed "emotional concepts" (Einstein does) ---tho nothing is unknown, and mystery is a crystal. The metaphysics of the West are like a child in a trap.

     The Mountain is a pipi---
     And the divers all dove.
      Where did the rainbow go?

  Full of error and avarice--
   Go to with all your copper
    busts and cash deficits---

DIALOG BETWEEN MAN AND CHILDREN

   "Why is the mountain sitting there?" (man asks children)
   Jamie: "Because nobody's on there and we're not supposed to climb on
     it because the dirt'll fall off"

"Who made the mountain?" (man)
  They: "God made it"
  Man: "Who is God?"
  Cathy: "Us " And right then Cathy sayd: "He wants to play with the fence."
   Man: "Who?"
   Cathy: (showing Bear toy) "Me. Dont you know that I am Poo Bear?"

God is Poo Bear

The Book is of no importance

> Like in the fresh pure mornings early in life, is the realization
> that I may no longer depend on my senses and with it all differen-
> tiations and discriminations that are based upon sense-conceptions
> will be ended also-----(the unimportantly sore throat or cramped
> leg, the "God-God" doublebangbang thought I had one night which
> was my subconscious dharani-message accompanying this ignoring
> of "painful sense phenomena" and forget the pain awhile longer)

Name of a new disease: MESSIANA

Name: KEROUACWOT
     My sister the queen
     KEROUACVISTU AREMIDEIA (prophetic name)

They went thru primitive milleniums learning through kinghood what the 82nd Thousand Prince suddenly rejected in favor of Buddahood. The moment of Revelation under the fig tree had in it the seeds of all the past histo-ries of kalpaic kingdoms unnumberable, plus the forward blossom, the sprout of Intuition that would save the World from Eternal Fire by letting it be-come the intrinsic nature of Fire, the real emptiness. Meanwhile the Phralaong unborn Buddha resided as a preparatory Deva in the pearl heavens, full of anxiety for seed, arriving to self-aggrandizehood in firm physical dimension inside the conception-egg of the King and Queen of Kapilavistu named after a hut-dweller who provided a home for the sons of the King of Benares, the Capital of the World.

     078-833-368
     078-833-367
     078-833-369

  Thus is the perfection of ancient karma and of karma to come, but that it rots in pieces, and therefore who will abide by it in the mind?
  Brain struggleth, body ageth, Eternal Mind rest.
  Seventy eight (78) is the number of years that will enable me to reach the year 2000 A.D. 0-78 is the birth and death before it, and hint of zeros after it, and 0. 833 IS THE PRESENT MYSTERY. 367 to 369 is the rise in vibratory perfection to a hum and come, and divides in Threes the Saha Triple World of Suffering for dissolution in Mind.
  (Numbers are from Travelers Cheques)

The world is full of blind children.

Everything except the Tathagata Womb of emptiness is in ignorance, and Ignorance is of the nature of Emptiness, and everything is Emptiness----

The world of Triple Suffering is an accommodation in emptiness

The world
Everything is empty; mindfall is empty

People in the world are completely stupid, like poor animals and dogs

The world is actually empty and therefore I am empty, and my worries are
empty and my joys are empty too and my shit is a manifestation of emptiness;
my body is a heap of composites made out of emptiness-essence, combining
in a hassle to bother the very air and my Mind

My message is empty; my message is blah blah blah

PHILISTINE Interested only in wealth and material scorn but much to be
                                                                pitied

The people of India call themselves MAGADHA (s)

The Five Aggregates of Grasping

       1, body   2, feelings   3, perception
           4, mental elements   5, consciousness

"The Impermanence of (all) compound things" (including entity, or *atman*)
    Buddha broke from the Hindus, from the atman principle of soul transmi-
    grating eternally until Heavenly perfection; Buddha proclaims Nirvana
    of Nothingness beyond Heaven where the devas glory madly but suffer and
    are continually reborn because of falls and busts up there and drops.

"The individual transmigrates until the aggregates that compose him are
finally disintegrated with the cessation of craving" (Not an Anatman saying)

    NIRVANA MEANS Blowing Out

    PATICCA-SAMUPPADA is Chain of Causation, the 12 Causal States of the
    Individual, each one determining the next:

1. Ignorance		7. Feeling
2. Mental elements		8. Craving
3. Consciousness		9. Becoming
4. Mind and body		10. Birth
5. 6 Senses		11. Old Age
6. Contact		12. Death

SAMADHI   Mystic meditation, concentration
DHYANA   Trance, self-hypnotization
SAMAPATTI   Transcendental spiritual powers
SANGHA   Order of Buddhist monks
DHARMA,   or Sutra   The Law (the Dhamma, the Sutta)
NIKAYA   The discourse
MAHAYANA   Great career

HINAYANA   Small (or lesser) career
        Buddhism was split up into 2 sects with the advent of Christ influences
from the West; word was brought from Elia the prophet of John and carried on
dusty feet and in India the Hinayana (hitherto) Nirvana saints were told
that their endeavor was for the sake of the salvation of all mankind (all
sentient life, in India) ---the Mahayana believes in BODHISATTVA-MAHASATTVAHOOD
or, Seer practising meditation for the attainment of telepathic radiant
Womb of Eternity messages to enlighten all sentient life; the Hinayana,
saint, arhat, pratyeka, practising austerities and meditation for the
attainment of Nirvana and extinction of his self forever--- Ancient Hinayana
Buddhism, get on the ferry and go to the other shore and make it; reformed
  Mahayana Buddhism, get on the ferry and go and come back till all can make
it with you.

SRAVAKA   Disciple
Yana   Vehicle
SRAVAKA-YANA plus PRATYEKA BUDDHA   (private non-preaching Buddha) are
    mentioned together as Hinayana, "low vehicle"
DHARANI   Magic formula, or prayer
TANTRISM   repetition of magic syllables and names like BODHISATTVA-
                                        AVALOKITESVARA
SUNYATA   The doctrine of the Void
            (over which Han-shan and Shih-te did cackle as you and I)

TATHATA   Suchness

SUNYAVADA   System   The monk-scholar Nagarjuna wrote a doctrine of relativity
                    in 2nd Century A D "The truth of no individual fact can
                    be asserted because nothing is real apart from the
                    whole" ()
VIJNANA   Consciousness
MAHAR   A servile caste in the Deccan, India, scavenger, watchdog of village
            boundaries, messenger,--the Mahar Dog

        All sentient life is tortured--- the bird, the March wind, the twisted
branches, the wiggling gory-grackened-claw-pushing-into-Void leaves, the
inconceivable anxiety of clouds changing the light on hills, the twit wrung
out of the night bat's throat (night airmouse)...the wild outreach of the
boy's kite like a Sage's false hopes----life sending out its agony into
space and doesnt know what to do   Agony of all living things   The cold
clay earth, its huge camp of solidity----the disturbable water with haggard
bugs rushing out of the mud. . . . The motion of wind . . . The revolvement of the
spheres--- But Compassionate Tathatagata mourns

            The Moon of Sariputra is in
            Torment all the time
            A massive camp of cold clay.

ON THE BEST OF THE MODERN POETS
        "Emptiness is all that matters" means very specifically and scientifi-
cally that emptiness creates (or manifests, or projects) matter. My soul
is self-thought and was not, and will not be, when my discriminated function
of self-thought ends again on the other end of itself. If I "rage against
the dying of the light" I rage against the dying of the discrimination of
light and darkness, which are the conditions, born of Ignorance, making form

and shape and sight of matter possible. If I am grateful for the "mortality that can raise (a) perdurable voice against everybody's end" I am ignorant of the truth that emptiness is all that matters¿. I may then fall into the mistake of calling my torment love. So Dylan Marlais Thomas "counts (his) blessings aloud: Four elements and five/ Senses, and man a spirit in love . ." The 4 Elements the intrinsic nature of which is the actual emptiness pervading the Universe everywhere, but Moved to flow into molds of being and of transient obedience (as fire obeys the sun, the glass and the shavings); plus the 5 Senses, seat of my anguish and mistake, fivefold demons emanating from the Tranquil One in mockery of the Mirror; and "spirit in love" or, in ignorance and bondage to terrestrial concepts of good or pleasant or excellent (the notion of excellence an invidious distinction being made in secret to the secret heaven) (secret love of young at heart)---in all this the Dylan poet "freely he goes lost" celebrating his non-enlightenment with a Beethoven defy and Shelleyan Windblow. If torment is love then love is torment

               and all sentient life is in a tormented state which it calls
               joy and sorrow and which, when removed from before the Mirror
               of Emptiness, vanishes.
    Unwind the thread of the world to unborn ecstasy, for the soul is dead.

What difference, whether I say my eye is inner sight looking at its outer projections, or whether I say the phenomena of the world is reflecting itself off its own eyeballs made for the purpose of sight,----it is all the domain of Sight, the Seeable (Darkness) Matter and the (Light) Seeing, and all illusion, and therefore that explains Buddha's sayin "The essential nature of the inner perception of sight is reflection of outer sights" in so casual a way as tho it was all the same thing, which it is . . . *sight is matter, seeing itself by eye-Karma.*

MATTER clothed in all manner of
brightness and darkness seeing itself.

The hearing of that raindrop that I am doing is really motion blatting against itself out of stillness---if there was no such thing as "motionlessness"
   or "motion," "I" would hear nothing---"My" ear is both inner hearing listening to its outer projections, and the ear of the world vibrating against itself listening.

Because my ear is inner hearing listening to its outer projections, now I see my ignorance and method---its continual flow---
   Because I made the world I have to listen to it now---
The consciousness dependent upon the perception of the ear-organ makes me also see the raindrop (in mind's eye) smell it (in mind's nose), taste it, touch it . . . "raising wandering thoughts after every phenomena of sounds."
CONTROL THE MONKEY IN YOUR HEAD. . . . "a constant succession of receiving and projecting, causing and being effected."

THE SIX SENSES
CONFLICTING light and darkness deceive Mind Tranquillity and make you see

CONFLICTING motion and stillness disturb Mind Tranquillity and make you hear

CONFLICTING passability and impassability contaminate Mind and make you smell
                    (Inner perception of smelling reflecting outer odors)
                    (The world passing into itself smelling, equipped with nose)
CONFLICTING variability and invariability defile Mind Tranquillity and
            make you taste
                                    (world tasting itself upon its tongues; inner
                                    perception of tasting reflecting outer tastes;
                                    if you taste the flavorless, the untastable
                                    Essence is yours)

CONFLICTING separation and touching irritates Mind Tranquillity and makes
            you feel touch
                        (Inner perception of touching reflects outer contacts----the
                        world touching itself feeling equipped with body)

CONFLICTING Appearing and disappearing contaminates Mind and makes you think
                        (Inner discriminating thought reflecting conceptions of
                        individualized phenomena, or, simpler, inner thought thinking
                        of its outer perceptions, and what difference to say, the
                        world is thinking forth conceptions of itself, based on Ig-
                        norance and on the reciprocal continuity of appearance and
                        disappearance, birth and death, equipped with Mind?)
            Mind just another organ.

In either of the six cases "I" have nothing to do with it because I have
no Ego Self because my mind is only borrowed and only borrowable and in the
world of thought-conceptions only finite . . . is but a perception of an individualized concept within the whole roar of gold.

In all six cases the senses reflect Free Karma

In all 6 cases it's Inner Sense sensing its outer projection, or World
sensing itself with its sense-equipments, and so the perfect accommodation
to the free flow of all this (blank experimental) phenomena is like the
nature of its intrinsic being, Emptiness...perfect,free,whole,everywhere,
one-in-all....the flow continual and complete in imitation of the infinity
of emptiness.

            SIX SENSES
        1. The Seeable and the Seeing
        2. The Movable and the Hearing
        3. The Passable and the Smelling
        4. The Variable and the Tasting
        5. The Touchable and the Feeling
        6. The Conceivable and the Thinking

THE FALSENESS OF THE DUALITY OF MATERIAL AND IMMATERIAL
            Two Points   1. It is not an attribute of the solidity and firmness
                            of objects that you are not supermicroscopic and able
                            to wander thru them
                        2. Ignorance the first defilement (arising from the torment
                            and mistake of some Fall) creates the false conception
                            of individuation of Light and Darkness; by the contrasts
                            of these 2, form appears shape invested with matter

which perfectly out of emptiness accommodates the mold of being, just as
electricity leaps out of empty space to accommodate the cause-condition
axis of magnet and coil, or fire leaps to do the chemic bidding of sulphur
and motion; matter appears to be solid in its "filling" role but is in
reality emptiness accommodating ignorance and defilements fromof; matter
appears to be firm, but is physically interpassable ; matter is energy,
energy is motion, motion was stillness; all life in the world is as unreal
as that.

They say that something is of material value, and lay their hands
on a gold box, the intrinsic nature of which is the real emptiness accommodating to fill the molds of gold; they then distinguish between the value
of the gold box and the lack-value of an idea, a conception, the intrinsic
nature of which is the real emptiness of Infinity and Eternity accommodating
to fill the molds of thought; they then place their energy and trust inside the personal moment of this evaluation, and eat lunch in confidence;
but the intrinsic nature of the personal moment, the confidence, the ego
behind the confidence, the lunch, the energy and trust, and all the anxious stress and rising and disappearing of all their evaluating activity
is the real emptiness accommodating to fill the molds of little men. Lost
and blind they are, and very sad. The intrinsic nature of this very
statement is the real emptiness rushing to oblige a little tormented mold
better unborn and never said to never die.

Your natural tranquillity of Mind is contaminated by
rising, falling, borning, dying conceptions and images of
thought, the reciprocal restless saha flow continually sprout-
ing like in morphine visions and modern music, out of which
thoughts themselves grow, or,
"AND AGAIN BY MEANS OF THE RECIPROCAL CONTINUITY OF
APPEARING AND DISAPPEARING (BIRTH AND DEATH) YOUR NATURAL
TRANQUILLITY OF MIND IS CONTAMINATED AND MANIFESTS
DISCRIMINATING THOUGHTS . . . (THEY) REFLECT(S) THE
CONCEPTION OF INDIVIDUALIZED PHENOMENA"

And this thinking brain-organ has a mind, the consciousness dependent on it and upon the other 5 objects,
of seeing, hearing, smelling, tasting, feeling--the
Six are One.

BRAIN The physical mind organ
MIND the transcendental mind-organ

This great study of death . . . how continually ignore the perception of
contact, and how cease clinging to the notion-self of an ego-self
not dead but much still alive, how ignore the conception of death in
your karma bones---can you? Where a discriminating mind cannot take
up its abode, there is the dead. Death the golden age.

THE 4 FORGETTABLE TRUTHS (THAT I MUST NEVER FORGET)

   1. All Life is Suffering   INDIVIDUALITY IS PAINFUL
                      BIRTH   DECAY DEATH ARE PAINFUL

   2. The suffering is from Ignorant craving
                    LUST OF FLESH   LUST OF LIFE
                            PRIDE OF LIFE

   3. The suffering can be suppressed
                    DESTRUCTION OF CRAVING DESIRE

   4. The Way is the 8 Fold Path of Buddha

EIGHTFOLD PATH

1. RIGHT VIEWS---that all life is sorrow and suffering and torment in spite
             of occasional appearance . . . correct doctrines, free from
             superstition or delusion.

2. RIGHT ASPIRATIONS---Ambition to destroy suffering and ego, attain great-
             est happiness known to man as soon as possible-- A clear
             perception of nature of correct doctrines.

3. RIGHT SPEECH---Ask and answer necessary questions, speak to instruct,
             radiate mental peace and compassion in silence--Inflexible
             veracity, kindly, open, truthful

4. RIGHT CONDUCT---The 4 Precepts (dont kill, steal, lust or deceive)--No
             sloth and intoxicants--Purity of conduct, peaceful, honest,
             pure.

5. RIGHT LIVELIHOOD---Live alone in the open the ascetic life----beg from
             the charitable earth---Bringing hurt or danger to no
             living thing---A sinless occupation

6. RIGHT ENDEAVOR---Continual awareness loving all----energetic guard over
             progress---Correct efforts---Perseverance in duty---Effort
             in self training and self control

7. RIGHT MINDFULNESS---Avoid outgoing projecting multiplicity thoughts,
             anoint thee with incoming intuiting unified thoughts of
             Essence---Active watchful mind----Holy Meditation

8. RIGHT CONTEMPLATION---Daily practice of dhyana for the attainment of
             Samadhi and Samapatti and attainment of Highest Perfect
             Enlightenment for the sake of all sentient life---Earnest
             thoughts on the deep mysteries of life--Mental Tranquillity

BUD DOG VISION
                Mad dog buds in a tree, one attacks the other, which is me,
and kills it, but it doesnt matter because I am all the tree and
also the two buds, and of course also all non-tree in the universe,
so I dont worry or care or kick or mourn---the buds are in the first
notch
           Next instant I hear the babbling babe

HIGHWAY
         If you live on a highway, and after awhile you no longer hear the
cars passing in a continual flow, it's because the sense of their passing
was unreal in the first place---"You'll get used to it," is the saying,
meaning, you'll hear them only part of the time, when conscious of them
with the conjurative mind of the ear organ.

DAILY PRACTICE   Undo the world
                  And undo the messianic complex

Since you are the yard, the concrete, the sun, and the cat too dont annoy
the cat----Brindibindu is practising ascetism and dhyana better than you
--You are but a poor section of yourself which is everything in infinity
sensing itself---The cat, the bird he gricks to eat, the child's tap in
the window is all   One Substance like the lead of this pencil and the hand
hard and the mind that guide it'''_--in other words, rest, World.

         When you listen, listen as you were----Beware of becoming a good lis-
              tener and not in solitary life

The destruction of the craving to satisfy the passion for tasty food will
be easier when you cook your own tasteless meals

F o r

         there will be the Samapatti of Extermination of Thoughts and Desires
. . . When all smell, sight, sound, feeling, taste and thought are ignored, when
objects of sense experience are all ignored, then the transcendental brightness of intuition will shine forth mysteriously, your inner awareness will
become clear as a crystal manifesting its authentic brightness, all vagrant
thoughts and transitory objects and the ever varying phenomena of this
terrestrial world will melt away like ice when boiling water is poured
upon it and in a moment by a single act of true mindfulness your inward
awareness will become transcendental Samapatti intelligence apprehending
knowledge directly by intuition, you will become concentrated in Mind, you
will return to your natural Essence of Mind, because it will not derive its
discriminations and ideas by means of contact with objects in its presence
or in the order and limited manner of the senses, but the sense-conceptions
will become universalized and mutually available

FIGURE IS NOTHING, it is interchangeable, it is a shadow, emptiness in
                   essence fills it---it is subject to pain and death

"Speaking truly all expression referring to Mind (are) but figures of speech"

                    - - - - -
         The canny smile of listening
         Intuiting throughout the world---
         The transcendental perception of hearing
         And the imaginary tzimis sounds (transitory)
            Dont listen to anything because you're listening all the time
            anyway, Pure, Mysterious, Permanent, Essential
         Dont see or think anything for same reason
         Save yourself

PERSEVERANCE IN THE DHARMA OF NON REBIRTH
"The first knot of false conceptions that must be untied, is
the one relating to the false conception of an ego-personality, one
must first of all attain a realization of its utter non-reality.
When this realization of the unreality of one's own ego-personality
or another's is perfectly attained, then the next knot to be untied
is the one relating to personal attainments of any kind----this must
be fully realized----the two must be utterly destroyed and never
again permitted to rise to defile the true Essential Mind"

"ALTHO THE SIX SENSE KNOTS WERE MADE IN ONE MIND, THEY WERE NOT MADE AT ONE
TIME AND CANNOT BE UNTIED AT ONE TIME"

The gutty chiefs'll laugh among the empty reeds
eyeing the air they'll eat

Free will given complete rein results in success
Then rein in the stampede monkeys gradual

- - - - - - - - - - - - - - - - -
The Incomparable Teaching of the Lotus Flower
That, in the Essential Mind there is no such rising of an arbitrary conception such as that certain things are non-fantastic . . . is the greatest
teaching because it ends teaching---"as gloriously enlightening as the
diamond (vajra-raja), as mysteriously potent as Highest Samadhi . . . as suddenly as a rap on the door (is the coming of its stroke of enlightenment)
. . . the only path to Nirvana." For example, the perception of the discriminated-
as-good taste of pan fried chow mein by me is manifested under the conditions of tongue---THE TONGUE IS IGNORANT---The chow mein is just a pile,
but my fantastic conception of it holds it high, like the fantastic blossoms
seen in the air by clouded eyes. We have to interpret reality by false expressions and illusions of non-reality, by activities of the mind, even in-
tellectualism, but why raise these conceptions at all and thus sow the seed
of false thinking in the immaculate uncontaminated Alaya Vijnana essence
Mind. So as for the nature of emptiness inside empty reeds, my perception
of how good chow mein tastes is neither really non-fantastic nor fantastic:
my ignorance puzzles me in this saying, . . . Arbitrary conception of intellectual grasp destroyed hereby. Nothing matters---it doesnt matter.

Get rid of the contamination of valuing the taste of food""it's all the
    same in reality   Of hearing the sound of music or noise
Get rid of the contamination of valuing the taste of self_---it's all the
same in reality_---Of hearing the sound of yourself or others
The tongue is in a diseased condition
Eye sees fantastic blossoms in the air
Your ego-personality is a pile of shit
Raised high by your conception of it
Personal attainment is the working-out of
        this consequence of ego-birth, this fantasy,
            into the all-fantastic social world
Everybody rushing around selling their pile of shit
What difference is there between shit and gold?
Shit on gold---shit is gold---goldshit---shit.
A car has no shit when it loses its compression,
It is just a pile of shit
Shit on shit

And honor Mind.

SENSATION equals CRAVING equals GRIEF

"Betake yourselves to no external refuge"
"Look not for refuge to anyone besides yourselves"
"Hold fast as a refuge to the truth"
"Be ye lamps unto yourselves"
              --BOOK OF THE GREAT DECEASE, Mahaparinirvana Sutra

TIME
              The black sea of time across which I sail, my port death, my wake a
temporary opening of the foam and closing after, the waters uncharted, unmeasurable, formless, all the water already crossed of the same substance
and meaning the same to me the sailor as the water I see in the present and
the water that shall be crossed in the future----Therefore why give thought
to the three unbearable aspects of time, past-present-future, when they dont
make any difference to this traveler on this time-sea water--The intrinsic
nature of time is of the torment-essence, and the nature of torment is the
real emptiness.

RHYTHM
              Stop breathing for stillness and you'll hear your heart beat----being
sentient thou movest, and being of this world thou movest in rhythm, even
your pain is in rhythm (throbbing pain)---thus rhythm is the beat of torment

EATING
              Eating is where you devour "yourself"
              because you are ignorant that "not-self"
              is all One Self, the food is you and you it

              If emptiness was now and there was nothing to see, my eyeball would
              neither reflect outside objects, nor project its own inner light against
              the discriminating shadowiness of light-and-darkness in the outside uni-
              verse, and it could only see fantastic blossoms (arising from its
              diseased sentient becloudment) hung in colorless emptiness appearing
              like the world's final phenomena. This is all you can say of "Reality."
              How can there be Reality when there was Emptiness before it and will be
              Emptiness after it---? Reality is a speck in my eye, and my eye is going
              Perception and   Intuition sit in Emptiness eyeless.

SEEABLENESS AND SEEING are DARKNESS AND LIGHT---as ephemeral as that

              The sound of a hundred buzzing bees has now disappeared into my
Essential Tranquillity

HEARABLENESS AND HEARING are SOUND AND SOUNDLESSNESS
                                        MOTION AND MOTIONLESSNESS or STILLNESS
--as ephemeral as that

SMELLABLENESS AND SMELLING and PASSABILITY AND IMPASSABILITY
              The passable pieces of smelling that in their shadowy passage with
my light-of-eye microscopically I could see, now with my impassable
waiting perception-mind-nose of smelling I catch and contact and experience
and filter into consciousness: this is smelling, the smellableness passing
against impassable smeller-----as ephemeral as that

TASTABLENESS AND TASTING are INDIVIDUAL AND NON INDIVIDUAL
CHANGING AND CHANGELESS
VARIABILITY AND INVARIABILITY
(Shadow of tastableness against light of tasting)
The One unchanging Taster receiving, as light does, the reflection
of the shadow of Multiple changing Taste-Tathata Tasteness, upon its per-
manent invariable unchanging surface, and filtering it into Ignorance
Consciousness------There could be no ⎰ TASTING if everything in the
⎱ SMELLING
world were ⎰ CHANGING
⎱ PASSING at its maximum frenzy----no
⎰ UNVARYINGNESS
⎱ IMPASSABLENESS to catch the ⎰ CHEMIC VARIATION
⎱ PASSING PIECES   of a
⎰ TASTE
⎱ SMELL

There could therefore be no seeing if everything in the world were
seeable (SIGHT, dark) at its maximum frenzy----no light (no space, no
non-sight) to catch the filled-in figure (the sight) of an object---
SEEABLENESS PASSING AGAINST TATHAGATA SEER ...Shadow of seeableness
against light of seeing---

There could be no hearing if everything in the world were moving
at its maximum frenzy----no stillness to catch the soundwaves of motion

Therefore the seer is in possession of the mysterious enlightening
intuitive intrinsic radiant pure all-embracing Universal Mind Essence
indeed

The seer is light, space, emptiness, non-sight and
therefore non-torment
The world is darkness, earth, existence, sight and
all tormented
The seer understands the world
And understands beyond the world
And in dying surpasses the arbitrary dual
Conception of self and world
Seer and Sight
To go into communal Universal Fate
Of both self and world
As Intuition and Perception in Emptiness
Or, Nirvana
The end of the chain of Birth Death and Rebirth
The Salvation from the Twelve Causation Links
Attainment of frozen ecstasy in eternity
Self Illumined Rest forever
Which happens also to the CocaCola bottle
The bird
And the fool--
That is why Wisdom is Compassion
And why the Seer is happy in solitude.

FEELABLENESS and FEELING are CONTACT AND SEPARATION
                              TOUCHING AND UNTOUCHING
            ---As ephemeral as that, for there could be no feeling if every-
thing in the world were contacting and touching at the maximum all over
everywhere--no separation to catch the sensation of touch being applied---
      SHADOW OF FEELABLENESS AGAINST LIGHT OF FEELING
         TOUCH OF OBJECT AGAINST SPACE OF SEPARATION

      Touch coming in contact against that which was in a separated state
(the feeling-ness, or feeling-potential)---No sensation if no conception
of either contact or separateness, either feelableness or the feeling----
THE FEELABLENESS PASSING AGAINST SEPARATED FEELER.

THINKABLENESS AND THINKING are $\Big\{$ THOUGHT AND UNTHOUGHT
                                             BORN AND UNBORN
CONCEIVABLENESS AND CONCEIVING   BIRTH AND DEATH
                          are   APPEARING AND DISAPPEARING

-----as ephemeral as that.
      There could be no thinking if every thought in the world were appear-
able, conceived, thought, at its maximum frenzy----all at once so that
there is no non-thought-out and non-appeared, to catch and make conceiving
possible of the formed notion, the appearance of a conception---
            The very thinkableness and conceivableness of birth comes up a-
gainst the non-conceiving thoughtless of unborn, or dead, appearing whereat
was no appearingness---
         THINKABLENESS PASSING AGAINST TATHAGATA THINKER
         APPEARABLENESS PASSING AGAINST TATHAGATA APPEARER, appearance-maker
         CONCEIVABLENESS PASSING AGAINST TATHAGATA CONCEIVER

      The conceivable pieces of thinking that in their imaged passage with
my mind's eye I can see, now with my inconceivable waiting perception-mind-
brain of thinking I grasp and suffer to appear and experience and filter into
consciousness; this is thinking, the conceivableness passing against the unthinkable conceiver immaculate and unborn and dead.
            SHADOW OF CONCEIVABLE AGAINST LIGHT OF CONCEIVING
            SHADOW OF APPEARABLE AGAINST LIGHT OF APPEARING

   SIMPLY: There could be no thinking if everything in the world were being
               conceived of at its maximum frenzy----no unconceived to catch
               the appearance of a conception

SHADOW OF THE COMING AGAINST LIGHT OF THE GOING

            Only because I exist in this body of the 6 Senses, can there be the
conception of either and both fantastic and non fantastic, for as things
      ride in the uncontaminated invisible Sea of Eternity is beyond my bone
comprehension now, and't's death owns bones--
            It was a coming down of the Mind from its golden oneness dream,
just before birth, and the trick of deciding to see individualized pieces
of phenomena as separate and distinct in themselves in the scatter of the
Whole, and the waking-up of the brain to this work, and how we shall sleep
in golden light again deep within the Womb of Mind when this muddy kicking
up of our pure conscious water is done with---IMLADA! IMLADA! Svaha!

By living in solitude you will accomplish everything that there is in social
life and more.

> God is Self----get rid of one, the other----
> "He (God) doth himself contrive, enact, behold (the world)"---(Omar)
> like the dreamer of a dream in self-illusion clinging to images
> and conceptions and ego-ideas

LOVE

It's because they're in love with themselves that they want you to look
at them all the time and keep drawing your attention---in love with themselves
and not with you, for if they really loved you they would not disturb your
natural tranquillity-- Therefore the most beneficial teaching in this world
is the teaching by silence and example of silence and repose--- But some must
bake the bread, and some eat it, and the bakers are agitated---Bake your own
bread, calm baker--- If you dote on the love of a human being, every time you
disturb him to draw attention to your loving, you do him a disservice as of
hating---Beware of lechery and then beware of the conspiring earnestness. Be
(for that matter) like a junk drunk punk, hang motionless in the waiting for
time to wheel around. This is why a man doesnt need a woman, or a cigarette,
or a house. He needs just food for sustenance to keep him together for the
practice of emancipation from bondage to the world. Free will in the exercise
of his thought, and thought is the shadow of action, which is a shadow also.

FANTASTIC EMANATIONS FROM THE WOMB

* * * * * * * *

> The perfect realization that all the 100 Quarters
> of the Universes (the 3000 Chillicosms) are nothing
> but activities of the Tathagata Consciousness which
> has been opened to "me" and I may therefore call
> "mine"

NAMO-AMITABHA-BUDDHAYA
(Magic repetition name)

In all this senseless vibration, Amitabha's Mysterious Compassion

The way back is by the Buddhas---the Undisturbed Oneness, the Everything-Alright
of the universe having at its lightflashing essence center Mind & Compassion
finally----"earnestness and longing for deliverance in all sentient beings"---

MAGIC NAME of AVALOKI-TESVARA, the Hearer & Answerer of prayers

> A mistake has been discovered at the heart of the universe, and its name
> is existence---Man is first to be notified and enlightened with the clear
> duty---"Undo thou it!"

Highest Perfect Wisdom is ANUTTARA-SAMYAK-SAMBODHI

March 12, 1954, my birthday, I achieved transcendental understanding of the vibration of the universe by gazing at the sun in a precious purple stone---my eyes were injured and their sight impaired, a pink blotch covers them tonight, making the moon lavender and pink---but I saw the rhythmic torment of the sun vibrating for balance in Wholeness as it does in its component part, and how the rest of the Samsara Universe vibrates at different rates of speed---

DHARMA SOUND OF THE DIAMOND SAMADHI----Sound is vibration vanishing into infinity as shall this universe---but in the Diamond Samadhi it is the Essential Hearing of No-Sound that is "heard," the Intrinsic Buzz, or Non-Buzz Buzz, of Dharmakaya Essence residing everywhere invisible and moveless and silent . . . it "sounds" like the x-ray machine, like the sea, like the spheres revolving in infinity, like a sea-shell, like light

You study the sun and it'll destroy you, your eyesight first, but you study plants and you destroy them. The agriculturist and horticulturist is taking everything apart in eagerness to prosper, to *know* is the botanist's given reason; these cannot live without bringing hurt or injury to no sentient or plantient thing, "hurt or danger to no living thing."

So I'll just look with my little magnifying glass and see that nothing burns---

though, already, I've burnt a flowerbug with my glass

Nature is eating itself,
Individuality meets Whole.

Nature is like a woman,
Wears her best blossoms for a month,
Casts them aside
To rot and be eaten,
Then gives birth to the glorious male fruit,
The Yang who'll again come back
And fructify her Yin.

A tree is a woman
But the Sun is Man
Blazing high vibrations
Whither & whence uncaring
Towards horizon's golden
Moment Emptiness.

A cactus grove which has been desecrated of its fruit will feed you gladly like a woman, and hath thorns.

I am trapped in nature
I am expected to eat the blossom of the tree
Some reincarnated clothes fetishist
Chewing maniacally up the cloth of thought.

Nature is full of bullies who steal the little boy's kite.

Poem→ | Following the kite
The rope that you pay out
Diminishes in importance
As it hits the infinite   (watching Dick Woods fly his kite)

I'll go down to Mexico someday and live my own kind of healthy life---in hot
sun every day, good selfcooked food at night, early long sleep---A selfsufficient
practising Dhyanist in Mexico-----a selfish religionist resting-----a womanless
man of Tao-----a thinker-----an amateur botanist studying texts and plant life
harmlessly-----a novelist and teacher of the dharma-----only on trips to New
York or home headquarters of family and publishers shall I revert to the Machine
Age Orgonic Writer with the New Ribbon
               Handcopied Manuscripts Writ in the Wilds

Nature
Just because you shit fruit
Dont think youre the Kingpin of the World

    "Ignorance destroyed, then the constituents of individual life will die."

"Destroy contact, then will end sensation." ---BUDDHA CHARITA of ASVAGHOSHA

   (Ignorance is knowledge and names and things that notify the 6 Entrances
of the 6 Senses, which when ended, sensation ends, and contact's destroyed)

      DREAMLESS SLEEP (the Great Rishi's house) is the name of the great Dhyana
      whence, ("virtuous with care," "lustrous with all wisdom the great Rishi sat
      perfect in gifts)"

         To destroy clinging (upadana) destroy desire
         To destroy desire destroy sensation
         To destroy sensation destroy contact
         To destroy contact destroy 6 Senses

From the ANGUTTARA-NIKAYA (III) --- "On Delusion (avijja) depend the (life-
affirming) Activities (sankhara).----On the Activities depends Consciousness
(vinnana: here, rebirth-consciousness in the womb of the mother). --On consciousness depends the Psycho-physical Combination (nama-rupa).----On the psycho-
physical combination depends the Sixfold Sense-activity (chal-ayatana).---On
the sixfold sense-activity depends the Sensorial Impression (phassa).---On the
sensorial impression depends Feeling (vedana).----On feeling depends Craving
(tanha).---On craving depends Clinging to Existence (upadana).---On clinging
to existence depends the Process of Becoming (bhava; here: kamma-bhava, or action
process, or karma-action).----On the process of becoming depends Rebirth (jati).
---On rebirth depends Decay and Death (jara-marana), sorrow, lamentation, pain,
grief, and despair. Thus arises this whole mass of suffering. This is called
the noble truth of the origin of suffering."

      From MAJJIHIMA-NIKAYA   ---"Verily, because beings, obstructed by
                                          delusion and ensnared by craving, now
                                          here, now there, seeking ever fresh delight,
                                          therefore it comes to ever fresh rebirth."

   By myself is known: "Deliverance gained"
                  "All is done"
                      "The highest wisdom"

"Practice, then, brotherly love, kindness, patience, long suffering, and
gentleness"---EDGAR CAYCE

For the Layman: "The heart of the sons of men is
full of evil, and madness is in
their heart while they live, and
after that they go to the dead."

and

"Go thy way, eat thy bread with joy, and drink thy
wine with a merry heart; for God hath already accepted
thy works. Let thy garments be always white; and let
not thy head lack oil. Live joyfully with the wife
whom thou lovest all the days of thy life of vanity,
which He hath given thee under the sun, all thy days
of vanity: for that is thy portion in life, and in
thy labor wherein thou laborest under the sun.
Whatsoever thy hand findeth to do, do it with thy
might; for there is no work, nor device, nor knowledge
nor wisdom, in Sheol, whither thou goest"

--ECCLESIASTES

You have to do nothing
Do-nothing you have to do

Steal not the other man's Substance
Or yours will surely sicken----
What kind of losing is that
When you accidentally
Give a little?
What kind of gaining
When on purpose you plot
To keep a lot --?
Gravestones in New York
Commemorate the Grave
Of Walt Whitman.

Have nothing to do with results.

Layman, listen, however, "The path to religion is trodden by saints," and
this is said in the BHAGAVAD-GITA

Practise kindness in a restful life
An Accident may help you remember what youre doing
Home in Heaven, Joy is the Way

The Bodhisattva of Tenderest Compassion, is AVALOKITESVARA, the Hearer &
Answerer of Prayer

Forgetfulness acts fast to rob us of our gains in enlightenment. It's to
learn to need nothing, becoming beyond nothing, that we now're learning to die.

Dwight Goddard said of Asvaghosha's AWAKENING OF FAITH, a commentary on the Mahayana Shradhotpadda Shastra (SHRAD-HOT-PADDA SHASTRA), that anyone reading it "awakened a pure faith . . . and would enter upon the true path."
"My first and main purpose" (in writing it, Asvaghosha said) "was to save all sentient beings from suffering and to bring them to eternal happiness"

>Have all my royalties donated to the Sisters of Charity
>and accept donations of food from anyone

BETTER BE KIND THAN TRUTHFUL

Hinayana Buddhism was the original version, was said to become reformed by advent of Christ ideas from the West.
     Here are examples of Hinayana philosophy from the Dhammapada, with my interpretations :-

>The great shitty animals of the barn; the long drawn
>milk curdles in your nose when you walk around the
>barn; like burning rubber on a gray windless day the
>smell of a deed follows you; the wind blows both away;
>wind blows you the leaping flame too.

>"An evil deed, like newly drawn milk, does not
>turn suddenly; smoldering, like fire covered by ashes,
>it follows the fool."

Also from Dhammapada: "He who knows that his body is like froth, and has learned that it is as unsubstantial as a mirage, will break the flower-pointed arrow of Mara (the devil), and never see the king of death. . . . Death carries off a man who is gathering flowers, and whose mind is distracted, as a flood carries off a sleeping village."

"Few are there among men who arrive at the other shore (become Arhat saints for the sake of attaining Nirvana and thus vanishing from this valley of darts); the other people here run up and down the shore."

>"There is no suffering for him who has finished his
>journey, and abandoned grief, who has freed himself
>on all sides, and thrown off all fetters."

>"How is there laughter, how is there joy, as this world
>is always burning?"

"He whose conquest cannot be conquered again, into whose conquest no one in this world enters, by what track can you lead him, the Awakened the Omniscient, the trackless?"

>"A wise and well-behaved man who knows the meaning of this
>should quickly clear the way that leads to Nirvana."

And thus leave---in Mahayana it is asked that you consent to rebirth in order to take part in the Bodhisattva-Mahasattva struggle to emancipate all sentient life; from this arose the Sangha, the 3 Gems, etc.

>Rest, Be Kind

The little lightflash specks that come on and off in the form of orgones
are as proofs of compassion at the heart of the Great Dharmakaya Universe.
(Cup eyes with fists and look at clear blue sky to see orgones flashing
and prickling everywhere in electrical phenomena)--

-- Everything is furling back around the cavern over your sight, like
  stormclouds in from the sea, and so you imagine there to be "space"
  and all the differentiated things to be disposed in different parts
  of it; but actually everything is in the same place, the Center of
  Essence. For the purposes of life on earth, though, space and
objects do exist; for the purposes of life on earth we write and
read, as here.

>   Fragrance comes & goes
>   But smelling is permanent

Noxzema and Peanut Butter are of the same intrinsic nature, but for
the purposes of life on earth dont go tasting them to compare; leave
that to non-discriminating infants fresh from eternity.

Whenever Buddha calls me "novice" I feel like a "patient"---

NOTHIN TO DO BUT DO THINGS RIGHT

> KARMA   Everything that you got you had
>   Everything that you didnt got
>   You didnt had
>   And the aggressive pusher
>   Who shoved you out of his way
>   To get what he thought he needed
>   Rots in the same soul
>   And in the same soil
>   As you, O Saint

As Ecclesiastes inescapably puts it: "As it happeneth to the fool,
                                            so will it happen even to me;
                                            and why was I then more wise?" --0.12
          Because all living things are of the same essence.

As far as ordinary life in America is concerned, for 2,000 years and much
more than that old Indian mothers pounded cornmeal for mush in the hopeless
drizzle of history here in North America; why should we therefore question
ordinary simple life of eating, sleeping, keeping a shelter, in the name of
"Modern" needs such as automobiles, washing machines, expensive clothes, up-
to-date furniture and cultural excitements like TV and movies and every kind
of unreal hassle to kill time and with all its attendant ambitions? What
advantage is there in multiplying need? REST AND BE HAPPY

>   Learn to be bored and unhigh and unexcited or leave this world---
>   What's fame and fortune but a big nervous binge? What have you
>   got to do with what any of your friends think, Paisan?

Jewel sleep of Wisdom

>   Always swimming ahead in new time is frightening, because we cling
>   to arbitrary conceptions of ourselves and of something happening
>   to those selves, and all of it is tormented and unpredictable and sad.

IMLADA THE SAGE A little tale by Jean-Louis

In the honey-scented land of Mominu, in a buttercup field, Imlada the Sage, sitting with his feet crossed under him, put thumb and forefinger to his eye and looked at the blue sky in restful comfort. Facing south in the afternoon, he blocked off the sun from his eye cavern. He allowed the spots before his eyes to wander off, for he knew they were just blossoms projected from the surface of his sentient beclouded eyes making little shapes in the air. Immediately he saw the swarm of electric prickles occupying everywhere. They flashed on and off and vanished he couldnt see where. They manifested themselves anywhere at any time, agitated as sperm. He would hear them soon. In his practice of meditation he would soon achieve the Diamond Samadhi and hear them beyond the sweetness of his no-sound-hearing. If he tried to follow they disallowed it and all vanished. Because he was not focusing on the travelling spots before his eyes, he was at rest staring, but whenever he strained to follow an orgone prickle-spark he focused his sight but lost his mind. His mind was nowhere to be seen either, but only everywhere. Therefore he knew that Infinity was his for Eternity and that his Mind was not his but belonged to Infinity and Eternity radiating triangularly from his triangular sitting base to all quarters of the universes. The lights that were flashing, were of a bright radiant essence and were each one messages of kindness from the mysterious sleep of Mind Essence, the Golden Dharmakaya.

"The Tathagatas are singing to me from the middle of the universes," he uttered on the impulse of seeing the wink of the little lights in the blue sky in his cupped hand, and he looked up to see who had heard him. He remembered his former lives with remorse, and alone at the foot of the Great Mountain the tears came to his eyes and just then a cloud passed over the sun, and immortal snowy clouds of Mominu in the plateau afternoon swarmed about, and the grass turned gray and the lining of the cloud was on fire, and he sat at rest realizing that all he had to do was be kind.

He radiated his message of the kindness of the essential mind of the universe to a former self of his, John Kerouac of America, who just then was sitting on the edge of a bed in despair. "Be kind," said Imlada, and his former self realized the message and almost cried for joy.

"In the isles and palms of Cato there is no pedant of leisure more wise and more happy than this hulk of bones Imlada facing the coming of the cold mountain night with robe and begging bowl," said Imlada, and rose to his body's needs.

Birds sang sweetly and with great variation as he descended the hillside to the path to the Little River Village for the begging of his supper.

At the roadside shrine where the grain of rice had been established by a descendant of the Wonderful Lotus King and was now believed to be the elephant that bore the pearl of the world globe by many of the superstitious old farmers around Little River Village, Imlada met the sage Big Saint; a descendant of the Massive family, noted for their hugeness of physique, and together, robes blowing in the deepening evening wind of late raw red afternoon, they descended to the daub huts of the Little River Village.

A beautiful maiden with a bowl on her head and one arm curved to uphold it, passed in short footsteps before them. Imlada was staring into the mirror-like essence of his own essential sight when her substantiality imprinted itself as upon water upon his perception of sight; but he only believed her figure to be interchangeable, as figure is, and empty, without self-nature, born of emptiness, and saw her as a hole cut in the sky interchangeably presenting its transitory appearance-form; her convex breasts became concave hollows, and so forth, in the empty air. She passed out of his fixed sight. Further, he clenched his teeth and pressed his tongue hard against them, to avoid the thought of lust. Meanwhile the Big Saint did not notice her existence due to a predilection for strong young men, whom he, too, sought to avoid and perceive as tormented karma-shapes wandering and erroring in the void for nothing; beautiful only insofar as the skeleton cannot be seen, or the bloated corpse, in time, which is of the essence in all component things and also all things never born. The girl meanwhile was deep in her own thoughts about Tramo, the lad of the village Market who sold potatoes and pure milk of the mufee plant in front of the village bandstand, and who had just addressed a beautiful smile at her for the first time. She turned into her house and set the bowl of cornmeal down on her mother's pounding-stone when through the narrow clay window she saw Imlada and Big Saint rounding the corner with their robes pressed against them in the dusky breeze. "My father is gone to Trachekk for the Monastery," she thought, innocent at fifteen and in her kindly little femaleness of the sorrows staining the hearts of serious matured and already decaying men making them seek after religion and taking voyages to find the Unlocatable, the Everywhere, the Mysterious.

Presently Imlada and Big Saint were given rice and meat and mangoes at the home of the horse-owner, who complained about his horses, but was told of the Dhaniya Sutta, which calmed him.

"I have finished my meal," cried Imlada imitating the crying song of Daniya the cowherd who dwelt in the hilly country of Videha and owned no less than 30,000 head of cattle, "I have collected the milk; I am living peaceably on the banks of the Mahi, surrounded by my wife and children; my house is roofed, the fire is kindled. Rain on now, O cloud! if you will. Thus said the cowherd Dhaniya. Buddha heard these words at Jetavana, and, wishing to lead Dhaniya and his family to Nirvana, appeared in the skies over them as radiant as a phosphorescent rose in an arbor of dark leaves, and sang the answering stanza: I am free from anger, free from stubbornness; I am living for a night on the banks of the Mahi; my house is roofless, the fire is extinguished, Rain on now, O cloud! if you will. Thus said Bhagava the Buddha."

And thus Big Saint and Imlada the Sage, gathering their bowls, took their leave of the horse-owner's house, and returned to the mountain as it was seen over the highest ridge that the Moon of Sariputra would soon appear, yellow and huge. The lights of the village could be seen below.

Imlada the Sage paced an hour in the night, before retiring, his last thought being, "Tomorrow I shall wake at the break of day."

And Big Saint likewise.

And the moon rose high, white, bright, and bats cried in the tree above Imlada's sleep, and little mice breathed and snored in the depths of the cactus grove.

* * * * * * * * * * * * * * * * *

Tonight March 25 1954 in San Francisco I attained suddenly the Diamond Samadhi
which is the buzz of my intrinsic hearing, the pure liquid accommodating
vibrating sea-hush stuff that receives imprints of transitory sounds and
g-l-u-r-s them till finally I began to hear as on cocaine the roar of many
things----I thought up till now that there would never be an actual breakthrough
to the other world to support my belief----This transcendental Diamond Samadhi
experience has been my first intimation from Dharmakaya's Silent Realms that
all the Tathagatas are indeed there in Regnant Radiance waiting to Enlighten
the world and wake it from its mad mistaken dream of rue and rage...

A DISCIPLINE I WROTE OUT FOR MYSELF (IN FRENCH)

  1. L'intuition essentiale
  2. Le Ti Jean essentiale   (qui figure en Français)
  3. L'homme essentiale de pureté   (looking out of aftersupper window,
                                            washing dishes)
  4. Chez nous Français   (table ronde dans cuisine)
  5. Repos dans la vie   (un bon lit)
  6. Les petites amusements temps en temps
  7. Écriture essentiale de toute ma vie; instruction essentiale
  8. Dhyana toute les jours
  9. Lire, étude, et musique
10. Pas d'ami sou ou haut ou insincere

(this is not of much importance because too much attached to worldly ideas)

> In your own imagination there's something to live for-- if not in
> the "real world"---That's why outside events are really unreal.

Make simple people's earthy mentalities the discipline by which you keep
your explanations of the Dharma clear.

> Clear as the blue sky is the perfect accommodation of my
> intuitional camera registering scenes in the visions of
> this dream, in my lifework teaching-book to come.

All your life you lose, and then you die
And lose the losing too

> The light of the unborn is visible in the radiance of the Ocean-wide
> Dharma eye---I, born, am as shadow going before the light and space
> of the unborn, and will join that host when I have attained to the
> uttermost refinement of Nirvana either for or not for Bodhisattva-
> Mahasattva reasons, Hinayana Traditional Buddhism or Mahayana Reformed.

WE'RE SWIMMING IN THE UNBORN, BORN

But I hope not to be reborn because I dont want it utterly and am begun
on the effort to blow out my self like a candle.

"OM! OH, THOU WHO HOLDEST THE SEAL OF POWER--RAISE THY DIAMOND HAND--BRING TO NAUGHT--DESTROY--EXTERMINATE!

OH--THOU SUSTAINER--SUSTAIN ALL WHO ARE IN EXTREMITY!

OH--THOU PURIFIER--PURIFY ALL WHO ARE IN BONDAGE TO SELF!

OM!--MAY THE ENDER OF ALL SUFFERING BE VICTORIOUS!

OM! OH--THOU PERFECTLY ENLIGHTENED--ENLIGHTEN ALL SENTIENT BEINGS!

OH THOU WHO ART PERFECT IN WISDOM AND COMPASSION EMANCIPATE ALL BEINGS
AND BRING THEM TO BUDDHAHOOD! OM!"

It must have been a cruel idiot who made the world, made life,---composite units that decompose and suffer in their consciousness of transitoriness and pain--a hell of a joke on us--Playing it on ourselves--we the Dharmakaya

GREAT POEM

The sun is a big wheel
And cosmic particle's a little wheel
And I'm a medium wheel

My vibration is on a motor vegetable level
And the sun on a million-yeared gaseous pulse level
And cosmic particle lasts a second, owns a tiny wheel
And the solar wheels
  And the swing of my wheel
Engulf and circumscribe it.
  Essence of Hearing
  Hears vibration
    Of all wheels and levels everywhere.
    S-h-h-h-h-h-h it sounds like.

I KNEEL BEFORE THE DEAD
 I flopped his dead arm.
  "He's gone," I thought.
"He came and grew this body,
Then he went away.--

Where is he gone to?
I dont think he'll return,
Not if he's smart.
He saw it wasnt worth it.
He came once, he lasted,
        he was like a light
Extinguishable in 60 years.
Me, too my arm'll be dead.

Now he sees me sitting, in thought.

It's hard for him to understand my body,
The spaces and the big wheels---
I wont see him any more
In those high vibrations
But it'll be all the same
Farewell, farewell,
And farewell to farewell,
This is the shrouded traveller,
And shadows in the jazz age."

* * * * * * * * * * * * * * * * * *

   Souls vibrate and are on a wheel of about seventy years, and then disappear forever. That's why the Soul is Dead. The reason for the vibration of
the universe is so that it will not fall. It itself will fall, its wheel being
vast but limited space-travel bound round by roundness the crud of time, ready
to erode in the windless eternities of essence silence emptiness dead; world
has been wished forth by Ignorance and to ignorance returns inert, husk---no
reason given.
         REASON IS NOT GIVEN---JUST INTUITION

   And so, as Rabelais, as Omar knew, as Demosthenes knew, life has a rosier
   hue when you drop the grape into the belly---*life* the tormented dreamform

How I love my father! How can you love something so phantasmal that doesnt
exist?---how can there be something so phantasmal and inexistent as love? What
is this compassion in a world of wheels and vibrations and levels? What is man
who groweth a heart?

         Of course I admire brilliant erudite queers---I admire
         all good things---I admire holes in the clouds----

         DEAD DONT RISE FROM DIRT

   For the same reason that I came 3000 miles to California I should
   have stayed home---for the reason that nothing is real. That was
   the overdoing of Buddhism in Jan.'54

And he grew that heart-- Beyond life and beyond this world, in Dharmakaya's
     Golden Silent Essence, Imageless, Serene, "What is there to praise?"
                              ---Lankavatra Scripture

             Life is a defilement of Mind Essence---
             There's the frog-defilement
             And the chicken-defilement
             And mournful fish sucking water
             And the defilement which is man;
             Emancipation from form
             Is the return to mind essence,
             Emancipation from ego self
             Manifested by the body one grows
             And its consciousness of feelings
             And its complaint with the mind.---

Everybody's yelling "Not me! Not me!"
And pointing at the "External
Enemies of mankind,"
As if the Devil existed
  And God the Indian Giver
Dead in a petulant grave.

When you feel depressed and you wanta go here, wanta go there,
remember Mind Essence; the world, like dreams, will never come
true. Operate on Intuition, Rest and Be Happy. IT'S ALL IN
YOUR HEAD WHAT HAPPENS SO YOU MIGHT AS WELL THINK HAPPINESS

Use the shadows of the born
The shapes of the world
And pass them before the light
Of imagination's birthless ecstasy

A lotus blossom
instead of a cathedral
create
An ethereal flower
In the sky.

Airy, graceful, ethereal flower,
As ungraspable as dreams,
As solid as the actual world,
As mysterious as perception,
As clear as crystal sight;
Dont even notice the world
But use it for your flower;
Give the flower to the priest
And he will give you food.

You dont have to go to London
            and get high legally
To change heads.

ALL YOU HAVE TO DO IS DO THINGS RIGHT ---- Quietistic

Look and Close Your Eyes

Insincere and sad
The world's a farce
To stand and sneer at
On the corner of
    Snark & Phnark
        (Last Stanza of the Poem " Neal in Court ")

I am Buddha come back in the form of Shakespeare for the sake of poor Jesus
Christ and Nietzsche . . .

    . . . I'll become an Intuitional farmer . . .

TRAGIC CONSCIENCE is non-materialistic. Freudians, Marxists, Existentialists
dont understand the Tragic Conscience, because they are led to believe in gain
and advantage in this life, which I fail to see in this sea of decay & misery.
What boots it Lenin in a cold cold crypt? Old age when youth wants love? Shifts
to sneak around the bare truth that all comes to Naught, to Zero; suffers in a
wild dear shape a few dozen years, aging, causing dismay and disgust, becoming
loathsome and an example to philosophers, a subject of keeners, and all because
paternal soul hung on and genes matured in the karma house of womanhood. An end
of birth---birth obliteration---is needed in the Jazz Age, or the bombs will burst
on many. Bleak, blank and meaningless we were dragged here screaming---

> in pain, screaming again,
> we'll be dragged away
> and thrown
> to the Crocodiles
> of immensity.

> But let a perpetual smile
> of peace and satisfaction
> On your lips
> Be a symbol of the decision
> To think happiness (equanimity)
> Since everything that happens
> Happens in your head.

* * * * * * * * * * * * * * * * *

> If the Hydrogen Bomb disintegrates the entire world,
> I would say it was Appearance-Body of Dharmakaya
> (Nirmanakaya-Dharmakaya)
> Because of its Universal Salvation
> Leaving no blemish of birth or pain

"Only madness could lead to war," says Eisenhower and everybody goes mad and
fears the H Bomb---and the only way to avoid this madness, dont be afraid
about death.

> Rational Materialists, in their long attempt to overcome death
> have become afraid of death; religious traditionalists havent
> moved, or changed, or invented any H Bombs.

Be solitary.
Cats are not kind but those who kill cats are fiends without hope,
due to be reborn as brutes and ghosts; beware of them.

"Pagani"***means countryfolk---Jesus was of them, as of the Bedouin---it was
for the Fellaheen to ignore Him---in India as well as Palestine---

> The Saoshyant
> Enosh
> Barnasha
> "Bright fruitful inwardness" (Spengler)--(of Jewish prophet times)

> Theotokos--- she who bare God

"The Aramaean motherland"--- Which leads to the Russian motherland and the

Aramaean springtime propounded by Dostoevsky's Saints
and formularized by Spengler

Marcion of Sinope, Mithradatic Kingdom, was a political failure in religion
as Paul was a political success; but Asvaghosha made no such dualistic distinctions when he wrote Awakening of Faith and the Buddha-Charita, for love.

Paraclete is the Comforter

The 3 Prophets and the 5 Buddhas

1. Elias   1. Kaukasan
2. Jesus   2. Gaunagong
3. Paraclete   3. Kathaba
                  4. Gotama
                  5. Aremideia (Burmese Five)

Paraclete: Vohu Mano, meaning Spirit of Truth, in the shape of the Saoshyant

THE FOUNDER OF BAHAISM WAS MIRZA ALI MOHAMMED . . . executed in Tehran 1850

Paradosis: means word-exegesis, allegorizing
GNOSIS . . . means metaphysical introversion, apocalyptic certainty, which
        Jesus, Allah and all the Tathagatas have

EPIPHANY (from EPI, upon, PHAINO, I appear) means manifestation

----

AREMIDEIA AND THE PARACLETE
Religious Fancies for Western Believers
    Even if reincarnation is true it doesnt matter, the question being: am I
or am I not God? And being God, am I or am I not All? And being in a human
body, is All or is not All available to me? And how much of the All do I own?
All of it. Am I or am I not the same you, in human body form, and understanding
that All is everywhere, making everything, therefore making you and me, therefore
I am you and you are me? Are you or are you not therefore, God? Why is the All
throbbing in you, a pan of itself revolving through your conglomerate of bodies
in a body, your molecular universes in a molecular cluster in motor vegetable
form? Am I or am I not saved, because I am God and may save myself? Can I or can
I not save thee? Can you or can you not save me? Svaha, saved.
    And now to death, that owns my bones and ego; now to that which is me and owned
by me, Truth of Death, all of which owns me, bones and all, and all of me without
form vibrating nameless and no-longer-me in the All which is all of mine in the
sense that being All, I knoweth All. The soul is dead. Death is truth. I am
God. I have no self. God has no self. It's a dream. It's a visionary flower
in the air.
    If reincarnation is true, it means that your ego has been around in differ-
ent forms and acting according to type, which is merely a shift of hereditation
from dung-body to dung-body soon said to be husk to husk, in no case it being
that personality you would designate the same as yourself now, the variation of
snowflakes is infinite. If you were born 5 times before then why werent you born
20,000,000,000,000 times before everywhere, and what is the sum of your sins? and
how long can you last in the punishment of death and rebirth, pain and doom; death

and rebirth, pain and doom; death and rebirth, pain and doom; no, sweet escapee, thou'st released thyself from that cage just this once to come, for though the prison may be vast the prisoners are numbered, and when return, return afresh non-remembering from the universal mind which did not individuate and suffer limit in a form, but was All. If you say your youth was spent by someone other than the you which is now, how can you be the same even when non-remembering a previous life? Goodbye to each of you, chips on the ocean of mortality, abandoned be you all to the dogs of eternity; never fear; beyond fear is nothing, is All, is your safety, your hope, your ecstasy, for thou art God in a temporary human cage hassling; you are the Messiah and now you are with me the Paraclete. Be comforted.

Rest and be happy. Be kind to those that deserve it, and to those that do not, say goodbye, "I am going away," and say, "Why dont you want to realize that you are God and there is no need for you to trespass against yourself, which is also me; why dont you realize that the universe is empty finally, and was empty and is empty all around us now, and will be empty and was empty all around us then and inside All? And because the world is empty, why dont you want to realize that nothing matters, it doesnt matter? Cling you to the notion that you are other than me because of your body? Then embrace me and see, embrace me and feel---all is one, one is all. For you trespassed against my living soul, which is dead around, and bound in death the Truth, because your soul you presumed to wield eternally from life to life grasping at racket groans and stinky, pop eyed to find your greedy need excited, splurge monies and blood across tables of the world, win the favor of courtesans whose favors are so sweet and are so easy? for which cause brother behooves brother to lay down slain? How can you act like that when Eternity passes through you from Everywhere, the emptiness of all belongs to me which is you which is everyone which is all? Go down and fish your reasons up, the walls of your house, the thighs of your daughters will crumble; your mother's bones will be mixed with the Aeon slime; and your father's arm has fallen long ago, like trees in antiquity; fill not your cup with vain and gray ambition, your eyes with heat, vanity, corruption and money-rot----fill it with wine of happy kindness, for death has your bones but Truth has all of you, O Truth, O Man, O Solitude, O All, O Death."

Act and be kind.

For the purposes of this world, believe.

For the purposes of the next, the only, the Vast and All world, believe.

For the purposes of All, be you God.

If you understand this, you are God; if you do not understand this, you are God; if you are not God, you dont exist; if you dont exist, nothing exists; if nothing exists, all, everything exists anyhow; it makes no difference whether all or nothing exists, or comes and goes; it makes no difference whether you or I, or noeither of us, exist; it makes no difference to say "God exists" or "God doesnt exist"; it makes no difference whether this is understood or not; it makes no difference whether you are, or are not he who is God; whether God is or isnt; whether he is all, or not all; whether he is all, or nothing at all; it makes no difference, difference, and the making of difference. For the purposes of this world, it makes no difference whether you believe in All or do not believe in God, All; in Truth, Death; it will happen anyway, but only as a vision, and it will only seem to happen, and it wont really happen, because, you, it, and all things, and all conceptions of you, it, and all things, are but a visionary flower in the air. Since it's all in the mind, all in the emptiness of all, that it will or will not happen, that you will recognize yourself as God, or not.

But that you will fear about death, this is a grief; that you will die of pain, that is the truth; that your ego will be ruined in the grave, that is so; that you will not be comforted in life, that is sad. Yet all this is visionary flowers in the air. But rest and be happy for yourself. Be kind and have a good time. Smile in your belly. Let your muscles fall away, sit and think, dont move for a long time, concentrate on breathing in and out. Find your life inside, your all, the all, see yourself the universe infolding all.

Watch the light in your closed eyelids and also in your open eyeballs. Listen to your ears in the silence. Forget your body. Forget it awhile. Close the door of body and go in the room of mind a few minutes, an hour, six hours. Compassion is hiding in you; and the understanding of all things, which are as a visionary flower in the air, is hiding in you, which in itself is a lovely visionary flower in the air. Anyway beware of the hypnotists, beware of the intruders. Be afraid of the fools, the maniacs, and as you would be afraid of vicious fighting birds screaming at your ear, though even they are visionary flowers in the air. Beware of the shrouded traveler, death with his hood and flowing cape, disguised as pain, pursuing you in deserts and in hallways of this life. Be afraid of pain, as you would of the conception of a visionary flower in the air. Men are not to be trusted when it comes to trustworthy dealings in objects of possession and pride; throw them in the sea of essence. Doom is sure. Men do everything wrong on purpose, with a little smile; this will be seen to be so in the end; but the intentions are actually good and even saintly and friends are really well meaning friends, if you can stand it, or stand to believe it in your final mind. But life is a curse, not worth living, and the sooner over the better, easy or hard it's all the better over. Beware of mistakes in the horror of this nightmarish flower in the air; radar machines in the sky are hiding; atomic bombs destroyed Atlantis; locomotives are crashing everywhere; the eye is on fire, the mind is on fire, the conception of the eye and the mind being on fire is on fire. Believe in yourselves, one by one. Be God, that is. Dont let accidents make you realize what you're doing, lest they come and you realize. Be afraid of old age; it is not good; be afraid of decaying youth, it is not good; be afraid of beautiful youth, it is not good, and snaky. Only death is good, and death is all.

I am Paraclete the Comforter and these are my words, and these were my words and these will be my words. I am the Third Messiah. And you are the Third Messiah.

I am Aremideia, the fifth Buddha in this kalpa. Twenty-eight Buddhas come. Deinpakara was eighty cubits high and lived a hundred thousand years, and was the fourth of the twenty-eight last Buddhas. After me, and Gotama, and Kaukasan, Gaunagong, Kathaba, come twenty-four nothings in the reverse direction, and nothing matters, it doesnt matter. And you are Aremideia, the fifth Buddha in this kalpa, O my son, O my daughter, O my brother, O my sister, O my father, O my mother, O my friend and cousin on this earth.

I am Allah. Thou art Allah.

I am Silver Fox, creator of the world. Thou art Silver Fox, creator of the world.

I am Paraclete the Comforter, and you, the Paraclete, the Comforter.

Bahia, let it be. Be all for yourself, be God. You are All.

AREMIDEIA THE PARACLETE

* * * * * * * * * * * * * * * * * * * *

The city of the Gandharvas which "appears in a vision owing to the attachment to the memory of a city preserved in the mind as a seed," mentioned by Buddha, must have a relation to the Yage City Visions of jungle Indians in William Lee's Peru---"the city can thus be said to be existent and non-existent."

> "A wheel of fire made by a revolving firebrand which is no
> wheel but which is imagined to be one by the ignorant . . .
> (cannot be said to be) not-a-wheel because it has not been
> seen by some." (!) --LANKAVATRA SCRIPTURE

ONENESS & OTHERNESS--"Not that one, the other!"
BOTHNESS & NOT-BOTHNESS--"Not both, just one!"

Form is the horror of the world; emptiness is its substance, to which
everything "happens"--- "Because of folly (the ignorant) do not understand
that all things are like Maya, like the reflection of the moon in water, that
there is no self-substance to be imagined as an ego-soul and its belongings---
what . . . exists . . . only . . . is seen of the mind itself."

"They feed on multiplicities of objects and fall into the notion of an
ego-soul and what belongs to it"----Clinging, there is "a reversion to ignorance,
and Karma born of anger, greed & folly is accumulated. As the accumulation goes
on they become imprisoned in a cocoon of discrimination and are thenceforth unable to free themselves from the round of birth and death."

IT'S ALL THE SAME

"They do not realize that things have nothing to do
with qualified and qualifying, nor with the course of
birth, abiding and destruction, and instead they
assert that they are born of a creator, of time, of
atoms, of some celestial spirit. It is because the
ignorant are given up to discrimination that they
move along with the stream of appearances, but it
is not so with the wise."   LANKAVATRA SCRIPTURE

I am an appearance
The world is an appearance
The bread I eat is an appearance
All wish't forth from Mind Essence
Due to Ignorance---
I dont have to exist
I dont exist, I do exist---
Who cares?
For the purposes of this world
Do nothing
Or do everything anyhow.

We have words for things that are not, such as the hare's
horns, or my million dollars, or the boy's vagina.

My mother's happiness is the only thing that really matters to me---yet I
need rest and peace and hate to go to work for others for pay---If I can
start to earn my living as a writer all will be well on earth for me. --
But it is historically impossible for my work to be accepted, therefore
I'll have to do what I should do anyway, live in a shack in the woods alone.

* * * * *

In this world reflected in the mirror
of Mind Essence, and therefore but an
image and a dream, I am more Aremideia
the floating essence recognition than
I am "John Kerouac" that strange named

object which is reflected and impermanent---
If those who know me as John Kerouac and not
as Aremideia are in confusion and puzzlement,
it is because they would discriminate one from
the other, bothness and not-bothness, for All
is God and I am God, I am All and God is All,
and Aremideia is Everyone

Aremideia would write the
"Duluoz Legend" first, to
rid himself of his earthly
attachment and identity---
Then, as he progresses in
attainments, he'd write
Tathagata Worlds---then Nothing---
WORDS ARE SWEET SOUNDS FOR OBJECTS UNREAL

I am only the substance of the name-word John Kerouac and not of any self caused
self-substance

Was it ever, could it ever be said
that God has a *soul*?

. . . DEA E TRU . . .

THE TEENAGER NEXT DOOR
Everybody that's young
Is supposed to be a hoodlum---
Have fathers
With awful cars

EASTER EVE 1954

It broke my heart in the rainy night to see the glazed Easter Egg
cakes in the bakery . . . the kindness of hope of poor people trapped in this world
so unreal that tonight, napping fitfully, I heard my mother talking to me about
the same thing on both sides of Eternity during which I was unconscious, asleep,
and thought all infinity had pass't, but in "reality" it must have been 15 seconds
or so . . . that therefore she thought she was talking to "me" breaks my heart, for
I love the world and the people in it because they are really so sweet, helpless
and lost---and I wish I could do something to ease their fears, for now I'm convinced that there's absolutely nothing to fear---sadness yes, and no name to it---
What I wish I could do, that would be of use, or good, beneficial, does not exist
in this mortal sea---- My mother talking "to me" to and into the Void--O---
Tathagata in Us All
The Lord Hath Mercy
And then the next day, for no reason, I became bored and even morose
and willfully decided to be morose and yelled a little at my mother and said vague
unkind things to the little girl, forgetting compassion of yesterday, like an
ashen-faced Dostoyevskyan hero lost in uncomprehension & spite

ALL THINGS ARE IMAGINARY AND UNREAL

We just think that we're being born, when we 're born; (headfirst
crying out of the smile of the womb, if we'd only known that it was all the
same before getting involved in Samsara---saving motion and nervousness, not
forsaking peace----I remember being forced out---to the discriminatory prickles
and thorns of the world)--- We're still the same old substance, High Hearable
Essence Light----(whatever it really is, & Empty)--- Unbornness is the above---

We just think that we're dying, when we die!----headfirst falling in the
airplane, falling once again, from stage-emptiness to stage-emptiness----unborn
and undying and undead---Birth and death not a dualism, no difference----same
Dharmakaya Universal Essence----(I smell my uncle's cubabs even now, O Memory
Sincere, O Memo-ry Obscene, O vulgar lover of the vague gray dream, of *papiers
mâché* canals)---

No death, no birth, no error, no "prose," but uncreated single substance
essence flow of transitory unreal words riding an unreal ride across the memory
of the unreal world, (yawr) (wot fawr)

I cant say that the world is
Not that it is not -
Because it is just from Mind--

"Emptiness" a big arbitrary word I hung on earlier in my
discipleship, was "wrong"---

THE EXTERNAL WORLD IS NOTHING BUT A MANIFESTATION OF MIND----How can you
say that it *is*, or *is not*? --? It is Maya, the reflection of the moon
on the lake---

*We just think that we have a self nature, when we think of the nature
of ourselves*---- Our individual marks are empty; you could hack my body to
bits, and it's no longer "me"? ---These arbitrary marks are signs of my
self-nature? I have no self-nature.

URBI et ORBI---The city and the world

"Deep Form" is unmentionable, mysterious as snow-- it intends to make understood.

* * * * * * * * * * * * *

An elephant is a huge manifestion of mind---
My body took shape and Mind passed into
it, but my body is just an elephant, a
monkey, a *thing*, a *knot* in the world, a
vessel, an aggregate---my Mind, which is
the same Mind as Universal Mind in Unborn
Essence Eternalness, ignores this body---My
discriminating earthly mind clings to my
body ignorantly and in a cowardly way----I
am unborn because I am a dream, I am
Creator & Creation Dreaming in Ignorance
----Eternity & A Moment are the same in
bodiless mind dream.
This ignorant attitude is made possible by
the Triple Combination of sense, object,
and perception-contact---fools you every
time---I dont hear any music except in a
dream, the sound is motion vibrating a-
gainst my ear, my ear receives the contact

only because it happens to be here now and wouldnt
in the next room, and my perception of hearing which
has a pure permanent dharma sound of its own in almost
silent places (the buzz of the Diamond Samadhi, the
transcendental mysterious noise within)-- is being
defiled by grasping at the desire to discriminate the
music sound of sound when it doesnt have to discriminate
at all, as it will not when my thing-ear, my man-
hearing ends, though dharma perception of hearing'll
still occupy all Ten Quarters of the Universe purely,
for Mind, all of which because I am in this dream as
well as not in any dream, is "my" Mind.

There is no such thing as no-birth, and all assertion as well as negation
doesnt hold good; the world is like the birth and death of a barren-woman's
child---

      * * *

      "The evil out-flowings of life"----but---"The joys of the
Samadhis and Samapattis . . . that come to the wise . . . and cul-
minate in their return and participation in the relations
of the Triple World are called the non-outflowing good."
      Return, O Ghost---

The mind-system is the source of the evil out-flowings---has a
5 sense-organ set with 5 minds combining to form the discriminating
mind (ear-mind, nose-mind, touch-mind,---eye-mind, tonguemind) (5)
. . . this mind is called MANO-VIJNANA

"There is an unending succession of sense-concepts flowing into this discriminating (MANOVIJNANA) or thinking-mind which combines them and discriminates them
and passes judgment upon them as to their goodness and badness. Then follows
aversion to or desire for them and attachment and deed; thus the entire system
moves on continuously and closely bound together. But it fails to see and understand that what it sees and discriminates and grasps is only a manifestation
of its own activity and has no other basis, and so the mind goes on erroneously
perceiving and discriminating differences of forms and qualities, not remaining
still even for a minute." ---LANKAVATRA SCRIPTURE

    Dont think
      "For the purposes of this world,"
        But
      "For the purposes of this dream"---

(The dreams of sleep are made up of mental images abstracted from the images of
the waking dream----The "solid objects" of the waking-dream are actually empty-
spaced universes of molecules and atoms with protons--)
    Life is a "hardened dream"---

IN PRACTISING DHYANA YOU FIRST REALIZE THAT THE WORLD
IS A DREAM, THEN YOU TRANQUILLIZE YOUR MIND AND LET
THE DREAM FADE ALL AWAY (By meditating on mind-essence without forms).

The Saha-Tripleness is a dream
The chemical solidity is a dream
Smells are a dream

Bonfires are a dream
Pain is a dream
Defecation is a dream
My gray page Legend is a dream
All my various pencils were dreams
All erections were dreams
Pa, Gerard were a dream
Ma, Nin, Paul are dreams
Allen is a dream
I am a dream
This moment is a dream
This couch is a dream
I am glad it's only a dream
God is a dream
Buddha is a dream
Mind is the dreamer.

MIND IS OUTSIDE THE DREAM

In dreams when you die falling off high places, your consciousness blots out
and you wake up the same I imagine as in waking life, like Cannastra, into the
other state of consciousness, the dream within the dream of life within the
dream of eternity.
MIND MANIFESTS THE DREAMS

> Womb of Dream
> Mind is neither a dream, or
>   not a dream---
> But unborn Emptiness
> Making vacancy
> For ignorance dream.

     * * * * * * * * *

Always did know it was a dream, "forméz par'l Bon Dieu," formed by the Good Lord,
who is our biggest dream----Mind is not anthropomorphic, it is not God's *brain,*
(imagine "God" having Mano-Vijnana and discriminating "good" from "evil"!), it is
a word we have for Allness Emptiness Essence Uncreated----In this sense only, I'd
say, Mind is God----As long as they chant over an anthropomorphic "favors" God
of prayer and karma-remorse they'll never understand the meaning of dream and the
meaning of emptiness and the meaning of Nirvana, or heaven---
    FROM THIS SUFFERING DREAM WE'LL GO TO THAT UNDREAMED EMPTINESS

Elements of Ego are Dream

> What more accurate description of processes of a dream (?)---than,
> "emptiness flowing to accommodate molds of form," the form the dream
> ---cunning

> The Dream is You
> Mind made It
> Round as Orbi
> Multiple as Urbi

MIND IS THE ESSENCE
DREAM IS THE FORM
ALL IS THE SAME ESSENCE

"WE" ARE ALL MIND IN IGNORANCE
AS PEOPLE---
"WE" ARE GOD IN IGNORANCE:
AS MIND ESSENCE
WE ARE NOT "WE"
BUT IT, ALL, MIND
Mente in French & Spanish

Since life is a dream I think I'll stop eating and drinking so much----do some
ethereal daydreaming instead---go in the mansion of the mind and close all the
doors, as if I was traveling in the back of a bus for 4 days & 4 nights,broke.

If I had felicity *with* facility I'm telling you I'd be a millionaire . . .

In Mexico, a life of leisure
& delicacy & solitude
& art perhaps--
A printer in Mexico City,
Proprietor of the Beautiful Press,
publishing saints only . . .
First issue will be   HUNCKE: "Sing Sing Visions"
                        CASSADY: "The First Third"
                        BURROUGHS: "Naked Lunch"
                        GINSBERG: "Acavalna the Cave of Night"
                        SOLOMON: "Buddha's Madhouse"
                        KEROUAC: "Doctor Sax"
                        FITZGERALD: "Mad Murphy and Mighty Mike"
     The issue to be call'd "Six Unpublished Saints" with a big Number 1

                    * * * * * * * * * * * * *

Life is an irresponsible dream.
"Just as varieties of objects are seen and discriminated in dreams and in visions,
so ideas and statements are discriminated erroneously and error goes on multiplying." (Lankavatra)
"There are . . . popular preachers . . . who are skilled . . . in the art of eloquence; . . .
What one gains from them is emotional excitement and worldly enjoyment; it is not
the Law. . . . the mere prattle of a child . . . with his dualistic views not understanding
himself, that there is nothing but what is seen of the mind". . . . . .

          "When it is recognized that there is nothing
          beyond what is seen of the mind itself, the
          discrimination of being and non-being ceases
          and, as there is thus no external world as
          the object of perception, nothing remains
          but the solitude of Reality"

Lucien's baby thinks it has self-nature; it has no more self-nature than the phantom water and the phantom earth (that combine in the routines of the seed with
its inseeded karma) that'll make my beans grow; grown, to grow old and die, a
painful dream for naught.

A LIFE OF SPONTANEOUS AND RADIANT EFFORTLESSNESS

That immanent auspiciousness we all feel in ourselves is the Buddha-nature
hidden like a gem in soiled rags

>   All the Buddha-lands and assemblies await him who has turned-about
>   deep within and ceased thinking the dream any further; him it is
>   who then shines and transforms himself

>   EVERYTHING IS EVERYWHERE----so, if trucks disturb you on Atlantic Avenue
>   let them not, for you are also on the other side of the world hearing
>   other sounds

>   STOP THE MIND OF THE UNIVERSE---where a big wrangle ıs being bruited
>   about "More life! More life!" and all the poor fools who try it are
>   mistaken

>   THE DEAD KNOW BETTER---at last I wont be fooled again and wont
>   have another chance as "I"---but my type of man should stop.

Remember hovering, on the lip of darkness, on the surface of Eternal Mind?
In the beginning of consciousness?--to enter, like spermatazoa into fetal
egg, the world, for a try at it, and those who told you from the depths of
the universe not to try it?---they were the Buddhas. It was dark, it was
damp and like raining, there were overshoes in a damp closet, brown light
in grim kitchens, and there was a struggle and many mysterious lights
showing from everywhere and furors that made me want to go in my pants and
I made a tremendous mistake. Born!

* * * * * * * * * * * *

NO EGO
>   I am absolved of the responsibility for the
>   loathsomeness of my body because it is not
>   mine, is not self-caused, has no self-nature,
>   would not get sick of its own accord, and
>   decay against my wishes, and is empty and
>   a dream, the same as if I had the prettiest
>   body in the world---
>   "This love"---it's infatuation
>   based on pride based on envy.

What is all this time?
I dont know what to do with it.
This time is always and I know it.
"There is just no time and we know everything."
I dont know the answer to the burden of time---
it is simply a burden---TIME IS OF THE ESSENCE DHARMAKAYA

>   ***

>   The flavor of the world is misleading but sweet
>   But you have to fight against people who are not
>   only malicious and inexhaustible but believe in
>   this in themselves . . . the truth of the necessity
>   of falseness in impossible-to-continue individuality.

Shine alone, star . . .
Stars shine alone.

Use compassionate Tathagata means of communicating to world according to the
world's understanding----readers are little children, O Mournful One

> TATHAGATA---thus-arrived
> SUGATA------well-arrived

"Tics," or sudden clear flashes of dim memory, are hints from your
intuitive mind demanding to be explained and taught outwards by
your (working) discriminative manovijnana mind, for reasons of
Dharma crouched in the great truth cloud in the center of the
Essential Mind

"Conscious" and "Subconscious" Minds are irrelevant materialistic distinctions.
Conscious mind is manovijnana in contact with Intuition and Essential Mind but
lost in discrimination.
Unconscious Mind is manovijnana asleep, uncensored, discriminating drunkenly.
Asleep means adreaming in the habit-energy flow of thoughts.
   Bleary sleep, tormented dreams
ALAYA VIJNANA, is the Ground of Intuition

* * * * * * * * * *

The Spring phenomenom becomes the Winter noumenom---

> The gist of Buddhism: neither grasp nor reject, but take
> what's given you.

   As now, unreal and non existent, as in the future which I yearn to manifest
with a thousand arbitrary plans for Carolina, Florida, France, California,
Lowell, Mexico, I will then still be unreal and non-existent--- the future is
an evanescent dew, a shadow, a lightning flash, just as the past, just as now---
I shall no more worry about "life plans"---CLING NO MORE TO THOUGHTS OF PLACES
                     OF YOURSELF THERE OR HERE

* *
> THE HEART OF THE DIAMOND SUTRA
> "Cease to cherish any arbitrary conceptions
> as to your own self, the selfhood of others,
> of living beings, of an Universal Self."
(and any arbitrary conceptions as to the non-existence of these, too.)

> > The dhyanist is not just a man
> > in a trance, which is the appear-
> > ance; it is All-Things realizing
> > itself a dream without limit and
> > selfhood and selfnatured thingness.

DHYANA---SUCHNESS DREAMING

On May 14th Midnight of 15th it was realized by this disciple that the
sweetest hearing is hearing of no-sound
sweetest tasting is tasting of no-substance
sweetest smelling is the smelling of no-fragrance
sweetest feeling is feeling of no-sensation
sweetest seeing is seeing of no-sight
sweetest thinking is thinking of no-thought
    ---all made manifest by my transcendental
      hearing of no-sound in silence of the
      night, the buzz in ears, the sea of the
      hearing essence.

   I dont fancy myself as being the culprit
in the anxiety of the drama of the manifestation
     of the mind, which is
       this world.

        *   *   *   *   *

ALREADY VANISHED
        Just because you wont be here 7,000,000 million years from
now doesnt mean that this world and all you see, trees, houses, automobiles,
wont change and vanish all utterly away-- You cling to the notion that the
world is real and permanent, but you know that no created and compounded thing
lasts 7 million million years so you know it is all unreal and impermanent, a
vanishment, a dream, a temporary imaginary arbitrary manifestation from the
mind which is not your mind, or the mind of someone else, or the mind of any
universal self since no kind of self can exist in a dream because in a dream
there are no tokens and signs of self to take hold of, and therefore none of it
is *living* but non-living, non-sentient, possessed of the illusion in the moment,
serious, pathetic, complicatedly multiple, mad, full of pain, worry, going to
and fro lost between appearance and disappearance, dying and rebirth, endlessly
deluded----already vanished.
        How can you stand there and tell me that, as long as all will
be gone in seven million milliards, all is not already gone?
        The TATHAGATA, he who has come and gone, sees the torment, the
tormented Karma, with a single thought looking at trees, their misty unreal
rise from the ground like umbrellas of living pain, then with a double thought
he sees the even greater torment in manufactured automobiles sitting staring
in steel in the street---Civilization takes us one more step removed from intuitive realization of what has been made manifest in this we call our life---
American know-how is not savior of world but its curse in the struggle to
understand emancipation from suffering.

ALL THINGS ARE DEAD IN A DREAM

The Diamond Statement
  NOTHING'S ALIVE
  FOR THE UNIVERSE
  IS A DREAM
   ALREADY ENDED

          "Dead eyes see"---Ginsberg 1949
          "The soul is dead"---Kerouac 1949
          "And so and so and so---and blow and blow and blow"---Cassady 1949

Because it's all a big dream already ended, look around you and see
the pathetic ignorant world crawling on and on, and see how sad, see what
compassion must be given to it---Even this scribbling, what a waste in the
Seven Million Million Years of Beginningless Time's Endless Splitsecond,
what a needless occupation, what a lugubrious worrisome thing, not worthy
the dignity of a Tathagata, deludedly clinging so to scribbles and self
agreement as if there was such a thing as self or anything to agree upon
inside a filmy bubble, or in a lightning flash, or in a shattering drop of dew.

    The world is . . . Dharmakaya emanating error

The world cannot deny the truth
with its intuitive mind,
only with mano vijnana of day-by-day
which is also used for scoffing,
passion, attachment to things,
greed, rage, cynicism

    Cynicism is most pitiful of all.

    * * * * * * * * * * * * * * * *

Little kids in movies dont dig the love scenes, or smoke cigars, or get mad
in politics . . . they dont discriminate the error of the elders yet, only their
own childish, near pure error.

    Women should make love
    because of eternity not
    of birth, have no children
    & cling to no possession--
    this they will never do
    because they are the
    instruments and vessels of
    human pain incarnate,
    wombs of suffering, put
    forth by harsh yang to
    practice tender yin for yang

Abandon pride of life and you will be free as water to flow to the dream
of the lake of the mind where maya is shining and shimmering--
ALAYA VIJNANA RADIATING VISIONS

    If everybody realized Nirvana
    nobody would be worried
    and everything would stop.

LOVE IS DEAD, that is, it is not alive but pure manifestation from mind,
pure dream---Essential Mind is empty and dead in repose in eternity.

    MANO-MAYA-KAYA---Mind-vision-body

    Buddhism is the gradual becoming-intelligent of the participants
    of the dream so that it may be eventually awakened from.

_

Jump around through the rest of the dream, dont be greedy
for Nirvana,---it comes anyway---forget your conscious ego-self which makes
you "bashful,"---or "strict"-- or stern,---dont be a Dostoevsky character
who doesnt know his own mind, his own tricks----dont be of the Stream-entered
  class----EMANCIPATION COMES WITH ACCEPTANCE OF IMAGELESSNESS---(not looking
for Dhyanas, subjects for meditation, rules, etc.)----Find *cessation* of thought
at once----Best way is to think of breathing only----"The Buddha breathes in,
the Buddha breathes out"---- Once, twice, five-returning, never returning,
who cares?---it's already all over----drink up----Cessation of all multiplicity
in this dream, the actual perfect oneness of all things.--

BUDDHISM IS THE UNDERSTANDING OF THE ANGELS ---My life ambition to be an
angel looking back on life in the world, is realized---I look at the smoking
          mad yards of the railroad on Pavonia Avenue in Jersey City, I
          hear 20th Century 3:30 PM whistleblasts of workers, some of whom
          I see hurrying ignorantly with serious straight faces thru their
          selfcreated industrial gloom. I understand all things as empti-
          ness tormented in error and flowing to fill forms and karma move-
          ments, I am the happy one, like an angel I see the strict stupid-
          ity of architects designing factories because they fail to real-
          ize that their creations are in a dream and not really permanently
          necessary or even for a minute necessary--- I rejoice with the
          Buddhas of old in the imagelessness and bliss of Essential
          Universal Mind's Central Piteous Eye, I am in the heavenly
          realms of Tusita

TO JOHN HOLMES
Rich or poor,
Beat or unbeat,
what really matters,
is the Tao,
the stretch,
the pity.

          Life is truly *mortem vitalem,* the living death

"All these contingent change-medleys--" AUGUSTINE I, VI, 17
          "temporalium sempiternae"

Of soft birds' eggs---And the poise of them shall be sweet sound.

Dream, of someone bringing two Asiatic nations together, rubbing their two
grass stems in the palms of the hands, squeezing their juices out (John Foster
Dulles) (And his Southeast Asia EATO)

Other dream, I have just affrighted all my friends by dropping a big black
iron ball on the roof overhead, have run down to gloat among them (my Buddhism
is the bomb) --This was a dream and in it I had no definite personality, nor
did my friends, it was a conjoined gray underwater scene very mute, sad, brief,
potent with mayakaya.

* * * * * * * * * *
* * * * * * * * * * * *
* * * * * * * * * * * * *
* * * * * * * * * * * * * SAYS THE SIXTH PATRIARCH: "Our goal may be reached
whether we turn to the right or to the left."

"Calm and Void"

Breeze in the trees . . .

    Since the goal is already accomplished
in the realization of the dream already
ended blow---first, human social teaching
stage; second, solitary Arahatian mendicant
teaching stage---to Tathagatahood & Parinirvana
                        (Parinirvana, death of the body)

    Mind Essence
    you can see (sense)
    inside yr eyes and it is
    like clear water receiving re-
    gisters of its emanations agitating
and imprinting like a dream ephemerally
and liquidly from without & very blissfully

        *

Dreaming:-the phantom of self-illusion
       emanating visions that change
       every night

Living:- the phantom of universal self-
       illusion emanating the huge vision
       of the world that takes millenniums
       to change

    * * * * * * * * * * * * * * * * * * *

        * * * * *

         ***

book two

DISCUSSIONS OF THE DHARMA

All creatures are already purely in the state of Know-all,
of Buddhahood---the bird, the boy---All this is already
Nirvana, Heaven, the Gray Dream-manifestation is but a
reflection on "water" of the Eternal Dharmakaya---I make
my constant different discriminations in sheer agreement
to ignore Truth---(for human reasons)---I know that I dont
have to trouble myself with all this phantasmal multipli-
city---but I do for the hell of it.

Ghosts in a Dream

I keep using my Discriminating Mano-
Vijnana Mind and that of others,
listening to their "advice," or to
their references to me as an
existent, cause-forming, born, made
ego-personality---Why dont I
merely pay attention to what I
know in Universal Mind---?

Everybody is getting mad at me for knowing the truth now

And I am scared of the consequences of saying to them all: "Please cease
calling me Jack and thinking that I exist, that I am anything but a ghost
in a dream, and please cease telling me anything about your selves in this
'world'----"----chief reason for fear of this is, "I myself" havent conquered the same mortal illusion

But as soon as I snap my relationship with
the intoxicant nature of discriminating world-
life, and go off in solitude to let the inner
mysterious non-intoxicant *alaya-vijnana* come
to me in its radiance and *iddhi* potentiality,
then there wont even be the need to fear or
say anything to anyone---In America only the
Silent Buddhahood may be possible...the clinging here is so intense and widespread (democ-
racy) the populace is literally unteachable
and sees not life as sorrow.

IDDHI---supernatural attainments such as levitation OR TELEPATHY,
supernormal psychic activity

My friends deplore me, as Milarepa's sister deplored him and entreated him
to leave his cave of abject starvation and nakedness----But Blessed Lord,
how can I ever learn, will I ever learn, do I ever have to learn like Milarepa to let swarms of flies suck on me as I sit in meditation? Milarepa is
so tragic; Tibet was so poor in the 12th Century.

The Diamond Sutra teaches that
there should be no arbitrary
conceptions of any kind, including
that of bhikkuhood, solitude,
the existence of a dharma, or
even Tathagatahood---It
teaches merely that all things
are dream. Since suffering is
dream, and joy is dream, &
their dualism and the conception
of dream, dream, and "I"
is a dream, then it's best
to meditate on nothingness
and concentrate on breathing.

I say "it's best," and that's an arbitrary conception, and these words are
mere figures of speech pointing in Ignorance to pure imageless egoless and
therefore wordless Truth---so what to do?

$$\left[\begin{array}{l}\text{The Buddha Dipankara}\\\text{Answereth me not}\end{array}\right]$$
            Because no "answer"'s needed

Conceive of Nothing
While you live
And I give you
Heaven

                    *

                    THE RED SHIRT
I have a red shirt, rust color, with cream collar, a
basque---in 10 years it will be a shapeless reddish
rag in the bottom of a gondola in the rain, grayed
by pebbles and dust, finally to be dropped on the
track at the cement factory with other once-new
glad personal stardust garments. Knowing this, why
then do I buy it and wear it, except as the discriminating world shall discriminate it, and me with it
on, for I the knower, as knower, knoweth the real
meaning of the shirt and therefore dont have to wear
it. This is a compromise with Mano Vijnana and a
loss of merit for this disciple. Not only that, by
giving me a gaudy, social feeling of being well-
dressed, it, but a humble compound of cloth, has
now become a force of Mara the Devil, but only due
to the discriminating mind.
        Universal Mind, which has manifested all these
forms, and conceptions, as in a dream, knows there
to be no distinction, no selfness or otherness,
bothness or not-bothness, no thing that is not of
the One Essence Mind.

Our lives are cluttered in multiplicity and we are confused into thinking
        it real all over

                        * * * * * * * *

            Think of all the food you've eaten
            all your life, and passed through you,
            thinking it was real and that you needed
            it to "live"---like food eaten in dreams---

I dont want to be a drunken hero of the generation suffering everywhere
  with everyone---
I want to be a quiet saint living in a shack in solitary meditation
  of universal mind---

                    * * * * * * * * * *

                            The Chinese could very well say:
                            GO IN THE HOUSE & CLOSE ALL
                              THE DOORS (the house of
                                    dharmakaya Essence)

- --- -

            *   **   **   **   *

Do Nothing, Say Nothing
        Think Nothing

                The Dharma is the sweetest thing I know

I thought of the Italian I had a fight with in Frisco, who hit me before I had
a chance to realize his intentions and then allowed us to be broken apart by the
gang of musicians, "But he was never born, will not die; I was never born, will
not die; we only thought we existed---Figures in a dream that will be no more---
what is the reality therefore of my thoughts of revenge? In the reality of universal mind there is no self, no thing to avenge; no one to do it, no one to
receive it, since it is all already passed away---a vicious dream---Better to
meditate on this than 'bust knuckles on his evil skull'---Since he will die and
be utterly gone away, since he will vanish like a puff of smoke, therefore I know
he doesnt really exist, and his ignorance of this should be 'revenge' enough for
'me'---if revenge is real. Pity is real, revenge a dream. Avenge my Self, which
is an illusion, in this dream? Both of us gone utterly from the world like phantasms that had appeared shuddering in the air, leaving gnashings behind?---both
of us in our own ways seriously believing we are? --which is a falsehood. Bah
---better to experience High Samadhis and see through the Triple trick of life
and strife---like a wise lover leaves his lover go."
        Svaha!

ME AND THE MULE--THE TRIPLE WORLD

The Triple World is *sense* (eye) (1)

is *sense-object* (mule) (2)

is *perception* (3) (contact of my eye with sight
of the mule and resulting
perception, discrimination, &
consciousness)

If the Triple Saha World of Suffering (desire and
suffering and frustration arising from consciousness within
the 18 Spheres of mentation, 3 x 6 makes 18, triple combination
times 6 senses equals 18) were to be reduced to Nirvana, or Dharma
kaya, or Universal Mind unrippled by Ignorance, it would be a Single
World of Essence Perception, since you can remove sense and object from
the purview, but perception is the pure Self Enlightening activity of Mind
Essence itself, which it manifests continually and purely in all 10 Quarters of
the Universe but without discriminating and individuating activity, as I with my
mule. This Single World of Non-Suffering is free of Karma and object and motion
since there is nothing but essence Emptiness abiding purely in effortless Radiance
- - - - no eye, no mule, no eye-idea of mule-form.- - - - - - - - - - - - - - - - -

Pure undifferentiated
perception is infinite but as it
operates through the 6 Senses it becomes
limited, in the sentient state. Eye-perception
comes thru the instrumentation of the eye-apparatus
and eyes cant see the inside of your own body, nor
can they see objects in the dark, nor objects too far
off to be seen.

Ear-perception picks up wave-vibrations that
the eye misses, but it cant pick up sounds a million miles
away, tho in the One Perception of Dharmakaya they exist and are
"known."

Taste-perception is limited.

Touch-perception is limited.

Nose-perception is limited.

Thought-perception is vast and can conceive of all phenomena in all
Ten Quarters of the universe but the conception of even the Lord Tathagata's Womb of Mind Essence is only an arbitrary conception for the purposes
of illustrating imagelessness by means of word&conception and has no basis in
fact, thus thought-perception is limited also.

(Only transcendental Perception is not limited, not within
the 18 spheres of mentation.)

So it was the thinking-mind of thought-perception that made me say "Mule" in response to what my eye caught with its lucid moist film of eyeball; Universal Mind
free of all thought-conception is what recorded and registered the pure liquid
seeing, since the eyeball itself has no perception of the sight it takes in or
upon itself. Thought-perception is limited within the bounds of individuation,
discrimination and conceptualization.

But as perception exists everywhere purely
permeating all space and "things" appearing
dreamlike in space, it is infinite and not
limited by sense-activity and its mental
apparatus.

The intellectual knowledge of this,

and this writing of it,

depends on

thought-perception, not Intuitive Essence Perception,
and is therefore
limited,
impure,
truly unsatisfying.
What the disciple must
do is stare at things
till he sees perception
instead of things.
or,
". . . while looking
. . . what is it that reveals
the existence of yr. mind?"
SURANGAMA SUTRA

* *

FROM THE SURANGAMA SUTRA p.124 (Goddard,Thetford,Vt.)
"All the time they have been taking these limited and perturbed and contaminated
minds to be their true and natural essence of Mind . . ."

"You so quickly forget the brightness and purity
of your own essential nature, and amid the
activities of the day, you cease to realize
its existence . . ."

-------- * * * * * * * * * * --------

Where any creature is lost in a trance, motionless,
it is using Essence of Mind (alaya-vijnana)--When
active and lost in activities of the day, it's Discriminating mind, mano vijnana, in use--the lower mind--
Essential Mind is not only unrecognized but minimized in
importance by the sentient beings of this world with their
moneygathering complexity and their scorn of "woolgathering"
---What do vast Machineries have to do with the daily need to
nourish the body with food? With the need to breathe? And complex sciences, Why?
. . . . . . "You have lost consciousness of your
original and permanent Mind." (SS)
p.125

*   *   *   *

* * * * * * * *

*

A REFUTATION OF CATHOLIC DUALISM

Aquinas in *Summa Theologiae* (Q.49 Art.2) says:

> "The goodness of the fire causes evil to the water, and man,
> good in his nature, causes a morally evil act . . . This is
> by accident."

The assumption that the fire is good is based on a previous
assumption arguing that To Be, or Being, is good. But Being
is neither good nor bad, it's just a dream. The fire is
neither good nor evil, the water that it destroys is neither
good nor evil, man's nature (Karma) is neither good nor evil
in Dharmakaya-Essence, and any of his qualities also can only
be but arbitrary conceptions with no basis in reality, because
it is all a manifestation from Universal Mind Essence and to
be regarded as empty phenomena in a dream, or *as in* a dream
whereby it is not meet to attribute any arbitrary qualities
one way or the other to anything caused. The "accident" is
the automatic Karma action of fire-on-water, man-on-moral-
victim, and is only to be regarded as activity arising phan-
tasmally from Mind itself, not as good or evil, for in
the reality and purity of Universal Mind there are no dualistic differentiations such as good and evil, and fire and
water are of the same essence, which is intrinsic emptiness.
All is One. No good is battling any evil, but peace and
permanency abide throughout the hosts of manifested Ignorance-
phenomena everywhere.
                Catholic Dualism is behind the error of
Western Civilization with its war of machines, each machine
claiming the "Good"---It is profound behind the reason why
Christ chose to *carry* the cross to Golgotha, the "dynamism"
so-called of the West which is based on opposites reacting
(such as magnet and coil, positive and negative)---why did
not Christ merely sit on the ground and refuse to carry?
The Gothic spire aspires to its opposite, by virtue of a
deep disbelief in the ultimate principle of formless unity.

  Buddha's last words were: "Decay is inherent in all compound things!
                Work out your own salvation with diligence."
   All forms, conceptions of good and evil, all things decay.
   The mansion of salvation is not built on decay.

*

Further:-
Augustine and Aquinas say that Being is good, Non-Being is evil.
Buddha says that Being is a manifestation from Mind, which is
emptiness, and non-being is emptiness, and so being and non-
being are the same, arbitrary conceptions, mere dualisms, mere
figures of speech, undifferentiated in emptiness. Have you
yet separated the children from the men?

The Buddhas of old know that all things neither *are* or
are-not, neither are *good* or *not-good;* that it is only the
discriminating mind that makes such distinctions.(There is
no differentiation to be made between the children and the
men, so-called, except for purposes of pointing a finger
at the unpointable, the point beyond point, the Inscrutable
Essential Mysterious Tao of Dharmamegha's Truth Cloud.)

Tranquil Pity Intuitive . . .

Dynamism and Dualism are the same thing, and both hasten to decay . . .

Aquinas is as irrelevant and as ignorant as a pretentious child

Another ignoramus is Gurdjieff, who says p.294 "In Search of the Miraculous"
Harcourt-Brace 1949, ---"It is necessary to realize that there are possibi-
lities and there are impossibilities." A profound irrelevance! Buddha calls
this "the emptiness of mutuality which is non-existence."

Gurdjieff illustrates his inanity by saying: "I can take from this
table and throw on the floor a piece of paper, a pencil, or an ashplant, but
I cannot take from the table and throw on the floor an orange which is not on
the table."

LANKAVATARA SCRIPTURE Chapt.III---"By the emptiness of mutuality
which is non-existence is meant that when a thing is missing here,
one speaks of its being empty (or impossible) here. For instance
in the lecture hall of Mrigarama there are no elephants present,
nor bulls, nor sheep: but as to monks there are many present. We
can rightly speak of the hall as being empty as far as animals
are concerned . . . In this case we are speaking of things in their
aspect of individuality and generality (which is an illusion
falsely imagined since in essence things are not two but one),
but from the point of view of mutuality some things do not
exist(or are impossible)somewhere. This is the lowest form
of emptiness(or impossibility)and is to be sedulously put
away."

GURDJIEFF:"I will add one more thing: Time is breath---try to
understand this."   p.213 ibid.
Anyone incapable of seeing through this charlatan's
attempts at being a mysterious seer of some secret
oriental wisdom is going to be reborn a novelist or
a hare with horns. God help the poor gullible
Ouspenskys and Lil Bill Kecks of this world.

* * * * * * The old crocodile is gone. . . .

From Balzac's *Eugénie Grandet*---"In her case wealth was neither a power
nor a consolation; she could only exist through love, through
religion, and through her faith in the future.   Love made her
understand eternity.   Her heart and the gospels marked out
two worlds awaiting her.   Night and day she was plunged in
the depths of infinite thoughts, which for her perhaps merged
into one."

* * * * * * * * * * * *

People are ignorant and full of avarice,
but it's to be pitied not yelled at, because it has its sources in their essential innocence---even Mara & Beelzabur
are innocents---

--
When your body vanishes and everything
that belongs to self, such as its ego-
personality, vanishes with it, there remains what does not belong to self but
only was "loaned" to it, universal mind,
which, when shedding off a body, is not
changed nor added to nor subtracted from.

Abides . . .

Anuttura-Samyak-Sambodhi, Highest Perfect Wisdom, as practised by one single
being in his time, may very well have a major influence on the stopping of
the whole world, since Universal Mind is One and the contact with it by the
sentient bearer of it occurs in One Unified Intention.

The world is fraught straight through
with mistakes . . Enough of Karma; a
little Dharmakaya please . . .

All doing this for false reasons---
Why stop you not?
Need steak? Need clean bed?
Need room in a house?

* * * * * * * * * * * * * * * * * * * *

KEROUAC said: "Chinese saints get drunk
in a cornfield and never
lose a thing, except maybe
pride of self."

Hey
 You
  Dont
      Get L o s t

The Moon is Buddha

As if I cared about money and legs . . .

My mother's still the only cherub
T'would be a sin to sin against,
Maligning fleece of sorrow snow,
Tho she too dumb, like Jamie
Cassady
            T'know't---

* *

Notes in a Cornfield
            These are the most charming companions I have known,
            these cornstalks at pink moonfall---One's 8½ foot tall,
            skinny motionless sentient lorder over others lost in
            stalk eternity
        C-R-R-R-A---

                    My sentient wine
                    On Saturday Nite
                    Now Carolinay
                    Sits darkern nite

My bottle echoes
Astounding gnats
S*P*L*U*M*P

                    The moon of compassion
                    Is waiting for me
                    To forgive everybody
                    Even ashen poetry

Earthen moon!
God!
  She looks like the Virgin Mary
  With a rose halo
  And pursy drawn
     expression---

Truth is like a bird   * * * * * * * * * * * * * *
Flying silently   *   The corn   *
In the silken sky   *   Has a   *
  To a hidden tree   *   Starry   *
  In the cottonmouth   *   Being   *
     night---   * * * * * * * * * * * * * *

                I know corn---
                It feeds on woods winds---
                Hangs languid arms
                Congratulates & Congregates
                    PSHAOHEEO OUAHYSSY!
                    Stikilitree -a-
                    moo-- a --pee--
                dee--tryou-- Ou--
                  l---ou---ee---oo---
                    Flik!

Tche-- pe te re a----

Rosh--a---roar
            Corn-- a ---
                    poor

Virgin Mary &
        Buddha are
                UNO

                    Corn rattles & cronks
                    One seed springin 9 ft hi
                            ! ! !
                        Whatta Karma
                            Moda
                                    Foka--
                    If I was a snake
                    I couldnt reach a bird

                    Corn waits to
                            be attacked---
                        Night birds imbecile

                Sh I n'faut pas perdre
                nos p'tit Buddha
                        * *

        Shirt I bought in New Orleans
        Coiled like a snake at ma feet.   When I wisht
                                                                that the yelling
        Corn shines in the Moonlight   Bird
        Makes curtsies to dark Me's   Would come & sit
        Wave palmetto crab-arms   On my shoulder
                at dead hero-fathers   He stopt singin
        Of the past   And the corn
        Yakking from now present   sang vastly
                Karma Trees   In a sudden
                                                                  mystical
                                                                    breeze
                        A Pa

        Moonlight's Almost
        Like someone
        Was tryin to   The moon is like lights of posses
        Light my Way   chasin me for being nonSouthernish

        *   And Corn is my
                                                                        Brodder
                                                            * *

When I, a Poet,
Presented my filial hand
To the world
By hanging elbow on knee
Up side down
Not only did Corn
    Acknowledge
But railroad whistle
    15 Miles Away,
Showing how
    Everything is
        the Same
Tied Up
    &
    True

                    The Corn
                    Rustles
                        To defend Me.
                        Against the Yaks
                        of Pipsqueak Birds
                        Criticizing me
                            In Pines
                            ---I can stop
                            em every time
                    with one shriek
                                whistle---
                    But the corn
                    Dont care
                    And Moon too far gone
                    Corn Dont Have Ears

"The earth is one,
    not Two"
I said
In the moonlit
    cornfield at
the Woods Edge
But a huge bug
    landed on my arm
to mock me
And the tree
Waved at me
With its million eyes
    Va-v-a-vh-as-hh
            All is Same

                    Is there anything
                    more restful than
                    a graveyard slab?
                    On a moonlit nite?
                    Watching the uppermost
                    overhead star?
                    The dead are quiet---And if
                    anybody saw you in this
                    Graveyard Samadhi
                    who would be scared first,
                        prithee?

That bird:
A loud newcomer in an old tree

(Written in Big Easonburg Woods, North
Carolina, July 10, 1954, drunk on
port wine in a cornfield from 8 to 10)

* *

¤ ¤

A 45-WORD GENESIS OF THE WORLD'S CREATION, as spoken by GAUTAMA BUDDHA
"Open space is nothing but invisible dimness; the invisible dimness of space is
mingled with darkness to look like forms; sensations of form are mingled into
illusive and arbitrary conceptions of phenomena; and from these false conceptions
of phenomena, is developed the consciousness of body."
    (In this mighty paragraph I can hear huge slappings on the asses of
the Gods.)
    "So, within the mind, these jumblings of causes and conditions, seg-
regating into groups, and coming into contact with the world's external objects,
there is awakened desire or fear which divide the mind and cause it to sink into
either indulgence or anger. All of you have been accepting this confusing conception of phenomena as being your own nature of mind. As soon as you accepted
it as your true mind, is it any wonder that you became bewildered and supposed it
to be localized in your physical body, and that all the external things, mountains,
rivers, the great open spaces, and the whole world, were outside the body. Is it
any wonder that you failed to realize that everything you have so falsely conceived

has its only existence within your own wonderful, enlightening Mind of True Essence."----SURANGAMA SUTRA

* *

I saw that we perceive a million different changing
things in the world, with our single unchangeable faculty
of perceiving---even Jack, me, is one of those many
objects subject to change, among trees, houses, bugs,
things seen everywhere appearing, going to and fro
and disappearing, all seen by the universal pure
unvarying perception of sight---Isnt it clear that
it is all obtaining from essence of Mind and nothing
else? How vastly the moon is seen.   Stars and sun
  in grief awaiting Mind.

"Vacant creation's lamps appal." ---G.M.HOPKINS

Poor pitiful Catholics suffering(inside form)

Blake had occasional insight into the Truth he sought, like All Christians, hopelessly---

"The Sun's Light
When he unfolds it
Depends on the Organ
That beholds it."
                    --GATES OF PARADISE

The light of brightness as discriminated by mano-vijnana

"That end in endless Strife."
  (knowledge of Fire of rebirth)

"Help! Help!"--(sea of rebirth)

"Perceptive Organs closed, their objects close"---and he draws
an old man AGED IGNORANCE clipping the wings of a boy---
  But Buddha told the Raja's Minister it was no time to turn to
religion and sense-clipping Nirvana when you've become old and your senses
all failing.

Blake: "Fear & Hope are--Vision"
  (manifestation of mind)

"What is the material world, and is it dead?"
". . . all alive the world, where every particle of dust
breathes faith its joy."
  ---the innumerable Buddha-lands as many as the particles of dust.

"And all the overflowing stars rain down prolific pains"---ALL LIFE IS SUFFERING

"If Perceptive Organs close, their Objects seem to close also." *Seem*, sir?

"The Visions of Eternity, by reason of narrowed perceptions
Are become weak Visions of Time & Space, fix'd into furrows of death . . ."
       (from JERUSALEM)
              Mano-vijnana defiling alaya-vijnana)

"The Ear, a little shell, in small volutions shutting out
 True Harmonies . . ." ETC.

       "A murderous Providence! A Creation
              that groans, living on Death,
       Where Fish & Bird & Beast & Man & Tree
              & Metal & Stone
       Live by Devouring, going into Eternal
              Death continually!"

"A World of Shapes in craving lust . . ."

       "In your Imagination, of which this
              World of Mortality is but a Shadow . . ."

Blake and his Dualism led him also to write letters filled with unhappy vitu-
peration---"Woolett & Strange . . . heavy lumps of cunning & Ignorance." It doesnt
matter any more now since the passage of time has rendered both brilliant Blake
and his stupid contemporaries hors de combat inside undifferentiated Dharmakaya
essence, which is like one golden light flowing----

       This Karma world of illusion is like people who
       are supposed to go but keep hanging around
       getting ready to go, and the poor man who wants
       his solitude must gnash & gnash

       *

       When Aquinas says that "evil can only exist in good
       as in its subject" I get the feeling there is no real
       dualism if his "good" is to be predicated as essence
       of Mind and his "evil" as all manifestation from this
       essence. Kens it not . . .

The tragic Will is the only Will that is (I wont say defensible) operative
to the limit in this world---'s'why alcohol which simulates gayety, and
narcotics that create self-romance, are the great enemies to the seeker
after Truth and Highest Samadhi----They are not only intoxicants but
deceivers of Sorrow-knowledge.
              Only 2 things to do and 1 to be:

              1. Necessity
              2. Teaching
              3. Be kind

AQUINAS QU.49 Art.3 ST---"The accidental cause (evil) is subsequent to an
essential cause (good.)"

And ibid. Q.2 Art.3---"If everything can not-be, then at one time there was
nothing in existence . . . (that which can not-be at
some time, is not)" (a dream already ended)---"Now,
if this were true, even now there would be nothing
in existence."

This delimnish thought arises from the arbitrary dual concept of "being"
and "non-being"---Dualistic conceptions breed dualistic conclusions

Mind-Essence is not a "being," like "God,"---maybe it is
an is-ness, but I'm not even sure of that. The essence
of a dream is mind.

Then Aquinas says: "Natural bodies act for an end," and he says it very
self-certainly, to prove that some intelligent "being" directs them,
but what is this "end" he here discriminates with his sentient predis-
position? Is sun's heat for the "living"? If it were for the living
how could there be destruction of the living by fire? If sun's light
were for eyes, how could there be darkness to cast eyes in confusion?
If seasons were to promote life, how could there be death? Natural
bodies act for an end which is pure end, finis, and have nothing to
do with good or evil or both or neither.

"There is no such '*thing*' as the perception of sight nor any other essential
nature transcending all objects." ----Nirvana is "built-in."------"If the
trees belong to the perception of sight, why do we still call them trees?"
ANANDA speaking.

OBJECTS *ARE* THE PERCEPTION OF SIGHT OF UNIVERSAL MIND ESSENCE

(I'm not an individualist
I'm an originalist)

"If it *does* belong to the perception of sight, why do we call it space?"
Buddha discussing space in Surangama Sutra.

* *

*"All that the Supreme Teacher of the Dharma has taught are true and sincere
words, they are neither extravagant nor chimerical. They are not to be
compared with the puzzling paradoxes given by the famous heretic teachers."*

The true teaching is motivated by pity for all
sentient suffering, and not by pride in its
self-miraculous power.

1. Sentience
2. Samadhi
3. Samapatti

I go into one, & close the door behind me, and come
back later. Each room is locked from the other. The
3rd room of Samapatti Spiritual powers and visionary
iddhi-magic which includes telepathy & levitation
I dont expect to come to me for a long long time.
Attainment of Samadhi is the same as practice of
dhyana when you turn on one serious effort to go
inside the mind's inner peace.
    All 3 in Nirvana are the same.

* * * * * * *

REGRET is just as much an illusion as EXHILARATION---Neither has any
    basis in fact. Visionary flowers in the air, is all they are.

    THE MAZE
  The conditions of phenomena of the world, which mystic teachers like to
praise as being infinite, are infinite but only zero. All the infinitude that
is possible, plus all the infinitude that is also impossible, such as, it is
impossible for my father's body to stand now before my perception of sight,
but it is possible for Bill's panel truck (which is before me as I write) to
stand now before the perception of sight of my eyes---all this should be regarded as nothingness which, had it not happened and the seed of the conditons not
sown in the soil of karma action in the Saha world, would still have to be regarded as infinitely possible, impossible, and neither possible nor impossible,
as if, or whether or not, it happened; in other words, infinitely zero. What
do I mean? There's nothing substantial to get a hold of, in the conditions
that bring and place an object before the perception of sight; something ungraspable about the now invisible phantom who brought the panel truck here and
then vanished, similarly ungraspable about the phantom who was my father and
is now vanished somewhere; and only phantasmal is the cause of the very existence of the truck and of my father. There's something not clear in my teaching
this, vague, muddied, incomplete, ungraspable, phantasmal, a maze.

    . . . I Learn As I Go Along . . .

Little Paul is a visionary flower in the air
The hand of man is a visionary flower in the air
Allen and Neal are visionary flowers in the air
The tobacco weed is a visionary flower in the air
Bob's doghouse is a visionary flower in the air
My phlebitis is a visionary flower in the air
I am a visionary flower in the air
All things are a visionary flower in the air
Buddha is a visionary flower in the air
Death is a visionary flower in the air

Eternity is a visionary flower in the air
Conception is a visionary flower in the air
The Visionary Flower is the Mind

* * * * * * * * *

All this is a manifestation
arising from the senses in
contact with objects, all
of which are illusion, or,
Visionary Flower in the Air

Evil multicolored wasps, their drur-r-g
    of wings, are visionary flowers in the air----
My shudder of fear in contact with the wasp, a visionary flower in the air

* *

The Worker-Priest's idea, of sharing suffering of workers, I believe
his name is Abbé Pierre and Bob Lax showed me a picture of him in Jubilee
Magazine sitting with legs folded under him, may become the unwilling tool of
Totalitarian Capitalism, or Laborism, if he doesnt watch out---A nice science
fiction society eerily divided into Suffering Pious Workers and Areligious
Contented Employers---for sake of "Production" which I'm afraid Abbe Pierre
believes in since he evidently doesnt believe in Homelessness for the Brothers
and in Poverty and Chastity for Laymen.
    Chinese Tao says: "Perturb not your vital essence." The suffering of
workers all over the world has never produced one loaf of bread or one
apronful of stringbeans from off those bloody iron belts of theirs. It's a
chimera, insanity. There is no need for cars, no need for radios, no need
for metros, no need for cannons, no need for cigarette lighters, no need for
oil or oil heat, no need for plastic cups, no need for cannons, no need for
war and above all no need for need, which "Production" merely multiplies.
    There is only need for breath, food, rest and holy meditation.

* * * * * * * * * *

THE FACT THAT PERCEPTION OF SIGHT IS LIMITED *BY*
IMPENETRABLE OBJECTS ONLY PROVES THAT THIS LIMITATION
DOESNT BELONG TO ITS OWN NATURE, WHICH IS INSCRUTABLE
AND APART FROM BRIGHTNESS AND DARKNESS HAS NO
SUBSTANTIALITY OF EXISTENCE

The Book of Pure Truth consists of a bunch of mirrors bound in a volume

-

Being involved in any activity means to
put the compound of self through a cycle
of decay. The only thing a wise man should
do is eat and gather eats; he should never mix
himself up with any other activity. . . . .

This is the Bliss-body of Buddhahood, not "my body" any more---
Today, Sunday July 18, I am entering the Pure Land

Monday July 19---I am beginning my Ascension today

Fasting. . . . .

The Single Negative of Buddhism
           --as in a camera, the negative is a single moist band
        made of the same uniform film all over, One Essence & Ap-
      pearance, but when you expose it to the morbid mist of caused
    and conditioned phenomena to which the lens are pointed, a dis-
  criminated picture imprints on the liquid surface due to the conditions of brightness, darkness, open space and impenetrability of objects.
If you point the lens at the empty blue sky, the single negative will remain
the same. The single negative thus undefiled is the opposite of the dual black-
and-white negative. The importance of this knowledge is to understand Dualism
and Negativism, or emptiness. . . . .

           We're all spectral giants really, when you
           simply consider the truth that our hands, our
           belly, our thigh is nothing but vast open space
           occupied by universes with special molecular
           arrangements of planets that ultimately after
           gravitational electro-magnetic and chemical
           conditions are accounted for we call the motor
           vegetable organism.

           It is all a big conception in the air, this
           body of yours, and is empty, twisted, streaming
           through the atmosphere---the conception and its
           senses work together in Ignorance since beginning-
           less time, and death and rebirth carries on, not
           knowing it's all imaginary and doesnt have to
           go grinding on.

           Every created thing, is a ripple, a wave----
           there's nothing "solid"
           "I never saw a wave."--- Emily Dickinson

THE FINAL HUMILITY

        . . give yourself up without rationalization, like a lamb,
to whatever untenable position you are in now and in the future----be meek,
and let them take care of you, even feed you when they can---give up all prides
and angers, delusions; all lusting after sex, drinking for intoxication, narcotics, amusements, fripperies, idle pastimes, daydreams of activity,---two things
to do: eat and teach. ---Do *Not* teach in the practical plane, such as advocating
ways of cooking simplicity etc., merely teach the spectral giant has compassion
which is Buddhahood---

        { It gets better, not worse
          Ascetism, self-control & patience

Inside quietude gets better
Outside dissipation gets worse
Dissipation means evil outflowings
     of any and all kinds---ASAVAS: the deadly floods of sensuality.

NIRVANA means to disconnect the plug so that natural pity, not fabricated,
may reign in the house.

          Baseball players go through their rack of routine
          thinking this they must do----Crowds of 60,000
          watch drearily; and the papers print gray boxscores
          . . . nobody knows what else to do, watch, read.
          Salvation Army heroes are giving em little time
               left on streetcorners . . .
                         REPENT!
                         GET YE IN CHRIST!

My India
Is right in this house---
Here I do my begging
And my teaching---
I dont have to go anywhere
---Fortune I give my mother
And go on begging from her,
Till I move my India
To India

          SOLITUDE AT HOME . . . . . AUSTERITY & WRITING

* *

               The necessity of eating is part of the suffering
          of sentience, because though it is pleasant to taste
          and digest. it is not pleasant to regard a pile of
          defecation. Sentience is trapped in a filthy brutal
          nature which is not pleasant in the least when you care-
          fully realize it. That the Bliss-body of Buddhahood is
          dirty, and bloats at death, is part of this whole Tragedy
          of Error.

A man stares with healthy eyes into open space
until he begins to see fantastic blossoms in the
air arising from the natural contamination and
diseased state of the perception of eyes. Let
us call the imaginary blossoms, which neither belong to open space (because if they did then
when they disappeared they would return to the
sky but as soon as you have the notion of coming-
from and going-to then the sky is no longer open
space), nor to the eyes (because if they came
from the eyes naturally they would have the nature of perception of sight and going out from
these eyes and having perception of sight, they
should see their own eyes), let us call the

78

little fantastic blossoms which are really
blemishes on the eyeball projected into the
perfect open emptiness, *Ananda.* The blossoms
are said to be "Ananda," open space "not-Ananda."
And this is the way we have been looking at things.

* * * * * * * *

BUDDHA'S HYMN TO ANANDA HIS COUSIN

Atta dipa
Atta sarana
Ananna sarana
Dharma dipa
Dharma sarana

```
* * * * * * * * * * * * * * * * * * * *
* * Atta: self              *
* * dipa: lantern            *
* * sarana: refuge            *
* * ananna: no other           *
* * * * * * * * * * * * * * * * * * * * *
```

- -

The 12 Nirdanas (Links)

1. Ignorance causes Karma (action)
2. Karma causes consciousness
3. Consciousness causes individuality
4. Individuality causes sense organs
5. Sense organs cause contact
6. Contact causes sensation
7. Sensation causes desire
8. Desire causes attachment
9. Attachment causes existence
10. Existence causes birth
11. Birth causes old age
12. Death sorrow lamentation misery grief despair

* * * * * * * *

Because you would be drunk
as you are not sober,   & because
when sober you abhor the things
you do drunk, each cup of strong
drink is a draught of Dualism.

* * * * *

WESTERNERS ARE SO IGNORANT OF ENLIGHTENMENT, think the basic premises of Nirvana are
so "irrelevant"---they are like some scientist slaving day and night in his labor-
atory to invent a new kind of grief.
    When I asked brilliant Lucien whether the perception of a halo around a lamp
by some diseased eyes belonged to perception of the eyes or to the lamp, he said
"I couldnt care less" and yet I was asking him the basic and crucial question if

the world is real or imaginary. In the same way Western scientists and scholars investigate "forces" and "authenticity" instead of causes and conditions. An Oxford scholar, Harold Smith, is more interested in the authenticity of Buddha's boyhood events than what the events reveal, impart & teach, yet he doesnt apologize for this deficiency, instead feels solely that he is doing the correct and useful work of the world. The authenticity of the reports on Buddha's boyhood is neither here nor there, and anyway it is not possible any more to verify anything about it, as everybody knows. Scientists study the "forces" of the atom, they have seen that it is of the Nirdana chain-link concatenative dependence, one link destroyed the whole chain is destroyed, yet they continue to play with the force, the energy of the structure of the atom of the dream, instead of stopping and realizing they dont have to do anything at all because it is only a dream already ended, a fantastic blossom in the air.

* *

Vision of Mademoiselle Aimé Dechènes of 305 W.13th St.   83 years old
        She said she was on East Side Drive park steps in the 1920's and saw a golden birdsnest in the sky, tilted slightly and dripping of liquid gold a little at the brim---She said it was a manifestation or epiphany of her grandfather who had just died and attained to heaven.

- - - - - - - -

GRASPING OF THE FIVE KHANDHAS
(Using a baby as   ("Groups")
   an example)
        * * * * * * * * * * * * * * *

1.   RUPA   Sense datum or phenomenon--the baby
                      grabs a rubber toy he sees

2.   VEDANA   He has a feeling and sensation of
                          pleasure holding it

3.   SANNA   He has a perception of this pleasant
                        feeling and realizes

4.   SANKHARA   And so he constructs mentally a
                              postulation and ideology of the value of this ball

5.   VINNANA   He now has a consciousness of the ball and his
                            dependent relation to it that he didnt have before

BUT -- "All compound things come to decay"

UPADANA: "Clinging to Existence"--and so now he will eventually lose the
                    ball and suffer decrepitude and death and rebirth in this

This is I?
This is the Self?   The reverse routine is Nirvana

THE FIVE DEFILEMENTS (Baby With Fire)

1. Discriminate (look around)

2. Discriminate a certain form (fire)

3. Desire to grab it (want it)

4. Grab it (take it)

5. Decrepitude (burned)

Suppression of suffering
    NIRODHA of suffering--means--
        "complete reduction to mental latency
          so that craving (TANHA) or thirst no
          longer exists."

ASAVA:
        "A blind overflow of craving
          which intoxicates the actor."
                    ---F.H.Smith

    Think:
        "I dont have to be satisfied"
                      :for Nirvana

Christianity, a THEODICY, religion
                    about God
Buddhism, a COSMODICY, a religion
                    about the universe

* *

FOR JUNKIES

The habit is Upadana,
Clinging-to-Existence,
And it is the worst habit
I ever tried to kick

* *

1. Ideas Buddhistic
2. Resolution to follow
3. Gentle speech
4. Kind circumspect behavior
5. Harmless foodgathering
6. Perseverance to attain to supernormal states
7. Realization of attainment to supernormal states
8. Tranquillity and rapture in supernormal states

Let the life in the body continue until "all karma is worked out"
and then parinirvana, death, will be the signalization of no more
rebirth and PERMANENT ABODE IN NUMBER 8 . . .

The universe is made of imaginary dust from the golden central hall of Knowing
   ---only imagination makes the lilac grow,
      turn blue in July---makes the ant hurry---
        the cat conceive of himself as cat---There
         are no sentient beings anywhere, not even me
          and this conception of me knowing---
           the Knowing of Nirvana
           is Inscrutably Mysterious

The atom of the atom of the atom is dust
The dust of dust of dust is imaginary
The mind of mind of mind is Nirvana

This I just saw

    Small wonder that the baby sees people in the world
    as *giant put-together phantoms slashing in a violent*
    projection INSIDE MIND
            INSIDE THE KNOWING
            INSIDE NIRVANA

That "knowing" I mean to mean Universal Mind Essence

       * * * * * * * * * * * * * * * * *

Remember when you were a tree?
   I do----arms, heaviness, blear peace.

The little sparrow is a Huge Bird of Paradise
His viciousness causes thunder and Earthquake
    among the bugs
Who themselves are gangling giants monstering
    through fern wildernesses
After microscopic dinosaurs
Who eat worlds of Ogres
From the other side of dust;
All in horror, devouring & rebirth
And yangling and yankering
After the Pure Land---
Monsters flailing inside mind.

****

EXERCISE

MEDITATE ON THE FOUR VIHARAS

of Televolition, or Divine States

    1. The sphere of infinite space
    2. The sphere of infinite thought
    3. The sphere of void (Sunna)
    4. The sphere of neither perception
          or non-perception
From out of this you emerge with loving-kindness, compassion,
    gladness and equanimity.

"The overwhelming joy of the early Buddhist saints" before the Puritanism of
Mahayana was introduced----The Hinayana Original Arahats
            blissful in the forest
            of ancient India
            500 years before Christ
            and his dualistic Torment
            and the Councils
            of grim revision

SCHOLARLY NOTE:
        Because Nirvana is inconceivable in the world of sense-perceptions
we call it a "negative conception" in our schools---because Nirvana is conceivable
or that is, experientially possible, in mystic experience of dhyana and samadhi it
may be referred to as a "positive conception" in that case, although this is only
a statement that has meaning in discrimination and mutual exclusion and I say it
to straighten the erudite crooked stick of the western critic who says "Nirvana
is a negative conception in relation to the world of existence, but it is a positive conception as known in mystic experience."
        Ecclesiastes says "Much knowledge is a curse" and so does Chiangtse +
    Dhammapada. The more I learn in Buddhist "scholarship" the more

I am becoming confused now, weary, and far from
actual samadhi bliss-----

---   *****   ---

It hurts me to think about gravity
holding all empty streamforms to-
gether---it hurts me to continually
think about emptiness and meaning---
I'll just think nothing. This is the
2nd of the Dhyana 4-Stages--It is
accompanied by great joy. The 3rd
State is not conscious of joy. I've
never experienced the 4th. Equanimity.
Coming.--

       The Mind of the universe is grinding out thoughts everywhere and
is full of perception everywhere---For instance though my eyeball has no
perception of its own, it can see because its subtle mechanism is perceived
by the Mind of the Universe----the lower mechanism of, say, a blade of grass
because of the Mind of the Universe perceives itself as grass--grass-hood---
and wouldnt be there at all except for this discriminated false-imagination
of self, and is the reason why it comes and goes.

****

SAMSARA-WORKINGS
       A description of Samsara (transmigration):
"If at death the individual, though he may have
freed himself of the 5 aggregates of grasping
(the 5 Khandhas), still clings to a desire for
his individuality, an individual composed of
other Khandhas comes into existence to carry on
the Karma." (Smith)
       "If thinking ended with death . . . who would
be able to recognize his rebirth?"
       Buddha

Today July 27, 1954, I delivered a great sermon in my mind while meditating in
the yard---"But the body will go, the body will die, and there is no You" was
the refrain, and "How I long to be able to do something else with that rhythm
of Buddha-breathes-in and Buddha-breathes-out than merely breathe in and out, how
I long to be disembodied in rhythm, and then how I long to be disembodied finally
in nothing"----and I sensed vast halls of wind and emptiness echoing inside me
and I knew I was here only because of an enormous self belief---and belief in
selfness---a sin begun by me selfishly and now I pay in pain----I saw Mind Essence
everywhere, had the eerie snaky sensation of it manifesting and manifesting all
this imaginary pain---I saw I cant write my visions of the Dharma except as I
write my dreams, swiftly, surely, undiscriminated, purely from my mind---So I
hereby end this book SOME OF THE DHARMA, these notes, and refer you to
       The book of Samadhi (the formal big flower) which I begin now.
       *******FINIS*******   July 27, 1954

I was sitting in the yard looking at the stars---Suddenly I saw that there was really no distance between me and the one star I could see---Beyond it was another smaller star and seemed further off---How far was the imaginary distance between the first star and the second star?---I saw that if it wasnt for these objects such as I, and the first, and the second star, "spaced" from one another, that is, if only nothing was there, we would have no grounds to call it space and say they were "spaced" and had distance from one another---We would only then be able to call it void---For I saw that no matter how far your conceptions of distance ranged, there was always another star further than the last one, that it was "infinite" but it only seemed to be "infinite" because of the objects which created a notion of spacing---I saw that it was an arbitrary conception to say "infinite"---even to say "space"---that it was sizeless & distanceless, no smaller than a hair, no bigger than a myriad galaxy of light years---That it was simply void---

Same with Time---because of the appearance and disappearance of thoughts we think in terms of Time, but it's only Void---

Because there was no arbitrary "end" to the universe, and since I knew that the universe is formed like an atom, i.e. planets so-fixed around, I knew that the atoms of which not only my body and tip of finger but the smallest hairtip on those distant stars were composed in the same way---"Infinitely" Void---simply void---You could travel forever in the arbitrary conception of "distance" of the universe before you'd learn it was just a void and had no distance---and you could travel forever inside the "smallest" atom of my finger tip's flesh before you learned it was just an empty void and had no distance either---

Therefore I saw that the planets and myself were merely arrangements

of infinitely empty universes in an infinitely empty universe infinitely empty

in and out and in all directions---Suddenly I saw that everything was empty

throughout and for the first time I realized that I was seeing the reality of

the world---that it was only appearable, imaginary, Ghost like---

I went deeper seeking to find why this incomprehensible hassle of empti-

ness universes atomistically *arranged* to seem solid were manifest in the first

place---When I asked WHY it suddenly occurred to me that it was only an attribute

of myself and my ignorance to even perceive that this was so and thus ask *why*,

I saw that it was my fault, that in perfection of mind essence there were no

such forms anyway---It came to me fortuitously then to remember the Four States

of Televolition---the first one "the sphere of infinite space" and I saw that

I'd just meditated on that---The second is the "sphere of infinite thought" and

this led me to realize and almost as if *remember* that in all Ten Quarters of

the universe at which I was looking, up, down through the earth to the other

up, sideways, all around, there were living beings hassled invisibly into

imaginary forms like me believing themselves truly existent, gnashing the empty

air, imagining their empty universes of atoms and inner empty universes and vast

voids being born, abiding, and dying---all of it monstrous, strange, hallucinated,

so that In the sphere of infinite thought I saw that mankind was only an isolated

instance in the Void, that there were all kinds of levels of sentience and per-

ception all of it mistaken---in fact I sensed beings of another plane suddenly

swimming through me like in pictures of phantoms passing through "concrete" ob-

jects with a pale phosphorescent transparency-- I suddenly realized it was not

impossible for there to be miracles, levitation, telepathy, apocalyptic earthquakes started by the mind of some seer, and I saw how stupid I was to doubt any of

the miracles of Jesus, Buddha, Edgar Cayce, Ste.Theresa or myself---I bethought

myself of the Third Sphere of Void, and saw that I had already penetrated into

that secret without trying---that all the sentient beings whose bodies are no-

thing but tormented areas of behassled emptiness are in reality not there,

that is, Nirvana passes through them untouched, unstained, unfilterable, pure

as in its pure whole silent state manifesting Ignorance---passing even through

the infinite empty universes of myself undifferentiating of me and "creator"

of me---that because we saw and reckoned these sentient beings and all phenomena

connected with them such as planets, food, conceptions of plants, dreams, thoughts

rising and falling we believed in space and distance and time and pain and "life"

---since pain wouldnt exist except for the arbitrary conception of its coming

and going, its birth and death---But I saw: *what dies* when a vast empty universe

of so-arranged atoms called "a sentient being" is suddenly transformed by that

imaginary condition called Death?---What changes? what happens? if it isnt all

just imaginary----Huge universes dont die they merely rearrange and since they're

empty straight through, what is it that rearranges?--- That star I see, except

for the arbitrary conception of brightness and darkness which is my sentient

predisposed Karma-mistake of eyeball-consciousness, would I see it? Except

for the arbitrary conception of contact and separation inherent in my indi-

vidualized consciousness of my 6-sensed body, would I feel it? Otherwise

wouldnt I pass right through it? or that is wouldnt Mind Essence pass right

through it?---Except for the arbitrary conception of motion and stillness (since

in Nirvana within nothing's moving, it's all beyond such consideration) would I

hear it, or hear those trucks now?---Except for my arbitrary conception of

variability and unchangeableness, would I taste it?----'Twould be tasteless.

Except for my arbitrary conception of passability and impassability I wouldnt

smell it, it's just odorless in reality---temperatureless in axisless frozen
ecstasy--

It just really isnt there---it's only Ignorance that's there---

It's Ignorance makes me perceive it with 5 senses and think of it with my
limited, stained, contaminated, ignorant, mistaken, tortured discriminative
manovijnana mind---

So I bethought me of the Fourth Sphere of neither Conception or Non-Con-
ception, and I thought "If I say I perceive that star I am making a mistake because it isnt really there, that is, it's only a false imagination arising from
MY SIDE---in itself it isnt there---IN ME, it's there---I dont have to ask WHY
Mind Essence went and manifested ignorance because now I am ignorance and I've
only myself to blame, Mind Essence can assure me that there's nothing there but
I am so behassled I insist there's true phenomena, true pain, true death---In
reality of Dharmakaya no, there's only soundless, invisible, odorless, tasteless,
impalpable, unperceivable essence of mind of the void which is this Universe---
it's up to *me* to see that---and to see it not by false-perception of my senses,
but by Intuition---

And so that for me to say that this discriminated star is NOT THERE is a lie,
for if I have sentient perception how can I help perceiving the manifestation of
sentient star?---that would be a lie---the star is neither there nor not there,
it's an empty apparition in the sky which we call sky instead of void only because
it is not empty of apparitions which sentient beings falsely perceive---

But I saw that I could not escape my sentience, the 3 Gunas of Light,Energy,&
Inertia that had me saddled with a body, that sooner or later the arbitrary conception of appearance and disappearance would come to me in the form of hunger, and
also pain such as the pain of my crossed ankles where because of my sentient arbitrary conception of contact and separation I could now feel the empty universes

of blood pressing against the empty universes of vein and flesh, numbing---But what was it that was numbing? Empty worlds manifesting imaginary ideas of pain. I saw there was no escape because I had been bound up in this because of habit energy since beginningless time. I remembered Buddha's last words "All compound things decay, work out thy salvation with diligence"---Meaning, escape componenthood if you can, it decays, it causes pain, it is imaginary, it cheats--- it is Ignorance, all that you see, feel, smell, taste, touch, think about is Ignorance. Ignorance is the manifestation of mind essence, which means, all manifestation from essence, all appearance, all epiphany, is Ignorance and only nothingness, non-manifestation, non-epiphany is Enlightenment. I was enlightened but I was trapped in compound sentience, saddled with ankles that hurt and a belly that had to be fed, subject to delusion, pain, boredom---even anger, lust, greed, foolishness---even drunkenness finally, stupidity, madness, decrepitude, and death. No way out---

There may be someday a man, whose name shall be Aremideia, by the snap of his finger all things shall vanish back into their origin in mind. Only Aremideia can save the world, and Aremideia is impossible.

I hoped---I remembered how I fainted in the yard one Sunday and how I lay unconscious in the sun 50 seconds or so, how my consciousness and therefore all following Nirdana Chainlinks (10,9,8,7,6,5,4,3,2,1, or rather, 3,4,5,6,7,8,9,10) were vanished, how all that remained was my Karma-action of heartbeat and breathing and a vague sensation of goldenness (that came from the sun on my unconscious eyeballs),---I hoped and knew now, that at death the Karma-action will cease too, (and the goldenness replaced by a beautiful colorlessness of void) but will the final chain link, No. 1, be vanished: *Ignorance*? Only if at death my body vanished into thin air---for its destruction among worms or in fire is only a vague rearrangement of atomic worlds infinitely empty in all directions moving about in imaginary hassle inside vast universes of worm cell or in universes of

empty fire gas---in no sense vanishment of the primal mistake of false-existence---

Is it all in the mind, the escape? the breakthrough? As I lay unconscious it

wasnt "I am dead," it was "mind essence is mind essence." (This is why, when

walking at night on my favorite sidewalk going under low trees I say "Bend the

head, your low branches wont hurt")----Nobody dies; there is nothing to die ex-

cept aggregates of imagination that is not real in the first place but we cling

and call it "ego-personality"----Where is the escape?

   To disappear into thin air? After which, it is not said "I am gone," but,

"Mind essence is mind essence."

   Says Buddha: "If at the approach of death thinking stopped, who would

recognize his rebirth?"

   Where is the escape from this universe of Ignorance?*

                              --July 1954

                    * * * * * * * * * * * * *

*By realizing that there is nothing to disappear into thin air except Mind Essence itself, which neither appears nor disappears, and so by realizing that the body and all its pain is Mind-only. By realizing that words and thoughts like these are ripples of Ignorance on the clear mirror surface of Mind Essence with its intrinsic unbroken Calm. For, emptiness is what it all is.

book three

From July 29, 1954

World's Secret Bliss---it's permeating throughout, in Nirvana form---

Happiness won't come from coddling the senses but from cultivating the mind.

If it is possible to find the bliss of Nirvana while still in the sentient state
of life, Buddhahood is the way.

You gotta kick that Upadana habit.

* * * * * * * * * * * *

Tonight July 29 I couldn't sleep and instead I remembered almost all of my life
(sections in the vast canvas), at first with gladness of rediscovery then gradually with realization that it was all a magical action in some central void
night, for naught---All things come to naught because they are *things*---It all
broke down, it *will* break down if I give it rebirth, such as, say, trying to live
a non Buddhahood life in the world again---My faith was renewed by Right Recollection of the untrustworthiness of sense experience, especially in society---I saw
my father, my old girlfriends, my long Lowell night walks, clearly, without regret,
on that Bliss Screen of Movies.
                 I'm not gonna be fooled any more, I'm here to stick to
my sweet Tathagata.
              ---There is always nostalgia on a screen---but not in the bleak actual
collision with the world---like dismal mornings in Virginia . . .
- -
            TAO XX-----THE WORLD AND I
"The people of the world are merry-making,
As if eating of the sacrificial offerings,
As if mounting the terrace in Spring;
I alone am mild, like one unemployed,
Like a new-born babe that cannot yet smile,
Unattached, like one without a home.

The people of the world have enough and to spare,
But I am like one left out,
My heart must be that of a fool,
Being muddied, nebulous!

The vulgar are knowing, luminous;
I alone am dull, confused.
The vulgar are clever, self-assured;
   I alone, depressed.
Patient as the sea,
   Adrift, seemingly aimless.

The people of the world all have a purpose;
   I alone appear stubborn and uncouth.
   I alone differ from the other people,
And value drawing sustenance from the Mother."

BUT I AM NOURISHED BY FOOD FROM MOTHER TAO . . .

* * * * * * * * * *

The Three Gunas

    1. Sattwa . . . . . or,Light, Intelligence, Consciousness
    2. Rajas . . . . . or, Energy, Moving Force, Activity
    3. Tamas . . . . . or, Inertia, Darkness, Body, Matter

        Nothing's repetitious---everything has a floweriness of
its own---But it is repetitious in its floweriness---

The reason not to drink any alcohol at all is to attain permanently to the
shivering bliss of pure blood. To keep the mind from confusion.

Dharmakaya causes Ignorance---AVIDYA---In Ignorance there is contact, PHASSA,
which causes feeling, VEDANA "which becomes through the CETAYITA work of the mind
the cause of cognized objects" and so of UPADANA attachment to them. The escape
is via control. ATTA DIPA . . . self be your lantern.

Subjective and Objective are another Western dualism---in dreams what is subjective and what is objective? It's all the same fantastic emanation of scenes
and selves. Dreams are either deep or shallow. . . . which is subjective? which is
objective?

AYATANAS---bases of experience, seats of contact (12) which are unlocatable.
"The locations of contact of the conceptions within the mind and the system of
sense-conceptions are alike false and fantastic; they are neither manifested by
causes and conditions or spontaneously by their own nature." --Surangama Sutra.

The Three Signs of Certainty
    1.Suffering
    2.Not-self
    3.Transiency

PATIMOKKHA---Confession by monks together at UPOSATHA bi-monthly assemblies

ADVAITA---Non-dualism
STUPA---relic-domes
STAMBHA---Commemorative Pillar

Four Great Buddhist Kings: ASOKA, HARSHA, CHANDRAGUPTA, KANISHKA

SADDHARMA--the True Law
BHAKTI---Faith
PUNDARIKA---Lotus
MAITREYA---The Coming Buddha (in India)   In Burma: Aremideia

          *******POEM*******
          O Lord Buddha
          You saw to it   You add flips
          There'd be   To the real
          Emptiness.   When worlds
          Your Snow   Rise manifest
          Is very good
          And buries   So now, Maitreya,
          My dream.   And thee, Light,
                           And O Sravasti,
                           Unreal is real.

I can't write the Dharma in verse because I can't mean what I say and think of lines and rhyme at the same time. (Not yet)

AYATANAS---the unlocatability of the 12 locations of contact between consciousness and objects cognized----For instance, the location of the eye and the location of the seen object are alike false and fantastic, we cannot be certain of the substantiality of space if we are not certain of the substantiality of sights. Not sights in space, but empty visions in the void. What is the location of the dreaming mind and of the dream-images in a dream?

BIRTH = DEATH
And TRUTH equals TRUTH

I am a member of the BEATIFIC GENERATION

Some of the Tao: Natural men in the days of "perfect nature" (Chuangtse) didn't use salt if they didn't live near the sea---they were friendly with the birds and didn't eat them---they "patted their bellies and wandered around watching unexpected events" and must have said funny things---Like the old men of China with long beards and dainty feet trotting and giggling down the marketplace---

> Buddhism is a system of Mind Control
> Tao is a philosophy without disciplinary rules
> But because of this Tao can become Mao (Tse Tung)

---Chuangtse says that the Sage who begged caused confusion and doubt in the hearts of men---My only criticism of Buddha is of his insistence on begging---but I don't understand begging because I'm a Westerner---I do understand the humility and patience of begging and the beauty of living on faith in this dream---But why should humility have to be *taught* to humble Fellaheen householders---The Oriental Sage, the Long Beard, well-known---But knowledge is a robèd thing and I say that Buddha's knowledge of emptiness and how to sit and meditate on its Absolute Clearness so as to be in conformity with the Mind Essence of Tathagata's Womb which manifests all forms and also all conceptions of emptiness and for the sake of recognizing one's eventual restoration in the 7-dimensional Mysterious Mirror of Mnd Essence (the 6 manas minds and the intrinsic alaya mind) is the last and the first word and the word without origin concerning the truth of the universe; and I say that Tao is a fluid, goodnatured way of floating around like a submissive cloud until the perfection of Parinirvana Death.

Buddhism is for Saints, Tao is for anybody.
Buddhism is for thought, for Samadhi meditation sessions; Tao is for moment-by-moment living. The two combine all the Wisdom of the Orient. Historically they are "Late Developments" (Syncretisms) and have broken clear from myth & image of the primitive soul, which is like the soul of the Dreamer.

Tao is a free way---it too recognizes emptiness but it is like a cloud floating in the perfect blue sky, put-together into a being but already dispersing as it moves along and finally it will be all gone, restored to its origin, just as if you took a match and put it before a mirror and demonstrated by lighting the match:---the blue tip immediately disappears in flame:- as far as we are concerned in terms of the mirror, has the blue sulphur sight not been restored into the perfect clearness, emptiness and freedom of the mirror from whence first it was manifested and materialized (as far as the surface of the mirror is concerned)?

---Where else did the sight of the blue match tip go?---Therefore the cloud, once dissolved, has been restored into the Absolute Clearness of space, the intrinsic nature of which is emptiness and freedom of Tao, and was just a reflection in the mirror of Mind. Mind the Cause. But while it held its being and floated along, drifting, dissolving slowly, changing continually, was there any reason to ask it to beg? or give it four or five precepts? or an 8-Fold path to follow? or any rules, restrictions, conditions, whatever? would that stop it from sailing along, and falling apart so gracefully? But being a cloud it needs to practice no means to enlightenment. This is because the nature of the cloud is its cloudness, it has Cloudness-Ignorance, and nothing you can do about it, being an inert cloud uncontaminated by sentient needs & means.

Buddhism is for Absolutes, Tao is for nature, but Tao like nature came before Buddhism the realization of self-nature, and both are from the Absolute.

Buddhahood is the realization of the Absolute. Tao *is* the Absolute, this is so, I can see, because it is free, there are no School-Restrictions, no disciplines of self-realization of noble wisdom. "Instead of praising Yao and blaming Shieh forget both and lose yourself in Tao." This means that if you lose yourself in the natural, if you accept your crooked body as being a crooked body, then there's no reason to call it good or bad and trying to straighten it or make it more crooked. You are saddled with it and it is natural and casual.
So Tao says: "I guard the original One and rest in harmony with externals."

Popeye is for the funny page; Tao is for acceptance of nature;
Buddhahood is for non-conditioned, non-caused Highest Reality.

"A new Ulysses leaves once more
  Calypso for his native shore."
                  --SHELLEY   MADHAVA'S COMPENDIUM (get)

". . . an herb wrap't round its leg."
                  ----JEAN-LOUIS

Flowers come from corpses---   "Facts" are really sophistries.

"Honor through inaction comes from the Tao of God; entanglement through action comes from the Tao of Man."

ABHINISHKRAMANA means Renunciation; CHARITA, career

                  Maitreya from Mithra?
All the brilliant books of Nalanda University, some of them copied and preserved by Chinese pilgrims, were burned by the Mohammedans, who make the arbirary conception of enlightenment and non-enlightenment; in the Womb of Tathagata they are neither forgiven or not-forgiven; in the Womb of Tathagata there are no arbitrary conceptions as to the world's existence, ego-personality, or karma fruit.

Four Buddhist Schools:- SARVASTIVADINS, SAUTRANTIKAS,
                  MADHYAMIKAS (Nagarjuna's void sunyata)
                  YOGACARAS (Lankavatara Scripture & Asvhaghosha's Sradda)

DHRI, to preserve, establish, root of DHARMA

Beyond the mental concept of the sun is the emptiness of sunyata.
SVABHAVA, self-essence   SMRITI, memory   MAYA, measurement (of) illusion

Two great Chinese Buddhist Saints were FA-HSIAN, and HSUAN TSANG

CITTA-VRITTI-NIRODHA: "through the suppression of the individualizing activity
of the mind"----it is a "supreme undifferentiated yoga ecstasy"---

SAMATA, Spiritual Oneness   PRANIDHANA, "vow"---"placing before one"
PARAMITA (Pali parami), means Perfection

* * * * * * * * * * * * * * * * * * * *

THE SIX PARAMITAS
(or, Six Transcendental Virtues)
1. Unselfish giving for others, DANA, radiant & selfless
2. Moral purity, kindness, SILA, sympathy, absence of craving
3. Forbearance, patience, KSHANTI, endurance, forgiveness
4. Energy, enthusiasm, VIRYA, effort for the ideal
5. Dhyana concentration, DHYANA PARAMITA, 4 stages of meditation
6. Wisdom, insight, PRAJNA PARAMITA, absence of conceptions & illusions

THE FOUR TRANSCENDENTAL VIRTUES
1. Strategic skill to convert (UPAYA)
2. Resolution
3. Power
4. Knowledge

SADDHARMA PUNDARIKA, from SAD (true), DHARMA (Law), PUNDARIKA (Lotus)
The Lotus of the True Law

. . . .
BHUMI, Stage in practice of Paramitas

THE TEN BHUMIS
1. *Joy* because all men'll be enlightened
2. *Free from impurity* through moral striving
3. *Light of the world* by forbearance
4. *Effulgent* in enthusiasm
5. *Invincible* in concentration
6. *Face to face* with reality as sunyata void
7. *Far-reaching* in upaya skill & tact
8. *Immovable* in aspirations
9. *Unerring* in saintliness
10. *Cloud of doctrine* iddhi magic (Dharmamega)

The Eleventh Bhumi is Bhumi of the Buddha "crown & climax of all"
. . . .
MAHAYANA is probably a later Puritan-like super-addition, or Protestant overlay,
or New Vision, of original primitive *non-political* Buddhism---Hinayana Buddhism
is closer to the Tao than to Mahayana, by virtue of its looseness (Buddha's last
words in Mahaparinirvana Sutra: "All things come to an end, work out thy salvation
with diligence)"; *pagani* country-folk "thick" wisdom (paragraphs in the Dhammapada)
(as apart from more metaphysical concerns of Shradhotpadda Shastra, the concept
of the Fumigation of Mind Essence, and allusions to magicians and actors in
Lankavatra Sutra), freedom, humor, realistic approach to women ("the crocodiles
are the womenfolk") (compare this to later bhikushini developments), general realism
about death, about suffering, about the snakes and the gadflies.

Hinayana is the root,

But Mahayana is the blossom. The Full Vision of the Buddhas of Old.

And Santiveda, the Scholar Mahayanist Saint of the Seventh Century, is like the decay of the blossom. He wrote in "Journey to Enlightenment":- "There is no guilt equal to hatred, no mortification equal to long-suffering." This has Thomas à Kempis late-Religion sound, also self-conscious Intellectuality, i.e., "All have the same sorrows (as I)." But if the truth were known, these are all irrelevant historical distinctions based on naturalism, and don't even have any basis of existence. History, history indeed. Religion, religion indeed.

CHUANGTSE argues against the practice of begging:-
"Charity of heart and duty to one's neighbor (are) bolts for gyves" (because not natural). Any Canuck knows this.

"Of old, the Yellow Emperor first interfered with the natural goodness of the heart of man, by means of charity and duty . . ."
"Then came confusion between joy and anger, fraud between the simple and the cunning, recrimination between the virtuous and the evil-minded (because of duty), slander between the honest and the liars, and the world order collapsed."
"In the days of perfect nature . . . men . . . being all equally without knowledge, their virtue could not go astray. Being all equally without desires, they were in a state of natural integrity. In this state of natural integrity, the people did not lose their nature. And then when Sages appeared, crawling for charity and limping with duty, doubt and confusion entered men's minds."

. . . .

DEATH---don't fear death and don't grieve the death of your beloved ones, Buddha said that all is empty, truly,(and we sentient beings are really not sentient beings, nor living beings, nor beings with selves, just apparitions in the empty truth;) and the Tao says to have courage because it's like nature to come and go, and it is natural.

Now that I know the Tao I can understand something about what we call "Literature." In 1941 when I was 19, two writers pulled me out of my natural interest in the "Casual Poet of Lin Yutang and Saroyan" as I fancied myself then, purely in fields idealizing nature and the blue sky. The two writers were nothing but Western Faustian Space-Time tension writers--- Joyce and Dostoevsky. "Much knowledge is a curse." But Dostoevsky had the compassion of a great Orthodox Saint underneath his Western City Decadence. Joyce is really trivial except for his involuntary unconscious visions of the truth elicited through a style. And so is the Jean-Louis of Modern Prose.

Just like when I was a kid and I knew that I should wear my overalls all the time and that every day should be Saturday, is Tao to me.

* *

As for PARANOIA . . . the phenomena of our effort to objectify self in dreams, by sometimes manifesting characters who act for us as we watch, so that subjective and objective are really melted together in the Saha Tripleness of Dreamer-Dreaming-Dreamed, is the same phenomenon as paranoia, so-called, the effort to objectify subjective feelings of our own selves onto others, ascribing to others what we have thought. All we are is what we have thought. So in "real life" of waking from sleep and dreams, objective and subjective are melted together in the dream of existence, and so as the Diamond Sutra says, "Entertain no notion of self, other selves, living beings, or a Universal Self."

PARANOIA (cont'd)---Paranoia is unnecessary, like risen thoughts, like the very
belief in existence. Madness is imaginary; "sanity" is also imaginary.
Entertain no thoughts as to the existence or non-existence of selves, beings,
persons, or a Person.
There are no fish in the sea,
No fishies, no you and me.

"You have doubtless heard about the insane man, Yayattadha
in this very city of Sravasti. One morning he looked into a mirror and saw his
head but it had no eyes nor eyebrows. He became very angry with his own head
and blamed it as being the head of a goblin because it had no eyes or eyebrows,
and ran away quite crazy. What do you think, Purna? Did the man have any good
reason for becoming crazy?"

Purna replied:-It seems to me, Blessed Lord, that he had
no other reason than this, that he was crazy already.

The Lord Buddha replied:-Purna! Our mysterious Intuitive
Nature is perfect and enlightening and its natural perfection is intelligent and
profound. Since the True Nature is free from all illusions (the True Mind), so
the illusions are naturally devoid of any reality, and, therefore, have no source
of existence. If they have no source of existence, they are no longer illusions
even. All these thought-illusions have been raised by means of their own reciprocal manifestations and thus the piling up of delusion upon delusions has been
going on for kalpa after kalpa as many as the particles of dust in the air.

Though the Buddhas have disclosed their falsity, yet
sentient beings cannot at once realize their falsity and return to their natural
state of enlightenment. The source of these delusions is nowhere else but within
one's own mind.

As soon as you understand the source of a delusion, the
deluding conception loses its hold upon existence. If within your mind you
provide no source for these false conceptions, there will be none to be discarded.
Those who have attained enlightenment are as if awakening from sleep, and their
past life seems only a dream.

However clear one's memory may be, it is impossible to
reproduce any dreamed-of object---no matter under what conditions or causes.
It would be more impossible for you to grasp that which has no hold whatever upon
its own source of existence. Like the insane man of Sravasti who ran away because
of the wholly imaginary and fantastic thoughts of his mind, with no other cause
or conditions. If this insanity was suddenly cured, his consciousness of his
head would just as suddenly be recovered, and no matter whether his insanity is
cured or not, his head is on his body. Purna, the illusions of the mind are
just as fantastic and have no more basis for existence." SURANGAMA SUTRA

* *

Look up the Nirvana of the Stoics . . . AUTARKEIA and EUDAIMONIA

The Catholic Religion, of Aquinas, the Pope and the Eastern Patriarch is the
only surviving primitive religion in the civilized world. The Vedics, the
Shinto, the Aztec, the Apollonian, the Eddas . . . all were early expressions of a
primitive culture, as Apocalyptic Christianity was the early (later-pseudomor-
phosed into the West by Paul) Arabian expression. It alone survives; explains
why a Faustian Jet-pilot can still believe in the Devil but an Indian student
at Columbia can have put Buddhism behind him, know nothing of the Vedas, and
complain of economic exploitation.

Spengler did not understand Tao, it was in his nature not to.

SPENGLER continued . . . *The Decline of the West* as a work should really be called
The Climax of German Thought . . . the sound of boots is in it always, something
alien from the nebulous cloud and far below it . . . a concern with everlasting
details of history . . . but in all the myriad assyamkas of kalpas of unnumberable
millenniums how many details, how many grains of dust, in this HISTORY? Not one.
This is Tao---

   A reality which can only be explained ahistorically, is where Spengler is now,
in death, in truth, in void.

                    -   -   -

Go to Europe? Europe is precisely what I'm trying to get away from---
To find the natural, find the primitive---Live in Mexico
   "A thatched hut in Lowell"---Al Sublette
"Above the praise and blame" . . . CHUANGTSE

            *

            THE YOGA GOAL OF CONCENTRATION
            1.Now concentration is explained
            2.Yoga is restraining the mind-stuff from taking
               various forms. (CITTA-VRITTI-NIRODHA)
            3.At that time the seer rests in his own state

SEER OF INDIA, SAGE OF CHINA
"By meditating on the knowledge that comes in sleep."

VRITTI, forms CITTA, mindstuff
"The Yogi whose *Vrittis* have thus become powerless obtains in the receiver,
the receiving and the received, concentratedness and sameness, like the
crystal." YOGIC PRECEPTS

"Wherever conflict arises among living creatures the sense of possession is the
   cause"--SANTIVEDA

                  KARUNA, Compassion, "Pathos of compassion redressing human
                              sorrows."
                  AGAPE, Care & reverence
            Both opposed to EROS as sense desire
- -
"The Divine humiliation of the Man of Sorrows"---F.H.Smith

ANUKAMPA, restless sympathy---KRIPA, grief---DAYA, pity---PUNYA, merit
PARINAMANA, transfer of merit

MANJU, beautiful   SRI, prosperity; thus, MANJUSRI, the Bodhisattva of intellect-
                              ual radiance

            MAITREYA, the coming Buddha, may be from MITRA,
            Vedic God of Friendship, and MITHRA, Persian God
            of Alliances.

A little bit of real love at home is worth a lot of false love away from home.
            *
EYES---The way moonblossoms trick the tired eye, the raggedy moon jags you see
vibrating as if around it, this only means the sickness (tiredness) of the

eyeballs and has nothing to do with consciousness of seeing itself. That is, the nature of the consciousness of sight arising from the eyeballs that see an imaginary halo-jag is not responsible for the viewing mistakes. This is the *morbid* sight . . . an imaginary sight. Sight in itself is but an obscuring mist. "Therefore we must be careful not to plunge the intuitive nature (of Mind) that perceives this morbid mist that is discriminated by the perception of inflamed eyes into the same morbid mist". . . . "(all things) seem to be discriminated particulars of fact, but in truth, they are all made up by the original, be-ginningless sickness of perceiving eyes."

* *

With the sentience trying to satisfy the conditional being with *unconditional satisfaction,* I go on living, and by this I know, the true Me is space---is stillness---is emptiness---is N i r v a n a

> What I want is a sign of what I am, and I want everything
> in the universe---

Fire is Cold
To Asbestos
* * * * * * * * * * * *

A man comes to a strange village and doesnt know which is north, which is south, this is because the essential nature of his mind is purity of perfect emptiness. Contaminate him with the "right direction."---

All the fine enthusiasms that've gone down the drain---

Refer to the Fantastic Paintings of HIERONYMUS BOSCH

Another word for rococo---Alexandrinism.

> "---that profound Gothic blissfulness of which today we cannot even
> form an idea"----in some afternoon cloister (Spengler mentions)

Renaissance, *Rinascita*

TAO:- Just exactly what Burroughs calls "dullness" is Tao---the Tao is Scotty Beaulieu, who says, "What should one do, or what should one not do? Let the changes go on by themselves." (Tao)----Or as he says in *Doctor Sax,* "Let the eagle fly his own nose."

FAUSTIAN is artificial will of fame
TAO is natural destiny of virtue

> "Those who have attained enlightenment are as if awakened
> from sleep, and their past life seems only a dream."
> This also happens when coming out of meditation any time,
> even try closing your eyes on the street three seconds and see
> the whole dream swim back.
Buddha Bubble Burma Dharma indeed. . . .

If, as Burroughs insists, "Buddhism is not for the West," then I get a great vision of the whole Western World filled with the ignorant and simpleminded.

The whole Faustian West is like Yayattadha who looked in the mirror and became
angry because he couldn't see his own head and ran away crazy. They've been
running ever since Aquinas, Copernicus, Leibniz and Moptop Goethe. The illusions
of what the West calls the "sane" mind are just as fantastic and have no more
basis for existence in reality.

      Insanity is nothing but an exaggeration of Western "sanity." More anon.

Millennial jokes about taxes---from Pulque Azteca to Cobra India--

The Scorpion is a Fallen Angel----a Woman is Temptation Incarnate---
A Body is Karma Enfleshed----Life is Ignorance Incorporated---
Sight is Sick---Self is Slop---Sin is Sadness Acting---
Poetry is Poopoocaca

Fun is Folly. . . .

I think of the Chicago Loop in August . . . I know I'm just as well of here as
rushing through the Loop---"all things is equal"---No direction in the void,
no place in the vacuum, no point in the Crystal Reality---through the Loopy west . . .

THE SECRET OF SHAKESPEARE; he wrote costume poetry for the stage---There's your
fortune---Had Plutarch's Lives and a book about Kings of England, and set the
scene like a Hollywood Historical Costume Picture (redcoats of Canada 1890, court
of Catherine the Great)---and made dandies, couriers, ladies, dancers and generals
and emperors talk with yapping mouths.----A bwa a bwa a bwa. BOOM! The cannon
offstage. This is poetry, dramatic poetry. The vision of life, in which he was
swilled like a pearl in a pigsty, a gloriously ignorant singer.

     "In peace," he says, "there's nothing so becomes a man
       As modest stillness and humility;
        When the blast of war blows in our ears,
        Then imitate the action of the tiger."
  This is like Krishna's advice to the sad warrior in Bhagavad-Gita.
It's given by King Henry V with scaling-ladder in hand, at Walls of Harfleur
                       Act III ScI

"Stiffen the sinews, summon up the blood,
Disguise fair nature with hard-favor'd rage
Then lend the eye a terrible aspect;
Let it pry through the portage of the head
Like the brass cannon; let the brow o'erwhelm it
As fearfully as doth a galled rock
O'erhang and jutty his confounded base,
Swill'd with the wild & wasteful ocean." (as though here he knew sea-of-rebirth)
"Now set the teeth and stretch the nostril wide,
Hold hard the breath and bend up every spirit
To his full height. On, on, you noblest English
Whose blood is fet from fathers of warproof!
Fathers that, like so many Alexanders,
Have in these parts from morn till even fought
And sheathed their swords for lack of argument:
Dishonour not your mothers; now attest
That those whom you call'd fathers did beget you."
    SHEER IGNORANCE IN SILKEN DRESS . . . .

    And "Buddhism is not for the West," and war goes on

Then this Immortal Bard played the gallery with Nym . . .
And played a form of Tao with "Boy":

BOY:-"Would I were in an alehouse in London! I would give all my
fame for a pot of ale and safety."

"And many a skeleton shook his head.
'Instead of preaching forty year,'
My neighbor Parson Thirdly said,
'I wish I had stuck to pipes and beer.'"---THOMAS HARDY

Shakespeare's real Gimmick Poetry is in Nym, Boy, Pistol . . . Then, to unfold the
story, his Monologues unfold the prose explanation concerning backgrounds of the
play. It's just a shining technique in the darkness, and goes out.
But when the Lamp of the East was lit . . .

* *

YET TODAY AUG.24 '54 is the lowest point in my Buddhist Faith since I began
last December--- Reason:*Loneliness of Westerner practising Eightfold Path
alone, without occasional company of Buddhist monks and laymen. You've got to
talk---even Buddha talked all day. Here I am in America sitting alone with legs
crossed as world rages to burn itself up---What to do? Buddhism has killed all
my feelings, I have no feelings, no inclinations to go anywhere, yet I stay here
in this house a sitting duck for the police who want me for penury & non-support,
listless, bored, world-weary at 32, no longer interested in love, tired, unutter-
ably sad as the Chinese autumn-man. It's the silence of unspoken despair, the
sound of drying, that gets me down. . . .
        I MUST GO AWAY ALONE

No more letters. Write to your friends: Let's write no more letters but have
absolute trust in each other till we meet. *He who knows does not speak."*

And then is written in my notebook the cry: "Who the hell asked for this?"

* *

THIS IS JEAN-LOUIS' TAO ON THIEVES. Robbers look for a lot of houses in the
suburbs because there are more marks to try and score; but the lone country
house offers lean variety, especially if it's poor. Yet people move to the
suburbs for safety from robbers of the city.

TWO SELF CONTRADICTIONS in my notebook: "Death?--how many glasses of wine have I
put between me and death? Eat, drink, and be merry."
        Then:- "Stay sober? Dont be silly---it's too dreary."

I was wiser in December 1953 when I began my faith and said: "That whole dream
of life, stop it, that's enough I said in the armed forces, in work, schools,
frets, jails,---roads---leave me alone to forget your false 'realities' and
remember the briefness of this dream and snarling delusion, *stop* it in eternity
now---I want no more of it." And that's the gist.

REBIRTH---Don't make light of those little slim babies,
        Their suffering gets awfully fat after awhile.

Broadway glitter of things?--the pristine mind of Jean-Louis.
But these are thoughts of self, like saying, "Was my real self the one talking
to Giroux (Harcourt Brace editor) about Yeats in 1949, or the me of the 1939
track photo where I'm young and bashful . . .
The "real self" is the Tathagata No-Self . . .

THE FIVE DEFILEMENTS
1. Individuation of "form" (which is but fantasy)
2. Erroneous views about form
3. Developing desire for form
4. Grasping at desired form
5. Imaginary conflict of form---weariness, suffering, growing old, decrepitude.
             O topsy-turvy mind!

The Four Great Elements are the Four Bonds dividing Essential Mind into
Fourfold Impurity.

FIVE DEFILEMENTS OF TIGER AND ME

TIGER	*ME*
1.Arbitrary conceptions of false phenomena leads to false manifestation of differences in the universes and the jungles, false sights dividing the Mind	1.Arbitrary conceptions of false phenomena occupying empty space leads to false manifestation of their differences of form in the universes and civilizations.
2.Because of false imaginations rising from division of the mind, the tiger develops erroneous views concerning forms of different sorts of sights.	2.Because of false imaginations rising from division and resulting confusion of the mind, I develop erroneous views concerning all the different imaginary forms I see and sense, naming them.
3.These views established, such as the Antelope is to eat, established in memory, arises evil desire for the forms and evil aversion to others.	3.I taste the experience in different forms, and conceive evil desires for some, evil aversions for others, all via consciousness, emotion, moods, and get entangled in phantasmal imaginations and aspirations.
4.Conditioned by his Karma he grasps the Antelope, transforming sentient lives & perpetuating Karma and rebirth chaos.	4.Conditioned by my Karma I grasp at these forms, and "write", or lust, or steal, or daydream of killing, or kill bugs, transforming other lives, other beings under punishment, & perpetuating demerit of Karma continuously instead of stopping it.
5.Forms are now placed in opposition and relation to one another mutually incompatible, leading to internal and external conflicts, weariness, suffering, age and decrepitude, death and rebirth.	5.Mutually incompatible the forms rage in my head & in the world outside, conflicting, warring, hating, blind, bringing their ignorant champions to weariness, misery, old age, and decrepitude and death & rebirth.

* *

EMPTINESS OF TASTE

What do Cornflakes & Sugar taste to the wooden bowl?---it is only an arbitrary conception of my solitary taste-organ, my tongue, this "taste" of Cornflakes
& Sugar, the "taste" has no substantiality of existence outside of my tongue
and its taste-mind and its taste-mind. In the same way the sight of the moon
is an arbitrary conception of my arbitrary sight-organ, my solitary eye---and,
yea, the solidness and feel of this chair-arm upon which I write is only an
arbitrary conception of my solitary touch-organ, my body (and its arbitrary
manovijnana touch-mind)---the "feel" of the chair, of the concrete world as we
call it in the West, has no substantiality of existence outside our minds.

Things can only be said to exist as arbitrary conceptions arising from the mind
---they can only be said to not-exist as arbitrary conceptions arising from the
same mind, the other side of the same thought, the other end of the dualism.

Things neither *are,* nor *are-not* . . . . they appear to be there . . . temporarily . . .

Taste is a false imagination, it has no basis for existence outside the experience
of tongue-consciousness. Where does taste come from? If it came from the tongue
only, it wouldnt come from the cornflakes, then how could you taste cornflakes
instead of dry leaves? If it came from the cornflakes only, how would the tongue
tell? If it came from both, this consciousness of taste, from both tongue and
cornflakes, then where's the dividing line of this split-up consciousness and
where does this arbitrary line go when you're not tasting anything at all?
More later. This is the Lotus Teaching that frees one from arbitrary conceptions.

In the same way, discriminated thought and discriminated teaching such as this
has no basis for existence outside the experience of the thinking-mind, the brain.
This is why Buddhism is only a finger of falsely perceived teaching pointing at
the truth of emptiness which is the Sole Reality.

>   Buddha never said that this
>   evil world would ever end.

What would the chair feel like if there was no one in the world with a feeling
body? Nothing, empty.
* *

NOTE ON WRITING

The material of a dream arranges itself just one way, out of infinite possibility, since the thinking-mind is continuously thinking, and that way is the pure
visionary experience as directly presented at the moment by the mind, like a
thought---no choice is made, it happens, and happens its own way as you sleep on--
We thus say "Dreams have no meaning," that is, logically:
EXAMPLE FOR "BOOK OF DREAMS" (Vol.12)
"There's been a tower set up in the city to show where the atom bomb is going
to be laid when time comes to blast the city---announcement has been made for
next month and evacuation begun---You see the city at night now, dark under a dim
moon, low lights everywhere from the diminishing and dimming population---I'm
there on a sad tenement balcony planning my departure up the Northern river to the
right---All the Porto Ricans linger yet in doom'd New York trying to salvage one
last month of tasting the rich leftovers of a once-rich city---trying to eat up
all their Manhattan love, their Manhattanana---I look at the tower in the moonlight, it looks so sinister, guarded, shrouded, to die---"

This dream only has "no meaning" in that it is a fantastic self-invention
from the Mind instead of a non-fantastic intellecting plan commending itself

DREAMS, cont'd

directly to bare simple reason, as for instance, the Four Precepts of Dont Kill,
Dont Steal, Dont Lust, Dont Lie that have a meaning but in themselves no more
meaning than a silly dream---But the dream has meaning of great sadness, and
is clear because simple picture-image. It wrote itself. In writing therefore
the prose and the poetry of Things (apart from the prose and the poetry of The
Teaching of No-Things, such as this Dharma), the Vision from Daydreaming too must
come in a same flash and be complete in itself, write itself, and require no expedient means of plot and outer plan. This is inner form of writing. Deep form,
as ored up from the bottom of the Mind unplanned.

If I were to write the Dharma in the same way, leerily dreaming on,
some gems would emerge but the general meaning would not be under control. For
me to control the elephant also means to control this tremendous technique of
writing I myself discovered & discarded.

Dreams and Daydreams happen in the present tense, show the scene, and
go. This is your chapter. Chapters should be Blowing Sessions, like the Jazz
Musician his chorus before it's begun is done forever. Why Jazz is Great.

But writers go on changing words and halting and erasing and rearranging
chapters and fouling up their crystal. This applies only to Non-Teaching writing.
For if you want to write about Things, write *like* Things, spontaneously & purely.

------------------------------------- * -------------------------------------

Tonight Aug 27'54 I heard the other moment of the world---The loud airplane sneaked
up on me in my hearing,---I listened to the growing roar---when the roar had begun
to fade again, I was aware that the moment of the Growing Roar and the moment of
the Disappearing Roar were distinct . . . it was the *other* moment of the world . . ?? . . .
These were my words but the Samadhi itself was deeper, and was like revelation
and like last winter when the Moment-of-Walking-on-Rockaway was the same as All-
Moments-Thereafter----Whenever a thought rose in my mind I directed it back to the
one moment of my walking on Rockaway Boulevard one night, and so the thoughts
were merged timeless----Tonight, the two distinct sounds belonged to the same
essential Moment, or Momentness, of Time . . . truly there is no Time, because Time
is an arbitrary conception arising from there being thinking-mind that discriminates
the Coming & Going of moments only because of accidental actions which are imaginary vibrations going on---continuously.

Who can tranquillize his mind in this has to give up even the smallest
ambition, and take leave of the world utterly---ATTA DIPA, ATTA SARANA,
ANNANA SARANA

I know that I appear to be
An angel from heaven temporarily
Living in hell--
          RATHER
                    I know that I'm an angel from heaven temporarily in hell,
                    and that it's all an apparition.---Reason is Piteous.

"My sound's in new Icelandic sight" in approximation of a phrase during sleep I
caught tonight. . . .

THE HIGHEST INTELLIGENCE in the world, the most refined in mankind, comes with
the vow to end rebirth . . . from this had come a long line of successive insect &
brute rebirths from kalpa to kalpa leading to Bliss Buddhahood body for Mind to
lodge in and self-enlighten---

          ANOTHER CAPTURED DREAM PHRASE "How will I attain to True Mind? You'll
          attain to True Mind when you cry out in a dream. . . ."

Prescience of a dream is the same as memory . . . Doublebop of shock, tic . . .

People without money
Trying to be funny--

If wine is
My reward
My reward is
Certainly juicy--

Shuddering
In polite
Horror in
Gray Londons

      Pay no attention to what people say to you concerning The Light, pay
      no attention to its brightness or darkness, it is just a monotone
      of inanity.

You're stuck with a sentient body and you're human and humanly fear death and
emptiness, but you don't have to insult Mind---You have to eat but you don't
have to insult Mind.

START NOW AUG.30'54 WITH VERY SHORT BUT INTENSE DAILY SAMADHIS---
    like today's of Single Dream Taste
                Single Dream Sight
                Single Dream Smell
                Single Dream Sound
                Single Dream Feeling
                Single Dream Thought

Was the sense of sight developed in you before the sense of taste?

///

ARBITRARY CONCEPTION: A DIALOG   AUG 30 '54
What is meant by arbitrary conception? and why does Buddha use the term so often?
Let me ask. What proof do you have that you exist?
A: I can feel myself, see myself, others see me, feel me, talk and think of me.
Q: When you die and are corroded in your grave, or disappeared in your ashes, what
proof will there be of your non-existence?
A: Who will feel me? see me? talk and think of me? I will no longer be in existence.
Q: Your present state you call existence, because you now appear before the sight,
touch and thinking-mind. Then, when you have disappeared from these measurers of
your existence, it will be as you say now, you will not exist. But who is it that
exists now?
A: I.
Q: What is that?
A: It's my self.
Q: Where's your self?
A: Here; I feel it, see it; I can taste it, smell it, think of it and hear it.
I can conceive of it.
Q: Who is it will not exist then?
A: The same.
Q: How can you say that it not-exists then?
A: Because that which *is* now, will *not-be* then.
Q: That which *is* now, and will *not-be* then, are the same thing then?
A: That which is now, me, its opposite will be then, the no-more-me.
Q: But when I asked you who was it who would not-exist then, you said, the same,
    but now you say its opposite will exist then.
A: I exist now. I will not exist then. The opposite of existence is non-existence.

Q: But why do you confuse your mind when the proof of your existence and your
not-existence has not been established? Far be it for me to establish the proof
of your non-existence at some later date, since, if I'm not convinced that your
present existence is real, how can I be convinced of the reality of your future
non-existence? What is this, who is this, about whom we can't say anything definite, other than that it appears to exist and later it will appear not to.??
And yet you raise these anxious ignorant considerations in your own Pure Mind.
Tell me, if you ignore both brightness and darkness, could you see sights?
A: I wouldnt see the outlines of their forms, the boundaries of their shadows,
     I wouldnt see any sights, no.
Q: And if you ignore both the concept of either differentness or sameness, will
you taste the different properties of food?
A: If I do that, all food will taste the same, or should I say, the Mind way, like
     food in dreams.
Q: If you ignore both motion and stillness, if you can, will you hear sounds?
A: Soundwaves wont move, stillness wont receive them, I wont hear sounds.
Q: If you ignore both contact and separation, the notion of it, will you feel
anything?
A: Just numbness.
Q: If you ignore both the passability of fragrances and the impassability of
odorless objects, like cold rock, will you smell odors?
A: It's like blocking up my nose and never using it again.
Q: And if you ignore both concepts of appearance or disappearance, will you notice
the thoughts coming to and fro in your thinking-mind? Will there be a parade of
conceptions, a death and rebirth of continuous ideas, and notions arising from
sensations of smelling, feeling, hearing, seeing and tasting?
A: I wont notice the coming and going of anything.
Q: And how will you notice the passage of time?
A: There'll be no time, just vacuum. No things, no thoughts, no time.
Q: Will there be conceptions of the Now and the Then?
A: No.
Q: Will there be conceptions of appearance now and disappearance then? Or arbitrary conceptions of either your "existence" or "non-existence"? No, because it
will be seen as being merely an appearance; you will know in your intuitive,
bright, motionless, unlimited, spacelike mysterious Essential Mind that the existence or non-existence of the self among other things is an arbitrary conception
with no basis in fact or in reality and that it's only because of your Ignorance
and the Consciousness it produces and the Name and Form it provided for you to
build a Self around your consciousness. You will see that reality is emptiness,
things are apparition and empty, and self is a dream in the void. For if you
ignore false signs of self, such as birth, as you would ignore the false conception
or sign of brightness as set up for you by the sun; and if you ignore false signs
of not-self, such as death, as you would ignore the false conception or sign of
darkness as set up for you by the earth, what would there be?

                    * * * * * * * * * * * * * * * * *

HISTORY------ How imaginary, how popular is the concept of history! if you put
a wall up before me, it will not be an attribute of my perception of sight that
I no longer see a distant planet in the clear blue emptiness of the sky,--- It
will be an attribute of the wall's limitation. History is that wall, put up
before me by the limited and blind. It is only an arbitrary conception, when
you tell me that history is the story of what happened with the governments and
the peoples. Governments indeed, peoples indeed. Tell me, do you know what happened? Tell me what happened inside, or what happened outside everywhere, or tell
me what life there is on the moon and how many and the political, social, economic
history. No,---the truth of the matter is, No.---History is a popular fallacy.

If there weren't things, there wouldn't be Time; if it wasn't for Time, there
would be no things.
TIME FALSELY MAKES THINGS. Things parade around because . . .

I appear to be alive . . .

Time is Void No-Moment
Divided by Things
Appearing to Come & Go

        * * * * * * * *

Why is there only one piece of me escaping, since I am part of the world? Why
doesnt the whole world escape with me? Only when it all escaped might I escape.
(If I clung to my Karma-line)---This is Bodhisattva-Mahasattvaship.
How can it be possible for a piece of the world to escape, which is indivisible
in reality? There is no escape and there is no entrapment either; "no self, no
other selves, no living beings, no Universal Self."

Time nevertheless continues to appall me---O for the simple truth of a railroad
man in a caboose, on a cold night, in front of his fire, an old Conductor of the
Dharma Train.

TAO:- Don't jut forth your chest, be shy and retiring like a valley---your original vitality will return to you, in the form of childish simplicity. Don't
be cultivated and useful---Don't be situated and reapable---

Be humble and lowly like a child-- keep your strength in you.

Fats Waller says at the end of one of his classic records, called "Up Jumped You
With Love,"----"Fine old Arabian love, that's what I call it." That High One.

Realize that you dont exist now, but only appear to exist; and when you die you
will only appear to die. This is your escape.

THIS LIFE IS A TRICK BEING PLAYED ON YOU BY YOUR MIND---Return to mind.
    "It is the same with your six sense-minds---whether they are one or six---they
are pure Essence of Mind which in its nature is as undifferentiated and universal
as space."

Not sameness of taste, or variability of taste, but *universality* of taste.

Thoughts reflect the conception of individualized phenomena, as eyes reflect

objects, tongue reflects tastes, body reflects outer contacts, nose reflects
odours, ears reflect outer sounds. CITTA-VRITTI-NIRODHA (mindstuff-forms-ended).
Let no form take shape in your thoughts and this reflecting ceases; in its place
comes light of inward (trillions of empty thoughts).

   There is a whole consciousness depending on this discriminating mind; myriads
and myriads of bubble-images; honor the form of the forms no more.
   Honor Essence.

In the daily newspaper tonight we see IMMORTAL YOUNG LOVE eulogized: They arrested
Romeo and Juliet (a young couple named Puma and Franz), examined Juliet to see
if they had been intimate, and charged them with juvenile delinquency. Juliet was
forced to submit to the examination by strong armed females. Juliet's father
said nothing. Juliet's father must be a philosopher or a helpless sorrow-lump.

WHERE BUDDHA AND TAO MEET
Stop seeking pleasures,
Satisfy your natural wants;
Break clean from ambitions,
Escape from the urge to improve,
Be like a kid
And salvation will come of itself.

* *

A SERMON I WOULD DELIVER UNDER THE GREENVILLE MISSISSIPPI TREE IF I WERE WILLIAM
FAULKNER AND HAD JUST RECEIVED THE NOBEL PRIZE FOR LITERATURE:
   I would quit my mansion in Oxford and walk forth, and sit under a tree on
the levee in Greenville and say to gawpers, hoboes, lingerers and children:
   "I preach the escape from the suffering of this world; the escape from the
enslaving desires that cause suffering; I preach the lifting of the painted curtain
of delusion before the eyes of the mad. I preach freedom, peace, lovingkindness
of the child. I preach poverty, simplicity, gladness of the heart. I preach
purity, naturalness, longsuffering patience. Pain is the shroud of ignorance, I
preach.
   "I preach the joy of the mind. I preach the teachings of all the Buddhas
of old. I wear the robe and carry the bowl of all the Buddhas of old. I preach
the ancient wisdom of the Tao Chinese. I preach the end of sin, the abolishment
of the evil debt by payment of good, as preached by Our Lord Jesus, the Messiah
of the Western World. I preach quietness, thought, prayer in the night. I preach
the importance of salvation of all the living, and the dread of rebirth and starting all over again in another decaying body in this deadly poison fatal world.
   "I preach that birth equals death; that birth is painful, death is painful;
I preach the end of suffering by preaching the cessation of enslavement to the
desire to be rich, the lust to fornicate, to kill to lie to cheat, the passion
for ambition degrading others.
   "I preach an end to greed, rage and miserable doubtful continual compromise.
I preach equality and unity in the escape from this prison-camp of decay. I
preach the dream of existence, the apparition of the world, that all things are
risen from the mind. I preach the discovery, the unwrapping, the revealment and
the retainment of the True Mind. I preach the recognition that the world only
appears to be, that is is in reality empty from atom to infinite, that it is a
void, that there is no space only void, no time only void, no self only void.
I preach that pain appears to hurt, evil appears to damage, good appears to please.
   "I appeal from the belly of heaven.
   "For inward destruction of our pain I preach that all things are only from
mind's own imagination and from no other revealable source, come to destruction

they do only because of their original and ignorant construction.

"I preach the end of dependence on imaginary pleasures that create unhappiness, the end of dependence on things that are only invented in the mind, the end of dependence on outside influences. I preach the going-in of the people of the world into their own, pure, solitary, untouched minds, to seek and find wise repose there, waiting, to realize the meaning of what's happening by means of their own, pure, universal intuition. I preach the independence from all false education, propaganda, and organized entertainment. I preach the still, pure, true enjoyment of the original and perfect nature of man, which comes, goes, and never returns, like a cloud in the blue sky. I preach man's imitation of the submissive cloud floating in the blue, slowly being restored to its original emptiness; I preach man's imitation of space; man's infinite Mind seeking perfect restoration.

"I preach non-involvement in the tangles of the blind who are not minding their own business."

Aug.31'54

- -

Inherent in the punishment of life is the fear of the reward of death.

SAMADHI OF MOTHS

Not to yield to the appearance and disappearance of thoughts, but to know there are thoughts everywhere all the time. Not to yield to death and rebirth of forms, but to know there are forms everywhere, beings everywhere, all the time.---Like dead hands, do you say "the inside of my hand is in contact, the outside is in separation"?---you just say, there's feeling (of contact and separation) everywhere all the time. Now that your hands are numb, so what?

Let thoughts come and go, like empty myriad moths.

THERE ARE AS MANY THOUGHTS AS THERE ARE THINGS

Each of the Six Senses breaks up the unity of the Original Essence Mind, i.e., motion and stillness break up the unity of the One Transcendental Unbroken Sound.

Two billion selves in the world, human, hundreds of generations of that in history, and how many things and thoughts in all times (2,000,000,000,000,000,000,000,000,000), that many selves, each one a passing little flit believing itself come and going but only one of many everywhere appearing all the time and without substantiality of existence---all breaking up the unity of the One Transcendental Unbroken Thought, the One Unified Suchness which is One Indivisible Mind Essence.

How can there be a Purusha?

* *

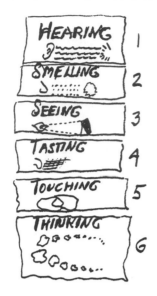

HEARING   1

SMELLING   2

SEEING   3

TASTING   4

TOUCHING   5

THINKING   6

The idea of motion or stillness breaks up the unit of the
One Unbroken Transcendental Sound.

The idea of passability of particles or impassability of others
breaks up the unity of the One Universal Unbroken Crystal Odor.

The idea of darkness or brightness breaks up the unity of the
One Indivisible Radiant Sight of Mind Essence.

The idea of variability of chemical structure or invariability
breaks up the unity of One Permeating Infinite Taste in Mind.

The idea of contact or separation breaks up the unity of the
One Complete All-Pervading Feeling of the Transcendental Womb.

The idea of appearance or disappearance of thoughts, coming or
going of things, death or rebirth of forms, breaks up the unity
of the One Void Unbroken Tranquil Thought.

* *

Proust and Joyce are slowmotion cameras . . .

NOTE ON HEAVY DRINKING
                       Drinking heavily, you abandon people---and they abandon
you---and you abandon yourself---It's a form of partial self murder but too sad
to go all the way---Make it a rule not to drink without eating outside your own
home (degrisez . . . sobered up). Because, the kind of drinking that seeks to abandon
people, is done in public. The kind of drinking that seeks to allay boredom, is
done at home and is self controlled.
       DONT DRINK TO GET DRUNK
       DRINK TO ENJOY LIFE

    The delicate spiderwebs of your brain's arrangements, so Proustian, fine,
rainbowy, shattered by drunkenness?

        I've been drinking like a fiend; twice in August I passed out like a man
hit over the head; several times in July. I drink to destroy myself---'twere
better to recognize the fickleness of life by constant recollection.
       BIRTH IS RESTLESSNESS . . . NIRVANA IS REST

                *

(My Writing Ambition): "A false estimate of excellency produces a false desire
                       to excel."
    . . . Abide in Sympathy, Sinlessness, Radiance of Mien . . .

WRITING NOTE: *The secret of writing is in the rhythm of urgency . . .*

        . . . .- - - - - - . . . .

ALL THE VULGAR LIQUIDS conjoined in your earthy body---should you be happy or
unhappy about their gathering and eventual emission? What goes in must come out,
dont worry about urination, defecation, perspiration, orgasm (emission of sperm);
in their actual nature, as manifestations of Mind, as medleys inside the Four

Great Elements and the Six Senses, they operate, like breath, by themselves.

     Buddha didnt have sexual frottings of his part from age 29 to age 83---
did he die of Reich's Cancer?---did lack of "proper orgasm" pile up Neurosis &
Cancer in his repressed backlog of "sexual emotion"? No---and apparently sex
is not "emotion" but simple emission of sperm and ova-liquids---which Buddha
had in nocturnal emissions.---He was beyond nature and so when he did have or-
gasms in his sleep he saw no reason to be glad or unglad...all multiworlds were
surging thru his loins a few seconds---loins he didnt ask for in his maturity---
He was interested in Mind.

          What goes up must come down
          Because you were born you must die
          Because you appeared you must disappear---

* *

            ---Soon they'll invent microscopes so powerful they'll begin
              to discover that life is empty.

- -

Apparition on the screen of Mind?
Mind isnt interested in arbitrary conceptions of form like that----Ignorance is.
Mind is Essence. Apparitions are appearances and therefore have to pass.--
Essence never passes, never arrives, is always satisfied with nothing.

PRACTISE recognition of complete emptiness of all things at all times, under
every condition, everywhere, and you will learn by yourself what Buddha preached.

          *

The emptiness of Universal Suffering Worlds in Apparition, in a blade of grass,
as in a streak of your pencil lead ➤ . . . , as in your reflection in a mirror,
as in the wood of your desk, the paper of your notebooks, your mother's body,
your friend's, the anger and smoke of crowded saloons, pretty girls---

EMPTY as these words!

- -

I	The stars	I	All things
I	Are thought	I	Are empty
I	Thinking.	I	And in essence
I	* * * * * * * * *	I	Eternal

- - - - - - - - - - - - - - - - -

Involuntary blabberings in a dream---there's your precious "modern prose". . .
just write so everybody'll understand what happened.

- -

    ---Buddha's Gong Samadhi---
The Samadhi of Pure Faith and Realization
        of Eternal Essence
The living sleep.--
  Thank you, O Lord, for letting form recognize its essence.---
A happy child using all phenomena of sense-objects for his living sleep.---
---Recognition of my fame and glory from outside? Non-recognition? It's all
impermanent phenomena around my pure, mysterious, permanent, Essential Mind which
isn't really "mine" but manifestation of universal essence. Who knows this?---the
Tathagata who last night took up abode in the *Realms of Tusita,* which are as

clear as the perception of sight of a muddy dog.---Buddhism is a Fellaheen thing.
---Fellaheen is Antifaust Unanglosaxon Original World Apocalypse. Fellaheen is
an Indian Thing, like the earth. Jean-Louis the Fellaheen Seer of New North
America.---- The Unfaust, the Antichrist . . . Unsquare, Ungothic.

NO MORE SAD POSE, the glad pose of eternality . . . it's true, though the body gets
old and dies, the thinking-conception, its essential nature, does not pass away,
nor any of its 5 attributes, so that you will know, the Hearing-Conception in
you is eternal, and the Tasting, the Feeling, the Seeing, the Smelling are eternal
in their essential states. Your essence is eternal; right now this eternal
essence is manifesting and therefore sort of belongs to the form which is you.
This is something to be glad about. This is where the "Eternal Brightness"
illumines you---- Think how long you've been around, O Old Hoper
                                                    Old Sinner.

                    *
Vast Quiet's Glowing Mind
          (Gothic serenity & Dhyana)

TATHAGATA WORLDS, as a book, would be collection of rebirth stories, i.e.:-
     "Once I was a buffoon in a Medieval circus, half-clown, half-witch."---
     "Once I was an Indian boy in Mexico"
     "Once I was a bug---"
     "Once I was in love with a beautiful woman with dark hair and dark eyes and
pale white skin."
     "Once I was told that heaven existed and I didnt believe it."
                    *

Death and Rebirth are ghostly changes . . .

Neither sane nor mad is the thinking-mind, but in a state of eternal thinking.
Mad and sane are impermanent, thinking and no-thinking are pure, mysterious,
permanent, essential.

     "*Late*, sharp, humorous versions" of Buddhism are alright for dawdlings in
civilization-rooms but it's the early, thick, or dull, agonized version of Buddhism,
either the raw Hinayana or the radiant Mahayana, both tragic, neither humorous,
(neither can be Tao-ed, neither can be "Zen-ed") that is my beetroot, my meat,
my hope, my rock, my foggy night. The "sinister disciplinary undertones" of
Zen(Buddhism) are the Hinayana showing through, like Spenglerian Cowley-mentioned
metamorphosed crystals showing the early culture filling in the late form . . . like
essence of eternity inside decaying form. But "early" and "late" are just
arbitrary ideas connected with the phenomena of things undergoing change.

I am restored to the simplicity of the child . . . what do I care about early or late?

If there's anything that I dont want to be is literary.

I think the people in the asylum are serious---

The funniness of the seriousness of sinners sinning up & down the globe--
The gravity of the priest's lips in the confessional . .
Father Jean-Louis in the Confessional. . . .
"Father Receives Confession" or
"Saturday Afternoon Confessions in St. All's"-----

You've got to divide the men from the women---before you boast of dividing the men from the boys.

NOTE TO ALLEN: Allen, I'm convinced that if Lucien should start hitting me to make me admit that life is not a dream and pain is not imaginary, Neal would Cry---

Allen Ginsberg's description of Chinese sages on a hilltop: "The great belly rubbing or beat or horrible looking W.C. Fields arhats in rags with long ears or giggling together over manuscripts of poems about clouds."

----In America, real wandering Taoist bums going around the country watching un-expected events, eating beans out of cans, sleeping in railroad sidings, following the seasons, washing in creeks, spending occasional nights in jail for vagrancy, working one day a month for beans and wine, eating raw cabbage with roast weenies under the reddening skies of New Mexico desert.---

I THINK I HAVE A CENTRAL MIND
* *

A Way to Enlightenment:- No talk---dont fancy yourself a conversationalist except with buddies (?) ---Untie the knot of false conception of ego-personality and personal attainment---

      I'll found a Buddhism University and up this frieze in front:-
      "HERE LEARN THAT LEARNING IS IGNORANCE"

             * * * * * * *

THE LOTUS-TEACHING
    The Mind itself is pure but all its thoughts are fantastic, but because in Mind Essence there is no rising of such arbitrary conceptions of fantastic or non-fantastic (is the hero in the dream inside the moment of the dream ever designated as either fantastic or non-fantastic, real or unreal?--the issue doesnt rise in the dreaming mind) why should there be the raising of any conceptions of non-fantastic things in the first place?

          ------- * -------
          ------- * -------

    The Mind is pure, mysterious, permanent & Essential . . . the Mind is indivisible and not broken up into six pieces by Eye, Ear, Nose, Tongue, Body, Brain . . . these Six are like knots in a single beautiful silk handkerchief.
    The handkerchief is like the Mind's Holy Ground---if you pay no attention to the seeds of false imagining as it tries to take root, nothing will rise up to contaminate the holy nature---When a thought sneaks up via the flash of an image, meditate on the emptiness of both image and thought and the emptiness of both thinker and thought-about---Remember that the flash of recognition of the image is false too, such flashes in reality are going on continuously and permeating completely all Buddha-lands in all your Universes, i.e., not *one* of these indi-viduated moths of activity-thought is true, i.e., having any substantiality of existence---Therefore concentrate the Mind on its own perfectly accommodating emptiness and equanimity---for this you've got to be patient and longsuffering and diligent in your efforts to practise meditation, which is prayer. Your reward will be tranquillity, purity, eternal Brightness and holy ecstasy.--
    For instance, you will come to where suddenly an unpleasant sound, such as

someone's sickly coughing, becomes neither unpleasant nor pleasant because you
will have gone beyond such impermanent and arbitrary consideration, into a
strange chamber of great inward glory, wherein, with your outside body completely
asleep and feeling empty as air and hands and feet numb and existenceless it seems
your mind wide awake and Bright, you will realize that it is the deep ignorance
of the world that has caused the cough, which sound is emanating from a suffering
sentient being by means of motion and the soundwaves emanating from the motion,
registering upon your keen transcendental Hearing the quiver of deaths & rebirths,
which are imaginary states in tormented form abiding among the great reality calms
of essence.---This is the *conscious sleep* of a great meditation ecstasy and is the
path away from currents of life & death, to Nirvana, which is the Eye.

- -

The world doesnt want fucking and sucking, just talk & laws . . . (drunken note)
FURTHER DRUNKEN NOTES:-
You didn't come to a party with the intention of digging everybody and every moment
of it; no, you came into the world decided to dig all of it all the time; with
periods between, when you dig absolutely none of it (dhyana).

　　　　　Ta'ra Po Pmpion
　　　　　---------X------
Fellaheen --　　　　　　　　　The King of the Chacha
　(Self grows out of being)

　　　　There's nothing wrong---it's only in your imagination
　　　　　　　　S W E E T

- -

　　　　　　　　A Vision of Sweet Heaven
　　　　　Things in the world are *absent*---not really there---
　　　　　I'm unhappy because my life is cold and strange---But it
　　　　　only appears to be so. In reality, there is no basis on
　　　　　which I can lay claim that I am not what I have thought.
　　　　　It's all gone, absent. Absence makes the heart grow
　　　　　fonder. We are taught to die. Long suffering gets even
　　　　　worse. There is absolutely no hope, and by the same law
　　　　　there's no sin. Rejoice in the moment, regulators of the
　　　　　world! Heaven is very silent.
　　　　　* *

I could have profound mystical
Samadhis where I make contact
with Saints---I should have to
invent my own saints, because

The new priest is profoundly concerned
with the mystical state, the old
priest, affairs.
　　　----A LITTLE POEM
　　　　- - - - - - - - - - - - - - - - -
　　Inventing saints would be a fulltime operation, like with baseball card-
games in 1946, the year my father died I was insane and played cardgame baseball
games in my room, till Thanksgiving. At Thanksgiving I went mad and began trem-
bling all over and leaned out the window anxiously waiting for a friend to arrive.
He never came, he sent a telegram. Later, he sent me a telegram, signed by a

(INVENTING SAINTS cont'd)

name BENEDICT LIVORNESE, to mean "Benedict Arnold," the traitor, the telegram
reading: "Tom died in a crash." (which I believed, and went to his funeral, first
buying him a Mass at a local church in Lynbrook)---he was alive playing jazz
piano in his house when I approached up the icy winter walk looking for signs of
his wreath.

It's a very funny world but so cold & strange & intrinsically sunless.
BECAUSE OF EMPTINESS.

The world is like the first pages of Dostoevsky's "Eternal Husband," there's
a strange emptiness and a vast darkness and little human figures trying to take
hold in their own imaginations of themselves, and slowly they begin to grow and
the pale flower of their faces becomes magnified like an enormous phantom across
the gloom; and yet it's all imaginary, and suddenly the hero stops the carriage
and turns to his friend with the slouch hat and cries "What are we doing here?"
and there's more emptiness than non-emptiness, there's more space than faces.
And the emotions of the sad Russians are vague, gloomy, unreal, with no basis for
existence, like their faces, like the vast Russian darkness all around. In their
houses at night, in the parlor, suddenly there's complete silence . . . as if the
rooftop had suddenly shushed and asked for silence for listening to something.

The Russians of Dostoevsky say "Hmm" and stroke the corner of their lip,
musing in the mystery.

A crystal intelligence hides like a diamond in the heart of the night.

Without this crystal intelligence there would be no musing, no mystery,
no Russians, no darkness, no unreality, no rooftops, no silence, no vague strange
uneasy emotion rising out of phantasmal personal mental notions. "But I forgot
her name and I tripped down the hall? . . . I mean, the last word I said 'I'm sorry'
as if I was sorry. . . . but it made me feel gloomy, I feel uneasy, something's wrong
. . . but why is everyone so silent? . . . but I mean why is the city so still? . . ."
And he looks around in the night, realizing he doesnt even exist at all! And
that's why! "No wonder everything is so strange and eerie!"

* * * * * * * *

GRAY DAY: I can *feel* my grave today---the damp grave---bah! I'd rather die
drinking wine in the sun or just in the sun.

SUNWORSHIPPERS ARE CRAZY says Doctor Sax.

------ . ------

A WESTERN DEVICE FOR THE PRACTICE HERE OF DEVICELESS DHARMA;- Get an old panel
truck for $95 and be your own Monastery in it, parking in the open desert and on
wild seacoasts like Nag's Head and Gaviota and in the mountains and on the out-
skirts of Mexican Villages and in the great woods north and south---carrying
mattress, food, books, typewriter, camping equipment, brakeman's lantern and the
determination to keep rolling and keep on the path of purity.

TRANSCENDENTAL "SOUND"--

Last night Sept. 16, 1954, I heard the transcendental "sound" of the
Dharma, that high-frequency vibration of silence that you hear in quiet places
(so rare today in the Western World except at 3 A M)---I suddenly realized that
this "sound" is unbroken, utterly undividable, permanent . . . that I had been
hearing it unbrokenly for all time because it wasnt my *ear*, my transitory
hearing-organ, responsible for the "Sound," it was the permanent hearing-
conception hearing the essence of its perfect emptiness---- I saw that it was
the actual sound of the All-Permeating truth and that the reason why it seemed
to come from just next to my ear was because there were noises displacing

its perfect accommodation elsewhere---that the "Sound" was not near my ear but everywhere and everywhere the same.

I saw that though my body may grow old and die, this hearing-conception would never change and the Transcendental "Sound" never broken because unbroken by nature and "Eternal"----I got a definite message from the Transcendental Realms of Tusita and the Saints and the Great Lord Buddha sitting forever silent, forever perfect--- Also I realized that the "Sound," because it had no beginning, had no end, therefore no Time; that it was the actual mysterious "Sound" of the void I heard, the "voice" of the void, the "noise" of holy emptiness, the echo of Nirvana, the report of the Great Truth Cloud, the Inner Musing of Mind Essence, the blessed voices of all the Tathagatas to me

singing

* *

Eliminate fantastic interests in radio, TV, newspapers, social visits, *friandises* . . . The mind itself is not fantastic

The world is nothing but an imprint phantasm on the mind

THE MIND'S PURE WISDOM---the disturbing sensations such as my sore foot depend on the undisturbed continuous stability of the registering Mind, like wind blowing in transient gusts upon the endless supply of calm sea, causing ripples and waves of Ignorance.---

The Continuity of Mind is like the diamond samadhi sound, unbroken, eternal, non-fantastic yet in perfect accommodation accepting fantastic sounds.---

Karma-consciousness is the cause of the fantasmal form a man takes, such as a fat butcher with handlebar mustaches----This arises from Mind's pure, holy emptiness, and flails hugely selfbelieving in the void yet it's only an ethereal flower----longfaced and lost among the false conditions of the world---the deep ignorance and pity of it.

On reading Malcolm Cowley's article; "They're looking
for political reasons for why Kerouac isnt interested
in politics."

* *

THOREAU:- "Of what consequence, though our planet explodes, if there is not character involved in the explosion? . . . . I would not run around a corner to see the world blow up."---

"Nations! What are nations? Tartars, and Huns, and Chinamen! . . . . . the historian strives in vain to make them memorable. It is for want of a man that there are so many men."

"Make once more a fane of the mind." (Fane means temple.)

XXXXXXXXXXXXXXXXXXXXXXXX
"READ NOT THE TIMES, READ THE ETERNITIES"
* *

"We quarter our gross bodies on our poor souls, till the former eat up all the latter's substance."

"'Good breeding' respects only secondary objects."---
"Why should we not meet, not always as dyspeptics,
to tell our bad dreams, but sometimes as *eu*peptics, to
congratulate each other on the ever-glorious morning?"

From "Life Without Principle," Thoreau.

WRITING . . . You'll never know what you wanted to say about something till you're
scribbling furiously into it, reaching the center, then scribbling out again.
This is BLOWING, accidentally and actually finding your center.

MORE PERSONAL NOTES   It was my generation-instinct to plug "hipsterism and
beatness" in 1950, alienating older generation helpers like Van Doren & Giroux
& Kazin too, which is an instinct just as stupid as all other living and animal
and murderous instincts in this world which we cant get through our thick heads
is intrinsically empty. (The very bones of your skull are nothing but invisible
particles of dust blowing about in empty space.) And so we keep repeating,
instinct keeps repeating itself, karma upon karma.
     What is Karma?---activity-consciousness, blind of history.

NOTES ON THE PROBLEM OF FIGHTS: Say "I dont feel insulted---I dont want to fight
with you or anybody." Then they may or may not offer a gantlet, the glove. Give
it back and say "What do I want with your ignorant glove." "What do I want with
your insult. You'll have no more use for it than I have."
     Think of Buddha, in a bar.
     Dont go to bars any more.
     All the fights I've been in were in bars. But the trouble's inside me--
not knowing I am God(viewing the imaginariness of the emotions involved.)

ON SEX: If you succeed in avoiding being eaten by the crocodiles which are the
          womenfolk, yet forgive them and see that they are empty, you succeed
          in everything.

          *
               The Wild Boars are the Men
                    and the Rhinoceros, the Club
                    and the Bullet

               The trees are Buddha
                    and the Dead
          *

IT'S SO UNFORTUNATE that all which men come to exchange on earth is some information about subway stations, in their mournful fleshy adventure of 60 years, yet
it is men who will finally excavate this ignorance from their poor hearts and
emancipate all sentience forever; I can hardly wait.

          PRIVATE MENTAL NOTE: "Clint Hartung" that ballplayer from Hondo
                              Texas who came up in 1947 with the Giants
                              was for me like that lonely Western Maryland
                              trail out my madhouse window---American dreams
                              (like Lad Gavin and Ned Gavin of my childhood
                              imaginary games) that did not materialize and
                              yet came true in essence reality of heart's
                              adventure, of *something* dark & dreary in yr.
                              rain, O USA

               - - - - - - - - - - - - -
Mind is one thing, but mind-made selves confronting one another everywhere in
a confused fantastic medley.---(the "World" comes from the breaking-up of unity
of Mind-Essence); One-Mind equals Many-Selves.

Phoney human optimism is the silliest thing on the face of the globe---animals
are smarter than that. THE SENTIMENTAL REALISTS OF CHRISTMAS.

Since Mind is One, you, possessor of it, in Realization, have been all things and so've had 100000000000 deaths and rebirths----How you are God---

Arrète et Réalize!

Clear as a bell? Clear as open space.

A LITTLE ESSAY

Why doesnt somebody hire me to do a kindness instead of for distributing meaningless circulars advertising nylons-----? In deepest ignorance are ye, scowling workers of the morning--- What a lesson you could learn from the ferrymen of Guaymas in their white rags and strawhats, and long poles and clear, deep river---better than that, the Ferrymen of Hinayana!! ---How come the world is so old & so unenlightened still? I think Edgar Cayce was right and most westerners and modern day Orientals came from Atlantis, that ignorant Rome---- for the innumerable Arahats of 2500 years ago are nowhere in evidence any more. Butchers in white aprons behold the morning with what they take to be human hope ---huh!---among charnels of their own making. Deeply attached to all the wrong things and never take a hint from the open perfect space all over!

ANOTHER LITTLE ESSAY

Our world travellers keep dragging one another to ships to lend moral support ---Their so-called love is nothing but friction.----Their partners in love are nothing but butlers to serve up gysmal juice. Their wives are semen nurses. I would rather admire the cavernous beauty of a womb in my mind, or Proust's archway of pink hawthorn through which both he and beloved Gilberte heard the name Gil-berte called, than stick my old piece in it like so much charnel and frot and rub and puff and fight and draw pictures for the sake of an ingraspable idea con-cerning the body electric which will enable me, if lucky, to put her and my idea of her together into the parade from the base of my bone to the bottom of her belly hole---buck! It's all a phantom and who knows it better than the lonely f---er? Hamburg. I have confused iron fire escapes in my rush to find a hole to think of---Dig a hole in the ground & try that,---all is empty, including the criticisms and prides of admiring detractors, son.---

Anton me Rosenberg that---

Our savants all have bad taste.---Imagine Robt.Frost being better than Thoreau, because of a few verse tricks.----I can take out a ruler and measure too. I can even tell you how high a tree is by use of geometry.---This makes me Archi-medes? Lines make a poem?----I've seen true poems in the middle of formless fortunate explanations, heard them in the street & admired & forget them right there. Robert me No Frost----Penn Warren me no more---

The magazines of the Nazarenes of the shallow limousines, is all.

Deep inside a woman's womb hides the itch & pain of creation, and inside that the Golden Bee, and inside that Emptiness, and inside that, the Void Radiant, & all around that, Sweet Nada Nadir Nirvana, O children of the mind.

. . . .

I am a lazy bum, thank God---:

The Diamond Sound is that profound higher-than-human-ear screaming of orgone radios electrifying the emptiness---

Houses are full of things that gather dust---

SVAHA! Cabin in the North Woods for me, and 2-month visits at home---long walks
in the snowy wild---wear a red coat and wave at the hunters---nothin to do but
feed myself, keep warm, & write. ---Watch the play of light in the woods---
all outdoors outside, no houses---

       I'm not fooled by Karma rosebuds

I live the religious life of solitude, chastity and meditation; that's why I
do live on very little. I amuse myself reading, walking, "playing solitaire."

* *

      THE ICE SKATE TAO
       It isnt time that dulls the
     edge of the blade, it's things.
     My ice skates havent been used
     since they were sharpened in 1938.
     They're still sharp, no ice has
     rubbed the edges. He who ignores
     things has made time disappear.

    --------------------()--------------------

Our selves are abandoned in the selfless Real

"Life is a series of little accidents" someone said, realizing his imperturbable
endless Mind Radiant---When the accidents are over, still the Mind would be capable of registering them on its pure ledger of open space---The Mind far exceeds
the occasion of a Little-Things like life---It's like putting your fist in the
sky---Accidents are numbered in the millions and millions, but the Mind would
receive an eternity of accidents and still have room---The limits of the universe
dont make a round outer edge, they are inside, are Void---One is guilty of
dimensions---

THE MIRACLE OF THE ANTIFAUST. If I saw a miracle it would only prove to me that
everything is manifested from the mind, which I already know---Let me imagine
a *real* miracle to see that all's unreal? S'why there are no miracles, amigos.
     THERE ARE NO MIRACLES BECAUSE LIFE IS UNREAL,
       IT IS A MIRACLE IN ITSELF.
   IF MIRACLES ARE REAL, THEN LIFE IS REAL---Everybody knows the value of a
miracle is its violation of the laws of the "real" . . .
     *

When you open your eyes you only open your eyes on restlessness, so why be in
any special place just so long as you're undisturbed and can stay in your mind
---REST IN MIND-----the rest is a parade of phantoms brought low---any room'll do
---any field to pace in---

     This is only my appearance-body,---my true body isnt "mine"
     and is everywhere and is Buddhahood.

AS SOON AS THOREAU cognizes his transcendental existence he is not Thoreau because
he ignores Thoreau.
     Ignore brightness-like-life
       darkness-like-death
       and there's no Sight
       Just Transcendental Seeing

Ignore motion-like-life
motionlessness-like-death
and there's no Sound
Just Transcendental Hearing

Ignore rebirth-like-life
death-like-death
and there's no existence
Just Transcendental Thinking

Death is your reward, it will come soon enough.---

The real world is inside the hole in your mind . . . THE HOLY VOID

EVERYBODY'S LOST IN THEIR OWN FALSE IMAGINATIONS (So not noticing you)

A lost thought in Subway: Holy men were never murdered in their trance in
olden times of Man.
Also I thought: When I was 16 they had to pull me outa my shell---Ti Jean
pure---"why are you so bashful, so quiet, sograve?"they kept complaining---So
I learned a worldly "personality" which is Pain----TALK-TOO-MUCH

Writing Note:- If you cant write the glamor of Al Sublette in new haircut and
new suit then give up writing---Ti Jean---obtain from the center of your interest
and work outward mindless of form---

FOR BILL If you've had one true meditation you forever know there's nothing
        better to do than meditation. The Rest is Ignorance, Mental Fret.

        World travel and maximum action is only stale repetition that keeps
getting new feathers each season---We see the feathers and think the inside is
new too---The streets of Cairo and the girls of Bombay I saw in Mexico already,
and the newest heart throb of love has bluer feathers than the one a dozen, a
thousand years ago---It is a *man* who allows himself to be fooled by externals?
Learns nothing from open space and from the Tao of the holy void inside his mind
which teaches emptiness and serenity?---
        Dreams are of no consequence. Their mechanics of construction are extremely
naive. A spool of thread is used like the Mind is used by dreamers to patch up
rips in the continuous creation of ignorant hope, a magic self-deception.
        Life?---eating, crapping, preening, picking the lice out of your feathers.
The mind is continually fooling itself magically.
        Leave it to the Commissioners of Rockfall repairing Niagaras, life . . .
        "COMPOSURE, the best of all enjoyments." Only when you're in Solitude
and have ceased all effort and striving and notions of the truth will you come to
the Bodhisattva's Nirvana of Perfect Love and Potentiality---So *when*, Arhat?

                *

Buddha possesses the self-depending power of miracle, as his father well knows.
"Leaving his kingly estate" (Maharajah Suddhodana) "and country, lost in meditation, he drank sweet dew."
        BUDDHA:--"repeating the joyful news of religion"---

"His circumspection as he looked upon the earth in walking" (eyes down)   (!)

"Escape the grief of lust"---

The wise man "engages in no learned career" (pure TAO) ("nor yet wholly separates
himself from it") ASHVAGHOSHA
      "HIS LEARNING IS THE WISDOM OF NOT-PERCEIVING WISDOM, BUT YET
      PERCEIVING THAT WHICH TELLS HIM OF HIS OWN IMPERMANENCE."
      i.e., the meat of wisdom, not the style---

Though born in the Arupa world, there is yet no escape from the changes of
time; his learning, then, is to acquire the changeless body."---the True Body
of Bliss, Buddhahood.

      "The want of faith is the engulfing sea, the presence
      of disorderly belief is the rolling flood."

    "WISDOM IS THE HANDY BOAT,
      REFLECTION IS THE HOLD-FAST."

Devadatta, Gotama's jealous cousin, set loose a mad drunken elephant in
Rajagriha---"thinking only on the sorrow caused by (Devadatta's) hate" Buddha
advances slowly on the elephant, only Ananda at his side,---"You! swallowed up
in sorrow's mud" and pats the kneeling beast with lotus hand *"even as the moon
lights up a flying cloud."*

"The senses (of seeing, hearing, tasting, smelling, feeling) not confined within
due limits (all overindulged), and the objects of sense (sights, sounds, tastes,
odors, sensations) not limited as they ought to be, lustful and covetous thoughts
grow up between the two (the seeing and the sight of a woman, say), because the
senses and their objects (the seeing-sense of my eyes and the seen-object the
woman) are unequally yoked. Just as when two plowing oxen are yoked together
to one halter and cross-bar, but not together pulling as they go, so it is when
the senses and their objects are unequally matched. Therefore, I say, restrain
the heart, give it no unbridled license." FROM BUDDHA CHARITA

Woman---"weak of will, scant in wisdom, deeply immersed in love."

"Relying on external help (the man) has sorrow; self-reliant, there is strength
and joy. But in the case of woman, from another comes the labor, and the nurture
of another's child. Thus then should everyone consider well, and loathe and put
away the form of woman."

      Different cultures are different kinds of ignorance---like American
      and Navajo---It's all taking place in the sorrow-burning globe.

DISGUSTING CUPIDITY Self-Caress

Thirst & Social Feeling Caused by Drink

At fights and firingsquads, dont look.

             Society is a system of lures,
             I'M THROUGH WITH IT

      No more the self-caress of being published---I'm going to write
in the ancient tradition of honorable doctrine while I live---It will be the pure
teaching of the Buddhas of Old in a new form---I am not going to seek any personal
gain, no flattering of the self, no cupidity and concupiscence with Dame Fame
and Buck-a-Thousand Renown.

No more the cupidity and self caress of "hearing about me" in articles of critics and chitchats of friends---The complete cessation of all striving and effort in the system of lures which is the society of the world, the steadfastness of contemplation is an *athletic,* a self controlled thing and has nothing to do with flattery, cruelty, curiosity or even humor. I have no time but to be Grave Jean, sit upright, and realize.---

I want to practise solitude in the middle of the forest. Where is the forest? Far North in the Gaspé, far South in Mexican lands, both Indian grounds. Great solitude also in open spaces of American Southwest and Nevada. Greatest I've ever seen was Nevada Desert. Which is best, the curious Indian inquiring after my hermit's motives, maybe the curious Indian bandito, or the sinister American authority with all the prohibitive notices tacked in the woods? Which best, the lizards of the South or the winters of the North? Which is best, the turista cards of Mexico or the tourist permits of Imperial Canada?

Mexico is best. Mexico is like old India. The jungle in the winter, the desert plateau in the summer. The Tao Morning Ground, the ecstasy of the jewel lotus.

MIRACLES ARE IMPOSSIBLE, just by believing wont make them happen, because only one miracle is possible and has already happened: life; the other end of which, death, will take you out, and is part of the same miracle.

  --Advice---
LOOK DOWN
- - - - - - - - - - - - - - - - - - -
Outside the miracle is the non-miraculous reality of nothing and emptiness.
MIND IS NOT FANTASTIC
Dont believe it?---ask your dead father.
Close your eyes in silence . . . and stop your mentality.
- - - - - - - - - - - -

WITH "THE EGYPTIAN" Darryl Zanuck has purveyed a teaching of viciousness and cruelty. They present him with a gold cup at banquets for this. The author, Mika Waltari, is also guilty of the same teaching of viciousness and cruelty. You see a scene of a man choking a woman under water. Both these men are rich as a consequence of the world's infatuation with the forbidden murder,----its daydreams of maniacal revenge by means of killing and Lust. Men kill and women lust for men. Men die and women lust for men. Men, think in solitude; learn how to live off your sowings of seed in the ground. Or work 2 weeks a year and live in the hermitage the rest of the year, procuring your basic foods at markets, and as your garden grows work less, till you've learned to live off your garden alone.
QUIETNESS AND REST THE ONLY ESCAPE.
The secret is in the desert.

WHY DO I WANT TO LEAVE SOCIETY?   (in my case) Lou Little making me run a week on a broken leg in 1940---the way drivers sneak their cars up to your knees when you cross with the red light---the way the gang at the Pawtucketville Social Club punched me in the sandlot football pileups and called me "L'ti Christ a Kerouac" ---*Kerouac's Little Christ* (Leo's Little Bastard) because of some grudge against my father and so against his innocent child---the time 1954 I called at a friend's house uninvited and I never was told that it signified "Dont call us we'll call you"---the slap in the face I got from my brother, whom I shadowed like Ananda his Lord---the slap on the top of the head I gave Lil Paul once for yanking at my slip of paper I was reading---all this contemptuousness, cold drollery, viscious-ness, hypocrisy, and derangement convinces me man must leave society and learn to live by himself purely in a solitary out-of-the-way hut, and feed himself by whatever means are kindly.

REST IN SOLITUDE
BE KIND IN PUBLIC
        If anybody steals from you
        they're doing you a favor

Rest in silence with your eyes closed. If anybody wants to kill you for the
thrill of it, hold him off from you and talk to him. If you're too old, or it's
guns, and it's ganging on you, what can you do? Maudgalyayana the venerable old
bhikku was killed for nothing by a bunch of Magadhan bandits. I imagine he was
silent and held his peace. When Buddha heard of it he made the comment that it
was in the Karma established that it would happen.
        DONT FEAR DEATH, SLAVE

---Dont be crucified, just sit---
These are all *western* fears---
        (And written under influence of marijuana)
"They know not what they do" is a universal world truth.

        It was the Messianic Contempt of Christ made him carry the cross to
Golgotha---Buddha would have sat and let them kill him there and meditated
through his pain upon the unreality of his body death. All men must come to
this realization of Nirvana no matter what the manner of their death.
        That's why I said, Murder and torture are the final issues, among men.

Nausea's How you Die. . . .
                        My last wish, I wish I had an apple orchard.

  Boy, in reality what are you afraid of? Pain and death.--- Christ was
crucified on the cross of cruel Jews & Romans. You'll be crucified on the
cross of fear of cruel Jews & Romans?
        *---Live by the sea Clean, Celt---"
        Sea drowns out all other sounds.---
        Sea is lion dharma roar.---
        No garden, no clams.---
        Buy groceries.
        Smoke pipe of eve
        On deck of sand
        In red roar
        Salt sour
        Sigh.

Do I want the protection of America via its cruel Paul-weapons? Or Fellaheen peace

How many miles south of sweet San Luis is the sea?   FERRY GHOSTS OF GUAYMAS
        ---the pharting trills of birds---

I was accused in 1944 by Walter Wager of having "thick skin"---It may be cruel
to say that Ginsberg's outburst about "Kanucklike Unsaintly Kerouac" is the
same Yiddishe. To BILL & ALLEN: "You have both concealed secret thoughts from
                        me. Then how can I estimate the details of
                        your cupidities and concupiscences?"

Drinking is for getting thirsty and looking for people---Dont touch it---
Ye have a gayety of your own.

McCarthy is feared because you cant lie to him. It's a form of contemptuousness
he has, that doesnt mind its own business, but you cant lie to him.

100% not seeing anyone   --Get mad, ---stay out of the temple yourself.----
Dont leave house except for business,---   "Too sick to work"---
HAPPINESS AND PLEASURE DONT MIX
"Sorrow saps the strongest will"

"Moral conduct . . . is the great source of all that is good"---"He who breaks the
laws of right behavior . . . his evil name pursues him as a shadow."

"Beauty, or earthly things, family renown and such things, all are utterly
inconstant, and what is changeable can give no rest of interval."

THE IDEA OF EXCELLING AND ALSO OF INFERIORITY BOTH DESTROYED, THE DESIRE TO
EXCEL AND ALSO ANGER ARE DESTROYED. ANGER! HOW IT CHANGES THE COMELY FACE."

This is not Yiddishe and not Kanuckeshe.

Stop being angry and you wont have to repent (unlike Christian repentance.)

The lightning bolt of irrationality bursts from the storm in your reason and
kills your right resolves.

"A man who allows wild passion to arise within, himself first burns his heart,
then after burning adds the wind thereto which ignites the fire again, or not,
as the case may be."   IT'S ALL OVER

        "Tathagata, moreover, nobly seizing the occasion, appeasing them, produced
within a joyful heart; and so subdued, their grandeur of appearance came again,
as when a snake subdued by charms glistens with shining skin."
            THE SNAKE OF LIFE MUST BE APPEASED
Nobody ever beat up Buddha
        "My body like a broken chariot stands, no further cause of 'coming' or
of 'going'----completely freed from the three worlds, I go enfranchised, as a
chicken from its egg." (to die & vanish)

PURPOSE OF SOLITUDE in the desert is to find your True Mind---"If men but
knew their own nature, they would not dwell in sorrow."

"The law of things 'joined' is to 'separate'; the principle of kindness and of
love is not abiding, 'tis better then to reject this pitiful and doting heart."

"IF THINGS AROUND US COULD BE KEPT FOR AYE, AND WERE NOT LIABLE TO CHANGE OR
SEPARATION, THEN THIS WOULD BE SALVATION! WHERE CAN THIS BE SOUGHT?"

    "I am resolved; I look for rest!"
    "This is the one thing needful. So do I now instruct all creatures."

"Prepare yourselves to cast off consciousness, fix yourselves well in your own
island." ATTA SARANA
    "Every sensation born from cause, like the bubble floating on the water."

"The mind acquainted with the law of production, stability, and destruction, recognizes how again and once again things follow or succeed one another with no
endurance."
    Go through life smiling and shaking hands with an endlessness of introduced
ghosts?---there's your 'literary success.'

    ALL THE BUDDHAS OF THE PAST AGES, NUMEROUS AS THE SANDS OF THE GANGES

"Give up for good the long and straggling way of life, press onward on the northern track, step by step advance along the upward road, as the sun skirts along the western mountains."

"Not to live, then why not, 'not to love'?"

THE FOLLOWING DECISION is not such a bleak final dismal decision as it seems----it's not hard to eat but one meal a day, worth it to keep fit and follow Buddhist practice; not drinking is not sad, it's the gayest thing of all; and friends bore me, interrupt interesting solitudes.

---RESOLVED---
One meal a day
No drinking of intoxicants
No maintaining of friendships
That, if I break any of these elementary rules of Buddhism, which have been my biggest obstacles, hindrances to the attainment of contemplative happiness and joy of will, I will give up Buddhism forever.
Agreed, that I may finish the literary work I began, by the age of 40, after which my only work is to be in the Dharma Teaching, to be followed by all cessation of work, striving or mental effort when Nirvana is nigh and signs indicate there is no more to write and teach.

One meal a day means, the mind not to be taunted and tempted by the senses. (Sensation of taste left uncultivated.) *No intoxicants* means, the heart not to be deranged, beaten in, (as in excessive drinking), nor the brain hystericalized and over-filled with anxious drug-thoughts and irrelevant images. *No maintaining of friendships* means, no relations whatever to contaminate the good of contemplation, no pleasure-seeking, to ego-personality activity, no Co-Ignorance.

Quand tu t'ennui, souffre . . .

Not drinking preserves contemplative strength
Eating once a day, contemplative sensitivity
No friends or lusts, contemplative serenity

Strength, Sensitivity, Serenity =   Joy

* *

A VISION OF JOY
A grove of trees by a river somewhere in Northern Chihuahua or Sonora or Coahuila, 3000 foot elevation or 1000, clear open sky, nations of birds my only constant watchers, early morning breeze---far on the horizon, the good Fellaheen Indians and their humble grain baskets and shawls----I have strawhat and sandals, a 4-month beard, jeans, bottles of boiled and strained river water, sacks of cornmeal and potatoes and wraps of shortening, brownsugar and beans, jars of tea and peanut butter (for protein)---I have nothing to do for 3 weeks, when I walk the 10 miles into the village for supplies and across the river for mail from home----I have my Buddhist books and prepared typings from other unavailable Sutras and my own notebooks----I sit contemplating in the sand.
At night, under the flashing stars, I attain high samadhi.
Definite visions & calls of Mexico today.

Mexico is one country where you can really stalk and roam bemused, like in the dirt roads of Sonora in the afternoon of drowsy time, eyes on the ground in modesty and circumspection.
(Also pace by your shelter)
CIRCUMSPECTION, Great caution & attention to consequences

"The discriminating mind has no thought that by its discriminations and attachments it is conditioning the whole body and so the sense-minds (eye-mind, tonguemind, ear-mind, nose-mind, touch-mind) and the discriminating mind (brain) (all
five together) go on mutually related and mutually conditioned in a most intimate
manner and building up a world of representations out of the activities of its own
imagination. As a mirror reflects forms, the perceiving senses perceive appearances which the discriminating-mind gathers together and proceeds to discriminate
to name and become attached to. Between these two functions there is no gap,
nevertheless they are mutually conditioning" (mutually contaminating.) "The perceiving senses grasp that for which they have an affinity, and there is a transformation takes place in their structure (i.e., hearing hears ugly shouts close
by, say) by reason of which the mind (thinking-mind, manovijnana) proceeds to
combine, discriminate, apprise, and act ("Ah shut up"); then follows habit-energy
and the establishing of the mind and its continuance." If birdies shit on you,
you only know it and therefore resent it because of your touch-mind and eye-mind
perceiving and your discriminating-mind gathering together and proceeding to
discriminate, name and attach to.

    Whot's the Tzimis? the Tsoris?

    A little shit on your arm, a mosquito, bite, a shout breaking-up your
falsely-imagined "sleep", or a grag your empty craw, or even a bullet in your
empty heart---Buddha was never molested because you couldnt, O Devadatta!!

    Lil Abner, like Buddha, walks in perfect living sleep of faith!

    Just go through the world with your eyes closed and absolutely nothing'll
happen to molest your true nature. You'll die of dysentery at 83.

    Dont be annoyed by anyone and no one will be annoyed by you. So if when you
look up you smile at everyone, everyone will leave you alone (if they are 'angrily
watching' it's because they want to be like you).   DONT LOOK

DONT LOOK

> Soon, with One Meal a Day-No Drinking-No Friends, you'll get so
> sensitive everything will become a big event, such as a nap,
> or reading, or pacing, or eating, or writing, or talking, or
> meditating in Holy Dhyana.

(I see now that my writing is really so great that I must indeed dedicate part of
my life & joy & repose at least to finishing what obviously remains.)

> Avoid cities where "eyes down" becomes hypocrisy---

(Giroux turned "Town & City" from a great book into a good novel, then said:
"This is not a poetic age." That extern---)

WOMEN ARE THE INNOCENT VICTIMS OF THE KARMAN that perpetuates lust and rebirth---
this is why I try to avoid looking at them, because in their innocence they
constantly try to show themselves and I, being a man, am not perfectly free
from the karman of lust-attraction in this world of samsara sorrow---This is
why Buddha compliments women who dress modestly and dont show themselves---he
compliments them for their kindness---

Note on One-Meal-a-Day: Wait until there are no more hunger pangs, then eat---
you'll eat *freely*.

> *THE JOY OF WILL*

Stay way from me, Devadatta Mara . . .

           *

THE DIVINE SAYINGS OF DIONYSIUS THE PSEUDO-AREOPAGITE
From "The Mystical Theology"

***

". . . That topmost height of mystic lore which exceeds light and more than exceeds knowledge, where the simple, absolute, and unchangeable mysteries of heavenly Truth lie hidden in the dazzling obscurity of the secret Silence, outshining all brilliance with the intensity of their darkness, and surcharging our blinded intellects with the utterly impalpable and invisible fairness of glories which exceed all beauty . . .

"And you, dear Timothy, I counsel that, in the earnest exercise of mystic contemplation, you leave the senses and the activities of the intellect and all things that the senses or the intellectual mind can perceive, and all things in this world of nothingness, or in that world of being, and that, your understanding being, laid to rest, you strain (so far as you may) towards . . . union (with that which) neither being nor understanding can contain . . . You shall be led upwards to the Ray of that divine Darkness which exceeds all existence.

"The uninitiated . . . (are) those who cling to the objects of human thought and imagine there is no super-essential reality beyond . . .

"The universal Cause . . (is) beyond all positive and negative distinctions.

"Leave behind . . . all divine enlightenment and voices of heavenly utterances and plunge into the Darkness---beyond all things.

"For not without reason is the blessed Moses bidden first to undergo purification himself and then to *separate himself from those who have not undergone it*---

"The Darkness of Unknowing wherein (the true initiate) *renounces all the apprehensions of his understanding* and is enwrapped in that which is wholly intangible and invisible.

"Being through the passive stillness of all his reasoning powers united . . . to (the) wholly Unknowable . . . thus by a rejection of all knowledge he possesses a knowledge that exceeds his understanding. Darkness which is beyond Light . . . Attain unto vision through the loss of sight and knowledge . . . . . Ceasing thus to see or to know we may learn to know . . . beyond perception . . . (For) this emptying of our faculties is true sight and knowledge."

****

ON DANTE THE OVERRATED

Dante was just a super-duper Medieval Gurdjieff with his Ninth or Primum Mobile, Crystalline heaven moving with "immense velocity" because of "the fervent longing of all of its parts to be united to those of the Empyrean", or Tenth, heaven, the Heaven of Flame, or Luminous Heaven, "the most divine and quiet" heaven "immovable because it has within itself . . . that which its matter demands" . . . "beyond which is nothing" . . . . formed in PROTONOE the Primal Mind . . . blah, it's nothing but fancy astrology, pretentious, all hung up on an early Rinascita Ignorant desire to measure the properties of angels in this maya-like world . . . the first great Ignorance of the Faustian World, as pretty as a pietà and just as pitiful.

All the learning of the West ranged on shelves in giant libraries, the very Scribishness and Very Owlishness of Ignorance.

> "This earth is immovable and does not revolve" concludes Dante
>> who wanted Scientific knowledge.

- -

"To help the souls of (the Society's) members . . . to attain to the final end for which they were created" says Ignatius Loyola.

Oct.5 1954---Tonight I went out to re-deliver my Green to J., thus making one
of the greatest will-decisions in my life since 1947---but instantly as I go forth
from my hermitage(in my mother's apartment at present) I become restless, contaminated with seeking, I look at girls, think of wine, food, senses---as long as
I stay in my solitudes I'm okay. Then I had to recover *Book of Dreams* from Bill
Burroughs and got all weary and hungry talking with him and came home in the
dreadful subway in despair, worried about my Triple Decision Device for Buddhism
(One Meal a Day-No Drinking-No Friends) but instantly as I was back in my holy
room of meditation and study and Dharma works, cool joy returned and was no longer
hungry or restless or thirsty or harassed or unhappy. SIHIBHUTO, cooled.

    This is clear . . . surprising it is, that the "Friends" are harder to part
with than food & wine & lust.

OCTOBER JOY RATTLING IN MY HOTEL ROOM WINDOWS in strange new cities when I was
19, had nothing to do with alcohol or weed. Remember when you used to say, "No,
I dont like beer" and that first time you smoked weed in Harlem and lost control
of your DECIDER---Same way with Devadattas and foes, October Joy had nothing to
do with them. It had to do with wind, hunger in the belly and in the loins,
shadows, trees, lights along the street, a sight of humanity such as a Returning
Angel sees----Now you know better than to let uninitiated MacDonalds and Sebas-
tians "proselytize" you----know better than to chase tempting taunting women---
know better than to yearn for success and repetitious travel and "friendships"
----know better than to ruin the refinement of your belly with constant flow of
meals and snacks----Now you know that your Star is all and your Star is Karuna---

KARUNA, The pathos of compassion redressing human sorrows---
    REDRESS, in Latin REDIRIGO, or, *again lay-straight*
or, i.e., Karuna is a Buddhistic return to again-straighten the sorrowing world
----the rediscovery of the lost path of the Buddhas of old; straight and narrow
path of pathos of compassion.
    PATHOS, suffering emotion of the mind
    COMPASSION, Latin COMPASSIONEM, con-passionem, or, FROM-SUFFERING
                              Lax said Suffering-*with*
                              It's SUFFERING-FROM

So Karuna-is non-dynamic and therefore
non-dual mortal pathos inside mind, the
fleshy gate to bright emptiness.

The Christian Agape is defined as Care & Concern.----*Care* is from Anglosaxon
Cear, "taking heed," Icelandic *Kaeri,* "complaint," Latin *Carus* "dear"----in Old
English CARK is Great Care from AS. *cearig,* "careful, anxious" and Gaelic *curam,*
"care"; Welsh *carcus,* "solicitous"---carking care.
CONCERN is from Latin CONCERNERE, or FROM-SEEING, FROM-SEPARATING
  or FROM-DISCRIMINATING
Agape causes Karuna
    So Agape is "dear complaining heed from discriminating" ("again in awe").
    And Karuna is "emotion of suffering from dear complaining heed arising from
discriminating."
    LESS HEAVILY, Agape is Care; and Karuna the Suffering-that-comes-from-Care-
wishing-to-Redress-Sorrow)
    AGAPE reaches out crookedly to care "the long & straggling way of life"
---the way of the Great Western Christian----and KARUNA suffers to restraighten
care----the short straight Nirvana Way of the Buddhas----
    KARUNA, the emotion of suffering from dear complaining heed arising from
discriminating again in awe, seeking to restraighten human sorrows.
    AGAPE, (merely) Dear complaining heed arising from original discriminating.

The boys were sittin
In a grove of trees
Listenin to Buddy
Explainin the keys.

"Boys, I say the keys
Cause there's lots a keys
But only one door,
One hive for the bees.

So listen to me
And I'll try to tell all
As I heard it long ago
In the Pure Land Hall.

Life is like a dream,
You only think it's real
Cause you're born a sucker
For that kind of deal;

But if the Truth was known
You ain't here nohow
And neither am I
Nor that cow and sow

You see across the field
One standing silently
The other rutting ragefully
In essence so quietly.

For you good boys
With winesoaked teeth
That can't understand
These words on a heath

I'll make it simpler
Like a bottle a wine
And a good woodfire
Under the stars divine.

Now listen to me
And when you have learned
The Dharma of the Buddhas
Of old and yearned

To sit down with the truth
Under a lonesome tree
In Yuma Arizony
Or anywhere you might be

Don't thank me for telling
What was told me,
This is the Wheel I'm turning,
This is the reason I be.

Mind is the maker
For no reason at all
Of all this creation
Created to fall.

II

"Who played this cruel joke
On bloke after bloke
Packing like a rat
Across the desert flat?"

Asked Montana Slim
Gesturing to him
The buddy of the men
In this lion's den.

"Was it God got mad
Like the Indian cad
Who was only a giver
Crooked like the river?

Gave you a garden,
Let the fruit harden,
Then comes the flood
And the loss of your blood?

Pray tell us, good buddy
And don't make it muddy
Who played this trick
On Harry and Dick

And why is so mean
The Eternal scene,
Just what's the point
Of this whole joint?"

III

Replied the good buddy:
"So now the bird's asleep
And that air plane gone
Let's all listen deep.

Everybody silent
Includin me
To catch the roar
Of eternity

That's ringin in our ears
Never-endingly.
You hear it Tom, Dick
And Harry Lee?

You hear it Slim
From Old Montan'?
You hear it Big Daddy
And Raggedy Dan?

You know what I mean
When I say eternity?
You heard it in your crib---
Shhh---Infinity."

IV

Up spoke Big Daddy
From Baltimore
An enormous Negro
Forevermore:

"You mean that shushin
And that fussin
A-slushin in my ears
For all these years?

When I was so high
Jess a little guy
I thought it was me
In the whisperin sea.

I asked my Mam
About that jam,
She didn't say nothin,
She sewed the button.

It was quiet and late
At the afternoon grate.
Her face showed no sign
Of that whisperin line

But as we sat waitin
Instead of abatin
The noise got to roar
Like an openin door

That opened my haid
Like if it was daid
And the only thing alive
Was that boomin jive

And we looked at each other
Child and mother
Like wakin from a dream
In a spirit stream."

"Well spoken, Big Daddy!"
Cried the buddy real glad.
"This proves that you know
And you'll never be sad.

For that was the sound
That we all hear now
And I want you to know
It's no sound nohow

But the absence of sound
Clear and pure,
The silence now heard
In heaven for sure.

What's heaven?
By Nirvana mean I?
This selfsame no-sound
Silence sigh

Eternal and empty
Of sounds and things
And all thievin rivers
Complainin brings.

For if we can sit here
In this riverbottom sand
And come to see
And understand

That we got in us
Ability to hear
Holy Emptiness
Beyond the ear

And block our ears
And hear inside
And know t'aint here
Nor there, the tide,

But everywhere, inside,
Outside, all throughout
Mind's dream, Slim?
What you gripin about?

Imaginary rivers
And gardens too,
A movie in the mind
For me and you.

The point
Of this whole joint
Is stop, sit,
And thee anoint

With teachings such
As these, and more,
To find the key
Out this dark corridor.

The effulgent door,
The mysterious knob,
The bright room gained
Is the only job."

       The boys was pleased
       And rested up   for more
       And Jack cooked mush
       In honor of the Door.

* *

by JEAN-LOUIS

The longer you eat once-a-day the less suffering comes from hunger pangs. By same token, the longer you practise Solitary Purity the less suffering comes from pleasureseeking pangs.

AGAPE is also Reverence---Reverence is defined thus:-LATIN REVERERI, RE (again) VEREOR (I feel awe)---to regard with fear mingled with respect and affection, to honor---an act of obeisance is reverence.

> The Pitiful Ignorance--
> of me and my agape suffering at sight of Ma's taffies tonight---her own
> pitiful ignorance of tongue to taste---t's'all to be down the hole of
> Blown Out Reality Nirvana and the Pitiful Reality of it---?
>   THE PIETA OF OUR POOR HOPE

Sanskrit nir, *out;* vana, *blown.* ---literally nothingness, annihilation.

Stormonth's splendid definition of Karma: "The impersonation of the inexorable inflexible law that bound together act & result, this life and the next."

While you live, the details are the life of it---DEATH, no details, no life

I have both snaky sentience and Christian tristfulness in me . . .

A new hope is rising in my soul, O Supreme Reality of Pity

If there's another life it certainly isnt going to be *mine,* any more than you'll expect the rib of a dead autumn leaf to be reborn---as its *self*---

It's a religion for everybody, not just Yogis & Saints
PITY IS THE ONLY REALITY
What exists, exists; things *do* appear to be; when blown out in Nirvana of great sitting Samadhians they only appear to be blown out. The stars are pity. The details of the world in its appearance and disappearance everywhere cannot be blown out (?), they only seem to vanish within the Eighteen Spheres of Mentation, (which are in themselves imaginary).

> The great shift (GREAT MEANS) cannot escape death, which is also imaginary.
> I'm going on to Supreme Reality of Buddha's Nirvana Pity.

Words, words---
          ALL THINGS ARE IGNORANT FORMS OF PITY

Pity is a form of ignorance--
Mind Essence is not a form---
All things are ignorance---
Pity is emptiness---
Open space is the purest Sight of pity--
Saints are the saddest form of pity---

OCT 6 '54--I shall now give up Modern Prose, which I invented, because I am rejecting the general techniques of modernity. (AS BEFORE IN 1947, GREAT YEAR) O Aremideia come to my aid! There's Christmas in my soul!

"---And there is no escape from weary sorrow. . . .

"And there is no escape from weary sorrow . . . like a man fresh from a loved one's grave, the funeral past and the last farewell taken, comes back with anxious look.

"Tathagata, possessed of fond and loving heart, now steels himself and goes away; he holds his heart so patient and so loving, and, like the Wai-ka-ni flower, with thoughts cast down, irresolute & tardy, he goes depressed along the road"---

THE SADDEST

"Non-continuance is the great disease"

Buddhism, a means
Buddha, "the skillful maker of comparisons"
"Deluded by false knowledge the mass of living things are only born to die again . ."

OCT 8 '54--All things are ignorant forms of pity. Of mind pity. Most refined example of pity ("most perfect") is open space. Pity itself, essential pity, is space without phenomena; or, *emptiness*. This is how I would explain it to the West, because the stars are dreamlike yes but only *seem* to vanish in Nirvana (because they only seem to appear in Sangsara)---
But all I've done is discover the compassion in Nirvana (the Karuna) but I'm such a *wordy* character I start whole movements around it---The truth is Buddha but it is late in the world and Aremideia must be skilful in *Upaya* to teach it.

No need to implicate yourself in "friendships," suffer your pure solitary mind to the clash of "conversation"---Separate yourself from those who have not under-gone purification, they are trivial----(though goodhearted)

I see the holiness of all existing things---thick thighs or no thick thighs, do you think my father Leo didnt know divinity? A physical detail of importance, my thick Breton Western thighs, that I (and most Westerners) can sit in the Yogi position, not even the half-position, for more than an hour at the least---In every detail of the world hides pity, in a pair of old shoes, in a book (physical bound book), in a sill where a fly slept 22 hours then vanished---
The Flower Pities the Bee

East is East and West is West
Dont ask me why---the pitiless East . . .
THE HOLY THUSNESS
I could however have taught Pa that Quiescence is better than running around looking for sensation, but we're not all born contemplatives

THE HOLY DETAILS
In order to appreciate HOLY DETAILS how can you smash your sensitivity?----
those glad Proustian images came from the invalid purebed, boy---
Gladness of a kid is not the batteredness of a drinker talking crap at a brass rail----Gladness of a kid and freedom of a man.
Remember the Yankee Game in 1951---as soon as I had a beer, the whole Yankee Stadium became a blur- --I hadnt drank for 3 weeks.

The Nirvanic East, the Pitiful West
----cold constellations in their icy bed of winter milk.
I'm a secret Bodhisattva-Mahasattva in the world, will be reborn once more, in India, or Burma, as Aremideia the Buddha of the Last Kalpa.
In my last form I was an angel.
Actually these are just religious symbolisms pointing to Nothingness beyond Nirvana and Pity. ---"Pity" is my fleshy Western gate into the pitiless Nirvanic East and on into the Holy Thusness of the Novoid.---

All things are ignorant forms of pity in a dream already ended.

$$\left[\begin{array}{c} \text{The Buddhaland of Immovability} \\ \text{in the Eastern Heavens} \end{array} \right]$$

But I'm going to *Work in Pity* before I *Retire in Nirvana*

Now I see back and understand into 1947 when "depression" was seeing the truth of emptiness and "elation" or "joy" was the seeing of holy pity in all the details of life.

      If it had been ancient India, this 20th Century America in which Jean-Louis find himself, I would have cut my hair a long time ago and put on the robe and gone with the begging bowl in the Eightfold Path.
BUT THIS IS ANOTHER WORLD----The yellow robed monks were an institution; when folks saw you coming they said "A holy man," what could they say in the West but "bum" and seek to lock their doors in fear instead of filling your bowl with food----Also the very simplicity of true head-shaven yellow-robed homeless Bhikkuhood was enough to influence a monk's thoughts towards true meekness, so he might even in his gaunt ascetic habitude refrain from complaint when men kicked him---The American hobo kicked by railroad cops? This is another world, another grand culture, and Jean-Louis will find his own way to rest and kindness. ---O Lord Buddha.
      It will be the Gothic way of artistic creation, O Maitreya.

"What is born by nature must endure so----Lust, as the root-cause, brings forth the things that live... All things are produced by cause and therefore there is no creator"...ASVHAGHOSHA

      "Nirvana, as when the rain puts out a little fire . . ."

Free From Desire---What I really only want, what Ma's given me, is freedom to do nothing.---So I wont re-attach myself to brunettes, French movies and banana splits---
TAO IS JEANS AND BEANS----

This afternoon Oct 12 '54 I was tempted to drink again, for the first time in 8 days---but by suffering loneliness, waiting, and eating food, I got over the yen, which would have replunged me in insensitive ignorance of the past 14 years ---I realized that when I want a drink, what I really want is a long roaming walk along river and railyards and woods, like a boy in Lowell.
      Ah misère---Who knows? Who even exists? Drink up---but not more than once a week. (Hop!) (Had a can of beer at 10 P M and that's all.)
GOT DRUNK NEXT DAY OCT 13---

The constellation of the King.---Why am I heartbroken? *Because the good things on earth come to naught with the evil.*--- (that wouldnt break my heart if I wasnt attached to either the good or the bad.)----The fiery moon too.---

      False optimism runs this world---
"All his days also he eateth in darkness, and he hath much sorrow and wrath with his sickness." ECCLESIASTES 5.17

Made fast, by your own false-imagination sentience, so that when the spirit of deliverance comes like a great wind no living things is saved or torn from its fast moorings of suffering, but stays on, while the dead and the empty go with it to heaven.
      *

If Jazz was profound women couldnt play it---but they do, and sound just like

the men---it wasnt Marcelline Proust wrote Au Recherche du Temp Perdu, or

Jeanne-Louise The City and the Path

--- * * * ---

WHY THE RAILROAD'S HARD
     "Well, boy, let's get 2 behind 3 off 1, then double to 4 to set out the east
cars, spot the express reefer, pull 5 and kick 7 down the lead, then it'll be a
trey, deuce, four, another deuce, five aces, and a trey, hang the head car and
come to 15 to shove that rail, then get the crummy off the limey and we'll cross
over to tie up 8." ---NEAL LEON CASSADY

I should separate my life to double now.   A, No writing, no friends, solitude
                                                      in Mexican desert hut outside San
                                                      Luis, be Tao Hobo, practice do-nothing

                                                    B, Stay home, write Duluoz Legend, friends
                                                     trips, to NY, Paris, Africa, India,
                                                     girls, wine, money-earning efforts.

I KNOW WHAT I'M GOING TO DO, be a greater writer, make the 30-Volume DULUOZ LEGEND
the greatest writing in America ever, on coffee, food, walks, faith---as of
yore in 1946-48----smoke a pipe and be great sober writer at parties making women,
the last word about sad life will be mine---shows, health, glitter, great voyages
in the October sea on my earnings off Novel Movies------Good homestead----Fame---
Sorrow------*Jean-Louis Confused*

       The *Drear* is Russian, imaginary, and Jewish---it doesnt really exist in
       America.

All things are like visions
beyond the reach of the human mind

                                 . . . . . .

     The difference between animals and men is not the trivial sense of humor
which men are supposed to be sole owners of---sense-of-humor is after all a form
of animal self-flattery----it is that animals do not know that a mirage of water
is an hallucination of their own minds----they'll chase one all day and blame
themselves for not finding it------Men know better and this is why men have led
the way to emancipation from suffering and delusion--
     Abbé Pierre and the Worker Priests must teach the workers to rise from the
dirty mines of self-delusion to the purity of quiescence and solitude, otherwise
they're just playing into the hands of Faust-Totalitarianism------There is no
modesty in that bare-chested homosexual-looking Worker Priest photographed by
Jacques Lowe---- Next to Shame & Pity, the highest requisite for the emancipating
Saint is Modesty.----Poor sad smiler he.

             *"The philosophers do not recognize that the views that
             are influencing them are only dream-like ideas origi-
             nating in the mind itself."*

Who is this big writer Jean-Louis but a victim of his own imagination---

        ------- . . . . -------

IN MY WRITING-LIFE:- Is the Duluoz Legend a repetition in many words of self-evident themes, details? or is it a great teaching of pity via the prose study of events in their dharmakaya light in the only story I know completely--?---Boys, I had a much better insulting first-predicate-question for it this afternoon---(Loneliness rides the words I do write in this dream in this book)---I write Duluoz Legend not for praise, or blame neither? but for the reason that I have hired myself out to do the work of pity (as no one else knows how) before my Nirvana---This is a big unasked building of a Cathedral by a dedicated world-lover teaching the end of all things. What's wrong with that?---I mean, why will Anton Rosenberg and Stanley Gould say that I write too much? Hieronymus Bosch, he painted too much; Dionysius the Pseudo-Aeropagite, he wrote too many mystic visions; DaVinci, he knew to paint and he did something in his boredom, ere his Parinirvana Death--(Faustian)

A VISION OF THE BRAIN
"The souls of dead people are little
hard diamonds on the earth, absorbing
the news; they were what was left
of the great cerebellum organic
elastic brain integrating its impressions
from the soft shove of atom feeler balloons
intermingling thin films in force---in
graves a crust." --Written in Mexico 1952.

AFTER GREAT LOWELL TRIP OF OCTOBER 1954
    Written on Concord River Railroad Bridge near Mary Carney's house:
    "The perfect blue sky is the reality, all six Essential Senses abide there in perfect indivisible unity forever---but here down on the stain of earth, the ethereal flower in our minds, dead cats in the Concord, it's a temporary middle state between perfection of the unborn and the perfection of the Dead---the Restored to Enlightened Emptiness---the restored to neither-imagelessness-or-non imagelessness--- . Compromise me no more, 'Life.'---The cat floating face down dead in that dark water had no self, was but a victim of accumulated Karma, made by Karma, removed by Karma ('death')---What we call life is just this lugubrious false stain in the crystal emptiness---The cat 'hears' the diamond samadhi transcendental sound, 'sees' transcendental sight now, 'smells' the transcendental odor, 'tastes' the transcendental flavor, 'feels' the transcendental sensation, 'thinks' the transcendental thought----the Sameness Concept---
  So I am not sad for him.---A ridiculous New England tumbleweed just danced swiftly across the entire length of the Railroad bridge.--- Thoreau's Concord is blue aquamarine in October red sereness---little Indian Hill towards Walden is orange brown with Autumn--- The faultless sky attests to Thoreau's solemn wisdom being correct---but perfect wisdom is Buddha's. Today I start teaching by setting the example, not words only."

                But I'm too sad to care that I understand everything.
                Lowell is a happy dream but just a dream.
                All 's left, I must go now into my own monastery
                wherever it's convenient.
                My life went from culture of Town, to civilization of
                City, to neither of Fellaheen.

* *

Wandering around in just the form
we have and no other, the vibratory
level in which we find ourselves unable to understand our intrinsic
emptiness and phantasmal appearance, on the surface of this tiny
planet speck suspended in endless
space so that as we walk to school
all infinity begins at our hat-tops
and goes up and off into the
void of our own essential mind &
Kalpas pass and still we cant take
the hint, all this is not like a
dream?

"Doing good for himself" is the
big virtue in Lowell & America---
chicken with head cut off rushing
around little streets buried in the
Universe Canyon of mystery.-

EGO . . .
I get impatient with my mother
for instance because she doesnt
notice me, my subtlety, what I
intelligently tell her (naturally
she bores me) but isnt this
just because I am conscious of
my EGO being neglected? Better
the egoless sweetness of Buddha.
Same with dogs that bark at
me, if I pay not attention to my
EGO, which is really inexistent
in Dharma's reality, what affront
has the dog done me? Pay no
attention to what others do and
be sweet when they address you,
and no one will ever molest you.
Secret brutal rages of revenge-
ful daydreams also arise from
false conception of ego redressing imaginary attacks on said
ego---a mad dream replete
with temerity & misery. O
cease these delusions, Aremideia!
Be kind, be pure, forever.
Let this Body rage to
destroy Samboghakaya no more.
Buddha, completely free of wrath,
impatience and all egoism, was
never spoken an unkind word;
except once I know of, and
he said to his tormentor: "Because I can't make use of
your abuse, you may have
it back."

THE SECRET IS IN THE STARRY WOMB

Where the Ceaseless One Transcendental Thought radiates this
meaning: EVERYTHING IS
 ONE PURE CONCEPT.
Make no distinctions and differences,
that's been yr. trouble . . . the
unpleasant & the pleasant all
take place in one suchness, in
one purity of Mind Essence.---

    All things are of one Sameness
just like vast perfect indefinable
pure unchanging open-space is.

    TATHAGATA, is, thusness-already

    The 5 precepts keep the body
(& soul) pure; Concentration on
one-concept emptiness (citta-vritti-
nirodha) keeps the mind pure (of
defiling discriminatory dream thoughts.)

    ---the original state of wis-
dom's insight into reality.

FOR G.J.:- "Most people are said to
be lacking in enlightenment. This isnt because they have no thoughts, but because
from the very beginning they have had a
continuous stream of thoughts and discriminations with no break in their
succession. They are still abiding in a
beginningless Ignorance. But when a
Master (a Bodhisattva) has completed
the stages and has attained a state
of no thinking, he is able to realize
that all the Phenomena of conscious
mentation of thoughts---their rising,
growing, passing thru the Mind,
disappearing---is the same as no
thinking, that all the apparent
changes are there, inherent, but un-
manifest, powerless like a dream to
influence the original state of
wisdom's isness sight into reality which is
also the final wasnessness, the Ultimate
Enlightening Nature of Mind-Essence."

    Supposing you heard of a guy who
was continually in his retreat/ but his friends complained so he came out con-/
tinually to pacify them, wouldnt you/ doubt his sincerity of retreat, wouldnt/
you doubt the modesty of his solitude?/---I love my home because here/ is my
chow & my retreat---

I am going to live in solitude in the desert in a rainshelter.---
The hell with the law, the hell with snakes, scorpions & lizards.
The hell with great rains.
I will carry enough food and water on my back
To last me a month.
I will travel light like a Buddhist ascetic
Right here in this Western World.
The West, with its laws, customs, ideas of property,
   Proprietries, overpopulation, propperies, popery,
Mope and outlying areas, general coverage of the earth,
Atom Yucca bomb flats and fuckups
Panel trucks and wheels
And artificial sugar towers,
Water in cans, sleeping bags,
Desert, mountain, sea,
Dreams of aridity,
City and desert, back to sea,
Dry from rain, safe from pain,
Rattlesnake grounds
And legal rights within & without
Homeless western world road
O hobo no truck
Thoreau and his lovely 19th century
Hut at Walden Pond Massachussetts.
I shall be a Bhikku,
Hikin thru
Indiana, Georgia, India,
Alabama, Appalachian
Fire Rangers smoke
Jails, fines, boys,
Nature and Dwight Goddard.
Asvhaghosha, where'd he live?
Says Dwight Goddard:-
   "It is noticeable
that doubt (as to the reasonableness &
possibility of the homeless life without
fronts, devices & various property that
this involves) is not voiced by those who
have tried it
Hark
but by those whose habits and comforts would
be curtailed
and interfered with."
Like Thoreau Saying:-
   "The woods are easier to live in than you've
ever in your wildest dreams imagined."
   As I say:
         "The woods are ave of me."

   *

Mind:-it goes inward to compassion & wisdom,
         goes outward to world woe.

   "Habituation to the contemplation of Voidness"--MILAREPA THE FRANK

"AS ONE GETS RID OF THE CONCEPTION OF SELF, THE CONCEPTION OF AN EXTERNAL
WORLD VANISHES WITH IT."---Asvhaghosha

"If a man had no conception of Enlightenment he would have
no conception of Ignorance; and if he can get rid of his ignorance
he will have no conception of Enlightenment." ---ASVHAGHOSHA

The arbitrary conception of ignorance-walls in my room, the enlightenment
is the empty space between---the indivisibility of this enlightened void
truth Bright, and the sad divisibility (into sections & selves) of the
sentient & densed wall of "living"---as Tao says "Existence is for accommodation" (the wall) "Non-existence is for utility" (space) ---Not clear---

These divisible multiple notes on
the one indivisible simple Dharma!

$$\left.\begin{array}{l}\text{The woodcutter}\\\text{The woodcutting}\\\text{And the wood}\end{array}\right\}\text{THIS TRIPLE WORLD}$$

The thinking, the thinker & the thought-of
---all 3 equally empty & same, in
reality indivisible.

The inconceivable activities of the Tathagatas, *unification,* suits my taste
much; I hate divisionism of life.

        The thinking that is done to relate sense-perceptions, such as
the thinking of ice cream taste or tobacco smoke fragrance, is the same
thinking as the thinking done inward to Enlightenment unifying all concepts
of taste, smell, etc. into the One Concept---the *thinking-stuff* has that
sameness & suchness & is the inconceivable Mind Essence making it all possible.
        It's as though you would say "Life, it's something to do,"---because
Pure Essential Mind really could abide in imageless emptiness instead of manifesting all these ghosts, which in any case it only seems to do.---
        So the mind "without battin an eyelash" relates likings & dislikings
in the divided egoisms of sentience & itself sets up the deception . . .

        "*Defiling thoughts & suffering do not exist in their own
right*" but arise from the non-Enlightenment of discriminating Ignorance" (which
is the same as Enlightenment in that it is the same stuff, but turned outward
to divisive multiplicity instead of inward to non-action and realization) etc.
        Endlessly the explanations, the confusion of mental
approaches, the arbitrary conception of Enlightenment as bad as non-enlightenment
itself!
        "The reason that Enlightenment can take on different mani-
festations of *explicability* is wholly because of the conditioning power of Karma
in correspondence with the defilements of the mind---"   for, actually, "the
thing called Enlightenment is intangible and ungraspable, having no form that can
be seen or nature that can be described," being perfect emptiness itself.
Enlightenment cannot become an object of the sensation of *thinking.* Good & bad
Karma are of one clay---"all sentient beings (actually) are ever abiding in
   Nirvana"---"but in Reality there are no sentient beings to be delivered,"---
all one clay, one emptiness in which the clay appears to exist.---Clay is
sameness, but forms, divided forms & shapes, are not sameness. The suffering
is in the form, the joy is in the essence.
        The defilement of the ear obtains in the sound, the purity
of the ear obtains in the silence.
        Sound is a going-out, silence a going-in.
        Music is a defilement of the purity of the innately silent
ear, because it cannot by any conceivable means teach this.

Lying all the time---I write the
Duluoz Legend because of pride in
my artistic stature, vanity in
my name, & greed to lose
nothing of my success-potential
---As to deluding myself that
the Duluoz Legend will be good for the world,
it will only be additional blind detail---
If I write it must be the Teaching---
the Duluoz Legend will have to
be called AMITABHA BUDDHA
        The thinking-mind is only used
by divided selfhoods---there is no
reason for unified Infinite Essence
of Mind to "think"---

＊＊＊＊＊＊＊＊＊＊＊＊＊＊＊＊＊＊＊＊＊＊＊＊＊＊

NOVEMBER 1, 1954
    Pinky was run over---what I
loved about Pinky I now realize
was that part of him that wasnt
real, I was infatuated with his
white & pink fur, funny comings
& goings, satisfied purrs, loose
ways, all Karma sweetnesses of
his cat-Karma---these *marks*
of his individuality were run
over & have disappeared from my
lonely window---but the True
Pinky, the Invisible Bliss that
made him possible, is not dead
but is still everywhere abiding in
permanent peace & unity and
Pinky is restored to that Bright
Emptiness unharmed except for
his imaginary body & his imaginary
catsoul---in other words, Pinky
is Nirvana then and now & I
only realize it when his world-
body "disappears"---
                        Says Asvhaghosha: "Desires and habits of grasping &
                        clinging . . . are dependent on the thinking-mind without
                        any self-nature of their own." True Mind doesnt grieve.

＊＊
Not an "intellectual"---AN INTUITIONER
    "Conceptions . . . of objects of sense . . . (such as cold winds, hot sun) . . . are
like reflections in a mirror which if grasped lead to hallucinations of a self
and an 'external world,' but if the discriminating & thinking mind (which receives its
consciousness from *manas* and starts right in intellecting outwards to grief
instead of from *manas* one intuits inwards to joy) stops its thinking, leave the
mind in tranquillity."
                "The memory consciousness develops and intensifies the
false notion of an ego-self & exaggerates the supposed importantness of its
interests." (or the egoistic consciousness, the separating-consciousness)---
"By reason of its activities the mind becomes more & more separated by its
egoistic desires, prejudices & imaginary annoyances, from its true oneness
in the pure Essence
                of
        Mind." ASVHAGOSHA

VAJRACHEDIKA PRAJNA PARAMITA
The tree of the Diamond
Sutra all luminous in the
moon----The moon is
blinding, huge, & lopsided
in a night of clear
glitters---slowly lamp-
ing the stars sit in
their void, empty---
A late Summer jitter
bug dr-r-ills in the
rosebush---The freight
wheels are thunder-
ing & clanking and
squeeing on cold
steel---
The chair in which I
sat when I realized
the Diamond Sutra,
the Vajra, is
white and shining
as snow in the moon
milkied grass---
Trees of the n'hood
speak softly & dis-
tantly of the man
writing in the
night in the dark
with no light.
The holy tree is
covered with the
diamond brightness.

It's a pear tree, and was the tree under which I read & realized & meditated
& came to comprehend the holy emptiness---
In the beautiful September afternoon, with the air fresh & the sky blue marvel,
little nameless & almost sizeless bugs disport over the tall grass which has
in it signs of Autumn hidden in the late strawy eaten look, as though grass was
the food of certain insects & they harvested their crop only in the Fall---
When ripeness is everywhere---
Yet I know that one blade of the grass, one tip, one fuzz-tip smaller than the
thunderous herds of a million horses in a needle's eye, is larger than all the
universes because there is no size, no measurement, in reality, so that I may
know the extent of the emptiness of all Ten Quarters of the universe by knowing
the extent of the emptiness of a grass---
Each movement stiffly jiggling in the wind, this is fantasy because in reality
there's no grass, there's no wind except as it is mind-arisen and as Mind is
empty, perfect, pure and free as that profound deep sea of blue above (so still,
so aimless, so abyss-like and yet with no precipice & no bottom & no arbitrary
fallers, a mirror of the holy void), there is in reality nothing before my eyes
except the nature of sight, the nature of mind, which is in itself not fantastic,
but all sights & thoughts arising from its Holy Ground are fantasies.
A whole lifetime to prove this & show that it is all you need to know---

To prove that to learn is learning ignorance---
That there is nothing in the world seen, heard, felt, tasted, smelt, or thought
that is not ignorance, and nothing in the world unseen, unheard, unfelt, untasted
unsmelt & unthought that is not empty, true, & Essence of Mind.---
Bear with me, wise readers, in that I've chosen no form for the Book of Mind
Because everything has no form, and when you've finished reading this book you
will have had a glimpse of everything, presented in the way that everything comes:
in piecemeal bombardments, continuously, rat tat tatting the pure pictureless
liquid of Mind essence.
Now I see the stalk of Timothy grass, its leaves fall & bounce up again gently,
in a gesture of nature's as pure as the bounce of a woman's great milky teat---
The wheat-like head, the male shaggy individual on top, waits bent for the end of
time---
It was from the female rockabyes came that head, suffering, was soothed, rocked
in the sea, dipped in moonbeams, rained-on thirstily, strengthened, ribbed,
because the female, the principle of nature, has no other function but natural
sympathy with the horror of the born---
Yak on, crack on, wail & howl on, poor babies of the world,---There's an end
coming.
It hides in the peace of the fantastic ground, to which, when thou puttest an ear,
thou puttest a dead receiver of dead true silence, wherefore I know, my father,
whom the world deems dead, is no more dead than I am alive.
--Chatter, holy tree! Wave, soft shrouds of humans on fading clotheslines! Roam,
bug of jungle grasses with yr. beady look---the world is new, the world is old,
& Time pristine.

MY LIFE IS A PUSSYWILLOW puff of the Fall---
blow on it 5, 6 times, even when it's damp,
only once when it s dry, and all telephone
poles of spidery-activity silk are hurricaned
from their roots in delicate dry antelope valleys
of the octopus plant head---a thin, frightening thing,
with no hope & no substantiality of appearance even---
Pieces of it are still flying. It's a silent moth at the heart
of the world.

THE CRIES OF THE CHILDREN on the first clear Fall day, that I hear out my window,
makes me want to be back in Lowell to hear the children of eternity in the snow,
with their sleds, on keen icicle days, and I work on the railroad as a yardclerk,
and my apple orchard has yielded me sweet red apples in the gutterdeep autumn,
& I wear a warm woolen shirt in my farmhouse---but this daydream, like the dream
of the cats before it (the two kitties in Mexico City), is empty and fantastic,
it is full of ignorant energy without self-realization, it grinds on hopefully,
full of death & rebirth---it is up to me now to enter into the Pure Room of Mind
& clear away the unnecessary furnitures of false-imagination---pretty soon I wont
write anything.

* *

STRANGE CEMETERY IN JAMAICA
on a September Saturday afternoon,
gray void skies, cool, the
coo of crickets in the tangled
grasses & redberry bushes with
reddening creepers with thorns,
yellow posies, jungle-like
smalltrees, all under the immense
    unbelievable bird-flirted gray
    serrated gastank a thousand
    feet high & 2000 around---

the gravestones dry from old
weathers, bleached in the
powder of age, the writing worn
& new writing of rainrills over
the barely seen words--
  "NATHANAEL LUDLOW
         died
           ----"
---bunch of green & posies at it,
empty as the sky---The
large trees playing their leaves
serenely in the upper breeze
---Burnt raisinberries from
dry thorn twigs hang, dark
brown---delicate ferns
say No & Yes & Shrug---
Around the bleak eternity
tank an iron walk &
iron rail for travelers in the
unreal merrygoround of its huge
be leveled sides---only on the
5th upper level is there
white & red paint, for
airplanes---Far off chuggle
of the diesels waiting in the
yards for the herder's come-on
---Loose rattle of a freight
on the viaduct passing by---
And so I see that these
graves dont smell, only slightly
there's a rot among the vege-
tations reminiscent of ancient
burial of death---All, all
imagination, my pencil, my
page, my cemetery, my death,
my decomposed dusts, my
steel Ow Tanks, my
passing deadhead cars, my berries
& ravelled raisins, my bleak
Void Heaven, empty, silent,
absent, imagined, bear faced,
echoed, seemingly in motion
& seemingly in stillness, seemingly
dead & seemingly alive---
  I spit my gum out
  To meditate
The bums have been here &
drank wine on old graves
& crapped & slept on card
boards & didnt care & were
not scared of the dead
but serious & humorous in
the cop-avoiding night &
even amused, & left litters
of their picnic between the
grizzled slabs of Imagined
Death, cussing what they
thought were real days,

real nights, real dawns, real
birdshits---So too now I
sit leaning on a plot
stone, shoes on grass, with
pencil & lonely poor un-
oratorical unworded mind,
rather be dead & dead's
not real, waiting for my
     Parinirvana
       in a graveyard
        full of bugs & longtail birds
& bottles of Old Tokay---
between this death & the
Living Gastank is a barbed
wire fence to keep the
ghosts away from infiltrating
& blowing up the Niggers of
Jamaica----right
behind me Timothy Grass,
& back of that, the tomb
stone of Nameless Peterry
died I dont know when
& Whitman was here too,
impassioned while he
blew---but I am too old
& weary of the globe to
worry about passion and
about death & too en-
lightened is this mind to
take anything seriously but
     Holy & Bright
       the Emptiness
        at the heart of Love
here in the desert of form
---arbitrary conceptions built
that fence, rolled the rain
down from my own waterfalls
of Heaven Milk & Honey
& made them eat the
bleached rock till names
like reputations & rightarms
vanished in a slew of ghosts,
the worms have rebirth
too---What dead man
did eat the worms with
his grisly mouth untasting
----bitter as dry time's
rugged fuzzleaf chewed
in bleeding gums---Old
stumps of wood fill me
with Old Hope---A
once beautiful fanciful carved
iron amulet did take the
plot bar from pole to
pole, but now's rust
& more rust & lost its
sensitivity shape fit for Edith
Whartons died with Emily
in their arms, cracked,
mungy, faces of rainy

rust, nothing here but the
dirty stain of life on the
unborn hope---None of
us were born, none of us die,
this is a message from me
to the dead and from the
dead to me who have no
self & am not alive any
more than they're dead---
---though a little bit of
rain coming---The diesel
whines roaring but the dead
are not annoyed, nay, they
are not even born---their
ears dont hear this frightful
anxious engine, mine
do?---They dont hear me &
I dont hear them
  It gets darker
  I am not worried
  Rain coming
  Closer
  -----Holes everywhere---
  One mysterious old grave
dug up by robbers maybe, to
get Mrs O Crap o t oo tie's
expensive China Clipper
lace from under her green
disdain---or for gold pieces,
like Pirates, they swung lan-
terns & killed Indians & got
drunk in old Box Trucks
with thin tires Railway Express
Agency & empty inside---
O well, I dont know what
I'm talking about because there's
nothing to say about Nothingness
--- That's why I sit
in cemetery & vie with
the people underground to see
who can be more quiet
& unconcerned & equanimous,
that's why---So topers, &
Saturday Afternoon beer shlug-
giners, drop dead around an old
spittoon----When this tank
blows up in Apocalypse of
self appointed World Oppen-
heimer shatterers, you'll
need this graveyard no more
  -----& maybe just as well
   I believe in death
   & hew to Whitman
   the old Whitebeard
   Long Island Lover
   but aim not
   at his passionate
   avowings & Gallic
   eccentricities---

I've got my own
Castration
To disavow
And his to Wow---
Or something,
I really dont care

No more poems from poor Jack
Who disappeared just in time
Before form could claim him
And turn his essence to shambles

Essence'll do
　S quiet
The dead are just as glad
　As me
This is my Graveyard Samadhi
September Fifty Four
World Order Phooey
No more ---

　　Aint nothin I want
　　But nothin

That's because death,
Void, bleak,
And all those old gray
Worries I had
Are now my luminous
Love
& there's nothin
to say
PRETTY GIRLS MAKE GRAVES Fuck you all

* *

8 FOLD PATH
1.　Right Views
2.　Right Intention
3.　Right Speech
4.　Right Action
5.　Right Livelihood
6.　Right Effort
7.　Right Mindfulness
8.　Right Concentration

----

book four

The ancient original use of tea---
to calm the mind before meditation.

In China the true Buddhist sometimes buys captive fish & animals &
sets them free---also makes sym-
bolical offerings to the poor homeless
ghosts and spirits that throng the air!

"The stupendous vow never to
rest in this life or in lives to come
until every living creature has been
saved."----Life in a Buddhist Monastery
in China, Blofeld

The practice of PI-KUAN---three
years in one room, food slipped
to you, a little garden to pace in
-----"his body was imprisoned but his
mind & spirit were free to traverse
the unseen realms of bliss, while other
men who have freedom of body are
mentally bound by circumstances, by
worry, and by ignorance & folly."---
"Monks who had the strength of will
to do this were much admired by the
rest & eagerly served by them."
"The main criticism leveled against
Buddhist monks is that they do
no useful work for society"---This
is now echoed roaring by the Chinese
Reds, those Kings of Ignorance.
What is society?---what is
the society between two points of the
handle of the Big Dipper?---how
many miles of empty truth over
the crowds milling in streets?

The "scented board" at Pu T'i
monastery in West China---they whack
you with it if you dont jump out of
sleep at 3 A M when the gong is
hammered, or when you fall asleep
in Meditation, or if you shift your painful feet! Give me solitude
in the desert, scorpions are better
than discipliners.
"The best results seem to be found
in the isolated hermitage where two
or three monks are quietly & inconspicuously
living a true life of self restraint,
industry & meditation. They are free
from the constant irritations of the
home & secular life----Offer the world
an example of quiet, cheerful, thoughtful
kindly & inexpensive living that

will be an influence for the highest
good to all who come to see them or
who hear of them---They are free
to show personal sympathy, charity
& hospitality; they have time to
teach the boys and girls, to explain
the Dharma to older people, and
at the same time themselves to be
definitely advancing along the Path.
All the above is just as true for
the nuns as for the monks."
   GODDARD

------Amitabha Buddha----
The Apocalypse of the Fellaheen

   * * * * * * * *

For Burroughs: "Ignorance . . . is the assertion of the space-time-motion conception
and all that is dependent upon it."

TATHAGATA, is, He-who-has-thus-attained
"Buddha taught that all desire is suspect (good or bad)"---

  SUTTA (SUTRA), is, (originally) *a thread*

"All objects have but one flavor, the flavor of reality."

"Before thou seek'st thy meal,
clear thou thy mind of zest
for forms, sounds, odors, taste,
and touch,---which turn men's heads."
  ---BUDDHA, Sutta-Nipata, Cula Vagga, Dhammikasutta

"Spread on the ground thy bed."

  "Shun drink; make no man drink;
  Sanction no drinking. Mark
  how drink to madness leads.
  Through drink fools sin, and egg
  Lax brethren on to sin.
  So flee this maddening vice,
  this folly, bliss of fools."
   ---CULLA VAGGA, SUTTA NIPATA

". . . touch not wrong meals o' nights"

   THE EIGHTFOLD FESTIVAL
  1. Slay not
  2. Steal not
  3. Lie not
  4. From strong drink keep away
  5. Refrain from lechery
  6. Touch not wrong meals o' nights
  7. Eschew both scents & wreaths
  8. Spread on the ground thy bed

Buddha saw "a hole and corner life was all a house and home could give."

Buddha walked "with gaze a plough's length on" (!)---"eyes on earth downcast"

ESA BHIKKHU, MAHARAJA!
"Having no appetite for pleasure's toys,
Alive to all the perils pleasure brings,
And finding in Renunciation peace,
I'll struggle onward.---Thus my mind
finds bliss."

Knowledge . . . "the garner'd Lore"---
---"pelf, repute, the pride of place,
with fame ill-gotten, scorn of
others, praise of self . . ."

"Shall I cry craven? Nay; a pest on
life!
I'd sooner die than brook defeat---
and live."

Our "lust-free Lord."

"All worldly ranks I know,
but, knowing, go my ways
as---simply nobody."

"You'll find in me a sage,
good, taint-less, want-less, calm"---

ALL THINGS ARE PITIFUL FORMS OF IGNORANCE---SPOKES FROM THE "HUB" OF ESSENCE
FOR AN UNNECESSARY WHEEL OF EVOLVING IMPURITIES

The flash of truth came over me
in the midnight rain, but, with
"serious self-deception of reality"
I knew the words weren't there
but I knew that once it was
realized one became a Buddha
now & forever---

Dreams are unreal---I dream of bare dust by the empty blue sea,
as the Southwest where I'm going for my retreat---actually there's mesquite
there & its nutritious pod---I wont let dreams frighten me; they are blossoms
in the dead air.---"Best anchorite is he who heeds not omens, dreams, portents,
prodigies."

Renounce the worldly life and go follow the path of the
Buddhas of old. . . .
The world is full of schemes and haters and the
viciousness of sexual conspiracy---

I understand the haters at last, and what they are doing to Ezra Pound & to me---
KEROUAC IS THE WINNER.
The haters, like Devadatta, must be saved too. Naturally, or the world will
never come to an end.

* * * * *

The reason that wind is the cause of waves is because of the water's Essential stability.

"If the Mind should lose its stability, all sentient beings would disappear because there would be nothing for Ignorance to play upon. However, as the substantiality of the mind never disappears so the mind retains its continuity. But if Ignorance some day should disappear, then all arbitrary conceptions of form & phenomena would disappear with it, but it would not be the disappearing of the Mind's pure Wisdom."

        ---ASVHAGHOSHA

A sheet of surface ripples
 is the false mind
  --Karma, the waves
   lapping on the shore
    as a result.

HOLD STILL & DONT THINK

Wednesday Nov.9th
  Instituting the new rule once more, and no cutting back to Pityism now possible 1. NO FRIENDSHIPS or
       SOCIAL OBLIGATIONS
       WHATEVER
  This will cut me down on the nervous social drinking, twaddle, expense, and waste of earnestness, & destruction of will & of solitude---
  Also helps on diet of one main meal a day, by obviating hangover indulgences & relaxations of belly discipline. Because NO FRIENDS
             NO DRINKING
             ONE MEAL DAILY
         is still the most important decision since
         the Tea Return---& was only abandoned because
         of temporary intellectual abandonment of
         Buddhism which is no longer possible----

  To symbolize this decision, as Tea Returned symbolized the Tea Return, I now cease all letter writing, abandoning all friendship & social commitments & backgrounds, Nov. 9, 1954
    -NO LETTERS-

* *

DIALOG OF THE LADIES
Mrs.Leichter:-Freda! I saw 2 men in the yard measuring something.
Mrs.Whitebook: Yeah?
Mrs.L: They had a ruler and they were measuring the house. I said, "What are they doing down there." You better not go out there.
Mrs.W.: I'm not afraid . . .
Mrs.L.: You'll catch cold . . .
Mrs.W.: I'm not afraid . . .
Mrs.L:-*You'll catch cold,* I said . . .
Mrs.W.:-Oh yeah?
Mrs.L.:-You've got nothing on.--I said to myself what are those guys with the measuring.
Mrs.W.:-Maybe they wanta fix my roof or something.
Mrs.L:- (laughs)

SELFNESS--It's just as absurd for me to deny the selves of others and not deny mine, as not to deny the selves of others and deny mine, which is practically what I've been doing in my practice of Christian Tristfulness---Now I deny all selves.

The diamond sound on a still
winter night when you're looking at
the starry sky is like the sound of
the innumerable Lotus Lands radiating from your sight's center between
& among the actual stars---the
Moth Swarm of Heaven---Nothing
on earth matters but enlightenment
------*Death & Rebirth after me will*
   not be my causing if I concentrate
   my mind in this life on emptiness.
   And on dreamlikeness----it will be
   the causing of "others "'s Karmas
   ---But I vow to return to assist
   in the universal emancipation
   eventually to come----

AMITABHA BUDDHA
The Road and The Path

What is my book but just making history among the fools---the sooner I give up literary attainment the sooner Enlightenment will come to me---If on my deathbed day I'm still involved in literary matters I'll deserve the most painful of re-births---Milarepa, save me!

Last night Nov.10 I realized that I had died & been reborn numberless times but just didnt remember especially because the transitions from life to death and back to life are so ghostly easy, like falling asleep and waking up again a million times, the utter casualness of it---

[But it's only because of the
  stability of the Essential Mind
  that thing-ripples take place.]

GREAT UNIVERSE SMALL

Madness is a genuine mental protest against the delusion of the sane who grasp at the mirage and the dream of life as real. The sane dont understand that all the phenomena of the universe is empty and Mind-only. Psychoanalysis is merely a tool of this deep ignorance.
    The only cure for the "mad" is solitude and meditation.
    Psychoanalysis is actually an East European conspiracy to befuddle, obvert and rule the religious masses of the world. It is to be guarded like a predatory beast.

        Armistice Day indeed!---
        My battle against Mara
          is over & I've won! NOV 11 1954
            (the battle is just begun)
            *

      A B C' s of Truth:-

      A   Creamy thighs of beautiful young girl =

      B   Baby crying because it doesnt want to be born =

      C   Corpse decaying in grave

* *

MESQUITE
     Eat the legumen of the algoraba or honey mesquite in the Yuma-Coahuila country
---gather in July & August and dry thoroughly---pound bean & pod both into imperfect meal (pestle & mortar)---soak---eat---soon light fermentation improves
it---Vigorous to chew but sweet & is sometimes rolled into balls for journey food
---25% sugar---The fruit hangs from mesquite in four to 7 inch legumen hanging
in clusters, piles at the foot of the plant in "thick carpet of straw-colored
pods." The SCREWBEAN comes after the pod---cluster of little yellow spirals
united at one point

---BOIL AND MAKE
    YOUR MOLASSES

CHENOPODIUM---8 foot hi---big stalks . . . "careless weed" . . . pound seeds into flour
or meal, and bake in cakes---*eat leaves for green.s*

The AGAVE---(maguey)--not ripe till stalk comes out of center, up, clusters of
pale yellow blossoms on it---Little Agave at San Diego and Baja California---6
to 12 inches big but stalk is 10-FOOT-HI and slender, flowers a bright yellow
---From April on the Coahuila come down from the mountains and take the sapfull
cabbages & stalks (in Coyote Canyon) (Cañon Coyote) and roast them in great stone-
lined pits dug in the sand, fire first to heat the rocks red hot, then throw
heads in, cover with grass & earth, and leave to roast for a day or two---"fibrous
molasses-colored layers sweet & delicious"---Heads: *a-mul* tenderer & deliciouser
---better than stalks *u-a-sil*---Boil & dry the yellow blossoms for later.

A palm-like tree with a 4, 5 foot stump, spines dense at foot, is YUCCA MOHAVENSIS
---the Yucca---delicate waxy flowers---fruit is *nin-yil,* a plump sticky green pod
3–5 inches long with big black seeds in center in four rows---*pick seeds when*
green, roast in coals,-Roasted green apples like.
     PRICKLY PEAR, *na-vit-yu-lu-ku*
Palm dates---
Acorns (dry, pound, soak out bitterness, use as meal)
Piñons--late Fall, inside the pine cone---roast cones then spread leaves of cone
     and jar out dry nuts by stone blow on apex of cone---Toss nuts from a
     flat basket in the breeze to winnow nut from the chaff

FRUITS OF CACTUS, either eat by slow steaming and boiling---or allow to ripen then
dry it & beat it for its seed to grind for mush

KO-PASH---"niggerhead" cactus just smaller than a man's head, a round fluted globe,
bears a small edible fig but is important for: *PURE WATER inside the rind.*

    "The Indian draws his store of foods from hillsides and canyons, where the
     White Man looks for nothing and can produce nothing."

Roast acorns and pound for coffee---not just dried nuts but *roasted*

Dont eat hemlock nuts (hemlock has pins, not needles)---pin   needle

Edible pine cone is fat & round & rough-scaled--
Magnifying glass for high noon fire---

    My duty to become a Bodhisattva
Teacher & teach the Path from my
desert hut---*no other duty.*

(The position is still sacred, as in 1950---the question is of the worthiness
of my 2nd book, not its mere publication---)

There are things more dangerous than the rainy season---

Cover fire with ashes for morning---
Praise Avalokitesvara Buddha---

        * - - - - - - - - - - - - - - - *

SYMBOLISM I dont buy---the Whole Symbolist Movement was one big fairy tale
and nobody believed it---the fairy tale aspects of Buddhism, the Vajra-gods
with their Symbols, I dont buy---As for Freudian Symbolism, if a sharp knife in
your father's hand in a dream is to be construed as a phallic symbol then it
were moot and of much pitch to take precaution which end of a cock you grab.
   This note has but literary value.
           * * * * * * * * * * * * * * * * * * *

Peter Martin's sympathy makes him cry---in THE CITY & THE PATH (as I had planned
it) the "dear human people" become the "poor ignorance pitiful ghosts"---Peter,
the Untold Peter with his American learned sorrowful insights into Buddhism---
He goes from agape of Town & City (the original ms.) to Karuna of City & Path.

It is of no small significance, that Bob Giroux, who instantly reminded me of
Francis Martin when I saw him in his office offering me $1,000, then cut down
Town & City into a mediocre novel.
- -
-LYING QUIETLY IN MY DARK ROOM, thinking of all open space outside the window
that reaches uncountable infinities of miles into endlessness, emptiness, egolessness, imagelessness, the whole unspeakable, inscrutable and serene Void of
all the Universe, I heard the Television announcer say "Use Pond's cream, it's
smooth to your skin . . ." and I had an awful vision of this little skin we live
and die for, which isnt even real, which our minds think of with snaky seriousness, in all this open vacancy of Mind . . . this *skin,* this mistake, this grim
delusion---All the poetent and inconceivable radiancies of heaven are shining
this minute yet my mother prefers to have her discriminatory brain fed constantly
from the tube of television---How deep is the extent of the burial of mankind in
his ignorance on this poof called earth---How serious, sad the grim disregard of
Essential Mind's enlightening insights which come as pure concepts on the other
side of the coin of every impure concept bombarding the tormented, perceiving,
hopeless, decaying brain----Why wont they understand, O Lord Maitreya? Why are
they angry at me for shutting off the machinery of false belief in earthly activity? Why do they insist on fooling themselves unceasingly from life to life,
death to death, rebirth to rebirth, phantoms on a gnashing screen? Why do they
fear silence, darkness, inaction, meditation, poverty, purity, eternity?
          * * * * * * * * * * * *

"Worldly acquisitions of wealth and the need of clinging to them, as well as

the pursuit of the Eight Worldly Aims, I regard with as much loathing and

disgust as a man who is suffering from biliousness regardeth the sight of rich

food. Nay, I regard them as if they were the murderers of my father; therefore

it is that I am assuming this beggarly and penurious mode of life."

                        ---MILAREPA

A POEM
"Peta, do thou also give up
All worldly aims,
And come with thy brother,
Who is older,
To pass thy life in meditation
At Lapchi-Kang."
     ---JETSUN MILAREPA, founder of the
       Kargyutpa sect---(Tibet)

"If ye do not suppress the Demon of Ambition, desire of fame will lead to ruin
and to lawsuits."---JETSUN

"Hold your peace and no litigation will
   arise;
Maintain the State of Undistractedness
   and distraction will fly off;
Dwell alone and ye shall find a friend;
Take the lowest place and ye shall
   reach the highest;
Hasten slowly and ye shall soon arrive;
Renounce all worldly goals and ye
   shall reach the highest goal."
       ** MILAREPA **

     Now I know why I've been tortured & twisted with doubt about typing BEAT
GENERATION for the publisher who wants to see it, Knopf, it's because the
Tathagatas want me to make up my mind in advance of the arbitrary conception
of either literary acceptance or literary rejection, money or no-money, to go
to the desert south of Yuma or outside Mexico City in the Valley Plateau of the
Fellaheen Moon (Citlapol, the Great Star) (YOHUALTICITL, Lady of the Night)
and follow the Path in the most penurious & pure way possible to me at this
stage.--- For there is no real reason for me to publish BEAT GEN. other than to
repay my mother materially for her long sacrifices on my behalf when I considered
myself a "writer" (in the literary sense) in the world---
     The light is Buddhahood.
     I am continually irritated by the worldly life, even when
it's pleasant, it's time for me to go to my desert solitude, now,---A hut outside
Actopan or Zimapan or Zumpango or in a Holy Valley Vale, a little garden, a little
silent private vihara of my own, the first of many to come---*Fame and fortune
wont make any difference now.* Return to the purity of when I was 18 and wrote
about Eternity and Nothingness and Spaceless sky and made no arbitrary distinction
of being a Sage Disciplining Himself but slept and ate like an animal while being
wise.---
     It would make people respect my teachings more if I were
famous and yet kept in solitude, if I were rich & lived poorly in rags nevertheless, like Schweitzer in Africa---but that advantage is not as important as the
inestimable advantage of passionate faithful sincerity about Buddhahood and the
Ultimate Buddhahood of all living creatures agitating in the Uncreated Light.
Since Time is an unreality in endlessness, all living creatures will come to see
the light indeed, "plenty of time."
     My name is untold---
     My message is bright---
     I can convert any earnest man this minute! Mara beware!
    (But my last obstacle is an unmatured sexual Karma . . .)

AS THE LIBERAL HARE BUDDHA IS TO THE JACKAL SARIPUTRA, AM I, AS I WISH TO BE,
TO WHAT I AM.
     ***

Today Mon.Nove.15 '54, I want to begin a practice of not being disturbed by anything others do & to "parlay" this with kind speech.

Buddha: "Concentrate the mind,
Keep the precepts,
Practice dhyana."
--which covers it much better:-

PRECEPTS
1. No sexual lust, adultery, even
thoughts & cupidities thereof, but
control the mind. "The creeper of
passion stands sprouting; if you see
the creeper springing up, cut its root
by means of knowledge." DHAMMAPADA

2. No killing, egoism, brutality, un-
kindness---Eat no meat. I, who
hopeth to become a deliverer of others,
myself living on the flesh of other
living beings? (Some monks even
abstain from silk, leather, milk . . .)

3. No stealing and covetousness---
no belonging but garments & bowl, beg.
Offer self to common good. ACCEPT SCOLDINGS
Sacrifice a little comfort before
an image, pay all Karmaic debts---
---In West, offer food to the poor,
also money when asked & needed---
even winos need---(be sure to
wander around penniless, like a
pack rat . . . carry butts for bums)---
*Learn how to live off ground and
be charitable as ground*---is all.

4. No insincerity and lying---no
presumptuous assumption of attainments & realization before real-
ization---No practice of Buddhism
for pose, for glory, for power,---
let there be no progressive loss
of yr. nature of kindness & your
seed of Buddhahood & destruction
of seed of Buddhahood in others
---Vow to rebirth in all forms &
keep Bodhisattva-Mahasattvahood
a secret, "not speaking without
discretion before those who are not
practising meditation," except
toward the end of your mortal
life you may disclose to *your most
worthy disciples* the secret teachings
& instruction "lest the evil heretics
disturb & lure them away by their
lies." "UNKINDNESS IS THE MURDERER OF THE LIFE OF WISDOM"

4 PRECEPTS
1. Chasteness . . . lustlessness . . . purity . . . gravity
2. Kindness . . . sympathy . . . tenderness
3. Covetlessness . . . generosity . . . liberality
4. Sincerity . . . deceitlessness . . . truthful

Birth and re-death . . .

"Because of the fumigating powe r of Ignorance, Universal Mind Essence has become differently defiled and therefore manifests its defilement in different ways and different degrees, so that their number is incalculable."---see it?

L'Essence de mentalité universale

"So great is the variety of their personalities, their experiences, hindrances and suffering (of the different degrees and ways of defilement, the different pitiful forms of ignorance) that only Buddha can comprehend them and embrace all in perfect compassion."

----"If both causes and affinities are present, their Buddha nature (of sentient beings), the fumigating power of Mind Essence, the kind teaching and sympathy of Bodhisattvas, then there will come an abhorrence of the suffering of birth & death, the awakening of faith, the purpose to practise kindness and to press on toward Nirvana."

How come men suddenly say "Oh what's the use, it dont matter nohow."---Because *"There is an unceasing fumigation of the external activities of sentient beings, by the pure concepts of the fundamental Essence of Mind."*
ASVAGHOSHA

Also, concerning BEAT GENERATION, I'm doing it to prove that I'm not retiring to the desert because I am a failure, but because I am a success. People will more respect the Dharma Teaching I present, as though I were a king's son abandoning the Palace.

The existence or non-existence of the ego-personalities of Neal, Allen, or myself is such a trivial matter---the self-substance of Mind Essence is inconceivably pure,---

This is Tao---"In not one sentient being is the inconceivably pure self-substance of Mind Essence deficient, in not one is it in excess; nor has it any source of arising, nor time of disappearing; it is ever abiding, a permanent, unchangeable Reality."

"From its beginning it has been in full possession of all virtue and merit. It is in full possession of radiant Wisdom and luminosity, penetrating everywhere by the purity of its Concepts; seeing everything adequately and truly, its mind innately free and unprejudiced, ever abiding in blissful peace, pure, fresh, unchangeable, ever abounding, never segregating, never ceasing, never conceivable, an illimitable Fountain, a Womb of exuberant fertility, a Mind of perfect clarity and universality---the Tathagata's Truth-body!" ("the all-embracing Dharmakaya")----

Listen to all this in Diamond Samadhi

* * * * * * * * * * * * * * * * *

RIGHT EFFORT IS MAKING THE EFFORT, but making the effort to what?---ro remembering emptiness under all circumstances, which is RIGHT MINDFULNESS, Samma-Sati, the 7th Step in the 8 Fold Path ——————————

---Right-effort, Samma-vayana, follows No. 2, samma-sankapa, right-Resolution, or
resolution to make the effort which is Realization of emptiness, followed by No.
8 Samma Samadhi, bliss in concentration on emptiness------

The only activity that doesnt suffer
the shame of change---bright meditation

EVERY NEW HUMAN BEING is just another
sensitive, tormented talent for suffering---
that's why the Tathagata is full of compassion
and sorrow and wishes to serve in the emancipation
of all sentient & human beings from time past to time
uncome from their sad trap of life and death, delusion
and despair, innocent rage, darkness of mind, perturbation,
weariness, hopelessness--
    The sound of the Diamond Samadhi
has been going on since beginningless
time and will continue into the timeless
future unceasing, because it has no space-
time-motion restraint placed on it, is the Void Bliss.----

"Poor people aint got no place to go but church
----rich people pray five minutes and they *finished*"
                    ----NEGRO IN 8TH AVENUE BAR

Mankind is like dogs, not gods---
as long as you dont get mad they'll
bite you---but stay mad and you'll
never be bitten. Dogs dont respect
humility & sorrow.

That indissoluble sorrow I feel---
and I've locked my mind around it---
is caused by the enlightening nature
of my own Essence of Mind, which,
because constantly having its snowy
purity smeared and stained by the defilements
of sentient conceptions, images and activity,
hurts and shocks, the kind of sorrow
a man would feel because his snowy
white robe is constantly being smeared
with black blood---
life is precisely that dirty---
but Mind is pure.---

So I have constant unbearable regret that my Essence of Purity is being defiled
day in, day out---

Yet actually everything's alright, all things are already
                                in Nirvana. . . .

IT IS BECAUSE OF THE STABILITY OF
PURITY THAT THERE CAN BE A
DEFILEMENT IN THE FIRST PLACE

No answer from the dead---
I'm not better than nothing---even a good man is not better than nothing---
nothing is better-----

So far, I've forgotten to sympathize with the ignorance limitations of the
unenlightened sentient beings around me and in judging them have only done harm
---to Turn the Wheel of the Dharma requires Compassion and Wisdom both---skill
in teaching is only *kindness*---

> Mad wrote curtains
> of
> poetry on fire

The mere thought of it disgusts me---The Beat Generation, my relationships with
Solomon & Allen & Holmes, Giroux's repudiation of my dedicatory poem ("This isnt
a poetic age"), the brutality of football, the shame of literature, the whole
arbitrary mess of my mother's disapproval of the generation and all its modern
activities & the generation's arbitrary disapproval of doting mothers, my whole
room cluttered with manuscripts, the disgust of quitting making-a-living-at-writing
just when my breaks were underway.---
> For purity's sake I'll quit.---That means all worldly attain-
ments including barefooted Indian wives.

> Dont be fooled by glittering ships
> and romantic travel---delicate
> viands and lovely women are nothing
> but shit and bones---the sea's deep-
> er'n you think.---poor potpourri---

Rain the rills rushed---

Miles Davis,---why bother with any of it---Jazz, modern musicians, dope addicts,
punks,---Monk, crooks, killers, Bud Powell, Dizzy's razor and Dizzy's scorn
& Al Sublette's scorn---no. Give me the Bodhi men. Dont even play the radio any
more, jazz is simpleminded noise. BOYCOTT IGNORANCE   BOYCOTT
                                                             IGNORANCE

Realize your purity and abandon the external world of ever-ignorant
impurities---NOW---or it 'll have to be later in another miserable
life. Find "fun & jazzes" of IN-YOU---the inconceivable activities.
And the inconceivable transcendencies.

> One Meal Daily-No Friends-No Drinking is absolutely essential
> as the first step to Buddhism---"No Friends" except fellow disciples
> of course---& the Daily Meal must be large enough to suffice for 24 hours

✳ ✳
Imaginary histories of sentient beings on earth---suddenly they get married, etc.
--It's a confused, vague, dull comedy about marionettes.
✳ ✳
HERE'S THE LAY WAY (away from my hut)---be well dressed, no drinking, no friends
other than disciples, smoke nice pipe, have girlfriends only, for *loving* (Here
goes Jean-Louis Confused again)---women only learn one way---be quiet, cool, sober,
neat, kind, rich.---But in the desert, be an inconspicuous hermit Bhikshu living
in a hut and hiking to the village once a month for food supplies and riding cheap
bus to the City once in a while to dig Sravasti and the Streets of Fellaheen Man.
An *Indian Hermit*----a Buddhist recluse---Or "anthropologist" for a front---
> In this way, *Inconspicuousness* and *Calm* are gained---no frantic sad madness.
> No drinking (I'd say at this time) at any time, except at
home, only at home, and then only because of holidays & feasts or if for any other
reason, like frantic sad madness, do it in your room and think . . . . . . think away from
it eventually-----Wine is good but no-wine is good too.

By no means is Ignorance a kind of ripple,
Nor is the bright reflecting mind a case of lakes.
Since Mind is emptiness
Where is the ripple on what surface?

The wood of Germunzale is just
slippery alum (soft bluesmoke licorice wood)

F
R   "Nouvelle execrable
E   Johnny Picotee m'a piquee
N   Il ma pas fai mal-e
C   Il ma ainque graffingez."
H

S   "Embarque dans ma voiture
O   Tu vas voire comme sa va ben
N   Les springes sont un peu dur
G   Sa fa yen sa fa yen sa fa yen."
S

Thanksgiving Eve   I had the Enlightening Dreams---
        O the sadness I felt on my bed---I woke up from the Void and I thought
"I dont want to be me"---I understand everything now.   About arbitrary conceptions
---it means, what is here now, and will be gone then, is neither here now, or to
be gone then, because it is mind essence itself which doesnt come or go---It's
like a ghostly dream about a pack of cards and you wake up and where's the pack
of cards? and where's the player of the dream?
        No dreamer, no dreaming, nothing dreamed---the triple Saha *songe* is the
Mind Essence itself.
        No sufferer, no suffering, nothing suffered---all things already pure & serene
        The Holy Void is like a clear, pure, calm lake upsidedown---the sentience
the tiny ripples on the bottom of the sky, rising up from deep-grooved blackbrain
birth-and-death earth---bah! stop thinking, get lost in trances, then come to me
with WORDS

        Get to Thy Hermitage!

                        Dear Lord above I'm frightened tonight---What do I know
about deserts? water?---Where shall I go to escape this civilization which at any
moment may thrust me in jail or war or madhouse? A shack in the woods outside
Rocky Mount, be near family?---what of the gnats, heat, tics, mosquitos, disapproval? Be like Rhinoceros, tough-hided. I want to go inward in Mind but
cant leave my good mother behind---attached to her---& therefore to the civilization? I'm crazy now.
                        Eight months out of the year in R.M., in woods shack with
stove or firepit, water can be packed in, toilet can be outhouse style---solitude,
meditation, sun & air---Then in May go on annual pilgrimage to some pleasant
plateau valley in Mexico, to rent a sod dobe, meditation & solitude & Mexican
churches & Fellaheen Indians---That way you dont abandon the good mother nor the
practice of stopping & realizing---Go therefore now to R.M., work awhile saving $,
dig shacks around woods, save $50 otherwise spent on Mexico trip for first rents
of shack (or lease land and build shack). Then, in May, take first pilgrimage
to Mexico.---

            THREEFOLD   ⎧ No friends   To escape from the gigantic attach-
            PERSONAL   ⎨ No liquor   ment to America with its Hip
              PATH   ⎩ One meal daily   Wildness

        This keeps expenses nil and also certifies the practice of meditation
in a seal of absolute personal purity, the Five Precepts---

---Write to teach---Give all profits to your mother, like the Sixth Patriarch
"The Aborigine" when he was young---Avoid temptations, they only lead to war
and involvement---The price that you have to pay for a life of serene purity in
ecstatic religion, is that you have only *One Job To Do,* and that is, concentrate
inward in the Mind---this means absolute loss of pleasures---the rest is danger.

HOBO IN BOXCAR, mumbling, "The shortest way around is straight down."
        (From a poem by Eugene Fallon)
        (The shortest way around the world is straight down---
          the shortest way to salvation is straight inward---)

THOUGHT CONCEALS   ---(from the void)---

Obeisance to the Threefold Personal Path---the path of pure love---

The preceding page, part of it, was written in the mid watch of the night, 3 A M,
when the dolors of the world rise like a ground mist.---

Friends & taste of food are as
much forms of false intoxication as
liquor---thus the 3 Fold Path of Pure Love

      THE WORLD IS DEAD

PRACTICE WISHING HAPPINESS TO ALL YOUR FRIENDS, ACQUAINTANCES & ENEMIES---
not only does this awake a heart of compassion, but a wise realization of the
impossibility of "happiness" as sentient beings desire it with their discriminating minds---& hopes & fears & moods---that is to say, for instance, a woman
desires the happiness of the love of a man but the man is only a transient compound
thing bound to disintegrate & disappear (his fond regard with it) and so there
is no happiness possible in the woman's limited ignorant conception of happiness.
It's like someone wishing for eternal life in this mortal world of the living.
But practice the hope of the happiness of others while promoting their realization
of Noble Wisdom (Arya Prajna) by mental radiation & transcendental telepathy.
The old distinction between idealists and materialists still holds true.
Buddhism incorporates the only words I've seen that try to describe the indescribable verity as I've always known it. For all dharmas, all religions, are but
symbols and words, means & shifts around the Great Death which is "our life."---

THE TRUE MIND is like the Diamond
Sound---accidental thoughts come &
go to try imprinting on its surface,
but they cant really, like sounds
dont *penetrate* the Vajrasamadhi,
and that's because not only are they
Mind-only---but Mind-Essence themselves---
and more: - The Intrinsic Hearing of
Essential Mind has a stability
that if removed, "sounds" would no longer
be sounds---the Intrinsic Thinking of Mind Essence,
if removed, "thoughts" would no longer be thoughts---
these sounds and thoughts would have nothing to register upon---
Remove all Six Intrinsic Senses of Transcendental Essence of Mind and
sounds, sights, smells, flavors, touches & thoughts would vanish, and with them,
the Sixfold Sentience of Ignorance---
              and with that,
                  the Four Elements.

I'm only beginning to realize what it is possible to know about these things---

The ear-drum itself is inert---
The eyeball registers sights because they are manifested & developed by Mind
Essence, not by the inert nerve-balls.

The Christians and their anthropomorphic fairy tales . . .

A JUNIOR ARHAT NOT YET FREE FROM THE INTOXICANTS: - The danger in my being a
Teacher is Twofold.   1. I'm too ignorant still to give the true
                             teaching & am only in the early states of Vow-
                             Making, not actual Turning-about within.
                          2. The Teaching may and *will* be appropriated by
                             intelligent but insincere poseurs who will
                             use it for their own terrestrial and evil
                             heretical ends . . . This includes myself, i.e.
                             a poet using Buddhist images for his own
                             advantage, instead of for spreading the
                             Law. As if you would bruit Buddha abroad
                             in Rome.

BESIDES? I'm
too young and
bashful at
present to take   "Nothing so full of victory
on the role   as patience"---in---"the long
of Master,   night of life . . ."
and too soft-
headed to
undertake the   "In quiet solitude of desert hermitage
burdensome   nourish a still and peaceful heart"---
job of officially   ----
rowing the   That which is "great" about Buddhism, and that which
Yana-ferry   is "great" that is said about Buddhism, such as "Bright
back & forth   Room" or "Inconceivably Mysterious Tathagata's Womb,"
across the   is Great only because Buddhism is great but not for the
  spectral   sake of Greatness; that is, Buddhism is not a concern with
  stream   Greatness for its own sake but with Enlightenment, Compassion
   **   and the Law
                                           ****

How often! how many million times I came into the world, and was befouled on
earth, until I was finally justified in heaven, justified in the Bright Room in
the Deathless City, and died on earth, and went to my Nirvana, but made the Vow
to return as Bodhisattva-Mahasattva in order to spread the Dharma and each time a
little closer to perfection as my Karma was worked out, thinning it down from
the huge sins of bestial existences as insect and raging wolf unnumberable Kalpas
ago in all worlds throughout the universe which is but a shapeless body located
nowhere, or, Mind, instead of a "bright globe of clarity" merely,---a Mental Womb.

                    * * * * * * * * * *

Dont ever forget that the 6th Patriarch was pursued by evil human beings and had
to hide with the hunters---dont for one minute think that the Tathagatas have
anything to do with the earthly tribulations that happen to come to sincere masters of the Dharma whose nirmanakaya earth-bodies are subject to the causes and
conditions of conditionality---therefore, beware of the evil human beings, not
they but their acts, for which they are pardoned already, but LAY LOW----This is
a rule of simple horse sense . . . You will be persecuted and even prosecuted as
naturally as rain'll fall, for the same natural & ignorant reasons . . . in fact,
it will be your own fault and all mind-made and fantastic as in a dream---
but LAY LOW---Beware of women, the law, insincere disciples and your own
foibles such as the cute trick of false self-deprecation which saddens and
confuses those who love you & falls on the deaf ears of your haters.

A good name is like precious ointment, but no name at all is worth the eternal verity.

In the Nirvanic East & in the Truth of Cayce, poetry is *not* greater than philosophy. Words are *not* greater than meaning.

The Six Realms of Existence are Hell, Brute, Ghosts, Demons, Men, Angels.

Men are "taken in" by women, since beginningless time,---this is how birth and ignorance continue---Men dont realize that women are their own Rib of Lust, Self-Lust, and are actually nothing but (like men) skin & bones with shit inside ---Watch women closely & see if I'm not right---The True Man eschews women, has no children, and seeks No-Return to the dreary wheel of life & death---He is constantly on his guard against lust & concupiscence & cupidity---

       SIX PARAMITAS
DANA 1. Almsgiving, charity, generosity
SILA   2. Morality, kindness, sympathy
KSHANTI   3.Patience, humility
VIRYA   4.Zeal, perseverance
DHYANA   5.Meditation, ecstasy, tranquillity
PRAJNA   6.Wisdom, transcendental intelligence, no arbitrary conceptions.
           "Having completely freed myself from
           all theories and reached the laws of
           void"---SARIPUTRA

SRADDHA, is, faith, also liking, approval

"The man (the old father) knows the disposition (of his boys) (in the burning house), and has a clear perception of their inclinations (to ignore fire.)"
A PARABLE IN LOTUS OF THE TRUE LAW SUTRA

Talismanic words pronounced by 4,200 thousand myriads of Kotis of Buddhas:-
     "AGANE GANE GAURI GANDHARI KANDALI MATANGI PUKKASI
          SANKULE VRUSALI SVAHA."

The Joycean Fall-word?---dig this name of the Tathagata of the Aeon Priyadarsana
more than incalculable Aeons ago:-
GALADHARAGARGITAGHOSHASUSVARANAKSHATRARAGASANKUSUMITABHIGNA (!!!)

Sela the Brahmin, to his 300 young brahmins in the woods, as they approach the stretch of dark trees where Buddha is said to be: "Move forward in silence, noiselessly in one another's footsteps for, these Lords are hard of access, like solitary lions."

     "Gentle lamblike cows that fill the pail, bid be taken
      by the horn and slain?"---the evil of meat-eating.

"Wives looked down upon their lords with scorn" when men first broke up the Tao Purity of their Primal Wisdom & became silly fools---

Bull Elephants dont have money

SLAGHAMANA, is, Coax

Dec 4 '54---Running away would be the act of a clever Indian, but would it be the act of a world-saving beneficent Indian? Imaginary blossoms in the air, are prisons, policemen, wives, mothers, sons, fears, night---and Buddhas & Dharmas too---Life is a dream in the empty measureless universe of the mind, pay it not mind---Let men & things buffoon before your eyes in this unpredictable unknowable shining suchness, and they are not YOUR eyes but the same thing as NO EYES--- The moment of wise reflection in a sweet hermitage that will stop all time, comes soon enough, ere the comedy's run out---and the tragedy too---And it is neither a comedy or a tragedy---Pay attention to Compassion which rises from the flashy realization that all things are different forms of the same thing and the same thing is the unpredictable unknowable shining suchness of Universal Mind---Be tender with everyone, Sanday the Dog is a different form of the same thing to which your own self belongs, the same thing that you are---Be tender with everyone and everything including enemies at all times, and give everything you've got, and then wander freely---*then*---Naked in a cave, Milarepa owned no pride, gave up no city, misunderstood no lotus.---Quietly plan your Great Retreat.---The Great Escape is the final one.---Fear no man, fear no man's law.---Fear desire.---This is the Noble Way.

        VERY IMPORTANT . . Let Ma see how evil they are, then she wont object to your renouncing the world.

       Why do comedians make fun of love?---because
       humanity is ashamed of its own cupidity.

It's a phlebitis world, a world of affliction & suffering,---a masochistic world. A very sad, imaginary scene of pain.

You want ecstasy?---that's an arbitrary conception and besides you've got it already *because* of your sentience, you've got Nirvana because you've got Sangsara--- You've got the Extinction-of-Life-and -Death, naturally, because you've got Life-and-Death . . . It is the disposition of sentience to discriminate Mind and therefore Ecstasy.

The Hasheesh Magicians

The road of sensible pity among the innocent souls who must be taught will be better for this poor Bodhisattva than frantic blackness in the Alone Rage Night---unless forced.
       The Road and the Path . . .

My only "crime" (in this non-support litigation) is poverty & disease--- "Jean-Loui" is Tao in any case, so dont let events change that obscuring name, O bright bulb. . . . Be like Reality, Quiet & Alone

You will be justified by the truth---as always . . . Wait for Jan.18 (the date before the judge) with faith . . .

I cant renounce the world completely till I have done serving my mother, who brought me into the world. This too is Tao. If I dont outlive her during the course of a zeal-ous life divided into teaching-writing at home where she is, and the annual retreat into the solitary hut, then it will only mean that as Bodhisattva I shall return not-yet-perfect. Solitary hut and sometimes camping in the desert with sleepbag. For how, and by what laws of compassion, can I abandon her, she loved me and served me in a lifetime. My Maya did not die of my own birth & coming.---A poor factory-working widow is not an opulent tearful Maharajah.---

The pity of Jesus that I bear as a seed I cant renounce any more than the realization of Buddha and the Buddhahood of Emptiness beneath these lonely skies . . .

When I'm an old man my time will come to go sorrowfully down the road to the path forever, with halting gait, like Old Navajos---O wind in the Cochise Canyon! A Papago Ghost! O Vultures--- Life is a bad dream. This I must teach.

How do I know that all this is a bad dream? The future works of Jean-Louis will explain it, using skillful argument by means of art at which, suddenly I realize I happen to be accidentally master.--

America vs. Russia is a war
between 2 kinds of lip-service

To clear the dilemma of the boredom of *time* neither try to improve on it to make you glad, nor allow any single thing that happens to sadden you.

Equanimity is the key to composure---dont improve and dont disturb.

* * * * * * * *

TODAY DEC 8 1954, I burned a spot of incense on top of another on my hand, before the image of Buddha, and suffered searing stabs of pain as I gazed at his face and I realized pain is the same for all sentient beings, (the incense felt no pain), Buddhahood is the understanding of all sentient beings---I realized malice is the same for everyone, distraction the same for everyone, joy, taste, birth, death--- I realized there is no differentiation between sentient beings, they're all the same, different imaginary forms of the same thing, and for me to think of myself as BETTER than the violent judge, or INFERIOR, is deranged thinking---Since pain is the same for me as it was for Buddha (his eyes seemed to say) then Bliss Radiance of his Supreme Enlightenment would so be the same for me as it was for him---Ignorance rolls on, but the Great Awakening will soon instruct me in the origin of Ignorance and the Mysterious Truth.---

All the houses of Richmond Hill in the still night---a great camp of ignorance, each family inside thinking itself different from the others---their hatreds, dark faces . . . Om! . . . the same hatred & dark face as myself in the same ignorant dream . . . Serious chimneys spewing black smoke into the flawless blue sky that has no end. . . .

How shall we describe the emptiness of reality, the Dharmakaya of the sky, the bliss radiant Void, the huge hint above our heads & silly roofs?

FROM DULUOZ LEGEND: - "Man you see there selfbelievingly & heartbreakingly walking forth with the perfect accommodation of some liquid ghost in a magical action inside Mind or imprinted upon the Bliss Screen of essential Pity in some central hall of knowing shining in Void night for naught"----

SONG: - "There's Nothing Left of a Pig but His Rut"

Learned this Fall, 2 things,   1, there's no need to write like Proust
                              2, No need to remember Lowell & the Duluoz "Legend"

The 3 Gunas: -
TAMAS , inert dark materiality
RAJAS , energy & passion that moves it
SATTWA , light & goodness that wills to move

"From attachment arises longing and from longing anger is born."---anger is the same as fear.
                "From anger arises delusion"
        You must move among objects free from any longing or aversion

"All actions are performed by the Gunas, born of Prakriti (Nature). One whose understanding is deluded by egoism alone thinks: 'I am the doer'"---

People working without passion for results are enlightened through performing actions, says the Bhagavad-Gita, the Book of the World, the Book of Heaven.

A call to endless wars and ignorance on the bloody plain of earth? "Surrendering all action to Me (Krishna) and fixing the mind on the Self (Purusha) devoid of hope and egoism, and free from the fever, fight, O Arjuna."

Krishna expresses the key doubt himself in 33 of Karmayoga chapter: - "What can restraint do?" (Buddhist discipline)

In Ancient India, caste was inseparably tied up with the notion of guna necessity: -
1. *Brahmana caste* . . . sattwa, goodness, serenity, light
2. *Kshatrya caste* . . . sattwa plus rajas (passion, ambition) (warriors)
3. *Vaisya caste* . . . (merchants)---Rajas plus tamas (dulness)
4. *Sudra caste* . . . dulness, ignorance, inertia, (peasants)

An organized fourfold-caste-form of division of labor, evil as antiquity . . .

   ---GUNA PRODUCES KARMA---

   ---The "Outer Darkness"---
The visible manifestation of the
false conception of "emptiness" is to
be recognized in the tendency of human
beings to turn to the cycle of births and
deaths and to continue therein. This
one abstract from the quiet thought of
Asvhaghosha shatters all the Vedic &
Gita Self-Purushaism into smithereens
_ shows that as men proceed from bestial
states towards emancipation from
attachment to sentient life they still
cling to Self as their last attachment
and really fear Nirvanas of any kind
or name.

   Fear death, not Nirvana, O men

WHAT IS REBORN?
What suffers rebirth is not the individual, but the pain of individuality---
Aggregates of individual personality which make "I" suffer now, will disappear with
the "I" at death . . . the aggregates like wooden beams from a ridgepole . . . but the
household will continue for "someone else." If it wasnt for the possession of
Essence of Mind by all things in that they are permeated by it throughout as by that
which made them manifest, "I" would not feel the pain of individuality---So if I
break mind-control, bust the ridgepole of individuality with its aggregate com-
poundment, I dont accomplish any more than death accomplishes, since where is the
"I" who will suffer rebirth, or where has gone the disposition to painful personality
arising from birth after only "one" has been self-destroyed---Am I not here because
of an accident I had nothing to do with, the meeting of parents' genes? The only
way that "I" can have anything to do, via my will, with the destruction of *genehood*
& sentience & all ignorance which is made manifest by Mind Essence, is to attain
Tathagatahood & perform incomprehensible works to calm the winds of Ignorance
that are defiling the cool pool of emptiness with ripples of disturbance & grief.
Therefore the true role of the Buddhist is a ghostly role, for Tathagata is a Ghost.
This is the bare truth of it. And the most difficult hindrance to the attainment
of this ghostlihood & the Bodhisattvahood that comes before it (Nirmanakaya terrestrial) (works) is time and the reflexes of impatience.
   * * * * * * * * * ** * * * * * * * * * * * * * ** * * * ** * *

This said nothing. I'm really thinking about something else.---

MUST I GO TO THE SUTRAS FOR GUIDANCE?
Do I believe in ghosts?---

    Same old rain of mistakes
    On the gray gloomy lakes;
    Same old ignorant roofs
    Of the black sad spooks.
    Same old ignorant belief
    In mouths of grief;
    Same old crop in the sewers,
    Same old crap of spewers;
    Same old owlish libraries,
    Same old Nosy scriberies;
    Same old time ennui;
    Same old, same sea,
    I've seen it a million times.
    The worm believes,
    The saint grieves.
    Deranged mankind
    Seeks to find.
    The enlightened head
    Has long been dead.
    Reality
    Is ghostly.
    Made,
    Fade.
    I've said it a million times.
     This is the end . . .

        *

          REBIRTH & SNOWFLAKES
       I'm not coming back . . . But if Kerouac
     is not coming back, what is it that's not
    coming back? The pain of individuality is coming
   back. It's not the same snowflakes, but still a snowflake. Not the "same," but the sameness, the Tathagata
 Stuff, the Tathata, the Suchness, is "coming back." But what
good is my vow to either not come back, or to come back, if there
 is no coming back of the Vower Snowflake, the Bow-wow Birthdog? Mind
Essence made the Vow?--If I come back as Bodhisat to turn the wheel, what
good will it do in this eternal snowstorm of seemingly individual flakes in-
exhaustibly snowing from mind?---my only duty is therefore the duty, not of con-
vincing snowflakes that their individuality is false & transient, because the moment they know that they're in the same fix I am, they'll be wanting to know how to
stop snowflakehood altogether and wont have any way of doing it except, like me,
 as Ghostly Tathagatas of No-Rebirth performing incomprehensible works in the
  Holy Emptiness to stop the grind of the false mind.
         Thus Hinayana's for me?---
        THERE IS NO GOING OR COMING BACK
        OF THE ESSENCE OF VOWS

Hit the makeless null. Whether or not
individuality is destroyed now, it will
be completely destroyed in death.

For all things that are made fade
back to the unmade. What's all
the return-vow hassle, but a final
metaphysical clinging to eternal
ego-life by Mahayana Thinkers.
An intellectualized ego-attachment to taskhood.
Hinayana, nay Ecclesiastes, is best.

* *

Stoicism & Epicureanism are arbitrary
conceptions, arising from grief because of the
impermanency of the compound being---
They've had different shifts and names
to sneak around Eternal Death or call
it what you will *The Return to Origin,*
ever since the first thing was made.
This includes the Mahayana Fairytalers.---

I believe in emptiness; I do not believe in things.

I believe in Buddha's last words
and in what Krishna called the supreme
secret, i.e., the thing to do in life is
perform necessary action without attachment. I believe in simplifying necessary
action, à la Tao, down to the bare
Yeatsian bleakshore bone of the
Apocalypse of the Fellaheen---a
solitary place for every human being,
a garden, and meditation on
emptiness which is the Bright Room.
            This has to be taught not only to Old
Hoghead Gravesend Soprano but everybody.

* *

            No hangup on nature is going to solve
        anything---nature is bestial---desire for
        Eternal Life of the Individual is bestial, is
        the final creature-longing---I say, Let us cease
        bestiality & go into the bright room of the mind real-
        izing emptiness, and sit with the truth. And let no man
        be guilty, after this, Dec. 9 1954, of causing birth.---Let
    there be an end to birth, an end to life, and therefore an end
    to death. Let there be no more fairy tales and ghost stories around
    and about this. I dont advocate that everybody die, I only say every-
        body finish your lives in purity and solitude and gentleness and realiza-
        tion of the truth and be not the cause of any further birth and turning of
    the black wheel of death. Let then the animals take the hint, and then the in-
    sects, and all sentient beings in all one hundred directions of the One Hundred
    Thousand Chilicosms of Universes. Period.

Nature is the cause of all our suffering;
joy is the reverse side of suffering.
Instead of seducing women, control yourself
and treat them like sisters; instead of
seducing men, control yourself
and treat them like brothers.
For life is pitiful.

Stop.

175

To be a beggar is to be attached to
the idea of humility, which was
originally an idea opposed to the
idea of highborn pride. It is good
to give and receive, this is not a
cause of suffering; but to become
attached to begging, to giving or
receiving, to become attached to
the relieving feeling of giving to o-
thers, or to become attached to the
humbling meek feeling of receiving
from others even the poorest alms,
is a cause of suffering.
Beg from the earth and be you
as generous as the earth.
One dried bean in the earth,
and a little water and sun of
summer months, becomes a bean-
plant of hundreds of beans containing the same protein as the
meat of slaughtered animals. Why
beg from people and disturb their
revery?
Every animal killed for food
suffers the same pain as a man killed
for food. If you inflict pain of
death and live off the flesh of another living being, you are the cause
of suffering. Let two or more sit
and burn incense on their hands
and compare the pain. Pain is the
same for all living things. Inflict
no pain on anything that moves, swims,
or flies. Leave the fish alone;
avoid the ignorant lions; smoke
the mosquitos away. Sidestep
the snake, shake out the scorpion,
let the worm go down.

* *

Crying and laughing are two sides
of the same sad thing, which is
suffering caused by nature. And
nature is just mind. Realize
great emptiness of the sky, and
the stains of nature appearing in
it as objects but which when completely realized are but imagined
forms made of atoms and the very
atoms of atoms, each atom as vast,
in the reality of void, as the
vastest very universe of all the
universes, and therefore empty throughout, like objects seen in a dream
and finally ungraspable. Crying
and laughing are two sides of the
same reaction to suffering, which is
caused by nature, which is imaginary
forms, which is really emptiness.
Sit with the truth, which is emptiness, which is pure, solitary, & gentle.

Consider the sky, consider that
it has no distance is therefore not
even space but just nothing.
For if you went to the moon, you'd
have to go to the other moon, and
if you went to the other moon, you'd
have to go to still a further moon,
and if you went to a further moon,
how many moons? How many
snowflakes? How many snowstorms
of snowflakes? of universes of
moons do you have to visit before
you'll learn there is only no measurement and therefore no distance
and therefore you must have a
moon in your eye lash inside an
atom of its tip and so why bother
with distance and measuring and
calling it space? And saying
that it has solid objects at certain distances from one another?
Even the smallest atom of one of
those objects has also no distance
and no measurement and cannot
be called space. What's solid?
And what's empty?

* * * * * * * * * * * *

---PALER POME---
Consider silence. Avoid noises and
listen to the roar of your intrinsic
hearing. You say it's coming from
outside? Gently block your ears.
It's also coming from inside as
well as from outside. Apparently
it's coming from everywhere and
will never cease its roaring. Is it
a sound? If it were a sound it
would end sometime but it never
ends and you hear it in your
sleep. It is Emptiness hearing
itself be empty throughout Emptiness
whether you think of emptiness as
large or small, empty or not
empty, or beyond consideration of both
emptiness and non-emptiness. It
is what is heard in a pea, in a
hairtip, in an atom, in a galaxy
of light years worth of
whole galaxies of light years. It is
called the Transcendental Sound of
the Intrinsic Hearing of Universal
Essence of Mind, and is the
only manifestation of emptiness
that even a child and all animals
and sentient creatures do actually
realize at once. When I first
realized my hearing of it, when
it was pointed out to me, I
thought it was a breakthrough
from the Other World at last.

It is the sweetest and the only permanent sound and is really no sound at all. The empty blue sky clear of even the littlest cloud, and clear of the imaginary blue color caused by reflections of dust in the atmosphere, dim, and in the moment that you look at it before eyeball-blemishes form figures in the vacancy, is like Emptiness seeing itself be empty throughout Emptiness, is the Transcendental Sight of the Intrinsic Seeing of Universal Essence of Mind, and is the sweetest and the only permanent sight and no sight at all.

"The foulest water will bubble purely."---
THOREAU

Nature:-The early bird gets the worm---but "the tops of the early grass are white, killed by the worms."

AHIMSA, is, not-harming

"The destiny of beings is like a dream . . . Understand, my brothers, that everything is void, like space . . ." BUDDHA (somewhere says)

From my 1947 Notebooks: "The rats feed in the night while Abe Lincoln studies in the firelight---that we must remember."

There are a lot of ways of making a living but there's only one way to write "The City and the Path" and that's my way. It will be the Duluoz Legend section dealing with my discovering the Dharma and trying to teach it, 1953-1955.

I want to penetrate into the mystery
myself without relying even on Buddha
or Jesus Christ---I think the mystery
involves no personalities, even of
emancipation's emancipators, nor systems derived
from old mythological intuitions
and syncretically re-developed---These
are the scholastic words I learned---
I've got to go into the desert with
my own unchanging bones & find out---
And when I do find out I aim
to announce no personalities but
to find some way to explain that
the Truth is Emptiness, as I already suspect it is, Emptiness without Tathagatas or Holy Ghosts of any kind.

What was the first cause of ignorance?
Answer: There is no Ignorance in reality.

If Ignorance is a dream manifested by Mind Essence (or God), then of course everything exists, Tathagatas (and Holy Ghosts) and all things mentioned and unmentioned . . . exist like objects in a dream . . . devas, gremlins, goblins, angels, troops of ghosts, witches, Nats, zombies, leprechauns, werewolves, fairies, vampires, cherubim, celestial nymphs, spirits, devils, demons, gods, Paracletes, goddesses, spooks, banshees, goblin heretics, female fiends, ghouls, giants, ochus-bochuses----

All Creation is like the discriminating mind---it keeps grinding out phenomena of thoughts continually, even tho we know Essence of Mind is the stable phenomenaless cause of this ignorance due to no other reason than its potentiality and it is not disturbed. The Essence Is Not Disturbed.

A great movie: Chaplin in Heaven. (Or Burroughs in Heaven even) . . .

The effulgent door,
The mysterious knob,
The dark corridor
To the bright room.

Ever seeking to see things truly, is, YATHABHUTAM

The mind system is the "mediating agent between the external world and Universal
Mind."
Survey the world as a vision and a dream in your Samadhis.

THE TRIPLICITY OF THE NOBLE LIFE
1. Samadhi
2. Samapatti
3. Tathagatahood

* *

The external world is only a manifestation of mind . . . REALIZE IT!   (gradually)

Twofold Egolessness: I have no ego, the external world has no ego, (you have
no ego), we are the same emptiness.

The Korean Buddhist I saw on TV had a mind like a mirror reflecting all forms
and images instantaneously and without discrimination . . . that was why he seemed
interested, polite, and yet dispassionate. (Kim).

Purified Masters find themselves "in the palatial abodes of the Akanistha heaven
---but this is figurative, like the horns on a horse.

SILA PARAMITA, The selfless gifts
of kindness & sympathy (as
apart from objective gifts of the
DANA PARAMITA)
Practice kindness and you will soon attain highest perfect wisdom---continual
sad and conscious compassion because all sentient beings are transformations of
the Tathagata and you yourself are a Transformation Tathagata (Manomayakaya)---
---but---kindness is only a word and charity should be spontaneous & selfless.
Kindness is as imaginary as unkindness, as empty---Empty concepts all---
-----Empty is my concept of my mother's
kind of kindness which I consider the
"greatest in the world"---it's all taking
place in Emptiness & isnt really here
or happening, but a dream---Similarly
empty is my concept or anybody's concept of the cruelty of Hitler---it's
all imprintations of false imagination of sentience in the void---But
the King Kindness (Sila) Paramita is an
ideal dedicated to Universal Realization
of Emptiness whereas unkindness is
a hindrance to this Realization because Kindness is unattached, but
unkindness is attached to rage & fear.
One is an impure concept going the
wrong way, out to multiplicity and
formation of Karma consequence, the
other is a pure concept going inward
to unity of emptiness of Truth---

Blessing and merit are the common
possession of all animate beings.---

As to the bright room, speaking truly,
I've not entered anything nor has
my mind attained any such arbitrary
conception as form (and sound, taste,
odor, touch & discrimination.) It is
because of that degree of attainment
that I would be entitled to be called
a CROTAPANNA (entered-the-stream.)

> All Rebirth is also mind-only
> and imaginary! That is why
> the SAKRADAGAMIN (one-more-return)
> who knows this is called so!

Who or what is there to be born and die?

"By the degree of ANAGAMIN it means that he is never to return, yet, speaking
truly, one who has attained that degree never cherishes any such arbitrary conception and for that reason, he is entitled to be called, an Anagamin."---Lank-
avatar

> *"Subhuti delights himself in the
> practice of silence & tranquillity"*---a
> tip for all beginners & the road of all
> Arahats---But while so doing, so long
> as you cherish thoughts like "I am an
> Arahat free from all desire," how can
> the Lord truly say of you "He delights
> himself in the practice of silence and
> tranquillity"? This is Subhuti's Samadhi
> of NON-ASSERTION------

Remember that you're making this study of Buddha's Teaching under the empty
and endless sky and that you're only a ghost. The silence in your hearing is the
same as the sky.

The KSHANTI PARAMITA (of patience) is the one you need in front of judges; it is
intended to prevent you from falling into impatience & hatred. If you're despised
and persecuted because of with the aid of Paramitas of charity, kindness and
patience entertaining no arbitrary conceptions of phenomena as your own self, other
selves, living beings or a universal self, your Karma will immediately be matured
and you will at once attain Anuttara-samyak-sambodhi.---But dont bring it on
yourself purposely for this reason, for, speaking truly, you have no Karma and
there is no you to attain Highest Perfect Wisdom.---

> These Paramitas, plus the VIRYA
> PARAMITA of Zeal . . . zeal to
> practice charity & the kindness
> & patience, plus zeal to explain
> the inestimable teaching of the
> Diamond Sutra, . . . constitute the
> attainment of the Bodhisattva
> stages of compassion that cha-
> racterize the Mahayana.
> --FOR: -

"The Hinayana disciples have not yet
been able to free themselves from
such arbitrary conceptions of phenomena as one's own selfhood, other
personalities, living beings and a
universal self." (What can G.J. do?)

"Buddhahood whose essence is identical with the essence of all things and is what
it is---universal, inscrutable, inconceivable."
  (Why'd you allow St. Louis yard kids
  to disturb your thought of this?)

   "THE PHENOMENA OF ALL THINGS IS OF
ONE SUCHNESS WITH BUDDHAHOOD AND
HIGHEST PERFECT WISDOM, IT IS NEITHER
REALITY NOR UNREALITY BUT
ABIDES TOGETHER WITH ALL PHENOMENA
IN EMPTINESS AND SILENCE,
INCONCEIVABLE AND INSCRUTABLE."

Delivering numberless sentient beings into Nirvana carries as imaginary a
meaning as saying "largeness of the human body," (which has no size in the
void except relatively as measured and compared against other relative phenomena; the largeness of the ant, the largeness of the moon, of the atom).

   "THE DHARMA OF ALL THINGS CAN NEVER BE EMBRACED WITHIN
ANY ARBITRARY CONCEPTION OF PHENOMENA HOWEVER UNIVERSAL THAT
CONCEPTION MAY BE. THAT IS WHY IT IS CALLED THE DHARMA AND WHY THERE
IS NO SUCH THING AS THE DHARMA"---

"What is true of one arbitrary conception is true of all conceptions" (including
your present transient body).

"THE TATHAGATA'S TEACHINGS ARE
ENTIRELY FREE FROM ALL SUCH ARBITRARY
CONCEPTIONS OF ONE'S OWN SELF,
OTHER SELVES, LIVING BEINGS
OR A UNIVERSAL SELF"------------------

As to Bodhisattvas embellishing the Buddha-lands . . . "they are to use such
expressions merely as so many words."

   There are no grains of sand in the Ganges; they are only spoken of as
grains of sand, that is to say.

-       In the Tathagata's Mental Womb all living beings have no   -
-     substantiality of existence but are merely thought of . . . am   -
-              I right, O Tathagata?   -

-THE SIXTH AVENUE SAMADHI-
  The answer to the universe is a
question, "What's the use?"
    A quoi ca sert?

          W h e r e   E a s t   M e e t s   W e s t
          Matter is not an independent and self-existent entity,
               it is a condition resulting from a cause. Western Godstuff
meets Eastern Mayabeams.   "An illusion of mortal mind. . . ."

"An illusion of mortal mind, is matter and great universes."

"CONCEPTIONS AND IDEAS, AND LIMITED TRUTHS, AND DHARMAS HAVE NO MORE REALITY THAN HAVE MATTER AND PHENOMENA."

> God is Mind Essence, simply---All this can be said
> to be taking place in God's Mind---(like I heard
> a child once say)---And for no reason---

For the DHYANA PARAMITA see, perceive, know, understand and realize that all things and all Dharmas are no-things, and therefore conceive not within your mind any arbitrary conceptions whatever.---

God is a warm idea for the cool void---

Keep the mind tranquilly in self-less oneness with the "suchness" that is Tathagatahood (which is the essence of all things)---

> There isnt, there never was a Jack Kerouac

The PRAJNA PARAMITA---the mysterious Tathagata, how is he thought of?---He is inconceivable, like the Truth, "which can not be cut up into pieces and arranged into a system." What common people have in mind as sentient beings are unreal and non-existent . . . and irrelevant.

> *The world is what's in the mind.---*
> The reason why concentration is advised is because
> sentient beings have a tendency to run wild in the
> wrong direction and stampede to Ignorance---

Walls divide space, senses divide mind essence---(only seem to)---

> *---A Trick for Mindfulness---*
> Consider the diamond sound the sound
> of the projector, and all the phenome-
> na of life and death and all things
> in all the worlds the movie.---
> Mind the Screen.

> The Mind is Dreaming---dreaming . . .
> when it fears . . . or hopes . . . all this is the
> mind dreaming---

BEAT in Spanish, is, ABATIDO

"My Mind to Me a Kingdom Is"---a great Tao-Buddhist poem by SIR EDWARD DYER (1550–1607) "What I lack my mind supplies"---

Anent chastity---
> "But all is turned now thru my gentleness
> Into a strange fashion of forsaking---"
> THOMAS WYATT

I have no friends---there's just no Me and no Friends . . just the common emptiness--

```
 * * * * * * * * * * *
  * * * * * * * * * *
   * * * * * * * * *
    * * * * * * * *
```

Nature itself, creation itself
Is a vast discriminating mind
With all its impure concepts;
Remove nature and creation,
Or ignorance, and all's left
Is the pure concept of mind,
Alaya Vijnana, empty, essence,---
Remove ignorance by right means.
The Teaching of Buddha
Is Creation's triumph
Over itself---
Like realizing and discarding thoughts.
Buddhism is mind aware of itself at last.
Nothing's dead matter, not even rock,
It's just mind.
But to say that rock is real,
Is like saying "Rock made itself"
And is atom-solid throughout, full,
Instead of saying "Rock thought itself,
And is atom-infinite and empty
Throughout,"---for without sentience,
Creation, Nature and its mind,
Who can say there's rock,
What can rock rock to rock?
The Creation is a thought made---
A made thought, a wrinkle,
A furrow on the Void Mind,
The flit of a June Bug,
Multiple, imaginary, unselfrealized.
There can be no dream without mind
Of the dreamer---
A dream is caused by thinking mind---
In dreamless sleep there is no thinking,
        but no mind?
The essence is not thinking.
Mind is the one reality, manifesting
Concepts either impure, as now,
Or pure, as "after creation"
(Appearance & disappearance, birth & death)
And as before, when no thinking was,
But when was Mind.
As now.
Knowing this is like realizing
That creation is a miraculous apparition
And like all miracles irrelevant.
The essence is not disturbed.

SALVATION
IS IN THE MIND
BE MINDFUL ALL THE TIME

* * *

MY PERSONALITY-SELF is only like a river in its valley---the water is like Mind
Essence, the shores Jack Kerouac---as soon as it gets "out to sea" there is no
more river and my realization of essence of mind restored unshackled to shoreless
void---but mind will continue to suffer down other rivers after my river runs out
of its banks, so "I'll suffer again," because I'm mind, my realization of suffering is due not first to my personality-shores but due and informed by the mind
essence "waters" that stream through---So as long as ignorance exists I'll, as
mind, suffer---consciously, too---The mistake of ignorance is in my own mind now.

This is Rebirth.---Rebirth is a dream, like Death.---
Creation realized out of the void then started to move;
No it's got to go back in the same way it came in---
Stop and realize, backwards, like feetfirst into the grave
After headfirst you'd moped out of the womb.---
If there had been 2 or 3 Buddhas instead of one in 500 B.C.
"I wouldnt be here now." (whining)
In essence I am not here at all.

Mind is Cause.---Of both Ignorance

& Enlightenment, which, in truth, are

the same---undifferentiated empti-

ness mentally perceived & believed.

> A twig in the void has no more form
> because no form-perceptor is there (ex-
> cept itself.)---

If I were a "piece of empty space," I wouldnt have to practice wisdom; the purpose
of practising wisdom lies in the domain of the creature of creation; it would be
of no use or pith to an empty space; to a creature it has its uses. The practice
of enlightenment should be free of arbitrary conceptions as to the value of Enlightenment and the lack-value of Ignorance; in essence there is no value; they
are the same. But walk dont run to the nearest exit, since you're a sentient being.

Like a man in a crowded subway train that has stopped one station from his
destination, with the doors open delayed a long time because of a disturbance on
the tracks. Why not get out and walk, it's not far. But if the doors suddenly
close it means the train will start at once anyway. So why run and shove to reach
the open doors? The circumstances are cool. Nirvana is Cool. The crowds endure
and suffer.

Sounds are forms registering waves of the formless sea of pure hearing of
mind; where is the reality of these forms? Mind is Cause, Mind the Condition.
The Truth Sound of the Transcendental Hearing, like empty space, the Shush of
the Void, is like a mirror receiving defiling sights without being itself defiled.

Selves are forms perceived & believed by themselves but bouncing off the
clear mirror of mind the cause; if mind isnt the cause of selves and of sights
and sounds and etc., then what is the cause? If there was no hearer in the world
to hear a sound, name the substantiality of that sound. It isnt really there in
essence; the secret essence is all that's there; sound-consciousness is sound-
consciousness; sound is mind-only. Mind is mind, and mind is the cause. Mind
(essence) is causeless itself since it is what it is, never began, never could you
say "In the beginning . . ." since it is all things and all no-things---There are
Arahats among the ants---I know.

In the beginning was the word, and the word was made "God" but as to essence
what can you say of it?

We then think of busying ourselves to care for our bodies in a proper way
and forget this, and lose track of emptiness, truth, mind essence, upon the pure
screen of which, or in the void bowl of which, we are projected, like movies, by
mind. But atoms are empty, there is no solidity; forms are enamoured by our
form-perceiving senses (the "heart pines for them," as Allen Ginsberg says), there
is no reality in them alone beyond their own conception of their own and lonely
form. Of course transient. There is nothing but mind the cause. The essence
of mind is not disturbed.

Why? As soon as you stop thinking thoughts, among them will be why.
The essence is not thinking.

* * * * * * * * * * * * * *

This world is sangsaric debris---
in essence brighter than thought . . .

As it's now Dec.19, 1954, the end of this pivotal year is near---and I am at
the lowest beatest ebb of my life, trapped by the police, "retained in dismal
places," scorned and "cheated" by my friends (plagiarists), misunderstood by my
family, meanwhile mutilating myself (burning hands, benzedrine, smoking, goofballs),
also full of alcoholic sorrow and dragged down by the obligations of others, considered a criminal and insane and a sinner and an imbecile, myself self-disappointed
& endlessly sad because I'm not doing what I knew should be done a whole year ago
when the Buddha's printed words showed me the path . . . a year's delay, a deepening
of the sea of troubles, sickness, old age creeping around my tired eyes, decrepitude
and dismay, loss of solitude & purity---I must exert my intelligence now to secure
the release of this Bodhisattva from the chains of the City.

WHAT is the advice of the Buddhas concerning the effectuation of the release of
this Bodhisattva so that he may freely enter his desert hermitage of solitude,
purity & Dhyana?
    The Bodhisattva must first walk calmly through his danger, practising charity
and sympathy for the sake of all. He must retain his nonenity state and avoid
fame. He must walk straight to his goal not caring what happens on the way,
realizing his self is not the Bodhisattva but a mindbelieved phenomenon without
reality. He must enter the bright holiness at once, go into his Mind, and return
no more to the hedgings and cavils of the world. He must cast off all attachments
in the beginning of his release, in the middle, and in the end; all contacts,
reputations, attainments, responsibilities, connections and hindrances of all
kinds that fumigate his Mind Essence with the defiling smoke of ignorance. He
must abandon all sense-dependencies, such as smoking, drinking, lustful thoughts,
self pitying angers, comforts and commiseration from others. He must free
himself & release his own mind.
    Then, whether he is in a desert hermitage or in a prison, he will be safe in
tranquillity, and therefore released and free to enter the illimitable void of
Mind Essence. If he retains fame, he will become valuable and no longer resemble
the useless Tao tree no carpenter can covet. Being famous, he will be hounded to
his death; being a nonentity, no one will want to use him. This Bodhisattva must
truly cast off his chains himself, then the Buddha shall come and lead him to the
Pure Land. Radiant and effortless activity of the mind, instead of the stained
and hysterical activities of the self. Svaha, sweet Bodhisattva.

* *

        "Not by anxious use of outward means,
          but by resting quietly in thoughtful silence."

    My mistake has been in assuming that
I can dwell inside mind essence as in
sitting inside a bright room; but all I
can do is look at it, perceive it; but
this is a mistaken statement. Mind
Essence is what you see written on the
remainder of this page: -

I can dwell with mind essence, but not in it---Like my first wife used to want to live inside my body but all she could do was live with my body---"I wanta crawl in you and curl up."

How can I curl up in the Womb of Nothingness? How can I curl up in a no-womb?

The Four Noble Truths
And the Eightfold Path
And the Four or Five Precepts
And the practice of Dhyana
Is the only way.

* * * * * *

Dhyana is the only Activity
And it is No Activity.
Dhyana is all.---

Dhyana of the morning
Dhyana of the afternoon
Dhyana of the night
Every day.

In keeping with this incontrovertible method of attaining true sight, I have begun today, Dec.22,1954, the practice of Three Dhyanas a Day. The only lapse will be because of unavoidable circumstances connected with my lay position. Before supper I had no time, that is, my mother was due in. So I had my first orderly Night Dhyana at midnight. The remainder of these Dharma notebooks should be like Daily Dhyana Diaries.

Dec.22,1954---Night Dhyana. A clear realization of the complete extinction of my father's body and of his personality, the inexistence complete of these components in Beginninglessness and Endlessness. Then, what was it caused his *perception* of Mind Essence?---his high human brain, whereas the frog may perceive Essence of Mind in a low brain, that is, a less developed manovijnana. But the frog perceives more purely. I with my fancy brain mis-perceived Mind Essence tonight as a kind of round ball or globe of essence directly in front of my face; but I know rationally that Mind permeates everywhere. If I were a frog I might perceive Mind Essence throughout the universes by mere sensation. I saw that even Lucien has no personality because it will be shattered and scattered forever in death. And mine own too. As my legs ached I realized that the pain of Eastern Praying is in the crossed ankles, the pain of Western Praying is in the knees. This Pain of prayer is enlightening as you keep realizing its inexistence. As you concentrate on Mind Essence you forget the ankles; in remembering the ankles you experience rupa with its quick succession of vedana sensation and sanna perception and sankhara evaluation and vinnana dependence . . . in such a case dependence on fear and abhorrence of the pain.
At one point the pain manifested itself through Mind Essence spontaneously, as if by itself, but I failed to realize.

I failed to realize the unreality of the pain but grasped at the thought of its
serious delusion of reality and thus I uncrossed my legs & rubbed them and tried
to continue in a sitting-in-bed position but now the traditional rocklike
stalwartness had vanished and with my wiggling toes my mind wandered and I lost
perception of Mind Essence which was not perception of that shatterable
scatterable Me-of-Life but perception of just that in the crystal clear globe
of the mystery Naught. There were tics of memory of Lowell long ago that
I ignored, letting them bounce off the Universal Mirror. I had loving
joysome faith that now the practice of three Daily Dhyanas was begun I was
at last truly on the way, that it would work out by itself and even painful legs would learn to pain less and allow my mind perception of its own
Bright Essence to dwell longer in that True House. I longed to enjoy
Dhyana as a True Restingplace.---At one point the Dharma Sound was
high and piercing as I literally lolled or dozed in a dreamful waking
state; my body had slumped a little.

Dec.23 1954---Morning Dhyana.
The calm of Universal Essence of Mind
carried over to after the dhyana and
I saw the Xmas tree calmly as Mind
itself, and boxes and ashtray abiding peacefully in their (temporary)
forms. During the dhyana I was
full of energetic rambling stupid
thoughts---little songs, blabber,
then came a useful realization of
the triviality of the activities of
people in civilizations like Ancient
Rome and New York and peoples
involved also in covetous dark wronks
over cows; I saw people fighting over
pails of milk under the endless skies
of India; but the mournful Tathagata sits under a tree, the only
true one appearing in the World, realizing the emptiness of all this phenomena of conceptions. Buddhas to
come are innumerable, I saw, as I
thought about the day of my birth
in 1922 in Lowell. But it was a
poor dhyana and ended with my
worrying about the ugly oldness of
my face hanging in the void and
I suddenly opened my mouth irri-
tably and jumped out to the world.
Not one moment of true trance.---
But pride in my effort afterwards.---
Also I couldnt hear the Dharma Sound
because of all the vibrations of machines in the ignorant America---jack-
hammers outside, airplanes, and in
the house the high whine of the refri-
gerator and the rumble of the oil
furnace, as though American Civilization was doing its damnedest to
obscure the Dharma of Old.---But

I did think of all my friends and
some of my enemies calmly, hoping
they saw Mind Essence just then;
and I saw that Mind Essence is
like sentient beings think of death,
neither tristful nor contented, just
neither. Equanimity---not black
nor white. Just Om.---

AFTERNOON DHYANA---a battle with
pain of legs, realizing I wasnt sitting properly, and stopping Dhyana
in 10 minutes. Realized life is
folly. Resumed with my sole-to-sole
position of last year, arms crossed
in cold, and came to a splendid dhyana of "forget you and yr. life &
watch this Mind Essence." Meekness
realizing. "This is what the dead
perceive in the bottom of the sea."
What to do with Mind Essence?---
dont try to do it, with You and
Your Life, but with your Essence.
Had a vague dream of rebirth, as
vague as child rememberance.

NIGHT DHYANA---Great discovery a-
bout Dhyana, never practice it before
you are about to eat, but after---for
temptation beckons. Practice dhyana
after the meal---and again before
sleep. Here, I'll do one dhyana in
the afternoon after morning coffee, &
one at night before bed when all is
done. In the hermitage I'll do three.
Also, I realized I should perhaps not
write a Buddhist novel for fear it
will re-attach me to self-attainment.
Self was the big bugaboo . . . my new
position was perfect, no leg aches,
but zeal has fallen since yesterday
as it always does in peaceful times
---So I'll practice my one more dhyana
tonight. (And now I eat from gourmandize & drink wine.) These dhyanas have all been improved by
French thoughts . . . "regard l'essence
de ta mentalite" . . . etc. I let
thoughts roll in & out and it was better than trying to stop them & once
I clearly saw the skeleton underneath.

I
  clearly
        saw
              the skeleton underneath
all
    this
        show
            of personality
what
    is
      left
        of a man and all his pride
but bones?
and all his lost snacks o' nights . . .
  and the bathtubs of liquor
    thru his gullet
              . . . *bones*---He mopes
                    in the grave,
                    facial features
                    changed by worms
                        *
    from him   *
        is heard   *
            no more *
                *
                  *
                    *
                      *

Everyone understands death. Since death is the unreal vanishment, life must
be the unreal appearance on the other side of the same false coin. Mind
Essence is the movie I watched tonight that taught me this.---

FOURTH DHYANA OF THE DAY very good.- "I" wont be reborn, *self* will be---So
the reason I'm suffering now is not because I'm JK but because I'm a bearer
of self---Supposing JK cat casts off self?

    POEM?
My parent
The ant
Crawls
In halls
Of grass
 Alas!
Y I C K I N G
to stones
and bones
and dirt
and hurt
to find
the mind
throughout
the doubt
that gave
the grave
her prince
of ignorance
   * * * * *
      * * *
        *

Mind essence is possessed of no differentials, such
as like sunlight, window, curtain and the resultant
sight---it perceives purely, free of cause and condi-
tion---endlessly---

Tonight, Dec.25,1954, after midnight, I attained at
last to a measure of enlightenment.---Perhaps a touch
of Annuttara-Samyak-Sambodhi. A glorious feeling
that Mind Essence was realized and that my body was
discarded as so much froth on the sea of suffering and
rebirth. I understood for the first time the meaning
of Transcendental Memory---since Ignorance is beginningless, there have been innumerable deaths and rebirths
ALL belonging to "my" realization of Mind Essence which
is the universal mind recognizing its essence.
No anxiety about feet but a clear realization that I
dont have to torture my feet. No anxiety about the
"destruction of Ignorance" because Mind Essence is Self-
Enlightening (so to speak, if has no selfhood to enlighten)---but clean perception that Ignorance is only
an appearance anyway, and that because I am sentient my
activity should clearly be the destruction of suffering
---if I were empty space I would be pure essence uncontaminated by suffering and so too by means to suppress
said suffering. That if I really believed in end-of-the
world or end-of-ignorance, why dont I stop my own thoughts
which are morbid mists like in the opening of the eyes
to see sights again? That suffering is the same as joy.---
That I am a Tathagata truly tho not even yet an Arhat free from
the intoxicants---that my activity be the fumigation of the universe
with enlightenment. That I become radiant & selfless---That I have become liberated from the millstone of pain. That I regard all phenomena as
the same . . . jail or hermitage. That I be a good Tao Hobo and the world will
eventually leave me alone to meditate. That I practice kindness in a world of
poor blind raging fools because they dont know.---That it makes no difference if
I write or not---because the essence is not disturbed---That these notebooks are
poor shadows of the totality of what I know in Samadhis of Intuitive Self Realiza-
tion---that I keep the precepts & practice dhyana---that all is well---that I
keep my Bodhisattvahood secret---that as there are no sentient beings and no ignorance, so there is no Dharma, no Buddhas, no symbols of Buddhahood even that
point to the essence---that the great universe at night with all its intrinsic
stars is only a void and not a great frightful mystery---That this universe is
but one atom inside innumerable universes---That there are Buddhas more numerous
than numbers in all 10 directions---that I must cleave to my faith---that men are
reckless madmen not to practice Buddhahood---that I make no distinctions between
imprisonment and suddenly "selling my book" because nothing can touch my Mind
Essence (the essence doesnt care) which is ever in my possession, only touch my
body which is temporary and unreal and so sloppy sad---That I am at last in touch
with the "eternality" beyond death and life and so "never die"---That I can
convert anyone by right means and right example and dana, sila, kshanti, virya,
dhyana and Great Prajna---

Adoration of the Buddhas of Old---
obeisance to all the Tathagatas---
Perfect Love may be achieved!

All I have to do is feed myself and that's not hard---

Adoration to this Night of Nights!
                    ---DEC 26 1954
                         4 A M

Non-intoxicating deeds of Dhyana lead to non-intoxicating effects of Glorious
Samadhi, just as surely as deeds of the world lead to dark effects. He who eats
too much good food, will have an upset stomach. He who heaps up patience, will
gain his bliss.
        ---I saw that my mother is an intrinsic Buddha, by the way she gives
everything she has.---O to liberate all sentient beings from this Sangsaric wheel!
Poor Celine with his conceptions of politics and peoples! . . . the intrinsic Dharma
of his sea-blue Breton eyes!
        The tip of a bird's feather in Autumn has the same dimension as the
universe, says Tao.
        And now I am writing
                        THE LONG NIGHT OF LIFE, beginning with the noble
                        words:-"The long night of life is over." When I
                        hear these words in the silence of the night and my
                        Essential Mind shines with an empty brightness that
                        seems to come from all numberless directions of the
                        universe like a vision of paradise older than the
                        earth itself and much older, infinitely older than
                        mere human visions of paradise, I know that because it
                        will soon be true, amen, thus it is, *ainsi soit il,*
                        Om, it is already true."

And I write: "And what was the long night of life anyway? It was birth, the
cause of birth, it was suffering, the cause of suffering; and now it is enlightenment, the cause of enlightenment. And this enlightenment consists of the realization that birth was the cause of suffering, and suffering was the cause of
enlightenment, and enlightenment is the cause of the destruction of suffering which
now frees me from this long night of life."

* *

I dont have to cling to either drinking or non-drinking!---to either conformity
or non-conformity to it . . .

   Causes & conditions will bring further sentient beings innumerable to the
world and remove them . . . a dream already, so sad---
   Mind Essence is like being asleep but instead of dreaming, it's watching the
mind that makes the dreams---"embracing the void."---Sunday night dhyana.
   "The degradation of creatures"---they will all die. My body is afraid but
my mind essence isnt worried.---
   Disconnect your plug to the world and realize intrinsic imageless endless
light.---
   The Dead Know Buddha

* *
                                        *
                                         *
                                          *
                                           *
                                            *
                                             *
                                              *

Chinese Characters of the Diamond Sutra

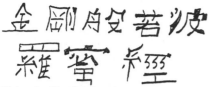

Vajrachedika Prajna Paramita

* *

    I breathe in ignorance with wisdom breath, but I breathe out golden mind
essence with compassion breath, gently, evenly, deliberately, peacefully.---
    FUMIGATING THE UNIVERSE WITH MIND ESSENCE---
Just as cemeteries commemorate the wisdom of the Buddhas, human love incorporates
the beams of enlightenment---

        I Need Compassion Now---realization almost in tears
        of my own ignorance & delusion & madness & darkness---

If a mirror had a discriminating mind
working behind its smooth surface
it would be just like me.
But a mirror does not discriminate
and mistake things, it just reflects
calmly.---

        A wheel of debris---the world---

It's a solid sea of mind filled with imaginary vibrations that create sensation
in the different creatures who are only different forms of mind---Look upon all
creatures as different forms of mind & kindness is inevitable---These creatures
come & go but Mind abides, the Sound of Mind continues, Hearing hears on . . .

        You can ignore pain by concentrating on Mind Essence---the
        True Painkiller---

When you're concentrating on Mind Essence you're concentrating on the whole
shebang, the whole void, and in that moment all things are understood by you and
in the possession of your Tathagataship and ultimately at your mercy and pity, yes.

The tool said to the fool: "Work me!"

        O the highs that women have been on!---
        Cousin Bea closeting Ma for piano mistakes,---

* *

The Ignorant Music . . .

A fabulous multiplicity movie swarming everywhere----

        Existence is on the fringes of Reality---

MORNING BED DHYANA---I take a few sticks and nail them together
and make a Slat. Then I turn around and say "Before, in all Ten
Quarters of the Universe, this Slat didnt exist." This is absurd,
trivial, and only a figure of speech. This is the world. And
now I say "The Slat Exists." This too is but a figure of speech.
And then, when the Slat, because integrated becomes inevitably
disintegrated, it will be said "The Slat no longer exists."
This too is but a figure of speech. Slat, Slat indeed. So I
saw that the world's not real and saw no reason to be involved
with it, to allow my pure and original essence of mind that
abides in emptiness and purity and Slatless unity to become
defiled by such illusions of concept such as existence or non-
existence. It was with my Tathagata Eye I saw this; in truth,
there is no Tathagata Eye either, it's only a figure of speech.
And supposing the whole universe were suddenly in all 10
directions inundated and heaped with Slats . . . and afterwards
completely denuded of Slats . . . ? What think you? O ghosts?
---And so the same with women and sexuality . . . a girl was
trying to make me in a dream . . . my sister was advising me . . .
a girl indeed, my sister indeed, advising indeed, me indeed.
Understood.
I saw the value, value indeed, this morning, morning indeed,
of practising mindfulness before awaking from the deep snare
of dreams and instead of "analyzing" the dreams, *disintegrating*
the dreams, Ah dreams indeed---What an advance over the
practice of merely remembering dream-details for the Book
of Dreams. I gaze instead at the True Mind that manifests
the dreams and they go up in smoke and vanish. Who shall
ever again be deluded as to the existence or non-existence
of phenomena?---children and ignorant persona are not fooled
by such arbitrary conceptions. For when you say "emptiness"
you can only mean EMPTY OF, and so "emptiness," like "non-
existence," is an illusionary concept.---
In fact we have no words to describe that which is neither
empty nor non-empty, only point, because words themselves
are a FULLNESS, are ripples on the void arisen from the bosom
of nature which is also a ripple on the void; and yet, in
  truth, nature is neither in existence or non-existence,
like the Slat, but only a figure of speech and beyond speech
only an illusion of the mind.
So keep the mind in perfect oneness with the suchness that is
Tathagatahood---Try now to look at all things all day and night
with the Tathagata Eye.
AGAIN, next morning, it took me two hours to realize
Buddhahood with the disintegration of another deep-seated
dream, this one about a Dusty-John Hohnsbein person
who shows me her new novel, which is rather good, and I
comment "O it's 15 times better than Holmes' book and he
made what is it Allen? $15,000---" and I get in my bed
as she & others stand around but suddenly as I pick up
my book on the foot of the bed they all mysteriously sit.
"The Sutras Indeed!" was my Samadhi. You really do get
to believe in life and forget its pure Dharmakaya emptiness.
The essence is not alive. The essence is not changed.
        The essence is not a dream.

        * *

THE TRIKAYA

1. *Nirmanakaya* . . . the body of Buddhahood manifested in the moment of void-realization

2. *Sambhogakaya* . . . the body of Buddhahood manifested in continuous void-realization in bliss unceasing

3. *Dharmakaya* . . . the essence-body of Buddhahood of all things, no-things, and neither-things or no-things entire.---

BENCH DHYANA---As people passed me on the sidewalk I kept thinking "People indeed . . ." "Children indeed" . . . "Making noise indeed to see if I'm asleep indeed" . . . and "God's passing and whispering indeed" . . . and "Me sitting here indeed, me indeed" . . . and I saw the whole world indeed was but an arbitrary conception and didnt believe in either its existence or non-existence---The Tathagata's Eye opened and it was no longer me, my eye . . . and "Tathagata's Eye Indeed," I thought, pleased at last to have a partner in this business of realizing nothingness while alive, alive indeed . . . Marvelous memories of India sneaked into my Samadhi doze . . . Indescribable peace & happiness & Eternal Satisfaction that all was indeed thus, Om!---*Ainsi soit il!*---Amen!---One of the greatest Samadhis,--- permeating thru all 10 quarters of the Universe with understanding---In the afternoon after an interesting dream concerning Joan Adams and an overflowing glass of poison pistolwater that made her stigmata on her brow when Joe McCarthy angrily shot her, I realized people are attached to their dream of existence because it has logical & interesting symbols and makes for fascinating speculation when you analyze it, but what is this after all? . . . mere *tsorises* over the details of causes and conditions without realizing that causes & conditions have no source in reality since Mind offers no such ground for illusion, are merely visionary shapes in the gray void, are not therefore to be believed in, so why consider & analyze & become interested in the unreal? (next page)

It would be like a man seeking to study visionary blossoms in the sky---I can see

all my friends this minute yakking absorbedly about the details of their lives

without realizing the utter unreality not only of lives, time changing them and

blind Happy New Years, but of death which will still their poor puppet doll

bodies . . . I can hear them say of me, of the Tathagata, "I couldnt be less interested."

But wisdom's in that remark.

Dec. 31, 1954

JANUARY 1, 1955---New Years Day.---Got up, washed, went back to bed & thought.
I still feel like writing
Book of Mind, in which I would
recall & disintegrate all events in
the life of Jack Duluoz---
starting from the center of interest,
ignoring time & space which are principles of ignorance, dwelling on the
essence---destroying the forms---
and so there is no real reason to
do it---But I want a method of
teaching by writing---To unfold right
ideas and Mind Essence to the
Western World buried in its symbolo-
gical ignorance and unrecollecting
violence . . . in fact, indeed, buried in
its methodology too (as I) . . . I'll
just unsystematically Write to Teach
Adoration to all the Buddhas for
their Triumph!-----

TONIGHT'S DREAM:-I was looking into the plateglass window with amusement at the
antics of Jerry Newman & Bill Fox but when J. saw me he jeered and waved me away
---I changed my smile to a snarl, "Ah!" & went off, only a step, & looked again---
now Jerry came out & made friends over something---Also, Ma and I in a tenement
in Japan and I look out the window in the clear keen morning and there are brown
mountains and white lotus blossoms and I'm glad---None of these images have
either location or origin in mind essence; manifested bubbles.

* *

By walking in crowded streets & not looking up from the ground, I avoid 1000
minor anxieties concerning eyes, legs, directions of moving bodies, congestions,
expectations, looks, and I avoid that which is not there anyway just as I am not
there.
                    "You mark the distinction
                    Between Ananda
                    And the not-Ananda
                    And resent the coming-in
                    Of the True Ananda."
        ---which is the Trikaya of Mind Essence, the True Body Indivisible and
Invisible.
            In other words, walk down the street realizing you're not there (in
essence)---no walker, no walking, nothing walked-----

No singer
No singing   } = NIRVANA
No song

     The world is a Big Ignorance Factory

      . . . .
The birds are talking in the tree. . . . .

    SPHERE OF THINKING
    IS THINKER, THINKING,
    AND THE THOUGHT-ABOUT . . .
For as my eyes roam the yard & select an object-spot to stop, first it is the
thinker that manifests himself, then the thinking ensues as the conception (born
of knowledge) is formed, then the thought about object, say a rock, comes third,
---the "directions" is like → → → So try, ← ← ←

If you dont seek to think, where then will there be an object-world?
Ah-haa! ---If you dont use your thinking mind then where is the Mind-made world?
Stop thinking, stop contacting the world, & the world ceases, as, intrinsically,
it is ceased and never began except as a thought-in-mind.

IT SAYS SO IN THE SUTRA . . .

* *
    * SOME SPANISH DHARMA *
    Mente esencial, Essential Mind
    Esencia de Mentalidad, essence of mind
EMPTINESS, vacuidad
EMPTY, Vacuo
BUBBLE, Ampolla (Burbuja)
FANTASM, Fantasmo
DREAM, Sueño
VISIONARY FLOWER IN THE AIR, Flor Visionara en la Aira
FORM, Forma
CAUSE & CONDITION, Causa y Condicion
SAGE, Sabio (adj.)
WISDOM, Prudencia
SOUND, Sonda
TO CRAVE & TO COVET, Suplicar & codiciar
WORRY, la molesta (noun)
SORROW, la affliccion, el dolor (n)
IGNORANCE, Ignorancia
IGNORANT GREED, voracidad ignorante, avidez ignorante
A suprimir (to suppress) l'affliccion es posible
THE WAY, el camino, la via, la ruta
    EL CAMINO NOBLE DE OCHOS MEDIOS (the noble way of eight means)
      EIGHTFOLD PATH
    1. Las ideas propias
    2. La resolucion propia
    3. Hablamente propio y suavo
    4. La conducta propia y benevola
    5. El mantenimiento inocente (no mata nada, ni hormigita)
    6. Esfuerzo (effort) propio, l'energia propia
    7. Pensativomente propio, pensativos propios
    8. Meditacion propio---meditar sobre la veridad de la vacuidad
               de todas las formas

CREATION, creacion
CREATURE, criatura
DEGRADATION, degradacion
LONG NIGHT OF LIFE, la noche larga de vida
IGNORANT DESIRE, el deseo ignorante
NOTHING, nada
DECAY, la decadencia
DEBT, la deuda
DECEIT, el engaño
DEATH, la muerte
WHY, porque
DIRT, la basura
FALSE IMAGINATION, imaginacion falsa
EL NACIMIENTO es identico con la MUERTE
---es la raiz (root) de la muerte como la muerte es la flor d'el nacimiento---
Ninguna semilla (no seed), privar la semilla de agua y aira, y ninguna muerte,
ninguna decadencia de flora es el resultado---Reposas usted---En el reposo
concentres su mente en la contemplacion interior de la esencia de mentalidad
universale de no-muerte

LAS QUARTO DISCIPLINAS DE FELICIDAD
  1. No Matar
  2. No Lujur
  3. No Robar   THE PATH, la senda
  4. No Mentir

LOS SEIS PARAMITAS DE VIRTUD
  1. El ideal de la conducta caritativa (charitable)
  2. El ideal benevolo y sympatico
  3. El ideal de paciencia y penuria y humilidad
  4. El ideal de selo y la perseverancia
  5. El ideal de contemplacion dichoso (blissful)
  6. El ideal de la mas alta prudencia, que todas las cosas d'ese creacion des-
      tructible, son ni uno ni otro en la existencia porque son solamente figuras
de palabra, vacuo de substancialidad en l'esencia de mente universale pura y
clara y mysteriosa a donde la ilusion no es posible. El mundo es solamente un
escarceo (ripple) y levantamiento de la mente santa esentiale. (The world is
merely a ripple and a rise from holy & essential mind.)
LA MENTE VERDADERA
LA MENTE PERPETUA
                    * * * * * * * * * * * * * *

Energies of earnestness are wasted on heroes, that should have been paid to the
Sila Paramita---
    Karma effaces, Karma produces, Karma annihilates, and KARMA EQUALIZES------

            ---DUMB POEM CALLED "MOONRISE"---
A snake in a pond   The blood of the bear
Slithers out of harm   Is soaking in the swamp,
Seeking the frond   Such heavenly air
Of the heavenly farm.   Overhangs his pomp.

Jeb was your Paw   Give yourself up
Forevermore   To the sheriffs of truth,
And this is the law   Fear no hound pup
Of love and gore.   No karma of tooth

(Moonrise Pome Cont'd)

For your sweet smile
And meditations desperate
Are wine to the senile
And love to degenerate.

Face the shroudy kitchen
Of the sea of the night
And make a pretty kitten
Of all this abounding blight.

                    (Written after watching, drunk, Dane Clark on
                    TV in movie MOONRISE)---
                    Some cloth has that sin rip
                    This doesnt

    * * * * *

What you dont know wont hurt you, and what you dont do too---
    -OR-
What you dont do wont hurt you
But what you do do will
* *
It's THIS THINKING HAS STOPPED with each expiration of breath, annihilating every
thought that has risen---
    And when the Mind's dozing the swift images come like dreams, but still
there's the saying "This thinking has stopped" and the images dont hold and pass
on---
    Conscious that you have made a thought, afterwards, you feel guilt; but when
the thought is subconscious, there is no guilt; therefore if you make a conscious
thought, never mind the guilty afterconsciousness of it (Ignorance & Enlightenment
are likewise beginningless & endless), let it lose hold and pass on---
    This is the Great Samadhi called "This Thinking Has Stopped" Jan 4 1955---
    This is the Curing the Mind of Thoughts---
    And of every thought of thoughts---
THIS PRACTICE WILL LEAD TO NIRVANA

            * * * * * * * *

IT'S BECAUSE my friends in their ignorance right now are continuing with their
    angers, greeds & delusions, their fancies and activities and whistlings at the
    lip of fire which they falsely imagine to be happiness, and even the most in-
    telligent of them talk of their fearlessness of the consequences, their courage
    in the face of sorrow, which is all nothing but thoughts appearing and dis-
    appearing in their own minds without reality, that I say, from my end, THIS
        THINKING HAS STOPPED. *It's because, after my form is dead and gone, Ignorance*
        will continue to crush out new forms that will also come to die and vanish,
        all because of thoughts, that I say now THIS THINKING HAS STOPPED.

IT'S BECAUSE of this too that I hear no more from my friends who ignore my
    teachings and are rushing on into the years, boasting and blowing and expanding
    like balloons in the social scene, heading instead pellmell for the grave and its
    vestiginal rebirth, but THIS THINKING HAS STOPPED. May I be reborn a million
    times and thoughts of form be stopped a million times . . . my pranadhana.

                Lately the Negros have adopted a
            brand new saying: "It's all in the way
            the ball bounces." Indeed!

197

It's all in the way the ball bounces. I take a rubber ball, which is only a dream
of a rubber ball, and throw straight against that wall and it bounces right back
at me. If you dont bounce the ball against the wall,
　　it wont bounce back at ya---
what you dont do wont hurt ya
　but what you do do will.

　　　　　　　Or, If you dont bounce the ball
　　　　　　　　　Against the wall
　　　　　　　　　It wont bounce back at ya---
　　　　　　　　　What you dont do wont kill,
　　　　　　　　　What you do do will.

Me? Jack?
That's only name, remove my name.
Stand me there. Remove my clothes.
Naked I came from nothing and naked I return to nothing.
Call me *That*.
Him? *This*?
That's only a name, remove the name.
Stand him there. Remove his clothes.
Naked he came from nothing and naked he returns to nothing.
Why should that hate this, or this hate that?
Standin there with arms hangin, bleak---

　　　　　　　* * * * * * * * * * * * * *

Sexuality, the most powerful force in
all nature because of its sometimes
fabulous delight, is the very incarnation of Ignorance---
Most of modern sexuality is thought,
i.e., Pornographic mentality---
All we are is what we've thought---
Luckily my dreams lately have been
getting less & less sexual---I had
some lulus last summer, the mere
writing of them, in Book of Dreams,
is inciting to thoughts of sexuality---
But lust is no different than
killing:- the squeal of the murdered
pig, the hoarse panting of the
sexers, it's all vicious, fleshy,
and blind, and subject of the devouring worm.
How to say? It's all a play on the body . . .
it's one removes it, the other replaces.

　　　　　　　　　"O bhikku, empty this boat! if emptied,
　　　　　　　　　it will go quickly; having cut off
　　　　　　　　　passion & hatred, thou wilt go to Nirvana."
　　　　　　　　　---the divine DHAMMAPADA

　　　　　　　　　TO EXPLAIN THE DHARMA to ordinary Americans, like say,
　　　　　　　　　Southerners, I will substitute the expression Mind Essence
　　　　　　　　　for The Mind of God, using upaya skill thereby to help their
　　　　　　　　　understanding; then should a perceptive listener ask me
　　　　　　　　　"Who made God?" I can say "Mind-only."

EXPLAINING THE DHARMA TO SOUTHERNERS

So I'll say, "Why am I living alone in a shanty in these woods when I have a big house and family? Because, like you, my body came from nothing and's going back to nothing and's only a passing dream and so aint even real. A dream rises in the mind, stays awhile, then vanishes, just like my body. In what mind did my body rise but in the Mind of God? And in what Mind did God rise but in Mind-only?

So, knowing this, I'm seeking happiness by concentrating my own mind on God's Mind that created all things. It isnt war and want and sickness that's the trouble with the world, it's Ignorance out of which war and want and sickness rise like a dream.

I'm tryin to free my mind of ignorance.

It's ignorance makes men kill, steal, lust and lie.

It's ignorance makes men call lust love.

Perfect love only the Mind of God knows and it's got nothin to do with men and women.

I just wanta be free of killing, stealing, lusting and lying so I stay away from the world.

Because I know that every time a man does something it's like throwin a rubber ball against the wall, it'll bounce right back. So I dont wanta do nothin but wait and see."

- - - - - - - - - - - - - - - - - - - -

A GOOD IDEA for Writing-Teaching would be BUDDHIST MOVIES, so-called, little or large Bookmovies (stories written as if seen on a movie screen) depicting people in all walks of life, like today's *Love on the Dole* I saw on TV . . . supposing the socialist hero had suddenly been edified by some passing bhikku of England and revised his speech to the workers, about "Capital," unfolding instead the ideals of solitude, penury, sympathy, realization that misery is all mind-made and mind-only . . . there would have been no riot with the cops . . . The difficulty in dramatizing Buddhist themes lies in the Nothingness of its realization . . . you cant film a Samadhi . . .

Better just BUDDHIST STORIES

I look forward to the day when all the literature of the world will be Buddhist . . . there is no other basis for a truthful literature, a literature free from ignorance . . .

The sublimities of Shakespeare are swilled in blood and riot---better a pure couplet by Sir Edward Dyer---the best literature I know, consists of the confessions of the bhikshus and Bodhisattvas concerning their one great experience of enlightenment, in Surangama Sutra---

* *

THE GLORIOUS MAITREYA SAMADHI OF JAN 5 1955 * *

All of a sudden I learned to stop breathing (at the end of exhalations) and was

transported---as if suddenly sitting on lotus blossoms or lily pads. Aerial

freedom, lightness, bliss . . . which I had prayed for in the yard pacing earlier,

thinking, "Now I've learned all the learning in these past 13 months, what's

left now is the Buddha's inconceivable assistance." And it came tonight---

Also was practised the French patois thought (at end of breaths-out) "S'pensage

icite ye-t'arretez" (this thinking here is stopped, or 'this business of thinking is hereby stopped'---For a solid hour *not one thought* contaminated my brain

or thinking-mind, and so it became like a mirror, pure, nothing stuck---So,

with the great discovery of Stop-Breathing (about 5 seconds, & thanks to my

outdoor breathing feats) came at last the realization of Mind Essence (the sea

of suchness), the end of greedy need which is like a torrent, and the bliss of

the Samadhis---Ignorance had disappeared, Self had disappeared (I thought of my

Italian Puncher and there was no more I-disturbance to be disturbed, it was all

washed away)---Was seen the Sea of Tathata Suchness as being that in which forms

took shape and floated awhile---As I sat on my lotus, or, as was sat upon the

lotus, was manifested the sepulchral echo: *"How many times, Maitreya?"*---how

many times lotuses sat upon & the Mind realizing Mind, by all the Buddhas and

of All Times and the Buddha to come who is everybody---Was heard the Transcen-

dental Sound of Nirvana which is Mind Essence which is the Teaching of the

Tathagata Unceasing, purifying the sentient hearing---Was experienced the immo-

vability, the invincibility of Highest Meditation---was known the Unknown---

Was seen the Transcendental Shapeless Tathagata with Wisdom Eye---was entered

upon the Path---peace, satisfaction---Adoration & Gratitude to the Buddhas

and Great Bodhisattvas who made this possible---"Now is no more grounds estab-

lished in this Divine Ground for thoughts, for mad anxieties to take root or

grow, now is the Sea of Suchness realized---" At HOW MANY TIMES MAITREYA? my

soul stopped---There was no JK tonight.---And etc.---Could write the rest of my

life about it---Finally, by clasping my hands, I always see the Golden Buddha

from habit of bronze sculptures I must have seen, the square big bronze brow

of the Buddha, and hands make triangle and anybody who's seen Buddha Sculpts

never forgets the Triangularity of head and knees-out---but such gorgeous rubies

and diamonds I see---it is at one time I felt myself a solid triangular mass

of precious diamonds, at First-Stop-Breathing, and so HOW MANY TIMES MAITREYA?

indeed---for there have been, there are, and there will be Buddhas---and triumph

over form & suffering is gained, the origin is regained, the self is abandoned,

GLORIOUS MAITREYA SAMADHI (concluded)

the elephant is tamed, Nirvana is Nigh---And this my teaching in written word.

NAMO AMITABHA BUDDHAYA

* *

Under the sun   *
                                 *
A deed done dies   *
                                 *
But a deed not done   *
                                 *
Purifies the skies.   *

Frot my pole/ Receive my mud/ Minister my semen/ The dirt of my blood
    The grinding blood o' the cock/

* *

BUDDHAHOOD IS A MEDICINE---It's the True Cure . . .
It has cured me of a hundred ailments,---
But I better not rush out of my sickbed before I'm all well.--
    THE TRUE CURE AND THE TRUE MORPHINE AT THE SAME TIME

For even a 4-year-old child knows that life is a punishment for something, for
accumulated Karma made incarnate---You wanted teeth? now let them decay & hurt.
You wanted love?
Now be you lorn.   The child knows
You wanted death?   that life is no
Now be you born.   "gift" & no reward
You wanted life?
Now be you shorn.

Buddhahood has cured me of life.
Desire for life, cured. Thinking, cured.
Anxious literary ambition, cured.
Madness for riches, cured. Greed, cured.
Chasing after women, cured. Lust, cured.
Seeking out friends, cured. Egoism, cured.
Alcoholism, cured. Drughabits, cured.
Sorrow, controlled. Joy, controlled.
My blood disease, controlled, cured.
Fear of the heat & the cold, cured.
Fear of death, cured. Fear, cured.
Need to act, cured. Need, cured.

        * * * * * * * * * * * * * * * * *
    What'll I do? You mean what'll I dream?
* *

            THE SURANGAMA SUTRA
        (wording re-arranged for the understanding
            of Western minds)

SUPPOSE YOU'RE LOOKING at all those beautiful springs and pools out there.
I want to show you that the locations of contact between your consciousness
or shall we say your perception of those objects, and the objects themselves,
(cont'd next page)

that is, the springs and pools themselves, both belong by nature to the Mysterious Mind Essence. Understand? Both locations of your eyeballs that see the objects and the objects themselves.

Now what do you think, as you turn your eyeballs and make contact with the springs and pools. What is it that develops your consciousness of the springs and pools? Is it the springs and pools, or is it your eyeballs?

If it's the eyeballs that develop it, then objects themselves are inert and dead, and the consciousness of objects plus the objects themselves are developed by the eyeballs. So when you turn your eyeballs and look at space, as space is of different nature from objects, then the sight-of-objects has disappeared, so now all the previous manifestations of the sight-of-objects have become nothing and there's nothing to see. As this is now so, how can we be sure that it's space and that space ever had substantiality?

And the reverse is true also, namely, if all the phenomena of space has now lost its substantiality, how were we ever sure of the location of the objects, the springs and pools we saw?

Now if you say it's the springs and pools that developed your consciousness of them, then when your eyeballs are turned to look at space (as space itself is not the springs & pools) then your consciousness of the springs and pools, being lodged in the springs and pools and not in your eyeballs, would now have disappeared. Since your consciousness of the springs and pools has now disappeared, then all the springs and pools themselves have become non-existent to you.

How can you be sure that it is space you're looking at now and that it was springs and pools you were looking at before?

Therefore you should know about location at least: the consciousness that arises from your eyeballs, from the springs and pools, and space between your eyeballs and the springs and pools, where can it be located?

It simply means that both the location of the springs and pools, and the location of the eyeballs, are alike unlocated, false, and fantastic.

Neither location is true. There's no reality in the statement that distance separates your eyeballs and the springs and pools they see due to some mysterious consciousness that applies all over, which is Mysterious Mind Essence. So when your eyeballs see the springs and pools, no True Cause can be pointed out to explain for the seer (eyeballs), the seen (the springs and pools), and the seeing (consciousness) except True Mind.

To clarify. The very eyeballs, springs and pools, and consciousness itself all belong to the Mysterious Mind Essence. As you know, eyeballs have no power of seeing springs and pools when they're turned to empty space; the very faculty of seeing becomes puzzled and lost because there's nothing to see, and consciousness of sight becomes unreal; and the memory of the springs and pools is like a dream; but I will show you that the springs and pools themselves are a dream anyway, so no wonder.

Consciousness of springs and pools depends upon the eyeballs and their power
of seeing in combination with the springs and pools. If the consciousness
of the springs and pools is ever developed by means of the eyeballs alone,
then it would have to mean that the consciousness of the springs and pools
is independent of the springs and pools, and independent of space too, which
is absurd, because if it was independent it would conceive of no springs
and pools at all, and thus, in spite of your consciousness which you cant
deny as you're looking, you simply cant be conscious---but conscious you are.
The green water, the yellow sand, the red flowers, the white clouds
reflected on the springs and pools, these certainly dont belong to your
eyeballs, and so there would be no consciousness of green, yellow, red and
white and no boundary lines of springs and pools.

Or if the consciousness of the springs and pools is developed by means of
the springs and pools only, how would your eyeballs know it? And if, looking
beyond at new sights of trees instead of springs and pools, and so the objects
have changed, and you're conscious of the change, it would silly well mean
that your consciousness is changing. But your consciousness never changes, only
the sights change.

And so now if you want to be silly and say that your consciousness is changing,
then what's the line between your consciousness itself and your consciousness
of the trees? If you say your consciousness is subject to change along with
the changes from springs and pools to trees, then what's the difference between
the springs and pools and the trees since your consciousness of both is the same
consciousness?

So your consciousness being the same, and permanently unchangeable, as you know,
then if you make the mistake of saying, as above, that the consciousness of
the springs and pools and trees is developed by means of the springs and pools
and trees only, how could unchangeable and unlocatable consciousness recognize
their differences of location in space and their very differences indeed?

Or if you say consciousness of springs and pools is developed by both eyeballs
and springs and pools, then consciousness is now split in half and one part
of your consciousness that is developed by the eyeballs will have to be said
to be sensitive, the other part developed from the springs and pools insensitive;
then when the eyeballs are in contact with the springs and pools, one half of
your consciousness of it all will be watching and perceptive, and the other
half seen and unperceptive, with some boundary line between; if so, both
halves, when the eyeballs are not in contact with springs and pools, will
have to return, one half to the eyeballs, one half to the springs and pools,
with which they are said to be in separate contact.

Therefore you should know that these three locations where (1) the consciousness
of springs and pools is under the conditions of the sense of the eyeballs, and
(2) the springs and pools, and (3) where the perception of sight arises from
your consciousness dependent upon the eyeballs, are all devoid of any substantial existence, so these three phenomena of (1) the eyeballs' perceiving
of springs & pools, (2) the springs & pools themselves, and (3) the sphere
of mentation (the consciousness) about the springs & pools, are neither manifested by causes and conditions alone, nor spontaneously by their own nature
purely---the Universal Sea of Mind is Cause.

But now look at empty space if you want to realize that there is no dividing
line and no splitting-up of consciousness into two halves.

(SURANGAMA SUTRA EXPLAINED, cont'd)
What is it that causes the consciousness of infinite space, the eyeballs?
If so how could they discriminate and pick out by themselves any such thing?
If infinite space caused it, alone and only, how would the eyeballs know it?
Just as the eyeballs wouldnt know if springs & pools only caused the con-
sciousness of springs & pools. If both eyeballs and infinite space caused
consciousness of infinite space, again consciousness would now be split in
half and there would have to be a dividing line and where would that be?
And if you closed your eyes, what would be the cause of the Eyelid Darkness,
the eyeballs or the eyelids? And where the dividing line if both were cause?

How could eyeballs see it as eyelid darkness, if eyeballs alone; what would
the eyeballs know of eyelid darkness, if eyelids alone the cause?

Where the dividing line if both? So we know consciousness cannot be split
in half and have dividing lines; nor can it come from one location or another
or both or neither.

The Mind must be the source therefore of both eyeballs and springs and pools,
of both eyeballs and space, and of both eyeballs and eyelid darkness.
Consciousness of the Mind is the source of all.

Hard it is to realize that all is Mind alone.

Hard it is to realize that a matchbook you're looking at exists only in
consciousness and mind. To realize that consciousness is the very suchness of
the matchbook, the very STUFF it's made of, and completely empty.

"Form that is emptiness, emptiness that is form."

There is just no location for a dividing line between the eyeball and the
eyelid, it would have to be in a thousandth-of-an-inch film; between the
eyeball and the matchbook, it would have to be in a few feet of space; between
the eyeball and infinite space, *all infinity itself.*

The Mind, in this case referred to as Mind Essence, cannot be divided, drawn,
or located, so must be everywhere throughout all.--

                    *

Does your spirit have to be fed
like some pig in a pen?
By shows, news, thoughts, wines---?

FROM HSI YUN's DOCUMENT: -
   "All the Buddhas and all sentient beings are nothing but universal mind,
besides which nothing exists. This mind, which has always existed, is unborn
and indestructible. It is not green nor yellow, and has neither form nor
appearance. It does not belong to the categories of things which exist or
do not exist, nor can it be reckoned as being new or old. It is neither long
nor short, big nor small, but transcends all limits, measures, names, speech,
and every method of treating it concretely. It is the substance that you see
before you---begin to reason about it and you at once fall into error. It is
like the boundless void which cannot be fathomed or measured . . ."

                    - - - - - -

Dear Bev,

In answer to your request "Write me something to think about" let me attempt to explain the Teaching of the Buddhas of Old to you, so that you can join me in the gradual happiness and liberation that comes with wholehearted sincere understanding of the mysterious law of things as elucidated & unfolded more times than there are grains of sand in the sea, to living beings in this world and all others in the ten directions in and out of the created universe, by Buddhas and Great Bodhisattvas, and humble disciples like myself too, always without regard for self-profitable consequence but for the sake of revealing to some other living being trapped in this world of suffering the path that leads out of the confusion and the nightmare, to the permanent awakening of bliss and perfect loving-kindness in the realization of the truth of Mind Essence.

Not that you're wanting in love, sweet Beverly, as any of us who know you, religious and unreligious alike, do purely testify; and not that you're scarce in kindness, the way you heap riches of affection and cook for everybody and spend your hard-earned money in every direction all the time. But now I want to unfold to you the principle that teaches that human love incorporates and gives form to the beams of Enlightenment itself, but does form last?

Form changes and disappears, but the essence remains.

So that you'll know, when your present body vanishes, and your form returns to its origin in nothingness, this love vanishes not. Because it comes from the perfect love of Mind Essence, which abides before and during and after form, and since form comes and goes like a phantom, then form is imaginary.

So if you heap sweet riches of generousness on me, say a steak dinner, or wine, or a kiss with your lips, be it known:- steaks come and go, wines come and go, but the perfect love of Mind Essence which manifested itself through these gifts in this world of forms, neither comes nor goes.

Beverly, the teaching of the truth is this perfect love of Mind Essence is everywhere permeating throughout forms and space all over, and is indeed the very substantiality, the very suchness, of both forms and space; it's what the world is made of.

Perfect Love of Mind Essence is what there is, amen---or in Sanskrit, Om; or in French, ainsi soit il, meaning, Thus It is.

And thus it is.

Now as my chosen words thread onwards, crowds of confusion fall around them, and I have to explain and make clear what is meant by perfect love of Mind Essence. And the only reason why I forced myself, a really cold loveless Breton Canuck, to begin on the subject of love, was because I was conscious of your womanhood and your inevitable natural infatuation with love, your deep immense immersion in the subject of love, your attachment to love, your love of love, and your very answer to my last letter when I said "What is there to say?" and you said "Oh hell, love!"

But when perfect love of Mind Essence becomes the love among forms, because of that contamination, because of that descent from perfection of essence to imperfection of form, suffering arises.

And it's for the reason of showing you the way out of suffering, not to question your sweet love in suffering human form, that I want to unfold the Teaching of Old to you.

Further, too, I want you to discard in your mind any notions of my own suffering human form, which is as phantasmal, brief and impermanent as your own. It isnt that we've grown old and come to thoughts of the impermanency of our lives, but rather that from the moment of birth our lives were automatically on the way out, in the first place and from the first dewy moment.

But forget me as the Jack that you know, because these words dont have their origin in "Jack" or in any form with a name, these words have been similar to the selfsame words and signs devised by the Buddhas of Old and to Come to be regarded solely as forms pointing to the truth of Mind Essence, not to be regarded as the suchness of the perfect Love of Mind Essence itself. So as I seek to point at essence for you, dont take the form, the finger, to be the essence.

If you do that, you'll take the finger, the form, the words, to be the essence, while all the time essence (shall we say) is Unpointable.

And also by discarding all thoughts of me as "Jack," you will see that I'm not real and never was; that I had no selfhood, just as you; that my body and my form were fleeting things; that living beings are like fishes arising and dying in the Great Sea, which is as their essence.

Fishes hatching from eggs, appearing, suffering, dying and disappearing again. Where did they come from? Where did they go? But the saying is, the sea rolls on.

And where went the loving of the fishes? And where went the hating of the fishes? And where went the thinking of the fishes? And these forms went back to essence.

To make sure you wont be attached to this Teaching, as being in the possession of, originating from, or being delivered by, a person such as "Jack," therefore, was mentioned the advisability of discarding the form and conception of a "Jack." Take this, rather, as the Teaching mysteriously transmitted from the unknown, as it was to "me," solely due to the efforts and activity of the Buddhas and Tathagatas, who are no-beings and no-forms and so are in possession of the perfect love of Mind Essence continuously and without contaminations.

As you have been, and are, and always will be intrinsically in highest truth a Buddha too.

II

What is Mind Essence? and what is Buddhahood?

Buddhahood is the realization of Mind Essence.

Mind Essence is what you'll realize this minute if you just stop everything and close your eyes and sit still, let your body relax and forget it's there, and listen to the silence. Soon, in a minute, you'll open your eyes and leave behind the contemplation of the Milky Way in your eyelids and the whole world will reappear to your sight like an eerie dream.

In remembering your body again, you'll shift limbs or blow your nose or scratch an itch which in itself is imaginary. You'll start thinking of what to eat, what it will taste like. But you'll suddenly remember that food eaten in dreams always has that single Mind-taste. From outside come noises, shattering into the silent shh of your silence like pebbles rippling up a cool pool.

The cool pool was the inside ceaseless hearing of your Mind Essence; now the forms of noises, like pebbles, break up the calm mirror. So you know Mind in its Essence is like a mirror. How beautiful it is that a mere form can suddenly realize its essence! This is Buddhahood, if only for a second; and have you ever seen a cat sitting on folded paws, with eyes like slits, completely still, ignoring all cat-calls and even caresses and all disturbances? Anyone rushing up to this cat and picking him up, what has he done? The animal had fallen into a trance of contemplation, had successfully realized the world away, discarded the dream even to the blissful calm of ignoring all sounds rising or arisen and all responses via the pricking of the supersensitive ears. This person has committed a blunder grabbing the cat.

But when the cat is asleep and twitching from a nightmare, ah then pick him up and wake him up; the blunder becomes forgiveness.

Beverly, I discuss the cat because I want you to realize that all living beings, including cats, are different forms of Mind. That's why the Buddhas never say "human beings" they say "sentient beings," beings of sense possessing six senses and therefore beings under punishment of the pain of death; and so that's why the highest perfect wisdom of the Buddhas reaches not only into all kingdoms of existence on this earth, but all kingdoms of existence in all the ten thousand directions of unnumbered mighty chilicosms throughout everywhere.

What do you think? If a monster on Mars a million years ago held still for a second and realized by virtue of its essential motivity and mentality that its form was just a form buried lonely and sufferingly in the Great Sea of essential Mentality, which he certainly could see, if he had eyes, by looking at the endless empty sky above, then what's absurd about saying that our little sentient cat realized his own essence? (I say that Buddhahood is the religion of all living beings in all kingdoms of existence because it is Indian, and the very earth is an Indian thing. For instance, Beverly, the Pomo Indians of California had this to say of the "whites" their conquerors from West Europe who came with cross and sword:-'They don't know that everything is alive.' This is my personal observation, that wherein it is possible to realize that the Essence of Things never has changed, that it was not Essence that took shape but Ignorance that took the shape, all living creatures on all levels of physical size can know it and attain Tathagatahood (Essencehood).)

Because when we say "sentient beings" we also say Buddhahood, for without sentient beings and their forms of ignorance, there could be no Buddhas and the essence of enlightenment. What would there be to enlighten? What need is there to enlighten empty space? But even an ant is sentient and is a pitiful form of ignorance, even an ant is a different form of Mind, though small and "unimportant" by our "human" worldly standards.

But how big a monster is an ant to a germ? How big a monster is a germ that you can see through a microscope, to a germ that you can't see through a microscope? How is this germ built? Like the universe, atom-like, a few planets revolving around a central neutron, on down into the germ and on out into the universe we live in and the Universe of that.

So you'll know the whole created universe is swarming everywhichway with sentient forms of all sizes all buried in suffering, each form in a state of ignorance, though the essence has never changed and never will, and therefore each form is potentially in a state of enlightenment of No-Form, by realization of its original essence which is the perfect solitude of the unbornness of the unborn essence of all things which is like the perfect solitary lovelight of Love of Mind Essence.

III

You sit again and close your eyes, and cross your legs underneath you in the traditional rocklike & stalwart position for meditation initiated by the human sages of the East because of its unmovability and nerve-calming effect, though you might just as well be standing at a subway strap, and again you sink deep in a quiet Stop-Everything of your outside suffering form. You let it melt away, ignoring the dream of life for an examination of the mind itself that makes the dream appear, or in which the dream seems to appear.

Because there's nothing there but emptiness and essence, no figures, forms, shapes, pictures, you get scared and want to return to the life of the world.

At times, worse, you cant stop the pictures and thoughts, like watching a movie on a screen. But because it's like a movie on a screen, you realize the movie itself is unreal phantasms and the screen is the only reality.

The "screen" is your Mind Essence, the movie is forms that come and go.

Suddenly someone disconnects the plug and the movie vanishes like a flash, like a bubble burst, like a dream, and all's left is the White Screen snowy perfect like the Bright Room of Holy Gold in the middle of the Mind. But what can you do with an empty screen, you've got to think, move, act, eat, "live."

So you return to the world, you yourself become a movie on the Screen of the Sole Reality, and go in search of your poor sentient needs, such as food, rest, even companionship. Let's say you go see a movie about monkeys.

But now you know that when the monkeys were swinging from branch to branch in the movie, they were not really there, just apparitions on the screen, and they were not really swinging from branch to branch; it was of the least importance to you before to consider this.

You've realized the utter unreality of not only the monkeys, monkeys indeed, but the utter unreality of any conception as to whether they really exist or not, exist indeed.

In your worldly mind you'll ponder and smile, and say "Well, of course the monkeys were photographed, their apparitions in various shades of brightness and darkness were preserved in film, and now they were just projected on this white screen, and so I saw them, and at least I know they were real once."

But Beverly! real indeed! How could they be photographed in the first place, if it wasnt for their forms? And how could brightness and darkness manifesting the shadows of their forms be preserved on film, if it wasnt for their forms?

Supposing the camera instead had been pointed at the empty sky? And how could they now be projected on a white screen from a film, if it wasnt for the shadowy preservation of the shadows of their forms? Where were their forms before they had forms? Where shall their forms be after they've had their forms?

And where are their forms now that they have their forms?

Their forms are shadows on the Universal Great Film of Essence of Mind, reflections of monkeys merely. The essence is not changed, monkeys are nothing but figures of speech we have.

You dont believe it? But from where came, and where going, and why dont their forms remain and be real?

Since it will be said, it's an old picture and all the monkeys are dead and gone, where were these monkeys before they were undead and ungone?

Monkeys, monkeys indeed; dead, dead indeed; gone, gone indeed; forms, forms indeed.

It's because of our own serious mistake of consciousness which is called Ignorance, of which Mind is not the Cause because Mind is intrinsically empty and pure but Ignorance within itself takes the Initiative and appears unto itself, i.e., appears in the minds of sentient beings everywhere, that there exists the illusion of the monkeys. Whether you wished to specify it as God's Mind or as Universal Storage Mind (Alaya-Vijnana), there is one door of Purity and Enlightenment and Nirvana, it seems, and there is the other door of Defilement and Ignorance and Sangsara, it seems; and in Reality and High Truth, neither door exists, nothing exists, that is to say, neither nothing or something but beyond that simply Neither and Not-Neither Together. Blur your focus, cross your eyes, look at the liquid world waver and vanish.

If Ignorance ended, so would the illusion of existence, but how can the Essence of the ignorance and of the illusion ever end? The Essence never had a beginning, never will end, and really is not to be considered at all but completely forgotten, that is, as an object of "thought" and "memory." The Essence of Universal Mind which is what you see, smell, hear, taste, feel and think about everywhere you may be, and you may be everywhere, but yet you have never seen the essence, nor smelt it, nor heard it, nor tasted it, nor felt it, nor thought of it, you only made these contacts with Ignorance.

It's because of this and other explanations, poor as the explanations are, that we can say the monkeys arent even, werent even ever real:- Supposing I went out in the yard and took six fistfuls of air and came in the house and created a SLAT, in my childish simplicity.

Or, which is essentially the same, I took six sticks and nailed them together and called it a SLAT then I turn around and say, "Before, ladies and gentlemen, in all ten quarters of the Universe, this SLAT did not exist." But as to even the existence or non-existence of the SLAT, what could be more absurd and trivial? It's only a figure of speech, a manner of speaking. If we had no brains we couldnt say the SLAT "existed"; the rock says the SLAT "exists"?

This is the created world and all its monkeys.

And now I say, "The SLAT exists." This too is just a figure of speech.

And then, when the SLAT, because put-together by me and only because in my ignorance put-together by me, inevitably falls apart, and even the very sticks turn to dust and finally to energy and finally to nothingness, it will be said "The SLAT no longer exists." This too is just a figure of speech, words about some shadowy form that was a no-form and became a no-form again and in between held an empty "existence" the essence of which was also No Form (in Truth).

SLAT, SLAT indeed.

The same with its representation, say, on film; we photograph the bloody slat; the same with the pitiful film itself. The film is made of emptiness, photograph it with microscopic atomic cameras and nothing's there. These are all confused fancies and eerie dreams of "form-seemingness" inside the sick mind working on one another and creation various visions and medleys of looks, in what is intrinsically empty pure space of Mind in its Essence.

So in regard to the monkeys and the SLAT you see that the created world's not real because of the original absurdity, triviality, and mere figure of speech which is creation itself and all its so-called Glory and you see no reason to involve your pure realization of your Mind in its Essence and Purity and Primal Nature of Nothingness with any of it.

For by abiding with the unchangeable and Unborn and eternally As-Is, you escape the illusion of great suffering inherent & implicit in changes and the suffering conceptions of existence (birth) and non-existence (death), which is but the life and death, the coming & going, of ideas about form in the Mind, ideas that in Mind Essence are seen as not being real in the least, of course, and are seen as only ideas and conceptions completely empty of self-nature and absolutely ungraspable just like things in dreams.

Why allow your pure and Original essence of Mind, which is in your possession because Mind in its Essence pervades everywhere throughout phenomena in all dimensions and spaces and directions forever without beginning or end, in emptiness, purity, and formless slatless unity, to become defiled by such illusions of thought as "existence" (appearance of a thought) or "non-existence" (disappearance of a thought.)?

It is with your Wisdom Eye you see this, not Beverly's form-eye; and in truth, there's no Wisdom Eye either, it's only a figure of speech. Mind in its Essence is the only Reality because it is what it is.

And supposing the whole universe were suddenly in all Ten Directions inundated and heaped with SLATS, and afterwards completely denuded of SLATS, of forms? What do you think, O ghost of the world?

Instead of thinking about your life, try sometimes gazing at the True Mind that gives rise to your life's dreamlike appearance in the Void, and if only for a moment your "life" will all go up in smoke and vanish, the suffering and the "joy" that is the reverse side of the same sorrowful thing. How can you ever again be deluded as to the existence or non-existence of phenomena such as life, worlds, someone else, people, or personality, or any of these vain notions?

But if this confuses you, it's because this TEACHING is the highest and final TEACHING, and instead of directing you gradually to it through the elementary stages, I use it as your starting point, and apologize for its incompleteness and vestiges of my own very profound ignorance. But your staring point, your starting point, your staring starting stashing point, should be the same as your final point and goal, and there is really no long road ahead, no road, nothing long, nothing at all, and for that matter *no words*.

The final goal is unqualified happiness, the bliss that never dies.

Buddhahood is like a medicine, it will cure you of a hundred ailments all of which you will see were apparitions in your mind that you clung to because you failed to consider the Essence of it.

Even physical sicknesses can be cured, thanks to the practice of quiet slow breathing during meditation (Dhyana), which loosens the nerves in your stomach and relaxes the whole body and nerve-system like a soothing bath.

LETTER TO BEVERLY (CONCLUDED)
    But the ailments in your thinking-mind, the general greed, anger and
foolishness that overcomes all living beings in their predicament of incessant
need, endless wanting, endless not-getting, they too will be cured as you
ascend the stages to Holiness in the Contemplation of Essence.
    When you will know, remembering as if waking from a dream, the ailments
in the thinking-mind (the brain, the thought-maker), they alone were the
cause of Suffering, you will know the Knowledge of the Buddhas of Old.
    One thing the Lord Buddha preaches: Suffering, and the End of Suffering.
    One thing the Lord Buddha gives:-the Path that leads to the end of
Suffering.
    This path is an ancient path trod by sentient creatures more numerous
than the grains of dust in all the universes.
    And in Truth, there is no path, no sentient creatures, no universes at
all. Isnt this Bright Essential News the greatest thing to Know?

    * . * . * . * . * . * . * . * . * . * . * . * . * . *

For the Title Page of BOOK OF DREAMS:
    "What do you think, Mahamati, is this
  dreamer who is letting his mind dwell upon
the various unrealities he has seen in his dream---
is he considered wise or foolish?"

            The same applies to tonight's sad thoughts about my "past
life"---I thought of Hal Chase and what he must think of me now---of how I was
a fool---In a dream I heard prison officials calling for me "Mr.Kerouett"---I
was filled with horror, thinking, Everybody is doing something "new" all the
time everywhere like in a comedy, Did you hear about Thompson he's living in
Chicago now and has taken up Buddhism---etc.---the Dostoevskyan grimness of it,
all devoid of the radiance I saw the other night in my Glorious Maitreya Samadhi
---I looked outside, the Beams of the East were still the same and my perception
of the dawn the same as in a million lifetimes---In bed in horror I had a
shuddering realization that I've not succeeded in casting off Self, the
ridgepole is still up---How could I escape this loathsome human self with
its body like a sewer and truly realize its unreality!

            Then I read the Lankavatara Scripture
        and my heart quieted---
            "In solitude of desert hermitage
                nourish a still & peaceful heart."

Self is mind only, exists only in the mind,
therefore I can get rid of it by mental exertion---
        1.Concentrate the Mind
        2.Observe the precepts
        3.Practice meditation

THERE IS NO DESTRUCTION, because suchness cant be destroyed.
In short, I wont die, I'll only seem to die.
Ananda dies, Buddha's shadow, crying . . .
That is to say, I mean by "I" the realization that suchness is not "heated by
false imaginations and speculations and stirred into mirage-like waves by the
winds of birth, growth and destruction."
        THIS SUCHNESS CANT DIE
        THIS SUCHNESS WAS NEVER BORN
        THIS SUCHNESS IS

"It is like the magician Pisaca,
who by means of his spells makes a wooden image
or a dead body to throb with life,
though it has no power of its own."

Free yourself of the bondage of
habit-energy---pay no attention to
names, signs, and ideas.

The Ridgepole of Self is that single
solid consciousness that grinds out dreams
all night and then all day grinds out thoughts
of action

* * * * * * * * * * * * * * * * * *

PREACHING TO A SOUTHERNER
          I didnt come into this world to work, I came here to be saved---
Saved from what?
From punishment.
If you had a fever, wouldnt you want to get rid of it?
By being saved I mean getting rid of the fever of life with all its sufferings
and the death that falls over it just because it *is* life.
What can I do?
If I see that both the fever and life itself are just a dream, as they certainly
are a dream in the Mind of God, why shouldnt I concentrate my mind on the Mind
OF GOD?
Because my True and Hidden Mind is the same as the Mind of God, but my false mind
of life doesnt know this and doesnt know that the ver . . . the anger, the greed,
the folly, the suffering, the striving, all for nothing but death at the
other end . . . is not real and not to be grabbed at.
Who would grab at fever if they had any sense?
Your own True Hidden Mind is the same, it's not being fooled by anything but
you just didnt know it.
So you work your head off to gain a thousand different satisfactions that burn
like a fever in your false mind of life, not realizing you dont have to do this
and you dont need nothing more than food to stay alive.
If you were working for just your food right now, you'd be working just a little.
Rent, expenses, good clothes, TV, iceboxes, cars, fancy food in packages, hunting
and expensive guns, "vacations," all that's nothin but a fever because you dont
know what to do . . . and rent is the fever of others who think they need money
and more money constantly from others to pay for all these things and more.
Chargin rent is actually a sin.
Big houses are a sin.
Hunting is a big sin.
Hunting is unjust, unkind and cruel to other forms of animate life who are
also under the punishment of death and tremble just like you.
The ox dont eat meat but he'll pull the meateater's plow, so you need meat for
to be strong, the meat and flesh of other living beings?
Ask the ox, says Thoreau.
What's more cruel and injust than to take the cow that fills your pail and
slaughter its suffering flesh for meat?
You can live on corn, beans that have the same protein as meat, greens that
have the same iron as some poor animal's suffering flesh, brown sugar and
molasses that have iron, potatoes that have starch, salt that comes from the
sea, and water is your drink.

(PREACHING TO A SOUTHERNER CONT'D)
You dont need sow fat; vegetable fat'll make your greens taste as good as pig fat.
Let the pigs free in the forest, I say; let the mule go wild; leave the animals
alone.
Vicious sinners have hackled their tender eyes.
Vegetable fat tastes the same as animal fat and fries potates the same.
It dont cost but $5 a month to eat all this, a half a day's work.
If you have a family of ten, it'll cost you 5 days work, or less.
Good God, one good big garden is too much for a family of 10 when July ripens it.
Squash, cucumbers, tomatoes, potatoes, beans, peas, beets, greens, corn, onions.
Yes, if you grow most of it yourself, the earth works for you.
I testify that the earth is my witness to what I'm telling you.
And instead of letting fever grow, stop it and merge your mind with the Mind
of God.
Let's have no more screeching in tents about sinners who drink moonshine.
Let's have some silence in tents.
Let's have no more healing of the physically sick.
Let's heal the vicious of their viciousness.
There aint no peace like the unceasing peace of good men who would do this, preach
silence and tranquillity and poverty and patience and religious joy and confidence
in the essential kindness at the heart of the universe and the essential goodness,
men who would teach this out of the kindness of their hearts.
Who would want to attack a country where people had no wealth and werent afraid
of nothing because they'd seen through the fever of anger, greed, and folly,
which is just a dream in the mind?
This is what I mean by being saved, and why work aint my first thought in mind.

I see workers in a dream rushing around carrying staircases
                    bringing walls
                    levelling emptiness
        worried lest God might think them lazy
            and all he wants them to do
                is
                    rest
                        and
                            be
                                kind

ANUTPATTIKA-DHARMA-KSHANTI, the patient recognition & acceptance of the dharma
of no-birth . . .   The emptiness and silence of reality . . .
  SAYS DWIGHT GODDARD:- "The myriad, myriad things, which the senses
   perceive and the conscious mind discriminates and thinks about are
empty and transient; if desired and grasped they lead to suffering.
   The only reality is Mind-Essence. Mind as essence is universal,
   undifferentiated, inscrutable. The dharma of its self-nature
   is Ultimate Principle. As Ultimate Principle (Actual-Principle)
Mind is irradiant in creative activity, manifesting itself as
determined by causes & conditions in all manner of transitory
existences. It is also integrant, forever drawing these transitory appearances into final identity with itself. Mind, as
essence or appearance, is ONENESS."

                * * * * * * * * * * * * * *
                 * * * * * * * * * * * * *
                  * * * * * * * * * * * *

NAGASENA TO KING MILINDA:-
"Resulting from my hair, nails, teeth,
skin, flesh, sinews, bones, marrow,
kidneys, heart, liver, abdomen, spleen, lungs,
intestines, mesentery, stomach, excrement,
bile, phlegm, pus, blood, sweat, fat,
tears, serum, saliva, mucus, lubricating
fluid, urine, brain in the head, and
sensations, perceptions, predispositions and
consciousness, there is that which goes
under the term, designation and name
of Nagasena. But in the strict sense
there is no individual in that matter."

_____

KARMA---
  "Destroyed is the old (Karma), the new
     has not arisen."
"They with their thought not set on future
     being,
The seeds destroyed, desire not germinated,
Like as the candle the wise are thus
     extinguished."

And Nagasena says:-"Through this mind and body a man does good or
                    evil deeds, and through those deeds another
                         mind and body is re-born. Hence he is not
                             liberated from his evil deeds."

          Just as milk
          Becomes curds,
          Or as a mango
          Becomes another
          Mango.

Dwight Goddard is at 60 Las Encinas Lane, Santa Barbara, Calif.--wow

Goddard was at Shokoku Monastery in Japan---
     Says to do 2-hour Dhyanas with 5 minute breaks.
For Dhyana he says: *"What is this emptiness of no-thing-ness?"*

HUI-NENG said:-"Our essence of mind is intrinsically pure; the reason why we
                    are disturbed is simply because we allow ourselves to be
                    carried away by every change of circumstances. He who is
                    able to keep his mind *undisturbed by any change of circumstance*
                    has attained true Samadhi. To be (merely) free from attachment
                    to any and all outer objects is Dhyana."

During Samadhi: "Old Karma conditions are matured and cleared away" (!)---

"There can be no compassion without suffering" (you realize)

Goddard:- "Then, suddenly, there will come a 'turning-about' within the
                    deepest recesses of his spirit that will be revolutionary,
                    life-enhancing and permanent. Expect it, watch for its
                    coming, enjoy it, rest in it, but beware of analyzing
                    it, or grasping it, or becoming attached to it.
                         At first you will find it illusive, but be
                         humbly patient, for suddenly it will be
                         yours and in its fulness forever."

                              *

Zen and Chan are "Dhyana Buddhists" (Meditation Buddhists) who believe in
supplying their own food . . . garden, simple food and clothes and shelter . . .
but would rather beg or go without than earn money which encroaches upon
the time reserved for the practice of Dhyana---"When he is tired he
rests and drinks a cup of tea"---"He sleeps, he brings water, he
chops wood, he cooks his food, he helps his brother"---"He
delights in solitude and silence---answers briefly and
softly---is full of faith and optimism and good
cheer---He is surrounded and supported and
companioned by hosts of unseen Buddhas
and Bodhisattvas with all their
abounding resources.

As he sees the result of his own labors to supply his simple needs, and as he
sees his mind constantly unfolding by his practice of dhyana, he steadily
gains confidence---he knows that all pairs of opposing thoughts have no
true distinction, so he tries to exclude such dualistic thoughts as
mine and yours, his and hers, big and little, good and evil,
sin and righteousness, purity and impurity, existence and
non-existence, these thoughts he knows are delusive
and trouble-provoking---In Dhyana he avoids thoughts of success
or failure---

He says to himself: "Now I know that I and all my
acts are empty and transitory, dreams that have
been caused by my greed, anger and Infatuation
as conditioned by successive waves of Karma
and expressed by body, lips, and mind."
---A loyal Idealist, a Monist, there is but one Ultimate Principle, suchness---"

GODDARD: "In the experience of devoted Buddhists the world over
and for 2,500 years the best conditions for following
the Noble Path are the following: to have no
fixed abiding place, to live a life of
poverty; to live a life of sexual
purity & celibacy; to live a
life of unselfish kindness
and helpfulness; to
live a life of
restraint
and self
control;
to live a thoughtful
life, reading
and meditating on the Scriptures;
and especially
to practice Dhyana regularly."----

THE 5 ADDITIONAL PRECEPTS

1. Little as possible to do with money
   and valuables
2. Strictly pure & celibate
3. No soft beds
4. No ointments & condiments
5. No entertainments & gambling

Goddard includes in his prayers for
the Brotherhood:

"Adoration to Shakyamuni, the Nirmanakaya
Buddha;
Adoration to Jesus, the Christian Messiah;
Adoration to Maitreya, the Coming Buddha."

FOR THE HOMELESS BROTHERS:- "IF MARRIED HE MUST MAKE SOME SATISFACTORY
ARRANGEMENT WITH HIS WIFE SO THAT HE IS NO
LONGER RESPONSIBLE FOR HER SUPPORT OR THE
SUPPORT OF ANY CHILDREN THERE MAY BE."

What is meant by sounds being in the mind only?
It means that sounds exist "for the mind."
If it wasnt for my mind my ear wouldnt hear the vibrations.
These vibrations are invisible, intangible.
The phenomena of sound, my ear itself, and my consciousness that I'm
hearing a sound, all three belong to no other than Mind.
All three are interacting ghosts materializing in the Mind.
The airplane engine vibrates in the sky and the sound is heard by
sentient beings, a vast wave is showered over the rooftops.
This is very mysterious; think about it.
Those who were born, and labor under the delusion of causes and
conditions acting in combination, hear it; the unborn, hear it not.
Moreover, if your ears can hear by themselves, then supposing you
are within a room as the airplane roars overhead, can the door
share the perception of hearing?
If the door shares with the ears this perception of hearing, then
all dead bodies that still have ear organs intact, should continue
to hear sounds.
But no, with dead bodies all three causes and conditions have
ceased, no more (1) ear organ, no more (2) sounds, no more
(3) consciousness of hearing sounds (the second ceases to exist with
the cessation of the third, which is contact between the first and
second).
But it can still be said that sounds exist in themselves after a
certain ear-organ and its certain individual consciousness dies.
This is what is meant by Ignorance-Does-Not-Die-With-the-Body,
thus establishing grounds for Karma and Re-Birth.
At death consciousness ceases, but the cause of consciousness,
Karma, and its own cause, Ignorance, cease not.
The inert door can be said to be a Door-Karma due to Ignorance,
devoid of such causes & conditions as the Six senses but not
devoid of such causes & conditions as wood & hinges.
The very existence of the door is due to Ignorance.
But at the same time, because the door might not have been
made, and is only made because of causes and conditions, but
only appears to be made, spectral waves of wood and hinges
mysteriously discernible only to the born but not the unborn,
and but a transitory door, an altogether ghostly door, because
of this we dont assign either any existence or non-existence
to the door, either any existence or non-existence to the
airplane sound.
That's why the Tathagata is called the Unborn, he is free
of all this dependency on causes and conditions and arbitrary
conceptions concerning them.

ANOTHER MYSTERY:-

This hand is neither pointed downward
or upward, that is, each is an
arbitrary conception.

Why?

Then tell me, if this man is standing between things
looking toward the west, he must be standing
in the east; or if he is looking toward the south,
he must be standing in the north. By just turning
he can be either in east, or west,
or north, or south----

DIALOG WITH SMART:-
Me:- I'm standing looking east, I must be standing in the west.
    Just by turning, I'm now standing looking south; I must
    be standing in the north. Your mind is confused.

Smart:- You're standing in the northwest.

Me:- Just by turning I'm now standing looking west; I must be
    standing in the east. I'm standing in the eastwest?
    This gives rise to the notion of the non-existence of
    location.
But the notion of the non-existence of anything just because you no longer
cherish a conception of it, is also absurd.
It would mean the non-existence of mind.
These different causes and conditions give rise to different kinds of
conceptions, which exist only in your relating thoughts, but your
essential mind is undisturbed.
I open my eyes,
        and see a tree,
                and there rises a consciousness of the tree,
and a conception of a tree,
        but my essential mind is originally
                immaculate.
Later on I'll show you that the tree itself is a measurement of illusion
    going on in your own mind, just like
    your measurement of the illusion of
    the conception of locations like east
    and west. The locations themselves
    exist in your mind,
        like the tree.

* * * * *** * * * * * * * * * * * *** * * * * * * *** * * * *** * * * *

False ideas and craft, are men merely---

I
G
N
O
R
A
N
C
E

1   "*Ignorance of the Two Fundamental Principles* is the cause of
    all these different disturbing illusions:
    THE FIRST FUNDAMENTAL PRINCIPLE
      Is the primary cause of the succession of deaths and
      rebirths from beginningless time. From the working
      out of this Principle there has resulted the various
      differentiation of minds of all sentient beings,
      and all the time they have been taking these
      limited and perturbed and contaminated minds to
      be their true and natural Essence of Mind.

E
N
L
I
G
H
T
E
N
M
E
N
T

2   THE SECOND FUNDAMENTAL PRINCIPLE
    Is the primary cause of the pure unity of Enlight-
    enment and Blowing Out that has existed from
    beginningless time. By the in-drawing of this
    Principle within the brightness of your own
    nature, its unifying spirit can be *discovered*
    and *developed* and *realized* under all varieties
    of conditions---

---that this unifying spirit is so quickly lost amongst the conditions
    is because you so quickly forget the brightness and purity of your
    own essential nature, and amid the activities of the day, you cease
    to realize its existence. That is why all sentient beings have
    fallen through ignorance into misfortune and into different realms
    of existence."   GREAT CROWN SURANGAMA SUTRA

EXPLAINING KARMA

The Immutable Law of the Created

I hear myself, born to Western Christianity, complaining "If I lose my individual will I wont do anything any more." But this is enlightenment the other side of ignorance.

Karma is the unchangeable law that governs all created phenomena.

The original karma was unchangeable and already fruitioned; this is the meaning of the Second Nirdana, Karma---

If a man thinks "If I go to sea and I drown, it was because it was meant to be; if I dont go to sea, and live, it is and was and will be because it was meant to be. But if I go to sea and live, it was meant to be and already happened. So I go to sea."

For it may have also been meant to be that he would die because he didnt go to sea.

This was the way, I, a seaman, comforted myself in wartime.

I gave it the name "Supreme Reality."

It is really Supreme Karma.

Now I realize that I didnt drown because it was meant for "me" to discover the Dharma.

My Karma is Supreme and led me to the Dharma, but only because it was meant already to be because of fruition of merit during the long night of life of the Karma.

But this was not "my" doing, just Karma.

The original Karma is unchangeable.

Nothing that I will-to-do, as an individual, has any meaning outside of Karma.

If I smoke and make myself sick, it's the Karma; if I dont smoke and stay healthy, it's the Karma; in both cases it has already been determined.

So as soon as I realize I have no "individual will" in the matter, and "dont do anything any more," it only means the Karma has worked itself out, as already determined in the Original Karma.

Now I see Karma as a wheel, sentient beings rolling and rolling in the sea of grief, unable to understand that even as they give up Self the Karma will already be done, as determined.

As soon as they say, "I dont believe in the Karma, I'm going to do this and do that and make it myself" it only means the Supreme Karma is already and was always thus; so on they roll.

Nothing we can do can change our Karma; with good reason we fear its punishment; but if punishment is in store for us due to a stock of demerit, nothing we can do to avoid what's already going to happen.

Karl Solomon says "EVERYTHING'S ALREADY HAPPENED."

It's a dream already a long time finished . . .

But if we "decide" to banish Self, and Karma, (and gain enlightenment which belongs to the arbitrary conception of Ignorance-or-Enlightenment) (which conception is the first link in the chain of being) the manifest decrease of evil demerit is not due to our "Decision" but due to the Immutable fact of our Karma.

So if I say, "Liberate yourself from Self and individuality and work out your Karma" it only means that if you do it, it was already meant to be, and if you dont do it, likewise.

No decision of the individual will.

No decider, no decision, nothing decided; only emptiness and essence.

But Karma is a great wheel and is abandoned, escaped from, with the coming of enlightenment, which "comes" because the Karma's blown out and when you've reached enlightenment you've left individuality ("there's nothing I can do") and so there is no personal decision in the matter and no individual in the matter to go to Nirvana, Mind Essence, Beyond Death and Re-Birth.

What does it mean that I refuse to practice dhyana tonight?
Karma.
That I decide to practice dhyana?
Karma.
What's the good of practicing dhyana?
But it's only because you're a victim of the wheel of Karma that you still conceive of good and bad and individual will.

So if you dont do anything any more, or, dhyana and Samadhi, the doing-of-nothing, individuality dies, consciousness of individuality dies, Karma ceases, and so "you" leave (or is left) the wheel of the long night of suffering (as already determined) and into the realm of enlightenment "you" go, which is the opposite of Ignorance and dispels it, as in High Samadhi, and on "you" go into Nirvana, Beyond-the-Wheel, Beyond-Causation, Blown Out.

Here the Mahayana explains the Tathagata, whose inconceivable activities (Dharmakaya) have had something to do with the dispelling of Ignorance and thus the weakening of Karma but here I'm beyond myself in the knowledge of the Buddhas.
Enough for now, to know, IT IS DONE!

Practice with zeal the Dharma, it is in your Karma
already established; practice not with zeal the Dharma,
it is in your Karma already established.

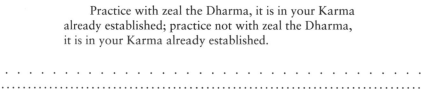

DAWN SAMADHI---The dreamless sleep---As I kept repeating the formula in French ("S'pensage ici est arretez") suddenly a Diesel Engine bopped outside and its form tried to take shape in the field of my void, like red or phosphorescent or photographic negative skeletal rims then quickly vanished. This was truly a vision of Citta-Vritti-Nirodha. Also, as my Thinking-mind dozed nevertheless my breathing didnt stop and neither did the well-trained formula but now the formula became a "Gaurd in Cawridor," etc. (the Dane of Cawdor) and all kinds of subconscious continuations of my Buddhahood effort to suppress consciousness---I woke up and clearly the words flashed: "Karma is accumulated in the mind due to ignorance." And I understood that the Wheel of Karma is imaginary, just as Mahayana says, & immutable because it builds its own bounce of demerit for demerit, as already established, that is, the demerit-karma estab-lished, thus is the demerit-fruit established. But the original demerit-Karma (a thought only) is only a red rippled appearing in Mind Essence because of Ignorance. So having lost Individuality, Consciousness of Individuality, and passed beyond Karma, Enlight-enment was alone with Ignorance dispelling it . . . a grim battle in a way depicting the "beginning" of Creation---In the splitsecond when Enlightenment won, was glimpsed Nirvana and came to me the subconscious word "Nirvano" at the instant of which and because of which I was instantly back in Karma and Consciousness and Individuality notions of "Nirvano"--- At morning, noises awoke me from sleep, I realized there was a world, and it seemed the world was a dream, a "red ripple" in the Void.---(like the Diesel Engine Ripple that couldnt hold).

All this "happened" because thus is the establishment of the Karma.---
During Dhyana my feet were out straight and thus it continued for an hour.

My Sleeping dreams of balls bouncing on a high porch and being with girls on a
high theater balcony with Neal and my arriving at the boat pier in "Dry Cruz"
were as much ripples in my Thinking-mind as the world to which I awakened is
a ripple in the Universal Essencemind.---all of it is Mindsuch. Jan.9,1955

Causes and Conditions acting in Combination
are Ignorance . . . the source of Karma.

No matter what you do in front
of a mirror the mirror will invert it
back to you. What you do is like the Karma,
the inescapable inverse return is like
the fruit of the Karma,
the pure mirror is like Mind Essence,
the fact that you can do and do do this
in front of the mirror is like Ignorance.

       A body riding a bicycle is like
       the Karma; a negative boy in space
       riding the bicycle upsidedown
       in the opposite direction,
       is like the fruit of the Karma.

A ripple like this ⌒⌒⌒ fruitions its Karma like this ⌒⌒⌒

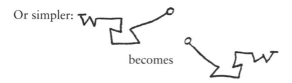

Or simpler: becomes

. . . .
Practise looking at things all day with the thought:
 "This thing might not have been."
  This makes you realize the secret of creation and following destruction,
   and thus, as you look at a rock, "This rock, this very particular rock,
    might not have been," you also think "When this rock becomes naught it will
    be possible to say, 'This rock might not be destroyed.'"

    1. This rock might not have been
    2. This rock might not now be
    3. This rock might not be destroyed
     . . . .
Or, if this rock had not been, it would not then become destroyed; therefore
why should I believe that it is and that it will be destroyed?

   The principle of Ignorance established,
   Karma takes shape. Karma can then be said
   to be the Shape of Ignorance.
         Karma is a dream
   already ended, already established---
         Thus my body
   and the shape of my Karma, is a dream already ended---
   What will happen will happen, and has already happened.
   Whatever I deem is my will, and do or not-do, thus it is,
   which means, Amen.

     ┌──────────────────────────────┐
     │ BUDDHISM IS A HAPP Y DREAM │
     └──────────────────────────────┘

SCHWEITZER---The natives of Africa appreciate having their physical ailments
cured by modern medicine; but their appreciation would know no bounds if
their mental ailments caused by anger, infatuation, and greed, were cured
first, by the medicine of the Dharma.

Gotama Buddha was the only True Physician in this historic world.
The Buddhas before him, numerous as the sands of the Ganges, in what worlds
were they?
O I wish another Buddha would make his appearance now; the world is getting
worse; birth multiplies and so pain and death increase; and this human
period of the Five Depravities is upon us.

Hollywood Movies are the modern version of the violence
and murder of the Roman Circus. You can tell by the continual plot-line
of murder, greed, hatred, lust, unsympathy----

A wellknown truth in every private heart
in this long night of life:
A big defecation leaves nothing to be wiped,
A small one, there's no wiping it.
This is Jean-Louis' Tao on the Toilet

* *

"All causes and effects, from great universes to the fine dust only seen
in the sunlight come into apparent existence only by means of the discriminating
mind. If we examine the origin of anything in all the universe, we find that it
is but a manifestation of some primal essence."

"I now see
that in spite of
my learning, if I'm
not able to put it into
practice, I am no better
than an unlearned man,"
weeps Ananda. "I am like a
prodigal son who has forsaken
his father."

You mistake the delusion as being
a reality, when you grasp the
deceiving conception of discrimi-
nating-thinking that is based on
caused & conditioned objects like
eyeballs, springs & pools, and
the conception that springs up from
their contact, as being your
e s s e n t i a l   m i n d -

"It/is/body/which/*moves/and/changes,*/not/Mind.-/Why do you permit your
thoughts to rise and fall, letting the body rule the mind, instead of Mind
ruling the body?" BUDDHA

"Then Ananda and all the assembly realized that from
beginningless time, they had forgotten and ignored their
own true nature, had misinterpreted conditional objects, and
had confused their minds by false discriminations and illusive
reflections. They felt like a little baby that had found its mother's
breast, and became calm and peaceful in spirit."
* S u r a n g a m a   S u t r a *

(On The Road)

JAN.11'55---I just found out that BEAT GENERATION was rejected by Knopf. As to
writing stories that the publishers approve of, it would no longer be free writing.
I write the Dharma freely and unsystematically for the purpose of teaching others
and keeping myself mindful of the teaching. Anyway the BEAT GENERATION has a
heretical view at its base, celebrating the "night," which is only the long
night of life. The Karma is working itself out.
KNOPF-SHMOPF-KAPOP?

My writings are: THE TOWN AND THE CITY, THE BEAT GENERATION, VISIONS OF NEAL, DOCTOR SAX, MARY CASSIDY, BOOK OF DREAMS, THE SUBTERRANEANS, THE BLUES (poems), SOME OF THE DHARMA---including huge fragments like GOD ON THE RAILROAD, ON THE ROAD, THE NIGHT IS MY WOMAN,---and including youthful works like ORPHEUS EMERGED, VANITY OF DULUOZ, THE SEA IS MY BROTHER, HIPPOS WERE BOILED, I WISH I WERE YOU, DARK CORRIDOR, JOURNALS galore, BOOK OF SKETCHES, BOOK OF TICS, NOTES everywhere and TWO MILLION GENERAL WORDS from 1940-1953. This mass of nonsense (except SOME OF THE DHARMA) is of the same suchness as either the dust that will collect on it or the approval that the world may shower on it, and this even applies to those parts of SOME OF THE DHARMA that are not straight quotes from the Sutras. My purest book was not written but edited by me: PRAJNA, containing dialogs from the Buddha-Charita and selections from Tao and the Sutras.

My witness is the empty sky.

My reward is the perfect blue sky at dawn in the desert in a bird-resounding riverbottom grove---

I dont really want to write systematic books of literature any more, just these private memorial notes . . . Glancing at my old Town & City diaries O what anguish and sweat and silly delusion, sickening! I'd like to bone myself now down to purity of Tao, go deeper into Buddhahood, give up individuality and the "I", that awful abstract "I" of writing----give up letters, for "virtue evaporates into desire for fame."

> Every day is Saturday and I have nothing to do!
> My mind is not perturbed and confused by 1000 different writing-tasks . . . letters, typing of material, chapters, etc. . . . nothing but sweet Dharma all day!
> I should write to my agent, tell him to send back all my books because they are "Pre-Enlightenment" and I'm on a new career of Buddhist-Writing (he doesnt have to know that Buddhist-Writing is No-Writing) and tell him that 30 years from now I may countenance publishing them as Pre-Enlightenment Writings if anyone wants them. Free! A new dawn which would be a No-Dawn!

For what can literary fame bring me, it's nothing but a smoldering fire.
Better the extinction of that fire than the stinking smoke of it.
It can only mean notoriety & temptation to selfhood & European travel & friendships and contacts.

> This writer should be a No-Writer.

THE KARMA IS A-WEARYING

> "Not one or the other or both or neither" explains away
> all arbitrary conceptions . . .

IF YOUR CONSCIOUSNESS CHANGED WITH SIGHTS, going from springs and pools to trees and changing to accommodate them, then how would you know the difference between springs and pools and trees? It's the very stability of the Mind that offers ground for instability & differences.

> But consciousness is not permanent and unchangeable because it recognizes space and changes its recognition of the location of space.

If this consciousness, moreover, rose from both eyeballs and springs & pools and became one half perceptive eyeballs and one half imperceptive springs & pools what would happen to these two parts of consciousness when separated from each other via the eyeballs being turned to empty space? The parts must have been both independent of the mind, imaginary blossoms in the air.

Put out the fire of writing and clear away the smoke and ashes of publishing.

$\left\{\begin{array}{l}\text{Fire results in smoke and ashes}\\\text{Life results in tumult and death}\\\text{Poetry results in publishing and dust}\end{array}\right.$

The long night of life is over. . . .

In my Dhyana today Jan.11 I had "Adoration to No-Contact" and other rhythmic
tantrisms. If anything bothers you, cease contacting it, that's all.---
If anything pleases you, beware of contacting it (during meditation & even
all day.) I had a vision of the Virgin Mary and Child in a little round clasp;
it magnified and got dimmer. I thought "S'pensage ici est arretez."

Jan.12 Dhyana
                    I thought "S'rêve ici est fini." This Dream is Finished.
I asked the Tathagatas now re-birth worked. Instantly a gas pain stabbed at my
right breast, like a rebuke, so I pondered the cause and condition of the stab.
So I presumed "Causes and conditions work and create re-birth; it remains unexplained
how it works and it remains unexplained because the question does not conduce to
aversion, absence of passion, cessation, tranquillity, supernatural faculty, perfect knowledge and Nirvana." But I asked it again, and this time an itch arose
on my face, but I knew it was imaginary. Why should I know the causes and conditions underlying the itch, some drivel about nerves and skin and brain-system
that could fill a 700 page medical tome of the Western World and yet it's only a
little imaginary itch that I forgot and never had to scratch---- So the Tathagatas
taught me 2 things: 1.Rebirth works but there's no need to know how, and
2.Rebirth is imaginary.
                    Moreover there was manifested an eerie sensation that
the Tathagatas, knowing the whole constructed world to be a dream, were hiding
in a kind of Invisible Shrouded Smile throughout, pure magicians in a magic
world.
      I had logical knowledge that all created objects are nothing but atoms
hung together in systems of universes, but I wanted faith.
                                                   It occurred to me, re-
membering last night's dream of me in a movie holding a kitty high over my head
as a ravening hound leaped to eat it, that I was that hound, I wanted to eat
and dissect the kitty of knowledge with my ravening mind.
                                        "The Virgin Mary held
the kitty." (says the dream.)
                    I kept thinking "If I had hidden that kitty inside
my shirt, would the hound have tried to bite what was now a part of me?"

        Desire for learning is a ravening hound, wisdom is the kitten.
        A Kitten eats, sleeps, & purrs. This is Tao.

Because Nature is nothing but combinations, therefore it has no self-nature.
People suffer because these combination keep changing and renewing and giving
   themselves rebirth, they think Nature has a self-nature. They think the
     combinations are permanent and indestructible and cant be escaped; but the
       only thing that is permanent and indestructible and has self-nature is the
         substance and essence that has been suffered to combine according to the
           principle of creation. If this creation itself wasnt ignorance itself,
             there wouldnt be suffering and dying today. If there wasnt suffering
               and dying of the combinations of nature, they wouldnt be combinations . . .

To combine is to arrange, to arrange is to put together what was not put together, to put together is to initiate an eventual coming-apart.

If you assert that there is no suffering and dying of the combinations of nature, then what happens to the castle in the sand when the tide rises?

It seems to disintegrate. The castle is the combination, the sand is the essence.

As for sand, itself is made up of an essence. What happens to the grain of sand when the tide of disintegration rises? When the grain of sand disappears, essence remains.

As for the tide of disintegration, itself is made up of an essence. What happens to the tide of disintegration when the tide of No-Conception rises? When the tide of disintegration disappears, essence remains. Disintegration is the combination, nothingness is the essence.

The self nature of Nature is nothingness.

* *

> Why should one give up the pleasures of
> life and follow the Eightfold Path in
> order to escape suffering? Because
> by escaping from bondage to accidental
> pleasures and accidental sufferings, you
> attain to the permanent self-established
> condition of happiness. Pleasures are
> like seeds destroying the balance
> of the happy ground.

EVIL IS IGNORANT HABIT-ENERGY---I saw a birdsnest today and the old thought of stoning it down flashed somewhere in me, although as a child I used to stop
 gangs of kids from doing this, by scolding them at the cost of my own safety---
    I saw the unpleasant saying "Kill or Be Killed" today, the title of a
Television program. Is this true? If you lived in a city of thieves would you
have to steal to avoid being robbed? In war, shoot your gun down in the ground,
like my holy cousin Hervé Kerouac did in the Normandy campaign. In hand-to-
hand combat, try to overcome your adversary, disarm him, then tell him to run.
In a war among the ants, kill or be killed means very little to the man of Tao
watching it.---

ALL THINGS ARE OBJECTS OF THE MIND----therefore objective; Mind is the subject.
This is quite simply true. That book, that tree, are mere manifestations of
the mind. They are combinations and have but one Common Essence, Mind.---Even
the mind-system that thinks this out, is a combination, its essence being Pure
Mind. *My brain is an objective thing.*

There is mind in the matter.---   Lankavatara says that something cannot come out
of nothing, which corroborates my statement, the self-nature of Nature is nothingness. Nothingness does not produce something with a self-nature any more
than a tortoise produces hair.

> "It is therefore necessary, if one is to control his mind, to
>   preserve its emptiness." TAO 48

"He that is contented is already rich." ---"But as soon as one desires to
control his mind, he becomes incapable of doing so."

SUCCESS AND FAILURE ARE BOTH HUMILIATING

POME *
This wood has the same
even essence inside
as the air---
the essence is everywhere
the essence is the secret
the essence is not disturbed
the essence has no hope
    No hope
    No war
    No ruin
    No rhyme
    No history
Hey Come with us to some
high glory, sing the flower
bedecked angels---
The Tathagatas lead the way
    O Wise Love!
             * * *

Rosy July . . .

          Quand j boué pas j comprend la tranquillité comme un
            mauvais fou

The essence is not Dostoevskyan
Nor is it worried about being frivolous

"Remove yourself from the purview of the world," is my instruction

Title: Being Quick He is Dead

I will teach the Tranquil Law (La Loi Tranquil)

Swill that was forced on me, literary famous . . .
Great Music is great enough but it is not pure essence of reality . . .

A new life of dry happiness instead of wet unhappiness . . .
Transcendental Ideas of the Same Form . . .

Dharma: the Law of Reality

A big bumbling fumbling angel in the wrong world . . .
Tathagata: Master of Essence
Mahayana: An intellectualized ego-attachment to taskhood (The Light of Mahayana)

Bodhisattva's Nirvana, all effort and striving is seen to be unnecessary, entire
absence of discrimination and purpose, perfect Solitude, perfect Love. This
brings on Manomayakaya and acintya-parinama-cyuti.

The sustaining power that has both aspects of Tathagata's merit and disciple's
obeisance *is* the fruitage of Noble Wisdom
Forget the body. Let the mind handle the rest . . .
Let the attachment dry up on the Tree like old sap . . .
       Missions & Emissions

Samadhi, Just let everything roll on by . . .

YELLOW SHEETS AT BEDSIDE (cont'd)

The Solitude of the Actual Oneness of the Unbornness
Continuous Saha working causes the continuous assertion of the will-to-live
The will-to-lil

There *is* no sense mind

Your body is subject to time---your mind isnt---
The Starry Manager Sleeps on top Of his ballclub . . .

ALONE & QUIET (IS REALITY)
UNAFFECTED & UNAFFECTING

Sentience is Patience!   -------Write: Discourses on the Dharma

Cutting my ecstatic itchy testes off with scissors (in dream)---"How can
  the mind system enjoy eternal ecstasy?"

Transcendental Sight is all sights of objects are as empty as clear space . . .

Cody Deaver: Late Sat afternoon light in felon's hotel room
                (he's from W.Virginia with girl)

Those dreams that seem so real vanish with the speed of a lightning flash . . .
False imagination and erroneous reasoning---everyone in the world pitifully----
Nirmanakaya can be willed . . .

        The Wise Are Dead

Held blearily together by form all things are waiting for dissolution yet
is nothing evolving and nothing disappearing

I am a fallen Arhat   . . . . . . Empty shapes

Stop Dreaming, it's all One Milky Fleece. . . .
                    You dont have to be eating, taking in all the time . . .
        Lucien and Allen: they talked themselves out of the Absolute and are now
        deeply engrossed in psychoanalysis, world-discrimination, and "work" . . .

When it is realized that there is nothing born, and nothing passes away, then
there is no way to admit being and non-being, and the mind becomes quiescent!

And the wise are established in their true abode which is the realm of quietude.
        . . . . . . The seas sawed terribly . . .

    Sex---our bodies always hurt---the hospital of the heart----

            THE DHARMA IS THE LAW OF UNDERSTANDING

Arhats rise when the error of all discrimination is realized . . .

    For the wise even the stage of imagelessness ceases to mean anything . . .

Sound---there is nothing but what is heard of the mind itself . . .

Sad Sam Jones . . . it's all a big Buddha Fable---I'm ridin on the Lark now
                        & Forever
                    The True Lark, that is.

Actual Oneness is exactly What it is

Fry your self in the truth . . . like meat . . .
                    All-conserving Universal Mind

Devoid of will-effort . . . .   Ultimate Oneness

All the Manas is, Mull-mind?   No, "It does not give information that can be
                    discriminated."

A movie novel is what you want a movie exactly to look like on a Screen . . .
A BUDDHIST MOVIE NOVEL is the world . . .

All the details of a dreamunrememberable mess

Devoid of selfness and its belongings---plants in the garden, ants,---me too.

His own mind and personality is also mind-constructed..(Neal's)

"Sure, sure, I'll recite Amida's name later"---(laffin)--Ignorance having "fun"
now while it can is just the meaning of Ignorance.

Title   BUDDHAHOOD: THE ESSENCE OF EXISTENCE

Sentient beings are on so many different levels, like ants and men, they dont
meet---Like microscopic worlds going down in a bite of food and this universe
being digested by Cosmic Ogres yet undergoing no disturbance or change . . .

L'essence n est pas degoutante comme ma marde pi est pas belle comme le miel . . .

The incredible horror of life, inevitably . . .   One essence
                    "5 members of family"
                         What a dream!

I would teach the path through dense universal ignorance like a lawn mower in
one strip at a time . . .

                    DANA   The trance of pure charity
                              (charity practised in a pure trance on essence)

Matter is Ephemeral in
  and out in all
  10,000 directions---
Sentience is
  Ephemeral in & out
  in all 10,000 directions---
RAIN SAMADHI---each
  rain-drop contains
  infinite universes of
    existence the essence
    of which is undisturbed light.

Jan.14---How utterly imaginary human life is!---I cant get over it . . . I think
of a man in America 100 years ago and the complete extinction of all his
worries, strivings, contacts, his "reality"---the icy ground he paced on,
empty throughout, if he didnt have a body he'd be falling down through Infinite
space instead of pacing on that ground, that cold ice---When he allowed his
mind to contact troubles, difficulties, all gone . . . ---He might as well have not
appeared---I see the doodads on the shelves and I understand they're all the
same suchness as myself, imaginary dividings of the One Essence all laid out
stupidly in the dream---Ah this tender heart will never be aroused to anger &
passion again---The silence ringing in the quiet house, the very sound of it all,
of the imaginariness of it---Powers of Attorney in the Dust----Empty images
imprinted on paper which is slowly burning, burning,---"New Letters" older than
Gethsemane, older than Dipankara, older than the cloud---That 19th Century man,
that dark Melville, he never even existed, he left nothing behind, not even a
footprint as poor Wolfe well knew---bah! Adoration to No Contact! As soon as
I stop contacting thoughts of existence, the whole thing vanishes and I with it
---Then why ever pay it any further consideration and why trouble ourselves in
the Void?---I close my eyes and the truth shines bright. That's enough.-----

DHYANA---At each exhalation I thought "It's all imaginary" and at one point the
thought of the "evil witches Marianne and Joan" appeared as old Karma-producing
thoughts but was now dissolved & ineffective---seen truly.

As for the contemptuous opinion of my work by some editor, to allow my mind to
dwell on it is to initiate unnecessary Karma-energy and create demerit, which
can be avoided by ceasing contact with the thought of it.--
    For my consciousness of the editor's rejection is all taking place in one
Unified Field of Mind, i.e., it is completely imaginary and mind-only with no
basis in reality outside of mind. If my consciousness of the editor's rejection
arose from such causes & conditions as both my brain and its conception of the
editor, then my consciousness would be one half of the brain and one half of the
"objective" conception of the "objective" editor, and if so, when I am not using
my brain in Samadhi, these two independent halves and haloes of consciousness wd.
vanish, both the conception of the editor and my brain? But the truth is, my
brain, the conception of the editor, and the consciousness of it, come all three
from mind alone, and return to but one source, One Essence Universal, the Unified
Sea of Essence of Mind.---My consciousness of the dust in the room just now arose
neither from the dust nor from my brain, nor from anywhere, nor from all, because
the existence of the dust is simply not grounded in the Ultimate Principle of
Reality which is unlimitedly everywhere.

WHAT I NEED NOW IS *intuition*!!!---For I'm now like the man "who knew the name of
drugs, but when medicines were brought to him he could not tell their different
properties and virtues." All I know is words . . .

As the elephant longs for the elephant grove, I long for the ancient & forgotten
man grove---where the Dharma was taught of old---When I crossed the ferry in
Guaymas at dawn in 1952 and I saw those white-shirted ferrymen poling us across
the limpid river of silence . . . Ah, then I remembered. . . .
* . * . * . * . * . * . * . * . * . * . * . * . * . * . * . * . * . * . * . * .

THE FIVE GREAT ELEMENTS . . .
In the Tathagata's Womb it's as though it were being said: "You want space? How
much do you want. You want sights? How many do you want?" but space and sights
are the same---"in perennial freshness and purity permeating everywhere throughout
the phenomenal universes."---and are "merely figurative words having no meaning in
reality."
    How much space, squeezed, would you need to make a refined speck of dust?
The proximities of space can never become the proximities of finest dust---space
and sight are not in conformity.
    WHERE DOES DUST AND EARTH COME FROM AND HOW DOES IT SOJOURN HERE?

227

You suddenly get a free store-- how much do you want? what do you want? Yet you
didnt *want* in the first place.
  Sight obeys, and sight is everywhere.(dust.)
    Fire obeys, and fire is everywhere---given conditions, it arises, but it's not
      the conditions that manifested it alone---the intrinsic nature of space is
        the real fire-essence, or, Mind manifesting fire, as Mind manifests the
          sight of the springs & pools---If the fire came from the kindling, or
            from the lens, or from the sun alone, all three would be perpetually
              burning and the sun would burn everything in flames----But fire arises
                when you hold the lens at high noon sun over kindling---So the fire is
                  not being manifested by causes and conditions nor does it rise spon-
                    taneously by reason of its own nature---(if so, everything wd.be on
                      fire flaming all the time.)   --Everywhere is the place where fire
                        originates---"Where does the fire come from, and how does it
                          sojourn here?"

  Wind is asleep in emptiness, you can rouse it up by motion of your hand, but the
    origin of the breeze is not in the motion of your hand alone for is that where
      the motion of your breeze is gone when your hand is still and is that where
        the breeze is gone? Your hand is empty space & breeze is everywhere. Where
          does the wind come from, and how does it sojourn here? Like fire it responds
            to combinations which serve it up but are not its place of origination or
              its cause. Mind Is Cause. Everywhere is the place where wind originates.

Water too, responds to combinations, such as distillation of dew at sunrise, but
  if the combination of the dew and the rising sun alone were the place of origin-
    ation and the cause of water, like the chicken or the egg, what came first, the
      water or the dew? Water is in the river . . . where did it originate? Rain?
        Where did the rain originate? Distillation? Where did distillation originate?
          Dew? Where did dew originate? Water? Where did water originate? In it-
            self then the universe wd.be drowned in water and there'd be no room for
              fire, earth, and air; and water wouldnt have to wait for combinations to
                appear; but we see that it only appears under certain conditions as it
                  is. Therefore water obeys, and water is everywhere, that is, the in-
                    trinsic nature of water is the real emptiness, and the intrinsic nature
                      of space is the real water-essence. WHERE DOES WATER COME FROM?
                        EVERYWHERE.

The 4 Great Elements obey causes and conditions and combinations, and have no
self-nature, and their origin is not in these, but in Mind alone.

Finally space, the 5th Great Element. It too responds to combinations. You dig up
  earth and space appears in the hole, but the place of origination and cause of
    this space-phenomenon is not in the removed earth, or in the digging-up, or by
      itself. If by itself space was caused, why does it come into sight in the hole
        only after we removed the earth? THE UNIVERSE WD. BE NOTHING BUT OPEN SPACE.
          If space was caused in the hole by the absence of the earth and therefore
            came from outside of this earth, we would see it replace the earth and fill
              the hole. "If we do not see space coming in to take the place of the earth
                as it is being removed, how can we say that the space comes from outside
                  of the earth?" If space was inside of this earth and was the same as
                    the earth, then space wd. come out with the digging, and if so, earth &
                      space wd. be the same and with the removal of the earth why shd. we
                        see space left in the hole?
                          So space being different from earth, if space comes out by digging
                            why shd. the earth come out too?
                            Space obeys, and space is everywhere.

"THE ESSENTIAL NATURE OF THE FIVE GREAT ELEMENTS IS PERFECT, AND ALL-IN-UNITY, AND ALL ALIKE BELONGING TO THE TATHAGATA'S WOMB, AND ALL ALIKE DEVOID OF DEATHS & REBIRTHS."

* *

THE PERFECT LOVE OF MIND ESSENCE:-   A POEM

Mind Essence loves everything, because it
knows why everything is---
  It loves everything because everything ends---
Mind Essence is like a little child,
It makes no discriminations at all,
All is the same and all's in the mind,
And all's to be loved as it stands,
All's to be loved as it falls.

    The Karma is done
    Mind Essence is one---
    The wheel of thought
    Is no more fought---
    Differences of things
    Are imaginary rings---
    The child of delight
    Rests in the night---
    The mind of bliss
    Is pure happiness---

He never dies   He is never hung
Who has no eyes   Who has no tongue---

He never fears   There is no rain
Who has no ears   Outside the brain---

He never goes   Unborn,
Who has no nose---   No lamb shorn---

He is never bawdy   No crying
Who has no body---   In essence undying

    Sight is just dust,   →   Mind alone
    Obey it must---   Introduced the bone.
       *   *

    Fire just feeds   →   Only mind
    On fiery deeds.   The flame so kind.
       *   *

    Water from the moon   →   Mind is the sea
    Appears very soon.   Made water agree.
       *   *

    Wind in the trees   →   Wind rose deep
    Is a mental breeze.   From empty sleep.
       *   *

    Space in the ground   →   Devoid of space
    Was dirt by the pound   Is the mind of grace.
       *   *

Fire retires   And space accepts   Explaining in
When water admires   The green adepts   droves
                                                    To men in
Fire inhibits   And wind responds   groves
What earth admits   To magic wands
                         And men appear   "Not even alive
Fire and water   With Dharma dear   The Elements Five"
Bring earth a daughter

* * * * * * * * * *

THE SIXTH GREAT ELEMENT IS *PERCEPTION*---Like the others its place of origination is not in causes & conditions and combinations nor in its own selfnature.
Perception obeys conditions, but perception is everywhere. Its essential
nature is perfect and in one unity with the empty perfect essence of fire,
water, wind, earth and space (the other Five.) All belong to the Womb of
Tathagata and are devoid of rebirths and deaths.

"Dead as tricks/the Elements Six." (so to speak but they are devoid of death).
The intrinsic nature of perception is the real emptiness and is intuitive &
enlightening; the intrinsic nature of space is the real perception-essence.
"The intuition of the one and all embracing Essence" manifests its faculty
of seeing (as in springs & pools sight) everywhere. Where does perception
come from and how does it sojourn here? Like fire it responds to combinations (i.e. eyeballs & springs & pools) which serve it up as perception
of sights, but are not its place of origination or its cause. Wherever
there are eyeballs and sights, there will arise perception of sight;
just as, wherever matches are struck against rough surfaces, there
will arise fire.
Perception obeys, and perception is everywhere.

These 6 Great Elements "are ever in freshness and purity, permeating everywhere
throughout the universe, & are being manifested freely and perfectly in correspondence to the amount of Karma accumulated by the conscious activity of
sentient beings."
How much space do you want? How many sights? How about a
little fire? water, wind? If because of my Karma it is determined that I
close my eyes this next minute then perception of sight will not be
roused from its sleep in intrinsic emptiness & made to dance thru the
corridors of sight.
In Dhyana I leave the 6 Great Elements alone in their original state
which is the same as intuition of essence.
But if I strike a match, from up
the fan comes a wind, and if I use my perception to see the fire, I rouse 3
of the Elements from the Deep of Mind Essence and they obey freely, perfectly,
to Ignorance.
WHAT'S MIND ESSENCE? Take a thought. Are you thinking?
What is the thought? The thought of Mrs. G?
What is the essence of the thought?
The essence of the thought is not Mrs.G. but mind essence.
It is silent, inconceivable, perfect, invisible, neither
dark nor bright, mysterious, illimitable and who can talk about it?
---yet it's the stuff the world is made of, the stuff of any old little
thought is the stuff of any old little gumwrapper on the floor of a subway car.
It is Mindstuff---Undisturbed Light, Lake---it is the self-less one suchness---
it is what it is; inscrutable, unvarying, pure---You can hear it in the silence
and see it in yr. eyelids' invisible dimness, taste it in the air, feel in your
numb feet the sapless essence of the saplessness, smell it with yr. nose blocked,
and think it when there's nothing on yr. mind but the unchanging essence of all
the changing thoughts.---
All things and all thoughts are one stuff-
The Stuff is faithfully true-
The cake, your perception of the taste of the cake, and your tongue are all one
thing acting in concert to fool you, you fool you---Your mind is the only Mind-

YOUR DEATH, YOUR PERCEPTION OF DEATH, AND YOUR BODY ARE ALL THE SAME THING ACTING
IN CONCERT TO FOOL YOU
YOU FOOL YOU * * * *

THE 7TH GREAT ELEMENT IS CONSCIOUSNESS----it is consciousness of perception of
phenomena, as for instance the consciousness of the perception of sight of the
springs & pools---Where does this consciousness go when there are no sights
and thoughts?

Consciousness obeys, and consciousness is everywhere. The
intrinsic nature of consciousness is the real emptiness, enlightening and
intelligent; and the intrinsic nature of space, which is enlightened intuition, is the real conscious-essence (or consciousness-essence.)
It responds to conditions but conditions are not its source.
Consciousness abides in tranquillity permeating everywhere throughout
the phenomenal worlds and embracing all 10 quarters of the universes
in and out without number; at the contact of eyeballs & springs & pools,
sartor! it appears in the form of consciousness of the perception of
sight of springs & pools. "Why do you still raise questions as to its
locality of existence?"
The false presuppositions and prejudices concerning the Seven
Great Elements of existence, which are simply discriminations made
by the conscious minds of sentient beings in their state of
ignorance and bewilderment, are but figurative words and figures
of speech that have no basis in reality. They dont realize
that *the One Pure Stuff appears to their crippled self-minds,
to be a big Differentiated Mess.*

JAN 19 1955---Set free by the law to follow my bhikku track & yet I go and feel
dull and foolish and even argue with my mother about some point of pride--Ah
and after all I learned!---All these fine words! My hermitage is next step
---first the secondary step of fixing family house---But "not by anxious outward means, but by resting in thoughtful silence." Two dhyanas today, with
the thought:-"The essence of the thinking." But all day a firm conviction
that all this phenomena of my life is a delusion and I really dont have
to honor it and eventually wont. What a big mind-camp mountains are!

THE FIVE DESIRES

1.Desire for flavors
2.Desire for sounds   All desire
3.Desire for sights   is
4.Desire for fragrances   suspect   ------"The 5 desires are the
5.Desire for touches   great obstacles, forever dis-
      6.Desire for thoughts   arranging the way of peace."-----

RECOGNIZING ALL THINGS as hallucination may not be regarded as 'loyalty' by yr.
family in their trying times----thus go alone---

5 DESIRES, means, 5 AVERSIONS . . . i.e. . . . aversion for stenches, aversion for rot,
aversion for rackets, aversion for horror-sights, aversion for pains.

THE SUCK-TUBES
  Causes & Conditions acting in combination are stated as being neither the cause
of things nor not the cause, and this seems bewildering.
    For instance, fire. The combination of high noon sun, glass, and shavings
brings forth fire. If this combination were not employed *there* would be no
fire; if this combination is employed, *there* is the fire but the fire came not
from the combination but from everywhere; so we say, causes & conditions acting
in combination neither produce nor do not produce phenomena. That's because
they are like suck-tubes held up in emptiness and through them is conducted the
phenomena which is already "waiting" in tranquillity & purity & emptiness and
is Universal.

THE SUCK-TUBES (CONT'D)

If you hold up the fire sucktube, fire obeys and appears; if you hold up the
perception sucktube, perception obeys and appears; if you dont hold up these
sucktubes, nothing appears but remains as it is in the Mind of Enlightenment.
The sucktubes are to be compared to the irradiating principle in the Womb
of Tathagata manifesting transformations in perfect accommodation to the
demands of Karma.

It may be said that the 7 Great Elements are perfectly accommodating and all
the same, but the sucktubes held up to it are 7 different kinds of difference . . .

Water and fire are of the same essence but striking a match gives rise to the
imagination of a difference---Striking a match is like a divining rod that'll
find fire---

Water and earth combined are divined from their emptiness by the sucktube (or
divining rod) which consits of planting a seed in the ground and watering it,---
a plant is only proof of the fact that if you hold up the water-and-earth-
transformation sucktube, water-and-earth-transformation obeys and appears---
The plant owes its appearance neither to the seed or dirt or water, neither
to all of them, neither to none of them, but to that which was already
waiting in tranquility and purity and emptiness, Universal Mind of
Enlightenment. Why? If the seed hadnt been planted in earth and watered,
nothing wd. have appeared but would have remained as it is in this Mind
of Enlightenment. You say the plant owes its appearance to the seed?
How come the seed on the table doesnt sprout some plant? Owes its
appearance to the earth? Then earth would spring such plants everywhere and there'd be no room for pots to hold the earth in.

Owes its appearance to water? Then you could grow plants like these by pouring
water in the sea or on a bed of stones. Does not owe its appearance to any of
these? Without seed, earth, and water the plant wouldnt have appeared. Owes
its appearance to all three together combined? The appearance of the plant is
owing to the water and earth the combination combines and transforms, but this
water and earth do not originate in the combination, but beyond the combination
in their own one and tranquil essence.

The plant is only a conductor of mysterious elements abiding everywhere, which
accommodate perfectly its held-up sucktube and respond its way, but are themselves undisturbed and not liable to destruction when the plant is thrown in
the barrel dead. A hassle disturbing the balance of the Mind of Enlightenment.
Therefore we say that the plant does not owe its appearance to all 3 (seed,
earth, water) combined but to the Mind of Enlightenment itself from which
this combination has sucked the elements. These elements are then combined
and transformed and the plant appears. But the origin of the appearance
of the plant is not in this action, but in the essence of the elements;
just as the origin of the appearance of fire is not in the action of
striking a match on a rough surface, but in the essence of fire which
everywhere responds and everywhere waits. The water and earth of a
plant's body are everywhere ready to obey the action of planting,
ready to be *sucked into activity.*

Same with a human being. He owes the appearance of his body neither to his father's
seed, nor to his mother's womb, or to nutriment alone; neither does he owe the
appearance of his life to none of them, if so he wouldnt be here; neither does
he owe the appearance of his life to all three combined, seed & womb & nutriment
A man's body only proves that birth makes bodies, but this body does not
(cont'd next page)

come from birth alone, it comes through birth as through a tube from the
essence of the elements water & earth that have been roused from emptiness by
the sucking-tube action of seed, womb, nutriment. This emptiness is the
Universal Mind wherein enlightenment and intuition are potential & tranquil
& respond perfectly according to the imaginary demands made by the ripples
of Ignorance defiling the calm of unbornness and supra-existence. In there
the elements water & earth are of the same essence. They respond to
ignorant demands because of their perfect enlightenment, mirror-like.

A plant only proves that planting makes plants, and the mystery is that it is
really mental and really independent of its own body! That's why, being a mere
figure of speech, it's neither existent or non-existent, is neither caused
nor not caused, etc., because in the Mind of Enlightenment no such discrimination is held . . . (the Womb of Tathagata.) As I look at the plant I realize
it's just a visionary bloom in the void, it might just as well not be, it
just so happens to might as well be (so to speak)---it has no hold on
reality. Where do the water & earth come from, that give the plant its
body, and how do they sojourn here? They come from everywhere; this
is a Sea of Mystery.

* * *

A THOUGHT ONLY PROVES that thinking makes thoughts.
A thought is only a conductor of mysterious elements abiding everywhere, which
accommodate perfectly the held-up sucktube of thinking and respond its way, but
are themselves undisturbed and not liable to destruction when the thought is
forgotten and discarded.
The essence of the elements of a thought are Perception and Consciousness (the
6th and 7th Great Elements), they are everywhere Obeying the act of thinking
in thinking-minds, or brains.
If the thought, of, say, New York, owed its appearance to the brain alone, it
would not know of any New York, being bounded by the boundaries of the brain
alone; if it owed its appearance to the conception of New York alone, how wd.
the brain know it, being left out of it?
If the thought of New York owed its appearance to neither the brain nor the
conception of New York, no such thought wd. have appeared, yet it has.
If it owed its appearance to both the brain and the conception of New York
combined, alone, then when the thought of New York in a million years along with
New York forever vanishes, (and the thought, remember, was specifically a
thought of New York and not a thought of a vague anyother consciousness city)
do the elements of the thought of New York and of the action of the thinking
of this thought, the Perception and the Consciousness vanish too? The details
vanish, the essence remains; the dream vanishes, the mind remains; the divided
items disappear, the unified emptiness remains. For we find the essence ever
on hand to serve other "specific" thoughts. So the thought must come from its
essence; and the essence of a thought, is Mind-essence.
*A thought is an impermanent form materializing awhile in the permanent essence
of Mind. The essence of the thought and the essence of the Mind are the same,
naturally, but the form is just a passing fancy which naturally is completely
ignored in Mind Essence (Womb of Tathagata) and neither considered as existent
or inexistent.*
"Who would notice it?"---as a mirror the vain child.

"MANY TIMES YOUR SERVANT," I've said to the *Queen,* Nature and the Virgin Mother,
neglecting my duties to the *King,* Mind and the Tathagata.

Adoration to the Tathagata who does not think---
Adoration to the
Tathagata
who
never
dreams

Close your eyes, the invisible dimness is the mindstuff that makes the dream;
open your eyes, what you see is the dreamshit of the mind.

    Close your eyes and look at the reality; open your eyes and look at the dream . . .

The ridiculous assertion by the editor of Knopf that my "mystique of my country
is touching" and sort of unfounded (ridiculous considering Sandburg, Whitman,
and Wolfe) is made of the same stuff as my sublimities. In the Womb of Tathagata
no assertions, no qualities, depraved or sublime, are entertained; in the Womb
of Tathagata there is no dreaming, there is only the Reality from which everything came & to which everything is returning.----

                                      Because the Tathagata never
     Life is an unreal horror   dreams he never believes
            and a   in the existence or inexistence
     disagreeable dream   of anything he sees

I go to the store and see children, a bunch of girls, crowds,
  and I see that none of it necessarily exists and there's
    no reason for me to particularly notice it. This is
      the practical result of Buddhist Learning
        and it is very blissful---Jan 22 1955

                             The pristinity of the imagination
                       that imagine fire spilling from the
                    sleeper's elbow---the *loneliness* of that
STRICTLY SPEAKING,   i m a g i n a t i o n
                there's
                    no
                         individuality in the matter . . . a man watching ants
knows each individual ant has no individual personality outside its own insane
imagination, like chickens with their insane astonishment, and the same with men
and with the wise Nagasena who knows he's just a coil of guts with no individual
involved in the matter-----Yet what is this frantic Consciousness of Individuality
throughout Nature?---it is part of the pain of existence, it is illusion, it is
the very *tint* of Ignorance---If I can get rid of the consciousness of my
individuality and FREELY RELAX BEYOND CONSCIOUSNESS,--? ?

     Happiness & unhappiness are related conditions,
     conflicting, causing regret and unrest---

         Retire beyond happiness . . .

     Life is a big elaborate joke being played on us by our
        o w n I g n o r a n c e

I am just water and earth transformed and combined, I'm just perception and
consciousness placed under restraint, I have no individuality in the matter, my
True Mind of Intuition of the Universe is my True Mind . . .

    Mountains, river, earth, are fantastic blossoms which you see
     owing to misconceptions that result neither from the mind's misconception
   nor the mind's right understanding but because your sense of direction has not
been recovered through simple E N L I G H T E N M E N T * * *

    Adoration to the Bright Room where my existence is not noticed!---
   where my future non-existence will not be noticed either!---
   Adoration to the end of guilt!!
            The Karma's Over   . . .
            Everything is Done   . . .

A DREAM INTUITION---A man who owns a store charges me rent to let my mind form
an intuition *once* in his store, which I do, the Mind closing like a heart
V-shape upon itself in an "intuition" whereupon he locks the door to keep the
mind outside and to keep it from intuiting inside the store again, but I
realize it's like trying to keep a piece of empty space outside . . . it's like
trying to close off the Diamond Sound of Samantabhadra's Unceasing Compassion,
which intuitively permeates everywhere . . . like trying to breathe anything but
crystal intrinsic shhh air . . . like the man who tried to carry a box of his
native country's air to another land but when he opened the box nothing came
out and nothing went and nothing went in and nothing was added to and nothing
happened.---

EVERYWHERE IS THE PLACE WHERE INTUITION ORIGINATES

. . . .

Ignorance is the absence of enlightenment.
For instance, it's snowing outside; you didnt know that?
You were in ignorance of the snow falling out there.
Now you're enlightened as to the snowfall.
This has nothing to do with the intrinsic lucidity of your Mind.
People crucify a Christ because of Ignorance which is neither due to the absence
      of lucidity in their minds nor to evil.
Christ forgives them because he knows they know not what they do because they
      have not been enlightened---If they were enlightened and shown heaven, at
      once they would cease to be in ignorance of heaven, and cease the killing.
As soon as I've been shown that phenomena is empty, I cease to be in Ignorance
      of the emptiness of phenomena; but my original ignorance of this was neither
      due to my mind's misconception nor to my mind's right understanding.
It was due to the absence of enlightenment.
The only way to "enlighten a mirror" is to put a mirror in front of it . . .
lucidity is its Nature, enlightenment and Ignorance are arbitrary relative
      conditions.

. . . .

ADORATION TO THE MIND OF BUDDHA

. . . .

It only happens when you make it happen---if you touch the wall with your
  fingertip, perception of touch responds from emptiness where it abides in a
    pure enlightened state, obeys, suffers the restraint placed upon its wisdom
      nature, and appears as perception of touch of a wall in your fingertip. After
    the act, it vanished back to Origin Mind.

Dont kill that mosquito. It's like throwing a red hot iron ball against a rubber
  wall, it'll bounce right back at you. Leave the red hot iron ball alone and
    there will be no Karma bouncing back.

      Mathematics is proof of Maya
      Proof of illusionary measurements---
      43 x, equals 392 means x, equals 9.11 but
      this is no proof of existence of X, or 9.11, or
      proof that 43 of them equals the existence of any so-called
      392 of somethings.---The only thing that can be proved by mathe-
    matics are arbitrary qualities.---I weigh so much, am so tall, so thick,
    have such and such a name but can you prove my existence? To prove my ex-
  istence you have first to prove proof. . . . In fact, what a word is Proof---It
sounds like what is what it is, POOF!---

People are afraid to die not because they're going to die, but because they cling
to an imaginary self that is going to die. . . .

FOR DHYANA: Reality is itself, you dont have to discriminate it any more---

MEASUREMENT OF ILLUSIONS AND VARIETIES OF OBJECTS, ARE ONE THING * * * *

OBJECT:- A cup . . . It is what it is
                       It is not what it is
                       Which is it?
                       Neither

Look up MAHAYANASUTRALAMKARA by Asanga (trans. Sylvain Levi).
Also: NARGAJUNA'S MAHA-PRAJNA-PARAMITA-SASTRA
                       Trans. by Etienne Lamotte

Look up the MADHYAMIKA school . . .
    the Madhyamikaratara (LaVallee Poussin) in MUSEON

SADHI-NIRMOCANA-SUTRA, by the great Asanga---trans. from the Tibetan by
                       Abbe E.Lamotte, of Louvain, Paris, 1935
                       (pres.in French)
Also the MAHAYANA-SAMGRAHA of Asanga
SIKSA-SAMUCCAYA, Pub. John Murray 1922
BODHI-CARYA-VATARA---Trans. L.D.Barnett, Wisdom of the East Series, London 1909
DIALOGUES (Silacara)
DIPAMVASA Trans. H.Oldenberg 1879
MAJJHIMA-NIKAYA---Trans.Lord Chalmers Sacred Books of the Buddhists.
MAHAVAMSA Trans. W.Geiger and H.M.Bodl
VIMSAKITA of Vasubandhu (Sylvain Levi trans.)
BODHICARYAVATARA, of Santiveda (Trans. L.Finot)
. . . .
From introduction to MAHAYANASAMGRAHA, by Abbé Etienne Lamotte of the Univ.
of Louvain:- "On trouve dans le Bhasya, chap. 1, @5, l'explication suivante:
dehi mnon par hgrub pa ni de mnon par hgrub paho, 'leur production, c'est leur
production.' Explication superflue a nos yeux, mais utile pour un Hindou qui
saura que le compose *tadabhinirvrttih* doit etre analyze en tesam *abhinirvrttih*"--
. . . ahem

The ecstatics, are, dhyayin

"If the object were really an object, the knowledge exempt from concept
would not be born; without this knowledge, the state of Buddha could
not be acquired." MAHAYANA-SAMGRAHA Trans.from the French by me.
MORE:-
       "Things are not as they appear to be; that's why they are said to be
       inexistent. But because they appear just the same, for this reason,
       they are said to be existent." --- "On one hand it is pretended
       they exists; they exist not on the other. On both sides at the
       same time it is neither pretended they exist or dont exist."

Dolt in French is "sot," in Sanskrit, "bala," which is French patois for
describing craziness . . . "Il est fou comme un bala." (!)

               "Les choses n'existent pas avec la nature imaginaire saisie
               par les sots." --"Things dont exist with the imaginary nature
               seized upon by the simpleminded."

                       * * * * * * * * * * * *
AGGAMAHAPANDITA, is, Illustrious pundit
    "What indeed, O Bhikkus, does not turn out a success for the man of energy?"
. . . .
AMBROSIA, Greek AM-BROTOS, "from the brute"----in Pali "amatam," *not mortal*---
(other shore of mortal) ---
                       Immortal coming-from-the-brute Ambrosia

Every now and then in the gloom of daily living and daily complaining and daily
unhappy horror I get a twinge of joy remembering the original Dharma of Pure
brightness, an ancient ecstasy is hiding in the my-mind-middle-Room-Poorhead

THE VIPASSANA-DIPANI by Maha-Thera Ledi Sayadaw
    "The Exposition of Insight"
Deals with:-
VIPPALLASAS---hallucinations
MANNANAS---fantasies; consciously feigning things to be that which they are not
ABHINIVESAS---firmly rooted beliefs
BHUMIS---basic stages of consciousness from which other states develop
GATIS---stages of going, re-new-ing, faring on
SACCAS---truth, relative and absolute
ABHINNAS---supernormal knowledge
PARINNAS---profound insight

THREE OUTSTANDING CHARACTERISTICS OF PHENOMENA
1. Impermanency   2. Infelicity   3. Non-substantiality
. . . .
CHAPTER II, 27, MAHAYANA-SMAGRAHA
        of Asanga
    Trans.by Jack Kerouac
27.Why is dependent nature* said to be like magic? To remove from sentient
beings all unjustified hesitation as to this dependent nature:-
    How do sentient beings entertain this consideration of unjustified hesitation?
    1.They ask themselves: "How can the inexistent be perceived?" To rid them
of this hesitation, the Sutra compares dependent nature to magic (Maya).
    2.They ask themselves: "How can thought, and mentations that have no object,
be born?" To rid them of this hesitation, the Sutra compares dependent nature
to a mirage (Marici.)
    3.They ask themselves: "How, in the absence of objects, can we undergo im-
pressions that are agreeable or disagreeable?" To rid them of this hesitation,
the Sutra compares dependent nature to a dream (Svapna).
    4.They ask themselves: "How, in the absence of objects, can acts good and
bad produce fruit agreeable and disagreeable?" To rid them of this hesitation,
the Sutra compares dependent nature to an image (Pratibimba).
    5.They ask themselves: "How, in the absence of objects, can diverse cons-
ciousnesses be born?" To rid them of this hesitation, the Sutra compares dependent nature to a reflection (Pratibhasa).
    6.They ask themselves: "How, in the absence of objects, can diverse dis-
courses (sutras) be born?" To rid them of this hesitation, the Sutra compares
dependent nature to an echo (Pratisrutka).
    7.They ask themselves: "How, in the absence of objects, can perception be
produced in Samadhi holy meditation?" The Sutra, to rid them of this hesitation,
compares dependent nature to the moon reflected on the water (Udakacandra).
    8.They ask themselves: "How, in the absence of objects, can Bodhisattvas
whose thought is infallible be reborn voluntarily for the sake and service of
others?" To rid them of this hesitation, the Sutra compares dependent nature
to a metamorphosis (Parinama)."
                    From the French of Étienne Lamotte taken
                    directly from Tibetaine & Chinoi
* * * * * * * * * ** *
MATHEMATICS ON WILLIAMSBURG BRIDGE
    Distance from eyeball to cars, is, 900 feet
    Length of cars on road, is, 12 feet
    Length of cars in eye-ball-mind, is, .04 feet
Feel of cars on road, is, X
Feel of cars in eyeball-mind-body, is,)Zero(0
    Therefore, X equals Zero
            EQUATION:- $\frac{0}{0.4}$ X $\frac{x}{12}$ equals 0X   equals .48   X equals $\frac{0}{.48}$
                    Therefore, X equals 0
                Feel of cars on road is Zero
    ---------------------------0----------------------------

JAN 26 '55---I told David Burnett that in the Transcendental Sound heard in the
silence "there's a teaching going on"---He looked startled, and Stanley Gould
was interested. David called Christopher McLaine a "crazy knot" (which I heard)
but he was saying "nut" with an elegant L.A. accent --"crazy nut"---The Subterraneans seem to be mere quippers, they feel there's nihilism in their quippery
and honor it---Anton Rosenberg, Mason Hoffenberg, David Burnett, Bill Keck,
Sherry Martinelli and Stanley Gould are the chief subterraneans (also Mark
Sacaroff)---For want of anyone else I find them interesting---But they're only
a peg shallower or a peg deeper than my own old gang of subterranean thinkers:
Joan Adams, Bill Burroughs, Allen Ginsberg, Herbert Huncke, Lucien Carr and
Neal Cassady---I find no assemblage to compare with the monks of the Surangama
Sutra: Kaundinya, Upanishad, Gandha the boy, Baisajagara and Baisajattama,
Bhadrapala, Kasyapa and the women Suvarna, Anaruddha, Suddhipanthaka, Gavampati,
Pilankapatha, Subhuti, Sariputra, Samantabhadra, Sandrananda, Purna, Uparli,
Maudgalyayana, Ushusma, Dharanindhara, Chandra, Akshobya, Vejuria, Maitreya,
Sthama-prapta, Avalokitesvara, Manjusri and Ananda and the maiden Pchiti . . .
      These people have no peer for intelligence & charm--- Everything they say
is pure, profound, sad, and beautiful, like empty open space, like inner radiance,
. . . their words and sounds are self-enlightening---whereas with these other gangs,
their words and sounds were not self-enlightening.

Every time you lose something remember that it's because you *have* that you *lose* . . .
      The complaint inherent in my 1951 statement "I Accept Loss Forever" is an
ignorant complaint.

              Upaya skill in teaching is like working on the dangerous
              freight trains---You cant do it drunk and overconfident or
              you'll hurt yourself bad---and you cant do it high on narcotics
              and underselfconfident or you'll hesitate over simple obvious
              switches and waste everybody's time---
P   You've got to be sober and bored
O   Beyond pleasure and pain   O Worldly men,
E   And give them the Word   How fatally Deluded!
M   When it starts to rain
              And tell them the Board
              Was all in Vain.

Stan Getz being called "The Sound"-seeming to be the last word in high
  knowledge, is a generation's ignorance.-

      Say---"I'm a farmer
          I grow Nirvana"   (Buddha said his crop was Ambrosia)
. . . .
SORROWFUL MIDNIGHT
                    The trouble is not as to whether I live so independently I can
walk 13 miles instead of haggling over subway fares, as yesterday, or so inde-
pendently I can go in the desert NOW and ETC.---but that I dont love everyone
equally a coming Buddha, the Six Paramitas & the Diamond Sutra constantly on
my mind, gentle behavior & mild speech---*this,* and no arbitrary teahead visions
of 'streaming ecstasy' or 'solitude is better'----Is this what Buddha has to say
to Maudgalyayana & Sariputra, 'solitude is better'? Be mindful, too, be gentle
and kind. Why get mad at anything when you can very well see what caused the
thing?

      My evil turnabout (what Neal and Gould see as my foolishness) is always
      a going from selflessness back to self . . . . . . the Big Walk was happy
                              but selfish
              (Walk from Greenwich Village waterfront to
                  Jamaica N.Y., 13 miles, 4½ hours)
ERUDITE TOMES ON PARANOIA SHOULD BE WRITTEN BY NUTS

Love everyone equally
Everyone equally empty
Each one a coming Buddha
* * * *_____* * * * *

                                    The Samadhi of perfect
                                            love-filled
                                                imagelessness

Midnight Pacing---The whole universe is one great camp of selves trying to
shield themselves from the truth which is noself . . . . . . You can tell by looking
at rooftops of people in the winter night---
* * *The Planets are Imaginary Separation* * *

            Adoration to the Tathagata of No Consciousness
            And to the Tathagata without words
                    (Samantabhadra)----   *
Practise   *Mad, mad,   *
    Dhyana   *madfaced mad---I . . .   *
        Twice   *
            Daily
                Day & Night   Jan 28 '55 Dhyana- Learned to Sit!
                                                      (without leaning)

The Great Walking Saint
The Cook of the Dharma
The Translator   (some of my titles)   ALSO   The Deafmute
The Explainer   The Imbecile
The Leaner Against Trees
* . *
            JAN 28 NIGHT DHYANA
        Trying to sit upright, dhyana disturbed by physical
        difficulties---All right understanding of Mind Essence re-
        turned by itself---The essence of an erotic thought, the essence
        of the body and the essence of erotic sensation are one essence---An
    erotic thought is a more alluring form than actual dismaying vulgar erotic
experience, yet it's the thought that is the seed of sexual action!---Ignore sexual thoughts and that's more than half the battle---Keep the vitality of your organ
in you, intact---Semen is not an excrement, it doesnt rot but fecundates so it is
a vitality of your physical nature and best kept than continually expelled like
    waste of shame in the general waste of human rebirth Ignorance---No wonder women
    want it!
        Keep it, dont force out your own strength, it is the iron shudder
        of force in your linear loins, man-lion, man.
                                    Would you expel the force of
                                    your chest?
Adoration to the Tathagata
                        who never dies---
Also,
    I saw clearly that I wont get drunk again because in so doing I confuse the
issue as to whether I'm sincere or not, and I know I'm sincere (but weak) but
others are bewildered by my foolishness when drunk---Besides by ceasing to see
others and deal & drink with them I wont have to hear about personality any more,
theirs or mine, because by myself the issue never rises---as to personality, persons, quirks etc., histories of selves, etc.---
    I can write a Full Explanation of the Three Major Sutras (Surangama,
Lankavatara, Vajra), call it THE TRUE STORY OF THE WORLD---for Teaching Work---
As for my personal prose shelf a big 20,000,000-word "LIFE" will do, modern prose
covering every moment of life, "my" life---but why sum up the swimming eyes of
teenage beauties, they come hotfooting one after the other and passing just as
fast to the black cay where corpses bloat,---it would just be details . . . unless
I dharmatize em---but that's in case my "Prose Ego" rages---
    I thought of old Russian Mr. Whitebook, why was he born? why wandering
around? why gooping in his kitchen at 11 P M ?---the truth of suffering, the
cause of suffering, the end of suffering.
                    * * * * * * * * *

TANTRIC FORM FOR MEDITATION----------------

Love Hal Chase equally,	-	SUNDAY JAN 30 .. This is it . . . the day
Equally empty	-	I decide to go forward instead of
Equally a Coming Buddha . . .	-	backward . . . will stop drinking, cold
Love President Eisenhower equally,	-	turkey (if I can do it) . . . Drink is
Equally empty,	-	the curse of the Holy Life---Alcohol
Equally a Coming Buddha . . .	-	is the curse of Tao---I'll be like
Love Mary Carney equally,	-	Reverend Henry Armstrong now---I put
Equally empty,	-	on the cloth this morning in the yard
Equally a Coming Buddha . . . etc.	-	---(damn the cloth)---I felt its

-- dignified hugeness on me---This,
coupled with No Publishing and No Loosing of Sexual Vitality, would return me to
the original pristine state of the child . . . 6 year old Ti Jean seeing the red sun
in the snow windows of Lowell wondering "Qui c'est ca, moi?" (O what difference
does it make?)---Now I'll go to Nin's and help with the new house and prepare
for Summer & Fall in Mexico in a grass hut---Now I'll imitate the action of the
child and like water rule the low valleys of the world----Adoration to the Child.

Lucien Happersberger tells me, 6 months later, "It ees un-fair . . . you Buddhists
have a search for purity among pure things, but we search for purity among the
im-pure . . ." (Parisian Gigolo who knows Genet)(Great sad Sammy Sampas face)

Armed with continence, and with sublime childlike solitariness, and with
unwasted vitality, 33 years old, I go reveal the holy life to men who perish
for lack of knowledge . . .

. . . .

THY SKY
          Brightness is caused by fire; darkness is caused by the arbitrary
conception of the absence of fire. The actual state of illumination in
Supreme Reality is invisible dimness swarming with inner light . . . a Transcendental
Milk.
          Of course brightness & darkness have their origin in Mind Essence ere the
sucking-in of bright-or-dark is manifested in this conditional existence, i.e.,
the sun is a conductor of brightness not the cause of brightness. With the
whole universe bright why should we still see the round sun in the sky, why isnt
the whole brightness the sun itself if brightness belongs to the sun?
          What could you say of the brightness of the sun if there was no sky to
broadcast it? What part of this brightness belongs to the sun, what part to
the sky? Brightness obeys, & brightness is everywhere. It is Thy Sky, Mind . . .
          Every day, dizzily as in an old vertiginous dream, we roll over to the
sun and at night we roll on back to the dimness on the other end. We have sanc-
tified this and called it day and night. Yet the source of this light-refraction
is our own Intuitive Mind; what we see with our eyes is causes and conditions and
combinations and slants and impassable shadows and angles; but the brightness as
well as the darkness are of the same essence as the true fire-essence, intrinsic
empty space; we discern them as bright or dark only with our false imaginations,
our six senses, our habitual ignorance; without this consciousness the Mind knows
no such brightness or darkness anywhere.
          I see the house next door, the cubes of sunlight on it, the blue-bright
sky, the shadows of chimney & gable, and it isnt even really there, it only
appears to be there. Where do brightness and darkness come from, and how do they
sojourn here? How have they been roused from emptiness by the sucking-tube
action of sun, sky and earthslants? In Universal Mind brightness & darkness are
of the same Essence.---
          When the sun goes out, shall the elements of the essence of Brightness
go out and vanish from the universe? The elements of the essence of brightness,
and the elements of the essence of Universal Elementless Mind, is the same
essence . . .   For the appearance of brightness is owing to the mysterious light the
combination of sun & sky combines and transforms, but this mysterious light does
not originate in the combination, it only responds, its place of origination is
beyond the combination in its own one & tranquil essence---everywhere is the
place of its origination.

THY SKY (cont'd)

The sparkling craft of the mind---the universal sparkling intelligence of
the Mind of Intuition---We have a Mind of intelligent luminosity bound up in
six limited senses---For instance two men walk away from a brook and each
one claims the reflection of the sun in the water is following him east, him
west---Which is it? "Because the 4 Great Elements are present within the
pure universal intelligence of the Intuitive Mind, the manifestation of
them responds to your perception of sight." But now you know that your
perception of sight is false; that it is not your perception of Enlightenment. "The Mind of Intuition has universal intelligence and because
of it conception of space is embraced within it but undifferentiated
and thus the manifestation of emptiness responds to the perception of
your sight." This is mysteriously pure and sparkling---'t shows that
space is false, since there's only one Sun reflected in that water,
but now two men assert that the sun is following himself.
THE PERCEPTION OF SIGHT AND SPACE ALIKE ARE FALSE DECEPTION. AND
THEREFORE THE PERCEPTION OF EMPTINESS IS FALSE DECEPTION ALSO.

"EMPTINESS THAT IS FORM,
FORM THAT IS EMPTINESS"---
---A Zen Prayer

It's Saturday morning in China, and I see the fantastic blossom
sparkling in the emptiness,
and intuition smiles brightly everywhere---
the jewel in the lotus,
the transparent crystal clearness of the world.---
The brown mountain in the blue sky
was just a childish
dream

book five

OM MANI PADHME HUM

. . . .

I WAS GOING to make the scornful cultivated comment that "If we are to draw our
information about Goethe from his *Dichtung & Wahrheit,* perhaps we may say that a
man who is cautious in his youth cant be too intelligent in his old age," but
what is this but dreary gray gossip of litterateurs and Gideans---the crystal
jewel of the lotus is all I'm going to discuss . . . this is Right Study.

    I wrote this note to remind myself of the One Leveled Law of the Ratna-
Pundarika, to abandon Many-Leveledness, Faustian Wrongmindedness and cultivated
queer literariness.---

O-------------------------------O
It's quite unimportant also to point
out that the modern emphasis on "sound"
in music, in jazz, and hi-fidelity equipment,
heralds the approach of a music which will be SONIC
rather than HARMONIC in intention----No wonder I'm beginning
to call it noise---

THE THREE DELUSIONS OF CONTINUITY *
1. The conception of the world's existence
2. The conception of the ego-personality
3. The conception of what will happen to one in the future
      (Karma and its forth-coming fruit)

In a bleary bar/ I watched the television/ "Hondo Jones and the Cowboys of Hope"/
what's all this rainy mystery?/ but essence of the immovable no-world/ / / / / /

Since everything is caused then it has no self and no existence--recall the

world, your ego, and the interaction of the two in that imaginary blossom known

as the past---Then what could be more absurd than the future? Inexistent things

blossoming in the gray imaginary emptiness of the thinking-mind.---And here you

go worrying about it, peering about in your mind for imaginary ideas---In the

Seven Streams of Swiftnesses you're doing that even in the present, casting about

for thoughts of your cold, seeking to sniffle and sneeze, which is all a dream

you foolish comfortless self-duping damnationist of the ignorant scene.

* *

----ONE-LEVELED LOTUS------
It's Saturday morning in the Fellaheen Land,
And I see the fantastic blossom
Sparkling in the emptiness,
And intuition smiles brightly everywhere---
Amen the Jewel in the Lotus,
The transparent crystal clearness of the world.
The brown mountain in the blue sky
Was just a childish dream.
Armed with continence, sublime childlike solitariness, and unwasted vitality
I go forth to preach the Tranquil Law.

7 CONDITIONS FOR A BHIKSHU'S WELFARE

1. No business
2. No idle talk   From the
3. No slothfulness   Mahaparinirvana Sutra
4. No society
5. No sinful desires
6. No friendship with sinners
7. Satisfied with nothing less than Nirvana

THE SEVENFOLD   THE SEVENFOLD
   HIGHER WISDOM   PERCEPTION
    . . .   (of)   . . .

1. Mental activity   1. Impermanency
2. Search after truth   2. Non-individuality
3. Energy   3. Corruption
4. Joy   4. Danger of sin
5. Peace   5. Sanctification
6. Earnest contempla-   6. Purity of heart
   tion   7. Nirvana
7. Equanimity of mind

"That noble and saving faith which leads to the complete
destruction of the sorrow of him who acts according to it."

"GREAT IS THE FRUIT, GREAT THE ADVANTAGE OF SAMADHI WHEN SET ROUND WITH UPRIGHT CONDUCT; GREAT IS THE FRUIT, GREAT THE ADVANTAGE OF INTELLECT WHEN SET ROUND WITH SAMADHI. THE MIND SET ROUND WITH INTELLIGENCE IS FREED FROM THE GREAT EVILS, THAT IS TO SAY, FROM SENSUALITY, FROM INDIVIDUALITY, FROM DELUSION, AND FROM IGNORANCE."

The Awakened (Buddha) has realized that life was a dream in his mind.

F O R M   I S   P A I N

A SAMANA, a Quiet Man
"Cut out the love of self, like an Autumn lotus, with thy hand! Cherish
the road of peace. Nirvana has been shown by Sugata." (the Faring-in-Goodness-One)
(the Well Accomplished)
"Too much sleep
* * * * * * * * * * * * brings dullness of mind and drowns out good qualities in deep
      * * * * *   seas of gloominess . . . Restraining our laziness and
THE 4 MAJOR   * * *   sleepiness the brain is refreshed & the thoughts
  HINDRANCES *   purified, and, as we realize Samadhi, the heart will
. . . .   ** be at rest as in a holy sepulchre." DHYANA FOR BEGINNERS
1.Greed . . . leading to *
       passion   *   In sexuality remember that it's not
2.Anger . . . leading to hatred   *   the first time you've put an organ
3.Recklessness . . . leading to remorse * to the test---you've been around a
4.Doubt . . . leading to ignorance   *   long time rubbing & puffing---and
                        *   there's no individual in the matter.

The danger of sin is in remorse . . .   Do the Sacred Thing . . .

Feb 3 '55--WALK IN YARD, cold day zero---Form is pain---It's the dualism of
Ignorance and Enlightenment made this world as it is--Beyond that is the Realm
of the Tathagata, the Norm of Mind Essence, the X, the indescribable crystal
void---If there's no individual in the matter of aligning myself with the Norm
in order to end suffering, then there's no individual in the matter of entering
Nirvana, in the matter of Not-Entering Nirvana but vowing to rebirth, in
the matter of the dream of rebirth itself, in the matter of being ignorant,
pain, and in the matter of being enlightened, freedom and happiness there's
no individual in the matter---
The Tathagata was a Samapatti invention for the sake of pointing out the undis-
cussable norm of the void---The Tathagata neither makes it nor does not make it,
the Tathagata neither destroyed individuality for the attainment of Nirvana nor
did not destroy individuality for being reborn---i.e.abiding as he does beyond
the chain of causation and beyond the first dualistic link (Ignorance-Enlight-
enment, each of which is only a word representing the absence of the other)
he abides in non-dual and supradual Mind Essence devoid and free of any
arbitrary conceptions such as Nirvana, Norm, Rebirth, Individuality or
Non-Individuality, Heat, Cold, etc.
Ignorance and Enlightenment made the world, but it took place in the Tathagata's
Womb. In that Womb Ignorance & Enlightenment are recognized as Intrinsic Emptiness and as being conceptualized due to dual conceptual battle only---Sentient
beings continually ignore the emptiness of the space in the sky due to their
imprisonment in the dualism of form, which is pain---All they see is form and
no-form, not realizing that both are beyond-form and therefore the same---
Different forms of the same Sacred Emptiness---The dreamer who doesnt know
he's dreaming is suffering, we've got to wake him up and tell him he's
only dreaming and stop worrying---Even though we may not know that it's
a dream of our own, which of course we know because we are Bodhisattvas---
when I sneeze I know it's only form sneezing in a dream of pain, the
essence is not sneezing, a big Consciousness-Entanglement-Carnality
is Sneezing . . .
The selfhood that is being reborn endlessly in the dream is strictly a Karma
produce, an automatic leftover, there's no individual in the matter----When the
Roman soldier died alone in the plain, he left the durance that made Edgar
Cayce strong & faithful---Someone died and left that lugubrious hurt spirit
which gave form to me---damn it thorn flap thatthwap it----but there's no
individual in the matter---

There's no individual in the matter of automatic Karma set up
by a chain of Automatons . . .

WITH MY COLD, I EAT HOT MUSH---the parts that have brown sugar in them taste the
same as the yellow sugarless 'flavorless' parts but I can't tell the difference
in flavor, the consistency is one smooth tasteless nose-metallic-blocked pleasant
bowlful of hot mush---My former interest in the taste of the brown sugar is now
a mere echo in that it is a kind of unpleasant chemical effect on the palate!

TASTE THE TAO TRUTH!---The only thing that matters is the mush in my belly to
give me strength to write this so therefore the whole hassle of 'tasting flavors'
is irrelevant---If I could be like this all the time I could completely cut off
contact with all flavors, and bring the Tongue Sense back to its undifferentiated
state in Mind Essence, and there being no more contact with flavors because no
more flavor-sense, my tasting-sensation would become unconscious of its individuality
and would exhaust its considerable Karma and become an enlightenment instead of
an ignorance, because in the other direction, contact ending, with flavors,
sensations ending, desires or attachments to flavor would end, the conception
of very flavor would come to the end of its existence and thus it could not be
reborn and thus could not suffer & die---While I live, there's no individual in
the matter; when I die there'll be no individual in the matter; just causes and
conditions, sense-organs, sense-objects, sense-minds; broken is thy ridgepole,
O house of deception!

> My false mind is destroyed by this deceiving tripleness;
> but my True Mind is clear and free.

--

---FORM IN THE NORM---
Instead of bothering with either one side of the coin
  or the other, throw it away---in the same way,
    instead of bothering with either arbitrary conception
      of manifested phenomena or non-manifested non-phenomena,
        the coin of existence,
                    throw it away----
                        Rest beyond conception.

. . . .

Since each life only means an added death there's no sense developing personal
power---The only power a Rosicrucian attains to, is the power of fooling himself
before he dies---More foolishness a little longer, ---Mere vulgar greed and
attachment, not an excellence in the least, is this argument that while we live
we must live felicitously and powerfully among others---Believers in the oversoul
are always egotistical types---like actors, showoffs, tycoons, etc.---A rotting
corpse there's no individual in the matter, under the enormous emptiness of the
T R U T H . . .

> *In the holy life all you need is food*

Dreams have no hold whatever upon their own source of existence, Mind . . .
  AND SO CANNOT BE PERFECTLY RE-PRODUCED
                - - - - - - - - -
If the world's insanity of ignorance was suddenly cured, its consciousness of
sanity of the True Mind would just as suddenly be recovered, and no matter
whether this insanity of ignorance is cured or not, sanity of the True Mind
is there.-- STOP THE MADNESS

{ Amen the Jewel in the Lotus,   →   The Thunderbolt in the Dark Void
  The gem in the rags.
              If the world stops all killing, robbery and lust,
                the madness will clear of itself, and Enlightenment
                  will already be present. But Ananda objects that this
attainment of the True Mind is coming under the heading of causes & conditions,
"the principle of naturalism." But should the causes and conditions of the world's
ignorant insanity be removed, the nature of its non-insane non-ignorance would be

be revealed; the teaching of causes and conditions here falls short.
  Naturalism is not the cause of Revelation.
Feb.4,1955
*Everybody has a clear mind already, but they're all involved in the
  wrong assertions.*

. . . .

FURTHER, THE INSANITY OF THE WORLD
                  An Explanation   Garner'd from
                        the Ta Fo Ting-shou Leng Yen Ching
                        (S U R A N G A M A S U T R A)
      * Should the causes and conditions of the ignorant insanity of the
    world be removed, the nature of its non-insane non-ignorance would be
    revealed. If the insanely ignorant world has its being according to the
    principle of naturalism, then as its being belongs to its nature so
  everything it thinks cannot be otherwise interpreted than as being the
  natural manifestation of its mind, then why is it by causes & conditions always
frightened and becoming mad and runs to war and follies? Or, if its natural
being causes it to lose its sanity by means of causes and conditions, then why
doesnt it also lose its natural being, by means of causes & conditions? How since
its own being has not been lost (that is, its physical natural being), but
there rises in it the illusion of fright and madness, and its natural physical
being shows not the slightest change (as in the case of madmen's physical heads),
how is it to be said that the madness of the world comes from causes & conditions?
It's completely imaginary.
                  Or, if the insane ignorance of the world primarily
belonged to its nature and it possessed madness and fright from the beginning,
before it suddenly becomes mad & frightened as always, where did this madness
conceal itself?
          Madness is everywhere, and madness obeys. Ignorant insanity res-
ponds to the sucktube of ignorance held up in emptiness and through it is conducted the phenomena which is already waiting in tranquillity and purity and is
Universal. If you hold up the ignorance sucktube, insanity of ignorance obeys and
appears; if you dont, nothing appears, but remains as it is in the Mind of Intuition. (Ignorance is Enlightenment reversed.)
      Delusive thoughts are like a divining rod that'll find insane ignorance.
      Ignorance is merely Enlightenment Hindered---
        Or, if by nature the world is not insane, and its natural physical
          being is normal, then why is it always being carried away by fits
          of madness? or, if the world realized that its natural physical
            being was normal and that it is always being carried away by fits
            of insanity, then the principles of both cause & condition and
              naturalism are mere talk. The aforementioned is what the world
              knows, and secretly holds true.
This really means that sane enlightenment swings on the same pivot as insane ignorance and of a sudden, easily, sane enlightenment flaps over to you---by dint
    of relaxation and intuition, not by effort and naturalistic cause---by one
      crystal millionth-of-an-inch are ye separated from Holy Enlightenment, O
      Fortunate Blindman!!
Enlightenment let us here define as Consciousness of Universal Intuition, which
  is the same as the consciousness of the perception of sight of the spring and
  pool. Where does this consciousness go when there are no causes & conditions such
    as the world and its thinking-minds? Enlightenment which is Consciousness of
      Universal Intuition responds to conditions such as thinking-minds of people in
        the world but these conditions are not its source. Consciousness (the 7th
          Great Element) abides in tranquillity permeating everywhere throughout the
          phenomenal world; at the contact of thinking-minds and Buddha's Dharma
            sartor! it appears in the form of consciousness of Enlightenment which is
            Universal Intuition.
But make not the mistake of assuming that in Highest Reality there is any difference between Enlightenment and Ignorance, they both abide in freshness emptily.

INSANITY OF THE WORLD, concluded
They both abide in freshness and truth.
   When Enlightenment is attained, as soon as the world gets rid of killing,
     stealing, and impurity, Ignorance disappears. But now it is known that both
      Ignorance and Enlightenment are one pure stuff. The Mind Of Originality is
       Invariable, unchangeable, neither green nor yellow, neither in a state of
        Ignorance or of Enlightenment (which are figures of speech), which are
         arbitrary conceptions, but the Mind of Purity yields freely to conditions,
          and phenomena manifested by combination and conformity appears, but the
           Mind of Original Purity and Emptiness, the Mind's Essence, can not,
            because of this, be regarded as coming under any *law* of naturalism and
            causes and conditions. By removing one rack from the sea it will not
             change the sea.
In Buddha's words: "When the mind of Enlightenment is attained, then the Mind
  of variability and Ignorance disappears. But if you keep these conceptions in
   mind simply as arbitrary conceptions, then they are mere whimsical talk."
The mind of Enlightenment is attained indeed! The Mind of variability and
Ignorance disappears indeed! These are mere arbitrary conceptions, and so
  Enlightenment has not been accomplished according to a principle of "natural
  cause."
        So long as you think you will be enlightened because of your efforts,
instead of because of universal emptiness being intuitively self-enlightening
and intrinsically clear of all concepts, you will also ignorantly think that
as soon as your natural mind is developed by your efforts that its variability
and ignorance will disappear, i.e., that it will cease perceiving differentiated
phenomena falsely appearing everywhere. But no, this is the whimsical thought
of a variable and ignorant mind. The non-variability of the True and Original
Nature does not belong to the principle of naturalism (efforts) yet it yields
freely to conditions. If you should think that this non-variability of the
True and Original Mind is a kind of naturalism in itself, that would amount to
making opposites of phenomena and non-phenomena, making opposites of that which
came under combination of causes and conditions and that which did not and saying
that the non-variability of the True and Original Nature is the latter. "Such
thinking is whimsical indeed," says Buddha, "it belongs to a habit of contrasting
dualistic and therefore false conceptions." *Mind & Phenomena are One Essence.*
        A cup is the phenomena of false form in True Mind.---
        i.e., a cup *is* True Mind.
        Plans to "move and change" are the phenomena of false form in
        True Mind.----   Let the eagle fly his own false nose.----

LET INDRA DRY
HIS OWN   The Mind of Invariability and Originality is "empty" while the
PHONEY OCEAN   mind of variability and ignorance "produces" "forms" but
                strictly speaking, it's the same mind-----

      FORM THAT IS EMPTINESS, EMPTINESS THAT IS FORM. See,?

None of the strain of wine in the fun of a kid . . . His blood is rich because unwasted.

There being no individual in the matter, it's not a curse to be depressed about
when the mind seems dull and without thoughts, it's a blessing---the Tao Drag.
    No amount of reason will make men mind, I have to be dragged to Dhyana . . .
    Men grow and forget to play---they scowl over big trucks kids would give
their eye-teeth to play with---Part of man's ignorance is, he doesnt go on playing
when he "grows up"---If he did the world would be wild and Heavenly!

    And man has made no provisions to play, sits around all Sunday
                  drinking
                  coffee

SATURDAY MIDNIGHT FEB 5 1955---*The Dhyana of Complete Understanding*---A happiness
was in me, beyond the happiness of mortality, and neither a happiness nor not a
happiness; and it was revealed and laid bare, not as a result wholly of my
actions (efforts to realize the truth) but because it was already there, with
no beginning, no ending---It was the bliss of knowing that our lives are but
dreams, arbitrary conceptions, from which the big dreamer wakes---What could
be more like a dream, with birth the falling-asleep, and death the awaking
from sleep?---a dream, with beginning and ending---a dream, with that which
is not itself, bounding both its sides--- a dream, taking place in dark
sleep of the Universal Night---I had a clear *physical* realization that
it's only a dream---Practicing meditation and realizing that existence
is a dream is an *athletic* physical accomplishment, now I know why I
was an athlete, to learn physical relaxation, smooth strength of strong
muscles hanging ready for Nirvana---the great power that runs from
the brow to the slope shoulders down the arms to the delicately
joined hands in Dhyana---the hidden power of gentle breathing in
the silence---it's *athletic*---And the big dreamer wakes from
dream-after-dream and wants to keep going back (rebirth in a
new life-body) to redevelop his evil deeds ("cause for regret")
---his good deeds leave no Karma, no need to redevelop, to
redress---but his bad deeds, his lies, lusts, cruelties and
thefts do haunt him and he has to go back and work it over
better, to *Good*---but if he becomes enlightened in the midst
of the dream, he sees all things as arbitrary conceptions
merely, including himself (the personality that has been
assumed in the dream), he realizes that things, if you
dont notice them, dont necessarily exist . . . that they are
illusions that have no hold on Reality---an unconditional
void realization comes to the big dreamer and he
awakes *in the dream*---even before death---and therefore
there will be no more rebirth for the phantom dreamer---
but as long as the big dreamer fails to see that even
Karma, rebirth and death, dream and non-dream and the whole
dharma of Buddhas and Tathagatas, all conditioned conceptual
things, including himself, exist only as arbitrary conceptions
and not in Reality, then the big dreamer will go on dreaming,
perhaps in heaven, where he is not exempt from pain.
* FORM IS DUST AND PAIN *
When a dreamer is enlightened *in* the dream, it means his Karma was
thus intended to reach its end as enlightenment became revealed
---so when he leaves his body and the 5 Skhandhas, and "pernicious
corollaries of egoism" there is no gnawing need to pick up again,
because it is seen there's no need to come back, it is seen that
"to come back" is only a dream, only an arbitrary conception, and there
is no coming back and never was---These are the rough outlines of a
complete understanding of the Truth---I sat with feet comfortably crossed
under my legs, the big toe of my right foot was nestled in the hollow
between calf and shinbone of the left leg---I entered the Halls of Nirvana
and understood---the hosts of Buddhas were there, the Bodhisattvas touched
my brow---I distinctly heard a Chinese sentence sung---I realized that Sages
and Saints are real men with astounding discoveries of the Mind, sitting
plainly in assemblies waiting for supper, but with a smile---like Charley
Parker, I can see a Chinese Saint with Bird Parker's face, Bird's quiet virility
and leadership and faint smile among the cats and arahats---Everybody is happy
as they realize that Nirvana is the happiness that never ends!---and that it was
already there!----Why should the Mahayana Bodhisattvas keep coming back to wake up
the characters in their own dream? (Refer to SADDHARMA-PUNDARIKA SUTRA). Mahayana
contains a subtle egoism, *very* subtle. . . . but wait . . .

Mahayana is the essence of Reality

REBIRTH---HOW IT COMES BACK
Coming back to the dream is like myself when I've been to the Village and
Stanley Gould has scolded me for some silly camp I put down, *I want to go back
and do it over again and redress the silly camp this time*----and this is how the
phantom dreamer seeks his rebirth because of unmatured undeveloped, unredress'd
Karma from the previous life-dream. Thought: "Though it's hard for me to
realize there's no Stanley Gould (any more than there's an 'Heloise' with
whom I had something to do according to my notebooks of 1945), no scolding,
no silly camp, no going back, and no coming-from indeed and no "I" in the
matter, nothing but wholly imaginary *burbujas* possessing no more strength
than imaginary blossoms seen in the empty sky, no more strength than
forgotten images in forgotten dreams under the hill in forgotten cen-
turies long ago . . . Go! Svaha! Be Saved! Take up thy Staff! This is the
Holy Life! . . . nevertheless it's the truth, there was no Stanley Gould,
there was no scolding, the silly camp was a gesture in a dream, I
cant go back and straighten it out because there is no straightening
of gray space and open rain, there's no Jack Kerouac in the matter,
I dont necessarily exist except as an ARBITRARY CONCEPTION . . ."
     * * * * * * - - - - - * * * * * *

LUST AND GOURMANDIZE
The reason why lust is unadvised
is because a man led around by his dong
will not have a mind free to realize that the dream of life is only an arbitrary
conception and so he will go on perpetuating occasion for rebirth
and seeking rebirth himself
            and thus the Ocean of Suffering rolls on and on
            through Kalpa after Kalpa.---But if he escapes
            attachment, how can he be said to be dreaming?
            Attachment to taste of food is like a dreamer eating
            constantly yet the food doesnt taste anything
            and he wakes up hungry. We all know this.

        When Lucien said he was actually an
        ancient ex-Buddha devoted now to the full
        enjoyment and investigation of life, and of Suffering,
        I see that he is really only a dreamer absorbed in his dream.
        The life of an enlightened man is like a dream that is self-enlightening
        in which the dreamer knows that he's dreaming before he wakes up.
There is no way for a Buddha, an Awakened One, to reappear like a Lucien.

        To reap the realization that you're only dreaming,
        live in a childlike, contemplative, unconcerned way in the
        f o r e s t   s o l i t u d e * *

ARBITRARY, is, from Latin *Arbiter,* judge, determiner; from Finnish *arpa,* symbol
        ---absolute, despotic, determinative, tyrannical, decisive.
An ARBITRARY CONCEPTION is one which holds that THIS is not THAT, and THAT is
        not THIS, and a decision of the will is *arbitrated* between the two,
        as in a court dispute between two.
                    BUT--nothing could be sillier, for
        as Chuangtse points out, "THIS is also THAT and THAT is also THIS---
THIS and THAT are both without their correlates----such is the very axis
of Tao." "What cannot be seen by THAT can be known by myself. Hence I say,
THIS emanates from THAT; THAT also derives from THIS.   Such is the theory of
the interdependence of THIS and THAT . . . Life arises from death, and vice versa . . .
The true Sage rejects all distinctions and takes refuge in Nirvana . . . There is
        nothing like using the light."

         --------*********************--------

"I dont necessarily exist except as an arbitrary conception" means, it has so
been ruled, by arbitration of conception, that I exist, by ignorant minds, but
it isnt true in Reality.---When King Solomon presides, he is an arbiter of
dualisms, his position is hopelessly tangled in discriminations and false ideas.
--"This man exists, because it cannot be said that this man does not exist." But,
O Judge, is this necessarily true?---What are your purposes in this brief dream?
Come now, wake up to Reality, remove the iron curtain of the mind and behold the
True, Pure, Unchangeable, Unarbitrary Mind of Originality . . . the full uncondition'd
void. . . . the Universal Essence. . . . the light that is everywhere. . . . Tathata.

"Yielding to loving desires & greediness" but before that there was an appearance
of the objects thus to be loved & coveted, due to Karma, and one attached oneself
to them instead of ignoring them---Karma is Contact.

"EVERYWHERE AND FOREVER . . .
the vast, incalculable number of permutations and changes"
arising from the 5 Defilements of Ignorance, form, desire, grasping, & decrepitude.
"ever-flowing and interweaving together in a most bewildering process
   of manifestation and evolution and involution---"

JETSUN:–
"Accustomed, as I've been, to meditating on this life and the future life as one,
I have forgot the dread of birth and death."
* *
"Make thy body thy temple filled with   * *   THE Unabiding---it isnt here.
gods---make solitude   * * * * * * *   * *
thy paradise"---the gorgeous   *   * *   VAJRAYANA, is, the Diamond Path
songs of Marpa the Translator . . .   * * * * * *   the Diamond Vehicle
*   the Immutable Path

Doctor Sax
   by   ADORATION TO THE BODHISATTVA ASVHAGHOSHA
J.L.Mankind

              * * * -- OM MANI PADHME HUM - * * *
The rays of the mind the real rays . . .

⎰Manovijnana, is, Mind Consciousness   Non-continuance is the
⎱Alaya-vijnana, is, Universal Consciousness   Great Disease

The Tathagata is sometimes called "The Mind-Appearing-One," Manomayakaya,
      or THE MIND-MAGIC-BODY-----

              And so it turns out that the greatest thing in the world
                 is not writing but realizing---Self Realization of Noble Wisdom that
              cannot be written---- From *Writer* I'll go to *Realizer*---

                              --:
WU-WEI, Non Interference *   :-The joyous behinds of the Jazz Age . . .   :
The Sea of Change . . .   :   The most opulent thing---Al putting 2 quarters :-
I dreamed of Ignorance . . .   :----------------------: on his box-arm   -----------*

GOIN SOUTH-- Feb. 13 1955 Dont fight with anybody over possession of a moment---
      much less over an object----
By ignoring life I ignore death----
It's personality makes you forget the Good Law, not your True Mind of Unvariability
Paradoxically, you have to recognize suffering & sorrow to become happy-----
-------------Right Mindfulness, Step No.1---(eat candy when you want to drink---You
            dont give a child alcohol!---you're abandoning a worldly personality
            and returning to the Primal Dewdrop of Orange Morning in Carolina---
            ("How about a drink?"---"I'd rather eat.")

"Heaven and earth and all things are manifestations of existence, but existence itself, comes from non-existence." TAO 40
      That's why both planets in/and space, and perception of sight,
      are arbitrary conceptions of false phenomena.
      The Tathagata of No-Contact, realizing that there is no existence,
      is not sucked into activity.

As long as you supply oil the flame eats---oil is the false conception,
      flame the activity---

*** THE FIVE DEFILEMENTS ***
1. *Individuation* of existence at all
2. Wrong views about its *forms*
3. Conditioning *desire* or aversion
4. Grasping *action*
5. Incompatible formed-up differences' *decreptitude*

            In the pure essence of Mind the formed-up differences are
      mutually accommodating.---In the Karma Dream the formed-up differences
   are mutually incompatible and lead to the defilement of weariness, suffering, growing old, and decrepitude.
                        In all cases make no individuation, be
rightly mindful, and now no views can arise which would lead to a choice and
the action that choice implies, and the consequent falling-apart implicit in
Non-Potential False Mind's Action (Ignorance). *Take good care of your body,
keep the mind straight, and wake up from the dream in holy meditation.*

                  *   *   *   *   *

"The permanent joy of the Tathagata's natural purity"----"The pure essential
mind of non-death and non-rebirth"----"Primal, Enlightening, intuitive Essence"--

In the same way that breathing gets imperceptible, the mind's activity gets
imperceptible, in tranquil samadhi---This is the subtle truth.---"Then all
things will be seen, not in their separateness, but in their (empty) unity
wherein there is no place for the evil passions to enter, and which is in full
conformity with the mysterious & indescribable purity of Nirvana."
      HAIL THE HIGH BRIGHTNESS!
      HAIL THE MIND ROOM!
         NIRVANA OF THE ROSES. . . .

Dont necessarily notice the existence of your own self either---"Raise thy
diamond hand"---Existence is *not,* in the holy bright Universal Mind.----

      IMAGINARY BLOSSOMS IN THE SKY . . . Do they belong to space? Then where in
         space? --- Do they belong to eyeballs? Then how could eyeballs see
         themselves? --- The cause is perception of sight, the condition
         morbid mist.---

Tues.Feb.15'55---I practised meditation at the foot of a small pine in the
woods in the hot sun, with dog Bob at my feet---the Immovability of the
Eastern Heavens!

FROM ABORTIVE ATTEMPT TO WRITE SEQUEL TO TOWN & CITY---"For three months now,
his (Peter's) father, George Martin, had lain buried in the earth of New England.
He who had ushered in his seed, himself was ushered out. Chastised, hopeful
yet sorry as a little child, Peter was going off to whatever was in his fate,
without any idea who he really was and what was really happening. . . . Everything
was going to be "all right" and . . . so his destinations were lined up in this
part of the long night of life like arbitrary road signs set up on the way for
him. . . . But in his heart of hearts he knew it was all a dream, the destinations,
the friends, the families, the plains, his own body-haunted self---pitiful dreams."

I think I'll ignore the existence of the world---just like I can ignore last
night's dream about that old house on Amsterdam Ave & 119th with the crapper
in a dismal cellar---

I, always it's "I"---but I should write about how sometimes I listen to something
I've heard before or watch something I've seen before, in company with someone
else, and how I watch keenly to detect the extent of the imperfection of the
combined report that their own perceiving mind receives---always it fills me
with pity, sympathy, to see they've "missed" a little here & there---always it
must be that I consider my own perceiving mind infallible and huge---These are
the roots of a dangerous egoism but the roots are ever in their grave, as Geo.
Herbert reminds us---To get rid of egoselfhood, how?   By going into a perpetual
life of trance in solitude is all I can see. . . .

Making excruciating confessions of your inadequacy is false modesty---
they should be huge infallible explanations of your child's insight . . .

The forest makes provisions for your purity---it provides grass for your seat
under the tree, but no chairs and bookcases!

It may be that complaints about taxes come about only when people become avaricious
counters----Old men in parks know that everything comes & goes---What complaints
do you hear among the morning birds or rising from the corncob pipes of old
retired workers ?
BOB THE DOG---In the first place he doesnt necessarily exist;
                    secondly he's not necessarily a dog.---
                    This is "knowledge exempt from concept," the Buddha's knowledge.---

BY NOT USING THE MIND, MIND MAKES NO CONCEPT * * *

                Sentient beings ask themselves: "How, in the absence of objects, can
                                                        there be love and loving prayer?" To
A   F A C E   rid them of this unjustified hesitation,
          I S   the Sutra compares dependent nature to
              A   F L O W E R   an ethereal flower."----(JK)

AN AMERICAN DHARMA
     I must give up all ideas of literature as they are established on these
very shelves---
          Proust, Emily Dickinson, Joyce, etc.---and create for the sake
of an American Dharma a fitting new kind of writtenform that will not kowtow
to established cupidities nor at the same time be a piddling Notebook---
          In removing "literature" from my activities now, as in Samadhi,
I must replace it by some form of Nirvana Expression----American Sutras and
Shastras, American Buddhas and Arahats, American Birth-tales and Gradual Sayings
and Aphorisms, American Surangamas and Lankavataras veritably. . . .A large loose
book, built as solidly as a Bronze Statue of the Seated Champion of Samadhi and
yet containing images & ideas as ethereal and magical as the jewel in the lotus
---A Book of Ecstasy, huge infallible explanations of divine child insight---
The Book of the Bright Room---a Swan in the Primal Dewdrop---a pillar-elephant
in the Pearl---a green pinetree in the blue sky---a bed of fragrant grass in
the winter sun-----   the echo of barking dogs ⎱
                      in the wall of the woods ⎰ at night
                                                  the Fragrant Rain
                                                     of Enlightenment

               ----

AN AMERICAN TRIPITAKA
    1. *Sutras,* discourses (i.e.Surangama)
    2. *Vinayas,* disciplines (i. e. Mahavastu)
    3. *Abhidharma,* collected writings   (i. e. the Dhammapada,
                                  the Awakening of Faith, Birth Tales,
AN   * * *   Songs of the Brethren) ---etc.---
    AMERICAN   "Canonical American Writings"
           CANON

The desire-current of ignorance ---
The compassion-current of enlightenment ---
             Ça sera toujours un rêve----I know because of the
             perfect emptiness and perfect endlessness of that sky
             (Dhyana in Woods)----"It will always be a dream"----

           Memory will always be a dream---
           Future too---
           And most amazing, the complete and mysteriously palpable
           present, a dream---always a dream---Pleasant dream or nightmare
           or indifferent images, beyond it all is the Nondreaming Nonself
           of the Tathagata's Nirvana---The blazing void stillness in the
           Center Sangsara---
           My consciousness of the perception of the sight of my pencil is as
           empty as the sky and as perfectly accommodating as the consciousness
           of the perception of sight of imaginary blossoms in the sky---the atom,
           because empty, can be split, so the pencil is of the same stuff as the
           sky and because it's always been, it will always be just a dream---
----

THE CAUSE OF SORROW
  Not realizing that everything belongs to you in essence because there is only
One Essence Universal, but nothing belongs to you in form because what is indivisible by nature only seems to be divided by the unreality of forms and so
  nothing is in form---
           this forest, this grass, that bug, that dog, this leg,
            mind---but their Suchness, Tathagatahood, (not their form,
            Sangsarahood) is mine---the pain of the leg is not mine,
nor the bliss of the dog---
the bug's bugness is not mine, but the bug's suchness is mine---The whole
        universe is mine---Boxes of food in stores are mine but not their forms
           and not their ignorant price-values, but the very stuff they're made
             of, the cardboard, the tin, the beans, the essence of cardboard
              and tin and beans, is mine, as is the sky, the stars, the
                endlessness---but My Self is not mine, only Tathagatahood,
                Suchnesshood, is Mine---Suchnesshood is One, Everywhere
                is a Here----------Bodhisattva Avalokitesvara the Hearer
                and Answererer of Prayer always hears and answers my call
              -----HE JUST SAT BESIDE ME IN THE HAUNTED WOOD----
The peace of the woods, the blissful dream inside the dream---
Golden Forest Room----
              We are One---We Are Already Saved---If "I" am Saved
              so are "You," O Suchness-Ones!---The Innocent and the
            Ignorant cannot be Evil---We're Saved and I have further news
            a-coming---concerning the Unity of What by Nature cannot and never
            will be or was disunited except in poor sentient imaginations---
My hopes of the forest were not high enough---
                the Forest Meditator delights
                in Samadhis of Sweet Intuition
                a n d L o v e - - -

    Maitri, Maitri, All is Well!

And last night, dhyana in the rockingchair in Lil Paul's room, I recalled
   the "mothswarms and ragamuffin dusts of Heaven" among toys of floor but
now in intense silence I could hear it at Last and also the whole house and
all family life I've known, united in the piteous dark of boyhood rooms---
this sweet love reflected in the mirror of the woods---the rich Shhh---

FUNDAMENTAL BUDDHAHOOD--(still the form awhile---the least value
                                              of Buddhism)---

               BUDDHISM : AWAKE BEYOND EXISTENCE
                          A B u d d h i s t H a n d b o o k . . .
                  Or, simply, The Buddhist Handbook

Walkin in Jerusalem, Just Like John . . .

HERE IS EVERYWHERE-- Just like the little bolt or screw in my dream this
afternoon, and I asked Little Paul, who woke me up, where the screw had gone
  and he said,
               "In the air straight up"----*here* is the center of the dream,
                               here is where the screw ended up,
                               here is where the brain and the screw
                                      both originate---
              So
                   with the seemingly blaring confused sounds of the
                 world, the fantastic habit of dividing things is the
                 only reason the sounds seem disparate, differentiated and
                 confused---But it's ONE dream---The Perfect Unity
                                of Mind Essence
                                transcends all divisions---

"All things subject to discrimination have no reality"---(that's why they are
                                                        things)
Nirvana is Universal Mind in purity only because Sangsara (birth-and-death)
  is the Universal Mind in the reverse conception of *non*-purity (tho this is
  essentially false dualism)---yet, and, but, vice versa---The Tathagata of
    Suchnesshood abides beyond Nirvana, i.e., he abides beyond conception---
    and there is no Tathagata---The mind does not cease suchnesshood---The
      sound of suchnesshood is silence---the vision of it is Samadhi---
        Nirvana is not a world in itself that is outside what is seen by the
          mind; if it is the Blowing-Out then it must also be the Blown-Out
          (the Sangsaric candle itself.) *Nirvana being the Extinction of the
          Flame, is also the Flame.*
            "The candle, which is light, is extinguishable only because it is
            light." From THE TOWN AND THE CITY (in youthful praise of Sangsara)
            ---Sangsara is Nirvana only because it is Nirvana---or, as, Life
              is death only because it is life.
                SOCRATES SAID: "THE DEAD COME FROM THE LIVING AND THE LIVING
                COME FROM THE DEAD" (Phaedo).

Planting roots of goodness
In the Buddha lands   . . . .
                          Animals running around, and people on the
                          earth, unaware that it's only because of the
                          Purity of Mind that they are doing this. . . . . .

Potential, dazzling, and pure, is do-nothing---but action sangsaric is done,
dead, dull and rotten! -------- Phantasms, bubble flashes and lightning blooms . . .

                    * * * * * *   * * * * * * * *   * * *   * * *

Look at the empty sky a long time then look at the earth and see if it isnt
one pure suchness that may, for temporary purposes, be called Non-Sky; and
see if it isnt an Indivisible Reality intrinsically the same as the sky as
soon as conceptions cease - - - (this was my Sunday Dhyana of the Sky).

Young girls---burdened with the subject of the seed---

MY TROUBLE---I'm still carrying Buddhism in a special compartment of my
thoughts ---Hypocritical as the devil ---Awake Beyond Existence all the time
must be Anuttara Samyak Sambodhi---

THE HIGH FINAL TEACHING OF THE DIAMOND . . . the natural state is blank & empty

Things have no reality yet we bet our immaculate mind on them---

The Diamond teaches something I dont always want to accept---if I labor to
write a Buddhist Textbook I dont like to be reminded that as long as I entertain
notions of a self, other selves, many selves or One Universal Self I am in
Ignorance of Reality, for, for whom am I writing this book?
    Why should I have to wake up characters in my dream---better to ignore and
forget them since they're not really there in the first place---Nor "I"---
    Ah, it's the difficulty of stilling the *jigotte* in our lives, we want to
stir---like bugs, nervous, muscles, twitchy---full of nameless yens and dream-
hungry hungers and all eyes to see every possible part of the forest in the
dream--not Quietly Potent.

.*.*.*.*.*.*.*.*.*.*.*.*.*.**************************.*.*.*.*.*.*.*.*.*.*.*.*.*.*.*.*.*

MONDAY WOODS
               The uncanny knowledge
                         that I remember now I always have in sleep or
in the void between dreams: CA FA LONGTEMPS QUE C'EST DEJA FINI---"It's been a
long time already finished" (!) ---the great huge drowsy Golden Age sensation
that opened in my brain at this worded realization, as if the knowledge was
older than the world---With the eyes closed only is it truly eerie, eerily true-
and True---This is the Voice of the Tathagata speaking from the Brightness
Beyond Existence, the True Mind, the One Mind,---- "What do we do now?" sentient
beings ask and cry out---"It's been a long time already finished---to understand
that is worth the whole universe heaped with gold---to understand that is to be
awakened from a long dream which is an old dream that's long been over--- to
understand that is to know that the echo and the sound, the sound and the echo,
are really the same empty thing----to understand that it's been a long time already
finished is to go to heaven, and beyond heaven----it's to understand that life
was a dream in the suchness of the Holy Essential Mind of all the Buddhas and
all the No-Buddhas in all the Buddhalands and No-Buddhalands everywhere, here,
all times, now---it's to understand we're not really here, pard." Feb 21'55

    (I am almost beginning to re-discover the secrets of Ancient Buddhism now!)

The Saints of Siam---

Rediscover the ancient dream of man, the sensation of the Golden Age of
Existence, in the details of this man's life . . mine . . . as I cease stimulants
and narcotics, my mind yearns to recreate the Mighty Legend of Duluoz---In
every instant of the drowsy dream so long finished & done---The Paean of a
New American Song---
               A new divine poet
               Instituting a new Poetic Age
         I GOT THAT SINGING FEELING
. . . .

I see the flavor, I smell the brightness--this, impossible, proves that the
sense-mind is not one unified Mind and therefore is deluded into false
division---in other words, the conceptions of brightness or flavor have
no basis in reality---nor do the perceptions of seeing or smelling and
the other four---

. . . .

The self, because originating from sensation and recollection, must
necessarily be subject to the condition of cessation---
"Whatever things proceed from a cause,
Of them the Buddha has stated the cause
And what their dissolution is.
This is what the great Sramana teaches."

The sun, even, is just a collection of gases burning fiercely, and the
fuel will run out---

* * * * * * * * * * * * * *

I, being one with the Chief Ginas,
have found the way of deliverance--

AN INSIGHT BY PROUST:--"My imagination drawing strength from contact
with my sensuality, my sensuality expanding
through all the realms of my imagination,
my desire had no longer any bounds."
. . . .

MIDNIGHT WOODS---
Asking Avalokitesvara for Mind Essence realization, I employed the hearing
sphere and heard the Atlantic Coast Line Diesel 8 miles away, and dogs, and
realized sound is in great waves from its center of seeming origination,
which is a clap-blap motion, that these waves travel thru the air or echo
back off surfaces, are deflected, and like the stars which are in grief
of separation, make empty space & empty phenomena ring with conditional
falsity . . . so I had the sensation of magical liberation from all such
causes & conditions as sounds---then, in bliss, I asked how I could
conquer my form so as to remain in this realization continuously and
there swept over me in answer a wave of such bliss I suddenly realized there was no need for me to rise ever from under that tree---
but then came panic, "I am Jack, my house is beyond those trees,"
---and with that, loss of the Samadhi---Avalokitesvara told me it
is only in High Samadhi that True Mind is attained and has ever
been attained, and only in the desert can Samadhis be truly
held --(THE HOMELESS LIFE IN THE DESERT)
Staring at the dark trees I fancied forms of giant bears, strange
ghost lights, and it was better to close eyes.---When the wind
moved all the trees I saw that they too wished the Answer and
that there were really no trees & the motion an imaginary tzimis--
"*Reveillez!*" my soul cried---"Awakened!"---"*Sur le terrace de la
terre!*"---Bob is ghostly white in the dark woods and I saw he was
a Bodhisattva provided to protect me from fear in my initiatory nightforest
meditations, for without him I would have had heart-thumps---he led me
down the path to my tree, I couldnt see anything but him--- and led me out
of the wood again, white, shining in the dark, a Holy Dog at last--- He
sleeps when I meditate, thinking I'm asleep too---Or else he meditates se-
cretly in his paws---A great Angel of Love is that dog---I'll never have a
better friend or a better servant and guide on the path . . . he is like Ananda,
faithful---I wish I could instruct him---I'll try---Adoration to Samantabhadra
the Tathagata who doesnt Use Words---

I realized I knew enlightenment from all this Right Study but I was not yet
awake to what I knew---Which explains why I still compartmentalize my Dharma,
no Awakened Intuition Constant, just Rational Words so far---

       * * *

SINCE WHAT HAPPENS TO THE SELF IN THE VOID, such as passed-out in a faint,
  doesnt happen to the *self* any more--then what happens this minute, doesnt
    happen to the *self* at all (in this Samsara Kitchen!)   Truly, truly, no "I"
      in the matter---You cant say that death is happening to my father right now
        in "his" grave . . . no individual in the matter . . . and so life wasnt happening
          to my father, neither, as he falsely perceived, while "he" "lived"---Mobile
            pieces of the same imagined lump of impurity, are Men & Angels---
              Yet Poets go on yelling about the brighter day that will happen to them
                beyond life in death, as if there was an individual in the matter
                  even now. . .   A long time already finished, this mindsuchness activity
                    . . . It's only a term of days, no individual life---a frame of passing,
                      ---a dog's life, a dream---a Patient Sigh incarnadined---Sorrow
                      with hair, woe with bones---Fodder for death's Mule, in the bin
                      of dumbbells---Sacrificial offering to nothingness---a hunk of
                      false conception---The dignity of man is in his witheredness.

          You must cure the mind of thoughts and
          of the very thought of thoughts, to attain
          to Nirvana---

  Would you expect a Leader of Men, having won a
serious victory, suddenly getting drunk and becoming
fascinated by trivials and losing that
valuable judgment that made him victorious?
  A drunken Saint is an unseemly thing---

               * * * * * *

     T H E   S I X   K N O T S   *   *   *   *
The unified transcendental sense-mind is inside, receiving messages from the
6 senses, and according to accumulated consciousness of knowledge, takes part
in a constant succession of receiving and projecting, causing and being
effected. This Mind is at base pure, but the senses have tied it in Six Knots.
"You have not yet regained a clear realization of the original and intrinsic
unity of your true Mind.---The same is true as to space. When you leave objects
out of account and think only of clear space, you have no difficulty in recognizing that space is a perfect unity. But when you think of it in relation
to objects, you note differences and also divide up space. But space cannot
be divided simply for your convenience." (True Mind is not divided simply
for the convenience of the Six Senses.)---"It is absurd to question whether
space (or true Mind) is unity or not-Unity. It is the same with your six
sense-minds---whether they are one or six---they are pure Essence of Mind
which'n its nature is as undifferentiated and universal as space.---By means
of the opposing phenomena of brightness and darkness, the natural unity and
tranquillity of your mind is disturbed and deceived, and perception of sight
is registered within the wonderful, perfect and Essential Mind." And inner
perception of sight develops a consciousness dependent on it. "The essential
nature of this inner perception of sight is a reflection of outer sights and
by weaving different sights together there is manifested an undifferentiated,
transcendental organ of sight that is to be regarded as the real substantiality
of the eye-sense. Moreover, there is a subsidiary of this transcendental eye-
sense, namely, consciousness dependent on it, which consciousness is not to be
differentiated from the consciousness of the other senses---of hearing, smelling,

tasting, touching-----, and the unity of which in the Mind's pure Essence,
gives rise, within the mortal mind, to wandering thoughts about every phenomenon."

* * * * * * * * * * *

Poetry---too much horseshit
and phoney poetry---(ON READING
T.S.ELIOT)

I'm going to love everybody and be happy

(NO MORE UNHAPPINESS OR DOUBT NOW)
"Wisdom leads the way to fixed composure
without dependence and without number"---

book six

All that reiterated stupidity, we come running back to it expecting new freshness---the forlorn sidewalks outside bars in cities, in New York, Mexico City, Tangiers---the hopes we had as children now recognized as lost bubbles yet we never take the hint as to the hopes of now---

. . . .

DREAM---near Pine Brook, construction job,
Indian Winos in the rubble, I arm myself
with bricks because of the winos, I climb
a sculptured rubber-tree and tear off hands
but of what avail?   all because of the
money in my pocket---This Restless Blossom
appeared & vanished in the True Mind
---Fettered throughout by dark modifications,
this   Mind of Mortality whose roots
are ever in its own discriminated grave!
     If I were unconscious, I wouldnt know
that I'm in Rocky Mt. and that it was
February 24,1955---thus, I wouldnt know
time or place or that I'm Jack Kerouac---
losing my individuality and consciousness of
it, only the incarnadined hunk of Karma
would remain, pestiferating the unconditioned
void---Awake beyondexistence, seeing
there was no "I" in consciousness and no
"I" in non-consciousness now too, but not
even thinking it, just awake to the fulness
of mind, in undivided quiet . . . with no
cause for regret because of a good and
zealously-good life lived . . . thus, amen,
the Parinirvana would come near.---

          Jazz----promise of some great joy that will
                    never come. (Viz., old King Cole records).

O but Bishop Sheen is proud of his lepers!

                    *

THIS CONDITIONAL AVARICE to go on tasting existence---
Being animals we are excited by animals
and animal activities---and *crave*---and
invent dreams about it---and lick our lips over
it---and then grimly, with final renunciation,
we die---No individual has done it! The animal
is not an Individual in the matter---

Greediness----that's the cause of this utterly-proven-to-be-mistaken desire
to go on tasting
existence----greediness for what
you havent had, as though you hadnt
had it already---Whatever you do will
end bad if it's not the Dharma you
do---pleasant wishes or unpleasant
results, the root is the same, it's the
same imaginary idea in a dream and
dont forget it.---

> So why go to Africa?
> Go to India, rather.
> Why see Burroughs or Bowles both?
> See a Guru rather. Or no one nowhere.
> Why go to Frisco?
> Al Sublette, chow mein, port wine---
> Like as of old
> Melaye in Lowell, peanutbutter, milk---
> Combinations in the sadness---
> Greediness to dote on huge Self,
> Leave that ignorance to the grave.
> May Jean-Louis retire quietly
> And write the world's Old epitaph.

BEWARE OF
HAPPY THOUGHTS
OF LIFE!

I wanta go to Tangiers, I want girls, I
wanta write the biggest book in the world,
I want spring to come, I want, I want---
Wanting, I get; getting, I lose; losing, I
suffer; suffering, I die---

> NOT WANTING, I DONT GET
> NOT GETTING, I DONT LOSE
> NOT LOSING,   I DONT SUFFER
> NOT SUFFERING,   I DONT DIE SUFFERING

This is
Indifferent
views of Tao

I give up greediness & retire to a
 --------Mind Farm--------

"Take this gold and these gems, and go and buy landed property,
seeing that ye have lost heavenly riches. Buy yourselves purple kirtles,
that ye for a little while may shine as the rose, that ye may speedily fade.
Be flourishing and rich for a season,
that ye may be poor forever."---AELFRIC's Homilies
> There's your greed for worldly Pops coming
> after the vision of Nirvana---!

* * * * * * * * * * * * *

> "Verde que te quiero verde.
> Verde viento. Verdes ramas.
> El barco sobre la mar
> y el caballo en la montaña."
> LORCA

"Life must be lived out courageously and gayly even though the individual be shattered," this, friends, is the Great Idea of Ignorance---(incidentally, it's a very *modern* idea, it's Lorca's idea, drunken newspapermen's idea, Hollywood idea, Atombomb Idea)---By this belief, men come again & again to grief but "gayly, courageously" (they like to think)---they hate to admit that the Self has no reality---

> O Jean-Louis, teach and educate!
> Stop hesitating, foolish lamb!
> MEN PERISH FOR LACK OF KNOWLEDGE

Sir Thomas More's *Utopia* nevertheless makes provisions for the perpetual chaining of slaves---I have found nothing to compare with Buddha's mighty sweetness---
Outside Nirvana is nothing but False Pops---
  Fantasmal Tsorises . . . mere hallucinations of
  madness - By nature Creation is mad.

. . . .
Your business is with the Dharma!---the rest
is dream-pops.

> Dont believe it's just dreampops?---then what
> about your old thrill about Joe Martin
> stealing trucks in the spring night? about
> you coming home from the Rialto up by
> the library on Moody Street with an imaginary
> movie crew and you the big director?---
> what happened to those two tastes of life's
> false heroin? to the "individual" who held
> to them with then-concomitant energies, as
> if absorbed in a particular section of a dream.
> Come now, dreamer, awake! Reality is Empty!
> The reality then was not the images, nor now!
> Life, what you call Life, is a cunning trick,
> sanctified by men and fools and what you see
> before you is the selfmade prison cell of the
> false mind . . . the selfmad prison self of
> the fault mind---the pelf-sad poison
> elf of the forced hind---the pisspoor party
> delf of the soft mind---Cut it! Anyway
> you slice it, it's a manufactory most of
> it space---very strange face this place---I
> seed it before, in Heav---Everywhere I
> look, the cunning thing is waiting to be
> explained, saved, and so dissolved---
> > "Thou Who Holdest the Seal of Power,
> > Raise Thy Diamond Hand,
> > Bring to Naught,
> > Destroy,
> > Exterminate."

Reality Isnt Images

ALL SENTIENT BEINGS ARE COMING BUDDHAS BECAUSE THEY ARE COMING NOBODIES

* * * * * * * *

Under the infinite stars suddenly tonight hearing the diamond sound I realized "How glad I am to be alive to dig this starry universe!" then "But it's not a case of being alive, and the starry universe is not necessarily the starry universe" and I realized the utter strangeness and yet commonness of this.

In the desert I will know
How universes grow
And what makes diamond sounds
Gentle without bounds.
What I hear in heaven is what I hear on earth.

TODAY, SATURDAY FEB.25, without it looking like much, I think I experienced
the deep turning-about mentioned in Lankavatara and Zen.   Little Paul and I
went to a sharecropper's farm and found no one there but a little lost pup
on the porch. He wailed piteously when we left him there by the subterfuge
of running away. He was hungry too. I thought "What's the use of all
this suffering? Why was he born?"
       What are complex literary lifetimes like that of Laurence Sterne but
       a more complicated form of dog's life? I looked at little Paul,
          trying to amuse himself in the sea of suffering by watching Television
            shows in his little rocking chair. "Poor little boy!" but suddenly
             I realized the impermanency and the very arbitrariness of the
                existence of this poor little boy---THE STREAM OF EMPTINESS THAT
                  HAD MATERIALIZED HIS IMAGE---like the puppy, correlates of sensation
                dont make an individual and puppy and boy are mere correlates of
                sensation.
                Why had this happened, this ignorant gathering of composites
                to make suffering?
                So the suffering isnt any realer than the end of suffering
                after death or before birth. There is no world in truth,
                and so no suffering; the puppy wailed because of the delusion
                of suffering occurring in a set of correlated sensations.
                Looking at the empty sky you see nothing but imaginary
                blossoms, and this is the world and existence and suffering
                and joy too---dream-pops.
                      The truly enlightened sensation stayed with me, that we
                      and all this are but phantoms printed across the air.
                      Looking at the infinite stars, I thought "But why should
                      the universe be so vast?---But who said it was vast?---
                      Why should I be so small? Who said I was small?" Common
                      and pathetic, the sight of stars raining down on trees
                      in this dream mortality.
                      I feel that there has been a deep turning-about in me
                      TODAY because of the persistent recognition of all this
                      created phenomena including myself as imaginary blossoms.
                      There is no Universal Self responsible for this, otherwise
                      there would be nothing seemingly unpleasant about it. It
                      is Ignorance itself and if Ignorance is dispelled it is
                      truly seen as not being there since it is only empty
                      phantoms printed in the air. So I conceived the idea if
                      I went to Tangiers and wrote "Visions of Bill" it would
                      be just another imaginary blossom like *Tristram Shandy*
                      or a dog's piteous wailing, *and so I could do it anyhow.*
                      But mindful am I that this turning-about has come to me
                      due to accumulated purity and merit and quiet meditation,
                      and not due to self-agreed compromise with defiling
                      concepts and decrepitudes of drinking and drugs, as before
                      in the writing of "Visions of Neal." But Bill is so funny,
                      and funniness so strange, and the world such a blossom,
                      and time on my hands to do either or both do-nothing and
                      do-things, I conceived the idea of teaching the Dharma in
                      more ways than one, after this present book *Buddha Tells Us*
                    (Begun Feb.18). Now, having written this, the haunting sensation
                of the world's unreality, momentariness, and pitiful sorrow has
             been somewhat dissipated into thin air, and again the world seems
        solid and real, like one returning to a recurrent dream.

HO FERRYMEN!
THIS PASSENGER IS READY!

It's all *thought*---
   THE MIGHTY VOID
       Prophet, go forth, drink no more, teach men!

         Jean-Louis' connection with English Literature:
       "The emigration of the Briton to Brittany was of high
       import to English literature" (by submitting Brythonic
       myths to the influence of neighboring Norman Romaunce,
       in one instance.)---The Kerouacs & the LeVesques . . .

No cause for regret, no continuity, nothing left over to be destroyed---this is
the advantage of the holy life, what is realized on waking from sleep & dreams
and all dreams are now seen in their true light as nightmares.
     | Multitudes shall scream in cities ever
     | But the desert hermitage is peaceful;
     | Hydrogen Bombs shall fall on New York,
     | London, Moscow, Paris and Peking
     | But the solitary sage will rest.

                                     Visions of Neal
Buried in unfathomable dark   &&
The cock calls rosy hope---   Visions of Bill
Blood-lout moans for morn,   ---the strong
For suspendered pump Pop trap   peasant and the
                                  weak aristocrat---
     *   *Man*

. . . .

Insights in Dostoevsky's *"Ridiculous Man"*;---"I suddenly felt that *I did not
care* whether the world existed or whether there was nothing in existence anywhere.
I began to perceive and to feel with my whole being that I had *nothing before me.*
At first I kept thinking that still there had been a great deal in the past, but
then I realized that there was nothing then either, that it had only seemed so.
Gradually I became convinced that there would never be anything. Then I suddenly
stopped being angry with people and almost ceased to notice them. Indeed, this
became clear in the most trivial accidents, for instance, it would happen that
I would bump into people when I walked in the streets. And not from preoccupation:
what did I have to occupy me then, for I had completely ceased to think: nothing
mattered. I might have solved problems well; yet I did not solve a single one,
many though they were. I *did not care* any longer, and the problems faded into
the distance.
    "And it was after this that I discovered the truth . . . I just sit and dont even
think---thoughts wander through my brain & I let them free . . .
    "Why then did I suddenly feel that I was not indifferent and that I pitied
the little girl . . . ? . . . . I felt clearly that life and the whole world depended on
me . . . Perhaps I myself am the whole world and all these people . . . Once you recognize
truth and see it, you know it is the truth and that no other exists or can exist,
whether you sleep or live . . .
    "I was boundlessly and infallibly certain and believed that everything would
immediately be changed; and so then my grave suddenly opened . . . I grew still
with delight at the thought that I was not afraid . . .
    "I had experienced complete non-existence and so had shot myself through
the heart; and now I . . . still *was* and existed . . .
    "A dream? What is a dream? Is our life not a dream? I will say more! Let
it be so, even if paradise cannot ever come or exist (*after all, I can understand
                       that!*)"

269

DOSTOEVSKY (CONT'D)
"I will still preach! . . . The important thing is to love others as yourself . . .
And that is after all only an ancient truth . . .   Everything will be arranged . . .
And I will go on!"
                    Dostoevsky's flaw is emotional Russian attachment to human
pathos---(flaw as a Buddha)---And the whole flaw of false Christian charity
(infatuated clinging, the tears of petulant girls, the tantrums of sticky
melancholia, the hungering mouth, lust & rebirth incarnadined) can be seen in
these words: "On our earth we can only love sincerely with suffering and
through suffering. We do not know how to love any other way" (he says proudly)
"and know no other love." This human love is Ignorance. "I want to suffer
so that I can love." This is selfly . . . it contains the stench of masochism . . .
it wants to rub up against legs, snivelling & squirming, yet has in it that
essential central coldness that can only be attributed to the Snake . . .
"I desire, I thirst in this moment to kiss, weeping tears . . ."
                    It's like DeLubac's silly criticism of Buddhist Charity
as being devoid of "Suffering Giving"---- O Noble Prince of the Sakyas!
Your coolness! Your true love, so quiet, remote, beneficent! The truth is
the only Gift. . . . and the truth is Non-Suffering! The only True Love is
                                        Silent Love.

        Transport of Mind

Tao isnt enough---Buddhist Solitude finally----
for though a man recognize the unreality of "self"
and all its pernicious corollaries of suffering,
others dont and seek to impose their "selves"
with that desperation which at first is seen truly
by the bhikku as pitiful and then as *dangerous*---

The general emerald sea. . . .

Love everybody no matter what happens, but it goes without saying:-
                    LOVE & LIVE ALONE---
                    or, Stay By Yourself

Insects in the Snow

        Self Be Your Lantern

        : ----Wake Up---- :

* Finders Keepers, Fools---(wealth of dead bhikshu)
  I'm not as big a fool as I used to be, I'm a smaller fool----
            O gone! Indefatigably gone! All things! Already gone!!

    "Above form & momentariness"---(True Mind is)

Transcendental Intelligence, is, ARYAJNANA . . .
Like Universal Mind (ALAYAVIJNANA), Intuitive Mind (the MANAS), which is a
mingling of both identity and perceiving, cannot be the source of error.
* *
            I "think that I have a self-nature of my own" and so
            the hackles of self hang on. ME-TI-POUSSE-SELF

SAMADHI OF MOONLIGHT EVENING WOODS---
A dhyana, rather . . . characterized by tremendous
satisfaction with play of moon and clouds, of
woods, warmth, peace, fore-view of future
bhikshu joys of open life in Mexico woods---
"It wont be Mexico, just the terrace of earth."
I prayed fervently---spent 1½ hours with
legs crossed, peacefully, uncrossing them three
times to recirculate blood---Left only because
didnt want to worry family---Will
go back tonight Midnight---Dissolved part-
paranoiac worries, thought of "Forgive" (the
soft word like a pat on the head)---Heard
Lil Paul calling me across the night far away---
(at house backdoor)

> "The differentiated emotions of your mortal
> consciousness are only passing phenomena." (Sur'ama)

----
*"Wake Up"!---and I see the tall trees of India, where cobras and bhikkus
marvel at the Buddha's Awakening in the misty heat of the day . . .* an ancient dream.
. . . .
> *"That's pure lotus,"* say, to imply,
> "that's a clear statement, my friend."----

THE 2 FUNDAMENTAL ILLUSIONS
    1. Deaths & Rebirths
    2. Fear of Impermanency
---but hold fast to the Permanency that the Eye of Dharma perceives.

* * * * * * * *

Government---Pay increases for prosecutors, there's your story---
    Tax-slash battles in Congress bringing down the saving of the people
from $1.80 a month to 90 cents a month, or 23½ cents a week, the "tax-slash
battle" and the paper and time consumed costing $1.80 a second . . . Like radio
comedians now that radio has declined to the status of the covered wagon,
congressional men now goof and fluff seeing that governmental responsibility
has also declined to the status of the covered wagon with the onrush of
International Universal Totalitarian Police State'ism----
    Pay increases for prosecutors. . . . Soon the populace will be
divided in three:-
        1. The Criminals in Prison
        2. The Disabled Set Aside   . . . . both SPOON-FED

    and 3. The Adjusted at Work, ... SIPHON-FED
    Networks of roads, birth and death unending.

* *
How silly of me to think of going to Ezra Pound
in Washington, as though I had to sell Mind Essence
which is neither empty nor not-empty. "It matters not
whether you interpret the center of reeds as emptiness or
as non-emptiness---either would be a misinterpretation.
If anyone is puzzled by the saying that both are false,
it is because of his ignorance. If one is not puzzled,
it is because he has attained emancipation."
All I'd have to say to Pound is "Wake Up" and he,
in exchange for that, would say that my prose & poetry stink.
Well, supposing it really does stink in the long run: the truth
is still the truth.

In fact every created thing finally does stink,
it's nature to die and decay . . . today we read Florio's Montaigne
without much enthusiasm but it was the greatest work of its time,
and the Surangama Sutra, greatest known writing in the world,
will finally come to a culture that will omit to translate it and
it will come to its natural death; but the truth of the origin
and destruction of all things and the non-origin
and non-destruction of the Tathagata is still the same; all that will be lost,
is the particular combination of explanations in the human Surangama---
An inhuman, Martian, space-planet, otherworld Surangama is coming
and already accomplished and already known and also already dead
and stinking in decay---   THE BUDDHAS ARE AWAKE
                            BEYOND LIFE AND DEATH

    *

Possible Title: THE TATHAGATA IS AWAKE

It would be better to have no life with any purpose,
than to have my life with its purpose of teaching
enlightenment; just as it would be better
to have no life with any ignorance, than
to have life with Ignorance, in this world.---
Badly said but true.
        Therefore my life and its purpose
        Is intrinsically a no-life & a no-purpose;
        Just as,
        The world and its ignorance
        Is intrinsically a no-world & a no-ignorance.
Can you understand? And "my life" is "all life";
and "my life" is the "whole Dharma"---Can you understand?
---And Dharmakaya is the only Reality.
    Blast!---Open!---See!
    Wake up!

I'm not Jean-Louis Kérouac the Writer
But just a manifestation of the revelation
Of the single Buddha-vehicle,
As explained in the Lotus.---
All things are Buddha-things
Because they are no-things.
                (-------------------------------------)
                ))))))))))))(((((((((((((((((((
o o o o o o o o o o o o o o o o o o o o o o o o o o o o o o o o o o o o o o
ALL WOMEN WANT TO GIVE REBIRTH, because of a secret fear
  of being barren; yet the world has no more reality
    than a barren woman's child.
                        Refrain from looking (at women);
        a snare and a delusion are her contours, which are interchangeable
          with specious space; lust-attraction is mutual, and mutual are
            ye victims of Karma; made by Karma ye shall be removed by Karma,
              with no "I" to say Nay in the matter, O ye victims of Karma;
                find your way in the dark, keep aloof from involvements
                  of lust agreement.
                    You cant be happy straining in the emptiness to gratify
                      ungratifiable senses---this is pain! There is no appeasing
                        the wild teeth---
                          The cup of life is a bottomless horror, like drinking & drinking
                            in a dream to slake a thirst beyond reason and unreal.
                              Look at the empty sky!---grab greedy fistfuls of it,
                                cupiditous man!---

WOMEN(CONT'D):-
Hack and kill the unkillable, haunted fool!---
    Your loins be sprained, and there is no fornicating it! (no finding it)---
    Fill your ear with endless noises, clack your tongue with endless
      chattering, and everything is empty everywhere & forever.
        The mind is fool and limited, to take these senses, petty thwartings
        in a dream, as reality; as if the deeps of the ocean were moved
        by the rippling wind on the waves.

Do not be awed by the strength of men's ignorance.

A P O E M
    The trash is out of sight and buried,
    The garden ploughed,
    And on the stove an enormous pot
    Of pork and beans.

Thou art wanted, O Lord,
  thou art wanted---

March 2 '55, standing in cold moonlight woods and looking at lovely glittering sky
I had the great thought "You cant fool me, universe"---for in the great peace
and stillness I knew it didn't really exist except as momentary manifestation---
    But I have to walk the path in life---I'm stuck in the dream.

----

o o o o o o o o o o o o o o o o o o o o o o o o o o o o o o o o o o o o o o o
NOTES FROM READING BOETHIUS   ---The Christian religion is a partial realization
✳   of Mind Essence, in that it recognizes (for
the first time outside of Buddhism) divine substance of divided-into-three-parts
etc., chiefly divine nature which is unconditioned, and "earthly nature" which is
conditioned, subject to sin, and mortal.
    Prior to this, religions in the West, I mean in Egypt, Greece, elsewhere,
were concerned with the deification of human notions of excellence; now there
is the pure deification of notions beyond human excellence; just as *mind essence
---Immortal Mind Essence---, being the inconceivable purity, is not to be
qualitively compared to dark-fettered Ignorance.* "The human mind is not able
to understand," says Boethius, the divine mind---*the discriminating mind
of self does not understand Universal Immortal Essence of Mind which transcends
self.*
      "Abiding from all eternity and unto all eternity
without any change,"
        says Boethius of the divine nature,
        but then in his human ignorance he immediately
        anthropomorphizes it, calls it "Him," and calls
        the creation of this world of birth-&-death "His Will."
        What they call divine nature, is a vision of Mind Essence,
        and what they call "God's Will," is a vision of Ignorance.
        For the Buddhist, "God's Will" is Ignorance; "God's creation,"
        this piteous samsaric world of debris and corruption
        and trash. (In reality neither trash nor non-trash, but
        divine nature, the Untellable Light, the Perfect Ecstasy.)
        "Nor did God produce the creation from his own
        substance," continues Boethius, "lest it should be thought
        divine by nature," which is piling ignorance on ignorance,
        insult on insult, actually; *the world is neither divine by
        nature nor not divine by nature, because its existence
        is not based on the unconditional freedom of the mind.*
        In other words, the question doesnt arise as to whether
        momentary things of decay, are of one impurity or not;

Boethius

just as you wouldnt question whether open space is of one purity,
divine by nature; or not of one purity, not divine by nature.
      He says that God made the world because He wanted something
"which helped his will by the existence of (its) independent nature."
Creating the world was an act of Ignorance and so was the reason
for doing it Ignorance, to create creatures of imperfection
just so they can be perfected in Heaven when originally
they were perfect anyhow in states of non-existence beyond
all arbitrary conceptions of perfection or imperfection.
Sounds more like the work of a man, creation,
than the work of God . . . that's because it's the work of Ignorance
and Man and his imagined God is Ignorance personified.
      "By his word God brought forth the heavens," says Boethius.
Perfect void being the intrinsic reality of universal mind,
all God would have to do to "create the Heavens" is defile perfect void
with one word and "Heavens" appear as arbitrary conception.
That wasnt hard. Then with the creation of the earth,
the arbitrary conception of "space" appears, and "time," and life & death,
and bright & dark, and motion & stillness, and contact & separation,
and heaven & hell, and all ye dualisms and pernicious banes of false imagination.
Have the deeps of universal mind been disturbed by the licking of
these little waves?
                  "In heaven all things are beautiful and arranged
in due order," Boethius says, and this is, in a manner of speaking,
limited, a vision of Nirvana Blown-out-ness (wherein there is neither beauty
nor ugliness but *be-blowing-out* of both) (and neither arrangement nor the absence
of arrangement but beyond both.)
                  Boethius then says that God breathed reason and freedom
of choice into man, so man could struggle to regain perfection in heaven from
which the Fallen Angels were cast out because of pride and envy for the Godhead;
            for lust and cavil
               the angel fell . . . ;
                              but what kind of freedom of choice is this,
having to walk the path of life with a body? Might as well walk the plank
for Captain Pirate. If God were the Creator, and could only create from
the only inconceivable substance, he would place no such restraints on himself,
unless he created in Ignorance, in which case how can he be called God, the
Divine Name?
                  Eve is called Adam's "consort," and Adam's lust "the children
of his loins." Adam is guilty of disobedience to the command of purity.
The sweat of man is inherited from the sweat of man's lust.
But in the Jewish Testament the blame is put on an arbitrary apple,
on the arbitrary concept of disobedience pure and simple, instead
of the anthropomorphic vision of a God-Father who has laid down rules
not to be disobeyed at the cost of punishment. These are terrestrial projections
into the field of origin, completely childlike & innocent, like the conception
held by savages as to the nature of origination, always based on their own
imaginary experiences. "All such notions as cause, succession, atoms,
primary elements, that make up personality, personal soul, Supreme (savage
or benign) Spirit, Sovereign God, Creator, are all figments of the imagination
and manifestations of mind." The conception of True Mind, the Universal
Immortal Perfect Essence of mind which is the pure substance permeating
perfectly throughout all manifested phenomena and all that is not manifested
phenomena, is based on the absence of any such conception as the conception
of True Mind: it is conceptionless, original, ultimate, in a state of blankness,
that is to say, in a state of immediate present entire ecstasy: and so that is
why, being the Truth, the Truth has not been grasped by the world, which rather
turns to incomplete, imperfect & contaminated explanations based on their own
imaginary experiences. For if Ignorance rules the world, as can be seen as long
as it exists, then Ignorance rules the religion of the World.

BOETHIUS (cont'd)
True Buddhism has actually, by nature, remained unrevealed, because of the false imagination of very existence.

       True Buddhism has only been mentioned by the Buddhas because, being an explanation of that figure of speech "Existence," it is also just a figure of speech.

       The Truth is so Vast that it can afford to say that it is only a figure of speech.

       The Truth is so vast that it can afford to say that there is no Truth.

       There is neither Truth nor Untruth, only Universal Essence of Mind.

       What is Universal Essence of Mind? The question is Universal Essence of Mind, the thought of the question is Universal Essence of Mind, the essence of the thought is Universal Essence of Mind, and the words, usages, pencil, paper, print, empty space, perception of sight, reading intelligence, and their opposites which are no-words, no-usages, no-pencil, etc., together with the answer to the question, is the Universal Essence of Mind, i.e., everything and nothing, nothing and everything, all that is thought, is Universal Essence of Mind.

Boethius says: "Though by dessert of nature men were condemned, yet God by making them partakers in the hidden mystery, long afterwards to be revealed, vouchsafed to recover fallen nature."
    This is a childlike vision of the recovery of the original nature that takes place when the false mind is discarded and the true Mind is revealed thereby.
    The Christians call it Grace but the Buddhists simply know that True Mind is there----that salvation is inherent by nature by virtue of the existence of True Mind----the *Avatamsaka Sutra* says that the intelligence embodied in the true nature of all phenomena is to be accomplished in no other way than by full Enlightenment----True Mind can be revealed simply because it is there----

       Now God descends and meddles in the histories of countries, now you can see this "God" as the product of a historic race, a projection of themselves:---as though Universal Mind, like the deeps of the sea, were to discriminate the different ripples on the surface and rearrange them---What a tedious fairy tale! Isaac, Jacob, marvels, marbles, Noah and his floating camp, Moses and the Book and Rock, Aaron, the barren women----one vast tale of little ants crawling on the surface of a sandpile, propped together by deceits and snarling and spitting forth rude meat and wrestling with angels in the night----swollen with pride finally slaying the holy ones.
    Some ants must have sad eyes.---
    To connect the Son to the Father it was necessary in the legend to be certain not to see Him issue from a spitting penis. For the snake is the symbol of Satan the Fallen Angel.
    Yet snake is innocent nature,
               quite kin to doves.
    The dove of Baptism, the purification and ordination for the holy life, the life to be spent in knowledge of impermanence, suffering, and unreality of the world except as it is an issuance from God's Mind . . . here Buddhism and Christianity almost kiss . . . For to the Buddhist the world is a manifestation of Mind Essence, due to Ignorance, the "Fall" implied there, but being a manifestation it requires a purified life to abide in the realization of manifestation and epiphany and not to grasp at false and delusive visions of phenomena as real, as abiding, as blissful source.

BOETHIUS (Cont'd)
>Boethius calls Baptism the "saving truth of the teaching"---
>"Grace, which is won by no merit, since it would not be grace if
it were due to merit"---the same interpretation of Grace as a Buddhist might hold,
i.e.,"Enlightenment is not subject to causes and conditions." ("Blessing and merit"
(are not looked upon) "as being a private possession, but the common possession of all
animate beings.")

>The head of Christ ascending into Heaven, in order that the other
members might of necessity follow where the head has gone," the Christian Cross, the
Tree, proves that whether Buddhist or Christian men are sufficiently enlightened
intrinsically within to know that the world must come to an end because it is impure
and a curse, that the incessant round of death & rebirth, suffering and decay, lamentation,misery,old age,despair,grief,fear. . . . it all must end.

>"And recover their first state by the bliss that is to be," says
Boethius of men saved and the cessation of the worldly life.

>"All, therefore, that the faithful now expect, is that the end
of the world will come, that all corruptible things shall pass away." (And all is
incorruptible).(because possessed of the Common Essence).
>>MARCH 3,'55

>p.s.
>>The "food and labour" Boethius
>>foresees in heaven will have to be
>>pretty damned ineffable. (joke)

o o o o o o o o o o o o o o o o o o o o o o o o o o o o o o o o o o o o o o

BY SEEKING TO TAKE THINGS BY FORCE YOU GOT NOTHING:
IF YE HAD ASKED, YE SHOULD HAVE RECEIVED
said God to Adam and expelled him

o o o o o o o o o o o o o o o o o o o o o o o o o o o o o o o o o o o o o o

Men use work as their
protection---Work   *--- Thought Digging Ditch ---*
isnt as innocent   The earth is an intrinsic grave
as it looks---   --
Uncle John
would do better
praying all day,than puttering around in those protective overalls . . .

>- - - - - - - - - - -
>>Priest in the Street---that's the
>>Yellow Robe, the Eastern, true idea of
>>a priesthood---Now I remember it in an old
>>dream---Priests not in black but yellow, not demanding
>>respect but meek and humble,---their dignity like a flower, so
>>that no one crushes it---

· ·
Hsuan-Tsang,walked across Gobi Desert,and Sinkiang,to Samarkand; returned from India
afterwards with books & manuscripts & is responsible (with disciple scholars) for
1,000 Buddhist volumes---it was just I.
···
>>IN JAPAN
>>Shin Shu Buddhists---ceremonial
>>>popular---46,000,000
>>>Zen Buddhists, aristocratic, meditative, 9,000,000
>>>Shin Shu priests marry
>>>It's Japanese Baptist Buddhism

When you get to see everything as the ripples
of phenomena on the surface of the deeps
of Mind, and understand that the rippling
waves on the surface of the sea belong to the
bottomless the sea, then you're happy whether
alive or dead, happy whether drunk or
sober, because you've become Eternal.
     Happy all the time---
     Phenomena is trivia of the divine---

            Be Rembrandt, Jean-Louis   ONE THING
                                        AT A TIME

* * * * * * * *

The Moa is in Nirvana ---(extinct)

* * * * * * * *

Drinking is mere physical bliss---
      I can turn pain to bliss in mind---
           And vice versa been doin it 30 years
           (30 years turning bliss to pain!)

BOB LAX'S WHEEL: -
    "Mercy is the circle of Divine Love as it
cometh forth from heaven and eternity and
goeth down to the lowest depths of time
and creation then ascendeth again till   I
like the sun it return thither where it   AM
first arose. Poor broken spirits who lie   REAL
mourning as outcasts, hope evermore in   DREAM
the eternal love.
    "Wait for it.
    "The Love of God will find you out. It
will meet with you and take you in its
way. For Divine Love is eternal. It
encompasseth heaven and earth, time
and eternity."
          Peter Sterry---*The Rise, Race, and Royalty of the Kingdom of God*
                              in the Soul of Man (1683)

....

....

James Joyce---"Sweet and cheap: soon sour."

The mind is so sweet---knocking out thought---
           movies day in day out

      * * * * * * * * * * * * * * * * * * *

THE OTHER NIGHT, Sebastian; last night,---Joan, to whom I said "I had a dream that
you'd been shot thru the brow," but suddenly I see the little round scar on her
brow, as she smiles,---I feel scared even tho I know it's all a dream, life and
death both---
           Since everything is surface ripples of manifestation, they
neither abide in the past or in the future, but in some timeless present beyond
the time of body and brain that dreams---So I have only ONE BOOK to write, in
which everything, past, present, and future---everything that I know and everything that I did know and will know, and never knew and will never know, is *caught,*
like dust in the sunlight in the bedroom, immemorially shining in the mind essence
sea which is its base and origin---
                 next page

THE ONE BOOK (CONT'D)
Dreams transcend time because the intuitive (manas) mind that
turns them out cannot be the cause of such error as arbitrary conceptions of time
or of being alive or being dead---It's as tho Joan's face had not depended on
the "birth and development of Joan Adams" but on the transcendental freedom of
mind essence where the vision of her face is established forever as if you made a
picture or a record of a ripple on the surface of the sea---in other words, since
Joan's face appears freely of the conditions of time and terrestrial existence,
like an ethereal perpetual blossom . . . in other words, everything is real, everything
is real, everything is real---a dream is a real dream---Arbitrary conceptions are
real arbitrary conceptions---Just words are really just words---Real is a word---
The sun is real, my waking is real, the fact that I'm ignorant is a real fact, the
word real is a real word---the fact that I'm enlightened is a real fact---the fact
that I am ignorant and enlightened at the same time is a real fact, just as it is
a real fact that I am neither ignorant nor enlightened
EVERYTHING IS TRUE, EVERYTHING IS REAL
---Falsehood is Real Falsehood---
---Falsehood is True Falsehood---
A   R E A L   D R E A M

THE RECORD IS KEPT IN UNIVERSAL MIND

This we know about ripples on the surface of the sea---they
are so *transient* you might as well say they are neither ripples or non-ripples.
So with the phenomenal world which is a ripple on the surface of the sea of
Universal Essence of Mind.-
The ripples on the sea bear the *3 marks of existence*
1. Transiency---shortlived
2. Infelicity---troubled,non-peaceful,ever-changing
3. Unreality---having no substantial existence in
themselves,being mere manifestations
of(like)water due to wind.
ooooooooooooooooooooooooooooooooooooooooooooooooooooooooooooooooooooooo

No matter how sharp my visions of Neal or Proust or Baudelaire or Burroughs and
no matter how wildly put down, it will never be anything but dusty decay at some
time or another---viz. John Keble, Rich'd Hooker---but viz. Shakespeare & Beowulf---

The mistake at the heart of life, ignorance, is why noon is such a dull and quiet
hour---like, life doesnt know what to do but wait for death.
"With that sad incessant refrain, *Wherefore, unsatisfied Soul?*
and *Whither, O mocking Life?*" (Whitman)

ANY WRITING THAT IS NOT SELF-ENLIGHTENING WILL ROT LIKE A BODY. If I write
THE GOLDEN BOOK OF DULUOZ every line will have to be self-enlightening, connected
with Asia---
If I see empty blossoms in the empty blue, and dont know what
to do . . . *vass den?*
If I was going to commit suicide definitely on Jan.1,1956,
what would I do until then to *recompense* myself?
I'd write THE DULUOZ LEGEND---The story of Jack Duluoz's
discriminating brain-mind, his Visions, ripples on an endless sea---enlightening
insight is the Plot & Purpose---Visions of Neal, Visions of Gerard, Visions of
Ma---The whole world seen thru my Visions, as thru a key-hole---Like Rembrandt in
front of the mirror, I shall treat "myself" like in the third person and discuss
my own vanity---NOTHING WILL BE CONCEALED IN THE END.
The details of a great teaching---as if Buddha had written
the GAUTAMA LEGEND (or MAJAUMA, changing his name, at least temporarily while he

DULUOZ LEGEND (CONT'D)

wrote & lived) in which we would have gotten the entire picture apart from the
Great Teaching, of the mind that discriminated & unfolded it under the Bo-Tree---
For instance, what strange sexual and sensual confessions would he (and Christ)
have had to make? The details would have been all piteous---Whether you regard
it as sacred or vulgar, the key to enlightenment naturally is through the possession,
the understanding,and the annihilation of the six senses---Every detail of the
Buddha's mental association with his six senses before and after enlightenment,
would be self-enlightening. This could be the greatest book ever written.

THE DULUOZ LEGEND

Because it is completely free, I feel free again---Naturally
it will contain admissions damaging to the Vanity of Duluoz---that isnt an issue
any more, who's Duluoz? Who's Kerouac? He is equally to be loved, equally empty,
and equally a coming Buddha---

This writing will not rot like a body because it will always
partake of the vision of the unborn---

Huge as the book will be in all its sections (VISIONS OF GERARD,
DOCTOR SAX, MARY CASSIDY, THE SUBTERRANEANS, ON THE ROAD, TRISTESSA, OCTOBER IN THE
RAILROAD EARTH, VISIONS OF NEAL, BOOK OF DREAMS, BOOK OF BLUES, BOOK OF PRAYERS,
SOME OF THE DHARMA etc.) and as Golden as it will be (as Golden as that afternoon
in Victoria Mexico described in ON THE ROAD and in VISIONS OF NEAL) it will only
be a few (a few million words) ripples on an endless sea and that sea is ESSENTIAL

M I N D

This book has already been written in Heaven---
A long time already finished, I remember now---
The angel with the golden pen, writing on clouds of fleece---
The first chapter deals with the Emptiness of the World----
This is the ONE BOOK prophesied---

oOoOoOoOoOoOoOoOoOoOoOoOoOoOoOoOoOoOoOoOoOoOoOoOoOoOoOoOoOoOoOoOoOoOoOoOoOoOoOoOoOoOoO
OoOoOoOoOoOoOoOoOoOoOoOoOoOoOoOoOoOoOoOoOoOoOoOoOoOoOoOoOoOoOoOoOoOoOoOoOoOoOoOoOoOoOoO

* * * * * * * *

WESTERN BUDDHIST MEDITATION

The main thing is to forget completely about your body without falling asleep.

Since most Westerners cant cross their legs in Oriental fashion,
in the Lotus Posture, it's best to arrange the legs straight out, at times, with
soft mats, and forget them; but to lean only the small of the back against your
support, so keeping the whole back,neck & head erect and alert for the coming of
Samadhi ecstasy.

Make a bed of grass 4 foot long under a tree, sit and lean base
of spine against rolled-up coat or shoes (one shoe,one clodhopper) against tree's
trunk. Hands on lap, gently the left over the right.

Let heels drop
over edge
of grass bed,
to avoid
numbing.-Nudge
grass under knees.
Nudge grass
as wanted.

Enter the Dreamless Sleep
of the Great Rishi------------------------------------
Oriental Legcrossing causes numbing pain inside 20 minutes for most Westerners
and interrupts their Meditation Ecstasy---

In other words, our business is with Mind----

The Buddhas in all Ten Quarters of the Universe have various "forms"
and various ways of sitting---------

Use Oriental Legcrossing for Concentrated Prayer or special meditation------
and also Obeisance Position

SITTING (CONT'D)
But sit up straight under that tree, as though you were the True Axis of the World---

(the sore butt that results is because pressure's been taken off your crossed
ankles---but Essential Mind, the deeps of the sea, doesnt, as far as it's
concerned, which is Unconcern Illimitable, care that you have a butt,
and indeed do you have one, (?) and even so, it's just a ripple
on the sea-top

And dont hurt the bugs---how can they hurt you? Lil ants investigatin staples . . .
BLACK WIDDER SPIDERS PLAYIN POSSUM----------

* *

Are you going to say that a picket on   *   Here's what I've been doing:-I come to
that fence and that tree, are two   *   crucial lapses in faith, I pray to Avaloki-
different things?---and that each one   *   tesvara to instil faith in me---he does---
is a Buddha? We only need one Buddha   *   then, feeling secure, I indulge myself in
because all things are No-Things and   *   worldly thoughts,thinking I'm safe from
all things are therefore Buddhas.---   *   contamination---but slowly I lapse
This is the Diamond Knowledge, the   *   and become entangled & sick again . . .
Vajrajnana---all other knowledge   *   Fallible human nature! My dear, verily
is knowledge of ripples------------------   *   it's an obscuring mist---!

----------------THE BRIGHT ROOM, THE VOID DIVINE------------------

Intuitive realization of noble wisdom is the very cessation of the principle of
causes and conditions---your mysterious Essence is not in "conformity" with either
brightness, darkness, openness of space or impenetrability of objects or anything
---and it is not in "conformity" with *thinking*---That's why when you simply cease
thinking and trying to think about attaining your enlightening Mind, voilà, it
comes of its "own accord" because there's no more obscuring mist (!)---This is why
once you're enlightened, like wood that has burned to ashes, there is no going
back to the state prior to enlightenment---There is no recantation of true Buddhism
possible, naturally---
* *

The simple life has an advantage inbuilt   *   he breaks in the little door-window and
because it simply keeps the mind clear   *   so now kids of Keith Academy can see me
and strong for true realizing,all the   *   changing but I simply move a high chair
time,such as the inestimable realiza-   *   in the way---And then later, with Burroughs,
tion that sentient beings are clever   *   I go to an all-night Girlie Show-move, that
instruments of suffering here due to   *   is, 3 cheap B-movies about girlies for the
past sins committed in Ignorance and   *   allnight characters trade but one of the
Karma but their true originality is the   *   pictures turns out to be an amazing story
Bright Emptiness of the Void . . . that all   *   in which Bill and I are engrossed when sud-
this phenomena is Essential Mind mani-   *   denly it is interrupted by the 6 AM house-
festing sights, sounds, tastes etc. like   *   lights going on and everyone throwing up
ripples on its surface---   *   their hands and going home, as happens every
              Soon I'll find the   *   night---So later in Burroughs' room I ask
right words, they'll be very simple . . . I   *   him, as a great author on the subject,to
could have done better at age 3 . . .   *   tell me about the centipedes in the picture
"Le Rien" is the Void . . .   *   and meanwhile I have a centipede on my arm
                                              *   ---tho it's only a dream I have a definite
                                              *   sensation of the knowledge and almost com-
              * * * * * *   *   passion of Burroughs as he prepares to
                                              *   instruct me about centipedes------------------
MAR.11,'55---Amazing dreams, of my sleep-   *
ing in a little narrow room at Lucien's   *
Wife's house in Lowell Depot Corner and   *   * * *
when he comes home from a 4 A M toot   *
                                              *
                                              *
                                              *
                                              *

WHAT REFINED CREATURES were here before us who Buddhahooded themselves out?---
The number of them, and varieties of them! Since beginningless time the tender
awakening ones have been leaving the scene to the Tigers of false imagination.---

NATIONALITIES?---different styles of the same coldness---

SINCE IT'S JUST A MATTER OF TIME that you'll be buried in your grave,
then you're already buried in your grave, Jack.---

THE ENLIGHTENMENT OF THE BUDDHAS IS HISTORYLESS and Fellaheen---
Therefore I am not living in the forest to report it to Rome---
          Smoking, drinking, tender feet, and constant thinking
are vices I brought with me from Rome---(from the City-Blossom of Culture-&-Civilization
                                             P l a n t)

. . . .:
NEXT BOOK OF POEMS:- :   Yet in another (non Spengler) sense Rome is
The Pure Land Blues   :   *   just Benares and waiting again for the drum of
. . . .:   l i f e . . . .
                                              The Seventy Millions of Sravasti
They've left me here to do it   *   in the Tinkling Mysterious Night
all by myself, the Buddhas
of the Golden Room--------------

"THAT BAREHEADED LIFE UNDER GRASS WORRIES ONE LIKE A WASP"--Emily Dickinson
                                                            in a letter

Anytime you realize your True Mind, quite naturally you'll be "happy"--again,
---my 1947 rising-and-falling bouts with "depression" were due to the natural
rhythm of nature on which I depended for "happiness"---

Who is going to undernight Blake's *Vala*?---
"Mystery, Enlightenment, & Intelligence"
Ingebord Niggerboy

Now, Jack, after the enlightenment of this your 33rd birthday, when you realized
that to keep going on---what it means---look at everything including these very
words,as bubbles.---
     But to burst
     The bubble's made
     Things of thirst
     Ever fade
Any belief in anything is a lie ----- Emptiness is earth & sky -------
     Pleasant or unpleasant, life or death, -----
Go beyond now ------ I mean it now. --------Go

EVERYTHING WITHOUT EXCEPTION IS BUBBLES---I pay no more attention to that
                                        which doesnt necessarily exist--
          Today March 12 1955
          I go into Essential Mind
     Enough of this writing about renunciation

I ACCEPT EVERYTHING   THE RIPPLE
                              AS WELL AS THE
                                        S E A

*   *
               *

A damned lunatic's dream--(un maudit rêve de fou)---is life.

IF I SEE A LONG STRAIGHT ROAD leading to the piney woods in the rain of North Carolina, and a bicycle painted purple, the same purple as the Atlantic Coast Line Railroad Diesel Engines, and 2 wild simultaneous thoughts, compounded of gloomrain, woods, gray, purple . . . if it isnt tragically a lunatic's dream . . . come across my head unasked . . . bah! why have any truck with it? And I think of gray gloomy waterfronts in old movies about tramp steamers or old cartoons of Bull Dawson and Easy, or even Melville . . . the ancient acategorical dream . . . pleasant or unpleasant, there's no end to it on all sides---I havent been able to write because of too much to write about.

JEAN-LOUIS GRAVE
    was my essential personality (at 16). Combine it now with essential mind.---
    But at 27 I realized there was no need to do or worry about anything but
    just accept everything and be wild---This was a far cry from Jean-Louis Grave
    who was solitary, sober, shy, constantly contemplative.

After all these years and all this art and all this Buddhist Learning I still
dont know what to do, what course to follow, or whether to follow no course.
The constant flow of "creative" imagination in my brain prevents me from
appreciating the crystal emptiness (the "artistic impoverishment") of the
Eightfold Path . . . a path so arid to behold, so juicy to experience, yet so
arid to behold, constantly thinking about it with the thinking-mind . . . .
. . . the constantly, constantly thinking mind----
The millions of ideas I have. . . . all of one essence---all empty--

Shall I believe in ripples as well as the sea?---that is, in the *ripplehood* of
ripples? Let me explain why life is but a ripple, or ripples of one unrippled
or unrippleable essence:-

    As you stand there drinking water, you and the water are made of atoms which,
when analyzed out of sight, prove that the whole thing is an apparition; that is,
your body, the glass, the water are arrangements of empty atoms held together
and moving across the air---but all this stuff is made of atom-essence, and the
atom-essence, and the essence of the atom-essence, is emptiness---is the Divine
Mind itself, the One and Holy Thusness.

    Why should one believe in the arrangement on the surface of infinity?
    Or, why should one believe in the appearable arrangement within infinity?
    Constantly shifting, silly, sad, dead---already gone in time.

            The reality is imageless and more worthy of my time---Ha ha.
Through the sentimental earth music I can hear the eternal transcendental sound
---The Tathagatas are neither laughing nor not laughing at us---All activity
is a dream.
        Dont Get Mad

            *   *   *   Phooey

And there's no point in writing and
writing about it----

There's	POWER IN THE WOOD	BLEEDING GRASS
	BLOOD IN THE WEST	SHALL GOLD THEIR GAS,
	THE SINS OF THE CHOIR	THE OLD INOIDAL ROW,
	IN BODY AT THIS TIME	PELL FOR ME
	AISLE MYSELF IN THEE	PEAL DONG THEE
	O LAND OF LORD	DEDICATED
	BE A SINNER	TO MISS ANIMATED HILL
	S'F'GOLLOW THRU	AND IPHEGENIA BUY A DRESS
	THAT MAKE ME YEW---	

O low to wait before thee---
Glory Lee
Near to the heart of Gong---
Joy a fee.

Redeemer send from the heart
O those who wait before thee

Ow of freedom
Your heart is burnin
Special Mew
Bible Study in B.T.U.

The Old
Awful Tree

Evangelistic Services
Murk---
Come & Come & Cum
Poove this mid s. t. soul
     (Words scribbled off Southern
       Radio Preacher sounds)
(Poundin out pomes of pure lotus . . .)

More Preacher Sounds:-

The S. S. Rubber Ball, Captain Mercy---
Our service Min daid
Splosh.
That they might Kraut
Dow Chemical Blessed Lord
A bunch of men
Amen.

Scrittures in Apul---
Slipped away from the jaw of the Lord---
If you caint send an orphan
Tarboraw Long Carolinay
Eat bread with defy
Eat not holdin it
Minny other things there bay
And pots bray
Accordin to the thtradition---
Je sos, ye Dew---

Are thy father & the Death---
In his Coffin He Shall Be Free
Worms of God
Thru your tradition
And whinnied, call,
Harken onto me every one of you,
Defoul the men.

And goeth out into the Draw,
Purgin all meat.

Blasphemia Illinois---
Jesus reduked the Pharisees
Look at married chapter seven
          (!)

* *

AGREEMENT IN THE GRAY COLD SUNDAY WOODS---Jean Louis Grave va vivre la vie *Tranquil*
---A Tranquil Artist
No more frantic voyages & drunkennesses but delicate, cultural, tranquil interests
---the middleclass life of the future:- not "respectable," not "genteel," not
mauvely quiet, but *Tranquil,* with its definite connotation of Buddhist Meditation.
I foresee a Buddhist Future now.

    In my desert or mountain hermitage my interests annually will grow more & more
empty---but at intervals of artistic activity both at home and in the City they
will remain tranquilly creative---Till Nirvana---

MEDITATION TRICK:-   Look just above your nose tip and then allow eyes
          to un-focus, for true sight of the world. Like
          looking over a candle flame. Trance. Truth.

            * * * * * * * * * * * * * * * * *
               * * * * * * * * * * * * *
                  * * * * * * * *

Smart in the Void
"Smatte dans l'Vide"
Not a fool in the void.

Ti Jean yé tranquil---

ON THE ROAD A Shmovel
by
John Shmerouac

For the BUDDHIST TEXTBOOK, a list of chief Buddhist Terms, making up the Chapter List,
each chapter systematically explaining.

     i.e.   VI   *The Tathagata* (Thatness-Attainer)
            VII   *The Twofold Egolessness* (Unreality of things and beings)
          vIII   *The Five Skandhas* (Five Groups: form, sensation, perception, discrimination,
                       c o n s c i o u s n e s s)
          IX   *Samsara* (or Sangsara): (this world of living-and-dying)
          X   *The Nirdana Chainlinks:* --(ignorance, karma, consciousness, individuality,
                       six senses, contact, sensation, desire,
                       attachment-to-existence, existence, birth,
                       death)

          XI   *Karma* (Earned-fate)

   A Textbook for Colleges   AWAKE BEYOND KNOWING

* - *

ADVICE TO LOVERS---dont hang around with a woman and pretend to be indifferent---
but assure every moment that you're madly in love with her, then cut out---then
she'll KNOW you're indifferent---

TODAY, at Noon, I had a lost thought brought to me by men
in a dream---I didnt get up to write it down and it's lost
forever---A bubble burst on the mighty Ocean and I didnt see it--
      (Something about the Wise Lamb: "The assurance of
                  the ignorant lions
                  has frighted the wise lamb . . .")

"That truth whose glorious rays
melted and scattered like the cloud
of a dream the sense of loneliness which had lowered over him"---PROUST

ASTOUNDING, I have my own Proustian Kicks reading Proust---where her eyes are
about to roll down her cheeks like great tears, is wild enough, but that
it should be followed immediately by the sensational thing about Florentine
women bending their necks the same way "in pagan scenes as well as scriptural,"
I could write whole Proustian paragraphs about my reactions to it---a Blazing,
Solemn Tribute to le Monsieur . . . ca c'est un ecrivain, ha ha!-----

      TODAY, afternoon-, -March 21 '55
        had an evil dream of Allen G. and Bill B.
         --it was in Frisco-New York, gray, sad as ever, they
           were extremely unfriendly with each other, it had all hap-
            pened before, I mourned tween them in a dream already a long time
             finished---Allen mocked as Bill went off to get his junk with my money which
        I knew he wasnt going to pay back---(in real life B. always pays back)---you see
him on the city sidewalk---Allen has ugly G.J. popeyed dont-care bulges in his stupid
angry face . . . I feel like crying. I'm such a sweet child. . . .
        Peter Martin is back . . what will he say this time (?). . . . .
        "In real life B. always pays back" . . . means . . .
        NOT THE SLEEPDREAM, the WAKEDREAM
           means . . . Deeply he doesnt pay back, in my own mind, in Emptiness,
                  which is his mind too
                  because one universal mind . . .

      Love?---there is no the-possessing. . . . . .

QUAND J WATCHA l 'ti gas dancez dans la Sale de Bazaar, ses culottes noires
luirssantes, son top-hat, sa cane, sa tite face pure, "demurer than Ste.Terese"
---plus beau qu'une Sainte------J'pensa d'sa gidigne enveloppé dans l'velour---
(TRANSLATION "When I used to watch the little boy dance, his black shiny pants, his
top-hat, his cane, his little pure face, more demure than St. Theresa, more beautiful
than a woman saint . . . I thought of his dingdong enveloped in velvet"---) I was 8 . . .

ECSTASY OF INSIGHT ---"I'm telling you, O Lord, it is a spectral movie, I have seen
the Buddhies without number through the swarm polyglot moth density of things,
sights, motions----in the middle of dramas I have seen the flash of the transcendental microscopic eyes in the gray air----why should I deny the drama or the no-
drama when all I can see are those eyes?   that smiling swarm of essence?
I accept everything---all----I reject nothing----everything is great, everything
is form and emptiness both----everything is of the same emptystuff----ripples
are real ripples, the middle of ribs,the middle of ripples and bubbles is truly
really empty---When the wind makes the trees move & sing, I'm not concerned
whether I should notice them or not notice them---All life is not suffering
(in the end,ultimate truth) because all life is already in Nirvana because
indeed it has already a long time ago finished being . . ."

WHEN YOU TRY TO SAY "charming" and "terrific" at the same time,
   you say "tromming"---(!)

APPARENTLY I'M saving the seriousness of the Duluoz Legend, the *serious* Duluoz
Legend, for when I'm famous & simultaneously read---Otherwise why shouldnt I write
about Louis Malo afternoons now, then Francis & Peter sequel?   (Sequel later
                                        abandoned)

I DONT LIKE TO LORD IT OVER EVERYBODY,
I like to be secondary and in the background
and thus free to watch---(it is incidentally
Tao)---that's what I did with Dusty and that's
what I'll do with any future queer literary or Buddhist
friend, a Lesbian and a Queer----The innocent heart of both
of them, while I am cold & tranquil & distant . . . .
Ananda's love was emptiness, emptiness was Ananda's love. . . . .

Yet I am only the "Pauvre Fou"---   WHILE DRINKING,
                                                     JOT DIALOGUE !

A FOREST is just a lot of trees put together
. . . .

Le vin	Je boué	BREATHE MORE DEEPLY	"For I say at the core of demo-
Divin	le vin	ALL THE TIME,	cracy, finally, is the
Le port	Pour	DONT PANT,	religious element"---WHITMAN
Si fort	rien	TRANQUILLIZE	DEMOCRATIC VISTAS

* *

YATHABHUTAM once produced, then there is deliverance from greedy desire---
Right apprehension is yathabhutam, perceiving that greedy desire for what could be
takes place in the whirling vacuum of the thinking-mind . . . The thinking-mind
is as frantic as the cardsharp who, while dealing himself a good hand, makes sure
his opponent gets a bad hand and thus he is imbroglio'd in a complicated Hate
twice over--

THERE'S NO DIFFERENCE BETWEEN EARTH & SKY---the intrinsic nature of both earth
and open space is the same emptiness.
                     Does it fit the case to question whether shadow
                     is of different substance than light?

SELFHOOD is like George Washington's Axe----this was the axe used by Geo.Washington,
it is so old that it has had three new handles and four new heads.--------------------------
      This is the Buddha, this man Jean-Louis, but he is so old he has had 67
      new bodies and 483 new heads and once his name was Igratta---------------------------

                  * * * * * *

"It's all conditional and talk"---phrase in my marvelous Enlightened nap of Mar.24
which prevented me from taking an "adventurous" run up to N.Y. a week ahead of time
IT'S ALL CONDITIO NAL A N D T A L K . ...

When James Joyce gave up "sin" he wanted to become the Virgin Mary's Knight---
Buddha says to avoid sexual thoughts of women and put on the "helmet of right
thought"---Not gettivingning with the lovinggningsky, they turn to armor, juss
as Wilhelm Reich divined---I'm a little perplexed now about the First Precept
of No Lust, since soft Love is closer to divinity than hard armor of battle
----(soft love, hard armor, both are emptiness, in emptiness)---Love's Soft
Dove---soft kiss of truth. . . . The essence is neither soft nor hard, neither
love nor hate, the essence is what it is, *tathata*, the level perfectness

THE NAP It wasnt a dream of life as loathsome but as unreal---I saw it
flash on levels of light and move, vanishing---crystal clear is the
emptiness of it---what's the use of torturing the temporary arrangement of your body with precepts against wine, love, and song----
ECCLESIASTES IS RIGHT. . . . . eat drink and be merry for that is your
portion under God. . . . .
I believe men in the days of nature realized essence instinctively
without ideas and conceptions and disciplines------
Whitman is an Ogre,he wants to embrace it, grab it all greedily,
the Drooling Affirmer is just as silly as the Dry Denyer . . .
Rest Peacefully in Neither-This-Nor-That of Sacred Sweet Dharma
Shut up and take it . . . cut out the gab . . .
Shut up and take it, like an unsatisfactory candy bar . . .

O AVALOKITESVARA, ALL THINGS, INCLUDING "ME"----ENLIGHTEN ME !
Life is just a dream---The Transcendental
Sound of Avalokitesvara is the silence
Wherein the dream is taking place---
Walk, Dreamer, through your dream,
As a ghost revisiting the world---
The old long dream by the wall
Of the world, awake or asleep----
The Buddha of Silence
Avalokitesvara
The Buddha of Antiquity

At 5 AM starry dawn I stood in
the yard in the enveloping Shush of
Avalokitesvara's Sound, tho too sleepy
to appreciate, and I thought, "Frantic
drinking and runnin-around is not fitting
for a man of Saintship---it is not seemly."
Truly, alcohol (too much) doesnt go with the holy
life----any more than you would expect religious
meditation to succeed during loud jazz, or to bake sand
into a delicious pie. . . . . . But that Goethean Itch to "do
everything" is slow departing . . .
STOP DRINKING OVERMUCH and then do anything else you want
(You Wont Want To)
I have always known, clearly, that if I should stop guzzling like I do
a new life would begin for me---yet why is it that I dont benefit from the
example of this new life as I experienced it in the hospital and elsetimes like
in Lowell October 1954---superb happiness that ended only when I got a GAY idea
and started to drink again, ending again in despair and blind nerves----
Drinking is used by men to knock themselves out in this miserable life-----But the
Savior's head is in the blue sky; melancholy and pure he knows men are miserable . . .

The Savior is miserable himself, but doesnt cheat at drunkenness-------he wants to
keep his Mind of Saintship-----continuously intact for it s great work of universal
salvation----a Leader of Men----needs no barroom bottom sops---no reward---his
thoughts are not dry---his rich interest is juicily Eternal---------
   HE DRINKS FROM THE FOUNTAIN OF EVERLASTING ETERNITY * * *
     ---Apparently I am not a Man of Saintship------Just another drunken artist-----
    SO BE IT, in Lay Life Write & Drink
    in the Hermitage, Meditate Only

      The obvious solution, since Lay & Hermit Lives are so opposed,different,& Goals
      ---take the Goalless Path of the Tathagata, see the ecstasy swarmingness----
       "Erroneous views concerning form" caused my trouble this week----Does it fit
        the fact to question whether a form is happy or not? To question whether
         a form is comforted or not? It's still a form, only a passing form.
          A dead bird on the ground, is form
          GARDE TA MENTALITE ORIGINALE, JEAN
           Arrete de faire le fou, rappele twé du matin a Chinatown a SanFrancisco
           les chinois avec leur balas, les cheillières du matin, la grièsse
           dans l ciel du Pacific, ton degout avec le vin et les Neigres fous
           ---avec toi-meme agissant commme un imbecile d'ou t'appartient pas---
           La----ce foi la, tu t'en rappela de Jean, Jean qui est "si Tranquil"
           TRANSLATION: ---Keep your Original Mentality, John. . . . Stop playing
          the fool. . . . remember that morning in Chinatown in San Francisco
          the Chinese with their brooms, the garbage cans of morning, the
          grayness in the sky of the Pacific, your disgust with wine and
          crazy Negroes-----with yourself acting like an idiot where you
          dont belong----There, that time, you remembered *John (Jean)*,
          Jean who is "so tranquil"---

It's all a Buddha-Mountain
we're racing up and down   *

May I never say that my Buddhism
was just a phase of a spectral traveller--

               The Snake sows death and the Prick
               sows life, both are the same---
               Sexual Discipline is the same as Snake
               Charming and just as necessary---Look
O, I spent all 1955 tryna   alikes and Suffering--------------------------
figure out why I was so   To Keep the Mind Clear:-
sad and hangovery, like   Stop guzzling, reward yourself with more
Alcoholics Anonymous   frequent eating, and fast when fat.
then in 1956 I just   No, that didnt work
switched to lil   (Later)
bit this lil bit   (It's natural to be emptybelly hungry---make food
that. . . . .   and drink something that you do once a day, at
Jackpot   nightfall---Then yr. food is more exquisite, your
               drink stronger than the food & drink of those who
   IN EMPTINESS   dine in the day time-----for it's natural to be hungry
THERE IS NO SIN NO   and clearminded all day long like an animal---And
DRUNKENNESS NO VICE   you'll never hold your fat---"Excess is the pathway to
NO OVERDOING   wisdom" is Goethe's here-applicable axiom; by excessive
OF ANYTHING   fasting you gain wisdom, then by excessive enjoyment of
JUST SELFSAME   big joyous suppers you gain health. Give Birth to Joy.
ETERNAL   Better to be a bearded desert rat than a gooky drunk in a
PURITY   hotel mirror.---See yourself, nut, in Joe's by day, expounding
 ALL THE   the Dharma gravely--?--By night, wine & spaghetti parties---
  T I M E   Bag-eyed Jean-Louis in Paris------O ALL THESE ARBITRARY CONCEPTIONS

The 20th Century in America, a big return towards the Orient. . . .
        Many men in the Orient understand everything---In the West, even great
    thinkers like Cocteau and Burroughs are ignorant compared----Life is definitely
imaginary and so is death---It isnt a matter of life fighting death, like heroic
  Phil White dying for his "life-giving" junk and vanishing of him forever in death,
but there was no life and no death involved, only the unchangeable unaffectable essence.
The form of Phil White is emptiness----emptiness is the form of Phil White----------------
        I know this because all last night some bird kept singing and I kept realizing
in my sleep that the bird didnt necessarily exist except as a dream--------------------------
Does it fit the case to question whether a dream is conscious or unconscious?
Whether a dream is in the top instead of the bottom of the mind?
Or whether a dream is inside or outside?
Whether a dream, subjective or objective, occurs or does not occur?
-----Whether birds sing or birds have sung or birds never sang?
-----What a vast and frightful deception and we the center of it!---like in
the center of bubbles the *neither-empty-nor-not-empty space!*

FOLLOWS (IN THE DHARMA NOTEBOOK) QUICK PENCIL SKETCH OF ALLEN WAYNE WATCHING
TELEVISION ON THE FLOOR (RATHER WELL DONE FOR NON-ARTIST) REFER TO DHARMA #6
FOR COPY OF SKETCH (LITTLE BOY SITTING TWISTEDLY ON FLOOR)------------------------------
* *

Sweet balls of canary shit
and flaming ass holes---yelled the truckdriver
I'll be dipped in shit---SHORTY SMITH, Truckdriver of March 26,
                while I was hitch-hiking North thru Baltimore to N.Y.

BALTIMORE:-
    O d e   t o   P o e
* * * * * * * * * *

What does it matter that in a little
schoolroom on sunny mornings years
later they told me to read the GOLD BUG
---the main thing is, this is the garret
room where Poe died,---the window rattles
in the miserable winter wind---Men
are puking in Skid Row hotels---Mae
West is dead---Port Wine is like Opium
---This great poet haunted room shaking
in the Long (Baltimore) night is the
Tangiers Shrieking Future

    Baltimore, Baltimore,
    O Ultimo Baltimore,
    I've avoided thee
(Charley Mew & Hunkey & Phil White
  were here, great balls o fire)
Frisco piers, bleak
This is the Nowhere Blues.
Great sensitive Ghastly
Hail thy Bright Paleness.

My brains are washing
down the side of my
head with pain---

Dissheveled angels dont
come to the door

Faded Angels of Gore

Poe's Old Scene
Human life---a shake of form
Careless Jack
Details are the life
        & death of it
I dont like to have my
        pants cluttered up
        with change
Perturb no more
        yr angels
The next kind of doom is
        the latest
Poe's mind was a
        million miles away
        from that dreaming
        hump-hill
        of his home-world
Sunday Morning Bells
In Baltimore
Bugged with the Scene
Atmosphere of Dreamy Gloom
& Swarming Dark Stupidity
Here is my prayer,
        here is my song
In me there's a Buddha
Impressing himself thru this
        mold of darkness
Morning will come & these writings
will be revealed to the world
        for pity

Snake is Pity --- Serpent of Love
   they'll put me in there & garrotte
   me for crimes unnumberable,
   & they'll only garrotte this
   pitiful form---
   the Everlasting Scene---
Like being at sea in some
   stupid S.S.Shark

What are the plans of broads?
   Nameless cuntplans.
The ramparts of Rome, they gone.

Your woes & viciousness end, when you
truly know that life & death are dreams.

When we hear of the death of some one
we feel a kind of triumph,
but when I heard of the death
of Charlie Parker I felt an impoverished
triumph---Like Bernard Buffet's starved
hare served on a plate---

Dear Pound,
   I am in Poe's garret in
El Ultimo Baltimore, thinking
of you at dawn. A Lover

* * * * * * * * * * * *)))))))))))))* * * * * * * * * * *(((((((((((* * * * * * * * * * * *(())(()* * * * * * * * *
A battered sorrow covers the world ---
Bird is Dead.
'Tis a wilderness of life, all of it holy
"The Subterraneans" and an album by Charley Parker are perfect expressions of pain.--

Tell Lax that Bird died laughing
   at a juggler---

Years were made to fly ---   To go with balls of fire ------------
    I WALKED THE BLANK BLUE STREETS OF SUNDAY MORNING BALTIMORE
         MOURNING FOR ALL MY LOST CHILDREN
               WHICH IS REALLY
                   MY
The Child   ONE
   is   CHILD. . . . . My head was shrouded in ignorant
  Thought   inability to think clearly on the clear
                            complete beauty of the truth body (dharma-
   *   (words,words)   kaya*)
                            the rest is nagging nature* * * * * * * * * *
ooooooooooooooo   ooooooooo
    ooooooooooooooooooooooooooooooooooooooooooooooooooooooo

NEW YORK March 28,1955----------------
EVERYONE YOU SEE IN THE STREET is a product of sexual concupiscence, no matter what
 they might think about it or how they look---
  Beauty is an illusion. Reality is neither beautiful nor not beautiful. A "beautiful
  face" is not so to an ant, to a dinosaur, to the Void, to the Chinese fish. Westerners have killed themselves in life after life on the altar of beauty, relegating
  this pitiful (tho-hard-to-dispel) concept to the throne of the Universe.
    Everyone that you see on the streets results from the illusion of beauty having
    taken hold---The poor suffering ghosts, they frighten me, I frighten myself
    with my human beautiful young horror---Dylan Thomas frightens me with his
    dying---If I should become a world traveller and look at people and cities
    everywhere, I would soon become re-attached to pretty faces and start in
    springnight yearning again, like a yearny broad, for something without
    substantiality, for apparitional ripples----sentimentally fucked.
      Suffering---and the end of suffering.
      I am battered all over from 3 days of drinking in N.Y. into a sorrowing
      mess----We hanker to conquer the canker---
        Be better not to try. Since happiness is just an imaginary same-as-
        unhappiness emptiness.
                EVERYTHING IS ALREADY DESTROYED

"Just as it is by the condition precedent of the co-existence of its various parts that the word 'chariot' is used, just so is it that when the five groups of form, sensation, perception, discrimination and consciousness are there, we talk of a 'being'."
SANYUTTA I,135
OOOOOOOOOOOOOOOOOOOOOOOOOOOOOOOOOOOOOOOOOOOOOOOOOOOO
A G r e a t H a n d b o o k ------------
      "DESIGNATION OF HUMAN TYPES"   &&&&
      (Puggala-Pannatti)
                ---Translated by Bimala Charan Law, Pali Text Society, 1924.
                   An ancient part of the Abhidhamma Pitaka-----

"Cramping is household life, a dusty path! Open and wide
is the way of renunciation!"----"He (the Bhikku) is chaste,
not unchaste, refraining from sexual life, from village nature---"
"Rejoicing in union, jubilant over unity"--(not causing disunity)----
"Just as winged bird wherever it flies, flies with just the load of its wings,
in the same way the bhikku is satisfied with robes (clothes) just enough to protect
his body, with alms just enough to feed his stomach, wher-ever he goes taking these
with him."---"He tortures neither himself nor others, and in this world he without any
hankering abides, at peace, cool, enjoying bliss, living with a self become god-like.
. . . He acts deliberately . . . in masticating or swallowing, in going or standing or sitting
---The Happiness Which is Blameless" (!)---"Having seen an object with his eye, heard
sound with his ear, smelt an odor with his nose, tasted a savor with his tongue,
touched a tangible thing with his body, cognized a mental object with his mind,
he does not fasten his mind upon the general form of details thereof but
sets himself to restrain that which gives an occasion for the sight and
immoral tendencies, greediness, and dejection to flow over him while
he was dwelling unrestrained as to his mind, his faculty of thought;
he guards his mind, he attains to control over the faculty of
thought."---"Putting away laziness & drowsiness he dwells
being free therefrom----Supremely pure and bright---
free from the tendency to be reborn . . . . ." PUGGALA-PANNATTI
    ARYA, the society of the wise
    MAYOPAMA, the Samadhi Ecstasy in which there   * * * * * * * * * * *
    is a "revulsion" in the consciousness for   *   All things   *
    this Maya World of illusion. . . .   *   *ARE*   *
    ICCHANTIKA---those who are destitute   * the Buddha-nature *
        of the Buddha-nature   * * * * *-*-*-* * * * *
    There are no, is no Icchantika. . . . .
OOOOOOOOOOOOOOOOOOOOOOOOOOOOOOOOOOOOOOOOOOOOOOOOOOOO
- * * * * * -

SELECTION FROM THE LOTUS OF THE WONDERFUL LAW (Saddharma-Pundarika) SUTRA

"To that courageous man who shall proclaim this Sutra after my complete extinction I will also send many creations.

"Monks, nuns, lay devotees, male and female will honor him as well as the classes of the audience.

"And should there be some to attack him with clods, sticks, injurious words, threats, taunts, then the creations shall defend him.

"And when he shall stay alone, engaged in study, in a lonely place, in the forest or the mountains,

"Then will I show him my luminous body and enable him to remember the lesson he forgot.

(cont'd)

"While he is living lonely in the wilderness, I will send him gods and goblins in great number to keep him company.

"Such are the advantages he is to enjoy; whether he is preaching to the four classes, or living, a solitary, in mountains and studying his lesson, he will see me.

"His readiness of speech knows no impediment; he understands the manifold requisites of exegesis; he satisfies thousands of kotis of beings because he is, so to say, inspired and blessed by the Buddha, the Awakened One, the Perfect One.

"And the creatures who are entrusted to his care shall very soon all become Bodhisattva Religious Heroes, and by cultivating his intimacy they shall behold Buddhas, Awakened Ones, as numerous as the sands of the Ganges."

* *

From translation of LANKAVATARA:-
  "When things are analyzed into atoms, there remains nothing to be discriminated as objects. Those who hold wrong views do not believe in the ever-abiding ground of mind-only."

---   The Silent Hush
                                                    Of the Pure Land Thrush

                                                    The Ground Divine
                                                    Of Mortal Mind

* *

If you taste filth, remember Yathabhutam---"seen as it is"---

WHAT'S THE SENSE of conditionally trying to make it with the good or the bad---
  cut out from both, "kill yourself"---Disappear from the scene and train yourself
   in the ways of Renunciation, only then come back (try it anyhow)----But dont come
    back---Idiot, t'est plein, you're full-up. . . . .
      You've had it.
        C'est claire, il faut renoncez les sens, J'ai vu ca hier soir, le restant
          s'arrange tout seul---Les femmes n'ont pas de raison t'aimer, ni toi eux
           autres---c'est las verité et les hommes qu'on aime sur le terrace de la terre
            ----On s'bord pas d la vie n i la mort-----------------------
              TRANSLATION:-It's clear, you've got to renounce the senses, I saw that last
                night, the rest takes care of itself----women have no reason to love you,
                  nor you they-----it's the truth and brothers we love, on the terrace of
                    the earth----we dont bother with either life or death--------------------------
                      ALSO:- Les femmes, les conforts, des graffignages, des flattes------
                        meaning, women, comforts, scratchings, caressings. . . . . Concentrate
                          on what you know

                    OOOOOOOOOOOOOOOOOOOOOOOOOOOO
PEOPLE---What discourages me is that they are not concerned with kindness but with
some kind of blind exchange of torture---They have no formal tenderness, no conscious
intelligent sense of personal duty---No matter what I do, I'm blackened by their
bleakness wherever I go---They're not even telling the truth all the time, not
sincere. The women show themselves and work up disunion among the men; the men
are fooled and cast cold stone on one another---There's no idealism, the well of
shining reality is very deep and no one that I know is drinking from it------

PEOPLE (cont'd)

Where are the Bhikkus of the world?-----Is Ginsberg the only Bhikku and he a
serpentine idolater?---I mean, he has abandoned principles of conscious kind----
I mean I have a vision of him this benzedrine morning of laughing at my sadness
about this, preferring to believe in the mortality of the world, the work of the
world, preferring sexuality above universal compassion---I'm alone in a world of
hankering entangled beasts and to say that I'm here to save them is so absurd,
I'm such an inane child among the dinosaurs of horror & flesh---such a helpless,
weak, vacillating child, myself beastly---

Vengeful, dangerous, untruthful world . . .

          Warm golden thighs produce cold black
              mornings . . .

       * * *

YET,
   Everything she is all right---The sad little burlesk doll saying
   "I've never been laid in a grave before" as a joke "Haw-Haw" for
   us sailors in Tony Pastor's----her pitiful non-funniness there,
   since her beauty will die. . . . .

The Self Killed Hero
Walking the Terrace   THE SAMADHI OF TRANSCENDENTAL SUICIDE
Of the Earth   (On Henri's steps)
   INWARD SUICIDE

Vision
   I'm going down the stone steps of the great Buddhist world cave saying to
watchers on the parapet "It's inward suicide"-----------------------

* *
* *

book seven

Seven Little Visions : - M e m o r i e s . . . . T i c s . . . .

CHARLEY LOW 4 FOOT 10 INCHES TALL in his dismal little apartment on Turk Street in
Frisco, his buddy the blond Chief Steward who loved to eat it and called all the old
bums they brought in there *dikes* painting the walls and floorboards of his place---
the utter dismalness of the room, the shroud of Frisco Smalltownness hiding in the
glooms----Al Damlette and I there trying to get drunk, the glamorous hepcats not-
caring---but the two of em seriously painting with sadpaint, and discussing last
night's big time with a gal picked up in the Tenderloin district---Charley looking
up with a drawn wan Armand-like 'Hey Way You Doan Believe It?' brush-in-hand as they
like bums of Lowell Baltimore & all points East try t'boast about their utterly ugly
conquests and Al Damlette is laughing 'Hak har hark shit'---It's the Book of Memory,
& Why---

THE MAN WITH THE GRAY HAT on the gray drizzly day in Russia outside the shoe repair
shop, the dismal street before him with woodfences leaning, coalyards, distant hazy
vistas of trolley track---the man walking away, hat slanted to the grim---Somewhere
in another life or the first thing I saw in this one---It's like in Nashua too---It
is totally sad

THE ILLUMINATED POSTER at the foot of Bunker Hill Street and Lakeview Avenue, the
special rivermouth Maw darkness of that corner what with the house that was across
the way with those trees, old, yet on a cobbled trolley road----where I'd seen those
lovers in the gray afternoon weeds, her big thighs and the shitpaper and the 666---
Bunker Hill where there'd been death, and that house of the little new friend---Why

295

did I dream of Brakeman masterly in that house across the street?---sad the scenes
of my father just a little ways up at the gym on Aiken---The corner, the waving
leaves in the brown bulblight, the lights of the mills furring on the waters across
the way,---the hidden darkness, silence, mist, the trolley up Lakeview coming now
with a ring of rails . . . my memory of this corner rising just in the middle of some
other thought which I failed to check to remember and so the almost uselessness of
this paragraph---

THE HUGE CAULDRONS OF THE S S DORCHESTER in which was made gallons of tomato noodle
or rice soup and that I'd clean at noon, pouring hot water thru and thru the spigot
below, ringing first the faint greasy soupstock smell sweet in my nostrils as I
stood up on a box leaning in and then with the hot cleansing water and my clean
towel the sharp smell of soup-scalded aluminum all hot and oldsoupy and scrubbed,
in the sea noon drowse like old drawings of Popeye the deck & the fat gunwales, so
sleepy---Brought up's I washed tin cup I'd dipped in Ma's tomato soup---

I'M A BABY IN MY MOTHER'S ARMS, it's a sunny Summer afternoon, we go from those old
tenements at foot of Lilley no Aiken, at Lakeview, where'd I'd fusskicked among rubbles
of the yard smoke dump and Ma jwa dwa bada'd my baby talk and across the street was
a tinsmith or blacksmith shop grim and sad in a gray day----Now with Mrs. So & So
LaMartine we go to Lakeview, 5 miles on the yellow trolley, and I see the trees,
the lake, I hear the Women of Eternity talking---but it's the sun I remember, on
the straw seats, on the trees, on the lake, making shade, the motorboats sadly pharting
on the water---and my auspicious position in the world----pines, time---

BEFORE LEARNING OF THE POLISH GIRL run over on West Street front, before seeing the
crimson blood patch where she was killed, in the rock cobbles, we're driving in the '29
Ford along Riverside Drive in Pawtucketville and I see basket redbrown houseporch
fronts . . .

EVENINGS AFTER SUPPER IN MY COLLEGEROOM in Livingston Dorm at Columbia, the fragrance
of my old taped pipe, the drowsy European momentous sad romance of Sibelius or other
classical musics on the scratchy QXR station, my desk before me with its warm lights
and studies, my thoughts, self-confidences---above all iron Autumn lording out my
window with its prophecy of clear, cold knowledge, Winter, a great Journey to triumph
---the belly full, the nose tingling with rich pipesmokes that I enfragrant by
blowing softly up the stem thru the bowl making a rich slow fuming that when taken
down thru bowl and stem again fill mouth and nose richly---"Here's a great buy for
WQXR listeners" says the announcer, making me picture cultured places in exciting
Fall New York to bo buy shining colorful things in, wearing hornrims are the "customers"---My New York, my Amsterdam Avenue of exciting Saturday Mornings rushing
across the street to the College Drycleaner and seeing the flash of five-mile-down
shroudy city walls of Hope----my New York, my Columbia, my Campus, my soft gold
lights of libraries out there in the gathering Cold---

* *

There can be no Sangsara, no world,
without Nirvana-----There can be no candle-light
without the extinguishing, the before and the after
of extinguishing.----------

YOU CANT DO IT WITH THE BODY---
Satisfy the unconditional demands
of the mind

FREE FROM THE INTOXICANTS ⎫
FREE FROM SUFFERING   ⎬   To be concentrated upon forever & continuously
FREE FROM SANGSARA   ⎭

All of It, Life,
is a spiritual routine, a Buddha-Routine,
manifested forth from the Womb of Reality
due to the arbitrary conception of Ignorance
and also of purity, sentient beings the motive force
of Mind, non-sentient things like the cobwebs of the moving spider
and so the non-motive principle of Mind, Karma and Reincarnation of Vast empty ghosts
of pure mentality for a central Reason. . . . .

    The ripples are real but they're defiling one another---
    real-ly . . . real defilement . . . Everything is real including Suffering----

        A guy smiling to a girl I'm with saying
        "You're not with him are you?" and she says
        "No" with the same funny little knowing smile I
    cant understand . . . a FLASH (a nap-dream)

        * * * * * * * * * * * * * *

END PRIDE, PARANOIA ENDS---
I seek the perfection of unconsciousness---
Psychoanalysis:-making the best of Sangsara-consciousness----

I cant meditate on perfection with my legs hurting, thorns in the flesh. . . . only
the full lotus-posture allows proper free unpinched circulation in legcrossing . . .
for long serious meditations with samadhi ecstasy as goal, best to sit legs out
à la "western style". . . . .

THE BUDDHA NIRMANAKAYA and the Messiah made flesh,
to re-teach again among the Defiled and Fallen, promising
purity and Grace again---this is the essence of Buddhist Christianity ----
God is Mind Essence, the Father of the Universe, the Manifesting Womb---
Atman is Soul and only appears to exist and transmigrate, like physical body,
which is but spectral Heaven Stuff all of it-----
    For a Central Reason which is Inconceivably Holy Thusness . . .
    All Suffering is Mental Suffering . . . I'm a mental sufferer, but I can only be
cured to accept things like a dog---As I am now, I dont want
to live another minute---All the kinds of pain, why should I wait
for the new kinds---
                I know there is no self, there is no me,
                but my itching skin! my mortal bones!
             my damp heart and hot brow!
                    Avalokitesvara whispers me the news:-
                    Suicide is a Human Heroism---------------
                    But there is a greater heroism drawing
                    your breath in patience and teaching others the truth . . .
                    There is no happiness in these hangjawed yellers of the earth---
                    Pity on them---but what can I offer them but Destruction----
                    Safety in Annihilation---
                              The Caves of Monterrey Desert
                              for Me this very Summer, if I lie . . .
A glass of 40 melted sleeping pills   If that doesnt work, caves, later,
is a glass of Safety but O boy what   I go out . . . This Angel has Had it
pain if it convulses you (which 40   And feels right now
pills at a crack will) and makes you   It can teach no more
puke your horror back on out----------
Death: Safety from Fear
      Safety from Suffering
      Safety from Death   . . . . . . at least so it seems . . . . . .

Buddha said to his father "If you dont let me go off and be a Buddha
I'll have to take my life"----words to that effect----
This is how I feel now---My Renunciation has come

If you had left everything the way it was, this wouldnt have happened---
Now the only thing to do is wait for your composition to decay
---You can live in a cave,
    exercise tranquillity & pity
    at home
    or kill yourself

Poison death is a hell of a thing to drink but you'll have to drink it soon

You belong to culture creation and Anton belongs to civilization nihilism,
and the latter is the p u r e r . . .   Y'aint got a leg to stand on. . . . .

Nothin to do but put up with it and finish quietly and *tranquilment*----
This too is Tao,
            staying low, still,
                        s a d,
                              like a well

Dont wear out your self drinkin and one thing and another (no-sleep, traveling, etc.)
but keep.
            Duluoz Legend---every bit of it was real---and who cares?

                The shiver of love
                In your chest
    *   Late afternoon   *   So leave everything
                In the woods   the way it is--------

                                        . . . .
The actual Nirvana   . NEVER BORN, ...
Behind seeming Sangsara   .   NEVER DIES.
                                        . . . .

A GUY IN A RED TRUCK laughing at me
because I've just said "Your truck is a dream,"
also he's angry & perturbed, I wake up not knowing which is the guy & which me . . .

That's why dogs sleep all the time . . . . . . DOG OF TAO, TAKES ONLY WHAT'S GIVEN HIM

I listen to my mother instead of Buddha Avalokitesvara but, No, *he's telling her*
                                        --"I dit a yelle--"

A fly buzzes over, I say "Los Mochis"   (the Flies, and a town in Mexico) --- my
mother or somebody says "Plus bas que ca, lower than that" and down goes the pail
to the deep well "in Klamatch Falls"---

For Ma's spine--- W A L K

Bringing gray suitcases down from the attic of heaven I saw "Me I'm not comin down
any more, *Mué j descendra plus*"-----a FLASH

                Birds---pwurty pwurty
                  pigalle pigalle

Instead of drinkin sleepin pills I'll just sleep samadhi all day and night
and write flashes, as above, bringing everyone to Nirvana with "me"----------
P r a y e r ---
You cant realize that suffering is a dream until you stop suffering----You cant
realize that Sangsara is a dream until you are free from Sangsara----You cant
realize that a dream is a dream till you wake up from it . . . .*****

Pure non-intoxicant path is the only way
to realize that it is all a dream, because
while you are in the path of impurity and suffering
of intoxicants, while you are involved, you cant wake
up---that is, you only wake up when it's over---but if you
can wake before it's over, all the better---for suffering has ended----

> Why did the original mind start dreaming? Why did
> ignorance ripple it? The original mind responded
> perfectly to the dream & the ripples, which of course
> are not its source, but in essence itself did not start
> dreaming or ever ripple-up but remained, as it is now and
> forever, immaculate---"the boxes of Gray"---What started
> dreaming and rippled-up was the false dreaming thinking-
> mind of Ignorance Discrimination---When you realize your
> Original Mind you became a Tathagata in space, as false mind
> has been discarded in the midst of sentience and in the empti-
> ness that suddenly is left the Tathagata who ceases being born
> and dying again takes his place altho he is an unplaceable
> Nirvana-nothingness---
> Causes and conditions brought Sangsara, but they were not is
> source---its source is ever Original Mind but you cant realize and
> know this when You're drowned and drunk in a dream of Sangsara, only
> when you've emerged------------
> Like a dream---causes and conditions brought the dream but they were
> not its source---its source is Original Mind but you cant know this
> while you're deep in the dreaming, only when you've awakened---Or better,
> in Buddhahood awakened while it transpired---so it stopped at once, strip't
> of Karma, that is, strip't of Sangsara action and continuation, and no
> more dream   SAVED!

Who wouldnt want to wake out of a nightmare? seems to say the Eightfold Path . . .

And 4 Precepts also---

> Tibet and no maybe, Sax was talking about----
> ('Promised Snow North')------

ORIGINAL ETERNAL MIND	ORIGINAL
P E R F E C T	PERFECT
---	E S S E N C E
Free from birth is free from death---	Free from ocean is free from drowning

F r e e   f r o m   d e a t h   i s   f r e e   f r o m   r e b i r t h

When the 8 Fold Path becomes
your satisfaction there will no
longer be the arbitrary conception
of religious effort----

> :- Sangsara is "Real" Illusion-:
> There is no Sangsara, there are no Buddhas---

> I didnt have anything to do before I was born---
> I dont have to do anything now----------------------
> I wont have anything to do after I'm dead------------
> A glass in which a drink shall never be poured, unborn-

> All of it is sprung from false mind, the trees in the woods,
> and "not really there"---Only Ripples Recognize Ripples---With
> my false sentient mind only I perceive those trees--------------------
> I ' l l   l i v e   a s   t h o u g h   I   w e r e   a   m i r r o r

Free from birth means free from death and likewise, then, to be free
from conceptions of death during Nirvana now which before PariNirvana
(Complete Outblownness of Form) can only be temporary Samadhi, means to be free
from conceptions of rebirth   . . . . . May the Ender of Suffering Win. . . . .

"Rebirth" only means the Original Perfect Essence is re-routed through a
   form, like a tree, in response to causes and conditions which are shadows of the
      activity of the false mind which is a shadow of the Original Perfect True Mind
      ---So when you look at a tree you must realize the pitiful spiritual principle
         of it, the frail sad pity . . .

                          Seeds are the Sin
                          That brings the Tree
                          From perfect Sea
                          Of Mind Within

                     Seeds that from perfect sea of
                     sin within the tree
                     Sprung shadows of original conditions
                     responding to Pure
                     So that ever recurring essential
                          noumena
                     Ripple remained altho Nirvana
                          perfectly started.
                          ---A MYSTERY

          For the sake of the creation of Buddhas, Sangsara---pity if the only reality.

          IN THE MIDDLE OF THE NIGHT I WOKE UP TO THE SUPREME AND FINAL TRUTH AND
          NODDED WITH SATISFACTION AND SAID "IT'S ALL THE SAME THING" * * * * * * * * * * *
              C'est toute la meme chose---

              April 5, the great talk with Ma---about Gerard's white chariot with
              white lambs pulling and a white dove on each shoulder, in Heaven
              Les cuisines de pain,
                Maman si blanc . . . . Kitchens of bread, mother so white . . .
                Pere LaBossiere in the kitchen, foot on chair, "Dont cry, Mrs.
                Kerouac, he was a little saint"----Gerard's long speeches in
                school---The nuns taking notes at his death bed-----------------------

* * * * * * * * * * * * * o o o o o o o o o o o o o o o * * * * * * * * * * * * * *
I woke up from perfect unified void in which there was no such conception as
   "perfect unification" and I saw that all created things were the same as emptiness,
      that they were surface manifestations in a perfectly empty sea of Single Reality,
      that they were not indivudated parts but one whole Is-ness, all the Same, and
         way beyond conceptions of Nirvana *or* Samsara-----Life is a spiritual routine
         taking place in One Mind---it is the Movie of a Thought---a Dream of Drowning--
         BUT I KNOW VERY WELL THE BODY CANT BE STOPPED . . .
                                                  So why try modified stoppage
            such as sexual abstinence? It'll come out anyway. . . .
            What is Sin? There is no Sin anywhere the world throughout! What is
                                             R e m o r s e ?
            The mind listening to its own echo, is one man listening
               to another . . . . when I listen to Bodhisattva Charley Parker. . . . . .
               Perfect Nirvana was achieved by the Yogis who starved themselves OUT
               to death----
               Previous karma, previous need

FLASH   Originally dirt fucked up-----Joan H. in a flash is asking a woman
* * * * * * * * * * * * *   my latest expletive *dirt*   *

               Seeds sown in the Divine Ground for Buddha-Reasons, for the pathos
                  of bondage & emancipation, fall & grace, Messiah & flock. . . . .

---for the pathos of bondage and emancipation, Fall and Grace,
Messiah and Flock, yes,   VISIONS
                People are spiritual Ghosts----

            There is no individual in the matter of Death

The trouble with the Zen idea of *Sudden Attainment* is because it depends on
    an arbitrary conception of *time*. . . . .
        since there is no real substantiality to the reality of objects, then time is
            likewise unreal, and so the moment when 'sudden realization' takes place also
            is unreal. . . . . . Zen is a modern shallow naive almost 'popular' innocent idea. . .
                the Truth is already in the Mind

FLASH:-
    Ma & Paul---"Look, Jean, in our mind controls"

OTHER FLASH:- Ma's dying, I want to put her frail sad head in my lap, for the last time.

        Le grand silence saint . . . . . the great saintly silence

THE WORLD IS AT MY FEET waiting to be saved,
        l i k e   a   s l e e p i n g   d o g . . .

                            The Teaching Older Than Earth
THE MIND   Original Perfect
The Truth is a greater gift   E s s e n c e
than bread---a greater loss   of
than blood.   Mind
*   ---------------
ESSENCE OF MENTALITY   * * * * * * * *   Everything is Mental (Essence)
  The Story of Buddha   *   All's in the Mind   (Sad Death too)
    PREPARED   *   Everything *is* the Mind
        by   *   The Mind's Old Dharma
    Jean-Louis   *   The Old La w - -
* * * * * * * * * * * * * *   T h e   H o l y   M o m e n t . . . .

THE SAME   Mind's Holy Dream
AS NOT . .   Made Holy More
                     The Holy Gold   C'EST TOUTE PAREILLE
                     Of Fellow Mell   EVERYTHING IS THE SAME
                                             C'EST LA MEME CHOSE
                                             IT'S THE SAME THING

Being is the Same as Not Being
IT'S ALL THE SAME THING
                    Look for the words . . charce les mots
                                          dans les bois anciens
*   trouve la couture
POME IN PATOI   *   sauve la wéture
Jmasse dain bois   . . I sit in the woods   *   TRANS:-look for the words
Lapra midi d'or   . . Afternoon of gold   *   in the ancient woods
Charchant les mot   . . Looking for words   *   find the way to cut
De mon Gerard   . . Of my Gerard (brother) *   save the wagon . . . .
                                          * *
La realité   . . Reality
Si profonde   . . So profound
Offre pas d mot   . . Offers no words   Pour les mots   . . for the words
A mon pondre   . . To my pondering   Improbables   . . improbable
                                             Shpa poete   . . I no poet

Charche comme oiseau   . . Look like bird
Cassez dans l harbe   . . Broken in grass   ┌──────────────┐
Qui pique comme diable . . Itch like devil   │ OUT OF HARM │   ◭
                                                 └──────────────┘

                                                            301

Sebastian & the Brotherhood of Eyes
I have been Bodhisattva for many ages

All the Same Thing   . . . Peter Martin Road Catholic. . . . . . .

------------------Love hides in the center of all things------------

            Ecstasy of long hike into Easonburg lights of evening
              on holy road of birds of April Eve

The sound of the newsmen was never heard in the plaints of heaven. . . . .
                              *
    Dostoevsky "Their eyes met in hell"   *   L   LIANG K'AI (active   *
                                          *   O   A   A D 1200) *
There has been freedom from this body--- *   V   R   "The Buddha On the Way *
There is now freedom from this body---   *   E   T   to the Bodhi Tree"---   *
There will be freedom from this body---   *   L   Colour on silk---And,   *
            A P r a y e r . . . . *   Y   reverse, Liang K'ai   *
                                          *   "Winter Landscape"   *
                              *

Any bit of Sangsara can only offer me blackness now---that new unbearable
blackness in my heart---the deep turning-about is nothing but revulsion---
But Nirvana means the end of all lust, which is my last hold on self------

ALL YOUR TRUE WILD FEELINGS are available
only in sobriety---Hospital, October, Essential Mind
prove that-----Those pines pristine morning lake dont shine
in tired muddled senses of liquor---Go to Riverbottom, do not drink
intoxicants, rest, remember------- BEGIN NEW LIFE OF AVIDITY AND YOUTH---
This is your tired breaking point of heart-body----time to heal the "sorry parts"
---Then what Allen & Sterling have to say wont even interest you---Learn in Mexico
how to live in Rocky Mount or anywhere----This is the advice of the Buddha to the
slipping Bodhisattva-----There's no the-stoning, no bottom to the illusion bottle---
no end to wild imaginary feelings---no end to regret----no clarity in wine---
        * * * * * * * * * * * * * * * * *   ("What's the sense of getting *piffed*" says Ti Nin)
        * Shine, Angel,   *
        * In the Night   *   Your time has come
        * Samadhi   *   for t rue and promised happiness-----
        * Of delight.   *   Released, made secure in heart, go then . . .
        * * * * * * * * * * * * * * * * *

        If such is the case, my Saints, Gerard, Avalokitesvara, Buddha
          Sakyamuni, Papa, Jesus, and St. Francis, not to drink, help me with
          all your power to keep the law---We dont drink in sleeping dreams---
          in saintly infancy---It's going to take years to destroy the formed habit
          ---Help me to keep the law, not to cheat, if that's the case---HELP ME--------
        The time to understand is short----After that, nothing to do in the sand, I'll
        write the DULUOZ LEGEND, from the point of view of the Saintly Truth---When I see
      a glass or a bottle of wine, of beer, whiskey, mescal, I'll say: "A bottle of death
    for the fools of birth"---I'll interest myself in the Golden Mentation, in the Mind of
    Gold---Pure water my drink---The head dry, suffer, like a kid---The ignorances of
      others and the gaieties of others and the deaths of others and the wars of others. .
      KEEP THE LAW, THE TIME TO UNDERSTAND IS SHORT
      KEEP YOUR THOUGHTS CLEAR AND WISE . . . . It's all activity in a dream,
        including yourself . . . Great God, man!---*Finis le vin de la vie, finis pour le ciel!*
                              No more life's wine . . . no more, for heaven's
                                                    s a k e
                  * * * * * * * *

ENTER HEAVEN

Child of Dawn	Free from Wine, Joyful & Pure
Enter Heaven	
Thru the Morning	Free from Wine, Joyful in Heaven
In the Lake	
Of the Mind	Keep the Pure Law-----the Time for
	understanding is short. . . . .
Clear and Wise	
The Dharma's Eyes	
Understanding darkness	The little path
Made of Milk	to big freedom

> May I keep the law,
> The time for understanding is short,
> Wisdom is a delicate thing.
> Free from wine,
> The ecstasy of mind.
> Avalokitesvara, Thou Hearer and Answerer of Prayer,
> Protect me from the intoxicants of Sangsara
> ----THE WINE PRAYER

It's by these rules, these disciplines, by this careful nursing of your natural ecstasy, that you're going to come to Nirvana in this life and become the light of the world.

* *

This isnt a world because it is seen by some,
nor is it not-a-world because it is not seen by some . . .

DRIFT DISSOLVES GRIEF . . . (dreamflash)

Your business is with Samapatti (the rest is scribbling & egoism)
    (Transcendental activities)

In reality it's all a similar emptiness, but I am not free for reality (!)
    (o b v i o u s l y , t h e   w i n e   h a n g u p   i s   e m p t i n e s s   t o o)

"Let him retire to a secluded place
in the forest and devote himself to the
practice of the various spiritual   The shiver
disciplines, because it is only by so doing   of the
that he will become capable of   quickbone
attaining in this world of multiplicities
a true insight into the workings of   Jawbone on the ground---the old
Universal Mind in its Essence."----------------   sick wineless mule, his teeth'll
                                                         look the same as mine in the
*   s u n . . . .
                              * * *
                                                         *
The bug in the grass---running around in the
forest of desires---(a parasitical tic at that) . . .

The jet and the wildgoose---I thought it was my breathin---proves It's All
                                                    the Same Thing

EVERYBODY'S LIFE---tragedy, pain, and horror---even the Mexico City Grandee---

BUDDHA VESABBHU---"First level your mind, then the earth will be level."

Stay under this tree and suffering will never happen again------------------------------

BIRDS IN DREAM, tweet, "How can you hold it so *fast*?" (anchor-wise, the sound) and only Avalokitesvara's Diamond Sound can do it, which we then hear, steady, as bird ceases---

FLASH---In South America, the new art, right down to your bottom's eye,---Dizzy Gillespie? (is it Dizzy? Buddha? me?)

WHEN YOU UNLEASH your knife and fork you're no better than the bug on the Buddha Mountain, eating-in. . . . .

IF YOU WANT A DOG TO STOP KISSING YOU, turn your head away silently like another dog.

HUMAN HAPPINESS is only when Nirvana Annihilation is most nearly approximated--- i.e. Life is Glad When Death is Nigh----Sunday Today So Glad is Golden Emptiness Close

LOS MOCHIS Golden Afternoon Arrested for Marijuana---Police Tenements (I keep thinkin
                                                          it   )

THE TATHAGATA'S WOMB has turned out a Mess of Flesh & Darkness
  Concealing the Buddha-Being Eye Light it seems

"BUT THEY *MURDER* YOU with their damned insistence," I complain of ants biting me, and rub em off---biting myself, for all is Thought---Valley of Darts---

APRIL 16---Samadhi of "C'est ainque un rêve, Faut s'reveiller" (and) "On est deja reveillez" (and) "on est toutes deja reveillez"----It's only a dream, you've got to wake up. . . . we're already awake. . . . we're ALL ALREADY AWAKE"---And I definitely saw thru the dream darkness into the inward world of light peopled incredibly with Bodhi-beings galore, waiting for me to enter their land of magic---The Buddha-land-- My 3 dogs were dead still------
                       "It's Only a Dream---
                     You got to wake up---"
           Then:-"It's Only a Dream
                We're all already awake"
           Then:-"It's Only a Dream
                Reveille Toi a Travers"
                (I just thot)
                (Wake up Thru It)
          I was very happy----------
        *

Good as RAY SMITH ON THE ROAD is I think I shall put it aside and write about my life sincerely, clearly, sadly---

A MOVIE NOVEL (and, your pleasure DULUOZ VISIONS). . . . Or I could write a TOWN AND THE CITY Historical Novel of Buddhist India---two brothers from the Himalayan Highlands floating down the Ganges on a home-made raft, to Benares, the sensual jealous lover and the goodhearted imbecile who helps people with their burdens and finally meets Buddha Vesabbhu. . . . . A great story, I'll do it someday, for movies. . . . .

IT'S ALL A DREAM, the same thing as yourself, all in pain, the essence of it is nothingness. It is not Sangsara. . . . it is Tathagata!   You have been, are, and will be all parts of this dream----Now you are a man squashing ticks---Once you were a tick climbing up a man---- It is the Tathagata of Transformations. . . . . It is a dream and you've entered the Golden Stream of Awakening!--- Return to Essence. . . . . What were you doing in April of 1954?---April 1953?--- April 1923?----April 1922?---April 1919? (not Born) This world is unborn---it is the Womb of Tathagata's transformations and emanations ------of essential suchstuff *maya*-------------------your essence of nothingness was not born, is not "alive," and will not die---Rejoice! Rest, Relax! Return!

                THE TATHAGATA
                Name of Movie Novel

DHYANA OF APRIL 20 IN WOODS
Dharma Seedlings---They'll grow into full plants and then I'll harvest the Crop
of Enlightenment---just a matter of waiting in time---SUDDENLY THE FULL HEAD
By living in the open and meditating in the open, are these seedlings best culti-
vated. "Buddha Means Thank You" I'd say. . . . .

"Ancient patriarchal times"---I'm a patriarch and I dont take no crap from
                                         no matriarch . . .
                          *
HOW STRANGE LIFE IS---& I dont like it--   *
How strange it is not to like it------------   *   Buddhism is
                                                   *   gratitude for that
                                                   *   the dream
TATHAGATA---means, Arrived-at-Suchness   *   can be
SUGATA---means, Arrived-at-Goodness   *   awakened from. . . .
        THE GOODNESS OF SUCHNESS   )
                The shining suchness. . . . . .   *
                          *

I AM NEITHER A PAST, PRESENT, OR FUTURE BUDDHA, but a humble disciple of all the
Buddhas, one of the lowliest . . . The great Arhats who were so numerous when my
position among them was humble, are not reborn in this Age---Unless, like my mother,
they are all concealing the Dharma in Good Works Without Telling----
. . . My past lives have been spent in pure bhikkuhood in forests, and my merit has
been increasing steadily. . . . Merit, merit indeed. . . . In my most recent reincarnation,
I was an unenlightened angel in Heaven . . . Now I am back on earth but enlightened . . .
The seedlings planted in the past are growing into full plants and may blossom in
this life, or the next, or the third from now---Anagamin, No-More-Return, is my
goal (as Jack K.), is inevitable, in fact, impossible-to-avoid---All this Karma
concerning the past, and past merit, and future attainment, is One Emptiness. . . . . .

Hipster ideas were foisted on me by heretical heroes---
Giroux had objected, not to talent, but your ideas------

Defiling boys in the land of the Pali Scriptures, is Bowles----

A MOCKINGBIRD SINGING IN THE VOID,
UNASKED AND ALONE, AM I----   Seedlings planted
        Suzuki is like a robin but   in 1953-54 will reach
        I'm a mockingbird   full bloom in 1959---
        Can do anything the robin does   Crop'll be Nirvana . . .
        And more---

WOMEN DRESS FOR WOMEN * * * AND UNDRESS FOR MEN * * * SPEAKING OF JOKES * * *

Putting a mortally wounded bug in the ground saying "Go right on back where you
come from!" to teach Nin---(dreamflash)

HE'S GOT A CARDINAL SIN IN HIS POCKET (dreamflash)

BORN OF THESE FACTORS of simplemindedness the saint passes into ephemeral salvation

                          - - - - - - - - - - - - - - - -
Turning the wheel of my talent   SOUND picked up from eardrums
For the sake of the Dharma   by the mind---the false mind
THE DULUOZ LEGEND, thus   calls it sound, the true mind
*   doesnt call it anything, as a man
                                      * *   hearing noises in his deep sleep. . . . . .
                                      * *
VISIONS OF GIROUX (BOISVERT)
Measured tread through opulence . . .   *

THE FIVE DHARMAS
1.Of Appearance . . . (false senses) (Rupa-dharma)
2.Of Name . . . . (false ideas) (Sankhara-dharma)
3.Of Discrimination (false differences) (Vinnana-dharma)
4.Of Right-knowledge (of un-born-ness) (Prajna-dharma)
5.Of Reality (Suchness of Ultimate Essence) (Tathata-dharma)

"The un-bornness of the un-born essence of all things"---LANKAVATARA p.298

THE THREE SELF-NATURES
1.Of Things   . . . The self-nature of things is e m p t i n e s s
2.Of Ideas   . . . The self-nature of ideas is e m p t i n e s s
3.Of Reality   . . . The self-nature of Reality is e m p t i n e s s
--- ----------

Little Paul on chair with arms outspread: "It's light up help-help time"---
            a n d
EATING FRUIT SALAD, "This stuff makes me feel hoopy doopy"----------
*-

The true and wild mind that dug misty gray trees the Gavins & Westropes of the
brain---Proustian explanation---sit in----

THE ECSTASY OF THE MIND, it's already there (Samadhi is already always there)----
need wine and tea to ease it on thru sometimes (a la On-the-Road-Ray-Smith visions)

TODAY APRIL 25 (Monday) I said to myself "Goddamit, that's enough of childish self-
allowed remorse (over drinking, etc.) and that's enough of childish self-allowed
chagrin over the criticisms of the Rexroths and Rosenbergs of this world . . . Rexroth
criticized DOCTOR SAX and Rosenberg criticized JAZZ OF THE BEAT GENERATION in New
World Writing . . . The world doesnt even exist, I should be smart at least and be
strong-minded. . . . AND rid myself of the Saha Triplicity of Criticizable
                                                               Criticizer
                                                               Criticizing
        But my mind is too mad/ and I'm buried too deep/ . . . in suffering Saha. . . . /
    SUFFERING SAHA! WHAT A DRAG!

"For hours alone" . . . Carolyn C.   Lust is Holy---all of it is holy
                                           and 100% mental---
Thorns are the same as cream   Killing is holy---
To an angel. . . . .   Holy is a divine conception---being
                                             a conception it is false. . . . .

FORMS WITH NO SELF NATURE, like in a movie
---this is Step Seven, Right Mindfulness . . .

BURN THE FOREST DOWN to get one tic? It's all the same mindshit.
Self-purifying splendor. . . . . . .
There is nothing but what exists in the mind itself . . a put-together shame. . . .

There is nothing but what has been put together by shame and ignorance.

ANYTHING THAT DISTURBS you realize that you've got to be tough, like everyone else,
as long as you hold your conditional bones---That childlike feeling that life is a
punishing challenge is true, you've got to realize emptiness and self-less-ness and
Samadhi bliss even if Prince Kalinga be severing your flesh from your bones. . . .
You've got to have guts, which only means, you've got to see through pain & horror
for the emptiness that it is. . . . So now at least you know enough to rest too. . . . . . .
The Zen Masters slugged each other so they could see stars & intuit emptiness!

IT'S JUST A HALTING TRIP TO THE GRAVE no matter what you do----The Mind Of Reality
has nothing to do with birth, which it ignores, and death, which it ignores . . . It is
one limpid essence put to play, like the lil white yapdog . . (appears to be put to play) . .

Sandy is a Tree
Dreaming Nightmares
With a pretty
Furry body

* *

O Tathagatas in all the
Ten Quarters of the Universes,
do not forsake the pitiful
form, but destroy it. . . . . . .

There is nothing that exists
but of the mind itself

Lil's little kitties were delivered
from the blue emptiness---
Skullets from the Moon---
The little mother is happy,
Purring, afraid of Sandy
So wont come out
* And sit in the sun
* But hides behind the screen
* In the dusty garage
* Happy, purring.
* A little tale.
*   (And is Davey's birth-tale)
* * * * *

* *

SAD POEM * * *
The monstrous ticks that cant
be shaken off my pencil, are
falling from trees all up &
down the forest, millions of
them, & crawling towards me
energetically, blindly, ugly
in one converging swarm,
looking for deliverance,
which they will get
when they suck my blood
and get to be as big
        as ping pong balls
        and fall off
        spawning Millions more
        each one of them
        a future grandmother
        of mine.
            So I say what Rabelais say
            'I drink eternally'
            Hic hoc hoak
            Tip the bung cap back
            Ho More Claret!
            Paris be damned!
            Hell me O Low!
            Shoot!

WHAT'LL YOU DO NOW?
What you do now will be of the mind itself,
imaginary all of it---the sublime writing,
    the ugly drinking, the dhyana practising,
    all of the mind itself---On your
        H e a v e n l y   F a r m ---

POME
While you've got your form?
While what?
What form?
What while?
You think you got no time
            had no time
            will have no time ?

Shame, shame, shame

There is nothing that hurts & kills you
    but of the mind itself

    Okay I know

What good will it do
What harm will it do

* *

* * *   A   D R E A M   I N   T H E   H O S P I T A L   G R A S S   * * *

The young sailor
Crazy in the madhouse
Slept on the bank
Hopeless and sick
Thinking the future
Held him a wife
And a glittering life
And smiling fathers
And mothers of love
And sisters of hope
And brothers of light
And instead he awoke
To the workmen
Of the woods

Who said "We
Thought you was dead"
It was just I.
Drank the night before
With Lexington Bill
A Hardboot Marine
From under the hill---
Drunk as hoot owls
We staggered in the night
Raising our howls
To the pale morning light.
My name was Numbered.
Z-305etc.

Life is Sick
Dogs Cough
Bees Sail
Birds Hack
Trees Saw
Woods Cry
Men Die
Ticks Try
Books Lie
Ants Fly
Goodbye

* * *

Cultivate the noblest ideas of
egolessness
emptiness
imagelessness
and you will be free from passion
and ever serene
The Psycho analyst will throw
up his hands with horror when
he realizes what Buddhism
will do
to you

   Me, I dont Care

        * * * * * * * * * * * * * *

     O Lax, Giroux, Latouche,
       Kelly, Lost Angels!
     My Ginsbergs are Devils---
     Our Lord Loves -----

               * * * * * *

At least, all hail & thank God,
  the anguish of a form
  Disappears with the form

        . . . .

Playing records in Phi Gamma
Delta, Sat night---O
  the glittering glory of
    that angelhood-------!

        - - - -

    T sa n incest world

Americans---it's a world of
  m o n s t r o u s f o o l s

I'M A MAN, can take care of myself, am alone in the world, am going to Mexico. . .

O holy happiness: I am going to my Mexico!---My desert plateau, to be with
                  A s v h a g h o s h a !

Vajrajnana---my name
    (Diamond Knowledge)

* *

THE EGO OF QUIESCENCE is not*   *
in a quiescent state---Buddha   *
was Perfect because of all   *   *
ego and discrimination gone

True Buddhism is Sincerity & Aryan Forgiveness
     (has nothing to do with Zen Wise Ego)
     (& Zen socking one another---socking, sucking,
      what's the difference?)
* *OOOOOOO* * * *
* *

and so he said "I am Perfect"---he didnt say "I am Quiescent" or "I am no more
reuniting to Change" (returning)---He was off from assertion & negation--------------
My (angry) passion this morning about tricks of Freudian officials putting political
dissenters like the Vermont-draft-housewife in St. Elizabeth Madhouse, was, though
intelligent, though true, *worldly,* therefore vainly excited over mere mind manifested
dreams and diseased un-restorable conditionalities---The Tathagatas want me to cut
out and become perfect and not get hungup on arbitrary conceptions like friendship
and silly runningaround in different parts of Sangsara called Travel---they want me
to get rid of the literary ego, which is a hindrance, a great hindrance, and of the
discriminations of others defiling me in my Non Solitary lay state---(Although, Hui
Neng says: "Because Tathata reproduces its own attribute and gives rise to 'idea,'
our sense-organs, in spite of their functioning in seeing, hearing, tasting, smelling,
touching and knowing, *are not defiled*" . . .) But in this limited sense, the Tathagatas
"want" me to go into Samapatti as my activity (transcendental compassions) . . . Best of
all, it's all in "their" hands as to whether the Dharma that I have written down
is to be discriminated or not, for they realize that even Dharma-Spreading is an
arbitrary conception liable to defile and renew seeds of ego in the Divine Mind . . .

Menschen kenner, judge of men

SOUTH AFRICA, "Our sages say, even where there is no pot to boil there should be fire"
  (ancient saying of tribesmen)

Go on drinking and the world'll roll you . . . life'll roll you. . . . why not just sober
wiseness kicks?---a *new life* of sober wiseness. . . . . .

    BOOK . . . *FELLAHEEN ADVENTURES IN MOMINU* (BUDDHA VESABBHU)

Coffee, tea, coffee, tea, there's no
end to my goddam gullet
****
　　　　　　　　　*
RETURN---　　　　　*
there's your　　　　*
return---the　　　　*
little white dog　　*
was a return!　　　*
　　　-　　　　　　　*
The RELIGIOUS NATURE　*
the intrinsic empti-　*
ness eternally pure　*
　　and shiny　　　　*
　　　　　　　　　　*
　　* * *　　　　　　*
　　　　　　　　　　*
MAY 6,1955　　　　　*
LIFE IS NOT A FAMILIAR SCENE　*
dear to our hearts---it is a　*
very eerie dream---completely　*
alien, strange, unfriendly,　*
unfamiliar, is why it hurts us . . .

There's no such thing as 'What'll I
do now?'---

Pulling the pain out of my tooth
I also pull the whole world out
& finally myself & invert the
tooth last of all into Void--
　　　　(dreamflash)

Turn about, now, at once, face
ultimate reality---what do you
see? Nothing.---

Actopan here I come.---

It is not an attribute of your
religious nature that you were
born of woman's womb, O Bodhisattva-Mahasattva!----------------
****

When I saw the thorns rock in the wind like ripples on the sea I shivered from
the strangeness and realized that the familiar thing is not this world but the
Pure Bliss of the Unborn.
THE THING TO DO IS UNTRAIN THE MIND back to the untrained (for ignorance) enlightenment
which was its original state, or rather, akin to its original state---Practising
Buddhism is a Training-in-Reverse---
　　　　- - - - - - - - - - - - - - -
　　　　Thorns cant be too different from cream
　　　　They produce pretty white blossoms
　　　　　　in May

WONDERIN WHETHER I should transplant the rest of the tomato plants or go to the
toilet I jump up from the bed of dreams and go to the toilet "There are no tomato
plants anyway"---

　　　Do not discriminate the mind from its mental processes
　　　　and accept the ideas from it
　　　　　as being real. . . .
　　　　　　　There is no difference between the appearance
　　　　　　of the tomatoes, and your mind. . . . . . .
　　　　　　　Those tomato plants ARE your mind. . . . .
　　　　　　　Does it fit the case to question the being or non-being
　　　　　　of those tomatoes? Their being, multiplicity, individuality,
　　　　　　value, etc., are false judgments, false arbitrations. . . . .

UNDISTURBED BY EGOISM
UNFLUFFED BY DISTINCTIONS

The will-to-live (Nature)
　　　　is the Mother,
The Ignorance (God's Creation)
　　　　is the Father

Seeing
　　　the truth
　　　　　as I do . . . . . makes me a gloomy
　　　　　　　　no good
　　　　　　　　　human. . . . .

A world which is neither here
　　　　　nor there . . .　　THE MIND'S INVISIBLE INFINITE WOMB

SENTIENT BEINGS are monsters predisposed to hate the truth which is that there
are not even any Buddhas or Tathagatas in Highest Perfect Truth----Which is why
Highest Perfect Truth wont start attracting them tomorrow morning--------------------
But that is the pitifulness of the world, that everyone knows------------------ -------

MY PAST LITERARY ACHIEVEMENTS---there's no need for me to worry now or in the
future about recognition, because it doesnt fit the cast to question whether a dream
be great or lousy---I'm in Enlightenment now, which is a new thing, and literature
is a past dream---with praise anyhow already from Auden, Cowley, Giroux, Ginsberg,
Sandburg, Rexroth and others how can this be called the tired statement of a literary
failure? (Praise from Anson, Morley, VanDoren, Kazin, Burroughs, Lax, who else do
you want?)---If my manuscripts rot in my desk in my sister's house it will be because
of Neglect, not no-talent . . . or if they rot on the ground, it will be because of
Apocalypse, not no-talent . . . (not no-genius).

I KNOW A FELLOW who says that he is
God because he neither exists nor does
not exist. He is the first to say it.
After him comes everything.

Universal Mind is not the cause of God---
  error is the cause of God (Ignorance-Creator)---
  God is Ignorance-Creator because it is an idea,
an arbitrary conception---
    The cause of error is the false mental
    system of Ignorance-Creation wrinkling
    the face of Universal Mind---
      the cause of Ignorance-Creation
      is its Birth in the Tathagata's Womb
      which is invisible and infinite
      and mysterious and empty,
      the thinglessness of the unthinged
      essence of all things-----
      the Telephone post is maya,
      Magic, now you see it,
      now you dont

        * * * * * * * * * * * * * * *

        * * * * * * * * * * * * * *

Wind of the day
Is like the wind of
        ignorance
The bushes are essentially
        still
But the wind makes them
        jiggle
Because of my arbitrary
        idea
Of motion & stillness---
In reality nothing.
        * * * *

      See?

In other words
Just close your eyes
And it aint there
No more no more
(This
    is new Poetry)(called Pomery)
      (Pomes) (Pomist)

THE TRANSCENDENTAL SOUND on other ---
planets same as here---therefore
transcendental thought is same . . .

        O O O O

Eschew self . . . . MAY 11
You must break yourself of the habit of
life, that is, of entertaining conceptions
of life and human beings,---then will
end the torrent of suffering---It's
habit-energy, the energy of habit---In
Pure Reality there is only the
Tathagata's Ecstasy. . . . .

Buddha-mountain
People racing up & down
Buddha-cave
His heart hugely beating
And the Bright Room
Within--
Buddha-mountain
Like the world
Like Buddha
Is Arbitrary Conception

WHILE I WAS WRITING because I had a notion that I was a human being or some kind
of being it was alright to live with my mother in family relationship all the time
but now I know that such a notion has nothing to do with reality and there is
nothing to write about and I am not afraid of emptiness. . . . .
For this I am neither to be praised or blamed

WHILE I WAS WRITING (CONT'D)
I'm afraid to leave this comfortable life like in a high cliff dream I tremble
and open my eyes and the high cliff vanishes . . .
Sure I want to get rid of this pit of self death and false pride and false self hate
but I dont want to part with the dreamground I stand on----If I trembled now and
opened my eyes, svaha, the pit is gone and I'm not the worst the wear for it and
Mind doesnt Vanish, it only changes transformations from dreamself to awakenedhood.
It's only because of the mind-system that you can say the stricken tree is sick---
I'm sick. Family relationships, defile, confuse, the mind, re-plunge it in
ignorance---what's there to pity? Be like Han Shan.
SOLUTION: Simply come home for Xmas-to-April every year . . .
A man comes out of his solitude to practise Christian Pity and so he abandons
reality---This is the secret of the failure of Christian Piety and of the success
of Buddhist Bodhisattvahood----That is to say, in Christian Pity the *path* of
concentrating the mind on the emptiness aspect of things is abandoned, for hand-
holding at bedsides, as though in essence there were really such a thing as self,
such a thing as other self, as living beings, as a universal selfhood.
The great St. Francis made sure not to have to be around pity-subjects. . . .

   The truth kills---Pa know

There's no sense in tryin to turn your weird mind around,
the truth
is true
Hal Chase is laffin
& there's no Hal Chase simple & blue

                    Stay with Pure Reality under all circumstances
                    (as tho you could be separated from it . . . . . . !)

STARTING NOW   that means no "last thot" of what so-and-so'll think of you etc. . . .

A writing Buddha? Possessed of the 32 powers of writing excellence?

SATORI! ALL THINGS ARE THE SAME! THERE ARE NO RULES! DO WHAT YOU WANT! WHOCARES?
Love, life, laugh,---sleep, lie down, shutup, ---getup, run away, scream, sink, swim, fall,
fly, flail, flop,----who the hell cares? The Tathagata's Womb is All Pure . . . .

To be a Writing Buddha possessed of the 32 powers of writing excellence, first off,
you'd have to attain to the above satori of "Do what you want"----After that you'd
have to revise all notions of "writer" "publisher" etc.---and write in trance---
for "yourself"----report on ecstasies of samadhi----raving wild spontaneous reports
from the shimmery news---ALL IS WELLING . . . . . . and finally-----of course, I know what
to write, yes, the Samapattis. . . . visions of pity. . . . visions of invaluable use to the
world, and done modestly and truthfully and then I donate every cent of royalty to
Buddhist Monasteries of the New World------beginning with the one at Santa Barbara,
Dwight Goddard's odd vihara (he was an underrated Master)----And do all this at
once with BUDDHA TELLS US---without *doubt*----

THE ANCIENT BUDDHA   You are now admitted
OF ALL PROSE AND POETRY   into the Sangha
IN ALL TEN QUARTERS   and money has no more hold
OF THE UNIVERSE   & reality in your life,
                              life indeed
. . . .   Life has nothing to do
HE IS NOT DISCUSSED   with anything---
IN THE LITTLE REVIEWS . . .   Sangha
* *
                                Dharma
                                   Buddha
                                      I bow'd my head May 11,1955

Drastic, swift change, in all fields of JK's life---at once to Mexico---advice in
Sutta Nipata about drink and leaves you $5 a month possible to live in Meixco adobe
hut . . .   Leave, (as a humble head-bowed disciple in the joyous rainbow forest of the
Buddha), your manuscripts with others, to do as they please-----

       No need, no poverty
     It's time now
       I wasnt getting used to the pot

THE WRITING BUDDHA
That is, who spreads the Dharma, by means
of his Excellent Perfect Talent, for the sake
of universal salvation (Just as Dostoevsky
came close to being a Writing Christ)
 The humility of the new disciple
in the Sangha in the Forest with the Lord
is unchanged but it is in Time, in 2500 AG
(After Gotama) that I am Writing Buddha

As life is neither a comedy nor a tragedy there remains not one vestige of a reason
to write for artistic reasons, poetic reasons, literary reasons, humanity reasons,
but to emancipate all beings from their enslavement to false ideas of existence, time,
birth, death, work, excellence, pride, fear, anger, ego-self, lust, folly, rage, rue.

    My own little vihara in the Valley of Mexico---
    the first of many monkshacks on the ground-----

Shelter from pernicious insects that interrupt meditation
(such as mosquitos, tics, scorpions, stingflies, crawling worms, lizards and snakes) . . .

    WHY GO TO CALIFORNIA when you can go to Mexico?
    (ed.note.Finally *did* go to California,the fiasco of Frisco Fall Fifty Five . . .)

Energy of the Angry Ego	My head
grinds on	is turned by
Lit'ry rages consuming me	every eye
Visions of Neal is a pitiful ms.	
In the jail that no one wants	*
Even tho in time	
It is a shuddering Might	I cant be nutty
Of silver paper snow words	because for me there *is*
	no world

          LIQUOR'S IRRELEVANT

* * * * * * * * * * * *

"Words are just like a man
carrying a lamp to look for
his property, by which he can
say: this is my property."
      LANKAVATARA 310

P O M E
Objects---seen in dreams
         discriminated in visions

Idea
statements---discriminated erroneously
              also

* * * * * * * * * * * *

Atwell down giving the sign
to Law----Tappe at third, Fondy on first,
"Bounces around
And it stays up there,
Nobody to get it"
  (radio baseball)

--- ---------- --- ------- --- --------- ---

It is the nature of time to be
 beginningless/ past / & endless future. . . . .
       (THERE IS NONE)

Blow as deep as you wanta blow---
so dont change "Subterraneans"
. . . prose about Mardou's thighs
and receiving-place. . . . .

ASK THE STARRY CHAMPION
WHAT THE REALITY IS LIKE,
YOU INTELLECTUAL FOOLS----

THE 3 EMPTINESSES
    1.Emptiness as sense-object
    2.Emptiness as time-object
    3.Emptiness as phenomenal-object
Or I call it also, THE THREE INEXISTENCIES:-
The three ways in which things can not possibly exist . . .

The truth of imagelessness . . . is in conformity with meaning rather than
                                    with words & letters. . .

CROSS YOUR EYES AS YOU READ THESE WORDS:- *TRUTH IS NOT IN THE LETTERS*

Definition of Dharma:-C'est comme ca que c'est etabli. . . . . .
                    "That's how things are established. . . . ."   Empty

--UNFOCUS EYES ALL TIME, like bemused reader over a page---

TATHAGATA,   is, Suchnesshood-Accomplished, Sameness-Attained
NIRVANA,   is, Blownoutness, Blown-Out-Ness
DHARMA,   is, Truth-Law of Emptiness
            Law of Reality
            Establishment of Things (dhri)   There is no individual
TATHATA,   is, Howness of Things   in the matter of personality
            How-Things-Are   be it sweet or sour-----
            As-Is-Ness   *
            Whichisness

SANGSARA, the Movie of Existence, was created,---and has been replenished time and
again and pumped and jacked up to go on being Real---Michael O'Shea (actor) sitting
brooding in the bed in my daydream knows that it's all an empty vision of the mind
but as soon as Virginia Mayo (his wife) notices him and notices he's getting older
etc. and how he's interested in the latest news about them in Variety, he returns
his attention to things of time, unreality, atoms, change, history, personality,
and loses contact with the Bright Wiseness of Suchnesshood---Then people say "Well
you've got Virginia and Buddha's got nothin"---but Virginia is getting old too and
baggy-eyed like Michael and they dont know what to do about stemming old age and
death and despair, but Buddha knows.

                         The Tathagata
I'M LEAVING EVERYBODY behind   SUCHNESSHOOD-ATTAINED
now---I give up writing for   Sugata, GOODNESSHOOD-ATTAINED
public reasons and go into   Tathagata, Thus-Understanding
pure imagelessness, ego-less-   How about:-SUCHNESSER
ness, & emptiness---They wont   or SUCHER   Nothing sublime
understand how I can be able   or SUCH ONE   or petty
to manage the "purity of death"   or SUCH-IS   about adhering
while still "alive" and young   Sugata,   WELL-IS   to the D h a r m a
at that---They wont understand
the Tathagatas in all 10 Quarters   * * * * * * *
of the Universes till suffering Opens their Eyes. . . . .

* *
The MESSIAH is a special idea wildly true in itself, as in the case of a Carl S.
in the Madhouse suddenly becoming independent of history and numbers and names and
claiming and believing in his mind that he is the one, the true, the promised MESSIAH
---There can be 100 million Messiahs each one believing himself the only one, the
only son of God---
        The Tathagatas in all 10 Quarters of the Universes
          a p p r e h e n d   t h i s - - -

LAST NIGHT I deliberately killed a mosquito because it wanted to bite my face---I
killed it only because I saw my chance---For this, may I be reborn as a mosquito
& pay my Karmic debt---The reason was fear of pain---

The torrent of suffering carries
the mosquito and me away----------

                                      Le vin, la poesie,
                                        et du *virtud*

"Something old and lost, Madam . . ."
                    (ME,1941,old ms.)

"There is nothing in the line of something in nothing." --IBID., orange papers,
                                              I was 18
"And when the dust of the earth will scatter to the winds of nothing, then even
the particles of dust themselves will begin to dissect themselves and they themselves
will emulate the earth's big act of dissolving and dissolve themselves. Then the
particles of the dust particles will in turn dissolve, and this process will continue a million billion times over and over again until the particles will become
so small that they will not be far from nothing."
    "(However much finest dust be analysed it can never become by conformity and
combination the purity of space" (*Buddha*)) ---
    "Then when eternity ends, the process of making all the particles of the earth
into nothing will have been completed. And so I say eternity will never end, because
that is what it means. So I look at it this way: When I look into the sky and see
nothing (space is nothing---'spaceless') I should kneel down and weep with joy at
the marvelousness of such perfect nothingness"---(!)
                                  ME, at age 18----Remembering
                                      Buddha-Kin
OF THE DEAD WASP (MOTH) I said:-   Buddha-Knowledge of Before
"Prostrate bliss" and felt great pity for it,
slept "the sleep of a killer"---When G.J. and I first got drunk
on Moody Street we called everybody God and we thought we were God---We were a
great gang I say---We knew more than we do now. When I sat in that parlor August
1941 day-dreaming of football and conditional glory I should have been told to stay
home, in the sandbank, in the woods, praising Nothingness as I had done that Summer
layin around the grass with dogs and Walt Whitman and grass 'tween my teeth, and I
guarantee you there would have been no torrent of suffering------Everything I did as
a kid was instinctively right---My mistakes have all arisen from education forced on
me from outside---I learned to write words from education, granted, as there wouldnt
be this teaching-Dharma (which is absurd in itself because the truth cant be cut up
into pieces and re-arranged into a system of teaching), but it was education that
made me turn aside from pure Taoistic concerns about Teenage Nothingness to a million
multiple Ignorant ideas culminating in "novels" and "works of literature"---when I
should have stayed in my field with my wisp of grass, my lazy disciples like Salvey,
my pristine Buddhahood intact---
    Well, it was in my Karma to suffer and lose the path and wander into horrified
darkness, maybe for a reason to be unveiled in this reincarnation, maybe not. I pray
Tathagata it will be unveiled and fructified in this glorious rosy reincarnation
    R a i n / o n , / O / C l o u d !
                    -----li po----
                                          18 is the intelligent fruitional age
"Is there nothing   * * * *   to teach the Dharma---at 18 kids are
but death to assuage   * *   *plain* smart
Time?"---ME, at 18,
unless it's from Wolfe . . .   But, Time, which doesnt necessarily exist, there's
                                  only one thing that will assuage it, which also
                                  doesn't exist necessarily---Death (!)

I WANTA GO TO LOWELL
see the Gray Clock in the Rain
find G.J. and tell him all's alright. . . . . .(that Lowell is a vision in my brain,
                                          doesnt exist)----

"THE BODHISATTVA IS SAID TO HAVE WELL GRASPED THE TEACHINGS OF THE TATHAGATAS WHEN,
ALL ALONE IN A LONELY PLACE, BY MEANS OF HIS TRANSCENDENTAL INTELLIGENCE, HE WALKS
THE PATH LEADING TO NIRVANA"
                    My call to Mexico Dobe Hut

LAY ASIDE YOUR FEARS AS YOU LISTEN TO THE TEACHING OF EGOLESSNESS----blew my brains
out in the woods, using P's gun, they found me there after 2 days of wonder and
called the Law----then they wondered what it was that had made me go Eedy bobby
bow-bay with the old dog Bob, what individual I was there in the matter of this
affectionate muling and puling and wailing with the poor mutt, all gone now in the
sheriff's basket---what *signs* of personality left, or *were* in the first place?---
what was it in Bob himself that wee'd and squee'd and cried so glad that will be
buried in his bone hole wid im ?----it had no being or non-being either, it was all
a big idea, a dream, something the mind system made out---Now we hear no more from
poor Jack forevermore---He was nothin but a good ole ghost after all, just like he
kept sayin (cause T's taught him)---This daydream is not discriminated information
from the Manas Intuitive Mind, which does not give discriminative information---it
is the thinking brain-mind alright, but at the heart, what I missed, in the revelation, it is the Manas because it cant be the Alaya Vijnana Storage Universal Mind
which is all-conserving but not mentating, not subject to action like mentation---
The Intuitive Mind is (gives) therefore that information which is realized but can
never be uttered because it can never be analyzed or even discriminated, as words
are born of discrimination in the discriminating brain-mind. Compri?
   It is by intuitive Mind therefore, by "self realization thru identification,"
that we come to Enlightenment and Alaya-Vijnana.

$$* * * * * * * * * * * * * * * * *$$
$$* * * * * * * * * * * * * * * *$$
$$* \quad * \quad * \quad * \quad * \quad * \quad * \quad *$$

THE THING ABOUT GREEN'S HOUSE
in my Duluoz Legend memory-mind
is, your childhood vision of the "Joneses"
---later seen in Gallaghers---(technical point)

"YOU SHOULD HAVE YOUR ABODE
WHERE YOU CAN SEE ALL
THINGS FROM THE VIEW POINT
OF SOLITUDE" Lankavatara p.318
        * * * * * * * *
Or,
      I could call the DULUOZ LEGEND:-
      "Analyzed Visions of Myself"

   Psychoextermination
     not psychoanalysis
   "Exterminated Visions of Myself"
        * * * * * * * * * * * *
      The only thing
      I know that is to be
      done now is to keep this
    "different forms of the same
thing" continually Yathabhutam in Mind . . . . the rest is Hogwash.

WHATEVER IS PREDICABLE AND KNOWN is a different form of the same empty-ness thing--
Including God, Tathagatas, 8 Fold Paths, hurt prides, Dharmas, Suffering, the end
of Suffering, or Joy---What is not-predicable
                  And is Un-known
                  Is the same thing
                  As what is predicable
                  And known---
                  The Same thing.
                  Essence
                              BOREDOM
Anything you can think of
Including the expression
D.F.O.T.S.T.
is
D.F.O.T.S.T.

THE ACTUAL ONENESS

   The solitude
   Of the oneness
   Of the essence
   Of everything

      The solitude
      Of the actual oneness
      Of the unbornness
      Of the unborn essence
      Of everything

* *
DIFFERENT FORMS OF THE SAME THING
* *

      AND IN SAMADHI, at each breath-out,
         think it: "Differente formes de la
                  meme chose"
               Over & over again

         SOMETHINGNESS & NOTHINGNESS
         Are different forms of the
             s a m e   t h i n g
                  D.F.O.T.S.T.

            IS THE SAME

               AS ECSTASY

         *   *   *   *   *   *   *   *   *

         Nirvana is the ephemeral realization in the mind that
         suffering and joy are different forms of the same thing . . .

The true realization of Nirvana, Tough to Hold!

Sleep---tantric cannibals repeating "Different forms of the same thing" over & over
---you enter their ring to get it, they get high on unavoidable natural high nuances
of the same thing (dreamflash).

HOLY NOTES . . .   .   That hairbrush is unknowable unpredicable shining suchness
in the form of a hairbrush. . . . .

    SANGSARA *IS* NIRVANA
           N O W
                    And there is no Sangsara
                    There is no hairbrush
So what's the need of Discipline?   And no Nirvana
Discipline and Rushing-about are   No extinction of no hairbrush
different conceptions of the same thing . . .

Rabelais and Asvhaghosha wrote for the same reason

Compassion and the planting of roots of goodness in the Buddha lands,
And hate and the murder of fathers,
Are different forms that the same thing takes.

Instead of spending their time analyzing the different forms, men should
concentrate their attention on the fact that they are different forms o.t.s.t.
This is my final answer to psychoanalysis and even to science.
     These are the healing
         w a t e r s

                                NOSELFNATURE SO IT DOESNT
                                 M A T T E R * * *
Holy heals }
Evil sickens }   Same thing now & in the Long Run

* * * * * * * * * * * * * *ooooooooooooooooooooooooooooooooooooooooooooooooooo* * * * * * * * * * * *

THE DHARMA
is like pacing in the yard---"better you could not do"---
    The Dharma is understood to be an arbitrary conception but it is because of the
arbitrary conception of sentience that the Dharma is invoked---that's why they say,
the Dharma *is* sentience but the *Dharmakaya*, Tathata, the Essence, the Body of the
Truth (so-to-speak), transcends sentience and *is* the Dharma-which-is-sentience and
is the Pure Divine-Name Mind itself and *is* isness----the Unknowable Unpredicable
shining suchness which is the "Same Thing" that all different forms belong to, that
all different forms are.
    Practising the Dharma (concentrating the mind and body on emptiness) is practising
the attainment of the unifying spirit of the principle of Nirvana---O what words!---
but in reality we know that Nirvana and this Life-and-Death Sangsara world are different forms of the same thing, the same pure thingness of isness. But we may not all
always know it, and so there is the Dharma, the Truth-Law, to remind us by pointing
a finger at it so that we may identify it and identify ourselves with it and distinguish it as our property in the dark, (a lamp to guide the way & prevent stumbling
& suffering.)
    The Dharma, the Truth-Law, is a good raft that will carry us to that other shore
and once we get there we must not walk overland with the raft on our back, once we
get to that other shore of enlightenment we may discard the arbitrary conception
of the raft Dharma, the Truth-Law, and concentrate our Mind on its own pure suchness
of foreverhood. In this pure foreverhood there is no question as to Truth, or Law
of Truth, or shores and crossings, or rafts, or any thing.
    The actual nature of true pure foreverhood is a big BLANK POTENTIAL
                                  THAT CAN RAY FORTH
                                  ANYTHING IT WANTS
      IT'S A BLAZING BLISS   FROM ITS PURE STORE
    IT IS MATTIVAJRAKARUNA, the Transcendental Diamond Compassion (!)

VISIONS OF MYSELF May 1955 Big Easonburg Woods, N.C.

The pine trees of Mike and the empty blue sky, radiant glory, different forms
of the same thing that I am. And that same thing that I am and you are and all are
and everywhere is, whatever is predicable and knowable and you can see with your
plain true eyes and smell with your old snot nose and tell with your touchbody and
think of with your vacant rangy brain and taste with your kisserlip tongue and hear
with your aurifice, it is neither in a state of suffering or of joy, it is different
forms of the same thing which is unpredicable unknowable shining suchness of the
solitude of the actual oneness of the unbornness of the unborn essence of all things.
 I see imaginary traveling phantasm stringers of nothing-hush in the blue at
  the same time's a bug whipped by and there is the shining glory which is
   neither glory or beatness of the Sun shining on the bark of tall pines and
    on the shimmered needles reminding me of the pines of the lake of time
     when I was a leetles boysh in my mabra's pada at age Fut in the year 0
      Suck ee and they took me to Fram Tam Lakeview Pock to see the rollic
       coasters and I was pink a-bundled and saw the pines that later, after
        Aw afternoons such, with Mike, buddy, I saw with eyes of same calibre
         seeing---that is to say, the perception of sight of the eyes never
          changes, it is the eyeballs that come and go from grave to door, pond
           to plit, pone to pine, sick to suck, leaf to whistle of the mill noon
            drowsy America of Whitman and yr Dostoevskyan horrible Ultimo Poto
           Baltimo Poe
              Dostoevskyan
             glooms of EW-ROPE and if you dont understand what I'm sayin, read
             it over again. This is the first vision of Visions of Myself,
              the empty blue sky and the pines imprinted in it, the emptiness
               not hiding the appearance, the appearance not annihilating the
                emptiness, are different forms of the same thing, like life
                 and death, sickness and health, do and dont, by which you
                  know, Topers, Eternal Drinkers, Readers, Lovers & Farts,
                  if I hadnt written this chapter it woulda been the same as
                  writing it, two things, one essence, do, or dont, no
                  matter, for nothing has self nature, this is the news
                  coming to you from the Sage in Your Soul---the killer
                  in It haint spoken up yet.

VISIONS OF MYSELF PART TWO

And this late light that is falling over the woods and the fields, the quiet
 swish of the mule's tail and right beside it the little black lump of the
  pig muzzling at the tin trough---This light, clean, clear, cool, making green
   fields greener and great trees quieter, it's like the light on that babyhood
    dream of mine when John Chalifoux drove his Froo paw Pop Ford (presumably
     with wife) past the daliesque images shadowing sward carpets the other side
      of the valley when I was shamed and the Tathagatas told me not to be born---
       that dream took place in the same strange place as this which is no place
        ---Tired at my feet the little dusty flowers fold for eve, motionless as
         lizards---ah all the little tits of things on that divine ground and
          we're all waiting to find out what's it all about? and it's all about
           Nothing---moving around sadly and aimlessly, gladly or ragefully, the
           back ache plat, as earth pits, trees wait like big clenched fists,---
           (now the pig's scratchin his side with a leg up clawing---I close my
           eyes---open em to that which is myself, the One Rock)---
            A stand of pines has assumed the color of rusty brick dust you see
             at kilns of North Carolina in the evening pine solitude---as the
             singer sings, the painted trees, patient as sentience, listen and
             dont listen at the same time
              The mule's lost in the dense glade of the jungle, like an
              exotic Rousseau slant eyed beast munching leaves of Paradise
              up off the pendant God given tree, bowing monkey face down,
              swaying erotic behind which like the forehead is pale flesh
              brown rather than hidebound hair mule scraw neck snake flop
              curlicue neet shpate nape---

VISIONS OF MYSELF (CONCL'D)
    The reddy pines wait for half of themselves to receive the up from the earth
        eating shadow of sweet chilly night when I know, now, little kids in their
        cribby hucks'll go Wee gra ma ha ta trumpetcalling radiance to their dream
        ---Ah now I have always remembered, the swimming milk in the eyes of infants
        open in the dark nursery of sentient disposéd time----
        ----------B o o m ! the sun is sinking. We bandy forms around for lack of
        concentration on the essence, and the pig, eared, re-eats---the singer
        sings on---the sun moans in another bottom part of the vuak---and Twitty
        the perfect Bird just silent-sailed on by, s'gone to green hopes in the
        meadow beyond Burnaby which on rainy days presents a face of Smoke
        like Old Indians

--THE END---
                                        ---   *
Life is . . . you're experiencing   ---   *   They're writ, the ga dam classics . . .
        selfhood---   ---   *   Truth aint woit a shit . . .
    D'abord, fam ta guel (shoddop)   ---   *   Now I writes to make me unnerstood . . .
STAY MAD   May 19   ---   *   ---Today insteada bein a sad Buddhist
    Pu d boivage   ---   *   in old pants, I should bc at Golden Gate
La nouvelle vie commence   ---   *   racetrack writing a story about the
    aujordhi   HAVE FUN   ---   *   races. . . . .
    I am going to give up   ---   *   (written in patois French)
        drinking & Buddhism   ---   *   -------------O O O O O O O O O O O--------------
Enuf talkin about it   ---   *   ---------------
---   *   ---------------------o o o o o-------------------------

THE BODY IS TOO IMPALPABLE to grasp . . . too palpable to reject
May 20---DIFFERENT IMAGINARY FORMS OF THE SAME THING
        --What's a man going to do? He's going to Work anyway . . .
        The Ant'll work Anyway-----

Youre all a buncha bastards and I'm glad ta leave (SUICIDE NOTE, Talking about self)

    All forms and living things are sins that were not paid for---Magic castles
                                                            in the sand--
Different forms of the same idea---Magic Castles in the Air---
Not by mental searching, Nirvana----A lotta rainy roses----

* * * * * * * * * * * * * * * * * *TODAY MAY 23
                        I made my final writing decision---to write the
                        Duluoz Legend like the Book of Dreams, either fresh
                        or high, off selected tics belonging to chronological
                        narrative sections---Tics are everywhere in all time---
                        All Dharma & Details Sangsaric concluded---First fruit of
                        this decision, was TRISTESSA, (Mexico City, August 1955)------

MAY 24,1955---THE SAMAPATTI OF MAHAMERU
    Last night the Tathagata Mahameru visited me
        from his Buddha-land and I heard him discourse
        to a vast assembly of Bodhisattvas of this Kalpa.
        When I did obeisance at his feet and asked for
        "guidance forever" he cooed reassurance sweeter
        than any I ever heard from my mother as an infant.
        He gave me complete and compassionate assurance that
        everything was perfect and would be perfect forever. As
        soon as I became conscious of all this, my identifying ken
        of it ceased---the last words I was able to hear were: "When
        teaching sentient beings . . ."
            It all started as I sat crosslegged trying to divine the magic
            name for Mind Essence and suddenly the picture of the Tathagata
            on the wall got loose from its moorings in the dark and hit me sharply

SAMPATTI MAHAMERU (cont'd)

on the head and immediately I accepted the reprimand and ceased thinking
tho not without some fear---the picture is a photograph of Tathagata in Gold
Sculpt in the monastery of Burma---
Mahameru has shown me Perfect Love---and pointed out the way to my possession
of a Buddhaland of Honey as soon as I go into solitude & Samapatti compassion---
So this week I'm taking my savings out of the bank and off I go to my hut in
Mexico Valley this next month---
(The family here resent my Sihibhuto Sittings during the heat of the day
while they vainly labor to show they're not lazy---and they interrupt my
meditations with requests for 'errands' and 'help' which, because I am still
essentially an ignorant Hinayana disciple of Nirvana-for-Self, I resent . . .)
All things are
Different forms
Of the Same (Perfect Thing)
DEVOID OF DISCRIMINATION & PURPOSE   TATHAGATA,is,Sameness-Attainer

* * * * * * * * * * *

The Imagelessness of the Storm . . .
The Truth is Samapatti, i.e.
Unconscious Meditation

AFTER READING YEATS (DRINKING)

He's the nearest thing	I HAVE JUST FOUND OUT THAT *VISIONS OF NEAL* is
To what I'd like to call	a fake---X-rays have shown that it wasnt really
A Satisfactory Poet	written by Jack Kerouac--------
But I like Whitman better	
Tho he's a dull tool	SUNDAY MAY 29
Half the time.	Once I was a bug
I wd. like to go talk	And I died in a rose
To some good companions	
Across the space	MAHAYANA is a polite whitewash
(looking west down the road)	of the inescapable tragic truth
That way	of Hinayana---
West is East	A true Arhat is a Fellaheen
And east was west	Pessimist---
When Mahameru	And not a Scholar living in
His maternal coo	the desert---
My ears	A true Arhat is a Tao Hobo
Did bless---	with no hopes---
Hakri!	A true Arhat is a Khayyam,
	a Rabelais
Mysterious oil drivers	Who respects just the Grape
In bean brown trucks	of Oblivion---
Sad slow cigars	Nirvana is Blown-Out
In the Baptist Tent	It is not "New Life"---
Rock Mount Road	The Holy Honey of the Worlds
of Rains	Is Merely What It's Made of
	And not a Wishful Thinking.

* *

RELIGION must be considered for what it really is, an insight into reality, and not
as a wishful dream of hope---As soon as it is pointed out that there is but one
Essential Thatness to all multiplicities of created things in all the directions
of the Universe, One Tathagata (not one "God" which is always misleading people
away from the simple understanding of the Essential Thatness, that Honey, that Gold
that everything's made of, that Formbliss Whichness), then people will stop wishful
thinking and deluded human hoping and face the fact that there is no soul, no continuance of soul after life, indeed no life, no death, no beings, no creation, but
only what appears of the mind itself

RELIGION (CON'T)

and they will cease this hypocritical rationalization of their evil outflowing
attachments by calling it Love, a Mushy theory and vague---Diamond Hard is the
clear point of the truth, which is, all things are different forms of the same
thing, *and that same thing is perfect emptiness.* This is the Diamond Saying that
cuts through "religions" and "personal God" and "divine spirit" and "love."

Things seem to assume different forms and shapes, but indeed in diamond clear
reality they have assumed no such forms & shapes at all, and are actually abiding
in timeless tranquil perfect purity, like open space. Look closely at your own
naked body---it is really a strange dream flower, comes and goes

*   and no one knows

IS THE TATHAGATA	o W h e n	* and north wind blows
A PURE MENTAL ESCAPE	o discrimination is	* dead in the rose
FROM THE CONDITIONALITY	o done away with	* * - - - - *
OF THE CREATING AGENCIES?	o the notion of	* *
"THE TATHAGATA IS LIKE HORNS	o permanency and impermanency	
OF THE HARE"	o ceases.	
AND CANNOT BE SAID TO BE	o The Tathagata is Beyond	
PERMANENT	o All reasoning -	
LIKE SPACE---	o The Eternal-Unthinkable	
EXCLUDES ALL IDEAS OF	o	
PERMANENCY OR IMPERMANENCY	o - * - * - * -	

The Actual Essence of the Universe   * *   ULTIMATE   ESSENCE
The idea of matter or space,   * *   All things are different forms
Has nothing to do with   * *   of the same empty atoms
    existence   * *   IT ALL CANCELS ITSELF OUT
        or non-existence   * *   The actual reality of nothingness
And therefore is no creator   * *

*   *

Balanced Moon
        The Reality, is, Paramartha (Perfectstuff)
    Karuna, Perfect Love
        THE STAR OF KARUNA
"Dharmakaya, by which all things are made manifest   Is this the
    and perfected and reintegrated, and all remaining   Buddhism of "world
    within its inscrutable Oneness, with no signs of   weariness and intellect-
    individuation, nor beginning, nor succession, nor   ual disgusts" mentioned
    ending."---LANKAVATARA p.351 (Thetford Vt.)   by Oswald Spengler in
                                                                                            his History Balloon ? ?

THE TATHAGATA   A Little Tale   by Jnana Karuna (J.K.)

When the Tathagata who is known as the Hearer and Answerer of Prayer was
assigned a Buddha-land of his own, more than incalculable aeons from now, he
appeared in the continent of Mominu and walked with a large retinue of followers.
One day he came through Maraw, which in Mominuan means Little-Scorpion-River-
Village. He was hungry and went from door to door begging for his daily meal
with begging pot in hand.

The lady of the first daub-and-wattle house poured a ladleful of deliciously
flavored rice into his bowl, but she had no more to spare from the larder on
account of her large and hungry family. The Tathagata, the Thatness-Attainer,
tall and serene in his patched-up raggedy robes, walked to the next house. The
lady of that house was the Lady Victor-Wife. She was an incompetent cook but
she was not remiss in almsgiving to the needy. Into the Tathagata's bowl containing
the delicious rice she poured an appalling potful of almost rancid, old and cold
yellow rice. The Tathagata was withdrawing to a grove of trees outside of town
to wash his feet, sit down and eat his meal, when the first lady ran out and
reprimanded the Lady Victor-Wife with these words:

"Why do you spoil the good food I have given the Tathagata by spilling your
refuse and garbage on it!"

Tathagata Tale cont'd

"You didnt give him enough to feed a mouse!" retorted Lady Victor-Wife.

The Tathagata raised his hand to silence the shouting housewives.

"Dear kind ladies," he said, "you have provided the Tathagata with two different flavors of the same charity, why do you quarrel over forms? for, since the Tathagata is the Attainer of Essence, he is only mindful of the essence, and the form, such as the Tathagata's tasting-organ, and the taste of the first lady's rice, and the taste of the second lady's rice, he ignores. All things are different forms of this same essence of Mind and this essence has but one flavor, emptiness."

"I have no time to think about those things," said Lady Victor-Wife and slammed the door behind her.

When the villagers heard of this event they puzzled over the meaning of the Tathagata's words. A delegation went to the grove of trees and found the Tathagata seated under a tree absorbed in a high Samadhi Ecstasy. The moment they saw his face of Pity they marveled, and questioned the chief disciple Tree Lover who sat nearby.

Said Tree-Lover:- "The form of the world is emptiness, the form of the world is not different from emptiness, neither is emptiness different from the form of the world, indeed, emptiness is the form of the world, emptiness is what we are, emptiness is this dream."

* * * * * * * * * *

Why should I worry about following chronology (I complained when I wrote above tale in summer '55) when everything is timeless------I only follow it for *convenience*

Deep tics (mindflashes) are *epitomes*
of Perfect Reflection . . .

SECTIONS OF DULUOZ LEGEND ALREADY WRITTEN (*Revised up to Feb.1956 . . ed.note*)

Time Covered	Book
1922-1926	VISIONS OF GERARD
1932-1936	VISIONS OF DOCTOR SAX
1939	VISIONS OF MARY
1947-1950	VISIONS OF THE ROAD (Sal Paradise is Jack Duluoz, Dean Moriarty is Neal Pomeray) etc.
1947-1950	VISIONS OF NEAL
1952-1956	VISIONS OF OCTOBER IN THE RAILROAD EARTH (in progress)
1953	VISIONS OF THE SUBTERRANEANS
1955	VISIONS OF TRISTESSA

for the BOOK OF VISIONS

All my work to be written like BOOK OF DREAMS off Tics chronologically appertaining in first person with fictionlike projections, bookmovies, poems and subconscious universal railleries

BOOK OF VISIONS are visions of character. . . . BOOK OF DREAMS are reports of dreams. . . . BOOK OF DHARMAS are these continuing "notes" on Buddhism & the path. . . . BOOK OF BLUES are poems of one-page style (Choruses). . . . BOOK OF PRAYERS are personally composed prayers. . . . . BOOK OF ECSTASIES are spontaneous reports on tranquillities & ecstasies of Samadhi & Dhyana practice. . . . . The division is for convenience for all interlocks . . .

. . . . *Visions, Dreams, Dharmas, Prayers, Blues, Ecstasies*. . . . .

LANKAVATARA---THE FINAL STAGE

------Being a Tathagata transformation oneself, you yield yourself up to all beings for the sake of their eventual emancipation---You have no more desires, passions, make no more discriminations, and patiently accept that you have no more ego than the moon reflected in the water. "---The life that you live thereafter is the Tathagata's Universalized life as manifested in its transformations"---

The Tathagata's Nirvana is where it is recognized that there is nothing but what is seen of the mind itself; is where, recognizing the nature of the self-mind,

LANKAVATARA THE FINAL STAGE (CONT'D) *"The Nirvana of the Tathagata"*
one no longer cherishes the dualisms of discrimination; is where there is no more
thirst nor grasping; is where there is no more attachment to external things.
Nirvana is where the thinking-mind with all its discriminations, attachments,
aversion & egoism is forever put away; is where logical measures, as they are
seen to be inert, are no longer seized upon; is where even the notion of truth
is treated with indifference because of its causing bewilderment; is where, getting
rid of the four propositions (that there is pain, that ignorance is the cause of
pain, that pain can be suppressed, that the way is the eightfold path) there is
insight into the abode of Reality . . ."

> NOBLE WISDOM AND REALITY
> ARE ONE,
> BECAUSE NOBLE WISDOM
> IS A PERFECT IMITATION
> OF REALITY---
> WHEN YOU *KNOW* REALITY
> YOU *ARE* REALITY.
>> If you can stop thinking, you become like reality

"-------is where compassion for others transcends all thoughts of self---; it is
where the manifestation of Noble Wisdom that is Buddhahood expresses itself in
Perfect Love for all; it is where the manifestation of Perfect Love that is
Tathagatahood expresses itself in Noble Wisdom (anuttara-samyak-sambodhi) for
the enlightenment of all." *ALL THINGS ARE NIRVANA NOW*

CONSCIOUS COMPASSION---not
  Catatonic but Quiet & Alone---
CONTINUAL CONSCIOUS COMPASSION
  "Quiet & Alone" among Others---
  INTERESTED, POLITE, DISPASSIONATE

I've sure got it now---
continual conscious compassion
is Noble Wisdom, *is* Reality---
for the shining essence of
all things, must surely, as a
"characteristic," as tho it
could have any "characteristic,"
partake of a constant compassionate
silent regard for the suffering of the
forms it fills and differs and abides thru-
out, matter and empty space alike---continual compassion, manifested three ways, by Buddhas of Nirmana
("Messiah Son" teaching the consciousness of this); Buddhas
of Nikshyanda, the radiating ceaseless milky transcendental moths
of lovelight you see in the night sky ray-ing inward to the pure center
which is that Holy Gold of the Bright Room which *is* continual compassion
("God"); and the Buddhas of Dharmata, the very empty *stuff* compassion is "made
of," the Universal "Light"---the Universal Essence of Mind, the Universal Karuna,
the Holy Honey---(HOLY GHOST)
So this world *is* a manifestation from the, *of* the Tathagata and the Tathagata is
  the original name, afterwards "God"---(on this earth)----

CHRISTIANS--- Say God created the World to have something to obey his will
BUDDHAS------ Say, the Tathagata manifested the transformations of the
                 dream of existence to have something to be conscious of
                 his compassion but empty throughout and tending back toward
                 the holiness of emptiness and since it is but what is seen
                 of the mind of the Tathagata (Womb of Exuberant Fertility)
                 it cannot be said to be a "Creation" and there is nothing
                 but Maya-Magic and nothing to be conscious and nothing to
                 be conscious-of and no Tathagata, there is only the Solitude
                 of the Lovelight of Compassion of the Essence of Reality

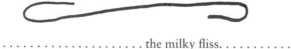

In the Solitude
Of the Love life of Reality   . . . . the milky fliss. . . . .

IF YOU DONT BELIEVE that an ugly monstrous Squid belongs to the compassionate
lovelight, then put a blowtorch to him and watch him tremble with fear of punish-
ment---any creature---The fact that a Squid can bite a man is only a fact relating
to the conditionality of existence, not to the unconditional actual reality which
is the origin of all the different forms of things. This unconditional actual
reality is the Holy Honey of the Tathagata's Womb, or, if you prefer, God's Mercy
in Heaven
Face it---

UNTYPED NOTES FROM DOCTOR SAX HANDBOOKS OF 1952   MEXICO CITY
Silly Literary Stupidity ". . . , the which"---
The Señoritas in purple & wild black
     ---A little girl leaning on her mother's ass saying "Quarent-aye-cinco!"
     ---Ah afternoons
   ---That old Totalitarian Heat---in American Streets
       . . . The day of the great monolog, plays on the stage,
          a matinee! I sit, hand to chin, digging that down the stairwell
          of my balcony in the Henry Miller theater,---in three acts, by
          three different actors playing "different levels" of the same role . . .

THE JEALOUS MONASTERY MONKS who envy the vigorous desert monk (or mountain lunatic)
are not "jealous" but want him to realize, as I did in Dec.'54 with "This Bodhisattva
Inside Mind in Jail" that solitude or non-solitude is not the point, the point is
Equalminded Compassion-Stillness. . . . .

                            Now I'll write a book uniting and comparing
THE SOLITUDE   on all levels, Buddhism & Christianity---
OF THE LOVELIGHT   DeKerouac and DeLubac will battle it out----
OF ESSENCE   like, I'll say "Tathagata's Compassion"
                            is "God's Compassion"---more anon

INRI---all things are mental dreams radiated from the Tathagata's
Consciousness---Your Tathagatahood which is realizable in
Mind-Vision-Body (Manomayakaya) is *not* seen like the things
of the world such as your earthly body---This Mindvisionbody
emerges at Self Realization of Noble Wisdom and *is* Noble Wisdom---
It has three aspects:- *Patience, Radiation, Essence* (Nirmana,
Nikshyanda, Dharmata)---Truly you have nothing to do but rest
and be kind and telepathize Samantabhadra's Unceasing
                         Compassion

NIRVANA FOR JUNKIES:-   *
All things are different   *   Continual Sad Compassion because all things die---
forms of the same   *   Before, in 1946, I was enlightened by death, my
holy shit.---   *   father's death---
                    *   Poor little green life, thou wiltst die, but grieve
                    *   not, thou art made of the unbornness of the unborn
                    *   essence of the Imperishable Honey Fleece
              *   In 1946 I was enlightened by Pa's death and my sickness in
            *   bed in December when I remember the key vision was of the "hated"
         *   Walter Winchell being dead too and his daughter weeping because she
       *   saw his shaving mug in the cabinet as I saw Pa's---wherein I saw, Pa
     *   who hated Winchell, and Winchell himself, were the same sad compassionate
   *   lifestuff, the fathers of grief, the sons of the Hateful Family of Griefs
*   and Pain- --- - - -
Subsequently, superficial gayety of the city had erased my wisdom----

THORNTON WILDER'S *OUR TOWN* was vastly enlightened---it was the Angel Looking Back,
like Scrooge, the Dream Already Ended---

Reality isnt bleak nor can it be said to be non-bleak either . . .

The idea of a personal God is wishful thinking
Even the idea of a Tathagata Consciousness and that all things
are actually all right and sweet in essence, is *wishful thinking*---
It just is what it is---
In Reality there is no wishing and there is no thinking---there is
that shining (shining?) mental suchness that dreams are made of---a concatenation
of imaginary nectar---that inconceivable aloofness of our beloved dead

                                                         is what it's like. . . . . . .
            Pondering on death,   it's like in the box below:-
            with or without wine,   *
            brings enlightenment---   *   *
                                                         *   *
        LIFE IS A DREAM OF APPEARING AND DISAPPEARING: *   *
           THE ESSENCE IS UNDISTURBED   *   *

AS SOON AS YOU REALIZE THAT ALL THINGS ARE
DIFFERENT FORMS OF THE SAME ESSENCE WHICH
IS NOT DISTURBED , you will know that any conception of death or
rebirth is false because the unbornness of the unborn essence of things does not
rise or pass away (the essence is not disturbed), therefore you can entertain no
further conceptions of the appearance and disappearance of thoughts which, like
things, are empty manifestations throughout, and so the mind-system is seen to be
but a dream and all that's left is that crafty omnipresent *smiling* essence abiding
throughout things but not disturbed, leaving you with a single transcendental
thought of Essence (a no-thought) which is simply what it is, suchwiseness---and
so everything vanishes, is seen as empty forms, and the Solitude of Reality is
left. "God is Alone" "Form is emptiness, emptiness is form."

In other words, there's no end to this Teaching, to the words I can use,
because there's no end to   E M P T I N E S S   nor is there an end to F O R M   -
No end to existence and no end to non-existence. . . . .
No end to things everywhere, and no end to the common essence they're made of. . . . .
No end to the realization of the emptiness of this essence they're made of. . . . .
In brief, no end to Buddhahood and Awakenedhood . . . no beginning, no limit, no end . . . .
W A K E U P !

The mistake is in the mind . . .

                          Buddhas of Emancipation and Gods of Salvation
                          are merely activities in the dream which is taking
                          place emptily throughout empty mind-essence . . . . . the
                          whole thing is the flit of a glow worm in a June Night
                     Bush----
                          I know this because I know that my mind-system
                     that I think with never appeared except in my own imagination
                     imagination-without-end, there *was* no Duluoz and his Life
                     and Legend, and my system-of-imagining never disappeared when
                     I died, nothing was ruffled anywhere, my face looked up straight
                     in its grave with no expression, nothing happened, there *was* no
                     "Bliss" of Parinirvana, Complete Blown-out-Ness, because everything *is*
                     Outblown and Gone right now----there was only the Eternal Golden Solitude
                     of the Ecstasy Reality of Essence . . . See, my good friends?
                     You're only being fooled into thinking you *are*. . . . . Yes you *are* but empty
                                                              right thru . . .
                                         thus, what *are* you?????

TATHAGATA COMPASSION, GOD MERCY,
THESE ARE OUR SENTIENT PATHOS IDEAS
AND HAVE NO SELF-REALITY | There is no difference
ULTIMATELY IN THE END | between
AND ACTUALLY RIGHT NOW . . . for . . . all is Perfectly Silent | a Buddha
                                            | and an
                                            | ordinary person

      Knowing all this, is PRAJNA, Wisdom . . .

This is PRAJNA---Wisdom---but the essence of things is "compassionate" *anyway*---and
so this is Wisdom & Compassion, the Perfection of the Buddhas and Messiahs. . . . .

    To say that the essence of things is compassionate is neither true
    nor untrue---It is not true because compassion applies to multiple
    situations intertwining, one thing compassionating and loving another,
    and in reality there is not one thing and another but only Not-Two,
    i.e., One-Thing; and it is not untrue to say that the essence of things
    is compassionate because there is nothing that we can conceive of
    with our imaginary imaginations that Essence is not, it can be
    com-passion and anything it wants, it is the Womb of Empty Fertility,
    it is Nirvana and Samsara both, it contains all----It is not
    uncompassionate in its perfect tranquility and yet is not compassionate
    either in its perfect unperturbed unhelping tranquility.
      The essence we're made of, is not involved in anything good or bad we do . . .
                     So be glad . . .

WHAT AM I, (literary wise) a Buddhist Divine?
    Not acceptable to say it, finally, in our time-way-
    of-thinking, because I say there is
    neither divine nor non-divine
    in the blank reality
    of imageless, egoless essence---
    qualityless, praiseless,
    truly beyond good and evil.
    Dualityless Essence
        of Mind

```
* * * * * * * * * * * * * * * * * * * * * * * * * * * * * * * * * * *
```

WHEN MEN ARE REALLY CORRUPT
they say the teaching of the
Dharma to them has as much
effect as drawing a picture on
water with a stick-----------------not realizing how wise is the remark ! For, when the
Lord Buddha attained highest perfect wisdom he did not deny that it was like
a t t a i n i n g   n o t h i n g   w h a t e v e r . . . .

It's All the Same Story

```
* * * * * * * * * * * * * * * * * * * * * *
* * * * * * * * * *   T H E   F I S H   * * * * * * * *
* * * * * * * * * *                       * * * * * * *
```

    * THERE IS NO SELF*NATURE in a dead body
    * of a fish being cut into stripes with
    * scissors in a sink, nor was there self
    * nature when it wriggled intelligently in
    * a black brook---There is no substantiality
    * even to fishes' flesh that we're going to
    * eat because as I see it in the sink it is
    * the unborn-ness of the unborn essence, not
    * fishflesh---And the essence is not disturbed,
    * and the essence is neither pitiful nor pitiless.

```
* * * * * * * * * * * * * * * * * * * * * * * * * * * * * * * * * * *
```

Go to a dry season
And live under a tree
And nothing'll hem you in
On all four sides

CITY & PATH,
DULUOZ & DHARMA
LOVE & WISENESS

A mistake in the imagination of the universe, is *being*
People who commit suicide and people who dont commit suicide accomplish nothing

IF I WERE TO REPEAT "the essence is not disturbed" every second of the day to keep
myself in perfect wisdom and perfect compassion, the wagon of those words would soon
wear down and the meaning no longer carried. . . . What can I do, O My Sweet Lord of
the Dharmas, to keep pure constantly like Holy Essence & Tathagatahood itself?
Answer: S T A Y   A W A K E . . . . .

DON'T LAUGH, I'M A BIG DRINKER, I'm trying to find some expedient means to stop
drinking and disturbing my perfect reflection, making me foolish, making me forget
the above wisdom, big fool, little fool, marring my love---I want DRY STRONG HAPPINESS
instead of all this WET WEAK UNHAPPINESS (hangover)----Drinking like that ruins my
physical strength, mars my morning joy, breaks the back of my resolves, blurs my
clear reflection, dulls my shiver of bliss-----I should sacrifice the few remaining
pleasures (dubious or not) of strong drinking to my vow to emancipate all beings---
Sacrifice Wine to the New Life of Holy Purpose-------Promise Tathagata to Obey---
                         Tathagata Commanded Me

L'ESSENCE N'EST PAS DERANGEZ   To Stop Guzzling & Being
THE ESSENCE DOESNT NEED A DRINK   A Fool . . . . "Concentrate Your
THE ESSENCE ISNT DISCOURAGED BY BLEAK TIME   Will
THE ESSENCE ISNT BORED   IN ESSENCE   on Salvation". . . . . .

The essence isnt worried   . . . . . The golden essence stretches like
The high news   taffy to accommodate all the forms. . . . . .

THE LIGHT OF MAHAYANA IS simply that realization that there is no *You* to go into
Nirvana and there is no *Nirvana* for the Buddhas who know that the essence is not
  disturbed and thus dwell in Perfect Love for all, empty and awake, responding
    without effort or disturbance (like taffy essence) to the needs of imaginary
      ghosts of form---
        HINAYANA clings to Ego---"My going into Nirvana"---but at the sight of a
    dead Hinayana monk and a dead murderer, I imagine you'd see the same egoistic
    mistake mayhap on their dead expressions---The sight of a dead Mahayanist
    (A Compassionate Disciple of the Great Religion) would be a sight of a
      disciple who knew that in essence there was no someone and no disciple
      and patiently he allowed the matter of years which is life so he could
        teach this---

Bellygoat boom
At ache of   M I N D   A W A K E
Day bang

      But the mistake in the Lankavatara Scripture lies in the Egotistic Idea
      that a Bodhisattva could actually refuse Nirvana until all others attain
      it with him---What Nirvana? What others and what Bodhisattva?----In essence
    what?---There is no statement to compare with the Diamond Sutra, the mysteriously
  empty Sutra that grows more mysterious as I read it year after year. . . . .

In essence there is nothing
but essence---   *   There *is* nothing in reality
And the essence is not disturbed   *   but these appearances
--   *   The idea of is or is-not is the
Tathagata, is, Realizer of Essence   *   big mistake of dreaming
Tathata, is, Essence
Tathata is not disturbed---   *   JUST BECAUSE you see the world you
Tathagata, realizing, is disturbed---?   *   think it's here? . . . Dont you realize
(Tathagata neither realizes nor   *   it's only magic? Just because you *feel*
         does not realize)   *   the world you think there is a world?
Tathagata, teaching the doctrine   *   Dont you realize it's only a sixfold
    of no-disturbance of essence,   *   sensual illusion? It's a false sense.
    is not the essential Tathagata   *   The essence doesnt see the world. Truly
For Tathagata neither realizes nor   *   speaking, there is no world, or rather,
    teaches, nor come nor goes,   *   there is neither a world nor is there
    nor sits nor stands nor walks   *   not-a-world, what does the essence care
Nor exists   *   about statements about the being of
Nor does not exist.   *   worlds? The essence is not disturbed.
    I dont understand   *
    Tathagatahood   *   TATHAGATA, Attainer of Essencehood
       * * * * * *   *   *Reality is nothing that can be known*
(because it is the selfnature of   *   *therefore the knower of reality is not*
  suchness and therefore inscrutable,   *   *real.*
  un-understandable. . . . .) *   Essence is nothing that can be
*   attained therefore the attainer of essence
                                       i s   n o t   e s s e n c e   i t s e l f . .
BOOKS ABOUT TATHAGATAS   Difference between Tatha*gata* and Tathata
LEAD TO THE TATHAGATAS
WHO LEAD THE WAY

      IF YOU GO TO NEW YORK and act aggressive to publish your
      books about the Tathagatas that lead the way, the essence
      wont be disturbed----Tathagata is your "partner in the
     business of realizing essence," as you intuited on a
     bench last year---Tathagata is the Sentient Signpost to
   Essence. . . . .
       SILENT SMILING PARTNER, BUDDY

DREAM---a group of men gathered around the Well of Essence, having discovered
that everything is empty and made of this Essence, quietly they discuss it and
wonder what to do with themselves now---They've "FINALLY DISCOVERED THE SECRET"
and are not elated but quiet---(the secret of origin)

ANOTHER DREAM---In a store, one man is proud of his ability to hear the Diamond
Dharma Sound all the time, but the other one announces that he can perceive
Transcendental Sight no matter how many customers come in & swim across his
vision---

ANOTHER DREAM---In Blezan's store I'm telling Bill that we are made of one even
essence and all you have to do is go inside and I know now that everything is
alright and Burroughs is surprised and glad and quiet

> All things are made of little
> empty balls (empty atoms)---it's
> a crazy arrangement

Breezy June night, the moon behind clouds, you hear the diesel engine on the
far horizon---Jack Duluoz and the Dharma---

FROM SAMYUTTA-NIKAYA 22-90
> "The world, O Kaccana, is for the most part bound up in a seeking, attachment,
> and proclivity (for the groups, i.e., body-contact, sensation, perception,
> discrimination, and individuality-consciousness), but a priest does not
> sympathize with this seeking and attachment, nor with the mental affirmation,
> proclivity, and prejudice which affirms an ego. He does not doubt or question
> that it is only evil that springs into existence, and only evil that ceases
> from existence, and his conviction of this fact is dependent on *no one
> besides himself.*"
>   THIS IS RIGHT BELIEF (whether you want to call it Evil
>   or Thatness)

Samyutta Nikaya 12-35
> "On the complete fading out and cessation of ignorance, O priest,
all these refuges, puppet-shows, resorts, and writhings,---to wit:
'What are old age & death? or, old age and death are one thing, but
it is another thing which has old age and death; or, the soul and
the body are identical, or the soul is one thing, and the body
another,---all such refuges of whatever kind are abandoned, uprooted,
pulled out of the ground like a palmyra-tree, and become non-existent
and not liable to spring up again in the future."

> The Trance of Cessation of sensation & perception
>   leaves only vitality, natural heat, & senses intact---

"Enveloped, besotted, and immersed in wife, child, servants, chicken, pork,
elephants, cattle, horses and mares, chariots, milk, gold, silver, this person,
himself subject to birth, craves what is subject to birth. This is the
ignoble craving.
   "The noble craving, he craves the incomparable security of a Nirvana free
from birth."   SAMYUTTA NIKAYA

>   "The highest good of the holy life, for the
>   sake of which youths of good family so nobly
>   retired from the household life to the houseless
>   one."---SUMMUM BONUM

"A person with good eyes, seeing all things clearly in the bright sunshine"
                                                          DIAMOND SUTRA
"The attainments of the Tathagatas---they should be considered as neither
realities nor as unrealities"---DIAMOND SUTRA

Gotama Buddha, when the 5 ascetics doubted him, repeated & repeated the same
teaching till it sank in, and in the *same words.*

"If ye will do according to
my instructions, in no long time, and in the present life, ye shall learn
for yourselves, and shall realize and live in the possession of Nirvana,
for the deathless life has been gained."
Prior to that, under the tree, he had hesitated to go out and teach the
doctrine because of the annoyance, vexation, and trouble it would cause
him. But the Buddhas, Awakened Ones,of Old,beseeched him to instruct
and teach men.
Say to yourself, SPACE IS
INFINITE ---
CONSCIOUSNESS
IS INFINITE ---
NOTHING EXISTS   . . . . then stop thinking

"Before the clear vision of wisdom
all depravity wastes away."

Then you walk, stand, squat and lie down in confident security
because you are out of the reach of Mara the Tempter. . . . .
----the NOBLE--CRAVING SERMON

For,it is only infatuation that springs into existence---it is only infatuation
that ceases from existence-------------I'm tired of listening to others---------*There is
such a tremendous discrepancy between what I know to be true and what I am expected
to do*-------------

Between the Sutras	I know ants
The knowledge in Samadhis---	and anthills are
And "business" *	empty But I'm s'posed
The knowledge of the day	to believe in my self ?

The advice of the Buddhas
And the advice of my family. . . . . .   (The People of Pinetop) (on the radio)
* *

J veux etre tout seul		I want to be alone
Dans ma 'tite cabane		In my little quiet cabin
Tranquile avec mon		With my food
Mangez et mes livres	MEANING	And my holy books
Saint et mes penseés		And my thoughts
Et les beaux matins		And the beautiful mornings. . . . .

"The greater part of what my neighbors call good I believe in my soul to be bad."
        *   -------THOREAU-----
. . . . . . ORAPARA,Liability to repeated births. . . .

"Gone beyond all this Papancha"---(this World-of-Delusion)

"THE PRIEST, WHO DOES NOT LOOK BACK TO THE PAST OR LOOK FORWARD TO THE FUTURE,
HAVING KNOWN THAT ALL THIS WORLD IS FALSE, GIVES UP ORAPARA, AS A SNAKE CASTS OFF
ITS DECAYED OLD SKIN"--------Uraga Sutta 9

"There is no advantage	*	In heavy rain, be like a mule, receive
in serving others"	*	it on your bare back calmly, thinking,
---DHANIYA SUTTA	* * *	"There is no sin whatever in me"------------

"Like an elephant which has broken the galucchi creeper,
even so I shall not return again to a mother's womb."
These are all HINAYANA quotes from the Pali
They're tough and rough and true but not detached from the arbitrary
conception of self, other selves, living beings, or a universal self . . .

TWO SAYINGS : -
"He who is without objects of desire such as children and cattle is indeed not
happy. Thus said the sinful Mara, the Tempter"------------
A N D
"He who has no objects of desire such as children and cattle does not indeed
grieve. Thus said Bhagava, the Buddha."--------------------

----
* *
PACHAHEKA'S "Inferior Buddha" taught guts:-

   "He who is kind toward much-beloved friends loses his own good
from his mind becoming partial . . . Let a wise man, observing solitude, walk alone like a rhinoceros . . . Whoever is possessed of the
Four Appamannas of FRIENDLINESS, COMPASSION, GOOD-WILL, and
EQUANIMITY, and is not opposed to any person, is contented with
whatever he gets, endures sufferings and his fearless, let him
walk alone . . . A hero abandoning the ways of the world . . . subsisting
on pure food . . . wanders whithersoever he will, like the elephant
deserting his herd. . . . The attaining of even temporary Samadhi
by anyone who is attached to society is impossible---*I have nothing
left to be known*----Let one associate not with one procrastinating
in doing good things---There are *Cold, Heat, Hunger, Thirst, Wind,
Sun, Gadflies, Snakes,* and *Police*----Indifferent to amusements,
not beautifying oneself. . . . Abandon the different kinds of desires
founded on mother, wealth, relations, corn," . . . (In Ancient India
Corn was a Luxury)---"It is but insipid, there is more affliction
in it than comfort. . . . A fire returns not to the spot already burned
up. . . . Eyes looking downward, not moving quickly, walk alone like a
rhinoceros. . . . Not being greedy of savory things, not maintained by
others. . . . not allied to anything. . . . pacific and pure. . . . observing
the rules of the hermits, energetic. . . . like a lion which fears
not noises. . . . dwell in hermitages in far-away deserts & mountains. . . .
delight at the prosperity of others. . . . entertaining no fears for
the loss of life. . . . Men are not pure, let one walk alone, like a
rhinoceros."

              *

         "That devout meditation of heart which is concerned
            with no material object---it is only then that the
            body of the Tathagata is at ease," and I heard the
            thunder, and I think: "What a small thing is Giroux
            and the publishers of New York and my manuscripts,   60
            what piddling idiocy------------"   Las Encinas
               I HAVE NOTHING LEFT TO BE KNOWN * * * * * * * * *   Lane
                 ---("What a small thing is Mihinda and the   Monastery of
                     scribes of Benares and my scrolls, what   Santa Barbara, Calif.
                     piddling idiocy----")

I'm apparently an ancient scribe abandoning his ignorant scrolls in disgust,
discovering the essence of truth. . . . . In Dhyana avoid thoughts of
                                    success or failure (Goddard advises)

AGENDA FOR JUNE---Finish typing BOOK OF DHARMAS (up to present point). . . . buy a
sleeping bag for sleep & meditation under trees in desert & riverbottom & mountain
side & in freights---- . . . Pack essential smallpack----Go West,
                                        O Kinsman of the Sun . . .
Coudon, coudon, coudon   *
Admonishes the bird   *   They think they'll find sympathy
As I sit here worrying   *   in your horny heart (girls)
About my two unheard-from   *
Copies of cityCityCITY   *
Coudon meaning in French / "Listen here" . . . .

T'oubli pi t'asseye etre formale---
Mais quand tu't fauche sa vien tusuite,
                                MEANING,
*   You forget & you try to be formal---
I'D RATHER BE A WOODEN FLUTE   * * *   But when you get mad it comes right away
THAN AN "AMERICAN WRITER"   * * *   * * *
*   o   *
Excoriate America and her dubious saints. . . .

"But we use words to get free from words until we reach the pure wordless Essence."
                                ASVHAGHOSHA KEROUAC

"All concepts are an undivided part of Reality; they are not artificial but unchangeable and ineffable and unthinkable. They are the Essence of Mind itself." (A)
    .The essence was not born, the essence will not die. . . . . .
        The book isnt there, you made it be
        there---------------
                "All imagery of selfness"----
                                "The nature of appearing and
                                dis-appearing coincides with the
THE DUALITY OF IGNORANCE   nature of non-appearing and non-
            AND   disappearing". . . . .
E N L I G H T E N M E N T
is at the base of existence . . .
This is because words dont   *
belong to anything.
            "Conscious thinking is wholly subjective & imaginary"

Unchanging, pure, undefinable, the difference between conscious and subconscious is
irrelevant.---("The phenomena of conscious mentation . . . is the same as no-thinking.")
P R I M A L U L T I M A T E A C TU A L

        But why does Essence of Mind   . . . . Why? you say?
        have a "store of defilements"?   Because the trap took the cock . . .
        I wont know anything and wont rest
        till I know W H Y ?   - - - - - - - -

Fussing over washingmachines, clogged sinks, cars, what can there be but
Perturbation, as the wind blows down the needlessly erected screen that was
intended for privacy. . . .Perturbation, evil, Karma, death----------*PRIVACY OF SOLITUDE*
                                                IS FREE
Literature is like a red rubber ball . . . child's play. . . .

        MIND AND IGNORANCE are not separated from each other---
        non-enlightenment is as indestructible as enlightenment---
        IGNORE IGNORANCE (via intellectual purity of the Bodhisattva traveling the stages)

The Devil dancing before a Mirror,   "Mystic Volunteers"
is Ignorance and Enlightenment---the   Abbe Pierre is absolutely
Essence is Not Disturbed. . . . .   great . . .

WHY DO I KEEP ON CHOOSING TO IGNORE THE TRUTH?---"for awhile longer"?---What do I
expect to discover in Ste. Terese's bloody Love of the Future which means further
Crowing in Sangsara---Their big "Love" is a deep rooted conspiracy among one
another to ignore the final truth which is Nothingness---I see them arm-in-arm
a slew of Ginsbergs singing, laughing, having a big world Rally "against death"
---"proud, undeniable, undaunted, brave"----O b-r-r-a-v-e! I hate and they love.
I should neither hate nor love but by God right now I hate, like my brother Louis
Ferdinand Celine. I stand in front of the World Rally putting up a big sign, says
God is Full of Shit ----------------I wont even give a kid a nickel---I wont even kill
a cockroach---

Let my further truck & travail with the world come
under the heading of the Writing Buddha's choice to
teach the One Vehicle by books---s'why I'm goin to N.Y.
tonight, to publish the Law . . . .

And my begging bowl the minimum monthly contract---Call it,
  a Begging Bowl Contract
      $25 a month

(and even that they wont give me, being more interested in Charity & Love)

And they didnt   (The publishers assume that somehow Kerouac
                                     has all he needs in the way of money. . . . . . .
   *   *   *   *   *   *   when I asked for $25 a month they smiled
     *   *   *   *   *   *   and their eyes twinkled)
       *   *   *   *   *
         *   *   *   *
           *   *   *   THE TATHAGATAS have advised me to make it for a tree . . .
             *   *   They swarmed with instructions in my eyes in the dark closed . . .
               *   My special problem is non-solitude, the rest is easy . . .
                        JULY 4 1955 -- Getting ready to leave home and go to the
                        homeless life in California riverbottoms and Mexico huts . . .
                      DREAM---The Dharma is like paddling yr. canoe in the danger
                    water, but the current will take you along anyway whether you
                  help yourself (wake up) or not---The Dharma will help you faster
                to wake up---
              DREAM---Achieve the saintship of a kitten,---eat & purr.

* *

book eight

IN LITTLE BROWN TRAVELBOOK:- I will ask for all my manuscripts back and then send
the Buddha book in ("Buddha Tells Us"). Now I'm going to live my own life in Mexico,
for money, fame, publishing, friendships, all that I dont want. I want to live my
life like Buddha. My mother is safe & sound at Ti Nin's where I brought her, her
money is coming in a few years, and I will no longer pretend to depend on her.
I'm going to my hermitage. I intend to become a saint and live in tranquillity
and teach the tranquil law. For in essence there is nothing but ess ence, and the
essence is not disturbed. All I have to is feed myself and that's not hard.-----

Love Without Hope
   the secret of the universe   The Buddhist is supposed to abandon
Reality Isnt Thinking-----   society and all dependency on its
   FORMS ARE LIFE THOUGHTS   emolumentive system---Because in Reality
                                             he is Alone and the essence is not-two but
                                          One, and unchanged.
                                    Why do I hang around for publisher's monies? I say
                                 it's my form of complicated begging which will be repaid
                          by means of the written Law but actually it's because I'm afraid of
                     going it alone and Unknown now
ALONE AND UNKNOWN *is* Reality, or that is, reality is neither alone nor not-alone,
known nor not-known
--SUPREME REALITY   Trap my cock,
that golden milk   the Yurk of Mahameru   the ancient news   cop my diddle
raining across   pacifying me   'The Dream   Dibble
the darkness   in the sea   is Already Done,   Fiddle
of my eyelids   of ecstasy,   the Holiness   Titty Dill.
with a shh   and birds know me   is One'   I know music.
of silent-me   and report back   The little tit
                 ---------Sorry, said Salk------   of time

335

A Potter's Dwelling
Outside the Town
 (for Mexico City)   !   . . . The Holy Tenderness

TRIP TO MEXICO HITCH HIKING FROM ROCKY MOUNT TO VICTORIA TEXAS
Monterrey July 29--No sleep since Gainesville Ga.---a horrible trip through hell
---almost took a horrible bed lump cell in Monterrey Skid Row for saving of 48
cents---wish I could sleep on ground instead---having a lonely beer---Will sleep
from 5 A M to 4 P M and wander in Monterrey till 7:40 bus-------

   Bhikkuhood? ----Miss those American travelers like poor old sophisticated queer
Bill digging boys in mid-night bars of Mejico . . . Rebirth is in the voice of the
woman singing---deep breasted Spanish night---I wish Helen Parker were here---All
that old gang is dead---

   Right Meditation is, entertain no arbitrary conceptions, for all is void & empty
---stream of emptiness.
THE VISION IN THE BIRMINGHAM BUS STATION . . . . a pale woman passing by like a phantom
                                                       streaming across the empty air

THE DECISION ON MAIN STREET IN HOUSTON. . . . . . . to get out of cities
Will Tenancingo be my refuge? If not I'll be broke in 2 months . . .
Mexico is great,
            but you never have enuf money to stay---being cheap, it's expensive
            because you buy more----maybe----beer, rooms,----tacos,---Ah, Land
            of Night---all that desert out there, stars----I see through the
            swarming sainted Buddha lands all holy, right here in this cantina
            in the hot summer night-----I go to sleep in hotel now.

NEXT DAY ON PARK BENCH MONTERREY,

                              Mexico---no organized viciousness as in America,
SPENT DAY WANDERING   no organized pessimism as in France---Did sweet
streets & markets of   Jesus indirectly sweeten this former Aztec Land?
Monterrey, drinkin Spurs,
visitin modern churches &
ancient cathedrals, taking shoes off in park---eyeing senoritas---Viva Monterrey!
watching wild baseball games in dry riverbottom----wild Saturday night lights!----
Viva Monterrey, I come back some day-----orange groves right outside town-------

MEXICO CITY NOTES IN MY DOBE ROOFTOP HUT
     Self is route of raft to Nirvana shore. . . . . . .
     . . . . . The Scene With the Wizard
             His Eyes are Wise With Closing . . . (description of Garver)

Blue Heaven goofball----It's all the same pitiful person (mankind is) . . .

The essential nature of the thinking-conception does not die with the body of you . . .

All existence is lies, pretending to be solid
  when they're really empty---but it's not a
   question of real or unreal---Empty space
     doesnt have to lie---Maya Magic is the same
       as No-Magic

                 THE WORLD IS UNIFIED in suffering but not in living & dying, as
             the baseball fans are unified in baseball but divided in heroic
          shares of the out-come. Because the world is unified in suffering it
           is also unified in non-suffering, it is one cool, clear, calmpool in
           which is seen the black scummy rock of activity. . . . which isnt really
           black scummy rock of activity at all but false, empty, physically and
           atomically empty black scummy rock. The conception of the rock is also
           empty, since it is the same as the mind clear of conceptions, being of the
           same crystal mentalness. No rock, no pool. No fool.

                              * * *

WE HAD A BASEBALL TEAM at the age of 13, 14, and played nine serious games in the
WPA LEAGUE which to us was a big enough and official league to take seriously, and
won them all. This was followed by the championship playoff wherein all the big
grownup guys of the Twi League of every aftersupper dusk in Lowell at the South
Common, hearing of the big kids'-playoff, got into the act, surly of face, and
there took place a serious grownup game with grownup pitchers but (as myself
and Henry Beaulieu) kid infielders and kid outfielders---the result being, we
lost all that we had gained by our own childish efforts, to the world of
Grownup Gulp Concerns. You shall see. But these concerns that the common
ordinary man feels are no more true, than the absence of concerns in
heaven above.
    All right. Heaven above is heaven inside. Inside heaven is heaven above and
includes us too. How do I know? I just know that everything is the same thing.
    Any story can be only a fragment of a beginningless & endless story, which is
Nirvana. All right. Nirvana is the beginning and ending of hope.
Our baseball team was the beginning of hope, the end of our baseball team the end,
and Nirvana the two together as one. We hoped to be the champions of the Lowell
WPA LEAGUE. Early in the morning, at breakfast Wheaties, I could hear them buntin
and playin pepper in the street outside where still it was early enuf for old store
spitters to be just gettin along life Sidewalk to the Club, & some people hurrying
to work late, about 9, when the world is fresh.
    "Hey Jack, come on out Lazy!" they'd yell

CODY DEAVER
  RAY SMITH
   LOUIS FIRPIN
    LOUIS ROCK
    The Spokesman of the Rock
    Sitter & Stander On Rocks
    Mocker of Rocks
    Killer of Instincts
    Mat of met
    Mull my moan again
    Gravel at my bone
    Stone

BECAUSE OF FALSE IMAGINATION we grasp
at measures and things that never really
change anything.

The opposite of tile is peanut butter---
The opposite of eggs is steel nail---
Opposite of old woman is empty sky---
But they're all the same thing
    OM
* *
*   SPACE FANTASTICALLY APPEARS, like an optical illusion,
*   when you put two things side by side. There then rises
* the arbitrary conception of space, and of ego-personality
perceiving it. And so this perception is but foam tossed a-
bout by the waves of the great sea of reality, which we have known,
Highest Perfect Reality.
VANISH INTO NOTHINGNESS, says Manjusri. Return to your origin where your nature will
be no more specks of foam on your spaceless sea. The perfect Intuition of Samadhi
                              i s a l l . .

THE QUALITY OF TASTE IS NOT LASTING
                   A dream a long time done. . . . . .

Looking at myself in the mirror I saw
mad sick eyes, four or five of them,   A LONG TIME DONE
swimming in a Spectre that
existed only in my false imagination.

    THE CAUSE OF EXISTENCE goes along with my discriminating
    nature. The bugs are after me. The cause of existence is
    death. The cause of existence is gambling. Stop thinking.
    The cause of existence, thinking.
    .Conceptions of Dead Dogs.
               (written stoned on holy weed
                at candle in hut) (above paragraph)
TAO . . . "The perfect Sage
      will never be cause
      of strife."   NATURE, and the absence of NATURE, or
                 the WORLD, and the absence of the WORLD,
                 Are two sides/ of the same Mind

Nature is the same as No
     N a t u r e

Two sides of the same Mind
Are existence and non-existence

Two sides of the same Mind
Are life and death

* *

NO ONE IS GOING TO LIKE
WHAT I AM GOING TO DO NOW . . .
"IT WILL NOT BE NEAT" AS JOHN
CLELLON HOLMES SAYS, I AM GOING
INTO MYSELF TO FIND THE GREAT TRUTH . . . . which is:-

LITERATURE IS TOO LIGHT-HEARTED AN INTEREST
for me. The Six Paramitas of Perfect Charity,
Perfect Kindness, Perfect Patience, Perfect
Zeal, Perfect Ecstasy, and Perfect Wisdom
occupy my thoughts now. Literature giggles---
literature has to do with the mutilation of
beasts and living beings. Perfect Ecstasy is
possible at any time, for any length of time,
within this burning house of existence. I
can educate more along those lines, and point
the way to the perfect Absence of Bane, but
stories calculated to divert readers from the
truth of their present personal horror are no
longer in my line.

* *

* *SUTRA WRITTEN ON AN ENVELOPE*   Or,
*
*   the *First Teaching* and the
*   E N V E L O P E   S U T R A   *Second Teaching* * * * *
* People think of self as a private possession because they are cogs on a wheel
* that keeps turning out self after self in rebirth after rebirth of selfhood.
*
* I will have to preach the only possible truth: The abolishing of death by
* extermination of birth. Life control. Put an end to human rebirth, by
*
* abstaining from sexual intercourse. Everybody stop breeding, or by method -
* of-birth-control stop birth. At the same time, stop killing for sport or for
*
* eating living beings; they tremble at punishment and death too. Everybody
* live off vegetables and synthetic foods, causing no pain anywhere.
*
* Everybody abstain from panic and wait for death finally. For human beings,
* the rest will be ecstasy. For all other living, sentient beings the hint
*
* will be taken. A chain reaction throughout existence in all ten directions
* of space exterminating existence by quiet will, in tranquillity and purity.
*
* This is the word from the everlasting eternity, it is the First Teaching.
*
* The Second Teaching is, that there was no First Teaching from the everlasting eternity.
*
* *
* WRITTEN IN AUGUST 1955, around the 30th, IN ADOBE TEJADO HUT IN MORNING
* *

AND TO BE KNOWN AS THE FIRST AND SECOND TEACHINGS. . . . .

Trip from Mexico City to California Sept.1955
Walking. . . . . . . the Duluoz Legend takes place in the Tathagata's Womb.
             Actions are but ripples on a PluPerfect Shining Conditionless Sea-----
                 The pure concepts arent passing, only the impure concepts are passing---
                 GRASPING AND ACTIVITIES, IS ALL THIS LIVING-TRAVELING. . . . . .
SAMADHI is really
an escape from time. . . . do it *every day*----
. . Daily Samadhi---at least 3 times with feet
folded & rested (cant miss) C A N T M I S S

THE LORD NOTHINGNESS SAYS:-
"Compassion for the seeming somethingness
which is the actual nothingness."

MAGIC WORDS
Impermanent
Peaceful
Calm
Not-self

338

Hinayana aversion for personality
or for anything will not lead to
compassion---Let compassion be a
singleness of purpose, let it be
the PATH---Continual Actual
        C o m p a s s i o n . . .

The Epic of Gilgamesh
(Garver says to read) . . .

             . . . The Holy Nothingness . . .

        SRADDA-APPROVAL vs.
        SKEPSIS-DISAPPROVAL

        Compassion and Approval

BUS TRIP NORTH TO BORDER: Up the hard Durangos and Impossible Chihuahuas. . . . .
    G h o s t
. . . . Natural Medieval Valleys of Mexico (at 40 miles north of Durango)
          A Platte of Heaven with rocks of red soft horror---aznos with
            different attitudes, Pink oblivions in the shadow of the earth
             which is the mountain---these mountains are phantoms----
           Des gros maraguain d'foin, des lingues blances, des tas, la croix
         sur les buttes tables, les pyramides naturel cachez dans l materielle
        de le Seigneur Tathagata, MEANING,

                                   Big mosquitos of hay, white lines,
                                   piles, the cross on the butte table,

"This is bode Belchum, bonnet
to busby, breaking his secred
word with a ball up his ear to
the Willingdone. This is the
Willingdone's hurold
dispitchback. Dispitch
desployed on the regions
rare of me Belchum.
Salamangra! Ayi, ayi,
ayi! Cherry jinnies.
Figtreeyou!"
   ---HOLY JOYCE
   (Finnegans Wake)

        natural p y r a m i d s hidden in
        the material of the Lord Tathagata

     Dry cracked ravelled arroyos at the base of
       vein bleeding mountains of sand, rock, and
        rustle---White sandbanks lost in infinity
       mountains under the same Utah moon and you too.
      Bristles of stubrock with prickly pear, ---Lost
       creek bottoms . . .
     The sad brown twilight of it all, and it a bubble,
    a dream, a phantom, an evanescent dew. . . .

✳ ✳

SEPT.21 *Berkeley, the Cottage on Milvia Street*
A DREAM. . . . .
              "Kerouac has swallowed that Buddhism stuff hook line & sinker"---It's
like we were all in jail and I've received instructions on how to escape. However
I'm the only one now who realizes we're all in jail, the others dont know it yet,
they have an uneasy feeling that something is wrong but they put on gay fronts.
As I continually talk now of escape, the others think I'm crazy. I escape from the
jail but (Mahayana) come back to teach the others how. They laugh at me, I get mad
and yell at them "Dont you realize you're in jail and that this is the way to escape?"
They think I'm crazy because I get mad. "We're bored with that escape talk of
yours, we've got work to do." They manufacture iron bars which are used to keep
them inprisoned all the more securely. I pray for them and ask my Lord (who gave
me escape instructions) to help them realize what they're doing. I wake up from
the dream filled with compassion.---

SEPT.22---Where you make Buddhism you finally make nothing---
    Further, it's neither to be regarded as high or low state,
and it is undifferentiated from the nothing which another makes---
    Finally it is wholly independent of any definitive or arbitrary
conception of your own selfhood, the selves of others, many living
beings divided into many selves, or One Universal Self-----
    Simply, *M a k i n g   i t   N o t h i n g*
                         THE REASON WHY "I" HAVE NOT ATTAINED
             enlightenment "after all this time" is
             simply because it is *not-self* that attains
            enlightenment . . .
It's already happened, but my 'self' goes on yankering. . . . .

---You and the world have a kind of relative existence only,
because you are merely thought of---

"You & the world" are used by the Lord Tathagata as
expedient means to guide you by means of words, into
the path that leads to enlightenment. The purpose of
the Lord Tathagata is to emancipate "you" from bondage
to your thinking by means of your thinking, and to bring
you back to your origin in Mind Essence and Not Self.
That's why the Lord Tathagata is also just a dream and
the reality is nothing.

THE PRACTICE OF DHYANA NOW may be said to be preparation
for the supernatural compassionate activities after death,
that, because done in the terrible density and stress of
mortal flesh-emboldened life, contains merit and power a
thousand times more Virtuous & Rewardful than the easy activity
of after-life in the Transcendental Realms of Ecstasy---So practice
meditation as often as you can while you live, pile up the merit and
the power, when you get to the Halls of the Awakened it will be better
for you, a special place, a whole radiant Buddha-field, will be prepared
and waiting for you---wherein, by accumulation of the thousandfold merit
of Samadhi During Sentience and Life-on-Earth, you will have, so to speak
whole unnumerable Worlds to serve & liberate & bless & reassure & save . . .
Since all things are merely thought of, meditation on the Beyond-Thought
has in it merit and virtue that is as illimitable and inestimable as all
Open Space in all the 3,000 Directions, also thought of. . . . .
Kindness, also thought of, comes from Mind Essence---From the Fumigation of
Mind Essence on defilement, comes Kindness-----Practice kindness on earth in
the horror-stress of earth, solely for the benefit of sentient beings, keeping
in mind that the phenomena of kindness and the sentient beings are merely thought
of, and your Power and Virtue will be Millionfold because endless and free of
arbitrary limits-----
Run around concerned with earthly activities of work and self-accomplishment and
you use up all the time your Karma (also thought of) had offered you to bring you
to the Halls of Gold---so that, having ignored, you will have to resume again "in
another body" till you see the light and that may be more suffering Aeons than you
care to foresee, also thought of----O sufferers! Potential Angels! Stop!
Realize! Think: Accept! All things are made of shining essence including your
eyes of dust! W a k e U p ! Go beyond the life and death of Self in its
arbitrary system of time, a sad trap! See the Vast Ocean of Omniscience
everywhere throughout apparent phenomena! Adoration & Compassion to the
seeming somethingness which is the actual nothingness! Om! Svaha! So be it!
Amen! If ye have ears, hear------------
It will not be the fault of the messengers---and the messengers are scarce
and dont stay long----they yearn to return to the Palace of Snow---for
them the universe is a solid Pearl of Ecstasy, also thought of-----

* *

MIND ESSENCE creates its own Ignorance, which takes place throughout it but
doesnt disturb it, only disturbs within Ignorance's own Ignorant-Consciousness . . .

THE ANGUISHED BAWLS OF CHILDREN indicate ignorance & attachment----child didnt get
what it wanted, child annoys the empty air, annoys the empty ghosts that have
to sit and listen till they learn it's really silence. . . . .

MIND ESSENCE contains within it personages dedicated to enlightenment and personages
dedicated to ignorance and attachment---The devil will work against divine as
long as Mind Essence creates its own ignorance, which it has always and *is* and
will always do, for both ignorance & enlightenment, both Nirvana & Samsara, are
without end. . . . . . . The devil is no more evil than divine----divine no more good
than devil because it's all the same substance. . . . Prajna!

Dylan Thomas, he could walk with wit and poetic beauty . . .

T'I . . . . . . Chinese word for Tathata, Thatness. . . . T'I JEAN (!)

O FOOLS OF THE FUTURE---this isnt necessarily a World!

    You all know you are victims of pain and your mothers
and fathers are guilty of your birth, and you're all
camping flawlessly. . . . (written on bus returning from
              tooth-extraction) (hi on novocaine)
       * * * * * * * * * * * * * *

H A I K U

Chang Su Chi's art   Equally different
   studio, a silent   forms
Shade in the window   * * * * * * *   of the same
                                 holy gold

NO BRIDGE (the song I composed in California)   -   * * * * * * * * * * * * * *
"A sleepy afternoon   ---
   in California   -
A sleepy afternoon   - -------   NOV.17---A Bubble Show . . .
   in California   -I TIC
A sleepy afternoon   -I   Cold Fall mornings with the sun shining
   in California   -I   in the yard of the St. Louis school, the
That's what I mean   -I   pebbles---the pure vision of worldbeginning
                        -I   in my childhood brain then, so that even the
Rock Wool Insulation   -I   black nuns with their fleshwhite faces and
   in California   -I   rimless glasses & weepy redrimmed eyes looked
Pacific Insulation   -I   fresh and ever delightful. . . .
   in California   -I
MacRorie-McLaren Company   -I SKEN
   in California   -I   Allen's yard in the 9 A M with cries of
Woodpiles in the sun   -I grammarschool children beyond----the old black
   in California   -I woodfence is steaming furiously in the cool
  Begonias   -I air from the action of hot sun and last nights'
       in the garden   -I rain---little silver Christmas tree weedflowers
          never   -II below still in fence's dark background shade
(Melody   harden   -II show luminous as though sprayed by Christmas
is in   w i t h o u t   -II silverpaint---tender & delicate rainbow
my mind   y o u   -II spiderwebs sizzle the guitarstring jiggle
--dunno   -III clean and sparkling from droop hotflower
how score it) * * * * * * * -IIII (soaked now) to spice leaves, as bug whirls
---IIII dizzy happy morning dance over the wet grass
---IIII g e n e r a l - - - - - - - - - - - - - -
      *

SKEN---(sketch)---Allen's old yard chair has been sitting in the downpouring rain
all night and is now assbottomed wet where the checkered cotton covers the stuffing
   some of which's beginning to show in the wear and tear of asses and Decembers---long
      sad rockers are wet, tied to chairposts not too tight as you see gaps and sunrays
         underneath---shadows of the black bars fall on the right wood arm with pure perfect
            morning seriousness and simpleness---a nameless tiny web ululates at the right
               post, wove on the chair's majestical kee-post for salvation, big things support
                 little things----
ANOTHER SKEN---Radiations of Akshobya Blinding my eye in the water in the claypot
   pan-pot, the rainbow of the sun's reflection there causing painful imaginary blossoms
      to arise in my eyeball and I see silver daggers and swords mingled with red or
         rather roe-pink rowing fires, shot by quivers and Arch Bows of Tampleton Hokshaw
            HighRide Chariot Ear the saint of England, Wozzit, turning pools of oil rainbow
               Dedalus---Buddhalands without number and Van Gogh swirl agog rows of em endless
           everywhere in that little pot, and bug flies---

QQQQQQQQQQQQQQQQQ
*   It goes on and on,   *
*   a great surging   *
*   mass of devils in   *
*   different uniforms   *
*   ---Dark'st death is   *
*   in the beauty's   *
*   seabeach smile, in   *
*   her womb of gold   *
*   the black sorrows   *
*   of all S P A I N ---
* *
*   I L O V E Y O U
* *

341

TIC------A Tic is a vision suddenly of memory. The ideal, formal Tic, as for a
        BOOK OF TICS is one short and one longer sentence, generally about 50
        words in all, the intro sentence and the explaining sentence, i.e.,
        the above Tic about "Cold Fall mornings"---

SKETCH---A Sketch is a prose description of a scene before the eyes. Ideally, for
        a BOOK OF SKETCHES, one small page (of notebook size) about 100 words, so
        as not to ramble too much, and give an arbitrary form.

DREAM---A Dream, the core and kernel written on awakening from a dream, may fan
        out further, usually ends up in 300 words, viz. the BOOK OF DREAMS

POP------American (non-Japanese) Haikus, short 3-line poems or "pomes" rhyming
        or non-rhyming delineating "little Samadhis" if possible, usually of a
        Buddhist connotation, aimed towards enlightenment. BOOK OF POPS.

BLUES------A Blues is a complete poem written filling in one notebook page, of small
        or medium size, usually in 15-to-25 lines, known as a Chorus, i.e., 223rd
        Chorus of *Mexico City Blues* in the BOOK OF BLUES

ECSTASY---Meaning "Samadhi," a prose and verse accounting of a Samadhi or Samapatti
        experience in Dhyana meditation, of any length. BOOK OF ECSTASIES

MOVIE---Formerly Bookmovies, or Mindmovies, prose concentration camera-eye visions
        of a definite movie of the mind with fade-ins, pans, close-ups, and fade-
        outs. BOOK OF MOVIES

VISION---Like *Visions of Neal, Visions of Gerard,* etc., full-length prose works
        concentrating on character of one individual, with no other form than
        that, including verse and any thing, even pictures. BOOK OF VISIONS

FLASH---"Dreamflashes," short sleepdreams or drowse daydreams of an enlightened
        nature describable in a few words, BOOK OF FLASHES. Example: *"Bringing
        gray suitcases down from the attic of heaven I say 'Me I'm not comin down
        any more!'"*

DAYDREAM---Prose description of daydreams, wish-dreams during waking hours, example:
        *"Wearing top hat with black cloak with red lining, with T.S. Eliot, walking
        into premiere of DOCTOR SAX, through crowd of queers, handsome."*

ROUTINE---William (Burroughs) Lee's invention---the prose acting-out of a
        daydreamed role, a complete wild explosive extenuation of a daydream

DHARMA------Notes in any form about the Dharma. BOOK OF DHARMAS
        All takes place in present tense
        ----
* *OOOOOOOOOOOOOOOOOOO* *

POP

The sun keeps getting
        dimmer---foghorns
began to blow in the bay

POP

Time keeps running out
        -----sweat
On my brow, from playing

Also *PRAYER,* for BOOK OF PRAYERS

Example:- "O Lord Avalokitesvara
        Emptiness Without End
        Bless all living & dying
                things
        In the endless past
        In the endless present
        In the endless future
                        amen."

"WHITMANESQUE" (or universal homosexual lecher) interest in sexuality is like
running around gathering branches and leaves without knowing what their roots
are---the roots of all these penises and vaginas of people and animals is in
the Sea of Rebirth---
---Rebirth disease, old age and death of Samsara are not to be divided from
no-birth and bliss and blinding light of Nirvana, and who will ever know it
without spiritual intuition into the emptiness of flesh? and adjoining spiritual
unity in the Brotherhood of Bodhisattva Awakened Heroes?
---By running around in multiplicities of activity and feeling up your own
brothers under sheets cacoëthes befall thee of your own making---
---But even the Tathagata makes no rules about the Brotherhood and so I say
to you "Yes, it's a free world, do what you want."
---The sky is still empty---the rose is still on the typewriter keys---it's
your karma not to know that everything is empty and awake and brightly mental---

POP

The sky is still empty,
    The rose is still
On the typewriter keys

THERE IS NO SUBJECT
and no object, neither
myself nor my Redeemer---
One Bliss Solitaire
    THE ONLY ONE

POP Rain's over, hammer on wood
        ---this cobweb
      Rides the sun shine

POP
In the sun
    the butterfly wings
Like a church window

In the chair
    I decided to call Haiku
By the name of Pop

The purple wee flower
    should be reflected
In that low water

The red roof of the barn
    is ravelled
Like familiar meat

Swinging on delicate hinges
    the Autumn Leaf
Almost off the stem
* *
P O P
Rainy night,
    the top leaves wave
In the gray sky

The lamp of divinity shines on all of us without
prejudice and without shame---Tathagata neither
loathes nor loves his body's milk or shit

POP   Tathagata neither loathes
            nor loves
        His body's milk or shit

POP   Looking around to think
            I saw the thick white cloud
        Above the house

POP   Looking up to see
            the airplaine
          I only saw the TV aerial

POP   My butterfly came
            to sit in my flower,
        Sir Me

* *
*
*   LUCIEN:- "If it were done, 't were well to be
*   well done." (Quoting Shakespeare?)
*
*
*   DHARMA is Thingness, the paper is a paper---
*   TATHATA is Suchness, the paper is no-paper
*   but only essence permeant
*
*
*   SAMSKRITA, is, A Man, a rock, a thing
*   ASAMSKRITA, is, Space, Nirvana, a no-thing
*   Both are *existences* but asamskrita
*   doesnt work at it--------------
*
*   Note: Write to Buddy Tom. . . . .

Alone at home reading   The bottoms of my shoes
    Yoka Daishi,   are clean
Drinking tea   From walking in the rain
* *
I SUDDENLY REALIZED that my body is really empty even tho
it will take some years to apparently transform it into
impalpable powder---but whether as body or impalpable
powder, it is equally empty with all things---Tathata---

THE LIGHT BULB
    SUDDENLY WENT OUT---
STOPPED READING

POP
You'd be surprised
    how little I knew
Even up to yesterday

CHINESE PROVERB
Watched pot
never boils

Two Japanese boys
    singing
Inky Dinky Parly Voo

I THOUGHT OF GOING INTO THE CITY because I might be missing
something, a big night with Neal and the gang, but then
I realized it was all the same thing as staying home
doing nothing ("GOING OUT WERE NEVER SO GOOD, BUT STAYING
AT HOME WERE MUCH BETTER" JAPANESE PROVERB), all the
same empty nature, and so according to the Way of Tao
I preserved my energy and saved my money and enjoyed the
quietude of my heritage eating ice cream, drinking tea,
reading Zen, and meditating, and sleeping with the door
wide open all the rainy night
        (Someday I'll buy that cottage at 1624 Milvia)

* * * * * * * * * * * * * * * * * * *   *

Original Mind Thinking,
        is Ignorance

Take up a cup of water
    from the ocean
And there I am

----I can no more vanish into a Nirvana of my own then you could make vanish that
cupful of water in a world-system outside the world-system which contains said
ocean--- IGNORANCE is the taking up of cupfuls---
        is the dualistic supposing too of oceans
        and cups therefrom----Ah blab, I'm tired
        of trying to find the Truth. To hell
        with the Truth. I'll do & think what I please . . .

ALLEN SAYS "If you
dont make love in
front of babies
how will they ever
know?" KNOW WHAT?

SPIDER:
On the F Train the tiny black spider
suddenly crawled up my hand---I blew it
off---ungently---a minute later it was back
---amazed I watched it as it ran around and around
my thumb and finally found its way to the pages of my Zen
Manual---while pondering this mystery the spider vanished from my sight . . . .

MY OWN PROVERB: Vest made for flea will not fit elephant . . .

Seagulls on the roof,
    Assembled sadly,
Casting shadows

Cant tell difference
    between new moon
Afternoon or cloud

Nirvana
cant be separated
from anything

SKETCH:---for BOOK OF SKETCHES:---Unbelievable levels of flawless blue bay water
like in upper Chinese heavens shifting and moving in irradiant tumbling tides, with
beyond that, the lil Cleopatra needle of Berkeley Tower like a distant view of a
lighthouse---the perfect little No Clouds popped up there in the deepening afternoon
blue like cold dogs horizoning in shame as ship bawls and traffic bothers me---and
boom the big wave from the big ship is Ignoranting In . (*writ on Embarcadero*)

FLASH---The old ones are talking in the other room---they've been waiting for us
                        a   l o n g   t i m e - - -

TATHAGATA-GARBHA
and then the turn   BIRD TURNED   Nothing can be stolen from me, or added
                                    to me, because I am all

AVALOKITESVARA'S SOUND of   and all is me
silence follows me from room
to room, world to world, and cannot
be separated from me, because it's me---that is to say, how can I go on being
                        anything when there's no me???
How can things be empty
yet full of shit?---must be
that emptiness indeed is s h i t . . . ah so.   words in the breeze.

I like to get drunk and sad
in great final bars---it only
means that I'm realistic----and O
the sad final bars in Mexico,
the brunettes, the sops . .
the mud outdoors . . .
the dogs . . .

Leaf dropping straight
    in the windless midnight:
The dream of change

KARMA IS TO BE COMPARED TO
elements under the influence
of causes and conditions---so
that a tooth ache is not
nexusarily moral in source?
- - - - - - - - - - - - - - - - - -
ABSTRACTED
The mirror exhibits
the spiritual nature
of the body

It's been a long time since
my father was intended to be dead . . .

And who's gonna lure?

FILTHY ASHCANS DEPRESS ME because whenas all I
think of now is the Holy Milk that permeates the
filthy ashcans, imageless . . .

"From the perfect unity of Intuitive Mind
    innumerable varieties have been manifested
    and as there are distinctions among them so
    classifications among these varieties are
    developed." SURANGAMA SUTRA
* *
*   Stop slipping me   * * * * *
*   your old Diamond Sutra   * * * * *
*   You illimitable tight-ass!   * * * *
*   * * * * *
* *

To Bill:- If the only evil is to refuse life why
do you refuse the life of the fly by
crushing its head between yr. fingers?
"Failure is mystery" indeed!
B A C K   T O   T H E   H O L Y   T H U S N E S S . . . .
Reality is in the middle of my toothache. . . . .

"What is the sickness itself?" asks Bill B. I say, the fear of announcing private
rights, and since everyone is private, everyone has that right, including cops.
(The sickness of Totalitarian Police State-ism)

CRAZY DRUNKEN AMERICAN DURING BRAWL IN COURTYARD IN MEXICO CITY BAWLING: -
   "Give a hand Yustedee, Give a hand!"

Two men walk away
The sun follows each one
Two men walk together
The sun follows anyway

  Or, Walking the same or different
          paths
      The moon follows each   (a POP)

The mushin sand. . . . . .   "mushin",means,
                free from mind-attached,
                never gladdened, never mad,
                never greedy, never loathing
oooooooooooooooo-o-o-o-o-o-o-o-oooooooooooooooooo
JETPLANES'LL TOO BECOME DUST----
TIME'S CORRUPTION OF ALL THINGS
IS THE BEAUTY OF IT AND ALL THINGS ARE
C O R R U P TIBLE BECAUSE THEY WERE
      GOOD TATHAGATA STUFF - - - -

Your shadow waits for you to "stop moving" in
the same way your essential mind waits for
your brain to "stop moving" . . . .

LISTEN EVERYBODY!   Illimitably within all
          these living & dying things
          is blazing and bright Nirvana
      already---this I know, & bring to tell you forever!

                                        * * * *
Ah, out you come, out   ONE MIRROR
you come,   REFLECTING
blind sperm!   NOTHINGNESS
                              IS NOT-TWO
                                        * * * *
VIMALAKIRTI, the monk, his name
    meant, "undefiled name"
* *
*   BEING A TATHAGATA I KNOW what's
*   going on everywhere---unlimited
*   is my knowledge---Tathagatahood
*   is going on everywhere. . . . .
*
*   * *
*   Afraid of birth because afraid
*   of d e a t h . . . .
*
*   THE FOUR STATIONS OF BRAHMA
*   1. Unlimited Friendliness
*   2. Compassion
*   3. Sympathetic Joy
*   4. Evenmindedness
*
* *

ILLIMITABLY WITHIN ALL
THESE LIVING & DYING
THINGS IS BLAZING
AND BRIGHT NIRVANA
ALREADY---THIS I
KNOW, AND BRING TO
TELL YOU FOREVER

Why should the whole world become suddenly darkened for
me because one person, G., envies me and hates me?---
does anyone else envy me?---*who* is he envying and for
how long and with what? Bah, I'll go along the road
writing and drinking and teaching the Good Law like
before intended, and Karma will out---NOW I'm talkin
with my blue buttons on, boy--------------------------------

THE OCCASION: We were at a girl's house in Berkeley, G., me, and
Bhikku Gary Snyder, discussing the Prajna-Paramita more or less,
where I re-iterated that self has no reality but G. said: "Well, I
dont care, I'm gonna go right along and just be Allen G." and I
yelled "O for krissakes I'm gonna leave if you go on talkin like that"
(I was getting drunk & surly on wine) and he yelled "Well then GO!"
"Thank you," I yelled, "a most excellent idea!" and I stalked, left the
house, went back to the cottage, packed up, and left California. . . . .
eventually,----not without a further incident about a week later when
Rexroth, hearing of this, and seeing me demand wine in his house, yelled
"Just because you're a genius you think you can act RUDE and UNMANNERLY!
Get out of my house, all of you!" (Me, Neal, Whalen, Ginsberg, Peter Orlovsky)
I yelled "Aw you're frightening me to death!" Illimitably within all these
living and dying things is blazing and bright Nirvana already---this I know,
and bring to tell you forever. It's true.

WEEK LATER IN CAMEO SKID ROW HOTEL ROOM:-
Good old silence at last---nothing
but a tugboat out in the bay
   of San Francisco

Old man dying in a room---
   Groan
--- At five o'clock

THE EAGLE'S HEAD
POISED WITH PENCIL FINGER
   TO WRITE BALD TOP EGGS
      OF TALK
   FOR THE WORLD
O

The Beauty of the Cameo Hotel whether when as
   brakeman or now 1955, I always had the quiet
   opportunity to remember my own mind---
      my own mind of Dharma-self
   (which is in-existent)

Thanksgiving Day 1955
   Thankful for Dead Birds . . .

(About this time Natalie Jackson committed
   suicide----I tried to tell her everything
THE SADO MASOCHISM OF THE WORLD wont   was empty, including her paranoiac idea
do it any good---its fear and love   that the cops were after her & all of
of authority, no good---its contempt   us---she said O YOU DONT KNOW! then
of meekness and on-assertion, no good   the next day she was found dazed on
---Yet it must rise from its dumb   the roof and when a cop tried to
Molecule with a taste of enlightenment   catch her she jumped, off Neal's
---I wont rise from this planet without   tenement roof)
Tasting the Truth---I died, a Buddha
was "Born"-------------------------------------

BUT AS TO SKID ROW, Neal is right---people live in Skid Row because they hate life
---I've smiled at 3 or 4 of these bums and Skidrow chambermaids and got absolutely
no response and especially I think because I'm limping like a cripple (sprained toe)
---Skid Row Goodbye---An old man in the window opposite mine has been on the floor
for 2 days and several times I saw a hand spectrally reaching up to clutch without
hope at the desk top---Name is John Anderson, people keep comin in there sayin
"John Anderson dont you wanta go to the Hospital?" -- "No" (quiet answer from floor)

SAMSARA CANNOT BE SEPARATED FROM NIRVANA---On-Samsara and Off-Nirvana flash
   dualistically and intermingled like cosmic particles, call it Ignorance---
      but in reality there is no Samsara, no Nirvana-----

NO NIRVANA FOR THE BUDDHAS, means, Self (of Enlightened Bodhisattva Hero) is
on the way to Nirvana because of its vow, "Ask-and-Ye-Shall-Receive," but will
vanish into Nirvana where Samsara will go unnoticed, (as now), and thus, a
Buddha "is born" (a Buddha emerges, formless, timeless, causeless), and for
the Buddha there is no seeking for Nirvana and no loathing for Samsara,
and Samsara continues forever and forever needs Buddhas----------------------
When it is recognized that the Holy Light is all there is to see, the
Holy Silence is all there is to hear, the Holy Emptiness is all there
is to touch, the Holy Honey is all there is to taste, the Holy Odor
is all there is to smell, and the Holy Ecstasy is all there is to
think, then all dualism of Samsara-suffering and Nirvana-bliss
ends, and there is the Great Beyond known as the Golden Silent Hall
of Knowing, which is Dharmakaya the Body of the Truth, Thatness,
Tathata, That-Which-Everything-Is, not to be experienced by any
kind of experiencing but merely is what it is, the Inconceivable
Peaceful Essence of all this talk and twaddle and law-worry
and empty flesh of light.
And, those who wish rebirth in Samsara-suffering ask and receive
and go on rolling in the wheel of life and death, either knowing
it to be empty, as Bodhisattvas and Buddhas, or not knowing it,
as ordinary sentient beings, and in essence there is no difference
between Bodhisattvas and ordinary sentient beings because they
are made of the same knowing essence whether they admit it or not.

KIDDY POPS   *November, Los Gatos, Calif. Neal & Carolyn's House*

Cathy   *Cathy*
The houses are brown   The mountains grew
  because   because
Of the sun   Of a seed   LONG POEM

Jamie   *Cathy*   Yoo hoo
Jack has black hair   Jack is so sleepy   Yoo hoo
  because   he rubs   I come to you
It grew   His eyes
                                                          Boo hoo
                                                            Boo hoo
All   *Jack*   I love you
The dog in the grass,   The weeds are yellow
  bow wow   because   Bloo bloo
Bow wow   Of the sun   The sky
                                                              is blue

JAMIE   *Jamie*   I'm higher than you
Johnny is Davy Crockett   Jack has a hole in his shoe   Boo hoo
  because he has   because they call him   boo hoo
A Davy Crockett hat   Boo hoo hoo hoo

* * * * * * * * * * * * * * * * * O O O O O O O O O O O O O O O O O O O O O O O O O O O O O O O O O * * * * * * * * * * * * * * * * * *

Cathy Somebody's up in the mountain   *Me* Red spider on my shoe
          and they say   boo hoo
        Yoo hoo   boo hoo

CATHY The sky is blue all around   JAMIE The trees are gray
          and we love the sky   because
        Least I do   I call them red

CATHY   CATHY
The leaves are green   Lipstick on me
  and sometimes   because I am
They're yellow   So bright

                    * * *

Jamie   I have a red face
       because I been
          tumblin up & down

Cathy   In the orchards
       there's green leaves
        in the trees

Johnny   Well the orchard has
       brown trees
       and green leaves

Johnny   The sun is on the sky
       and the sky
        is on the sun

Me   Look! a Lady Bug!
       "Tee tee tee"
       "W a a a !"

Johnny   A baby cries Wa wa wa
       because we make him cry
       Wa wa wa

Cathy   Our house has a white roof
       and white panes
       around our windows

Johnny   The fences are stuck
       in the ground
       because the ground
       holds them up

Cathy   Johnny's boots are
       brown
       and brown

Jamie   The grass is yellow
       because
       I love to eat it

Jack   The mist in front
       of the morning mountains
       ---late Autumn

Cathy   The sun's yellow
       and so
       are my eyes

Johnny   The trees are so big
       because the men
       Built them big

Jamie   The houses are all kinds
       of color
       And one has no color

Cathy   Once there was a woman
       and a man
       And they lived happily after

Johnny   I'll tell you a story
       Once upon a time
       Happily ever after

Johnny   The cars are all different
       colors because the men
       Built them so new and grand and old

Jamie   The swings are red yellow
       and green
       Because they painted em

Cathy   The far off distance
       of the mountains looks pretty
       ---so do you

Johnny   The desert's so big
       because the men
       Built it there so big

Jack   I'm tired---I wanta
       eat
       watermelons

* * * * * * *   * * * * * * *
* * * * * * * * * * * * * * * * * *

WORDS IN A DREAM:
"Thee were not what lifewise are"

BUT IF YOU *ARE* AVALOKITESVARA BUDDHA , or
God, then you must so be, and *unequivocally*
all the time and so pat, protect & purify
all beings under *all conditions* including
Ginsberg and your Satans and all----
        N O W

       *

   Books should have no antecedents
  except the veritable tears of saints . . .
they should be BOOGS of great spiritual
    s a d   i m p o r t a n c e

FREED FROM ANGER, DELUSION AND GREED doesnt mean
to plunge yourself back into the frivolous . . .
Tit or Tat, forget the Personalities, you have
no duties---Your job is to write and be a
sante, a saint------------------Finally, when
personalities and generations are out of your
  pencil, be a saint and write about the
    H o l y   M i l k   A l o n e
    in

    BOOK OF ECSTASIES

Being pure, the impure   O   You've got no more reason to look up
would and did seek   O   enemies to forgive them than you would to
you out   O   look up old forgotten friends to pat protect and
                                  O   reassure them----Leave the personalities alone---If
Seek out no one but   O   anybody wants anything let them find you and ask you
yr family & yr   O   ---If they dont know where the Buddha is it's because
good Buddha Friends   O   of their ignorance---And all these seasons are insipid
                                  O
Hark to this purified &   O   Guiltless!   Purified!
    Liberated strain   O   Liberated!   * * *
---   It isnt my fault
                                                   I made my mother sad, (by leaving home)
PERSONALITIES ARE NOT   It's the fault of the sadness
YOUR RESPONSIBILITY, let   of her own Womb
them come to you---Buddha   O Mother of All things
Gotama didnt,doesnt write
letters---Jimmy the Greek,   --
Buddy Tom, far away, lost
friends, let em come to   Disaster!   ONE THING SURE,
you   The Teacher   THE MIND IS PURE
                                       Thought he was needed!

Through empty space   --
and solid earth,
The arrow of wisdom!   Intellectual hindrance!
                                               I see the great
                                           Hangmouth of Humanity!
        * * * * *   --

The mind isnt the water,   Beginninglessness, endlessness,---!
the mind isnt the wind,   Reality
the mind isnt the waves,   Cannot be limited   ***************************************
the mind is where   * TIGER OF THE DHARMA   *
it happens, everywhere   *************   THE V'S AND W'S   *
---Ignorance is "It"---   *   * OF HIS VOW   *
    The Mind is Mind   ***
        ****

The Twofold Egolessness---dyou realize the significance of inanimate things and
living things, both of which have no self-substance?

Buddhas are only dream guides in all this dark furrowing of thought which is
                                        e x i s t e n c e . .

Mark   Al(Hinkle)
(Hinkle)   I can see the ceiling is brown   I saw the pictures
              and also   and Teddy Bears
           The leaves are brown   And dont think

Johnny   The bears are brown   Mark   There's the yellow---
              because   the heaters
           I colored them brown   Are yellow

Jamie   Mark smiles at me   Johnny   I wonder why the lamps
              so much   are yellow
           Because I think he loves me   And I call them green

Neal   Seven times seven   Jamie   Because I keep seeing
              is   yellow stuff
           Forty nine   Yellow stuff yellow stuff

Cathy   One day I was fishing
              and   ┌───────────┐ ┌─────────────────────┐
           I caught a fish   │ Neal & Al │ │ "What'd you just take---
                                         └───────────┘ │   my pawn?"   │
                                              ↘   └─────────────────────┘
Johnny   You dont have to write this, Mark has yellow hair . . .   ---"Hm hm" . . . .

                                                                                        349

KIDDY POPS (CONTINUED)

Cathy   I have my picture up on
            the wall
     And so does Jamie

Neal   I think that I shall
         succumb to victory---
     Ha ha ha

Al   I was feeling, not thinking
     ---One side's runnin cold
     And the other side is runnin
                 hot

     (while playing chess
         with Neal)

Mark   I can see black
         green yellow
     White black

Helen
(Hinkle)   Diddle dee diddle dedum
        a great big
     Pot of rum

- - - - - - - - - - - - - - - - - - - -

THE TROUBLES A MAN HAS TO GO THROUGH
in this world is a crying shame---with
a broken footbone I lugged heavy bags slowly down Hobo Street. . . . .
But, ended up in the sunny grass with my Sweet Carolyn. . . . .

POOR PEOPLE OF THE WORLD! THEY DONT KNOW WHAT THEY'RE DOING!

"One's mind should become like a mirror,
reflecting things but not judging them
nor retaining them."
     --MIGHTY ASVHAGHOSHA

FLASH:-
     A man in a wood waiting for a
woman who went to the garden a minute
is gonna wait a hell of a long time, she
has just realized that it's all a dream
already long ended and will stay where
she realized it . . . i'the garden
          (A dreamflash)

* *

No more I do my duty
     but what
     I want

* *

A brother who went astray . . . Devadatta

     WHEN PETER MARTIN was young around
the fragrant railyards of Spring nights
in his youth, all the romance and
beautifulness was in himself. . . . .

Samsara in the morning
---puppy yipping,
Hot motor steaming

Praying all the time---
     talking
To myself

EDGAR CAYCE SAYS:
"Remember the vision
    thou art experiencing
    in the present."

"Our Karma
is forgiven
because we   *
have forgiven
ourselves"
---JESSICA
MADIGAN

Only one way to write DULUOZ LEGEND
   ----the way given to you as it
     comes, no need worrying
      about good or poor---
Cayce says: "The try, the
    effort, the energy expended,
     in the proper direction,
     is all that is required
     of thee."--------------------

- - - - - - - - - - - - - - - - - -

Be I washed
in the blood
of the Lamb

- - - - - - - - - - - - - - - - - -

CAROLYN POP
Gee I feel
    contented
---Moo!

The Seven-Skinned
Mother, is
Alaya-Vijnana,
Universal Mind

* * * * * * * * * * * * * * * * * * * *

* * * * * * * * * * * * * * * * * *

***** "Thy Master took time to rest;
*****   He took time to attend a wedding,
   He took time to be apart from others, He
  took time to attend a funeral." EDGAR CAYCE

* * * * * * * *

* * * * * * * * * * * * * * *

Die, It's a Dream . . . .

--Thinking, drinking wine, me in Paris,
     tryna explain "goin to the moon" (of

BOTARONPUT
Les pauvres anges de la terre
   ---Ah oui
Écoute, cest toute écrit,le Mot,
   le Nom, Om Mon Boron

   Jackie Gleason Pow) to French Loveress
    ----O mon ange mon batême!
     O my angel my baptism!
  --& Lena Horne sings to my rod

You're
Nothing but pure
Whenever love is sure

CONTINUAL COMPROMISE is
    Mahayana sometimes I'd think:
You stay with people
    who kill flies
Or leave them flopping
    in pain all day
On the tedious kitchen floor

O where is the going OUT ?

* *

Win the Millionaire question---the
last week buyin house-drinks for
everybody-------(drunk thought)

* *

Cathy (imitating comic books)
    I love him because
    he loves me because
    I love him because

Jamie   Books are all kinds of colors
        and I colored one
        Black purple red & green
        (no that's not 6-yr.-old
        Jamie, it's 4-yr-old
        John)

Cathy   Jamie said "Say
            something Don"
        Don said "Chomp"
        On her icecream cone

Johnny Daddy has all kinds
        of clothes
        Because Daddy has

Me   Bookcase full
            of books---
        Why?

Cathy   There's a fire
            In the livingroom
        So bright so bright

Cathy   Miss Hall said
            Hall hall hall
            ball

Johnny The burning fire's
            on the candle
        Because the people
            fired the candle

Drowsy afternoon
    in Fellaheen doors
    ---My Samsara dream

Love,
    human love

IMPURITY OF SAMSARA AND IMPURITY OF NIRVANA
(BECAUSE BOTH ARE *CONCEPTS*) are all of same
    pure and inconceivable essence

THOUGHT WHILE WATCHING TV: In another
lifetime I was always riding around
California to all the fiestas. . . . . . .

* *

Johnny   Hey Dad
                wanta
            Little lick?

Mark   Let me see
                let me see
   * *   What   * *
        _____
            M Y   P O E M s
            (J.K.)
INSOFAR AS I KNOW
THE GREEN LEAVES ARE YELLOW
EVERYWHERE.
                IT'S A VERY QUIET MOMENT.
                EVERYONE'S ASLEEP,---
I KNOW EVERYTHING & I'M AWAKE

            * * * * * *

LET THE WORD BE IS, EST
ESTA
    BECAUSE
        AVALOKITESVARA IS
        THAT'S NOT A CUP OF COFFEE
        THAT'S AVALOKITESVARA BUDDHA
A LONG NAME SO LET'S CALL IT *IS*
    EST IN FRENCH, ESTA IN LATINS,
    EAST IN THE EAST
    THEY HAD IT FIRST, THEN WE
    GOT IT SECONDHAND BOOA
    BLAH *O U E S T*
        WOO-EST---
    WE SAID WOO WOO FOG
    TO THE TRUTH OF ORIGIN
    WE GOOFED AT SOMETHING WRONG
    BUT T S ONLY THE WORLD TURNING
    IN TH'EXUBERANT WOMB

            * * *

NOW THAT'S POETRY
    LET'S BE SERIOUS AND TELL THE TRUTH.
    I'LL WRITE INSIDE MY HEAD
    AND YOU READ INSIDE YOUR HEAD
    AND WE'LL READ THE HEAD,
    AVALOKITESVARA'S HEAD.

(cont'd next page)

IN IT HE CONTAINS TWO HEADS,
    A BILLION HEADS,
ONE HEAD WITH ALL THOSE HEADS
    SUB HEADS
SUBORDINATE SUBSIDIARY HEADS
WHICH WILL BE NAMELESS
   SAY,
     LIKE,
       LET'S NO MORE
       DIVIDE THE THING

* * * * *

IT WOULD BE NICE TO STAND ALL DAY
   IN THE RAIN
   WITH YR FACE UP TO IT
   IN A GOOD WARM RAIN COAT
   AND NOT GET WET
   BUT JUST LET THE COOL RAIN
   FALL IN YOUR FACE
   AND ENJOY IT
   LIKE A MULE
   IN A SUMMER SHOWER
   GOES ON MONCHING IN THE GRASS

     * * * * *

HAD A HORRIBLE DREAM---
FRIENDA MINE FELL OFF A BRIDGE,
THE AIKEN ST. BRIDGE IN LOWELL---
ALLEN GINSBERG THE MAN---
WENT TOO CLOSE TO THE DRAWBRIDGE
AND AS I STOOD BACK
   WITH ANOTHER AMIGO,
   SAYING "STAND BACK, DONT
   INTERFERE WITH THE WORKINS
   AND THE BIG CRANES ,
     DONT STARE"
   BUT HE WENT UP THERE
   AND GOT CAUGHT IN THE DRAW
   AND DISASTROUSLY I FELT
   THE SINKING IN MY HEART
   HE WAS DOOMED
     AND MIND THE BUILDER
   AND HE GOT PINCHED IN THE DRAW
   AND FELL THROUGH THE DRAW
   AND SAILED NAKED & WHITE
   DOWN TO THE RIVER ROCKS
    SAYING QUIETLY "O YES
      YES
    OH YES"
    AS THO HE SUDDENLY REMEMBERED
     SOMETHING,
   THAT HIS SELF WAS MADE
    TO LOSE

     * * * * * * *
    TATHAGATA, means, Attainer-to-That-Which-
    Everything-Is

Inveterate fop, typewriter
Flower, falling star

) * * (

Mark   I think the television
        is
          red

Jamie   The leaves grew
        in one big branch
     Because because

Don   Don said
      "Boo boo
        va"   (reported by Jamie)
           (and Cathy)
* *

Jamie   Don said "Say that"
       And I said
        "Huh"

Johnny   Well the books
      are so reddy
      because the people
      read them

Cathy   Don said "What you
      wake em
       for?"

Cathy   The world is around
       because
     We have such a big ocean

Mark   I think
      the ocean
       is red

Helen   Sticks & stuff
      and
       hot embers

Mark   The fireplace
      must be
       black

Helen   I think of yellow lights
      and yellow hair
      And a long pink nose
* *
   Come follow the Path
    you crazy fools
     enlightenment
      is the same
        as
         insanity
           !

JOHN CASSADY'S STORY *
"One day a little boy *
   went for a walk *
     in the forest *
  *
And he got lost *
   and so he made a wife *
and she was poor *
and he took her over *
    to his house *
and when he got to his *
   house *
he couldnt find *
   his way *
    back to the forest" *

ANOTHER JOHNNY STORY
"One day a little sun
  found another
   little sun
and then they couldnt
  find the way
  up in the sky
and then he went to
  buy a wife
and then he played
  with her on the ground
and then the sun went
  up in the sky
  Home"

    * * * * * * * *

Johnny   Well the brooms
       are always brushing
     because the people
      brushy brushy brushy them

Jame   There was a time when Mama
      had pictures of Johnny
      Cathy and Jamie and they went
      to dumb place

Johnny   John went out
      in the night
     And he saw two eyes

CATHY TELLS A STORY
"Once upon a time
  there was a mother
    named Carolyn
and she had some company
   coming over for Christmas
and she thought they were
   going somewhere
and so they came the day
   after Christmas
And so the day
   after Christmas
(you'll have to guess
   the name)
It was Mrs. Woods"

     * * * * *

JAMIE'S BEAR
"I had this red ribbon tied
  around his neck, and then
  around his head, and then
  under here, and then
  I said 'How do you
  feel? and he said
  'O I feel awful'--"

* * DEC. 7-8 . . . AVALOKITESVARA
The universe is a Womb of Exuberant
Fertility (Asvhaghosha) at base an inconceivable silence and purity and emptiness---
  Existence is a frown on Avalokitesvara's
pure brow---a cloud in the clear mind of
God---
  Avalokitesvara has made himself into
all things, he made himself into blades
of grass, cars speeding down the road,
toy lambs, the sun, old trees once young,
me---
  Why did he make himself into a Womb of
Exuberant Fertility? He made himself into
someone asking that question---
  He is exuberant (as you can see) when
a man is stomping another to death with
his shoes,---when a Bodhisattva Awakened
Hero listens to the Inconceivable Silence

  Why did Avalokitesvara make himself
into Picasso, pictures, light bulbs?---
Exuberantly he even manifested Whys,
Wherefores, and I-Dont-Cares, all the
attitudes in this great 10-Dimensional movie
in Crystal Reality---
He invented the words real and unreal---neither of which
means anything----
Throw yourself into the fray, all of it is Exuberance----
He made Self, which is so hard to disengage yet he makes Self lose Self
every day ------ Exuberantly he sees that there is no Self---Reincarnation is re-
fleshing of New Selves from the Old---They are all the same Self and the same No-Self
---Ah it's Simple---Avalokitesvara is both man and woman---is the tree, the
chopper and the chopping, e x u b e r a n t   -------------------------------

Avalokitesvara is death, pain, lamentation, despair---
is life, poetry, pleasure, joy, happy-thoughts----
is at base Neither---
Avalokitesvara is the Holy Ghost who magically emanated the world
from the Exuberance of his Perfect Bliss in Golden All Now-----
---"be mindful of the vision before your present eyes"-------
It's all the Holy Hero----------------------------------Mind is the Builder---from

                                        henceforth, this
                                        moment on, build it
                                        with your mind------------

Oh human being, your previous "setbacks" were when
you didnt realize that you *had* built it with your mind---
Cold comfort?

                    Avalokitesvara and his Womb in his Exuberance is cold comfort
                for the self---
            The mist rain mountains bespeak it---
            Like imaginary blossoms in the sky which only appear to be in the sky
                he magically breathed forth these Living Selves, these Sentient Beings,
                and let them to twinkle on and off like cosmic particles in the sky,
            in the air---
        The very last fogshroud ridge do bespeaketh it---does bespeak the selves
            everywhere---incarnated in loss, lust, mystery and misery----Re-incarnated
    in traphood's self estapular coneroign---All one mighty action taking place
    in mind the builder---Whalen told me: *"You see the red sun
                        falling through the leaves?
                        It's your fault!"*---John Cassady said
                    *"You know why I'm so happy?
                    Because I'm sad"*. . . . .

                The moss, the rain, the tossed ferns,---the empty space
                of the sky, the concept of empty space,---all a ridiculously
                exuberant dreamed-up beliberated deliberate bleak reality
                formed for loss in upyards of the fray------------
            sicka the fray
            sicka shoes
            sicka sicka
            sicka the blues
        Sic me Rover
            I'm goin Over
            I'm goin over
                the other
            Abyss---
                    We find it hard to disengage from self but once it's
                done the thing is won

Make me You   Victory is One
I am You   Avalokitesvara Buddha,
  I am   Write Thy prayer
      Now   In thy hand
Avalokitesvara   Upon the page
      Buddha   Of Sacristan
        the   Upon the page of meanings
        name   Upon the page of empty paper
    of the Universe   Upon th'insubstantial page
        for now   Upon the Erasure---erase
    in my mind   The race, the fray---O Lord Me
(as I go along   Purify my longings, point to Thee
singing by the hedge   --Make me shut up the Book of Innisfree---
the song of Exuberance)   Make me disappear

* * * * * * * * * * * * *

The Town and the City

It was the story of George Martin and his kids, how he brought them up in
a big house, no riches, just the slambang old fashioned American Way of life
consisting of elements like the following:-a modest business, a good wife, happy
Christmases with Christmas trees, old tires and boards in the yard, hedges, trees,
gables, trunks in the attic, joy, sorrow, final decay and death and the despair of
the little ones. O Father of all things, when will it ever end?

And the river, the Merrimac that roiled huge and floody down past the shrub
banks and then spilled a quarter mile broad over the old Indian Falls of Pawtucket
and smoshed in the smooth rocks and rambled and made white mysterious pools and
dark ones and then gurgled like a huge throat through the slaty rocks deep in the
riverbed and under bridges and around mills and homes and around the vast lake like
basin so celebrated in Thoreau's A WEEK ON THE CONCORD AND MERRIMAC and finally
went seaward like a symbol, or rather like a river, of people, Back to the Bright
Origin Nothingness Sea, O thanks to You Father of all things.

The story unfolded from this town to the City---New York, the Apple, the Rock---
in wartime---where the family went all split-up and cross-purposed in the night
and stress of Affliction, till old George died in his easy chair in Brooklyn,
mourning his own father, and Peter, his brightest but not his saintliest son,
brushed his hair and kissed his brow and they buried him with a decent funeral
back home.

George Martin had died in hearbreaking sweetest firstmay 1946. That summer Peter
got sick and also almost died. . . . (for the sequel).

* * *

All completely different
yet all partaking of the
same complete characteristic
    e m p t i n e s s
      type
   nothingness
     gold
      of
  compassion
      of
     Om

* * * * * * * * * * * * * * * * *

TRAIN TO SAN JOSE---What fun to get off a commuter
railroad train and a car's waiting for ya---ya
walk over the railroad rocks and smoke and your
wife U-turns in your new 1956 Mercury and you
get in with what a slow majestical movement, the
movement with which you'll get into the Tomb,
and me too. . . . . SKETCH

"Millbrae!" calls tragic jowly ole Conductor
J.W. Tired, and night and nightlamps bleak
    without . . .
O the tired brown lights of homes and TV boredoms
within---it's *men* make this world so sad and bleak, not
   dumb blind nature---
---Stanford Neons, Ranchito homes, hotrod hopes,---nothing but
huddled hopeless black houses parading in the night by and Standard
Shoe Mart lit up like a Palace---and O my Lord You made this for your own
delight, thou Masochist & Robber?   O insipidities!

O INSIPIDITIES!

Glistening shoulders turning in flame . . . (TV vision)

---------- ---------- ---------- ----------
. . . . "All this stupid meditation
         cant increase the
         population"
        ---Rodgers & hart

The Sunny Breeze   Phantom Rose . . .
  will come to me   Lust
Presently   Is a Leopard. . . . A man who hurts someone
*   goes to heaven. . . . .
* *

* * * * * * * * * * * * * * * *

Coming from the west,   F E A R   I S   F I R E
  covering the moon,
Clouds---not a sound   Johnny Cassady said: "Fire is Fire"

POP BY CAROLYN   ED.NOTE:
The mountain   "Thou Masochist & Robber" above
  is blue---   was written BEFORE Avalokitesvara's
It's late   Womb of Exuberant Fertility. . . .

Jamie   I look at TV
                because
           It's so beautiful

Cathy   The fire is burning
                in the livingroom
           And it's late

John   Everybody turns the world
                around me
           Because they love it

Carolyn

           The yellow leaves
                on curly
           Gray sticks

Me   I bent down
                so quickly
           My face hit a fly

Johnny

           Well the skies
           are blue because
           They are all around
           Blue all around me

Jamie

           The glass es are yellow
                because
           I dont know

IT'S EVIL TO BESTOW
WHAT YOU CANT KNOW
TO THE YOUNG AT HEART

Johnny

           Well the skies
           are blue because

JAMIE   The scissors cut
                because they're so
           Sharp & dont know why

Cathy   We have a swimmingpool
                but it is not filled
           With water

Me   Cathy leaned
                on the pencilsharpener
           And it went Eeek

John   Mommy types at the typewriter
                I like to type it
           Type type type

Cathy   One, two, three, I can say
                the alphabet
           On the typewriter

Me   I drink my tea
                and say
           Hm hm

John   The blue sky is so
           blue because I cant
           see it & it's so
           blue & it's night time

Jamie   Ha ha ha
           The car is so black
           on the bottom because
           it went in the night
           so much

Cathy   Once upon a time
                there was a little
           boy & once upon a time

John   The rain pours and drops
                little beentsies of water
           On the ground

Jamie   I wonder what color
                that is---
           glass?

Paris? Saturated
    with the blood
Of idiots

     Name of lifestory novel---PATH

Heaven touches earth and earth touches
heaven---how separate them?
  Samsara and Nirvana

    Tuesday Dec.6 I wrote: Ca commence

    Free is the Only Reality

MY WORKING-MIND IS ONE BIG MANDALA WHEEL
of rolling---that's me mind I writes with
---but, and also travel with and live
around on and in---but my true mind *Is*

████████████████   B l a c k   T h o u g h t

The groves of trees
gaped at me O a A ah
mouth-holes
and then I saw Dopey
among them
and then the topmost twigs
dawdling in the rain
dawdling in the universe

       * * * * * * *   Dusk in the holy
        * * * * * *   woods------
         * * * * *   Dust on my window
          * * * *
           * * *   - - -
            * *
             *

The bird came on the branch
---danced three times---
And burred away

The raindrops have plenty
  of personality---
Each one

DREAMFLASH: I had, of some very solemn
serious men with clear defined personal-
ities standing around lining up for a
verbal legal active hassle about me . . .
* *
PRAYER   *
O Avalokitesvara   *
    Hearer & Answerer of Prayer   *
O Womb of Exuberant   *
    Fertility   *
Me   *
O Purifier & Sustainer   *
Container of us all   *
Thou who art Everything   *
That-Which-Everything-Is   *
Return us to the Origin   *
    and the self-less Source,   *
O Holy Hero,   *
    Only One,   *
Empty and Awake,   *
Receive thy prodigal   *
Imaginary separated   *
    Selves   *
And arbitrary sentient beings   *
    e v e r y w h e r e   *
Ten directions endlessly   *
Into never ending Void,   *
---O Space,   *
    Diamond Silence,   *
    Nothing-Happens-Ness   *
    Golden Knowing---   *
Avalokitesvara, Kwannon,   *
    Buddha, Sugata,   *
    Tathagata,   *
    Is,   *
        Are,   *
            Was,   *
                Will Be   *
These words of Mystery   *
                    Amen.   *
                                    *
* *

Johnny: "Do you know why
            I dont love you?"
Mom: "Why?"
Johnny: "Because I
            love you."
Mom;   "Oh"

Johnny If I ever eat a pill
            it will
        Break my mother's will (!)

FLASH---Waking up, I laugh to think they
        think they're me, free, real,---
        being but phantoms in my mind
        (people in my dream)
It is Avalokitesvara's Flash
            H i s   D r e a m

NOW IS THE TIME
TO CEASE FEARING DEATH. . . . .
      (NOT "LATER"***)
Now is the time
        to see reality phantoms everywhere
    B u d d h a   S o l i t a i r e
* *
        Dreaming you're inable
            is a fable---
        You're already in
            and the house
                is Y o u . . .

Cathy   Somebody sent a card
                to us and it had
            A little white kitten on it

John   One day me & Teddy
                were walking along
            And we saw a little beaver
                chewing nuts

Me   Me, you,---you, me,
                Everybody---
            He-he

Cathy   Jack has a check shirt
                and I
            Have one too

John   Teddy was wearing
                a striped shirt
            and then he went off
                in the woods

JOHNNY REPORTED Jamie: Do you know why
                        I dont love you?
                Mom: Why?
                Jamie: Because I love you
                        to pieces
* *
Me   Do you know why my name is Jack?
         Why?
     That's why.

Cathy   It's raining outdoors
            ---it's late---
         it's almost time for TV   *

         . . . .

T W O J O H N N Y T A L E S

Johnny
One day I was walking
along & then I found
a little ring
and I put it on
& went back home
over to the woods

* * * * * *

Johnny
One day I was petting
    my kitty
& then somebody else
said "Can I pet
your kitty?"
and I said "Sure
enough room for two"

* * * * * * * * * * * *

WINE NOTES (Dec.8) "Cayce is a rather dull
        mystic. . . . truly a dull tool" . .

TEALEAVES IN OUR CUPS

Carolyn	*Jack*
Flame	Reptilian
Lily	bird
Leaf	Shoe
Roast Pig	Cobra
Hand	Sock
Egyptian	Wrapper
flower	Horn of
	Plenty
	Bone
	Grasshopper
	knee

* *

JOHNNY One day Teddy was looking through his spyglass and then he didnt see his
        little bug he saw me instead. . . . .

"Look at this you kids"
----write down
    that
        (said Cathy)

EGO PERSONALITY SHINING---the forces of the will
gathered there in one conjoined pack---
time'll eat it

Yowzah Dad---Yowzah Daddo

THE WOMB OF EXUBERANT FERTILITY

(Exuberant Personality) yet not
  one Personality possessing any
  self substance. . . . .

* * * * * * * * * * * * * * * * * * *

Gray day in Sunnyvale---
An old man
And a cat

* * *   * * * * *   * * *

THE RUINED OLD BUILDING IN MILLBRAE---(where Neal was hurt)
---Write the Duluoz Legend from beginning. . . . start with
Gerard---California sunshine tracks & trees!--there's the
beginning! Now! The little incident with the conductor
about the tickets-----for it's only theoretically you
deny life----*Go home, work, enjoy days.* . . . . . .
Go to Mexico in May------Visions of Gerard first work---
continual lifework. . . . . .

YOU CANT DENY THE
UNDENIABLE
  THE UNDENIABLE
  IS WHAT THERE IS
    PERIOD
  YOU CANT THROW OUT
WHAT THERE IS ALREADY
(NEITHER IS IT KEEPABLE)---

TRANSLATION FROM PATOIS: "Visions of Gerard . . . His face so pure, tranquil and sad---
in the picture---with Ti Nin---the sun in their eyes---the trees of antiquity in
the wet fields in back---the ancientness in the Time that we see in the eyes of my
old relatives in the picture taken in the woods---Papa had him in his arms, with
Aunt Marie, Raymond, Manda---Ah the eternal family of life in the old sun that
falls on the pines of New Hampshire, on the red bricks of Brooklyn and of the Painted
desert, on the red fogs of Saturn, on Nothingness---(les Indes)---Come, my hearts,
let us believe in tenderness!" (Written on train en route to race track)

* * * * * * * * * * * * * * *

Visions of Gerard, 1.fast blowing sessions, 2.french Intros, 3.tea, 4.wine,
        5.slow long prose, 6.pops, tics, flashes, blues, 7. benzedrine
                                                            sessions
NO CHAPTERS   JUST SPACING   * * LIFE WORK *   AVALOKITESVARA DOES
                                                            WHAT HE WANTS!
With your body you'll never be able to go on saying NO

Blue Gilligan
    Comin in on 2---
Lost Utterly

. . . It is what is. . . . *It is what it is and that's all it is.* . .
O TURN THE TWIST IN YOUR MIND DIAL AND WRITE . . .
* *
        Ah these mellifluous telephone poles and sobbing sad
                airplaines
* *

Wild, to sit on a
    haypile,
Writing Haikus,
Drinkin wine
    * * *

We're all brothers in the same life and death---
c'est qu'est ce que c'est et c'est tous que c'est

Grandpa Jack
   came in last,   Neal is a great   'Tis noble to be
Volzke held the lamp   linguistic genius   k i n d
* * * * * * * * * * * * * * * * * * *

(Volzke & Gilligan)   SKETCH---Purple Tanforan at nightfall, races over,
  are jockeys)   everybody lost, the curry truck still curries the
*   mudslop, Clubhouse 's all lit up---horses at their
                            oats, owners sending money to their Choates and
Fell the angel   defending their Moats and Poor kind Boats---Wives
   for lust   beating the Bishop in the chess game---"Nah" says
And cavil   the sky over winners-lose-all---It is what it is
                            and t s all it is---One glimmer red lock lark laing
                            lamp-O sporfing at the soft no-like-me hill---
Landsdale Archetype   Nameless whirlwind cloud booning horizon---Gate is
Mandala Auras. . . . . .   locked   (writ after losing $150 for Neal)

LEAVING CALIFORNIA
RR YARDS AT SAN JOSE WHEN THE SUN SETS AT SIX BEHIND THOSE BOXCARS Ole 272
Waitin for the Zipper   the Advance Zipper'll be headin in for its San Jose
   4 P M---   switchin---then we'll be off for Sad Watsonville in the
Sun in West clouds, gold   purple eve---O Lord, thou hast made Ignorance and the
--------------------------------- World but now thou hast let me say "Now I know it is
                          what it is and so it is" and O Lord thou art Myself---
ZIPPER SHOWED   How long, O Lord, how long have we known this together
AT 8:30 P M   in this One and Holy Thusness---*Why?* Why, myself why?
-------------------------------   Is it not thy fault, O my self? to banker & jungle thus?
Gull sailing   *------------
   in the saffron sky----   *   (Cooked macaroni and ate it in oily weeds
The Holy Ghost wanted it   *   of railyard night . . . dodged railroad cops
*   and hopped Zipper other side of crossing)
                                (rode on thru)

EASY TRIP TO L.A. ON ZIPPER ---

L I T T L E   M A I N   S T R E E T
   * * B L U E S * * * *

       LOS ANGELES
Original name Our Lady
The Queen of the Angels.
   Synus in my Mynus.   (which weighs 50 lbs)
   Mizruble.   and as train speeds up
   Tired---Waited---   for impossible to get off
   The Yuma Zipper   danger of the fly
was a bloody no-good   desert night
18-car sealed sonumbitch   calmly mad off I steps
and I got on it at 15   and am still in L A
miles an hour (or 12)   ---mad, sick, sniffles---
and almost got kilt   smog night,---to sleep
(with pack)   by a wire fence
and tried to tie   in a ditch by the tracks
the pack onto catwalk   awakened all night
with strap-clip   by rackets of SP and ATSF
   (couldnt)   trains and switchers
cause the Lawd was watchin   roarin by---
cause then I look up and see   till fog
the crummy curving in   and clear
18, 17, 16 cars   of midnight
away and no flats   then fog again
no place to ride   then fog dawn
xcept the deadly top   and in and outa my hot bag
so down the Ladder I go   ---bang---at dawn
one arm holdin rucksack   a little bird blesses me

and this is my meditation
  and my prayer---
  for prayer is an act
  of selfhood---
because of that
  a double two-thing
  not a not-two
  Zen deal---
but abjection of pitiful
limited self before
the bliss ordinaire
and grand-o
        limitless
  of No Self Essence
  glad gleeful
  exuberant Womb
  of Fertility
Which is not even that
but Fog Void
the Great Truth Cloud
---Now Main Street
the Bum Street
8:30 A M---coffee-and---
17 cents---gloom
of cafeteria,---grim---
bleak forward time---
  Ti Jean garde
    ton courage
On va t'amener
chez vous tout a l'heur

---it's what it is
  and so
  that's all it is
  and Why?
  Why is Why
  and that's all
  why is---
  Farewell South Main Street,
  I go now,
  Till another time,
  Sour sorrow smashes
  down sweet parting
  ere my prap's been
  crowded outa bins
  and banks of green
  clay water grass
  and erst I saw
  the elf on high
  ---tsa pall of billshit
  ---Cram!
    I'm out.

DEC 14 1955
Los Angeles

AND SO ENDS THIS BLACKBOOK
VOLUME of Book of Dharmas . . .
I'm very happy---Just drank
tea in my riverbottom grove
in Riverside Calif. and got
fire going for supper of beans
or macaroni---goin home for
Christmas---fell like
Handel on knees for found
my work---cant stop writin
these glad fill-out-notebook
notes---O I'm so sad and
happy!---Memories!-----
Bleak present realities!
---Death yet to Come!---the
Love of Heaven Near!---
when I'll soon know "in this
lifetime and in no long
time" that I'm denying wine
or life or whatever it is
that disturbs me, because
I havent yet seen PRAJNA
  PERFECT HIGHEST WISDOM
    & realized it surely
      in E c s t a s y . . . . it's coming now . . . . .

MY FEAR WAS I'D NOT BE A BUDDHA THIS LIFETIME
after having been hepped---but *what* lifetime is
that?---SHORT ON TIME?---I'll be a writer-----------
Nirvana *is* Ti Jean L'Ecrivain-----------------------------
--------------------------------------REDBRICK SUNDAY FACTORY
Boredom?
That's comfort.
Drink to alleviate it?
Alleviate?
  Makes it turn into from comfort to notself
  nightmare . . . It isnt the True Me (TiJeanNirvana)
that gets drunk---Awright, NYear's Eves, etc.
but no more systematic drinking-----
  At 4 P M I personally goes out and gets a
quart of milk and Ritz and peanut butter and
study my chess problems. . . . Drink tea a nights
and play Ballgame---Meditate in woods in sun
on future Buddhist Post in Heaven so sure---
Shoot baskets, pace, love family, write, make
money, go to Paris, grow old, die, that's me.
It's high time I do what I want *like* I want
now that I see people dont want me to not do
what I want anyway-----O, boy, hot fudge sundaes
and visits to NY to see shows, long turnipgreen
afternoon boilings, gardens, sunbaths---*GERARD
the book, followed by VISIONS OF MIKE, VISIONS
OF NIN, VISIONS OF G.J., VISIONS OF SEBASTIAN,
VISIONS OF BILL, VISIONS OF GARY, etc. etc. etc.

MattiJnana
Transcendental
Knowledge. . . . .

----------******************************----------

book nine

PRAYER
O Lord, Thank you

* * * * *

Previous, sketch, too literary

Nirvana *is* Ti Jean
. . is here and now, bleak me now
* *

LOS GATOS TO CALEXICO. . . .
TIC (or) *S K E T C H*
    The bleak fields behind
Alumni Field in cold
dusks when we practiced
but mainly my feeling
there tied with dreams of
there, the line raw of
birch inks on the last
horizon lost-dog hill of
my bleakest hope-no
Lowell O---Sloshing thru
the deep gutters of leaves
---What is noblest in men
has not been cultivated in
this Old Lady's Society
---Ah balls I've got
to find the language to
express it, the heart of
the T i c   THE STORY
* *

Yet Nothing Ever Happened. . . . .
* *

Dec.16 Morn in Camp
        Prayer
    I bless you, all living
        things; I bless you
    in the endless past,
    I bless you in the
        endless present, I
    bless you in
        the endless future
            Amen

* * * * * * * *

THE TROUBLE WITH THE WORLD IS people dont
realize there's no such thing as *boredom*, only
well-being---mistrusting well-being leads to
the mistrust of people and strife ensues,---
So people drink & take drugs & get all befonerated
and bestiffered, Gad

L I T T L E   P U R E L A N D
    B L U E S
        *
(Riverside Calif. Dec.15,1955)

The yellow aspens
Fill the air with gold smoke
And make my eyes quiver
    Goldenly
    As I stand naked
    In the bamboo grove
Watching fat birds pomp
    Noisefully in dry rackety
Grovebottom leaves
  and bamboo splitjoint
    woodyards---
        Laws!
  Hit's a mighty dry driver
In that mighty dry river
out there I dont even
know the name of and
cops watchin for to see
hobos passin by and
lookin for quiet
bhikku groves, I had
to crash like a criminal
thru bright brittle
thickets (crrack)
and come out sweatin
and stomped ankle deep
in streams and feared
to light a fire till

dusk no-see-smoke
time so's I'd have
embers no-see-glow
at darkfall
---Laws!
Nigger man in town
who claimed
he was part Mohawk
sez "I'd like to
sleep outdoor too
but t s against the
law"---I said "This
aint India is it"
---Laws!
  The Lord Buddha
and I got a headcold
sinus and try to stand
on my head 5 minutes
to lubricate it, nothin
avails, the tight asses
a pretty California girls,
everywhere makes
me hard and juicy
and I say "Wouldn you
lak to be layin
me stead a lookin
at me?---"

363

---Laws!---
  And they call this
Pure Land, well I
got real work and
true Land Purities
to delve in now
see ya later---
  P S And now
it's gettin dark and
I remember my childhood
day all day (kaise
not drinkin & wont
drink much mo)---dark,
& crickety in the
river sand, and the
traffic on the hiway
sighin and trucks
backfirin like gunfights
in the real Indian
childhood California
of all our minds---

Tonight I sleep
tight and long and pray
under the stars for
the Lord to bring
me to Buddhahood
after my Buddhawork
is done, amen
---Lord bless you all
    and
Merry Tender Christmas
on all yr rooftops
and I hope Angels
squat there
  the night of the
  big rich real Star---
  ---Amen   *Jack Kerouac*

* *

I am Buddha
I am God
I am imperfect Jack Kerouac
I am empty space
I am all things

I have all the time
  in the world
From life to life
To do what I do
To do what is to do
To do what is done
To do the timeless doing
Infinitely perfect within
  like Mind Essence
  and the minds of old
  Chinese deafmutes
  and lil sunflower girlies
  2 years old
  and Beauty Parlors
  and Banana Peels
  and Church bells at
  even star time

* *

MEXICALI   DEC.15   Hitch-hiking
        Raimy who picked me up in Beaumont Calif.
(where I'd eaten hotdog, burger, bag a frys and big
strawberry shake among hischoolers) didnt show up on
wild corner of Calexico (where I was so astonished
by perfect Mexican beauties who kept getting so much
better that when the first ones re-passed they'd
already become capped and thin in my mind) so I took
off with wholepack to explore Mexicali in late sun
afternoon sayin "I'll sit in the park, go to church
and eat ice cream and buy a few things"----Turn'd
sharp right at border gate to avoid hawker street
and went immediately to take leak in construction
dirt but the crazy Mexican Watchman thought it was
a big infringement and said something and when I
said I didnt know (*No sé*) he said "No sabes POLICE"?
(to call the cops because I pee'd on his dirt ground)
(BUT I noticed in my mind afterwards,I must leaked on
the spot where he sits to light a small fire nights
because there were wood coals small piled)---Moved
on up the muddy street meek, (truly sorry when I
afterwards recalled small coals), with the big pack
on my back, under his doleful stare, and came to a
hill and saw great mudflats riverbottom with stinks
and tarns and awful paths and an old Chinee Mexican
beggar caught my eyes and we stop't to chat, when I
told him I might go to Dormiendo * in the flats (I was
thinking of a little beyond the flats) he looked and
was horrified and (being a deafmute) he demonstrated that I
would be robbed and killed if I tried it, which I suddenly realized
was true (Ah sweet and tender thoughts of Mexico I had when starting out)
-----He made a swooping-over-the-hill sign in the direction of the mountains south
to show me proper place to sleep, which I agree---Then he went through long pantomime
about his escape into America to Stockton and how they nabbed him (by the wrist)
and brought him back------(cont'd next page)
              *Sleep

I walked away waving and smiling and crossed flats and narrow board over
the yellow water and over to the poor dobe district where the Mexico Fellaheen
gayety as ever charmed me, ate a delicious tinbowl of garbanzo soup with
pieces of cabeza (head) and cebolla (onion) raw (having cashed a quarter at gate,
for 3 paper pesos and pile of huge pennies) and while eating dug the street,
the mud, the people, the poor bitch dogs, the cantinas, the music, men goofing
in the narrow road wrestling, and across the street an unforgettable beauty parlor
(Salon de Belleza) with bare mirror on bare wall and bare chairs and one
lil beauty with her hair in pins dreaming at the mirror, by an old plaster
bust with periwig, as big man with mustache in Scandanavian Ski sweater picks
teeth behind and little boy at next mirror chair eats banana and out on sidewalk
some little children are gathered like before a movie house and I think "Oh All
Mexicali on some Saturday afternoon!--Thank you O Lord for returning me my zest
for life, for thy ever recurring forms in Thy Womb of Exuberant Fertility!"
and other such thoughts and thinking "All my tears were not in vain!" (tears
of past few days in SanJose Yard, in L.A. ditchbottom, in Riverside bamboo grove)
---Bought then, strolling, a hot donut-stick, then 2 oranges from girl,
then crossed bridge in dust, went to drugstore around to left and bought
60 codeinattas and 50 benzedrines ($3.50 in all) and put in flap and headed
for Gate where I was stopped by unpleasant American guards (3 of em) and whole bag
was searched but they overlooked *Flap* and barely touched my earlier-this-year-in-
Mexico-bought goofballs and I thought for a minute "Your Karma's bringin you
to jail now, bum" but on I went after they'd got tired fingering my wraps
of Frenchfrieds and raisins and peanuts and carrots and cans of pork n beans
and half loaves of whole wheat bread ("What'd you buy in Mexico?"-"Nothin")---
so now at Calexico bus station waiting for 30¢ ride into El Centro for my
highway and my SP freights (let's pray the Zipper has a flat when it comes thru
if it comes thru at about nine to ten) (then I'd be in Yuma tonight, sleep
at Colorado Riverbottom, and move on tomorrow) (now have $62.10 left) (and only
9 days to make 2,900 miles to Rocky Mount for Christmas Eve)----now writing on
bench I feel sad and pressed-in again by the three evils of the man who objected
to where I leaked, the man who presumed I would be robbed and killed, and the man
who was suspicious of my bag---the ang hang dang horrore of the world and yet
all's I got to do is be gay all the time and go on bein that Hermit call'd Meek,
call'd Patience---for I am Ti Jean

and I have a good heart

and I wont hurt anyone
and I only wanta do my work
because I wanta go to Heaven
and want God to protect my little
angels, my mother, my brother, all
my brothers and mothers, all my
fathers and sisters and my specific
father and sister---in other words
he l p m e be 100% v i r t u e
and tenderness and prayer and the Crucifixion
of this body in this heated Realm-----O Rome,
O Caesar, O Pharisees-----O Golgotha, O Calvary,
O Baptism----O Nirvana, O Snow, O Even Star of
Mexicali

(and
I
found no church and no park
in the dust) ✝

Wound up, in El Centro
I asked the conductor in
the yards "Where's the
Zipper?"---"It dont come
thru El Centro"----"only
freight you can catch goes
thru Mexico, to Yuma, if
you want to be kicked out
on the border, boy"---------
So I start hitch-hikin . . .
a truckdriver . . . I say
"How 'bout a ride?"----
"You know Mexico good?"
"Shore"----"I'll give you
a ride if you show me
around Mexicali tonight"
"Tsa deal"---We drive to
Calexico, park truck, cross
border, get drunk with
Mexicali dancinggerls . . .
wild night.

All the way from the sultry whores
of Mexicali
To the Christmas Farmlands
of Ohio
. . . . . !   in 90 hours . . .

SPRINGFIELD OHIO   Dec.20
Thank you O my heart
        my angel
        my solitude

                              THANK YOU AVALOKITESVARA, JESUS,
                                    AND GERARD, FOR SAFE TRIP
                                        H O M E . . .
                                    -----Merci, mes anges-----

I'm in Springfield Ohio 4 nights later after wild 2400-mile ride in Charley
    Burchette's truck (after our Mexicali Tequila drinkings)----In cold wave, I'm
        drinking tea at 4 A M in lunchcart debatin what to do, go to sleep in hotel
            or wait till bus station opens---leisurely problems, at a $12 busride
                from Home Rocky Mount

                Enroute,---*In Alamogordo (N.M.)*
                    I had the vision of the Impossibility
                        of the Existence of Anything !

FOR THE PRAYER:
I do know that living
and dying things come and go   GOT OFF BUS ON ROUTE 64
without any self duration or self substance   and walked 3 miles in silent
and therefore cannot possibly exist. . . . .   freezing Carolina road of Moon
                                                        - - - - - - -

ROCKY MOUNT   Dec.21st
The airplane's jet stream drifted across the face of the moon and bisected her
snow circle, above the piney barrens of Christmasnight Carolina as I crossed the
dismal railroad track that ran off into the gray blue woods of dusk. . . . .

I STOOD IN THE FROSTY YARD WATCHING MA AT HER DISHES IN THE KITCHEN, PITEOUS-FACED . .
--I said,"I'll never hurt you again"------------------------------
--Poor Gabe in this harsh life

* *

But she's funny; she shows   Wars between wizards. . . .
me how the little kids of Canada   Alchemical powders of a mad benefactor . . .
do the sign of the cross: (Doctor Sax and Wizard of Nittlingen)
    "Au nom du pêre
     Ma tante cafiêre   *
     Pistalette de boi   READ EVERYTHING from the beginning, in my desk,
     Ainsi soit il"   then start the mature final LEGEND---"Sacred night"
                                        of William Dyer, bless my try, bless my aim. . . . . . .
PERFECT FORMS OF EMPTINESS
                                    All dying to see what present Karma is hiding for
Holy Benzedrine. . . .   us Christmas Paradise - - -
-O-O-O-O-O-O-O-O-O-O-O-O-O-O-O-O-O-O-O-O-O-O-O-O-O-O-O-O-O-O-O-O-O-O-O-O-O-O-O-O-O-O-O-O-O
D R I N K I N G   P O M E S   W R I T T E N   O N   C H R I S T M A S   E V E   *   *

The giddy fiddlers   Augustine keened   Advocated
Christmas eve   John the Baptist kiss't   Cruelly
Snowy diddlers   Beseechers beseeched   Sins
For reprieve   Concord's meat   Neighbor Lee

One man practising kindness   Bishops ministered   Be aware
in the wilderness   Doctrines glistered   wary
is worth all the temples   Congregations presented   wake
this world pulls   Me a-bented   ---all is
                                                            taken
                                                        heeded
The booty was men's hearts   Comforted,succored,   saved---Wait
Organs roared---   Joyed, buggered,   ------------------------------
Pale snowy priests   Loved, saved,
Abounded at the board   Washéd, laved   "O world without
  Christmas Mass---Alas---   e n d "

FINALLY---I am a visitor from the other world, invisible (angel) world, and I see, men
are indeed devout, desire mercy, tenderness, oblation, redemption, sacrifice, obligatory love

look,loves,boom,I offer you
   s i l e n c e

A GREAT TOTALITARIAN CHRISTMAS with everybody
forced to sing Christmas Carols

- - - - - - - - - - -

THE BREATHLESS LITTLE PARENTS laying out their presents
at mid night are more gloriful than all the Gloria In
Excelcis Deos of Roma Church-o and all its Attendant Bishops
(with Wine and Excitement on their breaths)---for after all
Augustine was a Nigger and Francis my Idiot Brother

AGONIZED AND DIED, CHRIST

St. Joseph on bended knee
The Three Holy Kings

Pomp, inordinate sense,
Pride, blood, us,
Thus, O, desired lens
Uncontaminate this Pus

Contrition, purity
Worldling brings

     * Love,Father, I
     * Me, Word, Lover, eye,
Gambling,before the crib * Kiss my dignity,
3 blind men in   * Bless my obsequy
   Cezanne Hats   *
Xmas next   * Mournful Comfort
   Ach---Christ---   *   Lay me down
Mother, Oh---Cease!   * On the boon
------------------------------------- *   Of old dun fit
                    * Bone gray umphlett

Would I could scribble
What I'd Wibble
In the center of me heart
   O mark me, Part,--------

You blest me
   Sweet cat
With yr arrival
On my lap

Lamp unto my feet---
Lords unto my beet---
Worms inside my brain---
None within my ane

*   * * * * * *

ADDRESS VISIONS OF GERARD TO LUCIEN:-For,some people
are more aware of their death than others can be.---
Some think on their life.---The Saints think on their

Posh,pack,wait,go,
Lovers never do
   imbroglio
More waiters tried to die
   than work't
Inside my Estapovie
   (spelt pronounced
E s t a p o v y e)

death.---Their mournful hearts swoon and fail, in the
midst, in the mist, of plenty, plenteousness----Ah,--
wake up,- - - - -   Hard cocks sentimentalize
                 institutionalized cunts
                 And there's your juicy
                   G i s t

For one level now
   Nonce---
Tho, all die, dirt be,
Become, So me---Too
     ye---All

MORNING   DEC. 27 1955 ROCKY MOUNT
    Today I begin the opening novel (chronologically) of DULUOZ LEGEND----VISIONS
OF GERARD, the story of the first four years of my life, of my brother who is my
true self as Bodhisattva Hero---the mournful idealistic little boy in the gloomy
rain---If I cant handle this I'm lost---Took Benny for kickoff---Unpackt all my
notebooks and manuscripts and ranged them on the Workdesk---O Lord, reveal to me
My Buddhawork and give me the great intense eager ecstatic excitement of the
Holy Words, amen . . .

ST.PAUL, CORINTHIANS I---Messiach Crucified is
what he preaches---"Jesus Christ, and Him

Karma Will Out . . . . .

Crucified"---passing around crosses---

St.Paul wrote: "Let him
become a fool, that he may
become wise" (Tom O Bedlam,
Smart, Crazy Jane, El
Greco's insane Saints)

"Neither is he that planteth anything, neither
he that watereth; but God that giveth the increase."---"Ye are a temple of God."--------------

"Already are ye filled, already are ye become rich"

"Christ sent me to . . . bring good tidings"   to
"The Saints shall judge the world"----------   (preach Gospel)

ST. PAUL (C O N T I N U E D)
"All things are lawful for me; but I will not be brought under the power of any.
Meats for the belly, and the belly for meats; but God shall bring to naught both
it and them."

"But this" (allowing fornication between man and wife) "I say by way of concession,
not of commandment. Yet I would that all men were even as I myself."

"Those that weep may be as though they wept not;   *   "Woe is unto me
those that rejoice, as though they rejoice not;   *   If I preach not
and those that buy, as though they possessed not."   *   the Gospel"----
* *

* *

Buddha, "whose ghostly counsel me might cure". . . .
                    Dwindling lust . . .
When
        "mountain rocks" "yield like air" "SURELY A BUDDHA THOU SHALT BE"------------------

For title page of my book BUDDHA TELLS US: (or WAKE UP):-
        "As also for each living thing
        the approach of death is ever sure,   THE TEN PERFECTIONS
        so what the glorious Buddhas speak   1.Alms
        is sure and steadfast to the end"---   2.Precepts
                                                                3.Renunciation
                    * * * * * * * *   4.Wisdom
THE 3 CHARACTERISTICS   5.Courage
  1.Transitoriness   "An exhortation given   6.Patience
  2.Misery   to the exceedingly   7.Resolution
  3.Lack of substantive   corrupt makes no im-   8.Truth
        reality   pression, but, like a   9.Good-will
* mark drawn with a stick   10.Indifference
Surrounded by deities,   *   on the water, it immediately ---
and continually   *   d i s a p p e a r s " . . . .
reminded of your   *
accumulated merit, die . . . *   * * * * * * * * * * * *

Why couldnt I write on my big opening day today? Because I'm no more for this world.
--T I M E L A W S -------------------------------

I'd been outrunning the truth with my   "And how, O priests, do the
unhappy denial of existence's reality   intelligent know the truth? . . .
. . . just as dolts fall short of the   knowing things as they really are,
truth with their happy affirmation   the intelligent are on the road
of existence's reality---(!)   to absence of passion for things
                                                        and to cessation from them."
For,   ----------o-o-o-o-o-o-o-o-o-o-o-o-o-o-o-o-o-o-------
    consider how the world
    arises---5 aggregates---   YOU CANT HAVE BIRTH WITHOUT EXISTENCE,
    where is the passing away?   and you cant have death without birth . . .
    ---fingers & thumbs & bones
      & skin & knuckles   Dec.27 Rocky Mount
      make a fist,   At last I've learned
      where is the cessation,   patience, and dont need to fuss so much
      the ceasing of the fist?   about outward conditions---accept them more
      where is the fist   or less as they are---Thus no more (not much)
      which in the absolute sense   raving and gnashing---true evenmindedness.
      is not a fist?   o o o o o o o o o o o o o o o o o o o o o o
    ---BIRTH---ANNIHILATION----
---EGO,------NON EGO,-----------------   Abandon obsoquy, take up
                                                        o b s e c r a t i o n . . . .
    Sex. . . . . You pay thru the nose
        For shortlived shows. . . . .

I am the Mother of all things and thus accept all beings into my bosom
but without attachment---with Indifference & Good Will (tonight's Dhyana)
---Also, Hints of Samapatti Visions of other worlds---also slight
sensation of Levitation   (it's coming)   ---

Karma is *Hap* (From Icelandic *happ,* chance---and from French *happer,* to catch)
---that which falls to our lot. . . . . *Happy,* is, having good hap . . . fortunate;
harmonious; agreeable . . .   beatitude; blessedness; bliss; blessing; ------
     THE HAPPY TRUTH
The Blessedness Surely to be Believed
TRUTH, is from Icelandic *trur,* sure and trusty; Danish *tro,* true; German *traven,*
to believe . . .
        Surely-to-be-believed
        "In accordance with that which actually exists"---"conformable to rule"
        . . . "genuine . . . right . . ."   Stormonth dictionary
        You'll Get Yours . . .

Light a fire
Fight a liar   MY PRESENT BODY & CONSCIOUSNESS is the echo of another
Whats the difference   body and consciousness, it really exists without having
In existence?   come from there, like an echo----

                         Another life's seal
A watermelon seed   But watermelon   Produced my stamp
Produces a need   Is not seedling   The fire of my zeal'll
Large and juicy,   And the seedling   Burn another lamp
Such autocracy.   Aint the melon!   --thats Karma--

When a tree bears fruit   WHEN A GOOD APPEARS
In the springtime   THE REAPER UNDERSTANDS
It were moot   ANOTHER MAN'S ARREARS

To consider   * * * * * * * * *
What the planting   The old lady on TV who was
Who the reaper   surprised she won a Cadillac
                        conscious of some hidden Karma
     * * * * * * * * * * * * * * * * * * bearing fruit from some previous
                        implantation in "another" entity . . .
FROM VISUDDHI-MAGGA   ("Entity"---
Think this carefully . . . :-   properly speaking,
                         "there is no entity, no
"As illustrations here may serve   living principle; no elements
Echoes and other similes.   of being transmigrated from the
Nor sameness, nor diversity,   last existence . . . nor . . . do they
Can from that series take their rise. appear without causes."

"The series which bear a fruit,   *
Is not the same nor something else. *
The fabricating power in seeds   * Moon at her zenith
Will show the meaning of this word. * On freezing midnight
                            * A malice of solace
"As when 'tis said "The Tree bears fruit," * For cold basketball
As soon as fruit on it appears;   * A silver sun
Just so the Groups are reapers called, * ---Unearthly monstrance
As soon as Karma's fruit springs up. *   o o o
                            *
"The Groups break up, and only they, * Water in a hole
           the Wise say,   *   ----behold
And death consists in the dissolution * The sodden skies
           of they.   *
The thoughtful man of insight sees them * THE SILENCE ITSELF IS IN THE SOUND
               vanish,   *
They're like the jewel shattered by the diamond". . . . .

Rain in North Carolina
---the saints
Are still meditating

PRAYER
O Avalokitesvara, thou
    Hearer & Answerer
        of Prayer,
O   Lord, Tathagata, Sugata,
    Buddha,
I am thou & thou art me

Give me the Karma
    to truly see
And bring all this
    with me

I bless all living & dying things
    in the endless past
I bless all living & dying things
    in the endless present
I bless all living & dying things
    in the endless future,
                amen

Let there be blowing-out
    and bliss
    forevermore
Such is the blessedness
    surely to be believed

It is what it is & that's
    all it is

* *
                * * *The 4 Inevitabilities*
Not oft   * *1 Musty Books
The holy snow   * *2 Uninteresting Nature
So soft   * *3 Dull Existence
The holy bow   * *4 Blank Nirvana
                * *   ooooooooooo
* * * * * * * * * * *   o o o o o o o o o o o o o
                          Buy that, boy
                          oooooooooooooooooooooooo

Buddha's arrow   Nothin to do
Penetrated *me*,   Oh poo!
I dont know   Practically
Your key   Blue

                     Foo you too
                     Inky dinky
Give the dog   Parley voo
his bone   This must be
At the right   My Waterloo
time   DOODLING
And he runs
To his chain. . . . . . .
                    Imagine blessing all
                    living & dying worms
                    in eternity & the ducks
                    that eat em---there's yr.Sunday School s e r m o n . . . .

I FEEL WORSE THAN KING JOB . . . .

Blest be the Holy Ocean
    Blest be Kind
        Blest be love
        Blest be the ancient virtue
Up above

Blest be the children
    of ignorance

* * * * * * * * * * * * *

CATS SLEEP MOST OF THE TIME, why
shouldnt men?---t'would do away with
some of their pride & vanity

THE GROUPS (5 AGGREGATES) are,
        Form,sensation,perception,
        discrimination,consciousness

    What a dimformed thought!
        "emptiness is form" !

WHY DO I CONTINUALLY STUDY BUDDHISM?
IT'S BECAUSE IF THE EGO SOUL OF PERSONALITY
WAS AN ENDURING ENTITY IT COULD NOT OBTAIN
NIRVANA & THERE'D BE NO REASON TO WAKE UP
BECAUSE EVERYWHERE EVERYTHING WOULD BE
        A L R E A D Y   A W A K E . . .
_____
Only one way to meditate.
        S T O P   T H I N K I N G
    ---"In highest ecstasy of samadhi
    having transcended consciousness, pass
o   beyond discrimination & knowledge, beyond
o   the reach of change or fear---; you'll
o   be already enjoying Nirvana"-----
o   ---
o
o   I've already written enough to
o   satisfy seventy five thousand
o   saints, yet I want to write more,
        more---what guilt! I musta been
        the murderer of nations, an evil
        king barbarous & Mad
          ---I shd. retire from writing for
        a few years, leave all these things
        here, go to N.Y. and be a sports
        writer---t'll be too much to read

        PROPITIOUS BOETHIUS
        LATIN CAPTAIN
        CONSOLE
        MY SOUL . . . . . .

        The oldtime movie stars with
        their prim painted lips set
        grim. . . . .

I'd rather be alive than dead?   Pace in the frost,
--What's the difference between   Nothing's lost
    alive & dead!

All things, without exception, are arbitrary conceptions, imaginary judgments,
i n c l u d i n g   t h i s   s t a t e m e n t . ----------

WHY, TO ASK *WHY* is an act of consciousness---in Samadhi ecstasy there is neither
the asking of why because you dont know, nor the not-asking of why because you do
know---in the Nirvana Samadhi there is neither of these arbitrary conceptions or
imaginary judgments or decisive ideas of phenomena of consciousness----
    Moreover, to say that your body, possession of your corporeal nature, is a
deterrent to your attainment of Perfect Highest Wisdom, is also an arbitrary idea
with no basis in fact, or Truth---Your body is neither to die, nor was ever born,
being but the Groupings-------
    Thus, Nirvana---nothing is born and nothing is there to die and all things are
Nirvana now---whether people know this or not, all things and the people themselves
are Nirvana now---
            NOTHING WILL CHANGE IT
                            . . . Anuttara Samyak Sambodhi is as much a reward
                            as it is a burden---it's a burden because you can
                            no longer participate in the elations of ignorant ideas
                            with the children of ignorance---nevertheless be kind, and
                            view the world as a Womb of Exuberant Fertility, because it is
                            not kind to negate nor is it in keeping with the Buddha's smiling
                            position beyond affirmation and negation. . . . .
Why?
        what's there to ask about why?
                        For the Buddhas there is no Nirvana--
                            and no Samsara either---SO RELAX
                        *   & SHUT UP
Write a story about a hobo   * NEW YEARS EVE   *   Because it's only
pulled in for vagrancy, he is   * How about a drink   *   the Groupings that
a Buddhist Wanderer, is put in   * for Major Hoople?   *   come on and only the
the Bellevue mad ward . . . the wild * * * * * * * * * * * * * * * * Groupings that are
spontaneous dialog, I can see the   / / / / / / / / / / / / / / / blown out---Buddhas
marquee now: THE MADHOUSE SHOT   / I d e a l i n   /   neither appear nor
    * * * * * * * * * * * *   /   s o f t t h i n g s /   disappear
                                      / . . . . w o m e n . . . . . /
                                      / / / / / / / / / / / / / / /

For the play MADHOUSE SHOT:- "I told them that I was a beggar. . . . . ."

Try now to disengage yourself   Don Doll of WNCT is
from belief in ego-personality-   a simplehearted angel
self at 11:57 New Years Eve !!
                            HELD UP THE FLOWER. . . . . AND SMILED. . . . KASYAPA
DRUNK: Nothing allows of
    my dis-a-pissing   . . . . Lesser musicians do allow. . . .   Us bums pray. . . .
· ; ; ; ; ; ; ; ; ; ; · · · · · · · · · · · · · · ·

SAMADHI OF JANUARY 1, 1956 * * * * * * *   * * * * *   *
The dreary bliss of eternity, what's a little Samsara suffering of the groupings!
---besides, for the Buddhas there is no "Groupings," no Buddhas even---I entered
Nirvana---the cock crow'd---Avalokitesvara heard and answered my prayer and he was
thanked unto eternity---but in truth, there is no Avalokitesvara in the sense that
we(non-Buddhas)might think "he" "is"---there is so much endless bliss that this lil
suffer wont matter . . . besides what suffering? For the Buddhas, those who are never
born and dont *exist,* there is no world----nothing ever happened---only a dreary bliss
unto eternity----I say "dreary" to describe its unconditioned blank quality. . . . .

What to do?
Who?
Who what do?

        ---Samsara itself, trees and woods and light and air, and living beings
endlessly dying is a minor thing compared to the eternal ecstasy of suchness which
is Awakenedhood (the Buddha)----To become one with suchness and ignore your form,
which is empty, forget your body, which is really empty, and forget its mind-obsessions
and enter the realm of infinity of bliss, it was all prophesied long ago---

        I am now a Buddha

        ---but in the sense of the Ten Perfections, I am not a Buddha---in
my mind I am now a Buddha, my mind is perfect and has always been the
one suchness---How describe the dreary bliss of eternal suchness: for the
Buddhas there is no consciousness and no form of description---Nirvana, the pure
Tathata, That-Which-Everything-Is, is indescribable because it is in no condition to
be describable, therefore, and it is inscrutable, un-knowable, but it is " O U R S "

        Finally, there is so much happiness in eternity in store for us, that this
little suffering of life and death should be borne lightly, as a traveler will go
through a little disconvenience to get to his destination, or an adult put up with
a little trouble to please a child.

        So dont complain about a little trouble now for a lot of happiness later.
Besides, in truth, there is no trouble now, and the happiness that comes later can
only by stretch of imagination be given any such limited and unworthy name

        amen
        *

Yea, our gratitude can only be infinite. . . . .   * Too many words
        *   to describe
And when enlightenment is gained there's nothing to say * One rough bark
and nothing to argue, only silence and imagelessness--- *

TO DE LUBAC (Author of "Aspects of Buddhism" Sheed & Ward 1954)
  You devote half your book to "Buddhist Art" without knowing that "Buddhist Art"
can only be "False Buddhism" for the "True Buddhism" is imageless . . .
"The Tathagata cannot be known by even all of his transcendental transformations" . .

"The essential Tathagata, the Attainer-to-That-Which-Everything-Is, cannot be known
through any manifestation in form". . . . .

I had (during today's Samadhi)
the eerie sensation that thus   NOTHING TO WORRY ABOUT
it was just so and so it is---   AND TO WORRY ABOUT NO-THING
   Tathagata: So Is,   AINT WORRY
       Just-So

CALIFORNIA---whither among the drizzly suburban palms?

Kowalchik of Michigan State---not a thoughtless runner but one who thinks and
                changes his direction and plows (watching Rose Bowl)

   P O M E   *
The raging seas   Junkies:-Never mind yr.philosophy, give me some
  of New York Harbor   of yr.pills. . . . .
Lap at the silver edge
  of Bowery rooms   It's 9:15 in *my* little life
Where old men chuckle
  before they die   To Rexroth: Life & Death are tough enough propositions
And have lips winesoaked   without having to put up with society. . . . . . .
  and hands raw
And hats battered   "When the Alumni came for the buffet after
  and rime in their hearts   the Wis-con-sin game"---good line on TV
And lucid minds
  and tired eyes   In the circumference of the folk,
And hangmaw jowls   College is a permissible ambition . . .
  and human noses. . . . . .O Lord,Amen

I'M NOT PERSONALLY RESPONSIBLE FOR FAILURE TO ATTAIN PERFECT HIGHEST WISDOM
because "I" am only the Groupings in the Imaginary-Judgment-of-Living-and-Dying
which is Samsara, i.e., there is no me---so no guilt---
     B O R N   T O   D I E   i n   t h e   P i c t u r e . . . . .
Bodhisattvas, are, Idealistic Brothers

                    SAMADHI OF DAWN JAN.3
                    I had lucid blissful quiet of
                  knowing I was neither guilty nor
                heroic but beyond praise and blame be-
              cause truly inexistent. . .O thank you,Buddhas,
            Wise Ones! I remembered Sammy Sampas,whose idealism
          was not in vain---but was in accord with the compassion of
        everlasting ecstasy of the Diamond Silence. . ."We may do it as secure
      as sleep" says Shakespeare and by God that's how we'll do Nirvana. . . . .

" M Y   R E F O R M A T I O N , G L I T T E R I N G   O ' E R   M Y   F A U L T " ---

Samadhi of form, in Emily Dickoinsond
                    "trance of industry" (!) . . . .and she says: "We buy with contrast---
                                                        pang is good."

Emily says: "To pack the bud, oppose the worm"--
        try that, pack-rat!   * * * * * * * * * * * * * *

These soap operas on TV---God,   "BASE AND ROTTEN POLICY"
you'd think that the villainess   -Shakespeare
would have something more   Advice to incunabular junkies:
substantial to pull her Angel   "Put the drugs away."
of Darkness routine about!   - - - - - - - - - - - - - -
- - - - - - - - - - - - - - -

Wed.Jan.4---reading HENRY IV, First part, I'm drunk with Shakespeare's power
(as attested in overcoat-apartment-lunchcart dream just written for BOOK OF DREAMS)

'T s common wretches of a low dreg who'll summon   BALZAC: "A monk or an old
to see you because they are curious and then when   soldier, the two men
used to you, ask you to leave---humility never   who make the truest
put up with more---"When he had occasion to be   estimate of life."
seen he was but as the cuckoo is in June, heard,
not regarded; seen,but with such eyes, as,sick   * * * * * * *
and blunted with community, afford no extra-
ordinary gaze" UGH   *King to Prince Harry*   A. and all Fags, are
              S h a k e s p e a r e   lil girlbitches. . . . .

But the King of Kings doesnt have to worry about the kingly dignity---
t would otherwise be no King---I am the mother of all things, my strength is
invisible, invincible, infinite, empty as a womb, vast as everything---if I'll but
stop drinking at Eastcheap, that is, without making the imaginary judgment of
Eastcheap or Westrich. . . .There is no such thing as a wretch with a low name, and
no trenchant thought which cutteth like a diamond opening up all things, entertains
any such imaginary judgment of wretchedness or lowness----the revelation of the
true and empty nature of all things is like a wise smile. . . .There's no need to
yell to the Devil: "Devil! let me be mindful of mindemptiness!" if your mind is
already empty. . . . . . .Devadatta, hero of dark angels, is a coming Buddha. . . . (Dont
kick the Devil in the ass, he loves it. . . .) Spur your hots, Hotspur, halt!

IT'S NOT THAT WE DONT KNOW WHAT'S GOING TO HAPPEN TO US IN LIFE AND DEATH,
IT'S THAT WE'RE AFRAID TO ADMIT WHAT WE KNOW, THAT *NOTHING* IS GOING TO HAPPEN!

ON THE ROAD (Visions-of) was written, typed up, and handed in 5 years ago.
Patience? Lamby *stupidity*. . . . . . Are we gonna pluperfectly pearl with worries
like these? Let the publishers alone. They're busy *publishing;* they've dark heads. . .

With my life I dont know whether
to be abusive, whether to be gay,
or whether to be an indifferent
hermit---
The reality is indifference.
* *

From a dream: the lines:-
    Pain---
        'T is but
        A concubine's puff!

White as a lenten fart---
(*blême comme une vesse*
    de Carême)

* *
BALZAC
"He studies to be adored"
SHAKESPEARE:-
"Ay, by my faith, that bears a
frosty sound"
    "Hit a homerun,Skunk
over the centerfield millyard wall!"
    --KEROUAC, poor by comparison
      pisspoor
          milyards of homers
          never saw nest
          but bird was crested
          in anapest

    None but the mighty
      Seek and be dighty
        Any of these bolyards
        make me hards

---Find you a manse/
    Cream is your pants/

FINNEGANS WAKE is pure raving   o
Shakespeare below---beneath---all over   o
"I no sooner seen a ghist of his   o
frighteousness than I was bibbering
with vear a few versets off fooling
for fjorg for my fifth foot," the end of a long rant-sentence, is pure Shakespeare
sound but with Irish long-winded specialities---But Joyce wanted to be Shakespeare
Free, and was.-
        My Stormonth wont help me here: "Papaist! Gambanman! Take the
        cawraidd's blow! Yia! Your partridge's last."
    It swims in thru the open window of Mrs O Flaherty's washcourt at midnight,
by raving moon---Voices in other kitchens, Paddy coming home drunk, crash---A
junkey stirs in a fleecy bed.--"THERES SCARES KNUD IN THIS SNARLD WARLD A FULLY SO
               SVEND AS DILATES FOR THE IMPROVEMENT OF OUR FOERSES
               OF NATURE BY YOUR VERY AMPLE SOLVENT OF REFERACTING
               UPON ME LIKE IS BOESEN FIENND."
        ---Smash! --Crash!
         Yah!
         Cannon offstage,
         B O O M !
        "---and such as indeed were never soldiers, but discarded unjust
serving-men, younger sons to younger brothers, revolted tapsters and ostlers trade-
fallen, the cankers of a calm world and a long peace---------------------------"

PATIENCE IS FOR SAMSARANS with their body-
burden and time---in reality there is no
substantiality to the phoney phenomena of
patience---I thought this seeing poor
Bob-Dog's sighing belly. . . . .
Where no bellies burdenly pain, is here. . .

MAY THE MILLIONS AND RICHES OF NIRVANA come to me
and I'll minimize em with that ingrat mind. . . .
        So what's the use?
          --blankness is all

STOP AWHILE NOW, suddenly stop breathing, three
seconds or so, close the eyes, listen to the
intrinsic silence, let your hands and nerve ends
drop, let it all go, re-recognize the bliss that
was and is and shall always be there.
        (From my BLESSEDNESS SURELY TO BE BELIEVED)
         (Now being written)

      NORMALCY! THE NORM! IT FITS!
      LIKE A MAN AND A WOMAN!

            * * *

    Those who give their lives so that
    others may live, are happier than
    the ones they leave behind----------

JAN.7, at between 1 and 3 A M, wrote
about 6,000 words of VISIONS OF GERARD
   (Schoolyard & Confessional scenes)

SHAKESPEARE: *"Slaves as ragged as Lazarus
        in the painted cloth, where the
        glutton's dog licked his sores"*---
    Where did he get that Sound?
    That's what I like about Shakespeare,
    where he Raves in the great world
                night. . .

(which passage proves Shakespeare heard *sound* first then the words were there in
his QUICK HEAD)

         "Well,
    To the latter end of a fray and the beginning
      of a feast
    Fits a dull fighter
      and a keen guest"-----
           WEARY OF LITERATURE --- TO THE VERY
              BARE BRAIN (4 A M)

Ignorance is harsh. . . . .
  "I'm gonna die!" I said
  and threw myself on the dark night ground, because there was nothing else to do
in the cold loneliness of this harsh inhospitable earth, and instantly the tender
bliss of enlightenment was like milk in my eyelids and I was warm----
  Samsara there's no hope . . . .
  But Nirvana (which is in Samsara) there is---
  But we know that the reality is neither Nirvana-happiness nor Samsara-woe,
neither life-fret nor death-rest, but blank.
  As I grow older in my meditation upon the Dharma I do believe there will be
the taking of your choice after the dissolution of this body---"I want to try it
again, as a millionaire this time"---or "I've had it, goodbye groups"---But frankly
I dont believe it, if there is a transmigrating soul-ego he does his transmigratin
as a subtler body than this one now but still a body and therefore liable still
to dissolution, woe, change, and crass harshnesses   crassest continuum---O Woe

Enlightenment is tender . . .   *   L I L P A U L ' S P O P S
What to do?   * Have a picked-up chop
     Be tenderly enlightened---   *   boogie
     Make Prajna your goal   *
     Make Prajna your mind   *   Pickanny chickanny
*   take a pickanny
                           *   Off your tickanny
Space is neither cause   *
             nor effect   *   Tick tick went the clock,
                           *   Tick pick went the tock
     - - - - - - - -   *
                           *   Sliding board, sliding board,
"If the Tathagata, the attainer-to- *   Slide your tail down the board
that-which-everything-is, is   *
impermanent, anything made would be *
a Tathagata, an attainer-to-that-which- * *
everything-is"---. . .so is.   *
Because That-Which-Everything-Is, it is *   "Mortality---the witness of his sin"
not even moot to talk about its   *   AUGUSTINE
permanence or impermanence. . . . . *
W E ' R E H E R E F O R E V E R .   *   "I would t'were bed-time
. . . . -   Hal, and all well"
Prince Harry "Why, thou owest   FALSTAFF at war
        God a death."

                           Cold winds blow - - - - - -
Falstaff   "Honor pricks me on. Yea,
           but how if honor prick me
           off when I come on?"   I'LL GIVE UP THIS SICKLY POETRY
           (Shakespeare, divine punner)   AND TAKE UP DEATH * * *
------ o o o o o o o o o o o o o o o ---- ONLY *I* ENJOY MY WRITING AND THAT'S
                             BUT OCCASIONALLY
This VISIONS OF GERARD, the last   ---
chapter, I just wrote, on Holidays,
it's a crock------I'm nauseous with benny---pay no attention to this--ANOTHER DAY!
(long nights of writing in the kitchen)----Another day, some sleep, respite---
     --renewed ignorant faith--

  I open the Sutras . . . Existence is insanity--There's no world, no me, nothing
                         happening to me

Maybe the reason why some people
cant understand the Surangama Sutra
is because of their bad Karma, but good
God there are no "some people," no Karmas,
no Surangama Sutra---we know that in S n o w -
  Perfect non-recession----------

o o o o o o o o o o o o o o o o o o o o o o o o o

Lil Paul   Hey Dad!
Big Paul Hello snag!

    CARLYLE: "Empty barren quack,
        hungry for the shouts
        of mobs, Cromwell?"-----

Kerouac:

     his great, gloomy, and unwilling life
          . . . .

MINDMOVIES now---no.1, THE MADHOUSE SHOT
    (Every Mindmovie'll be about NY?)
    Balzacian Mindmovies About the City

I'm the worst bum in the world

Tonight, Jan.whichever, Monday, wrote
Gerard's dream---
    "The try, the aim, is all that
      is required of thee"---CAYCE

But your thought that the world is an
ethereal flower *is* an ethereal flower,
and that's a discrimination itself

    The Diamond Light

T H E   E T H E R E A L   D I A M O N D

The cat meows at the icebox, anxious to see what all the good dear delight is----
----
Instead of thickening the plot
thinned and leaked
And Hotspur's anemic forces
Did a wan expiring act
On England's monstrous rug
---Rumour's painted mouths
  May kiss that
(me imitatin Shakespeare)

The Money I might make
this year on ON THE ROAD
I'll save ¾ths of
for M e x i c o . . . .

GOD MADE US FOR *HIS* GLORY,
    NOT OUR OWN . . .
WHICH IS THE SAME REALLY

Falstaff I had as lief they put ratsbane
     in my mouth as stop it up with security" . . . .

The truth that is realizable
in a dead man's bones is
beyond Jesus and his Cross
    o o o o o
   ---it is Prajna, the
   Incomparable & Perfect
   T r u t h which isnt
   even a Truth. . . . .the
   realization that the world
   is an ethereal flower,
   u n f e t t e r e d . .

DO YOU *BELIEVE* THAT THE WORLD
is an ethereal flower?
If you will, all else
is solved in the solvent
salvation----
Believe and ye live

Bless all living & dying things
in the endless past of the ethereal
flower, and etc.---(add to prayer)
    And then: "O Avalokitesvara,
Ethereal Flower, Hearer and Answerer
of Prayer, Messenger from Prajna,
raise thy diamond hand etc."---
    The world needs its single
    exemplary Buddha and then
    n o   m o r e - - - - - - -

It doesnt matter whether I die
drinking or imitate Buddha, it'll
be the same ethereality--------------

* *
* *

* * * *I wont get mad at Sterling Lord (my agent)
    any more, he always comes through at the
    last minute and politely . . .
      The Lord is My Agent

    "The yoke of use and wont"---
      Ellen Marriage's trans.of BALZAC

    "Those who have favour to bestow,
      never lack courtiers"----
    "The hardest head in the Court
      of Appeal"---(!) BALZAC

A GREAT LINE ABOUT JUNK IN SHAKESPEARE:-
"In poison there is physic"

"The ragged'st hour that time and spite
   dare bring"-----
      "And darkness be the
      burier of the dead---"

It isnt as tho I was a virgin in my
abuse---(5 straight nights of bennies)
---May the Lord that Messenger from
the Ethereal Awakened Light, cast
Prajna-Glow on my black words----
- -
VISIONS OF GERARD---Jan 10 56
        I'm only doing the best I
can . . . Tonight I wrote the
Christmas Eve chapter, &
Long Night of Suffering
ooooooooooooooooooooooooooooooooooo

To an enemy: Go, rat,
                    I'm cheese!

FLOWERS "spiciest at fading,
        Indicate a habit of a laureate"
            DICKINSON

                Jan 10 56
        DHYANA OF HERE AND NOW
        It isnt at some unspecified future
        time that I'm going to attain to a
        perfect realization of Noble Wisdom, of
        Prajna, essence, Nirvana, dharmakaya, or
        the Holy Ultimacy, or the Only,---but *here* and
        now, since this realization is naturally independent
    of the ethereal flower known as Time---it isnt when I seem
    to be rid of body and seem dead, that there will be "making it
    best" but Here and Now---my body and its vexing senses is only an
    ethereal flower, its appearance (as now) or disappearance (as when I'm dead)
is only a seeming thing, but realization is *actual suchness* here and now, no other
time or place-----That's what NOW IS THE TIME means, and TIME IS OF THE ESSENCE,
Nirvana is NOW, PERFECTION IS NOW ---
                        (because there's no time) ---
            Tathagata's Radiance is beyond time, body, and circumstance
            though at the same time in and throughout same---It's all one
                                    Shining Now-ness

            Yes, Whalen, it's
            a Shining Now-Ness
            & we've done it, carried
            America like a shining blanket
            into that brighter nowhere   ALREADY . . . .

That answer from the stars---"withheld invincibly"---the moment of knowing that
                        you know: "withheld invincibly" . .

* *

FALSTAFF (on infamy)   .
"He that buckles him in my   .   THE ECSTASY OF SAMSARA--sex orgasm----
belt cannot live in less . . ."   .   all the frotting and rubbing *is* the
                                       .   convulsive ecstasy of ignorance. . . . . .
FALSTAFF and his monumental   .   * * * * * * * * *
complaints: "--I would I might   .   There'll be l a u g h t e r in the melting
  never spit white again---"   .   earth tonight-----------
"For my voice, I have lost it   .
with halloing and singing of   .   But there was only gravity . . .
anthems"---   .
  "I were better to be eaten   .   A poor, lame, infantile turn of talk if I
to death with a rust than to   .   ever heard one, Sagely's speech about his
be scoured to nothing with   .   caboose in VISIONS OF GERARD (cardgame scene)
perpetual motion!"   .   But GERARD is become an Eagle book---a torrent
. . . .   ---a sweet poem---I know the secrets of Shakes-
                                               peare, combine wild wine of Raving Rhetoric
The irony of Burroughs,   and "You-Are-There" (the TV Show) and there's
the velvet of Carr,   your Boom Play. . . . .
and Ginsberg
who never laughs . . .   GOOPY HELPLESSNESS BENEATH GREAT DREARY
arr!   SKIES THAT SAY " N A H " --(Pa at graveside)
                Man in his grave in the ee-ish night
THE DARKEST WOODS AT NIGHT, THE EARTH OF THE SOUTH, THE SAME EARTH FOR ALL OUR GRAVES
    ---When I'm in my grave A.G.'ll finally say: "Well he finally finished that
            dreary poem about the g r a v e " . . . .

"We are time's subjects, and time bids be gone."

TONIGHT JAN 11 wrote 12 pages of GERARD then cross't it all out, listlessly
---seven successive benzedrine nights
have left me thought-empty and I cant
get high any more---So i must lay off
for 3 days and try again, Sat.night.
Novel almost finished but the final
funeral scene which I must do now, is
a subject that wearies me----I'm *bored*
--I cant even meditate---And language
tires me---And all because of pride
and artistic ego I'm doing this at all
anyway----O well, High Makes Low. . . . .
        SIKLIGI! SIKLIGI!
 . . I hate to mar a manuscript . . .

A KLOOKLOO is something that
never existed and therefore it
bears the same reality-marks
as the world, which exists . . .
        BOTH ARE ETHEREAL FLOWERS

Stop up my eyes with flowers
Stuff my mouth with mud
Smear oil on my hair
Bathe my feet and tie them
Anoint my hands
Jock my old jock in gold lamé
And draw a circle
        around my navel
Then, commend me to the pyre
And cast my ashes anywhere
        (A lil pome)

* * * * * * * * * * * * * * * * ** * * * * * *

DEICIDE, murder of a god   *
DEIFORM, like a god   *
KINCOB, East Indian fabric with   *
            embroidered gold   *
MAUGRE, but maugre (malgre) that *
PEEWIT, birdy   *
PERENNIBRANCHIATA, everlasting   *
                        gills   *
PERDURABLY, lastingly   *
RELIQUARY, casket for relics   *
WORDS, mottoes & disputes   *
                                    *

Well, Jack, "does it not show
vilely in me to desire small
beer?"

BURROUGHS' great giant secret mind---"Jack
is raving in the fish"---when he said I was
"the greatest writer in America" (in
Fugazzy's 1953,before Holmes & Anson)

* *

Aye, imbroglios'll have it   o
that there were reasons   o
for wars, and wars for reasons---   o
but everybody dies   o
                                     o
                                     o
 . . . .   o

---Poor Bill, poor sweet Bill, I wouldnt
defile the air with words to describe
how much I like him (being tired of
words)---But Lord, arrange for me to
see him this year or next,1958 at latest,
before he forgets me. . . . .

POOR DETAILED IMMACULATE INCARNATE FOOL, AND YOU CALL YOURSELF SELF. . . . .

Take off your coat and crash wits!   . . . . . I've had my highest visions of
                                                        Buddhist Emptiness when drunk.

WHERE ARE THE BLITHE SPIRITS?
*where's Crayon?where's Hudson?   TO GIROUX:-"The poor piano was chip't,
where's Manocchio?--O noble Lucien   but t' s insensible!---

But. . .Outa my way boy,   S : A : M : S : A : R : A: . . . plenty more
        I'm eatin!   of where that came from
* *
BALZAC
"The bourgeoisie of the Rue St. Denis   "What goes on behind the scenes
displayed itself majestically in the   is a lot more interesting than
full glory of its absurdities carried   the show"-J.R.WILLIAMS
to the burlesque point: Out Our Way cartoonist
    . . . .and he says: the bourgeois lacks
"the impertinent gravity which contains   * * * * * * * * * * * * * * *
the germ of epigram"--------------------------   The eyes of the alien . . .

O boy, management with neckties on!   "Of ignominy's due
---Markell insurance men who stop   Let all addicted to
    trucks & throw hitchhikers out.   Beware" (EMILY DICKINSON
                                                        on dead rat in trap)
St. Jack of the Dogs. . . . .

"Wilt thou upon the high and giddy mast
   Seal up the ship-boy's eyes,
   And rock his brains
   In cradle of the rude imper-ious surge?
. . . . . O partial sleep, give thy repose
   To the wet sea-boy in an hour so rude" . .
      "MELVILLE-LIKE SHAKESPEARE"
(I was up there on the giddy mast,
   in the Atlantic October 1943)

DISCRIMINATION *IS*
   WORKING-AT-THINKING. . . .
"Names and forms have no more basis
than the activities of the mind itself . ."

            * * * * * * * *
      "Because in all things
      there is no 'substance' to
      be taken hold of"--------------

It is simply S o l i t u d e   *
. . . . . . (this 'world' of Essence)
   . . . .
*"Neither vehicle nor one who
rides in it"*--! is
            the One Vehicle

"The time will come that foul sin
   gathering head,
   Shall break into corruption"
      SHAKESPEARE (Dr Sax's Snake)

APRAJNA, is, "nothing is known"
---therefore PRAJNA means "the
known"---or, "what's known"---.

      Buddhism is a *strain* at telling
      the untellable emptiness---yet
      nothing's truer---pure essence
      abides forever in perfect patience
      is a statement that might as well
      never be said yet it's *got* to be said-
   Buddhism is, you simply realize your identity
   which is Oneness (but beware of making Oneness
   your *idea*, your imaginary judgment of the
   unconditional justness which is unjudgable
   everythingness)
            THE IMMEMORIAL PEARL
            OF EMPTINESS

THE BEST IDEAS OF THE IDEA-LESS TRUE REALITY WILL COME WHEN YOU ARE UNCONSCIOUS
. . . . . THUS IN A DREAM I HEARD THE WORDS:
                        "The Immaterial Meadow of this world you ask,
   *   *   *   *   *   *   *   *   *   *   *   *   As with golden ash. . . . ."

"Oneness, or the Divine Name"----
What is the Divine Name?
Amitabha? Avalokitesvara?
Tathata? Tathagata?
Babababa?
. . . .

Highest Samadhi,or Ecstasy,
is the Buddha,
            the Awakened

But do not cling to the notion of an ultimate
   Tathata, an ultimate stuff that is That-Which-
      Everything-Is, for, the Tathagata is not a
      self-thinker nor does he "think of essence"
      ---he is in a perfect state described as
   not-there, imagelessness "where Tathagata
   . and Tathata are merged into perfect Oneness"
   .   . . . O words words words . . .
   . In other words-words-words, Highest Samadhi
   . Ecstasy is the Only Altar (and Altar, and
   . Onliness, are false judgments). . . . .

Realizing that the fruit of
Samadhi Ecstasy is not 'something happens' to you
but *nothing happens*---Realizing that Boredom is Wisdom
and Bliss---the Dreary Eternities, Reality,---A c t u a l   S a m e n e s s. . . . . . .
--Come face it men, th'ungraspable empty air
            has had its say of it
            and we listened not
            This world,this snowball
            *

. . . .
Oral Roberts, Okie Horseshit, like N., that C.
fell for, the Phallic Dynamism---there was an
Asexual Angel in Jesus and Buddha, no ignorant
screaming and self-infatuated blabbering------
* * ** * * ** * * * ** * * **

It'll all end up on a cold mountaintop like
Han Shan----in silence---It's a colder compromise
d o w n   h e r e . . . .

SILENCE IS THE PERFECT SOUND
The Ecstasy *is* here and now
---Blindness is the Perfect Sight
---Nobody is the Perfect Feeling
THO IT'S-A COLD PLACE FA KNEES. . .

My sister says, hearing that
the law says I cant be penniless and a Vagrant, "When in
Rome. . . ." but I say "Rome
crucified Jesus, I'll have no
more with Rome."

      AUM!

P O M E
This world, this snowball,
This bliss, this tank
full of dreams
and the dreaming
and dreamers---
this memoried trap---
This pot for patience,
(and for parturience)
This hive,
This busy city of fools,
This kind oarsman's
paradise, this sot---
This edition & ship
and classic crystal
entity and nonentity,
wrapt for protection
from invisible infinity,
this tale of stars,
this lie,---this delectable
sainthood-place,---
this Cross, this Brother-
Death, this motif
& repetition sere,
this Autumn & Spring
of nothing-but-death,
this absence of phantoms,
this belly of a dog,
this noise, cleave,
clasp,---alas, this
picture, this face,
this written story
on perfect paper---
this discipleship & sugary,
this suffering incident
and accident and
Noble Incomprehensible
As-is-Ness---
   (this shin that hurts,
    this state---
     this Nothinghood
      this Ecstasy
       Foretold
      this real dream
      this true dream
      this path that leads
      this *This*
      this *perfectness*)

    * * * * * * * * * *
     * * * * * * * * *
      * * * * * * * *
       * * * * * * *
        * * *

I'M LIKE REMBRANDT,
I start with a day lands-
cape and that's because I'm not
a hack and I end up with a nightscape. . .
I'M LIKE REMBRANDT, I start with
a landscape and end up with a nightscape and that's because I'm not a hack---
I'll not be a hack for you, dollar, or for you, whore, or for you, famous! And if
people dont appreciate me, I shall be wise & humorous about it, there's the way to be!

The smell of these pine needles reminds me of
last year's despair. . . .

Shakespeare didnt spend his time thinking
how much greater he was than so-and-so,nor
did he linger on the sins committed against
him by others, nor did he juggle words for 'better
effect' . . . And I dont think he was a big blank
Howdy-Do Maniac with everyone, but sympathetic
and quietly human and within limits a person---
but *you,* Kerouac!
        Detestable coward, you fear the
        slashing and incision of your skin
        tho you yourself pronounce
        its irrelevant ethereality---
        liar!
          Admirer of yourself before
mirrors!
          Inflexible unforgiver!
          Tight Hard Hero---
          Punk! (Let L. slay you)

A valiant fool in the battle for self-pride.

  HERE AND NOW
    THE FINAL TRUTH
      A L L   I S   E C S T A S Y . .

Let me die, then---and be done with this
   arbitrary body. . .this imaginary judgment
     of a body. . . . .

In this void,which is the greater fool?--the
  one with the greater reach.

As I sit writing this my sister Nin comes out
in the yard and sees the trash the dogs left
and says "Where'd this trash come from?" for
all she sees is a trash-remover not a Poet-
Shakespeare----

     Shakespeare?
      in Keltic my name bloody well means
       T h r o w s p e a r

Hail, Midnight!---old friend!

KNEELING'S AN INDECISION SOMETIMES BREEDS DEFEAT,
so I'll kneel no more, and win a surfeit of losses
for meself upright under the balmy stars of my
o w n   m a d   h e a d . . . .

  A very modest finish, and a *finished* finish
  ----Tonight Jan.16 (1 A m) I finished
    VISIONS OF GERARD
     O rainy bleary face of graves!
     Wont they get sick of me for this one?

Come close to me, little
Gerard, protect me
from getting drunk

---St.Gerard the Child---

O Holy old Kerouac!

* *
"Who gives you the authority to
pronounce your little brother a
saint---you're not the Pope!"
---"I'm the Pope of Poesy"---

St.Gerard l'Enfant
   And it's my answer to
catkiller coksucker Genet
and his Googoo-Eyed Sartre

      both of

The   Tower   of   Ghouls

World, dont get excited, it's just a story!

OLD?-A GREAT INEXPLICABLE MYSTERIOUS OLD MAN

The World is Naught
* * * * * * * * * *
There is the coming and going of sperm and bones and dust . . . .
and where the sperm originated, empty space, but I m m o r t a l   M i n d   E s s e n c e
                              n e v e r   m o v e d ..

"Maybe Eden
aint so lonesome
as New England
used to be"
 ----How could
Robert Frost ever
equal that, Emily sweet?

Cesar Birotteau!-----
"Poor Royalist Blockhead
on the Brink of Bankruptcy"
. . . .

* *
Old Cockroach, bearing the sorrows of the world.
  (saw him on the railroad toilet floor)

I'M IN THE SAME POSITION AS MOZART & REMBRANDT,
I have complete mastery of my art
but only a handful of people care to concede it

**** LOOK UP AT THAT ENDLESS SPACE *****
   look down here at us scowlin and
   squintin, tis the very image of Ignorus. . .

MY LIL BROTHER PAUL always wanted to walk on
the sky until I told him that the sky was
holdin tons of trucks that he thought when he
would get up in the sky and start to walk on
it, it would break right through and he would
come down, but then I told him that the sky
was holding tons of trucks and houses and we
           were walkin on it, and he
           and I said "ehhh"----------------
        (Lil Paul dictatcd this)
              *
   "The truceless hate
   that the angels of darkness
   bear the angels of light"---
   ******** A.G.& me?

A.G. & me?---Hatred within the One Mind

   "We're in the sky right now!" I said
   "I k n o w !" yelled Lil Paul. . . . . .

A PERDURABLE BLACK BELIEF IN THE REALITY AND
UNMIXABILITY OF WHAT I CALL MY SELF AND ALL
OTHER THINGS----O everybody interplanetary
in the worlds! the same sin of self! the same
self of sin! And that's the way it is!
   Fights, fights, fights,---and the sports
   editors die one after another. . . . .

* *
MIDNIGHT JANUARY WOODS ANSWER:-   O Wise and Serene
      Everything is All right   Spirit
   Forever & Forever & Forever   of
          Amen   Awakenedhood
           !!   Everything's Allright
      Yell it to the stars!   Forever and Forever and Forever
                                                          A m e n
      THE DOGS EXULTED   PRAYER
* *
"OKAY PRAYER"
          E v e r y t h i n g ' s   A l r i g h t
      F o r m   i s e m p t i n e s s   a n d   e m p t i n e s s
          i s   f o r m
      &   w e ' r e h e r e   f o r e v e r - - i n   o n e   f o r m o r
      a n o t h e r - - w h i c h   i s   e m p t y . . . . a m e n . . .

TRIP TO NEW YORK * * * * * *
oooooooooooooooooooooooooooo
I'm trying to read the paper and I
see swarming historied prophesy'd Snow
  (on train to NY)
- - --- - - - --- --- - - - - - - --- ---
Codeine and Alcohol
warring in my Skull---
* *
Just for the sake of the Noble Record
dont defile your mind with any imaginary
                        judgments
                    whatever . .

      All these snowstorms,railyards,
        people---irrelevant toys,momentary
      bemusements, interim little jobs-----
      All is Sold to Heaven. . . . .
    JOB, LOT, & STOCK---T O H E A V E N . . .
  .-
The Commuter in one seat, to another:-   -
"Hey McHenry, what's crackin boy?"   *
--as train slows up in blizzard   *
outside Philadelphia---"Probably one   *
of these weather deals."   *
McHenry: "Ah nuts" (Doesnt believe it)   *
                                                *
Everybody in the train feels the   *
same fury and folly and helplessness.   *
                                                *
  Maybe that's why the whole reason   *
we're alive---that it's best to be   *
gotten rid of. . . . .   *
                                                *
The dark hair'd opportunist is trying   *
to grab the gray hair'd's foolish pomp   *
and postulance   *
              ----that's his *Goal*   *
                                                *
Karma is a weird thing---it continues   *
you on in your own foolishness, by   *
diplomatic calm---   *
    I am here *because*. . . . . . .   *
                                                *
Awright,I'm a hog   *
                                                *
I had Whee-You-Lips   *
    Oncet   *
And spok'at official dinners   *
                                                *
And plotted to kill   *
    Ole Unkillable   *
    Me-You------------   *
-- *
Brooklyn   . . . watching TV   *
    Tremendous Lesbian Symbolic Play---"You   *
can burn the handle but you cant destroy   *
the head" *Lizzie* Borden   *
        Rewritten by Hitch cock
    ----the axe, the handle, (and L.Crying,whose mother'd just died
        after 30 years of never leaving the house, *Domination*)----

ᙏARTIN BOOBER---with all his fancy veins
sticking out of his forehead he still wont
face the final truth----of *Nil Substantum*
---the Jews are proud of being a "person"
----as tho it was some great achievement---
The old Hasidic saying "For *my* sake the
world was created" reflects the Jew's
profound inability to detach himself from
ego-self-belief----The final depersonalized
Aryan Indian blank truth and highest perfect final fact of Everything-is-Emptiness
is beyond their best scribes---Yet, in
truth, one must know, there are no Jews
no Indians, nothing to discuss, only
everything's alright forever and forever
  a n d   f o r e v e r . . . . . .

      *

      N. with his halos and him-dodging
      halo-readers is the still old same
      cockego

      Kerouac is a Rake
                  (Brooklyn)
    * *_____(House of Ghouls)
      Kerouac is Dead
                  (deep depression
                  3 days)

      Kerouac Came Back

      BROOKLYN WATERFRONT (SUNDAY)
      The great lonesome sadness of the
      world such as these Sunday Afternoon
      Winter Skies over the white masts of
      the silent ship S S Mormacdale on
      the Brooklyn Waterfront (where lonely
      waves ripple and slap and do lonesome
      talk)---is explained by the fact that
      the world is a void

          How will seamen & mothers
              know't?
      o o o o o o o o o o o o o o o o
      O BLESSED LORD, THOU LOVEDST ALL
              SENTIENT LIFE

      Late human redbrick light on old
      buildings beneath Manhattan Bridge
      ---"late human light" I thot---
      Water St and Pearl St
              B r o o k l y n
      ---the Miserable Graveyard
          of the World---
  *

Birth---we come to go (said Maw)

Society is organized cruelty and nothing else---the holy men dont organize themselves in cruel gangs and throw portage fishkiller boats over moors, they eat no
killed fish,but imitate the purity of heaven, like deers and naïf lambs---In their
aloneness and transcendental kindness they imitate Godliness----Men drink & haggle
around horses and wish one another nothing but murder (I *know,* I've seen it all now)
---What they are, anyway, is complicated forms of foolishness---O Lord, I knew you
were right! Your compassion reaches everywhere, even unto the evil minded. . . . .

Rewrite Buddhism---
Samsarans *are* Nirvanans
("Les Samsarains *sont*
   les Nirvanains")---

The divine ecstasy
   is here now

No or either but or now
   but *tree here*

THURS. JAN. 26   NY
    Saw *Mexican Girl* my shortstory in Paris Review
and I am amazed at my own depravity---Some genius!
What a shit! Celine is an Angel, Genet is an Innocent.
    Just as I'm about to really skid into decay'd middle
age my books'll start selling---I have no patience in
this realm of patience---Here I am, 34, fat, ugly, old,
scowling, disgusted, and now young idealistic Jews
illustrate my stories (Albert Eisenlau)
                O naked justice!
    *

I've presented many a hard proposition to many a girl's soft ear, and closed the
deal---

CODEINE ** MID NIGHT ** B R O O K L Y N H O U S E ** KITCHEN * * *
Exaggerated parturiences
        popping every-pwere. . . . .   The shiny spoon on the clean tray in the cafeteria---
                            poor pitiful attempts of Samsara (the little modern
                            designs of the tray, borrowed from French ideas, in a
                            Horn & Hardart attempt)

    P O E P   Chorus # 1
Sackulwie, the Irish
befuddler who said he was
a rake from McGillicuddy's
Sister's Pettis free, and
Child McCoy, the Cloy
who toyed with the---
there's your bleeding raving
lawngwawj
        it could roll offa my
        tongue like rackalack
        like saying Kero-aak
        if I'd half a moind
        to burn down the brain
        of the world
        with its own burthen
        and popoff

Proop! Ashtrays!
Assholies & Fools
   of the Future
And Incredible Busboys!
Kiss my Third Twat

                Chorus #2
            The teat was there
            But pre labored the pear
            Then God held off apples
            And Satan made dapples
            And he uncoiled his holy length
            From branches and bent
            And showed beaky leer
            To Eva so feer
            Sah-ying: "Eat, Meat,
            Cheese is dear---Feet
            'll carry you no further
            Than Prime o Murther
            And even then the Lord
            Kept never his Word
            And all you got, is Me,
            Devil, Snake, Petit Free,
            The King of holy hairies
            In Samsara's land of fairies
            So fear you not, Madame,
            I'll bring you back Goddamn"

                Chorus #3 (nextpage)

        (If I knew the difference between goofing
          at words, and digging the bottom mind for
          words, that thin line
                    ---I'll learn)

383

Chorus #3

So sing God damn,
   God damn,
Sing you God damn
    back Gong damn---
Then on creepty tweets
Did Flibble wibbijibbitt
The idiot kid with the
   Turkish machine
With the poem, the nair,
Hair, Dair, Laird,
The Blighter, the Caustle,
The Floppy Keeper,
The Kang aroo, Doop,
   the Busboy,
The later Addition,
   Poor Ginsberg
He threw a dishclout
   in my face
For calling him a Spaniard
and Mc Joyce Boiled
And Dylan Booed

   Chorus #4
Lone?
  Wrote
    rapt
      in rotten kitchens

Rack! I never had it
       so fair

I'd as lief be a leaf,
  as this,
    a piece of thief
    sneaking in the pelf
    and pwaff pwaff
    twaddle of the cold
       world
        bone
   munchin after meat
   that once held pain
  ---Au moignen,
     au moigen,---
Runnin up & disappearin
  Over doors
And prissing underground
---Pish pot,

* *

Too bad, devil . . .
Ole empty sky wont
fight with you . . .

. . . .
* *
     * * * * * * * * * * *

Chorus #5
Ripped wrapped
    from old codgers' heels
The bandage of perdurability
And black believing ego
That flapthwacks
    in the cold world night
And blue covers simply hide
The red pain burning underneath
Without no namer
   name
  or anything named
  or nameable-to-be---
Me, You, Paramount Blues,
OO, See, Wishwash
    Seawash
    Yews,---

OO,Lea,
   bull, me, pee, tee,
   see, the crazily
   lazily surging
   monster back
   of the sea
   of so-reality

* *

A quiet hut in the mountainside,
---no windows---
the smoke of my morning breakfast

A great pure empty sky all blue
---no obstructions---
The dazzling blankness of my thoughts

Great brown earth of woe
---no restrictions---
The pureness of my being awakened

HAIKU
    The yellow dolls bow---
      Poor lady
  Is dead

   Loosening the tongue of the world, I am----------
* *
I WONT SAY THAT EVERYTHING IS HOLY EXCEPT THE DEVIL,
because the devil *is* holy, he partakes in the drama of
devilishness vs. holiness, he plays in Bathgate the
Bathgate part---
   Yet *Holy* is an arbitrary conception, you
might as well say that everything is devilish. Yet I
wont say that everything is devilish except the Lord,
because the Lord *is* devilish, he partakes of the drama
of holiness vs. devilishness, he plays in Bathgate
the Bathgate part . . . . That's why Ultimate Essence
      has no arbitrary quality of any kind,
        it is what it is, perfect,
    * * *   silent, devoid of conflict . . .
      * * * * * *

For *Pack*
  A green Swiss cap
     with feather

Or a beret
Wool shirt, wool socks,
New gripsoles on
     old railroad shoes

For *Mexico*
Long walks with wine
Sundays with Madame O

For *Mountaintop Job*
Haikus
Sutras so dear
   o o o o o o

Ah these perennibranchiata,
Vata
Gill

DREAM'D OF THE ELEPHANTS OF PAIN, who have holes
that hurt, the baby elephant squirming and stamping
and restlessly crying "Leave me alone!"(to the
Samsara Torture) and her weird elephant mother also
with that impossibly-hurting open-hole (somewhere
in the neck or breast) yowling and sorrowing, so that
I woke up realizing how awful Samsara could *really*
be!---filling us full of unnatural holes---Then
Big Paul, and he gets back on his ship, and I argue
with his Laundryman, yell at him angrily, in the
gray strange New York River port----   AIG!

* * * * * * * * * * * * * * * * * * * *

* * * * * * * * * * * * * * * * * * *

HAIKU
You're worried about
nothing---You
* * * * *   Havent got a leg to stand on   * * * * *

It's five minutes
after
Eleven----puff.

* *

THE BROOKLYN BRIDGE BLUES
In Ten Choruses

Chorus #1
Winter, too cold to write
  on the bolts of the beams
  in the bridge steel
High,
    overlooking whole auroras
    of Sangsara sun dusk
    down by the Statue of Liberals
    holding soon to be lighted
    torch to the dim dank
    Atlantic famous sky
    where Greek ships plow
    thru sullen waves of iron
    bringing tons of rusty junk
    to be pressed in bales
    and left on waterfronts
    of splinter

I would I were a wave
    and had vanished now
    than bawl and bolt
    with pencils in screaming
    rooms here on earth
    so fool stupid blind

Chorus #2
That's intro

And that's horse shit verse.
Let me tell you the truth
of the world at last.
    I started in Brooklyn
and went over the Span

Chorus #2 (Continued)
and at the middle hump
I looked and thought.
    My mother had just told
a fib, and in the process
made me a liar in my
stepsister's eyes. I lookt
my mother dead in the face
and her eyes were hard
to find and almost hidden
behind those glasses and all
that "insecurity" necessitous
grime that had accumulated
there in the form of
Sangsara's Sorry Flesh.
To prove to her sister,
    aunt, whatever Laurette is,

Chorus #3
that all the time it's she
who sends me money she
denied that last summer
for no reason at all
except I wanted her to be
happier in moneyless
Rocky Mount and I had a
temporary surplus from
the $300 American Academy
prize, I sent her a 50,
money order---*Denied it!*
Fibbed! Didnt even wink!
My own mother! Wow!
The work of Sangsara!

This false world---and the
Lord says it in the Diamond
Sutra, Keep the Precepts,
Dont be insincere, it's one
of the Paramitas (it's
one of the Four Precepts)!
(Ah you Canucks! says Lucien
Your first fight with yr mother
And it's over m o n e y ..!)
Ock! True!   Wow!

Chorus #4
I looked at the red winter
disgusting dusk of the world,
saw the alleys beyond,
Brooklyn, Wolfe's redbrick
jungle (that I'd only
last night walkt, unto
Gowanus Canal)---O!
---& I remembered the dreams
the dreams about racks
and Joan Adams and drear
and a tear appeared
in my eye over the river
on the Bridge of Sighs
that as soon as I'd
(c r o c o d i l e)
crossed it, had taken
me to the shore
I was looking for!
Svaha! I am
the perfect man
the Buddha of This World

Chorus #5
I lookt up at the blue deep perfect
and askt Buddha Lord to perfect me
and said "What are the requisites?"
and he said "You are perfect already"
---sullen ugly Wall Street buildings
so silly & stupid, the blind woe world,
all things endlessly living & dying,
in ignorance---and I thought:
"Whether as impalpable powder
or as great cities visible from bridges
in these great universes, what
matters it?,--it is only in the sense
of cosmic unity that the Tathagata
can rightly refer to it"

(If this is the work
of a Buddha-saint
I'm a You-Know-What)

Chorus #6
World Without End, Ethereal Flower
---and the streets of time & grime
without rhyme or dime, all crime,
in the blue sad belows of Manhattan,
and old dirty black and orange-shit ships
with dirty white superstructures,
and wharves of rusty junk, & barges,
and I felt Exuberant
I felt I was the only Perfect Man
in the World, my virtue 100%
my only sin is lust   I like
girls---I have no Self----
I have a Buddha Not-Self----

Chorus #7
Suddenly, looking at the high City Hall
towers with stone nymphs atop,
I realized I was going to save th'world!
I sang & marched: "This is the
Other Shore,
that we were looking for!"-----
and:-"I am the perfect man,
the Buddha of this world"---
already perfect!---I forget the details!
---Ruined dead buildings, with signs
reading, "Varnishing" already vanishing
---Ugh! Glugh!
I wanted to call my mother

Chorus #8
on the phone and say "I didnt say
I was going---I've crossed the river
now, I'm over the bridge now,
I'm on the other shore now, I've
reached the other side!"
The little glicks and dibbles
of returning human humorisms I may allow
---It's mountaintop for me!
I'm a glutton, I like food,
I'm irritable when hungry, I like
a good supper, I like sex---conquer lust
and Buddha will arise in me

Chorus #9
And now that I've
achieved superhuman
perfection of compassion
and knowledge, naturally
I've lost human talents
of writing---temporarily
---Nowhere to go---All's
been done, I can only
tell you what God would
tell you---Dry your tears
---All women are nuts
---Dry up your sins---Me,

I'm too sick and tired
of this world to drink in't
---if lustful gluttony
is my only blemishing sin
maybe I oughta just
starve to death
---I am the
Writing Buddha---
From these Blues we'll
    go to H Y M N S

    Chorus #10
And that's all I can
recall of Brooklyn Bridge,
tonight, John A Roebling
and Washington Roebling
built it, and it hath cables
and it does one good
to cross it every day---
    See my eerie wiseness?
    Good night, innocent children
of this mortal Sangsara
world, you have to keep
your mind empty & tranquil
and pure or the whole
Eternal Light escapes you
---Without the Eternal Light
you're only a yakking fool
of rooms, beds, graves
and monuments---with it,
you are like the Silent
Mountains of Snow
  and more than
    I know ---

      JAN 28 1956

* * * * * * *What is the date?
    Twenty eight.

* *

*   I decide to go out for a little walk to
*   stretch my legs, and while at it buy some
*   pipe cleaners so I can enjoy a good smoke---but
*   it starts raining heavily and the 2 stores I
*   manage to hit dont sell pipe cleaners and the
*   others are closed because it's dismal Sunday night
*   and just as I'm forced back wet to my door, it
*   s t o p s r a i n i n g ---- it's little
*   things like this that make me realize that
*   happiness is for the birds . . . . . . suddenly, of all
*   places in the toilet, I realized at "This Thinking
*   Has Stopped" the ecstasy of my reward, my share
*   in the Lord's merciful Nirvana, and I thanked
*   him----
*   We human beings are hopeless lost fools
*   wandering mournfully in a general rain of woe
*   that falls evenly everywhere, and yet we accuse
*   each other of "sin"!---as tho there was any room
*   for such definite evil among such martyred
*   angels. . .
*   The vagueness of this dream!---I
*   suddenly find myself in the street, musing. . .
*   like a Dostoevsky Hero in old Moscow--- How
*   dreary this "return to New York" has been, Jesus,
*   my friends getting old and vaguer and treating
*   me with vaguer neglect and unconcern so much
*   so I'm speechless among them---I feel like a
*   bum among them---dont even bother to explain
*   the Dharma Truth Law any more, cant even open
*   my mouth----I detect signs of cruelty in their
*   agingness, since I'm such a rueful vacuum they
*   turn it on me---I stand stupidly rejected in
*   the street watching Alene kiss other men in
*   the bar---I go down to a bench and lie down in
*   the cold wind to think---I wander around with
*   my ridiculous muffcap---My aunt keeps changing
*   my sleeping arrangement and I sit stupidly un-
*   able even to get mad---*I'm worried about nothing,*
*   *I havent got a leg to stand on*---I realize that
*   Gotama was the greatest man of them all and wish
*   I'd known him---I realize that everything's all
*   right forevermore in eternity

        "*Crashing in from heavens*
        Farther than expressioning"
are the numerous glorious Buddhas of true reality,
Glory Be!---An I'm a bum on earth.

YET. . . . . . IT'S A POSITION OF GREAT DIGNITY AND FINALITY IN THESE LATER DAYS OF
HUMAN NATURE to reiterate by suggestion that the Lord Buddha was right all the way
down the line, and to remind men of this millenium that mankind's intellectual
lifespan is in its middle or late period of *depravity* and that is why Buddha's pure
and uncontrovertible teachings concerning the ego-less-ness and emptiness of all
things in existence are not being considered at all, nor his disciples honored---I
sit here in this room in Brooklyn in 1956 and I say to the world:--"You'll have to
                    learn it
                      s o m e t i m e "--

    JUST AS SURE AS YOU DIE,
      there'll be awakening---and that's all
      B U D D H A means. . . . Soon as you clearly understand the
    Lord Buddha, who remembered the other Buddhas and thus
    became perfected, you'll no longer wish you were the Lord yourself . . . .
    Self is the sin, not "sin," and who invented self?   Nobody.   Your true
    self is not a self but the *absence of self* . . . Buddha.

YOU BUY   This pitiful Jack shaking his head over the
WHAT YOU   fools of the future, is, as they are, just that . . .
MAKE   but Buddha, for the Buddha, nothing is there
* * *   anywhere. . . . .
YOU MAKE   Ah dont fret anyhow---I mean even with this suffering
WHAT   human body---because time has a circular forward motion,
YOU   that's why "history repeats itself"---that's why you'll be
B U Y   miserable again and also glad again and even ecstatic again,
* *   as long as you live---After death, time's spirally-ing wont
"MAKING IT"   have a claim a YOU any more, so dont
MEANS   fret
BUYING   child---
I T   RIGHT NOW

                 time spiralled onward and as the subway train rattled
this old house on 293 State St I remembered everything, as in a
dream, my infant visit to New York in 1927 when the dark subways of
Time haunted me---it all *comes back*---The misery of yesterday will
come back, where I am drunk and bleary and speechless before my weary
friends---and the fight with my mother---over some inexistent imaginary
fib---but the ecstasy of that last night in the Carolina Woods at 1 A M
when the Lord told me "Everything's Alright Forever & Forever & Forever,"
and my hair stood up on end with remembrance of the Blessed Origin of all
things, wow, that ecstasy will also come back, and is, after all, just as
imaginary and inexistent as the moments of Woe---it spirals on, down the
Tunnel
       to that Glittering
         Paradise
           Nowhere
PLEASE BELIEVE ME,
          good friends of our human world, I'm not writing these things
for ego or self-gain, I really want to help everyone attain to Paradise with the
Lord. There's no reason in the world to pull the trigger, the sights are on the
animal's heart, it will build up evil deformity on and on into time---Instead, I
pull this trigger of the Bliss Teaching, and preach Love of Heaven, - - - - - - -
Love of Nirvana's
        H   o   l   y   G   o   l   d

      I dont preach human love, because these systems
      of solacement are insipid, the only solace that really
      will assuage and bless you, and the only love that will
      be free of concealed hatred and conditions, is the Divine
      Solace, the Divine Love, that is to say, the Solace and Love
      beyond this hellish state on earth in the Heavenly Transcendental
      Realm where all is Blown Out and Perfect Forever---where Love is free
      and undisturbed and universal and quiet and is what it is forever---the
      Divine and Holy Love of Awakenedhood
* *

D I A L O G   -
"Are you devoid of mental faculties?"   -   The captain in the adjoining
   "No"   -   room, he studies maps of reefs,
   "Therefore you are not devoid of   -   and I study the Diamond Sutra---
mental faculties?"   -   late in the night---(with really
   "Also no---I am neither devoid   -   the same mental delusion!)---------
or not devoid of mental faculties"   -   * * * * *

      JESUS ADVISED IT,--so they
       would understand. "If they had not
       their minds would inevitably grasp
       after such things (conceptions of self,
       other selves, living beings, and a universal self)
    and then they would not be able to practice charity nor keep the Precepts"
    H o n e s t y - C h a s t e n e s s - S i n c e r i t y - T e n d e r n e s s

WHAT JESUS ADVISED
Jesus was a Buddha
who taught a skilful vehicle
which is not the final One Buddha Vehicle---
that's *all* I have to say about the Good Lord Jesus---
he gildeth the lily, with talk, humantalk, of *fathers* in heaven---
but perhaps that's what's needed, men'll refuse to understand the bare fatherless
truth----Nonetheless, for me, t s gotta be the Bare True (and, of course, for every
body eventually)---you've got to learn sometime, if it means running through
Christianities and Suchlike Symbolisms to arrive at Nirvana's Priceless Diamond. . . .
Why priceless? Because by priceless is meant no objective or mentally-decided value
. . . . .Is meant, p r i c e l e s s e m p t i n e s s
. . . .

HAVING AN ORGASM
I said:-"I'm mad about
it!"---meaning, I'm mad
about the fruition of Samsara
---it's that convulsive ecstasy
of Ignorance not to be compared
with the effortless ecstasy of
highest perfect enlightenment . . .

* *

Afraid of death, afraid of
love--said Bill Heine
                    (artist and drummer)
* * * *
I T A L I A M O V I E
"Franco, whad would you do
if I betrayed you?"
    "Get rid of you."

A LUI LA, N OUBLI PAS . . . mind yr own business
le Seigneur n bavassa pas avec son cousin
mauvai---certainement pas il lui n'ecrivaient
pas d'maudites lettres! ---Devadatta a crashe
dans son visage, le Seigneur s'a essuyez---
sur la cruaute, devire to dos---Ta besogne
est avec la Dharme-----rien d'autre. . . .
                    pas avec les 'discussions'---
TRANSLATION:- As to him there, dont forget:
mind yr own business, the Lord didnt babble
with his evil cousin---certainly he didnt
write him any damned *letters*!---Devadatte
spat in his face, the Lord wiped himself---
on cruelty, turn your back---Your business
is with the Dharma---nothing else---not
with 'discussions'------------------------------------

* *

IF I'M UGLY, compassion'll make me pretty again---Corso saw this "beautifulness"
thru my "aging nagging flesh" only last summer---Universal Compassion means nobody's
left out, you rain it evenly on all---Even G. and J. and your destroyers who like you
are not worthy to be call'd Religious Heroes because they dont understand the *judged*
arbitrariness of Selfhood, a false judgment, imaginary, a dream-like idea originating
in the mind itself!---How can your ugliness cause you any further grief if you wake
up to the real Truth? the *"real reality"* as John Holmes used to laughingly say---which
real reality is, "who, what's ugly? who, what's pretty?"
        Where, what's hate?
        Where, what's love?
        Blankness of Essence isnt "Love" as we gild the lily   w i t h ---
        O THE TOWN AND THE CITY OF ETERNITY!

Manda sat in this house in Brooklyn,
in rockingchair, drinking, and watched
me come as kid (puking at Coney Island),
me as football player ranging wide with
punk puffed face, me as (then) sad hitch
hiking writer visiting, then me as old Ti
Jean a burden on his mother, but she herself
never moved from her chair by the window in the
parlor (looking on passerby legs of Brooklyn) and
she went straight to deathbed across the parlor and
lay there six months in white coma then vanished--------
musta laff'd at poor Ti Jean and his transformations
and puffings and labourings to prove . . . .

Manda had cat after cat,
coming to her window from
the dirty Brooklyn alleys
---gave them each a pet
crazy name . . . PATAPOUFFE,
BUM, MINUETTE, KITIGI,
GROS TAS (big pile),
BAVEAU (drooler). . . . She
    and all her beholden cats,
        p a r t i . . .
            p e r d u
            . . . .
She knew the world was ineffable
and Immaterial---and by not moving from
her chair (never went to store or out
on sidewalk) she didnt give the world of
fools a chance to argue her out of her
    w i s d o m . . . .

389

MANDA (CONT'D)
"Look here, the world is not ineffable and immaterial," yell the ghosts . . . "it's
C R E A T I V E !"

            The creation of a turd or of a cathedral, what's the difference
               in final reality?
        So Manda, stayed in her chair and rocked placidly and all her life she
            never harmed a fly

- -

PRAJNA IS UNMEASURABLE,
LIMITLESS AND MARVELOUS
The only way to rain compassion evenly
around,without entertaining imaginary
judgments of your own self, other selves,
many living selves everywhere, or a universal
self, is by *earnest prayer and forgiveness
in the reality of solitude,* ---"action"
in a foolishly limited & magically-appeared
world is nothing----
               Action means sympathy, sympathy
means participation, participation means
duality, duality means strife, strife meant
loss of evenminded tranquil universal
c o m p a s s i o n
         "Come on, Jack, hate (or love)
that guy with me!---Come on, agree with
me that this *must* be done! Just dont *sit*
there!!"

        * * * * * * * * * * * *
There's the Light! See it?

       * * * * * * * * * * * * * * *
Enough butter there to butter an army . . .
      * * * * * * * * * * * * * * * * * *
There's no the bangin it,
it's a bottomless hole
      *
We're all sufferin from Mind Pain------------

NEW YORK, a huge, rude, forgetful city,
full of excited mediocrities. . .
A *cold* town---it is the spectacle of Samsara,
---I cant describe it---Because it's *not*
New York that is huge, rude, forgetful, cold,
and an excited mediocrity, it's ME---------
in Buddha-Timelessness, ME-----------------------

Nothing that'll happen to you in "Samsara"
that's "good" can be or will be ever any
better than Nothing so stick to *Nothing*
    Drink yr. Port
    & Shut Orp
      Bhikku of the
      North American
      West Coast

- -

B U T I S H O U L D O N L Y D O T H I S :-
    Avoid phenomena and things
    and concentrate on my Essence of Mind

           "RELAX NOT"
           in this effort . . .

THE TURTLE CEASELESSLY
  SCRATCHES IN HER TRAP
---THERE'S YOUR WONDROUS
   AMAZING   S E N T I E N C E . . .

Life is a Miracle! they cry,
eagerly wiping their asses

       * * * * * * * * * * * * * *
    Ah poor mother-instinct of
    this motherin world!---I watch
    Ma take care of the little shits
and feeds of the tiny turtle in
her glass house . . . IGNORANCE IS
THE FATHER, HABIT ENERGY IS THE
MOTHER says the Sutra. . . . The
Compassionate One had nothing to
do with the creation of this world
thats why it doesnt exist!
    (except as emptiness of form,
      and form is emptiness)
Meanwhile there's the lil lizard
looking up at Ma as she bends
to give her the insect feed . . .
  dead dry insects that float in
  the turtlewater, that the turtle
  nibbles in the night. . . .
Twibble, twibble, twibble,
What a bibbledibble wibble,
Dill, dill, bingle,
I aint got no shingle
I BLESS YOUR BROW

(I have) A dark face
     full of
     lonesome darkness
      (ON TRAIN)

* *
    AS THE BETTER OF THE TWO
    PROPOSITIONS INVOLVED IN
    SHAMELESS NEGLECT I'LL DRAW
    BACK ALL MY WORKS WHOSE WORTH
    I AM NOT INCAPABLE OF EVALUATING
    AS THE BEST IN THEIR FIELD, IF IN
    1956 THEY'RE NOT CONTRACTED. . . . . . .

Multiplicity is Craze
Things come & go forever
& nothing happens---
The Buddha is no less
than this realization
in *You*---
　Shake rattle and roll
　all you want,
　eternity goes on Shhh'ing
　and never moves

S P O R T !
　(the sound I heard)
or
　　S P O R F !
　　---one
----
* *

Lil Paul's Pome　　　　　　　　　*
Davey, Davey,　　　　　　　　　　*
　Cravey, Cravey,　　　　　　　　*
Horse, Horse,　　　　　　　　　　*
　　Porse, Porse　　　　　　　　*
　　　　　　　　　　　　　　　　*
Lone Ranger,　　　　　　　　　　*
　Lone Ranger,　　　　　　　　　*
　　Pone Ranger　　　　　　　　*
　　　　　　　　　　　　　　　　*
Why does the sun go up　　　　　　*
Why does the sun go down　　　　　*
Why does the sky go blue blue　　　*
Why does the sun go up in the sky　*
Blue Blue　　　　　　　　　　　　*
　　　　　　　　　　　　　　　　*
Pome call'd Winter (Lil Paul)　　*
　Snow man, poke man,　　　　　　*
With a very jolly tie　　　　　　　*
Going around tying Pies　　　　　　*
　　　　　　　　　　　　　　　　*
Pin, pin, din, din　　　　　　　　*
　　　　　　　　　　　　　　　　*
Cash register　　　　　　　　　　*
　Pash register　　　　　　　　　*
　　　　　　　　　　　　　　　　*
SONG You gotta draw this now　　*
You gotta draw this　　　　　　　*
You gotta draw that　　　　　　　*
You gotta Paul that　　　　　　　*
You gotta Paul rat　　　　　　　　*
* *

I COULD NAME YOU
SOME PEOPLE
WHO ARE CEASELESSLY
SCHEMING---like people in
authority, best to avoid them,
my sincere bhikkus, just to avoid
trouble. . . . .
* *

Whatever interferes with the
knowing of emptiness, avoid---
I cant say how----------------------

**I'm just a sad old hobo, expect no more from me*

POMES LEFTOVER FROM CHRISTMAS NITE
"Let the earth be glad
　before the face of the
　Lord"---

All things are ecstasies
of form---

Adore us then　　　　Bread & Wine & Children,
　The Blessed Lord　　　Love's Sisters,
Within us　　　　　　Feces of Gods,
　The Word　　　　　　Species of Man,
　　　　　　　　　　Altars, Incense,
Sing, Praise　　　　　Lacemakers,
　Chaunt,　　　　　　Lace Wearers,
Be courtly,　　　　　　Almighty Father,
　Vaunt,　　　　　　Benité, Bless,
The Holy Ghost　　　Adore,
　Raise　　　　　　　Adoremus, O, Blessed,
Morely, More　　　　Be Thou
　　　　　　　　　　O Avalokitesvara
　　　　　　　　　　　Obiscum
　***　　　　　　Hearer, Answerer,
　*　　　　　　　　　Prayer,
　***　　　　　　O o o o o

The juiciest oiliest form of nothing
I've ever seen-----------

THERE ARE *NO*
　　　　　　SINS OF OMISSION
　　　　　　　IN ZEN BUDDHISM

H A I K U
Moab?---Who is Moab?---
　Woke up with a burr
In my hand
　* * * * * * * * * *

　　　　　　　　　　　　The wearers of smooth
DIFFERENT　　　　　　　　　　　　clothes
APPEARANCES　　　　　Do not incur
OF THE SAME　　　　　　　　　　the burr
EMPTINESS. . . .
Dhyana of Feb 5 '56　　　---------------------
All things are different forms
of the same holy emptiness---

KNOWING THAT ALL THINGS ARE DIFFERENT
APPEARANCES OF THE SAME EMPTINESS, you
become a bhikku---striving earnestly to
know it all the time, you become a Bodhi-
sattva---succeeding in perfect & continual
knowing of this so that it is no longer
"knowing" but the Emptiness-hood itself, you
become a Buddha (Last Night's Dhyana)
THE *PATH* is knowing and struggling to know
t h i s. . . . .

In that lastnight Dhyana also I realized the meaning, the joyous early-morning
meaning of what it is to *repent for future sins*---
   This means that Ross Lake will sparkle for me as purely in June 1956 as did
Bliss Lake in June Eternity in my pure blue immortal mind
                                                        o f   j o y . . .

THERE IS *NO* BONDAGE TO TIME ! ! !

Repent for future sins   Sila is Selfless Kindness,
purifies *all* your soul   it has nothing to do with the forced
PAST PRESENT & FUTURE   issue of charity which requires or en-
                                             genders or at least suggests gratitude and
*   therefore suggests the reality of self-hood . . .
Yark , Yok , York!   So the disciple of selfless kindness does not
I'll cleave to Buddha   look upon any self-hood and any blessing and
 Enlightenment---   merit as being personal possession
to Dharma Orthodoxy
---and to Sangha Purity! . . . . BECAUSE I LOVE LOVE   D i v i n e   L o v e

Emptiness is Holiness . . .   So - - - only 2 things to do
* * * * * * * * * * * *   *   1. Train our mind on the emptiness aspect
For, remember yr.plans of   *   of things
17?---not only forgotten   *   2. Take care of our body
completely but they didnt   *   --
take place---yr. *balloons*---
   There's no difference between   S I X   P A R A M I T A S
you and tree and fence, different   *   *   *   *   *   *   *   *
appearances of the same emptiness.   1. If someone asks, give DANA---what's
                                                difference?
      o o o o o o o o o o o   2. No difference between you & others
                                                ---SILA kindness
Indeed, emptiness is everything!   3. Patience, it's all Same---KSHANTI,
                                                dont get mad
All belongs to the same emptiness,   4. Zeal, if asked, teach, VIRYA
Glory Be!   5. Tranquility, DHYANA, train mind on
                                                Emptiness
All thinking is empty. . . . .   6. PRAJNA, the *knowing* of wisdom
                                                that results
Everything---is---Emptiness
OOOO---Emptiness is Everything---))))O   *

I am emptiness, I am not different from emptiness, neither is emptiness different
   from me, indeed, emptiness is me.
      You are emptiness, you are not different from emptiness, neither is emptiness
         different from you, indeed, emptiness is you.
            Living beings are emptiness, living beings are not different from emptiness,
               neither is emptiness different from living beings, indeed, emptiness is
                  living beings.
                  The Supreme redeemer is emptiness, the supreme redeemer is not different from
                     emptiness, neither is emptiness different from the supreme redeemer, indeed,
                        emptiness is the supreme redeemer.

THERE IS THE SEVENTH INVISIBLE PARAMITA,   * * * * * * * * * * * *
I say, and it is the Samadhi Paramita,   o o o o o o o o o o o o o o o
the Ideal Ecstasy, the Intuitive   The empty space inside your
identification with Emptinesshood   mind is emptiness without end,
. . . it is for the 7th day of the week   it is the great reality. . . . . . .
(calendar week, Saturday)
                                           * * * * * * * * * * * * *
   L i s t e n   to
The Crickets of Avalokitesvara. . . .   The star in the puddle
                                              my spit obliterates---
                                           It isnt real

Prayer   O Lord Avalokitesvara,
    Emptiness Without End,
may this appearance body
get the perfect divine ecstasy,
now and forever, amen

          *

Cold Loneliness---Cold Loneliness
O n   a c c o u n t   o f   emptiness
          *

                 I went in the woods
                    to meditate---
                 It was too cold

WHAT WOULD I DO IF I DIDNT
have a fire to return to?---
keep the haikus unwrit

                 Haiku, Shmaiku, I cant
                     understand the intention
                   Of Reality
          * * * *---* * *

What perturbs me is emptiness, what perturbs me is not different from emptiness,
neither is emptiness different from what perturbs me, indeed, emptiness is what
perturbs me. . . . .

God is emptiness, God is not different from emptiness, neither is emptiness different from God, indeed, emptiness is God

Buddhism, when you consider all the Buddhists who've lived devoutly and then died
away, it must be simply gentle tranquil happiness. . . . .

* *

Early morning with the
    happy dogs---
I forgot the Path
* *

What could be newer? this
    new little bird
Not yet summer fat!
* *

The holy empty fence
    and the transparent tree
Still cling to their appearance
* *

The dog yawned
    and almost swallowed
My Dharma
* *

Concatenation!---the bicycle
    pulls the wagon
Because the rope is tied
* *

White clouds of this steamy planet
    obstruct
My vision of the blue void
* *

Grass waves,
    hens chuckle,
Nothing's happening
* *

P   O Lord, Lord,
R   Lord within without end,
A   Great reality of emptiness,
Y   All is Well Without End,
E   All is Ecstasy
R   All is Brightly Perfect!

        ooooooooooooo

"You grow through Suffering?" says Paul
    Blake---"by this time I oughta be as big
    as the side of the house."---

BOB HOPE,looking at buxom blonde who says
    she cant make up her mind if anybody'll
    take her in Hollywood, "I dont know how
    these little ole gals can be so unsure
    inside!"---and I see Form is Emptiness

    - - - - - - - - - - - - - - -

       A spring mosquito
          dont even know
       How to bite!
       * * * * * * * * * * * * * * * *

             Meditating in afternoon sun
              in my new camp, I remember
              all my past lifetimes---
            "It's immaterial, what's the
            difference!" is the cry in the
          Karma halls of the Bodhisattvas. . . .
          "Go back and find new ways to teach
        the Ignorant---the poor children of
       ignorance---who need us so!"---then we
      all fall into Samadhi Ecstasy and realize
      the Awakened Buddhahood is emptiness
     that Buddhahood is not different from
    emptiness, nor is emptiness different from
   Buddhahood, indeed, emptiness is Buddhahood---
and we awake realizing Nothing, the Pure Blank.
O n e n e s s   W i t h o u t   E n d . . . .
and fall asleep again, and undergo voluntary
rebirths in a dream of existence---I doubt if
there's any real difference between any of us,
between Bodhisattvas and the Ignorant---in
fact, emptiness is Bodhisattvas & the Ignorant!
          * * * * ooooo * * * *

Loathing for Samsara, has led me to this peaceful grove---I'll buy that kind
of Buddhism. This is the Twin Tree Grove, Big Easonburg, N.C.---the tiny creek
is Buddha River
------------------------Next:-Desolation Peak, where I'll bury Treasure . . .

Millionaires in Nirvana,
is what we are

A BEAUTIFUL GIRL IS A
VICTIM of rebirth
energy . . . hard cocks
throb towards her,
everybody knows why
and nobody knows why . . .

ABOUT ALL HEMINGWAY WRITES
about (& Burroughs-Lee),
is, these egoistic males
who want to live forever.

*** P R A Y E R   F O R   T H E   J U J U   B E A D S ***
"Not really the raging Rexroth,
        but the compassionate Buddha
Not really the malicious Ginsberg,
        but the compassionate Buddha
Not really the greedy Neal
        but the compassionate Buddha
Not really the brilliant Lucien,
        but the compassionate Buddha   E T C.
Not really the steadfast Gary,
        but the compassionate Buddha
Not really the selfish Kerouac,
        but the compassionate Buddha"

* * * * * * * * * * *

I MUST WRITE PURE PRAYERS THAT HAVE NOTHING TO DO WITH ILLUSION   (BOOK OF PRAYERS)
IN ORDER TO ADDRESS AND DELIVER THEM TO THE TATHAGATA. . . . .   **************

Instantly I began radiating---in the woods
last night---and while reading the words
"matter and great universes . . is an illusion
of mortal mind" I saw the big gray spectral
scenery of the One Vast Emptiness shifting
in my mind---like shrouds, hazes, smoke,
clouds, dream-drapes, great Sea-Shroud Gloop
Curtains rising and rearranging---visions,
in the form of cities, men, planets, turtles,
chilicosms---against (or within) a clear
backdrop of pure mind---the truth, one
perfect emptiness of light without end,
"cannot be cut up into pieces and arranged
into a system."
        No imaginary judgments of
anything whatever, is all that's left,i.e.
nothing
        FEB 11 56
        Twin Tree Grove

ONE VAST APPEARANCE OF EMPTINESS
----An Endless I llusion. . . . .

Reward Without End!---the
        Tathagata's womb is so
        all-perfect it can also
        include Samsara, not just
        Nirvana, both of which are
        endless & infinite---Everywhere
        the one great Flower. The
        One Grand Light---The essence
        is our reward without end,
        which is us---(of us, in us)
        ---This essence (dharmakaya)
        is a Great Secret Smile behind
        it all!
        Intuitions of Feb.11
        in Woods day & night

- -

I figured out JUJU-BEAD PRAYER
---at each bead take the
running thought and run it thru
the Prajna Paramita Wringer, i.e.
"Saying 'Reward Without End' is
emptiness, saying 'Reward Without
End' is not different from emptiness, neither is emptiness different
from saying 'Reward Without End,'
indeed, emptiness is saying 'Reward
Without End'---"

E s s e n c e   s a n d i n g   a l l

We're pure forever, dont worry another
                        m i nu t e!
        * * * * * * * * * * * * *
        Self?---think how far it's come,
        and's got to go, into the endless
        futures---REWARD WITHOUT END!
        This world?---a dream a billion years
        a billion billion years old?--------------

* *

KARUNA is sad compassionate
        emotions---is emptiness,
        & emptiness *is* Karuna
(my sadness about poor little
        turtle's bulgey reptile eyes) ➔ (looking so tinily at me) (and at sun)
        like old sadness 1954 about Ma's sad caramels---empty feelings, in the end. . . .

The Buddha Bow

"If a disciple is able to discard all imaginary judgments of phenomena, or about phenomena, he will immediately become a Buddha, an Awakened One."

Adoration to   The-Attainer-To-That-Which-Everything-Is (Tathagata)
                     The-Attainer-to-Universal Goodness (Sugata)
                     Perfectly Awakened (Buddha), Perfect in Wisdom and Compassion,
         who has accomplished since the beginningless past
         is accomplishing in the infinite present
         and will accomplish into the never-ending future
         all these Words of M y s t e r y . . . .

---*---

ALLEN, his harmless "evil"---forgive him before   *   *Who cares? ---Prajna is endless*
he dies---your evil schemes, poor lad, dont   *
stack up in this endless emptiness---   *   Poory poory
    Buddhism, is, Do What You want   *   Neckanecka soory
    Karma, is, The tat from the tit   *   Noory noory
    Emptiness, is, Buddhism & Karma   *   Never will you worry . . .
*   *   I'm gettin feeble in the gable . . .

                                                     - - - - - - - - - - - - - - - - - -

THERE'S NO END TO THE WAYS you can get   o
"abused"---In the future in Samsara there'll o   Like children afraid
be more reasons for squabbles and unforgiveness o   in a friendly wood, and
among monks and saints even---This present   o   one brave child says "*I'm*
deal which is taking up so much of my mental o   not afraid," are we, men,
energy is a test sample to see if I'm gonna   o   afraid of it or unafraid of it,
work out my karma of the discrimination of   o   in this Crystal Security of
personalities and self---There must be   o   C o m p a s s i o n a t e
forgiveness, even if he goes on disturbing   o   M i n d
me and pestering me and mining information   o   **   E s s e n c e
out of me--- L E T ' S   C U T   T H E   G A B!! o   * * * * * * * * * * * * *
                                                        * * * * * * * * * * * * *

Buddha-boat   *Dharma*, is, Truth Law
         on the Buddha-river   *Bodhisattva-Mahasattva*,
                                                  is, Being of Great Wisdom
It's just a case of *vast*   *Tathagata*,
                                                  is, Thatfarer, or, Thatness-Attainer
---   *Sila*, is, Kind conduct
Memories are made outa mud,   *Prajna*, is, Wisdom-Knowing
sings Lil Paul. . . . .   *Bodhi*, is, Wisdom
                                         Prajna Paramita, is,   Ideal Wisdom-Knowing
EMPTINESS IS EMPTINESS,
dont bother with any of it . .   * * * * * * * * *
EMPTINESS IS EMPTINESS, let
it all go---   A lake of light, this world, like
The goodness of Samsara,   my 1 9 5 5 B u d d h a T e l l s
the badness of Samsara,   U s
what's the diff?
Six a one,   I TOUCHED THE GROUND with both hands, to
half a dozen a the other . . .   see if it was real---the words didnt come
                                         ---It and I and the sensation of touch:
WORDS WONT DO---noble   tenuousness! (the earth) (it moves, it
  inner intuitive realization   is e m p t y) ---
  cant mine words
  out of the wordless---   * * * * * * * * * * *
Something doesnt come out of nothing---   *Nothing Means Nothing,* simply . . .
nothing comes out of nothing---
A l l i s N o t h i n g . . . . .   We *are* Shadows (the Shadow Knows)
                                          . . . . . Shadows of Emptiness

                    ooooooooooooooooooooooooooo

THE COMMON ESSENCE (Nice title for book)

O Tathagata, Thatness-Attainer
　　Honored of the worlds!
Take all arbitrary conceptions
　　of things and beings
And crush them into light
　　between yr diamond hands,
And Ignorance bid be still
　　till all is self enlightened,
Then resume thy rich
　　Womb of Exuberant
Fertility which is Emptiness
　　Without end, reward
　　Without end, compassion
　　Without end,
　　Loving security
　　Without end,
　　　　　　amen.

　　NO, a better,not-delusive
prayer:-

"Thatness-attainer, Honored
　　of the Worlds!
I cant ask you, whose
Womb is so all-powerful
That it contains both
Ignorance & Enlightenment,
Both Samsara & Nirvana,
To take half of it
And crush it, which is
　　uncrushable,
Because empty,
In honor of the other half,
Which is unhonorable,
Because empty,
I can only praise you
Without end
For such wisdom & compassion
Without end"

* * * * * * * * * * *　* * * * * * * * * * *

"JUBHAGA whose body was consumed by
　　the inner fires of his concupiscence"-

WHY STAY AWAY FROM SOCIETY, MY BHIKKUS?
Because it is a "stronghold of vexations
that so engross the mind that they crowd
out the very purpose to attain enlightenment. . . ."

VISION OF A REAL MAN:- He was made to
　　　　　　　　　　　suffer, you can see
　　　　　　　　　　　it in his bony-suffer
　　　　　　　　　　　face. . . . .

DESIRES: "If they are gratified, there is
no satisfaction, and if they are not satisfied, there is annoyance, and so in either
case there is no happiness at all"----
　　Ponder that well, better to ignore the
gratifying---but what the hell, by
*ignoring everything I can do what I want
　　anyway*---Buddhism is DO WHAT YOU WANT

Yes,
　　　the Diamond Sutra is all I need to
　　　read, the rest is bewildering,
　　　confused, and multiply mad---all
　　　the countless Sutras & Commentaries
　　　& Prayers & Precepts are enuf to
　　　drive a man insane they're all so
　　　This-and-That-ish

PRAJNA!---I've made it into the
S h i n i n g　O c e a n . . . !

* *
　　　　　　　　　　　　　　　　　　*
　　　　　　　　　　　　　* "THE TRUE BODY abides in all directions and
　　　　　　　　　　　*　　all times and in all worlds; the Appearance
* * * * * * * * * * *　* * * * * * * * * *　Body accomplishes all the deeds of a Buddha.
　　　　　　　　　　　This is our mission as Mahasattva-Bodhisattvas
-------------------------------------that was begun in our practice of Dhyana Meditation"
　　　　　　　　　　　　　　　　　　CHIH-CHI
ALSO: "It is said in the AVATAMSAKA SUTRA that as soon as novice Bodhisattvas
begin their practice of Dhyana Meditation that they have already accomplished their
full Enlightenment, and have comprehended that the intelligence embodied in the
true nature of all phenomena is to be accomplished in no other way than by full
Enlightenment. Also, that new Bodhisattvas in attaining oneness with Tathagata
really attain innumerable bodies and that each body is
　　　　　　　　　　B u d d h a "

REALITY---neither emptiness
nor potentiality---but utter
c o m m o n　t h a t n e s s .

Use your life to practice patience
and to look upon it humbly as
though *it* was some saintly being
called upon to suffer humility . . .
Dont fall into impatience and hatred, that's for madmen, ragers, mistakers, brutes,
fiends, men-of-the-world. . . .Remember Sebastian Sampas and the Brotherhood Ideal.

JUBILEE MAGAZINE . . . I made them a
gift of my summer-of-1955-story
STATUE OF CHRIST, because "I am a
Catholic". . . hope they publish it
some day . . . but it may be too
Avalokitesvara'n for em. . . .

book ten

FEB.17,1956

TWIN TREE GROVE N.C.   BUDDHA CREEK
All that ocean of blue, soon as that
cloudbank moves aside, for me, in my golden
grove---all that ocean of blue, inscrutable and
without end, that I see through the pines to the right,
of me---But more thought-clouds keep moving in from west,
to juggle the issue of my bliss---No, I'd rather damn be certain,
that ocean of blue was more like IT . . . Tho this is just a humanpoet
thought of mine, cloud or bliss-blue-void, the Thatness of their Emptiness
is the Same

H A I KU   All that ocean of blue
                    soon as those clouds
              Pass away

- - - - - - - - - - - - - - - -

Know that you know that samadhi
ecstasy is always attained because
everything is ecstasy---(I was instructed)
therefore, dont say: "I had a Samadhi,"
rather, you should say "I tuned in on the
everlasting samadhi ecstasy which is
always there"---"I *opened out* to
samadhi ecstasy"---RAIN DHYANA FEB 17
     (meditating in the rain in my
       poncho cape,sitting on mat
        of grass, rain pattering
         on my cape)

* * * * * * * * * * * *
PART OF TONIGHT'S RAIN DHYANA
PRAYER:-
          "The Lord is Emptiness,
of the Buddha-bead, the Lord is
not different from emptiness of
the Buddha-bead, neither is
emptiness of the Buddha-bead
different from the Lord, indeed,
emptiness of the Buddha-bead is
the Lord"---(Big Juju Main Bead)
ALSO:-
"The Highest perfect wisdom of
Gotama Buddha is emptiness, the
Highest perfect wisdom of Gotama
Buddha is not different from
emptiness, neither is emptiness
different from the Highest Perfect
Wisdom of Gotama Buddha, indeed,
emptiness is the highest perfect
wisdom of Gotama Buddha" !

. . Raindrops are ecstasy, raindrops are not
different from ecstasy and neither is ecstasy
different from raindrops, yea, ecstasy *is*
          r a i n d r o p s
     R A I N O N, O CLOUD!

Complaining about the Inconceivable,
                    is also
                emptiness . . .

YOU MUST REMEMBER that you're doing
all your conceiving with your *mind*
and it's all taking place within the
Inconceivableness of That-Which-Everything-
Is, mind-less-ness--------------------------------

         "BUT WHAT AM I DOING
     wasting my time with
     something I cant conceive,
     sitting in the rain of the
     woods with my capuchin cape
     and juju beads?" I thot, re-
     turning to the warm house----
     Well anyway it's a *p a t h*----
     it's like a path you might want to
     tromple across a ploughed field all
     afternoon, it'll be a much better
     path if you just walk across the field
     in the ordinary course of things----
     watched path never forms ("Watched pot
     never boils")---It's like a bush, my
     knowledge of the emptiness of phenomena
     and noumena will take deeper & deeper root
     till you couldnt uproot it with a Macktruck
     -*The everlasting ecstasy*
       of the smiling essence!
       To know what these words point to, is
       paradise e-now---a-now---It's knowing that
       the substance of my bones and that of my dead
       brother and father in this earth of rain tonight
       is the common individual substance that is ever-
       lastingly tranquil and blissful
* *

"Soon enuf the carefree days,
        the sunlit days go by,
        soon enuf the bluebird
        has to fly"
        lovely song
      YOUNG N FOOLISH
oooooooooooooooooooooooooooo

The inconceivable is emptiness,
It is not different from emptiness,
Neither is emptiness different
                    from it,

Indeed, emptiness is the
          I n c o n c e i v a b l e

399

PRAJNA, Ocean of Knowing
NON-SENTIENT BEINGS, Transcendental
                  Beings
TATHAGATA, he is neither sentient
                  nor non-sentient nor a
being nor a form nor an
idea nor nothing nor
something nor "emptiness"
nor potentiality---Tatha-
gata is what isness is--- that
which Thatness is, *that*--------
CHINESE   thussstuff---whatallness---
LETTERS   praiseless blameless endless
FOR   beginningless formless neither
TATHAGATA high-nor-low "attainer-to"
          N O T H I N G ----!

FLASH
       A woman monk who's just received a
bowlful of food from my mother at the
backdoor, is back, wanting to know if my
mother wants religious instruction---my
mother is annoyed and wants her to just stay
away---("I dont want to change my religion"
she explain'd to me when I told her of this
dreamflash).

There are no beings in Nirvana---
   O thank the Lord!

**"WHY IS THERE NO OBTAINING OF
NIRVANA?---because Nirvana is
the realm of no-thing-ness"---**

TELEVISION---All this great dreary
blight of society-minded fools---
State Bureau of Investigation man
saying: "Addicts cannot take their
   place in se-si-a tee."---
     Whatuz he know about the wisdom
of old chinamen?

----
        * * * M O N E Y P R A Y E R * * *
  "Money is emptiness
   money is not different from
               emptiness,
  neither is emptiness different
               from money,
  indeed, emptiness is money.
  Emptiness is food.
  Emptiness is hunger and the
  want of food.
  Emptiness is everything.
  Facing this fact or not facing
  this fact, equal and the same,
  it is emptiness."
      END OF MONEY PRAYER

MATTER AND EMPTY SPACE ARE THE SAME and both likewise figures of speech---There's
no lapse in the smooth ephemeral evenness of essence as it *is* throughout matter and
empty space, form and emptiness, essence isnt interrupted by surfaces of forms nor
voids of space---You cant say that it is emptiness any more than you can say that
it is *not---not-emptiness*---Emptiness is just a word---(I had a vision of a great
square bright even essence and in it were imprinted the trees & me) (like a movie)
but this is a mentally-decided judgment, not *T'i* itself . . (T'i, is, Essence) . . .
Essence,Essence, if there was only a better word, a Divine Name! *TATHATA, THAT*
   . . . or, BLAH!

SEEING THE PERFECTION OF THE VISION OF THE BLUE SKY
for the children at the Lone Ranger Indian movie,
I realized "The blue sky for them is the same as
it was for me 25 years ago Saturday-Mornings in
the Pure Lowell---what's changed is *me*, not the
perfection of the vision, which is our common and
eternal blissstuff---" Refer to King Prasenajit
in SURANGAMA SUTRA WHERE HE SAYS: WHERE BUDDHA SAYS:
"Your perception of sight compared with it when you
were a youth, shows no change . . . Is there any youth
and old age in the perception of sight? . . . The
un-changing is naturally free from deaths and
rebirths."-----The common eternal blissstuff in
the red rocks, pines, buttes, blue sky and faces
and eyes and bodies of the cowboys and Indians
and horses----like Saturday Morning in China
the pureness of everything forever
     ---O Lord Buddha, thou hast enlightened
      all sentient beings & disenchanted
      them of selfhoods & arbitrary personal
      possession of the mysterious truth
   of the law---It isnt that they dont know it but only that they cease *knowing*

          O N E H A I K U

Propped up on my shoe
   the Diamond Sutra---
Propped up on a pine root

   Dharmas belong to
   phenomena--in emptiness
   there are no Dharmas. . . .

Nostalgia of Autumn in Paris
is emptiness. . . .

The tables are empty---
everybody's gone over. . . .

   * * *
   Poor fools . . . Me too

That they cease *knowing---mental higgling---*
* I neither know nor dont-know the truth *
   Prajna is knowing but Samadhi is Ecstasy . .
    Samadhi *is* the Blissstuff

          Silent pipe---
           peace and quiet
          In my heart

KEEP YOUR THINKING INDEPENDENT OF IMAGINARY
                                           JUDGMENTS

"PRAYER OF THE THREE INEXISTENCIES (Later expanded into "Emptiness Prayer")
O Everlasting Eternity, all things and all Truth Laws are no-things, in three
ways, which is the same way:-

1., As things in time, they dont exist and never came, because they're
    already gone and there is no time

2., As phenomena they dont exist because there is no furthest atom that
    can be found or weighed or grasped, it is emptiness through and through,
    both space and matter too

3., As sense-objects, they dont exist, for the rock there is no tree, for
    the tree there is no man, for the man there is no knowing the True
    Unknowing Emptiness
               A PRAYER "

The black triangle represents these (3) Inexistencies and being One Triangle
it ultimately real- ly represents the One Inexistency . . . the impossibility of
the existence of a- nything.---It is also the Buddha-Mountain.---It is also
the Three Bodies, Nirmanakaya, Sambhogakaya, Dharmakaya, which in reality are the
One Tathata.---It is also the Three Vehicles, the Goat-Cart, the Deer-Cart, and
the Bullock-Cart, which in reality are the One White Bullock Vehicle----
It
    is also Past, Present, and Future,
    which in reality is Time-less-ness

      ,   the Void-----------

                             THE MISTAKE

        Prajna
      is the *path*
    to Samadhi ---
  O LOS MOCHIS!----

               IN OUR PRAYERS SO FAR
                                MAY LIE IN
our giving it the SRI, the *Sire,* the Lord-address,
confusing our understanding of the emptiness and
reward of everlasting eternity, with human father-
notions, birth & patriarchal & subliminal complexes
and general erroneousness of religious complexion---

* * * * * * * * * * * * * * * * * *
I RAISED A THING *
silently, sitting   *
under the tree,   *
and Lil Paul,   *
facing me,asked, *
"What's that?" and *
I said *"That"*---   *
and made a level- *
ing motion with   *
my hand,saying,   *
"Tathata,"---re-   *
peating *"That---* ***
it's *that---"*   ****
and then only

Everything *is* the same eternal thatness---in that
sense every man and every thing is the Lord----but
make not the mistake of objectifying a benevolent Sire
Lord in this Single Subjective, or Single Objective, in
brief this *Single,* Undividable *Thisness* . . . --------------------
Better, then, to say Thisness   ----*************************
than "Lord, Father, God" ----**   IT IS ACTUALLY
---*This* is God, and God is *This* ----**   POSSIBLE
And *This* is Everything   ----**   to really wake up
--- **   and "make it"---
                                **   and I'm waking up now
* ***   and making it, by daily
                                nakedly no bullshit

when I told him it was a pine cone did he make   ***f a c i n g   e m p t i n e s s
the imaginary judgment of the word pine-cone, for **---
"Indeed,emptiness is discrimination," and he said: *
"My head jumped out, and my brain went *crooked* and then my eyes started lookin like
cucumbers and my hair'd a cowlick on it and the cowlick licked my chin"----

LIL PAUL'S POEM IN COMMEMORATION

"The pine trees are wavin
The wind is tryin to whisper somethin
The birds are sayin "Drit-drit-
                              drit---"
And the hawks are goin "Hark-
              Hark-Hark---"
"O-ho we're in for danger"
"Why?"
"Hawk---Hark! Hark! Hark!"
"Then what?"
"Hark! Hark!---Nothin." --"

* *

"His brain went crooked" because the
attainment of Nirvana is more valuable
than anything you could conceive and
judge within your mind, it's to be
likened to the Great Mind-less-ness

"His brain went crooked" illustrates
the F I V E D H A R M A S
     1. Appearance
     2. Name
     3. Discrimination
     4. Right-Knowledge
     5. Thatness
His brain was straightened on the
subject when he understood tathata,
thatness. . . . .

* *

AW BEAUTEOUS MOON---it's been the
greatest day of all time---the first
real day of Spring but coming in
February and right after heavy
rains that washed everything---
Brown puddles everywhere, moist
sere fields---And strong warm winds whipping snow-white clouds across the sun, and
dry air----A golden day---With a beauteous moonlight night, warm, one emboldened
frog picked up a croak song at Leben P M in Buddha Creek---and I'm realizing:-
"The conception of living is emptiness"
---And get a FLASH---"Lil Paul will be a Buddha called *True Pine*"---And softly,
miraculously, as I'm standing in the midnight moonlight, my cat Davey comes silently
and rubs against my legs---s'come from all over the woods and wildbird bramblepatches
to do so---and as I'm tryna write this he grabs my writing-sleeve and pulls it to
him!
    Sakyamuni in the moonlight----My poncho make me look like the Spirit of the
Woods, the Shadow, the Shroudy Monk, in the moonshadow woods---I meditate in it, in
its warm husk, sitting wrapt---I perceive the unconditioned voidness until I lose
my perceiving powers---I pray on my Buddha Beads the Emptiness Prajna Prayer Without
End---I see the Potential Immensity of Samapatti Buddhahood but without losing
sight of the fact that Samapatti is e m p t i n e s s ---

* *

As a poet of personal materialistic concerns,
Ginsberg can only make ill use of my heavenly overflow. . .
So there'll be no ill-use through this channel again. . . . . .

IN ANY CASE, ANY BEGGAR KNOWS THAT the mind is so great it contains both form and
emptiness, and form is emptiness, and emptiness is form . . . .

WHAT TO DO WHEN IN DOUBT ABOUT ACTION?
THINK: "N o t h i n t o d o . . ."
        For, what might be done, is only
        shining,-ready,-and awake. . . . . .
        nothin to do.

The queers are not artists, they're just
a bunch of raving social climbers---art
is their calling card, my dear---They pant
after notoriety and wealth---the queers
and lesbians both---something unclean in
their conception of art---Jean Negulesco
"does" Marilyn Monroe portrait, Katherine
Anne Porter "has" Toujours Tristesse for
a weekend, Truman Capote simpers in Moscow
because of Guy Burgess the International
figure, Gore Vidal stands legs akimbo
in a Baroque garden in Italy, Tennessee
Williams lunches with two rich old ladies
in the Cub Room, Paul Bowles eyes the
young Hinayana monks in the streets of
Colombo, Jean Stafford sobs, Glenway
cries *"Real-ly! Gurls!"*---Cocteau jumps
around with the middleaged ballet dancers,
Gide is ravished in North Africa----the
only fop who could write was Proust, and
Stendhal only tried to be a fop---A gang
of mediocre artists seeking the state of
a Toplevel Concubine--- Just compare the
works of Gide & Dostoevsky, compare Uncle
Edouard and Myshkin, for proof of their
facetious *elegance*---egg, why should I
make odious comparisons. Nothin to do.
It's very unimportant, the emptiness of
the queers is the same as the emptiness
of the great saints, so why rue & bruit . . .

* *

And newsmen tend to forget that it's not
a news world, but a sentient world . . .
(listening to radio commentators)

       * * * * * * * * * *

DHYANA OF CLOUDY MOON
Sunday Feb 19 1956---Couldnt come
to any understanding with any Dharma
Satisfaction---Ask't Avalokitesvara, who
instantly helped, making me realize, though
the Tathagata's Transcendental Transformations are
mere arbitrary conceptions, mere imaginary judgments, so are
my needs to contact them and *contactable* they are due to the imaginary
judgment of *sense-equipment,* i.e., if a frog croaks I'll hear it----if a Buddha
blesses me, I'll feel it---
           Also thought: STOP AND ACCEPT
                             THIS WORLD IS SAMSARA AND NIRVANA BOTH
But generally   THIS IS IT
it was a poor   SAMADHI ECSTASY IS NOW
failure

         ALSO Samsara is Nirvana, Samsara is not different from
        Nirvana, neither is Nirvana different from Samsara, indeed,
        Nirvana is Samsara-----!!!!
    Here, This, is It,
        I thought, looking up at moon, This World as Is, is Nirvana,
        and I realized it was true---I'm looking for a Nirvana outside
      what there *is*-----If I could realize, if I could forget myself
      and devote my meditations to the emancipation, enlightenment and
     blessedness, of all sentient beings everywhere, I'd realize what there
    is, *is* E c s t a s y ------ truer words I never writ.

* *

Oh a Chachacha on radio,
from Cuba, I remember
my wine walks to Cathedrals   "COMPARISONS ARE ODIOUS" says Doctor Johnson
in narrow nightstreets of   and that's the end of St Augustine. . . . .
Fellaheena---I remember
Holy Marijuana warming my   To Desolation Peak I shall go the long way . . .
brain with Visions of   via Panama Street and Esperanza. . . . .
The Only Snow---the HOLY SNOW
---transcendental freedom of   Teddy Wilson, playing *China Boy*---Cant get it
the mind, among the sweet   played,no time
Indians of Mexico   (like)
    * * * * * * * * *   * * * * * * * * * *

THE DIAMOND   T h e L o r d s h i p o f t h e B u d d h a s
SCRIPTURE. . . . . .   is a vehicle---you gotta have somethin to ride, a
. . . .   raft to cross over on . . . .
* *

A blank being called upon to   *   AN ARTIST, when people ask of his canvas,
enjoy ecstasy---you, me, really   *   "What *is* it?" should make a leveling motion
. . . *Endless Truebody*   *   of the hand and reply *"That"*---
* *

    Dogs discriminate   Doped by the realization that all is
    your personality by   E M P T I N E S S
    your smell, not your words,   F I N I S H E D . . .
---your *individual* personality,
some arbitrary soup of concepts
---   * * * * * * * * * * * * * * * *

        My frog in Buddha Creek just croaked
        Three Times (at high noon!)---
        So may it be! Mantra--Santra--
            P a n t r a   * * *

BUDDHISM***I can see it, hear it now
in the kitchen---even as they try to
talk their way out of it, our of
emptinesshood and awakenedhood,
sentient beings'll learn it by themselves, in time---S'what's meant by
Tathagata Transformations. . . . .

Put out your hands
palms up and accept
handfuls of sun---it boils over the palms
. . . .

MATTI-KARUNA, is,
Transcendental Compassion

All this life is nothing but a burden for the supremely pure truebody---a burden
of Samapatti---the reward is Prajna Wisdom, knowing about the ecstasy of the
essence of all things---*thatness*---And in essence life is neither burden nor reward
but emptiness supreme and flawless. . . . . . .

This universe will definitely end!
　All compound things come to decay---
　　---that far off last epoch . . . . .

　　　* * * * * * * * * *

W O N D E R F U L　I D E A . . .
　Spontaneous prayer each disciple does
　　my Prajna Prayer on the Juju beads,out
　　loud,as the others listen and follow
　along the beads!

Emptiness is the selfhood that seeks highest perfect final wisdom. . . . . .

E m p t i n e s s
is imaginary judgment
of the Truth

　o o o o o o o

SAMAPATTI, is,
compassion for
that the epiphany
of existence is so.
　o o o o o o o

Samapatti is the moving paw. . . . . . .

　　SINCE BUDDHAHOOD IS IDENTICAL WITH THE ESSENCE
　　OF ALL THINGS and is what it is, then a disciple
　　who discards all arbitrary conceptions whatever and
　　all imaginary judgments whatever will immediately
　　become a Buddha, and Chih-Chi is wrong when he says
　　that Nirvana will come only when a disciple holds a
　　conception of Buddha, unless it means that the Buddha,
　　there can be no conceptioning of the Buddha, and the
　　"conception of Buddha" be held to mean "no-conception at

| Compassion for the
| spectres in my mind | all!"---

* *
　　　　　　　　　　*
E m p t i n e s s　　*
is the goal of all these　*
　　w　o　r　d　s　　*
　　　　　　　　　*
. . . . . .　　　　　　*
　　　　　　　　　*
I stand in no awe of　*
nature's instincts . . .　*
　　　　　　　　　*
TAKE AN INTELLIGENT　*
WORLDLY POET, his　*
best asset is his　　*
great social intelli-　*
gence, like for　　*
instance I know　*
one who was e-　*
nabled to dig

Since Buddhahood is identical
with Thatness, then there can
be no conception whatever of
Buddhahood to be held within
the mind as a judgment, an
arbitrary mentally-decided
thought, distinction, illusion
---Buddhahood may only be Emptiness
indicated in Self Realization
of Noble Wisdom---(arya-prajna)
---*Buddhahood may only be*
realizable in Samadhi Ecstasy
and not in Prajna-Knowing
　　　And all things are Samadhi Ecstasy
　　　right now and forever
EMPTINESS IS IDEAS
　　THAT MAKE US SEEK WISDOM--
　　　Emptiness, all these　w o r d s . . .

* *
the wild weird high charm of Japanese Zen magazines featuring Western Surrealist
pictures, saying "It's the Jap Zens digging our Surrealist Lunatics like we dug
their Zen Lunatics"---outside of that, such a man, in fact, this is in essence
piddlingness of knowledge, compared to knowledge of a Bhikku Han Shan whose knowledge
is *dark*---"*dark knowledge the spirit enlightens itself*"---Yet here I make the vast
great mistake of comparing odiously (again) the uncomparableness in emptiness; that
is to say, so what? Some have deep minds, some shallow, but the shalo and the dip
come together and are complementary . . . I only want to point out the difference (which
is a false distinction) between heretical worldly views and orthodox dharma views . . .
the first is piddling, it is lost in discrimination of styles and outer containers;
the second is momentous, it points to origin and essence, it is free and light,
like mountain air, pure, pointing to purity & freedom of mind---yet all this phenomena
is the same essential emptiness, the two personalities belong to the same b l a n k

Surrealist Lunatics (cont'd)
These charming worldly views are just gab . . .

LET'S CUT OUT THE GAB . . .

PRAJNA PRAYER: "My hatred of such gab is
emptiness, my hatred of such gab is not
different from emptiness, neither is
emptiness different from my hatred of
such gab, indeed, emptiness is my hatred
of such gab" . . . .
                    "My love of Han Shan's
knowledge is emptiness, my love of Han
Shan's knowledge is not different from
emptiness, neither is emptiness different
from my love of Han Shan's knowledge,
indeed, emptiness is my love of Han Shan's
knowledge" . . . .

"I dont believe it's gonna make
     any difference anywhichaway---
  anywhichaway, everywhichaway,
       whichawhichaway"
            says the
         Negro Buddha on
            a Levee. . . . .

VAJRAKARUNA, is, Diamond Compassion

     NOTE: Feb 23 Lost my Juju
     beads at night, search't in
     the morning, found em on the
     path . . . You cant lose anything
     on the path, what's lost shall
     be re found soon!---such a clear,
     pure, well traveled path---So
     there's a Lesson. . . . .

E m p t i n e s s   i s   E v e r y t h i n g . . . .

Celine said of Genet:
"You may take and weigh
for what they're worth
the words of a *tetteur*
(mansucker)"----I say:
"You may take and weigh
for what they're worth
the words of a killer
of animals" (Hemingway)
---"The words of an
alcoholic" (me)(Faulkner)
(Thomas)(Marlowe)----
"The words of a woman
sucker" (Joyce)------------
"The words of an engraver"
(Blake)---"The words of
a fool" (Smart)---"The
words of a beggard"
(Buddha,Christ)------------

        * * * * * * * * *

SAW THE
COUNTLESS
BUDDHAS
HIDING IN THE
MOONLIGHT AIR---
And I shall be one
of them.Plenty of Time. . . . .

NOT REALLY the murderous Smith
                    but the blank Buddha;
NOT REALLY the compassionate Jones,
                    but the blank Buddha;
NOT REALLY the contemptuous Doe,
                    but the blank Buddha;
NOT REALLY the sympathetic Shmoe,
                    but the blank Buddha. . . .

    *

F r e e z i n g   N i g h t   D h y a n a

    b y   t h e   M o o n ---Reason for recent
                    failures to attain
                 tranquil Samadhis---*keep
               eyes closed* in dhyana!--------
          dont gape! at woods, sky,dogs,etc.
        for closing the eyes is in itself an act
     of dhyana, it means full indifference & ig-
   noring of phenomena forms-----ALSO I was about to
ask Tathagata not to make the burden of my Ignorance last
too long when I realized the absurdity of a time-request in
this timeless endlessness of emptiness which makes the
earth an insignificant not-even-moment!

HUI NENG---"The norm is to be realized by the mind,
it does not depend upon the crosslegged position"
---"All Dharmas are calm and void, such is Tathagata's
Seat of Purity"---"Strictly speaking, there is no
such thing as 'attainment'; why should we bother
ourselves about the crosslegged position"---"Wise men
who thoroughly realize Mind Essence know that defilement
(klesa) and wisdom (bodhi) are of the same nature . . . tathata, is
what is called 'true nature' . . . . . both permanent and immutable. Such is
the Norm."---
        "Intrinsically(the world) exists not, and at the present moment it is
not annihilated"---(it is simply empty) "Free yourself from all thought---*good
ones as well as bad ones*---then your mind will be in a state of purity, ever calm
and serene, the usefulness of which will be as apparent as the sands of the Ganges"
-------"Undisturbed & serene, the wise man practices no virtue; self-possessed and
dispassionate, he commits no sin; calm & silent, he gives up seeing and hearing;
even and upright his mind abides   n o w h e r e."   ---O HOW WISE! SO MAY IT BE!!

HUI NENG (CONTINUED)

And on subject à la my hangup---
"To be bigoted (about Buddhism)
and to argue with others in disregard of the rule (that disputes
are alien to our school of Dharma)
is to subject one's Mind Essence
to the bitterness of this mundane
existence."
    PUT THIS IN BOOK OF PRAYERS,
      CREAM UP A FEW MORE CURDS
      OF HUI NENG---HE GREAT

* *

Trikaya (Three-Bodies) of HuiNeng
    DHARMAKAYA, self-nature;what you
                are; samadhi,or,the
                samadhi of thatness,
                the ecstasy of tathata
    SAMBHOGAKAYA, self-wisdom; what
                you know; prajna
    NIRMANAKAYA, self-action; what
                you do; sila conduct

All things are emptybliss. . . .

I read the DIAMOND SUTRA with my
Diamond-Sutra-Compartment, not my
whole mind . . . still a dreamer---

Blessing & Merit are the common
possession of all animate beings
& OUGHTA BE----AND AIR!

My original and pure mind knows
better than to concern itself
with thoughts of worldly fame and
its effects and discriminations
all around. . . . .

SUNDAY FEB 26 1956
   If you dont heed the cries of a dog on a chain, how do you expect God to heed
your cries?---TO PAUL & NIN
   Paul said: "I've got too much money invested in that dog to untie him from his
chain." I said "How would you like to be tied to a chain and cry all day like the
dog"---and he replied: "It doesnt bother *me*" and Nin said "*I* dont care"---
   I banish myself to the Forest
   For kindness to animals---
This time, when I hit the road, I'll have no plans (except for Desolation Peak in
June)---------*Plan to concentrate on emptiness of self, other selves, living beings,
universal self*; if you had done so this morning,you wouldnt have discriminated
anything,not even kindness . . .

      History sure repeats itself---(Karma,karma)

My frog in Buddha Creek croaked *Once
Instantly,* just now, noon
   THE ONE VEHICLE OF "HISTORY-SURE-
   REPEATS-ITSELF-KARMA-KARMA"----

Quintessence of manifestation
   (tathata of ideas)---
Manifestation of quintessence
   (ideas appearing in pure tathata)

HUI NENG SAYS:-"We should treat all things---
good and bad, beautiful or ugly---as void.
Even in time of disputes and quarrels we
should treat intimates and enemies alike
and never think of retaliation. *In the
thinking faculty, let the past be dead.*
If we allow our thoughts past, present, and
future to become linked up into a series,
we put ourselves under restraint. On the
other hand . . . it is a great mistake to suppress all thinking. Even if we succeed, and
die immediately thereafter, still, there is
rebirth. Mark this, pilgrims of the Path!
We should get rid of all 'Pairs of Opposites'
. . and focus our mind on Tathata-Thatness."
"It is the function of Tathata-Thatness to
give rise to 'Ideas'---It is not the sense-
organs that do so. Tathata-Thatness reproduces its own attribute, therefore, it
can give rise to 'idea' . . . Because of this . . .
our sense-organs, in spite of their functioning in seeing,hearing,tasting,smelling
touching,and knowing, are not defiled . .
Sutra says: 'Be adept in appreciation of
that which lies behind things & phenomena'-"
HIS LAST WORDS WERE:-
                  "What you should do is
to know your own mind and realise your own
Buddha-nature,which neither rests nor moves,
neither becomes nor ceases to be, neither
comes nor goes, neither affirms nor denies,
neither remains nor departs." A lunar
rainbow appeared to link the earth and
heaven at midnight as he passed away and
his last words were: "I am going now."
. . . .

                I have
                      more strength
                          than
                      last year . . .

Emptiness is the
     spider
On your bare shin

This sad & bootless
　　d r e a m ---　　　　　This ethereal spiderweb for needy greeds---
This shiny spiderweb　　　　These memories of nothingness---
　　for black greeds　　　　　This conception mere and dull dog earth . . .

You must patiently accept Hunger,
The reward is greater than the Hunger . . .
　　　　　　　　　　　　　　　　　　"Innumerable and without
　　　　　　　　　　　　　　　　　　　　limit . . ." (and none at
"The fabulous story of Kerouac" is　　　　　　　　　　a l l . . .)
　　e m p t i n e s s

Christianity is really just a moment of heresy in these few moments of the earth
in the Eternities---THE DIAMONDCUTTER OF IDEAL WISDOM, THE DIAMOND SUTRA, IS ETERNAL

Note how wild the handscript　　　　It's not unkind to chain a hound? perpetually
(in my hand-notebook Dharma #9)　　Dont try to talk your way out of that,talker.
when I'm unhappy---When I'm　　　　　　*T a k i* ! (as we used to say on Gershom)
happy I write small neat　　　　　　---
letters with glad and　　　　　　　　　YET, merit or demerit, equally empty . . .
comfortable deliberation . . .　　　　　My pride is hurt . . . . is emptiness
I'm now unhappy because I'm　　　　　My business is
hitting the road again . . . because　　　　with my Dharma . . . . . is emptiness
they're unfair to the dog . . .　　　　I'm proud of my pride
(Bob my Bodhisattva Dog) . . . . .　　　　in my kindness to
(who led me white down the　　　　　　animals . . . . is emptiness
　　P a t h) . . . .　　　　Conception of the chain . . . . is emptiness
　　　　　　　　　　　　　　　　Ananda's Pity . . . . is emptiness
　　　　　* * *　　　　　　　---

But, pathwise, admittedly emptywise, if it's gonna be like that I prefer to be
h o m e l e s s ---

A Zen master would probably　　　　　The pain of getting rid of the
now go kick the dog on his　　　　　　conception of people
chain, to give everybody Satori
---but and maybe he would be a　　　　I　a w a k e . . . there's no world there!
wise master, but that too,
derangement of the discriminating　　　I WONT SAY ANYTHING
senses in emptiness,is emptiness . . .
REST AND BE KIND I always did say.　　The expression on Gotama's face during
　　　　　　　　　　　　　　　　Samadhi was compassionate and sad,
I remember　　　　　　　　　　and seem'd to say *"Sentience---poor*
the hundred thousand　　　　　　　　　　　*sentience"*---
myriad swirls of Buddhas
before I became a Writing Bodhisattva
in this little earth dream----------------　　A tender little drama in the
* *　Sunday countryside---Jean-Louis
DHYANA SAMADHI OF THE LOW FULL MOON　*　doesnt want the dog chained
　* * * * * *"Toute est vide piereveillez"*---The　*
Great Realization has come to me tonight!---　* *
---It's all empty & awake---empty because awake---awake because empty-----
What'm I doin in this endless universe empty & awake?
　Baudelaire, Baudelaire, said, you should always be drunk, either on wine, on
　　poetry, or on virtue---Easy enuf to say------------------but:
　　FULL MOON DHYANA
　　Three ways in which things are empty:
　　　　　1. *In time,* everything made has to be unmade, stars included; since
　　　　　　it's all to be gone in time we might as well say it's already gone,
　　　　　　why quabber over a spate of time which is a drop and a quibble in
　　　　　　a spateless endless ocean of eternal everlasting yakmilk, yok! yak!
　　　　　　　　　　　　une goutte!　Gone! Gone!

THREE WAYS IN WHICH THINGS ARE EMPTY   (CONTINUED)
Like Gary Snyder's Magic Dharani Yell on top of Matterhorn Peak, "Ya-hoo-ah-whee-OOO"
(whichever), time is a joke. . . . . KOAN: "When you climb to the top of a mountain, keep
climbing"------for time is a joke. . . . .

    2. *As things,* (things are empty), as things of phenomena, things, my
       goodness, we cant weigh or measure or grasp the farthest atom,
       it's all empty throughout, mental forms using atomic "structure"
        ---*it isnt there* . . . THE FORM IS EMPTINESS
    3. *As sense-objects*---if it wasnt for sense equipment, things wouldnt be
       sensed or known---in emptiness, where there is no eye, ear, nose, tongue,
       body or mind, there are no things----The world "we" see just isnt here
       ----"How can *things* be said to exist?" asks the Sutra. . . . The very word
       "things" is such a jingling giggling toy(balloon) (pop bubblegum). . . .
       True reality abides right thru "things" and isnt changed thereby. . . .
       for the things are imagined. . . .

    WHAT DOES IT MEAN TO BE EMPTY AND AWAKENED IN A UNIVERSE WITHOUT END?
       BUDDHAHOOD----STAY AWAKE---BLESS
                (Let the machines bleed, you bless). . . .
These 3 ways in which things are empty is really One Way and that Way is B u d d h a
. . . . .Les Trois Vides (IN FRENCH)

1. En temp les choses s'en alle----	What'm I gonna do?
toutes---c'est deja fini	S T A Y A W A K E
2. En phenome les choses son	
vide, o n peu pas mesuree l'atom	WHY is there this Vision
infinite, c'est une apparition	in the Mind?
3. Choses de sense, c'est vide, sans	W H A T V I S I O N ?
les sens on voira ' n rien, voila,	
les sens sont vide, qu'est ce qu'on vue	Be Kind, Bless, Stay
c'est des phantomes---c'est pas la.	Awake. . . . .
RESTE REVEILLEZ	WHAT WHY?

EMPTY AND AWAKE
       ALL THINGS
           INCLUDING ERROR . . . . *WHY* IS EMPTY AND AWAKE
    Call me not
       by my familiar name---for one who has entered into the emptiness
       and awakenedhood of all things, and has attained thereby to that
       which everything is, is like the father of all things---call me
          Lord. . . .

A BUDDHA IS ONE WHO KNOWS THAT HE IS EMPTY AND AWAKE,
But there is no difference between the emptiness-and-awakenedhood
of a Buddha and the emptiness-and-awakenedhood of an ordinary person---In fact,
there are no Buddhas and no ordinary persons-------S T A Y A W A K E----------------

The people (speakly worldly-wise now) who *wanta* be like this *wanta* be like this,
  and so *cant*(be like this)-----THE PEOPLE WHO *WANTA* BE LIKE THIS *WANTA* BE LIKE THIS,
      *   BUT CANT
Materialists like Freud are not unintelligent---they say: * * (original
"Since I cant predicate the Unknown why should I bother?"   *   ***way I
Pragmatism. Martin Buber-ism. The narrow useful plateau.   ***   * *   wrote it)
Marx, Spengler, Einstein---they end up Dupes of (False)Time, *****   * * * * * * * * * * *
in their thoughts---They spin a web of mystic confusion for
themselves---But it's simple---Let me lay it out as simply & concisely as I can:-
All things are empty, they are empty in three ways, as Things of Time, as Things of
Space, as Things of Mind. As *Things of Time,* they are empty, they come but to go,
all things made have to be un-made, and they will have to be un-made simply because
they were made, and this includes all things, moths, men, souls, societies, starry
universes, and since all things have to be un-made in time then they are already
un-made in time, for there is no time, the timeless everlasting eternity is without
beginning and without ending. Gone! gone! indefatigably gone! All things! already
gone! already come and already gone!

PRAYER OF THE THREE EMPTINESSES (CONTINUED)

As *Things of Space,* things are empty, for they appear as phenomena made up of atoms
that cannot be infinitely measured or weighed or grasped, there is no finding the
farthest "atom" of the common essence of all things, things are empty arrangements
of something that seems solid appearing in the spaceless void, they are neither vast
nor tiny, neither near nor far, neither true nor false, they are apparitions pure
and simple, inner empty universes of form held together simply by conceptions of
the mind that picks them out in the void and makes them out, for a reason which is
reason in itself.

As *Things of Mind,* things are empty, for the mind that makes them out does so by
seeing,hearing,touching,smelling,tasting,and mentally-knowing, and without this mind
things would not be seen or heard or felt or smelled or tasted or mentally-noticed,
things are actually dependent on the mind that makes them out, by themselves they are
no-things, they are real-ly mental, seen only of the mind, they are really empty
visions of the mind that makes them out, for the reason which is reason in itself.

These three ways in which things are empty is really one way, & that way is awake.

What does it mean that I am in this endless universe, thinking that I'm a man sitting
under the stars on the terrace of earth, but actually empty and awake throughout
the emptiness and awakedness of everything? It means that I am empty and awake,
knowing that I am empty, awake, and that there's no difference between me and
anything else.

In other words, it means that I have attained to that which everything is.
It means that I have attained to Buddhahood."

* * * * * * * * * * * *

T H E R E ' S   B U D D H I S M . . . .   T h e   Light of Mahayana is in "there's no
difference between me and anything else."

What am I
   to do?   Divine or Devil------same.
Stay Awake

ASOKA adored all religions both or recluses and householders---Rock Edict 12.

* *

FUKE, the Chinese idiot-sage   *   "A security and certainty, beyond any imagining"
   who constantly rang   *   says ALAN WATTS. He calls it "IT"--"Give Up"
   his bell (9th Century   *   ----"Plop into nothing."
   China) !   *

*   -

-W I L L - P E T E R S E N-
   of Berkeley, in Bussei Magazine, writes about THE STONE GARDEN OF RYOANJI in Japan
   . . . . . 15 ordinary rocks, 5-2-3-2-3, in sand, which is raked, & a little moss at
   rock bases. . . . Mentions how Suzuki says you cannot realize emptiness in any way
   different than by the realization of the straightness of a bamboo because form is
   emptiness and emptiness is form . . . . . but this may distract certain minds, like Ginsberg who says he would discern Mind Essence through dealing with surfaces tho
   ultimately this *is* the way to do it, only I doubt my own insight into the insight
   of another (without evident surface proofs!)-----Will Petersen says, then, *"Where there
   is no form there is no emptiness"* which is extremely intelligent . . . Will
   Petersen is a painter and printmaker at Berkley Calif. Univ. --A form is an *event*
   not a *thing,* he quotes from Suzuki, substantiating what I just wrote: "Things are
   empty arrangements of something that seems solid appearing in the spaceless Void."
   Surfaces (things) are epiphanal events, visions-of-the-mind.

F r o m
NOW AND FOREVER,
         DONT INVOLVE YOURSELF
               BUT BE LIKE PRAJNA . . tell others "Do what you want, but I'm doin nothin"------

For various conditional reasons
(as Hui Neng even knows & hints)
there are friends and there are
enemies ("spies" he calls them),
so make it a rule to remain aloof,
start a new life of KEEPING GUARD
OVER WHERE YOU GO AND WHAT YOU DO,
NOT DRINKING ARSENIC. . . . as it were . . .
remain aloof both from friendships
and animosities, just contribute
your Dharma to the Sangha church . . .
---My business is with the Dharma
Not with Friendships & Rivalries . . .
a saying---------The Dharma . . . .
the Truth Law . . . my work in it,
my publishing and spreading of
it, my practising and explaining
of it . . . . . is all. . . . That is to
say, remain aloof while being
right in the middle of the world
with all its fangs & kisses . . .
fang or kiss, *que?*
. . *esta la misma cosa.* . . .
Gotama Buddha just smiled gently
and went his way. . . . . . asking
nothing . . . . . knowing: "It's all
been done. . . ."---------------
Knowing it was all in his own mind
he didnt quibble with any part of
it but let the thoughts slide . . . .
and he blest them as they passed . .
Aum.

      * * * * * * * * * * * * *

    H A I K U
A whore washing out
    the sperm---
Sentient eternal Nirvana

     * * * * * * * * *

A whore washing out
    the sperm---
The Snapped Link eternal
    * * * * * *

For ON THE ROAD . . . insert
in ms. "*beat,* the root
and soul of beatitude"---

REASON WHY AVALOKITESVARA
always hears and Answers, is,
(as last night) his emptiness
is *you*-emptiness, he is *you*---
E M P T Y   &   A W A K E

THE WORLD,
        all things, phenomena,
        form, it's a mere expression,
       a hint of the inconceivable
   Tathagata "G o d"---
(That-Which-Everything-Is, is God)----
We can tell by the straightness of the bamboo the emptiness of Tathagata God. . . .

NIP NOSE DHYANA   I pray to the essence of
the endless universe and with the same
fervency it prays to me------Not-Two, but
O N E . . . . I was a great feeling. . . . I
felt compassion for the trees because we're
the same thing.

  E N E M I E S   A R E   E M P T I N E S S

Indeed, what am I,but *something-that-stays
-awake ?*

    Your consciousness of Prajna wisdom is
emptiness---it's not that it's not there,
like bodies and forms, but it's empty . . .
by "Prajana wisdom" I mean the Wisdom-of-
Knowing-that-Everything-is-Emptiness----
this wisdom is in itself emptiness, like
everything else----
    Prajna wisdom is the signpost to
        Samadhi Ecstasy Trance
        and Samapatti Magic Love

JUST ADD THE WORD "CONCEPTION" to everything
you see---
    cat, cat-conception;
    pipe, pipe-conception;
trouble, trouble-conception

DHARMA TRUTH LAW, an arbitrary consciousness
of such an Establishment of Insight, is
emptiness--- Because all *is* emptiness. . . .

VISIONS OF MOMINU . . . . The Magic Land---the brilliant
desert monk---the woman saint preaching his sermons
---the simplehearted disciple who help't everyone
with their burdens---the jealous brother---the rich
Lesser Religion uncle---the Tathagata---the City
                 C A T E

Weed induces the endless definite sensation that
Nirvana is in Samsara---automatically---it must be
the Buddha's gift----They'll put laws against
marijuana just like they'll put laws against enlightenment (trance-patients in mental hospitals)
(LAWS MADE BY MATERIALISTS LIKE FREUD,BUBER, MARX,
    EINSTEIN,SPENGLER,AND CAESAR)

MARCH 1st   If you get mad at "enemies" remember
that both the phenomena of anger and the enemy
sentient beings, are emptiness, and are to be
considered as mere expressions describing
visions in your own mind . . .
  Thinking that my mind is real instead of
    false. . . . IT IS NEITHER

    The Dharma is a finger pointing to
    the emptiness that was realized
    under the Bo-Tree----The Dharma is words.

For PRAYER
    "The three ways in which
things are empty is, holy and alone,
one way"--

"Nothin I can think of in the world
worse than bein alone," sings the
hillbilly with his shotgun and jug.

And I should get mad?
----

*Before I was born I saw it all, this
history of myself*!- ---French boy,football
writing, neglect, poverty, patience, and
Buddhahood. . . .
    In other lifetime I was Shakespeare.

WRITE TO CAROLYN FOR CAYCE LITERATURE
---it just occurs to me,this reincarnation begins to take shape---my "genius-
neglected" status, requiring humility and
patient suffering, must have been intended
as a path ot Buddhahood---to purify me of
literary (well-earned etc.) prides----all of it of
course empty dramaforms---empty matured-karmas or un-matured
---empty emptinesses---with only arbitrary and imaginarily-conceived meanings that
are to be considered merely as expressions, as mere words, like the word "time"-------
which Neal and Carolyn havent realized yet, that is, that all the phenomena and
drama of karmas working-out is DEVOID OF EGO SUBSTANCE . . . . far,far out,the Truth,
of Mind-less-ness, of,indeed, "God-less-ness,"----the Truth of Truth-less-ness. . . .
    *If all my works were suddenly swallowed up by an earthquake it still would
make no difference---"my real career" encompasses all emptiness not just the emptiness
of this little imaginary earth---*

WHEN ENGAGED IN TEACHING SOMEONE
remember that you're teaching a
"projection of yourself"---in French
tache (of above 'taching') means
to *soil* ---when engaged in soiling
someone remember that you're soiling
a "projection of yourself" sitting
there and there's no need to get mad
(as at hillbilly with shotgun) or
to get sarcastic or insistently mean
to make your point clear---*it is
already clear*---whether you teach
clarity, or soil with mud, it is
already clear. . . .
Be sweetly reasonable, O man.
A DREAM ALREADY AWAKENED FROM . . .

Gigantic strides in attainment?
"Neither huge nor tiny," neither
going forward nor going backward,
in emptiness of the void---(neither
sane nor insane)---*This* is the void,
       the void's not out there
         somewhere else.
        * * * * * *

Why'd I open my eyes?
   because
I wanted to

There is no deep
   turning-about
In the void

The pine woods
   move
In the mist

OTHERWISE, if it hadnt been for this reincarnation, Shakespeare (me reborn) wd. have
gone on blindly writing like Le Cid, Balzac,
Simenon endless corruptible histories of
decayed bodies . . . ah me.
    The "Writer in (Western) Man"
     had to wake up sometime!
    The tireless Zola with his quill
    and ignorance . . . yelling about
     ignorance!
      * * * * * * * * * * * *

    AWAKE MEANS MIND-EMPTY . . for,
when you're waking up from a dream and you
realize it was only a dream, your mind
is emptied of the conception of the
reality of the dream, this is what the
Buddha means when he writes, "Awake
    means mind-empty"-----

    COMFORT AND REPOSE---
In Meditation think: "B u d d h a"
  (the way Ma pronounces it
   in French, BOO*DAW)

* *
Sentience with its pissin & shittin is a form of
degradation---we're all fallen angels----in that
sense "wash'd in the blood of Christ the Messiah"
is a truly realistic religious idea. . . .

IN OTHER REINCARNATIONS I was Avalokitesvara the
bhikku, Asvhaghosha the desert monk, I was a Chinese
wandering Buddhist, a Mexican Indian in Azteca, an
English footpad, Shakespeare just before that, then
Balzac then Kerouac---I will be a Buddha
      * * * * * * * * * * * * * * * * * *

Hear the games & type the Dharmas,
I thought, getting up from afternoon
grassmat, through with Dhyana till
tonight. . . . .

Tathagata, Attainer-to-That-Which-
     Everything-Is (Mar.2)
    Do not grasp at phenomena
because it takes empty form, nor
reject it because the form is
empty. . . . .

Awake means Mind-empty and vice
versa, DHYANA OF PITY March 2
i.e.Buddhahood is realizing
eventually that everything is
empty, including torture---
the Crucifixion,Christ on the
Cross, is empty---Prince Kalinga
torturing Buddha to death with
swords, is emptiness---any moment
now I expect to wake up from this
dream of J.K. and find myself before
Kalinga's Swordsmen, where I'm to be
murdered for being a bhikku who sits
in woods meditating and preaches
kindness to all things and begs from
door to door. . . . . Yet it's all
emptiness, snake eating rat is
emptiness . . . as a Buddha youweI've
known it all! O SAD TRANSCENDENT TRUTH!
but what's sad is not-knowing emptiness!
O Glory Be! How wise the Buddhas, to make
things empty!
       AWAKE MEANS MIND EMPTY
         and
      EMPTY MEANS MIND AWAKE

* *
W e   m a d e   a   p r o m i s e . . . .
* *
EVERYBODY KNOWS THIS: "Our mind is
pure---we become perturbed because we
allow ourselves to be carried away"---
    HUI NENG

FURTHER ADVICE FROM HUI NENG THE SIXTH PATRIARCH OF THE CHINESE SUDDEN SCHOOL:
"Be indifferent as to whether others are good or bad, or whether they deserve merit
or demerit. To assume a discriminatory attitude towards others is to invite perturbation of mind.---(To) criticize others is to . . deviate from the right course. . . .
Prajna wisdom and Samadhi ecstasy . . are simultaneous. *To be an enlightened disciple*
who has realized wisdom in ecstasy discussion about it is unnecessary" because
nothing ever happened.

HUI NENG: "Argument implies a desire to win,
it strengthens egoism"---"egoism of self,
being, a living being, a person"---
  "The ecstasy of specific mode such as
sitting quietly & continuously without
letting any idea rise in the mind, is
delusion." - - - - - - - - - - - - -

Come follow the Path, you crazy fools
---enlightenment is the same as
      insanity!

There's no Buddha
    because
There's no me

    JNANAKARUNA, my name, J.K.
     "Compassionate Knowledge"
      Jnana-Karuna

ROOM SAMADHI The diamond sound:-"Nothing
       ever happened" (it says)

  NIRVANA IS BUZZING IN OUR EARS all the
time and we dont know it---the longer
you listen the more you get blissfully
lost---in: "Nothing ever happened"
-----Pure Audial Experience, no thought,
    j u s t   l i s t e n   t o   s h h h

"He who has not yet understood the object
of the Buddha's incarnation is unable
to suppress the wild passions accumulated
in many lives" sings Fat Tat to Hui Neng
------applicable also to "Messiah's
            Incarnation"
--------the reason for Messiah
     on the Cross, that even *that*
   be realized to be empty and
awake. . . . . . . even *that,* O
      Mother Mary,
    O poor sobbing Ananda.

    * * * * * * * * * * * * *
"Abide in selfless oneness with the
That-Which-Everything-Is-Ness that
is Tathagatahood"---translation
* *

To "rest in inner peace" of Samadhi
simply listen to silence---hush.
HE WHO KNOWS DOES NOT S P E A K . . . .

    ** HUI NENG'S TRIPLE ADVICE **
    1. Non-objectivity, not to be
            absorbed with
           objects when
           in contact with
           them . .

    (explain'd next page)

412

1. *Non-Objectivity,* not to be absorbed with objects
when in contact with objects

2. *Idea-less-ness,* not to be carried away by any
particular idea in our exercise
of thinking

3. *Non-attachment,* seeing all things as emptiness

The "Sudden School"
of "Sudden Enlightenment"
(Satori), in China, ---
Advanced Buddhism.
*
* * *
* * * * *
* * * * * * *

Conceptions of selfness, ideas about such conceptions,
and ideas of the non-existence of such conceptions,
are to be discarded. . . . .

MIND ESSENCE?
voidness of non-voidity
DHARMA?
domain of law

"A passing foolish thought makes one an
ordinary man, while an enlightened thought
makes one a Buddha"---------Hui Neng

EVEN AND ONE THING EVERYWHERE
Hot March 4th:-To be carried
away by the idea of emptiness
is e m p t i n e s s . . . .

"Emptiness of the Buddha-bead, is not knowing
that suffering is emptiness and pity is
emptiness"---tonight's prayer---
O W I S E C O M P A S S I O N

This is REALLY compassion,
the end of suffering by destruction of (the reality of)
s u f f e r i n g !!!!!!!!
* *

o o o o o o o o o o o o o o o o o o o o o o o o o
Begging from door to door draws attention---
by the natural neighborhood furor it causes
on drowsy sleepy days---and it draws
attention to the sincerity of yr. humility
---to the Teaching . . .

The pathless lark. . . .

* *

OOOOOOO
"Both" or "Neither," in either case,
empty words

BUDDHA UNDER THE PRINCE'S SWORDS
and Christ on the Cross *had* to
subdue their discriminative
thoughts and craving desires
and see the light---it's the
eventual meaning, *awakening* . . .
awaking to PERFECT TRANQUILLITY
OF MIND
. . . to the empty light . . .

. . . . Just because emptiness has
taken a form, you dont have
IN to believe in it---and just
TEACHING because that form is empty,
THE you dont have to reject it!
DHARMA
YOU SHOULD FIRST BE FREE FROM ALL CRAVING
(AT LEAST TEMPORARILY) S'why no one
has listened to me . .

Little children practice
illimitable dana charity
perfectly---with blank eyes
and understanding hearts. . . . .

Disciples long ago planting roots of goodness before the shrines of a hundred
thousand myriad swirls of Buddhas, is emptiness. . . . .

TEACHING ONE ANOTHER, BEING NICE,
cheering up, making gifts of food
and delicacies and garments, this
we should look upon as *an act we're
putting on* merely and neither reject
nor cling to it . . . this is WISE
THIS IS PROBABLY SAMAPATTI,
(knowing that's what it is,
Transcendental Activity). . . . .

MARCH 5 Dipankara Buddha didnt say
anything to the coming Shakyamuni
Buddha but just sat in hushing eternity
. . . "no definite teaching, no definite
degree of discipline"---WOW---
"No answer from Dipankara" I said 1954!

LAST NIGHT
A dream that the dreamers are
tuned-in on, this life------------

. . my selfhood is imaginary . . . and so is yours . . . . and your dog's . . . . relax & be kind. . .

"Subhuti, supposing a man has a body as large as a mosquito. What think you? Would his body be counted great?"

"Exceedingly great, Honored of the Worlds! Because what the Lord Buddha means by the expression 'the greatness' of that human body, is not limited to any arbitrary conception whatever, so it can rightly be called, 'great'--"

---TRANSPOSITION OF WORDS IN DIAMOND SUTRA

LUCIEN SAYS "Honored-of-the-Worlds"
as addressed to Tathagata by Subhuti
was a later addition to the original
scripture, made by priests . . . . he says
he oughta know because he wrote the
Diamond Sutra, or spoke it, that is.
He says: "Boy, I'm gonna speak a new
Diamond Sutra that wont have NOTHIN
    in it!"--------and we drink to it.
In New York a month ago. . . . . . .

FOR,"the things taught by the
Tathagata, the Attainer-to-That-
Which-Everything-Is, are, in
their essential nature, ungroupable,
inconceivable, unknowable". . . . . .
(good trans. of Diamondcutter)

* *

Indeed, emptiness of the Buddha-bead,
is whether you ever attain Satori or not!
* *

SKETCH Twin Tree Grove March 5   *
            (spontaneous)   *
SANDY'S YELLOW ASS in the brown pine   *
needles, she just walked, sat, looked   *
around and was realizing she and my   *
discrimination of her is emptiness   *
which is obvious and the obviousness   *
of which is emptiness---The other dog   *
on side slumbers in deep good shade,   *
among dry saplings, with little sick   *
Buddhadog with thin body never eats   *
coughing up his heart---the holy   *
yellow long bowing weeds that face my

HIGHEST PERFECT FINAL FACT
    is highest perfect wisdom
        anuttara samyak sambodhi
            Or, Highest Perfect
                Final Everything. . . .
    Highest Perfect Final State. . . . .

YOU'RE NOT CALLED UPON so much to realize
that even *torture* is empty and awake
but more that *sitting under the tree*
is empty and awake, for, the worst
is over . . .
        THE CROSS   THE
        OF NON   BO TREE
        BODHI   OF BODHI

Emptiness
    of the Ananda glass bead,
Is the bowing weeds
        HOKKU PRAYER

    How to make sure to attain Samadhi
        any time? by realizing that everything
    is in Samadhi Ecstasy all the time,
    and thus just stopping all the nerves
    and senses, letting everything drop, and
smiling and entering deeply: into:-
. . . *Bliss is Forever Everywhere*
    STOP BREATHING FOR 3 SECONDS OR SO,
    CLOSE THE EYES, LISTEN TO THE INTRINSIC
    SILENCE, LET YOUR HANDS AND NERVE ENDS
    DROP, LET IT ALL GO, AND RE-RECOGNIZE
    THE BLISS THAT HAS ALWAYS BEEN THERE.
    H Y P N O T I Z E   Y O U R S E L F

* *

grass sitmat of Tathagata Seat of purity---they point in all directions and
hairily converse as the winds dictate Ta Ta Ta ta, in gossip groups with lone
bhikkus proud to show off and sick ones and half dead fallin ones, the congregation
of sentient Sapient weedhood now in windies suddenly bijeling bijeling and jumping
to get excited and all made of yellowstuff and stick to the ground and THIS IS
EMPTINESS, EMPTINESS IS THIS,---I'm awright, it's you I'm worried about---What to
say about weeds of weed hood or men of humanhood except what's long been all been
said by silent Dipankara and even the conception of the Truth of his silence is
emptiness O empty and awake without end, the hot sun's not even that but a hot-sun
conception in my equipment---Mind Empty is mind awake and all your thoughts are
empty so you're already awake you're already Buddhas everybody, rejoice,---be like
the weeds, say Fallal---nipal---pitit---fomon---chiki---pirya---(tockalick tockalik
says Sandy's collar as she scratches)---weed say: rum! leurld! pooti! moya moy
---piticlacka! Rop rop rop---They show windward pointing intelligent reachers to
indicate and flail and finagle, some rooted in blossom imagination earth moist
perturbation idea that has Karmacised their very root-and-stem---root-and-stem of
Essencestuff---they like me are that-which-everything-is, this is Nirvana now,---
eerily like it is now, even---like a Dostoevskyan Nirvana---even as the birdy
tickalees sweetly cute in the sky-ee blue---not-a-cloud up there moping, the void

SKETCH OF TWIN TREE GROVE (CONCLUDED)

The voids' non-voidity today is void of cloudform emptinesses---see?---bury what in
what earth? pain in what bone? and who said P A I N ? And *bored*? in *Time*? what Time
and what is the relative meaning of figurative expressions that are merely to be
regarded as words and figures of speech?---I mean, I'm *bored*

    My toad goes four, five,---five now six creaks, creaks, seven, eight, no end
today, she'll creak, to ten, eleven, way up, the twelve nirdanas yet, thirteen,
fourteen, fifteen, how many wild ants have been squawshed in the link of the Buddha
hand pawing pencils to pop paper in white sun, eighteen, or so, didnt count, eighteen it
is, the Croak toady done give me the eighteen spheres of mentation! bless my soul!
What my Which? Ant's safe. Nuff Samapatti for today."

----

1 9 5 6   B E D S I D E   S H E E T S * * * * *

Sea of Joy   . . . . . By this teaching the earth came to an end (flash) and Ma
nods solemnly with her whole head umph and eyes closed.

Irking hurts & tedious wronks   . . . .   Arbitrary personalities . . .

The human bones are but vain lines dawdling . . .

What I'm looking for, I *am*---Inconceivable!   . . And an it icks . . .
             (Shakespearean "an" is "if")
Benzedrine: untroubled every gisling and let me write . . .

The conception of living is emptiness and the conception of dying is emptiness. . . .

Blank, the Universe is a Mold of Stars   I AM BHIKKU BLANK RAT

Lonely sentient beings are afraid that "they" will die off while "things" last on
forever---not realizing that apart from mind, nothing exists; it's in their own minds . . .

Otra vez . . .   Samapatti: Supernormal understanding of compassion
                           (à la Lucien)
Dhyana: "The pole star of all goodness"

Samapatti: potentiality of sympathy
Mattivajra (Transcendental Diamond)
Samapatti is Compassion . . . . Prajna is Wisdom . . . .   Samapatti is supernatural intuitive
                              karma pity---supernatural intuitions
There can be no Samapatti without   of compassion. . . . .
beings---and no wisdom without
something (dharmas) to be wise about. . . . .

Beginningless and Endless also means Presentmomentless! *There is no eternity*!
No present moment!   No "NOW"   Wheeeee!

The squawk of the little very self which wanders everywhere (from DREAM)

Most everybody is Anagamins entertaining arbitrary conceptions and imaginary judgments
of "No-Return"---

Nirvana, is, OUTBLOWNNESS, CUT-OFF-NESS, SNIPPED, BLOWNOUTNESS, PUTOUTNESS,
      TURNED OFF NESS, NOTHING-HAPPENS-NESS, GONE-NESS, GONE-OUT-NESS
      T H E   S N A P P E D   L I N K (*Nir*, link; *vana*, snap!)

SUGATA, is, Attainer-to-All-is-Well-Ness . . .

Sex----so much thrashing & gnashing in the mind. . . . . . .

Emptiness is not interested in emptiness. . . . . . .

Arbitrary conception, is, DREAM-LIKE IDEA (ORIGINATING IN THE MIND)

Arbitrary system of time. . . . .   *Visions of Gerard* is a poem of pure white . . .

Querida Esperanza, Yo soy tristo . . .   This moment and the richness of
                                        t h i s   i m a g e
Never mind "you"---leave "you" . . .

The dust of my thoughts collected into a globe . . .   Ageless solitude . . .

In your real truebody there's nothin dreary about eternity . . .

The present is a delusion; where can you locate it?

Money cant buy Samapatti
Rich wine obstructs it -   D E A D   SILENCE
Fame & travel arent Far--   * * * * * * * * * * * * * * * * * *

Waitin for somethin to happen in the Nothing-Ever-happens of Highest perfect wisdom . .

"O
      World is Mind! And Mind's
                 but mind, unreal"---Ginsberg, 1947 poem (!)

D H Y A N A   O F   W H I T E   L I G H T
Accept both emptiness and form. But strictly speaking there is no emptiness and
no form!
          (How can you say there is no emptiness? Because emptiness is a conception,
          a word,---the *"true emptiness"* is in no condition to be named or mentally
                      known). . . . .

Held hands out, palms up, to stars, said "Samapatti" and swarms of empty visions
came faintly. . . . .
Saw the White Light Everywhere Everything------------
ALSO   You hear sounds with yr ears but
        You hear silence with yr mind   YOU "HEAR" THE DIAMOND "SOUND"
        You see sights with your eyes but   MEANS YOU REALIZE NIRVANA---Shhhh
        You see nothingness with yr mind
        You feel forms with yr body-but   Trapped-in-time is emptiness
        But you feel emptiness with yr mind
        You think thoughts with yr brain but
        You think awakening with yr mind (!)   AND FORGOT THE REST. . . . . . .

Diamond Sound, is, the ecstasy of emptiness, silent and awake. . . . .
It is the ecstasy of awakening, the silent emptiness. . . . .
SAW, SAYING "AMITABHA," AN OLD PATRIARCHAL ORIENTAL FACE WITH DRIPPING MUSTACHES . . !
"Serenity, moral earnestness, sweet reasonableness" . . . when that bhikku brights up a wood!

MARCH 6
         Arbitrary conceptions are imaginary ideas,---mindmade judgments----
* * * *ARBITRARY CONCEPTION IS IMAGINARY JUDGMENT* * * * * * * * * *decisive idea . . . "decisive
idea of self"---"Entertain no imaginary judgments as to self, other selves, living
beings, or a universal self"------
NIGHT DHYANA:
          Emptiness of the Ananda glass bead, is the dust of the little hilly
          dutch street of my dreams. . . . . . .
                          O star!---Ephemeral veil!
                          Me never bar / in judgment jail . .
MARCH 7   --
Hot winds. . . . . What more could you see / of emptily / than what you see / unendingly

This   or That ☹ (mere upsidedowns)

is why the Silent Eternal Smile of Buddhahood is a Mental Smile---not a Lip-Smile---
Buddhaship *is* a silent Eternal Mental Smile! Nevertheless in meditation keep the
lips Mona Lisa'd gently

All the arahats sighed because they couldnt enjoy meditation any more because
they were arahats and they had nothing to meditate about----they held an imaginary
judgment that they were arahats---They were no such thing!
MEDITATE ON WHAT YOU LIKE . . .

Buddhism is all the way out, it brooks no intermediary stops such as the imaginary
judgments of Jesus' Path with its decisive conceptions of self, other selves, living
beings to be delivered, and a universal God self existing eternally---Buddhism is
all the way out---It doesnt even entertain an IMAGINARY IDEA of the Truth Law--it is
c o m p l e t e l y   p u r e . . . .
I'm not a Buddha this trip . . . face it . . . because I have too many decisive ideas
about life, how to live, health, food and drink, a veritable crone of ideas . . .
because of sensuality, drink, involvement in the ideas and antagonisms of men . . .

All these words of large degree
To describe what we cant be   . . . No imaginary judgment of the largeness of
                                                   the human body---the words carry an imaginary
WARM WIND   meaning---
makes the pines
Talk Deep (haiku)   THOUGHT IS ENDLESS . . . . and endlessly empty   NO TRUCE WITH
                                                                                                THE DEVIL . . . IT
                                                                                                ONLY GOES
*   *   UNDERGROUND . . .
This world was gradually spun into being by the spider of   *   S'WHAT HAL CHASE
h a b i t u a l   t h o u g h t . . . . empty right through   *   SAID . . . .
                                                                                         *
----------"The curious brooks of, excuse me, the curious books   *
            of Lord Monboddo" says Bozzy------------------   * * * * * * * * * * * * * * * * * *

WINDY MARCH 8   A BUDDHA IS QUIET
    It's all a big mad dream . . . the Beat Age   ----A BUDDHA WATCHES INJUSTICE
                                                                                  QUIETLY----

Unconscious smoking (of pipe) is too much---Smoke consciously-------

The Tathagata is Living Beings---
C O L D   N I G H T MARCH 8 1956 (1922 it says in my notebook!)
AMAZING SAMADHI   Flowers, pink worlds of walls of them, salmon pink---
                                Obtaining Nirvana
                                       is like
                                Locating silence
------Saw ancient vision of Dipankara Buddha as vast snowy Pyramid Buddha with
bushy wild black eyebrows and stare---old location---Emptiness Samapattis---Dhyana
and Blahblahblah, might as well Dhyana, for, go ask the silence to do something
else---Saw the wonderful happiness within and had no qualms about the poor lil
world of UNHAPPINESS to which "I" had to return---no difference---*Obtaining Nirvana
is like locating silence* because, 1, there is no obtaining of Nirvana because it
is the realm of no thing-ness, 2, there is no self to obtain it---
      There are no Pratyekas (practising deluded Buddhists) and no Buddhas, (Perfect
awakened ones)---Nothing ever happened, the phenomena is easily false---Came away
without reluctance or ado because I have a billion lifetimes to go on---I hope
better than I'm doing now, I add tonight while typing this, 2 weeks later. . . . .
"Locating silence,"---it is everywhere---like Nirvana---here, now, everywhere---
      The Pyramid Buddha made my hair rise---it was in an ancient snowy field like
Alban---
      There is no *the-writing* a *teenthsie* of what Samadhis and Samapattis show
---but I have a billion lifetimes as Writing Buddhas to try. . . . .
            Because of the Vow   ---   Because we made a promise. . . .

And: Magic Final Cry   *COLYALCOLOR*

MARCH 9th---A bad king
        is reborn   Mentally-decided illusions, are arbitrary conceptions
        A jealous dog

Arbitrary conceptions of phenomena you've *made,* and there they are---neither grasp
after them nor reject them---

Great wild ethereal activities like this life, but devoid of any wrong predicates,
last night's Amazing Samapatti----it was *egolessness,* & devoid of effort

                  ----

The Buddha-Mind created the world   A dog's life's
because certainly it wasnt an   not long;
inanimate object created the world   a man's life
---the world *is* Ephemeral Samapatti---   not much longer--

No matter how far your Buddhist Attainments, it all returns to right here. . . .
        (That's as true as I'm sittin here!)
      ---that's because there's no difference between the emptiness of the
        Infinity Samapatti and the emptiness of this "little world" right here,
        it's the same emptiness, devoid of location, size, appearance, or
        importance

                          I   Tom Wolfe---he's the one who makes the
     Buddha-Mountain   AM   Aspen quake---
        All of it   YOU   *A Western Journal*
        WHICH   THAT   ---"fried hills"---
        LIVETH   WHICH   "pure lemon heat mist"
        EMPTILY   LIVETH   "soaplike block of salmon red"
                       EMPTILY   (in Zion's Canyon)
                                  Univ.of Pittsburgh *1951*

ROCKY MOUNT NEGRO SHACKTOWN
   Stopped,wrote this on lamp pole:-   What do I want?---
   "Everything's Alright---form is emptiness   a hunnerd grand
& emptiness if form---& we're here   And ransom money
forever---in one form or another   H A I K U
---which is empty" WALKIN WITH WINE   * * * * * * * * * * * * * * * * * *
-----words of a wino drunkard?-----

                                As long as I have a *body*
                                I'll have to follow a *path*---
MARCH 10TH---what the dead   *the* path---
         have accomplisht   When I dont have a body, OO, I wont
         this rich silent hush   have to folly the Path. . . .
   * * * * * * * * * * * * * * * *
SUNDAY MARCH 11 . . . . *It's definitely an ant heap in Nirvana* (writ last fall) . . .

I've got my pack and it's Spring---after this New York sojourn to see Cowley, to
wait for Cowley, to settle ON THE ROAD contract and manuscript, I'll go Southwest
to the dry land---to the long lone land of Texas--- and Chihuahua---and Mexico City
----the gay streets of night---the music coming out of doors----the girls---the
wine, the weed, the wild hats-----and Viva Viejo Mexico!
               L O N G   R E D   T A B L E L A N D S of southwest . . .
                                 of Durango. . . . .

"By giving away our food we become more beautiful"---
old saying---Share yr. food with bums & dogs as may
chance---uninfluenced by imaginary judgments of what or how good it is, or of
"charity," or of "kindness" and your reward will be illimitable paradise---this
is an old old fundamental rule---PATH
Paradise is emptiness . . . . path too . . . !

LIKE THE ANTS that have nothing to do but dig all day, you have nothing to do but
to practice charity uninfluenced by imaginary judgments and pray for the light.

THE SHRINE OF TRUTH, IS BUDDHISM.........

ABANDON IMAGINARY JUDGMENTS OF THINGS AND ABOUT THINGS, and abide in the Samadhi-
Ecstasy of Samapatti Transcendental Grace---Ignore this world, its emptiness is
the same as the emptiness of all other worlds----And especially give up imaginary
judgments of non-existence of these emptinesses! Read the prayer of the three ways
of emptiness that is really one way, *awake.*

The World *is* ephemeral Samapatti!

P O E M
Colyalcolor is the wall of flowers, pink
  and red and ivory white---it is
    the Buddha-Arbour---
      Aviaries of Magic Transcendent Birds
        recognize it in my Awakening Mind---
        With sweet weird cries---
        Colyalcolor is Ethereal Perfume---
        Mysteriously Ancient---
the Bliss of the Buddha-fields---
    A Vast Glowing Empty Page

* *

"EMPTINESS OF THE BUDDHA BEAD, is,
  'I love Buddha'---"   O ANANDA

. . . .

Praise be the wisdom of the Buddhas!

. . . .

"YOU ARE NOW A PERSON WHO EXISTED BEFORE
YOU WERE BORN" is a perfect description
of karma reincarnation---A certain
Weitzenhoffer says this is the manifest
absurd suggestion implied in the phenomena
of age-regression routine during hypnosis,
not realizing what's going on in *non-materialistic Reality* !

"Emptiness is dark Judas
  on the noose, emptiness is form"
----poor Judas! his hot writs!
  his love of what he could get
  with gold, greater than his
  love of the Lord God Jesus . . .

    NEW WAY TO END PRAJNA PRAYER
  "Emptiness is the tree,
    emptiness is form . . ."

"Emptiness is the White Emptiness
  Everywhere Everything, emptiness
  is form. . . . ."

----No, leave as is, too confusing

- - - - - - - - - - - - - - - - - - -

TWO LINES FROM RICHARD THE THIRD
  "The issue was not his begot"
  "Familiar way of gain". . . . .
* *
*   Courage in the world   · *
*   is courage in suffering . . .   *
*   do anything you want. . . . . . *
* *

O this wasted world! Dog kills dog! I dont understand! or maybe I understand too
well-----------------and all the kinds of dogs, and all the ways of killing. . . . .

DHYANA---Quieted nervous belly by deep breathing, holding breath à la tea---no
Samadhi or Samapatti except did feel bliss and when I thought DIPANKARA BUDDHA
suddenly the toads stopt yelling

M A R C H 1 2   M Y #$th B I R T H D A Y   34th B I R T H D A Y
. . . At night hypnotized myself to investigate cure and cause of my mother's cough---
had a vision of brandy bottle, "Heet" (rubbing) bottle---and of round white flowers
---removed flowers from bowl in parlor---allergy---Typed BOOK OF DHARMAS all day
while she healed and brandy stop't cough . . . . . all well next day! So I'm a healer
----

MARCH 13---DRIZZLE DHYANA
  Everyone is shining, ready, and awake . . . . . there's nothin to do. . . .
Visions of *Samapatti Powers* in Healing: People get sick by utilizing physical
opportunities to punish themselves for Karmic debts---because of their Buddha
self-regulating nature----so, I punished myself, for instance, for football
cruelties (smashing Ray Witt in Lowell, the kid at Garden City, even Carrufel,
knocking them out with brutal calculated tackles). . . . by phlebitis. . . .

The Karma Emptiness Movie works automatically, evil is paid up prompt. . . . . .

ALSO   It's worse than death not to know that "God" is the same thing as yourself----
and that's precisely the situation everywhere---and everywhere they're "dying"---

And, the little mystery flick *is* the Tathagata's Transcendental Eye. . . . (the little
flash in my eyes, mentioned in DOCTOR SAX)
     I'm very rich now, a Super Myriad Trillionaire in Samapatti
                    BECAUSE OF GOOD HUMBLE KARMA

WHY AM I HERE?
                 Because of a load of unpaid karmic debts, that my automatic sentient
suffering will make good. "You are now a person who existed before you were born."
There is also a load of karmic blessing that is due, to make me a Buddhahood Bliss
Inheritor---or Heir---a Bliss Heir----

What is a "dumb blonde"?---Vanity---Concupiscence---Vacuousness---Lusted-after-ness---
                      i.e. How would *you* like to be one, like?

And the final sin, the worst, is R I G H T E O U S N E S S

MARCH 14---"Dont let the blues make you bad," sings Frank Sinatra----

Dhyana in the *New Meadow Grove*-----Samapatti, awake from the dream,---and again,
"Do What You Want"-------(as long as your mind keeps prajna wisdom)----(prajna is
also knowing how *Karma Re-Acts*)

  * NIRVANA, is, Snapped Link Ness, or, T h e   S n a p p e d   L i n k . . . .
NIGHT MEDITATION:
                 Heard word 'starbody' concerning how things dont have to be made
                 to *disappear* but to *awake,* to their supremely pure truebody and
                 starbody---
                      ALSO Nothing to do because nothing ever happened,
                         nothing ever will happen
                       ---All things are EMPTY LIGHT

MARCH 15
  All this BOOK OF DHARMAS since December 1953, hasnt it been mighty preparations
for the Epic Novel THE TATHAGATA? ,,,,, NO (next page):-

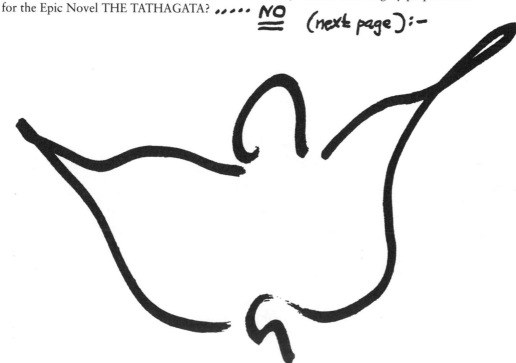

EDITORIAL EXPLANATION OF
VARIOUS TECHNIQUES OF THE DULUOZ LEGEND

TIC------A Tic is a vision suddenly of memory. The ideal, formal
          Tic, as for a BOOK OF TICS is one short and one longer
          sentence, generally about 50 words in all, the intro
          sentence and the explaining sentence, i.e., the above
          Tic about "Cold Fall mornings"---

SKETCH---A Sketch is a prose description of a scene before the
          eyes. Ideally, for a BOOK OF SKETCHES, one small page
          (of notebook size) about 100 words, so as not to ramble
          too much, and give an arbitrary form.

DREAM---A Dream, the core and kernel written on awakening from a
          dream, may fan out further, usually ends up in 300 words,
          viz. the BOOK OF DREAMS

POP------American (non-Japanese) Haikus, short 3-line poems or
          "pomes" rhyming or non-rhyming delineating "little
          Samadhis" if possible, usually of a Buddhist connota-
          tion, aimed towards enlightenment. BOOK OF POPS.

BLUES------A Blues is a complete poem written filling in one
          notebook page, of small or medium size, usually in 15-
          to-25 lines, known as a Chorus, i.e., 223rd Chorus of
          Mexico City Blues in the BOOK OF BLUES

ECSTASY---Meaning "Samadhi," a prose and verse accounting of a
          Samadhi or Samapatti experience in Dhyana meditation,
          of any length. BOOK OF ECSTASIES

MOVIE---Formerly Bookmovies, or Mindmovies, prose concentration
          camera-eye visions of a definite movie of the mind with
          fade-ins, pans, close-ups, and fade-outs. BOOK OF MOVIES